A TESTIMONY
TO COURAGE

A TESTIMONY TO COURAGE

The Regimental History of

THE ULSTER DEFENCE REGIMENT

by

JOHN POTTER

'The only thing necessary for the triumph of evil
is for good men to do nothing.'
Attributed to Edmund Burke
(1729–1797)

LEO COOPER

First published in Great Britain in 2001 by
LEO COOPER
an imprint of Pen & Sword Books
47 Church Street, Barnsley, South Yorkshire, S70 2AS

Copyright © 2001 John Potter

ISBN 0 85052 819 4

A CIP catalogue record for this book
is available from the British Library

Typeset in 11/12pt Garamond by
Phoenix Typesetting, Ilkley, West Yorkshire

Printed in England by
CPI UK

This history is dedicated with admiration and gratitude to

THE FAMILIES OF THE ULSTER DEFENCE REGIMENT

who waited and worried, shared the dangers, cared for their wounded
and disabled, mourned for their dead, yet never lost heart.

Contents

APPENDICES

Preface

Some people may feel that this is not the time to revive old controversies, now that Northern Ireland stands on the threshold of a new dawn. This is a time for forgiveness, however hard that may be. To forgive, but not to forget. Northern Ireland would never have arrived at this threshold had not The Ulster Defence Regiment played its part in holding the line against a violent terrorist campaign. That must never be forgotten.

When I retired after serving for thirteen years in a UDR battalion, followed by a further eight as Regimental Secretary, I was deputed by the Colonels Commandant to compile a historical archive of the Regiment. Since at its height there were eleven battalions, always evolving and constantly on operations, this archive became very large – four volumes in fact. Comprising as it does official papers, it is held by the Ministry of Defence and will be treated in accordance with the requirements of the Public Records Act, emerging therefore in due course into the public domain.

Once I had completed it, I felt there was a great need for a shorter, less detailed account that could be published now and which would tell those who had not served in its ranks what it was like to be a member of the Regiment. Hence this book.

During my research I have carried out some 125 interviews, ranging from generals and chief constables to private soldiers. I am grateful to all those who talked to me so openly, some recalling events the memory of which was still painful, and to those who took the trouble to write down their reminiscences for me. In some instances I have set down their stories in their own words, others I have had to abridge or leave out to keep the length of the book within reasonable bounds. However, everything I have heard or read has helped enormously in the telling of the Regiment's story. I have not related the circumstances of every death; there were simply too many. Instead I have included a Roll of Honour of all the serving and former soldiers killed in terrorist attacks. Sadly, with a few exceptions where the people mentioned have given me permission to name them, I have had to leave out the names of those who served in the Regiment and are still living. I could not run the risk that even now by naming them I might put their lives in danger.

I have been granted access to some official documents and have made extensive use of the annual historical records that every Army unit is required to maintain. In the UDR the standards varied in accordance with the enthusiasm of the record keeper; some were excellent, some cursory and uninformative, and in some years in some battalions there is no record at all. From 1984 onwards the standard improved and the records were considered by the MOD to be among the best in the Army. If some old soldiers feel that events in their battalion have been covered inadequately, the blame lies with the keepers of their historical records. I must also emphasize that the opinions expressed, where they are not attributed, are my own, formed by my own experiences in the Regiment.

A book such as this could not have been completed without the help of a great many people; the transcribing of taped interviews, the typing of the archive, followed by the typing and retyping several times over of the manuscript. I owe a debt to my daughter Nicola who did all the early transcribing and typing and then decided to have a baby instead; to my daughter-in-law Suzie who then took on the transcribing until she accompanied her husband on posting to Zimbabwe; to Jimmy James, Chris Johnston, Lyla Hanna and John O'Neill; and particularly to Brigadier Dick Trigger (ret'd) for his help in processing the text's clearance.

Glossary

AAC	–	Army Air Corps
ACC	–	Assistant Chief Constable
ADAT	–	Army Dependents' Assurance Trust
AIS	–	Army Information Services
ANFO	–	Ammonium Nitrate and Fuel Oil (a type of home-made explosive)
APWT	–	Annual Personal Weapons Test
ARA	–	Army Rifle Association
ARF	–	Airborne Reaction Force
ASU	–	Active Service Units
ASVU	–	Army Security Vetting Units
ATO	–	Ammunition Technical Officer
BAOR	–	British Army of the Rhine
BFT	–	Battle fitness training
BLESMA	–	British Limbless Ex-Servicemens' Association
BWO	–	Battalion Welfare Officer
BW	–	The Black Watch
BZ	–	Border Zone
CESA	–	Catholic Ex-Servicemens' Association
CGS	–	Chief of the General Staff
CID	–	Criminal Investigation Department
CIE	–	Coras Iompair Eireann (National Transport Company of Ireland)
CLF	–	Commander Land Forces
CLOE	–	Compensation for Loss of Employment
COIN	–	Counter-insurgency
COP	–	Close Observation Platoon
CO	–	Commanding Officer
CPTA	–	Cinque Ports Training Area
CQMS	–	Company Quartermaster Sergeant
CS	–	Call Sign (used on radio communications)
CWIED	–	Command Wire Improvised Explosive Device
D and D	–	The Devonshire and Dorset Regiment
DERR	–	The Duke of Edinburgh's Royal Regiment
DHSS	–	Department of Health and Social Services
DMSU	–	Divisional Mobile Support Unit (RUC)
DPP	–	Director of Public Prosecutions
DUP	–	Democratic Unionist Party
DWR	–	The Duke of Wellington's Regiment
ECM	–	Electronic Counter Measure
EOD	–	Explosive Ordnance Disposal

FAC	–	Firearms Certificate
FFR	–	Fitness For Role (inspection)
FRG	–	Federal Riot Guns
GAA	–	Gaelic Athletic Association
GOC	–	General Officer Commanding
GPMG	–	General Purpose Machine Gun
HME	–	Home-made Explosive
HMSG	–	Home Moves on Security Grounds
HQNI	–	Headquarters Northern Ireland
HQUDR	–	Headquarters Ulster Defence Regiment
IED	–	Improvised Explosive Device
INCREP	–	Incident Report
INLA	–	Irish National Liberation Army
IO	–	Intelligence Officer
KOSB	–	King's Own Scottish Borderers
LCPL	–	Lance Corporal
LI	–	The Light Infantry
LMG	–	Light Machine Gun
LSGC	–	Long Service and Good Conduct Medal
LZ	–	Landing Zone
MACM	–	Military Aid to Civil Ministry
MM	–	Military Medal
MOD	–	Ministry of Defence
MP	–	Member of Parliament
MPH	–	Musgrave Park Hospital
MRF	–	Mobile Reaction Force
NAAFI	–	Navy, Army, and Airforce Institute
NCO	–	Non-Commissioned Officer
NICRA	–	Northern Ireland Civil Rights Association
NIO	–	Northern Ireland Office
NIREP	–	Northern Ireland Report
NIRTT	–	Northern Ireland Reinforcement Training Team
NV	–	Negative Vetting
OCS	–	Officer Cadet School
OIRA	–	Official Irish Republican Army
OP	–	Operation or Observation Post
OUP	–	Official Unionist Party
PAC	–	Provisional Army Council
PD	–	People's Democracy
PIRA	–	Provisional Irish Republican Army
PPW	–	Personal Protection Weapon
PRUDR	–	Province Reserve (UDR)
PSF	–	Provisional Sinn Fein
PSI	–	Permanent Staff Instructor
PVCP	–	Permanent Vehicle Check Point
QGM	–	Queen's Gallantry Medal
QO HLDRS	–	Queen's Own Highlanders
RA	–	Royal Artillery
RAMC	–	Royal Army Medical Corps
RAOC	–	Royal Army Ordnance Corps
RCB	–	Regular Commissions Board

RCIED	–	Remote Controlled Improvised Explosive Device
RCT	–	Royal Corps of Transport
RGJ	–	The Royal Green Jackets
RHA	–	Royal Horse Artillery
RMAS	–	Royal Military Academy Sandhurst
RMP	–	Royal Military Police
RPG7	–	(Rocket Launcher)
RRF	–	The Royal Regiment of Fusiliers
RS	–	The Royal Scots
RSM	–	Regimental Sergeant Major
RSME	–	Royal School of Military Engineering
RSO	–	Regimental Signals officer
RTE	–	Radio Telefis Eireann
RTR	–	Royal Tank Regiment
RUC	–	Royal Ulster Constabulary
RV	–	Rendezvous
RVH	–	Royal Victoria Hospital
RWF	–	Royal Welch Fusiliers
SAM	–	Surface to Air Missile
SB	–	Special Branch
SDLP	–	Social Democratic and Labour Party
SDC	–	Sub-district Commandant/Sub-Divisional Commander
SIB	–	Special Investigation Branch
SLR	–	Self-loading Rifle
SMG	–	Sub-machine Gun
SNONI	–	Senior Naval Officer Northern Ireland
SPG	–	Special Patrol Group
SOCO	–	Scenes of Crime Officer
TA	–	Territorial Army
TAOR	–	Tactical Area of Responsibility
TCG	–	Tasking and Co-ordinating Group
TD	–	Territorial Decoration
TISO	–	Training, Intelligence and Security Officer
TSMG	–	Thompson Sub-Machine Gun
UD	–	Ulster Defence Medal
UDA	–	Ulster Defence Association
UDR	–	Ulster Defence Regiment
UFF	–	Ulster Freedom Fighters
USC	–	Ulster Special Constabulary and Ulster Service Corps (from 1977)
USCA	–	Ulster Special Constabulary Association
UUAC	–	Ulster Unionist Action Council
UUUC	–	United Ulster Unionist Council
UVBT	–	Under Vehicle Booby-Trap
UVF	–	Ulster Volunteer Force
UWC	–	Ulster Workers' Council
VCGS	–	Vice Chief of the General Staff
VCP	–	Vehicle Check Point
WRAC	–	Women's Royal Army Corps
WOI	–	Warrant Officer Class 1
WUDR	–	Women's Ulster Defence Regiment

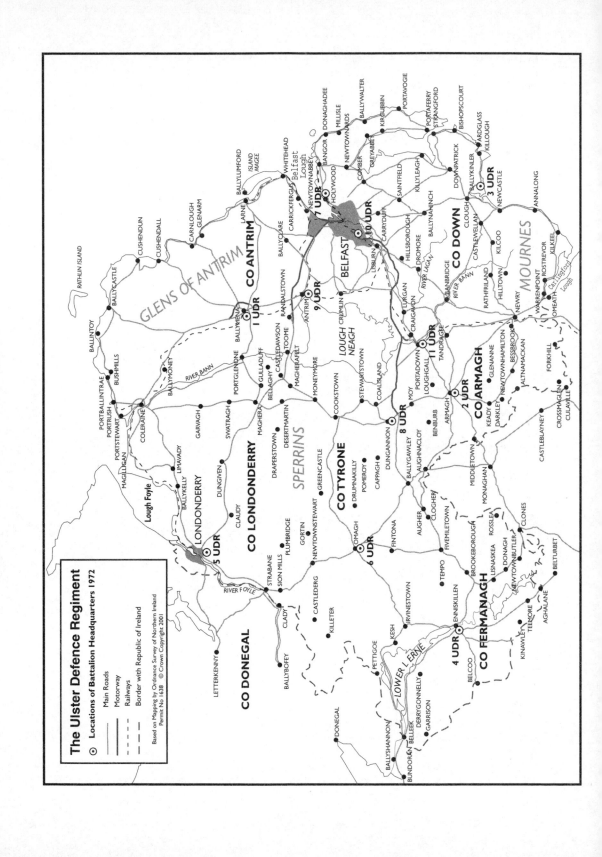

The Ulster Defence Regiment

⊙ **Locations of Battalion Headquarters 1972**

	Main Roads
	Motorway
	Railways
	Border with Republic of Ireland

Based on Mapping by Ordnance Survey of Northern Ireland
Permit No 1638 © Crown Copyright 2001

CHAPTER ONE

The Ulster Special Constabulary

Warminister, in Wiltshire, the minutes ticking away to midnight, 30 June 1992. Rain has been falling steadily since a thunderstorm broke in the afternoon. In the white light of searchlight beams soldiers of the 1st Battalion The Royal Irish Rangers and The Ulster Defence Regiment (UDR) are drawn up in front of a mock fortification. The Commanding Officer of the Rangers gives the order "No more parades, march off". The two guards wheel and march away, the band and pipers playing the marches of the two Regiments. The gates of the fort close behind them. From that moment the titles of the Royal Irish Rangers and the Ulster Defence Regiment have ceased to exist in the order of battle of the British army.

It is exactly 22 years and 91 days since the UDR came into existence, 22 years and three months of continuous operational duties. In that time a Regiment that began as a largely untrained, amateur part-time body of volunteers, motivated by their duty to protect their country against terrorist attack rather than by any enthusiasm for military service, had developed into a professional force, half of them full-time soldiers, and all of them regarded in their anti-terrorist role as the equals of the Regular Army soldiers sent to Northern Ireland on emergency tours. Successive General Officers Commanding (GOCs) have said that without the UDR the forces at their disposal would have been inadequate to contain paramilitary violence. The aim of this history is to gather together the story of the Regiment before memories dim and old soldiers fade away.

The UDR was unique. Never in modern times had a part-time force been raised as an integral part of the British Army to carry out military operations in its own country. Inevitably mistakes were made, by no means all the fault of the Regiment. Wherever the blame lay, the UDR came under sustained criticism throughout its existence. Much of this criticism was politically motivated, over-stated, and too often a distortion of the facts. So this history has a secondary aim – to set the record straight and to do justice to the loyalty, courage and steadfast determination of some 40,000 men and women who served in the ranks of the Regiment. Thirdly it is an attempt to describe to others what it was like to be a member of the UDR.

In December 1918, a month after the Great War had come to its weary end, a General Election was held throughout the United Kingdom. In Ireland the results were a decisive victory for Sinn Fein. Refusing to take up their seats in the British House of Commons, the successful candidates assembled at the Mansion House in Dublin on 21 January 1919 to set up the first independent Irish parliament, Dail Eireann.

Coincidentally on the same day a group of volunteers of the Irish Republican Army ambushed an explosives convoy at Soloheadbeg. It was not a very grand 'convoy', a horse and cart, the driver and a second council employee, and two policemen of the Royal Irish Constabulary. The two policemen were shot dead; their shooting was sanctioned in retrospect by the Dail. The first shots had been fired in the bloody Anglo-Irish War.

Initially the IRA concentrated its attacks on the Royal Irish Constabulary, a force composed of some 70% Catholics under a Catholic Inspector General. During 1920 176 policemen and fifty-four soldiers were killed, forty police barracks attacked, fifteen totally destroyed, and 351 of the smaller barracks, abandoned by their detachments, had been burnt out by the Volunteers.[1] The Constabulary, depleted by these attacks, by intimidation and by the inevitable drying up of new recruits, was reinforced in March 1920 by the Black and Tans, a paramilitary force composed mainly of ex-servicemen recruited in Britain, and, later in the summer, by a small Auxiliary Division of 1,500 ex-British Army officers. Their coming saw the beginning of a campaign of terror and counter-terror, with the excesses of one side matched by the excesses of the other.

In the Northern province of Ulster, and especially in the six counties which collectively had a Protestant majority, the IRA had been able to mount only limited attacks against the police. The main threat was the savage inter-communal rioting, breaking out in Londonderry in June, then spreading to Belfast. Violence erupted across the City and in July eighteen people were killed, some 200 injured, shops looted and homes destroyed. The Army and the RIC were heavily committed to restoring order, leaving the rural areas vulnerable to more IRA attacks. Fearing that these attacks would escalate and that events in the South were deteriorating to the point of anarchy, the Protestants in the North set up their vigilante groups, lacking any central direction. When the IRA stepped up its attacks on the police and rioting flared up again, in Lisburn in August and the city in the autumn, there was a very real fear of civil war. The military authorities in Dublin, recognizing that the RIC in the North was under intolerable pressure and that the Army was insufficiently strong to deal with both the riots and the IRA attacks, authorized, in the northern counties only, the formation of a Special Constabulary under the provisions of an already existing Special Constabulary (Ireland) Act.

There were to be three classes; Class A who were to serve full time and to be armed and equipped, uniformed and paid at the same rates as the RIC; Class B, a part-time force acting under the orders of the police; and Class C, who would be available for call-out in an emergency. Recruiting for the Ulster Special Constabulary (USC) began in November 1920. It expanded rapidly into a formidable force and by the summer of 1922 the total strength was 5,500 Class A and 19,000 Class B, plus a substantial number of Class C who were seldom used but allowed to keep their weapons at home.[2] The insurrection reached its height in the first six months of 1921, with some 50,000 British forces, including 35,000 Regular Army, ranged against a total IRA strength of 112,000, of whom some 2,000 were actively engaged in the flying columns; but the columns' weakness was their shortage of arms and ammunition.[3] In Britain press and public were becoming increasingly disturbed by what seemed, so soon after the Great War, a continuation of a senseless slaughter, and by brutal incidents perpetrated by both sides. Influential members of the Establishment and the Church, including the Archbishop of Canterbury, spoke out forcefully against the policy of 'authorized reprisals'. Parliament passed a bill, introduced by the Prime Minister, Lloyd George, the Better Government of Ireland Bill, under which two Home Rule Parliaments would be set up in Ireland, one for the six counties of North-East Ulster, the other for the remaining twenty-six counties. Elections were held in May, the Unionists in the North obtaining a commanding majority. A month later, on 22 June 1921, King George V came to Belfast to open the new Northern Ireland Parliament. The King had been deeply distressed by the war in Ireland. In a moving speech he appealed for reconciliation. The effect was immediate and dramatic. The President, de Valera, invited members of the Unionist government to a meeting in Dublin and on 11 July a truce was declared. It was an enormous relief to both sides. Over the eighteen months since Soloheadbeg some 600 members of the British forces and 752 IRA Volunteers had died and the total wounded exceeded 2,000.[4]

In October 1921, three months into the truce, Lloyd George and members of the Cabinet began a series of meetings at 10 Downing Street with an Irish delegation, led by Griffith, the Irish Foreign Minister, and including Michael Collins, who during the Anglo-Irish War had effectively controlled IRA operations. The British offered Ireland Dominion status within the Empire for the twenty-six counties, provision whereby the government in the North could opt out of the new state, a Boundary Commission to decide where the line between North and South should run. It was not the republic that the Irish had sought, but the delegation believed that, once they had gained independence, a republic would follow. They were right, though they had to wait another twenty-eight years. Indubitably they had won their central demand. Ireland, less the six counties, was a free country at last.

However, de Valera, who had taken care not to be a member of the delegation so that he could not be blamed if it failed, was bitterly opposed to the treaty terms. The country was split between Pro- and Anti-Treaty factions. The Dail voted for the Treaty by a small majority, a Provisional Government was set up and de Valera resigned from the Presidency. Within the IRA a powerful group of senior officers disowned the treaty. They formed their own military units and in April took over a number of buildings in Dublin, including the Four Courts, the centre of juridical control in Ireland. In June the army of the Provisional Government attacked the buildings, using two artillery pieces to bombard the Four Courts. The Civil War, which had been building up for two months, began in earnest. The pattern of the war was much as it had been against the British, with government troops organized in military units hunting down flying columns of Irregulars dressed in civilian clothes.

The terror and counter-terror returned on an even worse scale. The Roman Catholic Church issued a pastoral condemning the actions of the Irregulars: "They have done more damage in three months than could be laid to the charge of British rule in three decades."[5] It had no effect. The Dail introduced emergency powers stating that anyone discovered carrying arms would be shot. Seventy-seven were executed, three times the number executed by the British in the Anglo-Irish War. Some 13,000 Republicans were interned. When the Civil War ended in May 1923 it had cost the new Free State £17,000,000 and an army of 60,000 men had had to be mobilized to defeat the Irregular forces[6] The Civil War had achieved only many more deaths, great bitterness and an eighteen-month delay in forging ahead with the establishment of the new Ireland, the Irish Free State.

The truce, followed by the Treaty, did not bring peace to the North. Violent inter-communal rioting continued. The authorities were concerned about the threat presented by the IRA. Despite the outbreak of fighting between the Pro- and anti-Treaty factions, Collins, now commanding the army of the Provisional Government, and Lynch, the chief of staff of the Irregulars, agreed they must act together to bring help to the Catholics in the North, whom, they believed, were the victims of a Protestant pogrom. Officers who had gained experience of guerrilla war during the Anglo-Irish War were sent North to reinforce the local IRA. In May 1922 attacks were launched across the Donegal border into Londonderry and Tyrone, as well as from the Glens of Antrim and the Mourne Mountains. Police patrols were ambushed, barracks attacked, communications cut and the homes of prominent Unionist families burnt down, whilst in Belfast, following an attack on a Protestant funeral, a week-long gun battle was fought out between the Army and the IRA. Towards the end of the month an IRA force crossed the Border and occupied the isolated north-west corner of Fermanagh. Two Regular Army battalions, supported by artillery and armoured cars, counter-attacked and reoccupied the area without casualties, though the artillery had to be used to clear the invaders out of the old fort at Belleek.

Apart from this one deployment, the British government agreed that the Specials should be responsible for the defence of the Border, whilst the Regular Army garrison in the North should be held in reserve. It was a strange abrogation of responsibility, but the Army, still commanded from Dublin Castle, was in a difficult situation. The withdrawal of units from the South was well under way and the military authorities were anxious to avoid any action which could precipitate renewed IRA attacks on their depleted forces.

By the time the Treaty War ended and peace returned to Ireland forty-nine Specials had been killed. With the police committed mainly to dealing with inter-communal rioting, first with the RIC in disarray and then the new Royal Ulster Constabulary in its infancy, and with the Army reluctant to become too deeply involved, there is no doubt that it was to a large extent due to the courage and determination of the Specials that the new state was not plunged into a Civil War as bloody and pointless as the war that ravaged the Irish Free State. Inevitably they came to be regarded as anti-Catholic, charged with being the instrument of a Protestant government designed to subjugate the Catholic people. Although initially it had been foreseen that Catholic platoons would be formed to operate in Catholic districts, only a handful came forward to enlist. In the end the Specials gave up any attempt, little as that had been, to persuade Catholics to join them. In truth they were relieved not to have them in their ranks; the Royal Irish Constabulary, they believed with good reason, had been weakened by traitors in their midst. One of the most notorious was a detective in Dublin Castle. But, as time would show, by adopting that attitude, the USC sowed the seeds of their own fate.

The USC was retained over the next forty-six years but reduced to one Class, the part-time B Specials. What kept them together as much as the ever-present threat of a resurgence of IRA activity, was the opportunity for participation in competition shooting. The standard of weapon training was high and a shooting competition was held annually in which all sub-districts could participate. On occasion elements of the force were called out on temporary duties, such as in Belfast in 1931 when sectarian riots broke out again around 12 July. Shots were fired, the Army had to be brought in and the Belfast Specials, who, unlike the rural platoons, were trained more on the lines of normal special constables, relieved the police by assisting with routine duties and guarding barracks. Another eleven dead and 574 injured were added to the tragic litany of victims of two communities who, in the mean back streets of the city, could not learn to live together.

In the first half of the fifties the IRA carried out six major arms raids in military bases in Britain and in Northern Ireland. Most were highly successful, resulting in a boost to morale, an increase in funds from Irish -Americans in the States and an influx of young Volunteers. By 1956 the Army Council felt the organization was sufficiently strong to mount a new campaign across the border.

Some 150 volunteers took part in the opening night on 12 December 1956. A BBC transmitter in Londonderry and the TA drill hall in Enniskillen were blown up, the court house in Magherafelt burnt down and two bridges destroyed on upper Lough Erne. Next night two Fermanagh police barracks were attacked. A similar attack on barracks in Brookeborough on New Year's Day proved to be a disaster. The RUC sergeant, a former Irish Guardsman, repulsed the attackers with bursts from a Bren gun, wounding six, two of them mortally. The failure of the raid epitomized the state of the IRA at that time, enthusiastic and determined but in-experienced, inadequately trained and poorly organized. Some 1,660 B Specials were placed on full-time duties, whilst 12,000 part-timers patrolled the roads and the Border and guarded public utilities and police barracks. The Regular Army were hardly involved, though a reinforcement RA regiment was sent over from England.

Five years on the IRA was losing heart. Volunteers had set up over 600 incidents, but most were of a nuisance value – bridges, drill halls and USC huts, electricity transformers and telegraph poles. They had failed to enlist support on either side of the Border; in the Republic 130, including a number of the leaders, had been interned. In February 1962 they called off the campaign. Casualties had been light; six police officers and eight Volunteers had lost their lives.

With the failure of the IRA's campaign, the future for Northern Ireland looked more hopeful than at any time since its inception. Substantial progress had been made in encouraging major British and American firms to bring in new factories to replace the waning shipbuilding and linen industries. Since his election as Prime Minister in 1965, Terence O'Neill had done much to improve relations between North and South and Protestant and Catholic. He had invited the Taoiseach, Lynch, to visit parliament at Stormont and introduced him to the Cabinet; he had been the first Prime Minister to visit Catholic schools and in the General Election in 1963 he canvassed in both Protestant and Catholic wards of Belfast. The election results were an emphatic endorsement of his moderate approach.

In 1963 a new figure had appeared on the political scene. The Reverend Ian Paisley, the 37-year-old son of a Baptist minister, had established the fundamentalist Free Presbyterian Church. A commanding figure and a skilled orator, he was a virulent opponent of the Roman Catholic Church and implacably opposed to O'Neill's policy of reconciliation. When the Northern Ireland Civil Rights Association (NICRA) was founded in 1967, it was mainly Paisley who rallied militant opposition to the movement.

Membership of NICRA was open to all, but the majority of members were Catholic. A new breed of middle-class Catholic had grown up, teachers, lawyers, university lecturers demanding an equal place for their people in the North. Their basic demands were the introduction of 'one man, one vote' in local council elections, the ending of gerrymandering in the drawing up of electoral boundaries, fair allocation of jobs and public housing, the appointment of an Ombudsman to rule on complaints against the authorities, repeal of the Special Powers Act, introduced at the height of the troubles in 1922, and the disbandment of the USC.

Northern Ireland, born out of insurrection and with memories of sectarian killings still fresh in the minds of the older generation, was not yet sufficiently stable or mature to cope with the concept of peaceful protest. Londonderry was ripe for trouble. Discrimination in the alloca-tion of housing and blatant gerrymandering in the drawing up of ward boundaries convinced the majority Catholic community that the Unionists were determined to hang on to control of local government at all costs.

In September 1968 NICRA proposed to hold a protest march into the centre of the city. The Loyalist Apprentice Boys applied to hold a counter-demonstration and both marches were then banned. NICRA determined to go ahead. Some 2,000 people gathered at the railway station, including a number of prominent Nationalists, among them Gerry Fitt, MP for West Belfast, and, at his invitation, three Labour MPs from Westminster. The marches had gone a short distance when they were confronted by the police. Batons were drawn by some police officers without explicit orders, and both Fitt and McAteer, the local Nationalist MP, were injured.[7] A cameraman from RTE, the Irish Television service, filmed the violent scenes. The pictures were shown throughout the United Kingdom and abroad.

Since the foundation of Northern Ireland the British had left the government of the country largely to the Parliament at Stormont. Now it could no longer ignore the fact that all was not well in the Province. There were further disturbances, with NICRA attempting to hold marches in Dungannon and Armagh, and Paisley and his supporters holding counter-demonstrations. In November Stormont introduced a number of reforms, including a points system for the allocation of housing, the appointment of an Ombudsman and the setting up of a Londonderry Development Commission to replace the City Council. NICRA called off further marches for the time being and the Unionist Parliamentary Party gave O'Neill a vote of confidence. For a brief space it seemed that the downward spiral into disaster had been halted.

But a militant Left-wing organization based on Queen's University, Peoples' Democracy, in a deliberate attempt to heighten tension, decided to organize a protest march from Belfast to Londonderry. The marchers set out from Belfast on New Year's Day 1969. Their numbers varied between around forty and seventy. It was a typical Irish coat-trailing exercise. It might not have attracted much attention if the Paisleyite faction had not decided to oppose the march at every town en route and the police had been more resolute in ensuring that the marchers had a clear passage. On the fourth day, as they neared Londonderry, they were viciously attacked by a hostile crowd at Burntollet Bridge. The official toll of injuries was thirteen, but that was probably an underestimate. When the marchers limped into the city that night they were greeted by cheering crowds lining the streets. From then on Peoples' Democracy effectively hijacked the Civil Rights movement. Later, as a result of a series of parliamentary questions, two serving and forty-seven ex-members of the USC were identified as having been among the attackers at Burntollet.[8]

In February 1969, encouraged by the widespread support he had received from both communities after a national television and radio broadcast, but faced with a growing backbench revolt within the Unionist

Party, O'Neill called a general election. A number of pro-O'Neill candidates were opposed by nominees of local Unionist Associations. O'Neill
himself was opposed by Paisley and a prominent member of PD. The
results exposed the extent of the split within the Unionist Party, with one
third of the successful candidates being Unionists opposed to O'Neill's
moderate policies. From then on O'Neill's days were numbered.

At the end of March an electricity sub-station outside Belfast was
damaged by an explosion, followed four weeks later by attacks on the
pipe-lines from the Silent Valley reservoir and Lough Neagh, seriously
interrupting the city's water supply. O'Neill believed rightly that the
attacks had been carried out by Loyalist militants determined to force him
out of office. With his party turning against him and the militants resorting
to violence, he decided to resign. Before he left he persuaded the Unionist
Parliamentary Party to agree by a narrow margin to accept the most
emotive of all the reforms, universal franchise in local elections. He died
in June 1990. His obituarist wrote, "Although he was a man of bravery,
outstanding decency, liberal instinct and accurate analysis, he was felt to
lack the drive and ruthlessness necessary to cut through the atrophy,
simmering sectarianism and long-standing injustice that had festered away
for years under Brookeborough . . . He went too far and too fast."[9] The
same criticism had been voiced by friends in the Unionist Party in his life-
time. "Little did they realize," O'Neill wrote, "that we were doing too little
and too late."

Under the new Prime Minister, James Chichester-Clark, the government
pressed ahead with the reforms already agreed by the Unionist Party
under O'Neill's leadership and in addition declared an amnesty for all
those who had been charged with public order offences. NICRA
announced a temporary suspension of its civil disobedience campaign.
For a while, though tension remained high, an uneasy peace reigned.

The Apprentice Boys of Derry is one of the Protestant Loyal Orders,
taking its name from the thirteen apprentices who, at the start of the siege
of Londonderry in 1698, slammed the gates of the city against the army of
James II. Each 12th of August it holds a parade to commemorate the relief
of the city and the end of the siege. In 1969 the Minister of Home Affairs
was in a difficult position. If he banned the march, the government would
be accused of giving in to the Civil Rights movement and as a result might
fall, in which case the reform programme would probably collapse. If he
failed to impose a ban, then there was a real danger of a fresh outbreak
of the rioting that had broken out in the city in July. After consultation
with the RUC and several influential local citizens, he decided to let the
march go ahead.

Some 700 police were deployed into the city. Initially the day passed
peacefully, with the traditional service in the cathedral. However, as the
procession crossed Waterloo Place, between the city walls and the
Bogside, young hooligans began throwing missiles at the police, and then,
increasing their fusillade, at the Apprentice Boys. The crowd became

more and more violent, pulling away the crush barriers. The police mounted a charge into the Bogside, came under a barrage of missiles and petrol bombs and were driven back to the city centre. In danger of being overrun, they used CS gas to force their way back into the Catholic enclave. The Battle of the Bogside, with the police trying to restore order and the locals fighting back to evict them, lasted three days.

Since its formation nearly half a century earlier the original establishment of the RUC had been increased only once, from 3,000 to 3,200. Bearing in mind the principle that to cover every duty three men are required, in normal circumstances there were only 1,000 police officers to maintain law and order in a population of one and a half million. In the first seven months of that year nearly half the force received injuries requiring hospital treatment. Unlike the police in the rest of the United Kingdom the RUC was unable to call on neighbouring forces for reinforcement. The only back-up was the USC who, since the ending of the IRA campaign in 1962, had been reduced to a strength of some 8,600.

The Specials had received no training in riot control. They had no helmets, shields or batons. In a riotous situation their only weapon was the .303 rifle. The RUC was well aware that to commit them to the streets against a Catholic crowd would only heighten tension. The General Officer Commanding the Army in Northern Ireland had made it clear that military units could not be used to restore order until the Northern Ireland Government had deployed all the resources at its disposal, and that included the USC.[10] Thus, the B men, through no fault of their own, were thrust into a situation for which they were untrained and generally ill-equipped. Disasters were almost inevitable.

In order to overstretch the police and ease pressure on the Bogsiders, NICRA called for diversionary demonstrations. Rioting broke out in other centres, including Armagh, Coalisland, Downpatrick, Dungannon and Newry, whilst in Belfast the Protestants, fearing that this was an IRA-inspired uprising, began attacking Catholic areas of the city. In Dungannon, where fires had been started, due to a confusion of orders and a lack of liaison between police and Specials, the USC opened fire on demonstrators as they were dispersing and three Catholics were wounded. In Coalisland a party of Specials opened fire without orders on rioters making a determined attack on the police station, using petrol bombs and a mechanical shovel. The attack was repulsed, but some of the rioters were wounded. On the following night in Armagh the Tynan Platoon, reacting to the inadequate orders of a Chief Inspector, became involved in a riot and one of the rioters was shot dead. The Scarman Tribunal, set up to investigate the disturbances of that summer, had no doubt that the fatal shot was fired by a member of the platoon. The men compounded the suspicions against them by returning straight from the scene to Tynan to clean their weapons.

That same night during the inter-communal rioting in Belfast the Specials played only a limited role. Caught up between the two opposing sides between the Shankill and the Falls they were completely out of their depth. In the words of Scarman, "Whilst evoking the hostilities of the Catholics, they were unable to restrain the aggression of the Protestants." In some instances the Protestants came unasked to the aid of the Specials as they tried to hold back the advances of Catholic crowds. Scarman recorded two such instances. They were sufficient to perpetuate the belief that on that night in Belfast the B men spearheaded Protestant mobs in attacks on the Catholics.

At 4.45 pm on the 14th the Inspector General of the RUC sent a signal to the General Officer Commanding Northern Ireland requesting the assistance of the Army in Londonderry. The Home Secretary, James Callaghan, had flown down that morning to RAF St Mawgan to discuss the worsening situation with the Prime Minister. Harold Wilson had flown in from the Scilly Isles where he was on holiday during the summer recess. Callaghan was on his way back to London when the news of the Inspector General's request was signalled to his aircraft. He scribbled "permission granted" on the message pad and within minutes the first sub-units of the Prince of Wales's Own moved into the Bogside to relieve the police.[11] Next day the 3rd Bn The Light Infantry took over from the exhausted police in Belfast and were warmly welcomed by the Catholic communities.

It is easy but unfair to condemn out of hand the record of the USC that summer. There were many instances in which they were used to protect Catholic property and to maintain order in Protestant districts. Following the commitment of the Army, 250 Specials were tasked for street patrols in the Protestant areas of Londonderry and to man checkpoints on an outer ring around the city, whilst in Belfast another 485 were used to guard police barracks and Catholic property. Amongst them was the Carryduff platoon, brought in from the outskirts of the city. They were distributed in twos and fours, alone and with no radio communication to summon help if they came under attack. Four were detailed to guard Catholic-owned shops in the staunchly loyalist Sandy Row, near the city centre.

> "There was quite a hostile crowd," their former SDC recalled, "and these Specials were just standing there on their own without protection other than rifles. Another four guarded a Catholic church up near the Holywood road that had been attacked a number of times. They were there for four days, most of them would have been Orangemen, but those boys would have died defending that chapel, because that was their orders. Some of the Comber platoon were petrol-bombed whilst they were guarding Inglis's bakery because Catholics worked there."

Other platoons were used effectively to restore order in Enniskillen and Newry, two of the few times when they were deployed under firm police control and equipped with riot shields and batons; and when Lynch, the Taoiseach, apparently persuaded by his own hard-liners that he had to be seen to be doing something, announced at the height of the riots in

10

Londonderry that he was moving Irish Army units to the Border area, several Specials platoons were detailed as a precautionary measure to guard Border police barracks.

On 19 August Chichester-Clark, accompanied by Andrews, his Deputy, Brian Faulkner, Minister of Development, and Robert Porter, Minister of Home Affairs, attended a meeting at Downing Street to discuss the crisis. They agreed that the GOC, Sir Ian Freeland, should take over responsibility for security operations, including the USC. Harold Wilson asked what the reaction would be if the GOC recommended the disbandment of the Specials. Chichester-Clark advised that any such action would have to be taken very slowly. So far as the Stormont party was concerned the possibility of disbandment had not been seriously considered, nor had the United Kingdom ministers made any such recommendation. Before the six-hour meeting came to an end Wilson left to speak on television. In the conference room some of the members gathered round a set to watch. To the amazement of the Stormont delegation, Wilson said the Specials would be "phased out of their present role". He did not return to the room, so they could not protest that, back in Northern Ireland, this unfortunate phrase would be taken to mean that they had agreed to the disbandment of the USC.[12] In any case it was too late. The damage was done. When they flew back to Aldergrove the media were waiting "en masse" to ask the Stormont Ministers whether it was true that they had agreed to the disbandment of the Specials. Their denials were treated with suspicion and when, in October, the disbandment was announced, their credibility was seriously undermined.

The Newry branch of NICRA had received the telephone call from their central executive requesting their help in diverting police from the Bogside. Enlisting help from supporters across the border in Dundalk they erected barricades in the town, whilst roving bands of hooligans caused widespread damage to property. At the request of the RUC, Major Desmond Woods, the County Commandant, moved 250 of his County Down Specials to the vicinity of the town, where they were issued with batons and shields. Patrols, composed half of Specials and half of regular police, under RUC command, succeeded in removing all the barricades that night, restoring order throughout the town with relatively minor trouble. Woods described it as one of the most successful operations the Specials had ever carried out.[13]

George Chambers, SDC of the Dunmore platoon, was one of those on patrol in Newry with his men. A woman pulled him into her house telling him to come and listen to this. Harold Wilson was speaking. "There we were being pelted with stones and bottles and doing our best in difficult circumstances," he recalled, "and we were going to be phased out because of our sectarian, uncontrolled behaviour. That was the moment I said to myself 'Well I've had enough of this'." Since returning posthaste from a family holiday in Mayo, he had been on continuous duty guarding a timber yard in Belfast, defending the RUC station in Downpatrick against a violent crowd, assisting in the removal of the Newry barricades. Now this.[14] Understandably this sense of disillusion and betrayal was felt throughout the USC. The men were not only angry and bitter, they were astonished.

The following night Chambers, with a reinforced platoon of about fifty men, was given the task of guarding the Belfast Harbour estate, including the fuel tanks, the aerodrome where all the buses of Belfast had been parked for their safety, Harland and Wolff's shipyard and the harbour power station. The task was so enormous that in some places men had to be posted singly, and they had to remain on duty all night. "The thing that really got me," he recalls, looking back to that night, "was that my instructions were to detail two men to walk up and down the Sydenham bypass to protect the oil tanks. They could carry their revolvers, but only so long as they were hidden under their coats. It was no longer acceptable for two constables guarding two million pounds worth of fuel to be seen carrying arms."

Next evening Chambers decided to resign. His platoon said they were completely disillusioned and would resign with him. They loaded all their uniforms and weapons into a van and rang RUC Downpatrick to warn the Permanent Staff Instructor that they were bringing them in.

The news of the Dunmore platoon's decision was received with dismay. If other platoons followed their example, either a large number of troops would have to be moved into the Province or key installations would be unguarded and wide open to attack. Fortunately for the moment none did. A message sent out by the GOC, with instructions that it was to be read out to all platoons, telling them that he had assumed command and control of the Specials and that he had no intention of disbanding or disarming the force in advance of the findings of a government committee, provided much-needed reassurance.

The details of the committee were announced that day. Its terms of reference were "to examine the recruitment, organization, structure and composition of the RUC and USC and their respective functions, and to recommend as necessary what changes are required to provide for the efficient enforcement of law and order in Northern Ireland" At Harold Wilson's suggestion Sir John (later Lord) Hunt was invited to chair the Committee. As a serving Lieutenant Colonel he had organized and led the British expedition that had conquered Everest for the first time, the news reaching London on the morning of the Queen's Coronation. Although he did not reach the summit himself his brilliant initial military appreciation and plan made a major contribution to the success of the expedition. A gentle, courteous, rather reserved man, he was very different from the ogre of Loyalist mythology. The two members were Robert Mark, the Deputy Commissioner of the Metropolitan Police, and Sir James Robertson, the Chief Constable of Glasgow, chosen at the request of Stormont.

The Committee, with only five weeks to complete their task, began work immediately. They made a point of meeting the USC County Commandants and members of the force and listening to their views. Lieutenant Commander Jack Reilly, County Commandant of Tyrone, recalled that they were very courteous and very pleasant to talk to. But Hunt gave the impression that he had made up his mind before he arrived in the Province, and it was obvious that the decision had already been taken to disband the USC.[15]

Porter, as Minister of Home Affairs, had no input into the study. Indeed he and the Cabinet did not see the report until 8 October, 24 hours before it was due to be published. They protested that they needed more time to study it and publication was postponed until the following day. The main recommendations were:

> The RUC should be relieved of all duties of a military nature, and should cease to be equipped with armoured cars and certain types of weapons;
> they should cease to carry firearms;
> their strength should be increased as a first priority;
> the USC should be replaced by a police reserve force and by a locally recruited part-time military force, under control of the GOC.

The committee believed that a strength of about 4,000 should be sufficient for the military force.

> "We believe that this recommendation and the setting up of the police volunteer reserve should provide full opportunity for all sections of the community (not least members of the USC who are both physically and educationally qualified to do so) to serve the community in whichever of the two roles they prefer."[16]

Porter for one doubted whether the Committee had intended to recommend the inclusion of a military force. He believed the recommendation was mainly due to Victor Morrison, a Civil Servant from the Ministry of Home Affairs, appointed as assessor to the Committee, who argued that, if the Specials were to be disbanded, a locally recruited military force must take its place in addition to an unarmed police reserve force.[17]

The reactions to the Hunt report were predictable. In general the RUC welcomed it. The Committee had accepted many of the recommendations made in the report submitted to them by the police Central Representative Body, including "the phasing out of firearms as soon as this is compatible with the safety of our members."[18] The Unionist Parliamentary Party accepted it by twenty-eight votes to seven, with two abstentions. The Opposition at Stormont welcomed it. They were delighted by the recommendation that the USC should be disbanded, feeling that Nationalist complaints and accusations against the Specials over the years had been vindicated.

Paisley roundly condemned it, calling the report "a complete capitulation to the murderers and looters in our public streets. This is a sell-out,

and a government which proposes to introduce such dramatic changes ought to resign immediately and submit itself to the electorate."
The *Belfast Telegraph* was cautious:

> "Whether Hunt is being too optimistic in hoping to enlist sufficient Protestants and Catholics to both forces, when there is no tradition of mixing religions at this level, remains to be seen, but the worst thing would be to end up with two auxiliary forces, one under Army direction, which were as sectarian in composition as the force they replaced. This leads to the conclusion that Hunt is good in theory but weak in suggesting practical means for producing the desired new look. It advocates encouraging Catholic recruitment, but there are few suggestions as to how this is to be achieved."

The *Newsletter* was gloomy:

> "The recommendation is a victory for the Roman Catholics and the Civil Rights Movement, who demanded the Stormont Government abolish the all Protestant Specials. Opposition will come from the men themselves, many of whom took part in the 1956–62 bloody border battles. They take pride in their principal role of defending the border and vital points which have previously been the targets of sabotage and attacks.
>
> "With this inbred tradition, the elders are unlikely to want to renounce what they consider to be a vital duty for the preservation of the Province. It is unlikely that they will respond to the invitation to join a Roman Catholic – Protestant volunteer force."

The Shankill Defence Association called the report "a capitulation to the Civil Rights agitators" and warned, "Let Porter know that a day is fast approaching when responsible leaders and associations like ourselves will no longer be able to restrain the backlash of outraged Loyalist opinion".

In that they were right. The Hunt report was published on a Friday. On Saturday night after the pubs closed a vicious protest riot developed along the Shankill Road. Callaghan, who had come over to the Province for the publication of the report, described what happened:

> "A large crowd gathered in Townsend Street at its junction with the Shankill Road. At first about 200 policemen armed with batons and riot shields tried to stop the mob, among whom were many drunks, from advancing down the Shankill towards the Catholic Unity flats at the bottom.
>
> "But the crowd, waving Union Jacks and singing Loyalist songs, hurled bottles and bricks at the police who retaliated with CS gas and linked arms across the street to stop the crowd's advance. The mêlée grew worse and suddenly a fusillade of shots rang out and Constable Victor Arbuckle, standing in the front line of the police, fell to the ground with a bullet in his head. He died almost immedi-

ately; the line was instantly restored unbroken. Two other policemen were injured by the same volley. This was a signal for the Protestants higher up the road to throw up barricades of paving stones and over-turn lorries from behind which came a hail of machine-gun bullets and sustained sniper fire. At 1.45am the troops opened fire in self defence.

"These were the first shots they had fired since taking over eight weeks before."[19]

The *Belfast Telegraph* described it as the worst fighting since 1922. The first member of the security forces to be killed in the troubles had died by Protestant hand, and the first time the Army opened fire had been against Protestant gunmen.

Within the USC the final confirmation of their disbandment was greeted with dismay. The Glenwherry Platoon Sergeant attended a meeting with the Antrim sub-districts and their County Commandant.

"It was very noisy and rowdy. Our Sub-District Commandant made a proposal that we should hand back our arms and uniforms and walk out. The proposal was seconded and a vote was about to be taken when I stood up. I reminded them that the USC had been started by our fathers and grandfathers and it had been an honourable force, a disciplined force. It had carried out its duties faithfully for fifty years and if we showed any indiscipline in the last months we would be letting down ourselves and our forefathers. Someone seconded my proposal and it was carried. This did not make me a very popular fellow. The head instructor for Ballymena District was threatening to thump me on the way out and for a long time after my SDC would barely talk to me. My theory was that we would be better stopped by people we knew than by English or Scottish or Welsh soldiers. I thought our country was in trouble and it was our duty to protect it. We had an awful lot of feeling from some of our local councillors from Ballymena and when we started to patrol with the UDR we used to get stick from them.

"I had 23 years service in the USC; there were some, such as my platoon commander, who had over 40. Now these were people who had faithfully upheld the law without fault or favour through hail, sleet and snow for very, very little pay. Of course it seemed a great insult after all those years to be considered unsuitable to do our duties."

All the platoons that had threatened to resign agreed to withdraw their resignations, including Dunmore, except for Chambers who felt he had burnt his boats. To their great credit, the USC set aside their understand-able resentment and bitterness and served on until the UDR came into being at midnight on 31 March 1970. On the day after the Hunt Report riot the Assistant Staff Officer to the Special Constabulary at RUC

Headquarters persuaded the GOC that if he gave him permission to detail twenty Specials a night to patrol the Shankill there would be no further trouble. Permission was granted and for the next six months these Special patrols kept the peace in the district. Elsewhere the platoons continued to carry out the essential task of guarding key points. On 30 April 1970 the force was finally wound up. Despite the concerns of the British government and the GOC, all the uniforms and equipment and every single weapon was handed in.

The disbandment of the USC was inevitable, as inevitable as the introduction of universal suffrage in local government elections or the reforms for the allocation of housing. Inevitable because, like those other issues, the USC was seen as part of the whole business of discrimination against the Catholic community. For 50 years, apart from the last few months when Protestant extremists began blowing up public utilities, the only threat to the continued existence of the state had come from the Republican movement, and the Republicans were Catholics. At no time – until those last months – had any armed Protestant posed a threat. The USC was not anti-Catholic, but they were created to counter a threat from a Catholic-based organization. Of all the Specials interviewed, not one said he felt any hostility between himself and his Catholic neighbours. One recalled how a neighbour offered to look after his dairy herd whilst he was called out on duty during the August riots. Another, who lived in a predominately Catholic estate in Newry, used to walk out of his flat in his uniform and carrying his rifle, get into his car and drive off to duty. Chambers said that in Downpatrick District prior to 1969 there was no feeling that the USC was an anti-Catholic or sectarian force. "I can think of all sorts of situations where we were completely interacting with Catholics and the atmosphere was completely friendly, there was no feeling of hostility." A constable in the Newtownstewart platoon had no hesitation about going into the Catholic shops in uniform. "You were treated as normally as any civilian." He maintained he never saw any of his men being antagonistic towards the public. "If you stopped a local Catholic you waved him through."

Nevertheless there is no doubt that there were occasions, particularly in areas with a history of IRA violence, where individual patrols were guilty of roughing up people they suspected of being IRA sympathizers, sometimes on the basis of inaccurate gossip, and the sum of such incidents led to a general climate of fear and loathing for the "Bs" amongst the Nationalist community. A Nationalist MP, speaking in one of several acrimonious debates in Stormont in 1969, recalled how a member of his family had once been arrested for breaking curfew by a Special Constable with whom shortly before he had been playing a neighbourly game of cards. That was the problem; the existence of the USC drew a demarcation line between Catholic and Protestant, neighbour and neighbour. If one section of the community is armed and the other half is not, it can be a source of antagonism; not a personal antagonism, but a general charge, in the case of the USC, that the force was an instrument of a Unionist Government and the Orange Order. When the USC made mistakes, those who made that charge exploited the mistakes by demanding the force be disbanded. The making of the mistakes made it all the harder to resist the demands.

In their final years the USC failed. The failure was not entirely theirs. In the half-century since their formation no attempt had been made to modernize them. They had been neglected. They were still equipped to fight the terrorist of the Twenties. They had neither transport nor radio communications. Discipline was, in the words of an Adjutant, "laid back and existing on good will and respect for the individual in charge". Some officers were selected not for their leadership qualities but because of their standing in the Protestant community or because it was "Willie John's turn next". Administration was lax. One Regular Army major, on posting to a UDR battalion, was appalled by the conditions in the key points guard-rooms. Accommodation was frequently damp, lit by candlelight, bereft of any rest facility and with inadequate communications. Another found that the ammunition dated back to 1940 and would have been unusable, even dangerous. One of the B men's strengths was their local knowledge, but the force had no central system for collating intelligence. Above all liaison between the police and the USC had been allowed to deteriorate, with the former making little effort to oversee the activities of the latter. Undoubtedly this was a factor on the several occasions in August 1969 when platoons were tasked with inadequate orders into situations in which they should never have been involved and for which they had neither the equipment nor the training.

These shortcomings were not a reason for their disbandment, but if they had not been disbanded they would have been unfitted to cope with the new breed of terrorist. The Hunt Committee was right; the protection of the Border and the state against sabotage and armed attack was and always had been a task for a military force under the GOC, not a para-military constabulary under police control. The reason the Specials were formed was that in 1920 the Army had failed to take on that role. Fifty years on there had to be a radical change. However, had it not been for those B Specials, officers, sergeants and constables, who, despite their sense of betrayal put loyalty to their country before personal bitterness and applied to join the UDR, the Regiment would never have been ready in time to counter the threat from the emergent IRA.

CHAPTER TWO

The Formation of the Regiment

When they saw the Hunt Report for the first time, Chichester-Clark, Faulkner and Porter had decided that the military force should be called 'The Ulster Defence Regiment'. Callaghan had agreed, but later there were second thoughts in London about the wisdom of incorporating "Ulster" since the historic province included three counties in the Irish Republic. At a meeting with Hattersley, the Minister of State at the MOD, the subject was discussed. Porter argued that there were precedents, the Royal Ulster Rifles and the Royal Ulster Constabulary for instance. The CGS supported him and the title was accepted. During a debate in the Lords, Hunt regretted that the force had been given a name which was anathema to many Catholics. Bearing in mind his damaging criticism of the Regiment twenty years on, one must wonder whether he was fully convinced of the need for the military force, despite the recommendation of his own Committee. A working party was set up under the chairmanship of Major General A. J. Dyball, the Deputy Director Operations at Lisburn, to make recommendations on the organization, strength and equipment of the new Regiment.[1] Members included a staff officer from the Ministry of Defence, Morrison from Home Affairs, who had acted as assessor to the Hunt Committee, Lieutenant Colonel S. Miskimmin, the staff officer to the USC at RUC Headquarters, and Captain M. H. Armstrong, District Commandant for Armagh to represent the part-time officers of the USC. They met on three occasions in the following week. County Commandants were brought in to give their views on the number of men they would need to carry out the tasks that had been performed by their Specials. The figure was 6,000, 2,000 more than the 'off the cuff' strength suggested by the Hunt Committee. The working party recommended that the rank of private soldiers should be 'volunteer'; that the dress for operations should be combat kit and for parade a uniform of the same dark green as worn by the WRAC, a peaked cap and county shoulder titles. Initially they suggested that the cap badge should be the Red Hand of Ulster, but when Dyball produced his former Royal Ulster Rifles badge, snapped off the motto "Quis Separabit" and suggested that that should be the new badge, the other members agreed.[2]

They recommended that within each battalion there should be a mobile force of two platoons, each equipped with a Landrover fitted for radio plus three manpack sets. It was a very modest bill. Far too modest, for it showed little understanding of the need for mobility in the new force.

In fact it seems that the Working Party was no more than a means of giving the USC the impression that their views on the structure of the new Regiment were being take into account, for, after the three meetings, the members were summoned to Headquarters Northern Ireland on 12 November to be told that the Government White Paper was being published that day.

The White Paper confirmed that the new force would be known as The Ulster Defence Regiment. It would consist of not more than 6,000 all ranks, in lightly armed companies, grouped in battalions, the boundaries to co-incide with county boundaries. The task of the UDR was:

> "to support the regular forces in Northern Ireland in protecting the border and the State against armed attack and sabotage. It will fulfil this task by undertaking guard duties at key points and installations, by carrying out patrols and by establishing check points and road blocks when required to do so. In practice such tasks are most likely to prove necessary in rural areas. It is not the intention to employ the new force on crowd control or riot duties in cities."

The force would be part of the Army and would come under command of the GOC Northern Ireland. The force commander would be a Regular Army brigadier. Battalions would be commanded by "local members of the force".

> "During its early life these appointments may be filled by present County Commandants of the USC, almost all of whom are ex-officers of the regular forces who have had much experience in dealing with the tasks for which the new force is designed."

Other points covered by the White Paper included:–

the appointment of a Training Major from the Regular Army and a small administrative staff for each battalion;
enlistment open to all male citizens of the UK and colonies normally resident in Northern Ireland;
normal engagement for three years, but might be extended subject to recommendation;
lower and upper age limits to be 18 and 55, but as an interim measure persons with previous military or similar suitable service might be recruited or allowed to serve beyond 55;
all recruits required to take the oath of allegiance to the Queen;
the basic weapon to be the rifle;
combat dress and, at a later stage, a form of parade dress would be issued.

The White Paper concluded by saying that the Regiment would start to form on 1 January 1970, to be operationally effective from 1 April.[3]

That afternoon Porter rose in the chamber at Stormont to announce the main points of the White Paper. The Opposition welcomed the statement. John Hume for Foyle and Austin Currie for East Tyrone said they would encourage all sections of the community to join the new force. Ivan Cooper, the member for mid-Derry, said

"There is no point in honorary members of the opposition putting forward demands for a fair and impartial force unless it is supported by all the people, and my greatest hope is that it will have the support of the community."

Even Patrick Kennedy, the Republican Labour member for Belfast Central, agreed that members of the minority should be encouraged to join, though he looked forward to the day when the UDR would also become redundant, since there was no need for it. "There is no IRA. It is a figment of the Minister's imagination."[4] (In 1971 he was to introduce Joe Cahill to a media conference as leader of the Provisional IRA.)

The reaction from predictable sources was less enthusiastic. At Westminster Bernadette Devlin, the fiery young MP who had played a prominent part in the Battle of the Bogside, asked,

"Do you really expect me or any other member or anybody in Northern Ireland to accept one solitary word of the whitewash and eyewash you have produced? Can you give me one concrete state-ment that it is not the USC under the guise of the British Army?"

It was an accusation that was to be repeated time and time again over the years by critics who made no attempt to understand the changed struc-ture of the new Regiment. It was untrue.

The *Belfast Telegraph* declared.

"In no sense can the new Regiment be regarded like the old USC, as a vigilante force and virtually a law unto itself. Inevitably the members of the new force will be provided by present B Specials. And just as inevitably it is already being smeared in some quarters as simply the old force in new uniform. Every effort must be made to ensure that this is not so. No one must be able to put a denomi-national tag on the UDR and if one of the senior officers in the force happened to be a Roman Catholic, so much the better . . . The estab-lishment of this new force should be regarded as a turning point in the life of the community."

A few days later the leader writer returned to the subject,

"The civil rights protest was for equal rights for all. With these rights go obligations, and we would appeal to all Catholics who want to demonstrate their full citizenship to respond to Mr Hume's appeal. If they do not they will indeed fall into the trap which will prove to some people that there are responsibilities which Catholics are not prepared to shoulder."

On the day the White Paper was published Miskimmin handed out to fellow members of the Working Party copies of a letter he was sending out to all members of the USC, explaining the Government's proposals and enclosing an application form which they were asked to complete if they wished to join one or other of the new forces.[5]

When Stormont met a week later for a two-day debate on the Hunt Report, the atmosphere had been soured by this revelation and by the wording of a government advertisement calling for recruits for the two new forces. Ironically the debate was based on a motion supporting the recommendations of the Hunt Report, proposed by the Opposition. It was an ill-tempered debate, opened by Hume accusing the Government of giving priority to members of the USC to enlist in the new Regiment by sending them personal application forms; that these forms had been sent out in advance of the publication of the White Paper; that the advertisements for recruits published in the press had been directed at the USC, thereby discouraging applications from Catholics; and, according to another opposition member, the establishment ceiling had been raised from 4,000 to 6,000 at the behest of the government to make sure that the force would be composed predominately of ex-B Specials.[6] In his reply Porter expressed his disappointment at the Opposition's changed attitude in the course of a week. He reminded them that Hunt had expressed the hope that ex-USC members would agree to join one of the forces. The Miskimmin letter had not been sent out in advance of the publication of the White Paper. It had included a form, but, he explained somewhat weakly, its purpose had been to ask each B Special whether he had any previous military experience and which of the two forces he would prefer to join. It was not an application form.

The 'application forms that weren't' had three side-effects. The Ministry of Defence issued instructions that the Miskimmin version was to be ignored and that the USC must use the same form as any other member of the public, and that they were not to be issued in bulk to USC districts. Healey, the Defence Minister, wrote to Porter that as a result of the controversy the passage of the UDR Bill might prove much more difficult than it would otherwise have been. To avoid any further misunderstanding, future public pronouncements by the Stormont Government about the UDR, such as recruiting advertisements, letters to USC members or MPs in circumstances that might lead to publicity, should first be cleared through the MOD or the GOC.

The third side-effect was the most telling; it sowed in the minds of the Nationalist MPs, and therefore the Catholic community, the first seeds of distrust about the new Regiment. It was the first mistake to be made in connection with the UDR, and, like others that were to follow over the years, it was not the UDR's fault.

On 31 October General Sir John Anderson was attending the London dinner of the Royal Army Education Corps, of which he had been Colonel Commandant, when he was approached by Field Marshal Sir Geoffrey Baker, Chief of the General Staff.

"After dinner he pulled up his chair and said to me confidentially, 'I think I have a little job for you. We are starting a new Regiment in Northern Ireland, and I would like you to be Colonel Commandant.' Naturally I touched my forelock and agreed."[7]

General Sir John's appointment was announced to coincide with the publication of the White Paper. A month earlier he had been appointed Pro-Chancellor of Queen's University. Commissioned into the 5th Inniskilling Dragoon Guards in 1929, he had had a distinguished career during and after the war, including Deputy Chief of the Imperial General Staff, Military Secretary and finally Commandant of the Imperial Defence College. In 1968 he retired and returned to County Down to settle at his mother's house at Ballyhossett, between Downpatrick and Ardglass.

From time to time there comes a man or woman who it seems has been chosen by destiny and groomed by ancestry, intellect and experience to fulfil a vital role at the time of their country's need. Winston Churchill was such a man. John Anderson was another. He was the ideal choice: an Ulsterman living in the North, an experienced soldier with contacts in the senior echelons of the Army, still of an age, and fit enough in the beginning to take on a very demanding task. He was respected at all levels and in particular in Downpatrick where he was active in charitable work to support the care of the mentally handicapped. He was President of the Army Art Society and a competent amateur artist who had had two pictures exhibited in the Royal Academy. He was a man who believed wholeheartedly in the ideal of Protestant and Catholic serving together in the new Regiment. He never spared himself in promoting the cause of the UDR. He was a regular visitor to the battalions and was known and held in great affection by all ranks. It is rare for soldiers to know their General, but they all knew Sir John. In a talk to Belfast Rotary Club in August 1971 he told members how in the five months between his appointment and the formation of the Regiment, and in the first months thereafter, he set out to encourage enlistment:

"When I was canvassing people, both lay and clerical, Catholic and Protestant, who I thought could help us in the early days, I said that it was well known that Irishmen of all persuasions had served happily together in the British Army for decades and indeed centuries and that community relations within the Army had always been outstandingly good. Here was our new Regiment, an integral part of the British Army, and so surely we could make a 'go' of it too on these lines, and on that basis we set out. Here was a real chance for us to make a positive contribution to a purpose so necessary to us all. So, to make the new Regiment succeed, and succeed it must, it was essential that both Protestant and Catholic should join it and no effort should be spared to this end. This would entail courage, hard work and persistence."[8]

For the past year Brigadier Logan Scott-Bowden – 'Scottie' to his contemporaries – had been attending a course at the Indian National Defence College in New Delhi. It was due to end in November and he had obtained permission from the Ministry of Defence to drive home overland with his family. He returned from a visit to Nepal to learn that the permission had been cancelled, on the grounds that he was needed urgently for a new appointment which for legislative reasons could not be disclosed. Once Parliament had approved the White Paper he learnt what his future was to be – to raise and command the Ulster Defence Regiment.

"Being isolated in India," he recalled wryly, "I was the only Brigadier in the British Army eligible for the appointment who had not heard about it on the grapevine and so had no opportunity to present reasons why I could not take on the job, such as the long-lost cousins in the South of Ireland who would be put at risk. For me it was too late."[9]

The Brigadier and his family flew to Bahrain where they had a two-day wait for an RAF transport. "They were wonderful peaceful days, and I guessed they would be the last we would have for a long time." On arriving home he spent a day at the Ministry of Defence being briefed by the Director of Military Operations and the Adjutant General on what had already been agreed as regards personnel, finance, recruiting, pay and legislation. Coming fresh from India,

"I had no idea about the turbulence and argument that had already occurred in the Ministry about the raising of a new part of the Army for operational duty in support of the civil power, including the controversy over the title of the new force."

So when he said he disliked the inclusion of the word 'Defence' on the grounds that "no battle, campaign or war was ever won by being defensive," his comment was not well received.

The Scott-Bowdens arrived in Northern Ireland just before Christmas. Such was the rush in which the Regiment was being formed that initially the only quarter available for them was in Omagh, almost the other side of the country from the Regimental Headquarters in Lisburn.

Like Anderson, Scott-Bowden was another soldier with a distinguished war record. As a young major in the Royal Engineers he had served in the Special Forces' Combined Operations Beach Reconnaissance and Assault Pilotage Parties. In January 1944, five months before D-Day, he carried out a reconnaissance of the Normandy beaches, landing from a midget submarine, accompanied by a Commando sergeant. On the day itself he accompanied the US 5th Corps in the perilous landing on Omaha Beach.[10]

His senior staff officer, Major Arthur French of the Royal Irish Rangers, remembered him as:

"a living caricature of a peppery senior Army officer and much loved by the Regiment. Although he looked ferocious, with red face, bristly white moustache and white hair, he had a heart of gold from his mid-morning cup of coffee onwards. In the early morning he was intolerant and would start a day with a programme of interviews with unfortunate staff officers from HQ Northern Ireland for him to devour. His PA would then go in, soothe the troubled brow, tender a cup of coffee, adjust the telephone, and all would be sweetness and light for the rest of the day.

"He knew little about Northern Ireland when he arrived but he took a great deal of trouble to understand the problems and the personalities so that the transition from B Specials to UDR could take place smoothly.

"He was also tireless in visiting all possible potential UDR bases throughout the land and later meeting the men assembled at night for operations or training. Even so he did not always get the temperature right, and I remember the Specials County Commandants selected to be the initial Commanding Officers of the seven battalions being stunned at an early briefing by his declaration that he supported civil rights."[11]

French and Major James Barden, Royal Artillery, set up Headquarters UDR on 1 January in a small bungalow behind the NAAFI shop in Thiepval Barracks, Lisburn. Scott-Bowden moved in a few days later. One of his first tasks was to confirm that he would accept the USC County Commandants as Commanding Officers for the six county battalions, and the deputy staff officer USC at Headquarters RUC to command the Belfast battalion. All had had service careers, five in the army, the other two in the Royal Navy. The GOC left the decision to Scott-Bowden and he had no hesitation in accepting all seven. In fact, it was the only practical choice. The County Commandants knew their areas and they knew their men, and, if they had not set an example, it is likely that few of their ex-Specials would have agreed to join the new Regiment.

During the debate on the unopposed second reading of the UDR Bill Roy Hattersley, the Minister of Defence (Administration) who had been made responsible for overseeing the detailed planning in setting up the UDR, informed the Commons of the appointment of an Advisory Council. The Council, which would be composed of influential civilians drawn equally from both communities, would review general recruiting policy and would report directly to the GOC. It met for the first time on 5 January under the chairmanship of the Colonel Commandant. The meeting opened with a presentation by the GOC, who said there was much the

Council could do to establish the Regiment as an effective, non-sectarian body and to get it accepted by all sections of the community. Anderson said it was vitally important for the Regiment to be established as a viable force as quickly as possible. There was a threat to the security of the State and this had to be met by a trained and organized force, which could only be effective if it contained members from, and had gained the sympathy of, all sections of the community. The Commander reported that to date there had been 182 applications to enlist, of which fifty-seven were from Catholics. Some members expressed concern about the selection of County Commandants as Commanding Officers, but accepted that for a limited period it would be necessary for practical reasons that some at least should be appointed.

Recruiting began on 1 January. Advertisements were published in the local papers: "There's a new Regiment in the Army. We want you to help us to form it." Applicants could fill in a coupon or they could pick up a leaflet and application form at any Regular or Territorial Army unit, at libraries, post offices and police stations. A press conference on the first day was attended by some thirty journalists, including BBC, ITN, RTE and representatives of the national and Irish newspapers. Ivor Richards, the Parliamentary Secretary of State for Defence, told them that the first two men to fill in application forms were both Catholics and that the government regarded the success of the UDR as a vital part of the process of reconciliation.

The name of the Regiment began to be heard frequently on radio and television. A one-minute television advertisement was compiled, which included a personal appeal for recruits by Scott-Bowden. As a result, with his distinctive features, he became for a while a well-known public figure, one of only two Commanders to achieve that doubtful, but nevertheless useful, distinction. As a result of all this publicity, a steady stream of applications began flowing in to Lisburn. The problem now was to vet them.

Hattersley had made a special point of spelling out to the Commons the arrangements for recruiting and vetting: "I want to make it absolutely clear that recruiting will be carried out by the (Regular) Army who will do the screening." Never at any time did the UDR have any responsibility for vetting. Battalions might complain that mistakes had been made, good men turned down or unreliable men accepted. Little attention was paid to these complaints, even though some may have been justified. Occasionally COs who persisted that a man's rejection could not be justified would be told in strict confidence why he had been turned down. The applicants themselves were never told. As Healey had warned, some men who had been involved in discreditable incidents in the previous year were rejected, including, it seems, the whole of the Tynan USC platoon involved in the shooting in Armagh.

False rumours were circulated that applicants were being turned down because they were members of the Orange Order. No doubt such rumours were begun by people who did not wish to reveal the real reasons for their rejection; and no doubt for some the allegation that they would be rejected because they belonged to the Order became an excuse for not applying to enlist.

The Army Security Vetting Unit (ASVU) arrived at Lisburn at the beginning of January. It consisted of some thirty-five vetting officers, mainly retired officers from outside Northern Ireland with no experience of local nuances, including a Vice Admiral and several Major Generals. They had been given an impossible task. They were under pressure from the staff at HQ UDR, who were worried that the Regiment would not be operational by the target date. Every applicant had to nominate two referees. Normally the vetting officer would interview both of them. In addition the application would be referred to the RUC Criminal Investigation Department and Special Branch. For the moment it would take far too long to adhere to that system. Instead it was officially agreed that applicants would be divided into three categories: those who were apparently acceptable and could be cleared without further ado; those who were obviously not and should be rejected; and those about whom there was some doubt. Only the third category was subject to a more detailed vetting. It may seem to have been a rough and ready system, but at that time the only Loyalist paramilitaries were the few in the Ulster Volunteer Force (UVF); the Ulster Defence Association (UDA) had not yet been formed and the IRA was only beginning to attract recruits.

On 13 January the seven Training Majors, one for each Battalion, reported to HQ UDR and assembled for a group photograph. According to one of them, they all had three things in common. None had previously served in Northern Ireland, all had come at short notice with resultant domestic upheaval and, perhaps most importantly, all had a sense of humour. The photographs were published in the *Newsletter* and papers in the Republic together with names, regiments and UDR battalions. Geoffrey Hill, bound for 6 UDR, recalled how Scott-Bowden "beamed at us like a benevolent Father Christmas and chuckled; 'The problems that you will have to face are enormous but not insurmountable. It is all quite simple. Go forth to your counties, recce them and raise a battalion, to be operationally ready in three months'."[12]

Despite the Commander's assurance, those first Training Majors were given an impossible task, to raise a battalion in less than three months and ensure it was operational on the day, without being able to give the recruits any prior military training. The Commanding Officers could give only limited help since, until the USC stood down on 30 April, they must continue to function as County Commandants. In four battalions the Adjutants designate were the USC County Adjutants and heavily involved in the winding up of their districts. So for the most part the Training Majors must manage on their own with a wholly inadequate staff: a Regular Army WO1 posted in as Quartermaster; a Corporal Clerk seconded from a local Regular unit and changed over every three months; a Civil Servant Clerical Officer as Chief Clerk, and a typist.

From the conference in Lisburn the Training Majors drove out to the barracks where they had been told their battalion headquarters were to be based:

Major G. D. Isaac RRW to the guardroom of the Depot The Royal Irish Rangers, Ballymena to form 1 (County Antrim) Battalion.
Major P. R. Adair Coldstream Guards to the former Depot of the Royal Irish Fusiliers at Gough Barracks, Armagh to form 2 (County Armagh) Battalion.
Major G. J. Entwistle RRF to a hutted camp at Ballykinlar, built during World War 1, to form 3 (County Down) Battalion.
Major K. W. Battson RWF to the ladies' rest room of the Territorial Army Centre in Enniskillen to form 4 (County Fermanagh) Battalion.
Major L. S. T. H. Pelham-Burn Coldstream Guards to the former Anti-Submarine Warfare School in Ebrington Barracks, Londonderry, to form 5 (County Londonderry) Battalion.
Major G. B. Hill King's Own Borderers to the education building in Lisanelly Barracks, Omagh to form 6 (County Tyrone) Battalion.
Major R. W. Wilson RWF to Palace Barracks, Holywood to form 7 (City of Belfast) Battalion.

Their first problem was to find a building for the Battalion Headquarters. Entwistle took over the guardroom of the Weekend Training Centre, a wooden hut that was at least half a century old. It was damp, and the lighting and heating were inadequate. At least it had toilet facilities, unlike the two huts in Palace Barracks where the staff, male and female, had a long walk to the facilities in the Sergeants' and Corporals' messes. So far as possible, accommodation for the companies was found in military barracks, including TA Centres. There was a reluctance to use USC platoon huts, for to do so would have been to give further ammunition to those who were claiming that the UDR was to be the USC under a new name. Some did continue to be used for several years, simply because there was nowhere else. Most importantly it was essential to ensure from the outset that Battalions were organized on the same basis as any other infantry battalion, with control of operations, training and administration central-ized at Battalion Headquarters and exercised through company commanders, unlike the Specials where command had been exercised at platoon level through the Sub-District Commandant.

During January applications began to flood in to the Vetting Unit at Lisburn at a rate of eighty to 100 each day. When Hattersley flew over on a day visit three weeks after recruiting had begun and had lunch with the Advisory Council, he was able to tell the press that so far 1,345 applica-tions had been received. About a quarter were from Catholics, 40% from members of the USC and 30% from men who had previous service in the Regular or Territorial Army. These were "ideal proportions", the Minister said. Soundings taken among some 200 people in Londonderry about their attitudes to the new Regiment had shown that a substantial majority of Protestants rejected the idea, but among Catholics, other than the Republican elements, over 60% were at least tolerant towards the UDR and a significant number were thinking of enlisting. The headmaster of an intermediate school was encouraging his pupils to join when they came of age.[13]

Meanwhile the County Commandants, with the help of their Adjutants and Training Majors, were spending their evenings visiting their districts and platoons to explain to their Specials how the UDR would be organized and to encourage them to obtain application forms. The response was mixed. Farmers were concerned that the Army would be less accommodating about excusing them from duties at times of milking or for the harvest. In some areas attempts were made to discourage the B men from joining. In Fermanagh the attitude of an influential member of the Orange Order did much to discourage enlistment. An SDC from the Antrim area was alleged to have ceased to give duties to any members of his platoon who volunteered for the UDR, telling them they would be better off joining the UVF. In Londonderry recruiting was so slow that when 5UDR became operational on 1 April, the battalion had only 200 men for the city and 300 for the county, compared with 600 and 1200 in the USC.[14] One County Adjutant, who was spending his mornings winding up the Armagh District and his afternoons as Adjutant designate of 2UDR enlisting recruits, visited the USC platoon at Bannfoot on the southern shores of Lough Neagh. They poured out their complaints about the way the USC had been treated, but refused to allow him to tell them about the UDR. "So I got into my car and came home. If I had stayed any longer I would probably have ended up in the Lough." It was Woods in County Down who faced the greatest problem. From the outset he emphasized the fact that Catholics would be welcome in the UDR. This did not go down well with some of the Specials. He encountered outright opposition from his County Adjutant, an ex-regular soldier. He had served Woods loyally in the past, but once the disbandment of the USC and the formation of the UDR had been announced, he began to campaign to discourage the Specials from joining the new force.

> "He started going round the Sub-Districts telling them to have nothing to do with the UDR," Wood recalled. "There was nothing I could do about it. Had I recommended his removal there would have been no one to ensure that all the weapons were withdrawn and the stores handed in. But it meant that at a time when I needed his backing, he failed to give it to me."[15]

Scott-Bowden himself addressed a number of gatherings of Specials,

> "explaining what would be required of them as soldiers, stressing that Protestants and Roman Catholics would serve with each other

and under each other. In some remote country areas my reception was far from friendly."[16]

The largest number of applications from the Specials came from the Border counties, Armagh, Fermanagh and Tyrone, understandably since they had practical experience over 50 years of the threat of IRA raiding parties crossing over from the South. Some three-quarters of the B men in Tyrone volunteered. Until two years previously the County Commandant had been a retired Brigadier and, perhaps more than any other county, they had been run on military lines. As 6UDR, they were from the beginning by far the largest battalion.

The smallest numbers to apply were in Down, mainly because of the County Adjutant's efforts to discourage them from doing so, and in Belfast a mere thirty-six had been accepted. The City Specials had always been more akin to conventional special constables than a paramilitary force and it was natural that they should feel more at home in the RUC Reserve. Overall by 1 April 2,424 Specials, 29% of the USC, had applied to join the new Regiment. Of these a thousand had had to be rejected, mainly on grounds of age and fitness. It was due to those who were accepted that the UDR did achieve the impossible by taking over operational duties three months after recruiting had begun.

It is a strange fact that, in such a small country, different areas of Northern Ireland have different characteristics as varied as the countryside that shapes them. This, coupled with the manner in which battalions had been raised in the first instance – those who were mainly USC and those who spread their net more widely – meant that throughout the 22 years each battalion had its own distinctive character. It was a wry joke among the staff that if the seven battalions were asked for an opinion, back would come seven different answers.

Every battalion was successful in attracting some Catholic recruits, some more than others. Many were ex-regular soldiers, pleased to get back into uniform. Scott-Bowden's first staff car driver was a former Corporal in the Royal Irish Rangers living in Ballymurphy. Once in an absent-minded moment he drove the Brigadier, in uniform, down the length of the Falls Road. Of the two companies raised in Londonderry, half were Catholics. One recalled that his application form had been signed by Hume who told him to go out and get all the decent Catholic people he could to enlist. No records exist to show the percentage of Catholic recruits to enlist per battalion, but by 1 April they numbered over a third of the total enlisted strength. By July Catholic recruiting in Belfast was very good; in Londonderry, Down and Antrim reasonably good, but the situation in the three Border counties gave cause for concern.[17]

Hattersley took a personal interest in the rate of Catholic recruitment. If it was successful, it would show that Protestant and Catholic could serve in harmony together. HQ UDR had to produce weekly returns for the Minister. According to French, they became experts in presenting statistics,

> "so that our political masters could be given the information they wanted to hear without straying from the truth. In our opinion the politicians were more concerned about what we called the 'spiritual breakdown' than about the military efficiency of the UDR."[18]

It was of course a concept alien to the Regular Army, where a man's religion is a matter for himself alone, but in these particular circumstances it was essential information. Nevertheless the Advisory Council doubted the wisdom of giving too much publicity to the breakdown of recruiting statistics lest it should lead to repercussions against Catholic recruits. It proved a perceptive comment.

An urgent problem was the recruiting of officers, for without Company and Platoon Commanders the sub-units could not be formed. Since there was no time to train them and they must receive instant commissions, they had to be men who had held commissions in one of the three services, including the Reserve forces, University Officer Training Corps or the Army Cadet Force, or else had been officers in the USC. Many of the Platoon Commanders were found among the Sub-District Commandants. They had no military background and were never conventional Army officers, but they did have the necessary leadership qualities, men respected within their community, who in times of crisis exercised a calming effect. Scott-Bowden foresaw that many of them would only be a stop-gap and would have to be replaced after the first year, but he admitted that when he returned to Regimental reunions in the years to come he found that a number had stayed on and had been a great success.[19] The fact that they had been accustomed to the relaxed discipline of the Specials meant that they brought to the UDR a kind of discipline that horrified subsequent Commanding Officers and Regimental Sergeant Majors, and yet it did no harm. It was one of the special qualities of the UDR. Frequently soldiers would be addressed by their Christian names. In many cases they were neighbours in the fields and at work benches, and often members of the same family. Some were employers and employees whose roles were reversed when they came on duty. A member of the Peerage, who was also a junior officer in one of the battalions, went down to breakfast one morning to find he could not have milk with his coffee as the milkman had not arrived. When he did come he scolded him for being late. That evening the Earl was due to go on duty, but was delayed and arrived late, to be reprimanded by his Company Commander – the milkman.[20]

In many cases the Sub-District Commandants were too old to take over command of the companies. In 3UDR, for instance, only one joined the battalion. The other three Company Commanders were a wartime Royal Marine Officer and two from the Territorial Army, one a Catholic. In 6UDR a former Sapper Officer in the Bombay Sappers and Miners was appointed to command two companies, Strabane and Castlederg, because of the shortage of suitable officers. The Cookstown Company Commander had served in the Fleet Air Arm, and a retired Wing Commander, a Catholic, was appointed as a captain in the Larne Company. In 7UDR eleven of the officers were ex-Regular and Territorial Army, two had been in the Indian Army, one in the American Army, one in the RAF and three in the USC.

The first recruits to be enlisted in 7UDR on 18 February were symbolically a 19-year-old Catholic and a 46-year-old Protestant with six years' Regular Army service. The GOC, the Colonel Commandant, the Commander and some members of the Advisory Council were present at their enlistment. The Training Major, Bob Wilson, administered the oath of allegiance, and the ceremony, held in the Northern Ireland War Memorial Building in central Belfast, was covered by press and television. Photographs of the two men were published on the front page of the *Daily Telegraph* and the *Belfast Telegraph*, the latter also including their names and addresses. Personal security had not yet become a concern. Among the nineteen soldiers sworn in that night, four were members of the USC.

In 6UDR the first man to be enlisted was a Catholic from Strabane. Reilly, the CO, had wanted his former PSI in the USC to be the first, but Scott-Bowden insisted it must be a Catholic, and he was duly enlisted. Three days later the battalion received notification from the vetting unit that the man was not cleared for service. Deeply embarrassed, not least because the man's name had appeared in the local paper, Hill, the Training Major, persuaded the vetters to rescind their decision. But it was too late, the recruit had heard of his rejection, stormed into Battalion Headquarters, threw down his equipment and told the staff what they could do with it and the UDR.[21]

Although the number of applications was reasonably satisfactory, the business of vetting and of persuading applicants to arrange for their own doctors to give them medical examinations was a slow process. On 12 February Porter wrote to the Minister of Defence and the GOC saying that, bearing in mind that to date not one recruit had enlisted in the UDR, Stormont Ministers were very concerned that the Regiment would be insufficiently strong to take over from the USC by 1 April. They were firmly of the opinion that the Specials must remain in being until the effective strength of the Regiment was at least 4,000. Since he, Porter, saw little chance of that being achieved by 31 March, he intended to review the position in mid-March with a view to putting back the USC stand-down date. Healey and the GOC sought to reassure him that any shortfall would be covered by the Regular Army.[22] In fact the government had seriously underestimated the time it would take to enlist and vet 4,000 men, but politically it would have been unacceptable to put back the date. By 1 April only 1,606 had been enlisted.

The daunting task of ensuring battalions were organized and ready to take over operational duties in less than three months' time fell to the small battalion headquarters staff. The typist in 7UDR's headquarters in Palace Barracks, Holywood recorded how

> "The CO, Training Major, Adjutant, Corporal Clerk and myself all shared one office. There was no office equipment worth talking about, and we all worked at camp tables. The application forms were placed on the floor in alphabetical order. The heating consisted of a coke fire but it was generally not lit as there was no one but ourselves to lay and light it. It was just a case of everyone muscling in together. It created a great feeling of comradeship."

Details of recruits were passed down from Headquarters Northern Ireland as soon as they had been cleared for service. Enlistments had to take place in the evenings as men were at their civilian jobs by day. The men were interviewed, allocated to companies according to where they lived, and those with previous service were noted as potential NCOs. By day the Part 2 Orders bringing them on strength had to be typed out, duplicated using the old-fashioned and very messy rotary duplicators (it was at least two years before photocopiers were issued) and despatched to the Infantry Manning and Records Office in York. Uniforms were issued, the same olive green combat kit as worn by the Regular Army, green berets with the new gold coloured badges, steel helmets and '37 pattern webbing equipment. In addition there were two pairs of hob-nailed boots, puttees, two shirts, drawers cellular and two pairs of 'long johns'. The puttees caused the greatest mystification. One soldier, reporting for duty for the first time, on being asked why he had failed to put them on, replied that he thought they were bandages. The long johns caused derision; "Rather strange things with a big opening at the back; me and my wife could have climbed inside them and there would still have been room to spare." Some of the webbing had been dyed black for issue to the USC, and, to ensure uniformity in battalions, instructions were given that all equipment should be in the same colour. One soldier, misunderstanding the orders, duly black-dyed his webbing and his uniform, shirts and underpants. Standing Orders had to be written covering duties and discipline, and orders for each key point guard. The MOD had drawn up 'UDR Regulations' They were based on regulations for the Territorial Army, yet, contrary to what some branches of the MOD continued to believe for a long time into the future, there were only passing similarities between the UDR and the TA. As a result parts of the regulations were irrelevant, others ambiguous, and Barden, at HQUDR, made frequent flights across to London to seek clarification. Crates of pamphlets were received from Ordnance, made up in accordance with some standard list for an infantry battalion, regardless of the fact that some, such as loading plans for RAF transport aircraft, were irrelevant. Those that were essential, Queen's Regulations and the Manual of Military Law, arrived unamended, accompanied by a stack of amendments as large as the books.

Training Majors visited the key points to assess the size of guard each would require and, from that calculation, the capacity of the battalion to guard them. Those that the battalion was as yet too weak to take on were handed over to the Regular Army. Later some guards which the Specials had been providing nightly for years were discarded as unnecessary. The reservoirs at the Silent Valley in the Mournes and Seaghan Dam south of Armagh were so substantial that the RAF's Dam Buster Squadron would have been hard put to it to damage them. The Carnmoney Company spent many a night guarding the pumping house at Lough Mourne reservoir until the Company Commander asked to be shown where it was, only to discover it had been demolished months ago; his men had been guarding a hole in the ground.

> "It was a nightmare," the Adjutant of 2UDR recalled, looking back to those early days. "Seven days a week, I would be signing on recruits until midnight, getting home at 1am, leave next morning at quarter past eight and not finish until midnight again. Literally there were times when I did not know which day of the week it was."

With days to go Ken Battson in 4UDR was faced with an urgent problem, a shortage of ammunition, "so I put the word out, no questions asked, I needed some. Goodness knows where it came from but the response was overwhelming and I did not need to indent for ammunition for a long time." On 31 March he went into Woolworths in Enniskillen to buy torches for the next night's patrol.[23] That night Frank Jones, the SDC for Portadown, was on patrol as usual with his platoon of Specials. At midnight they stopped to change from their black police uniforms into the Army olive green and went on with the patrol.

In the early hours of the morning in 6UDR operations room Geoffrey Hill and his Operations Officer celebrated their achievement in getting the show on the road.

> "I remember putting the cork back firmly in the bottle and telling them, 'This is only the beginning. We are on again tonight, tomorrow night and every night. There is no turning back, we are on a tread-mill, and we're on it till the end of time'."

The same night, and for two nights following, the Army was involved in fierce street battles with rioting Catholic youths in the Ballygomartin and Springfield Roads. They were the first major clashes between Catholics and the Army. For the first time in Belfast extensive use was made of CS gas and thirty-eight soldiers were injured by stones and bottles.

CHAPTER THREE

1970–1971

On 1 April 1970 The Ulster Defence Regiment joined the order of battle of the British Army and became operational on the same day. Hattersley came over from London to watch patrols from 7UDR being mounted in Palace Barracks. Entwistle, the Training Major of 3UDR, determined that from the outset his men would have better accommodation than the Specials, spent the day moving in army bin lorries to use as guardrooms. A sergeant in the Downpatrick Specials, now a sergeant in the UDR, was commanding the guard on a pumping station on the water pipeline from the Silent Valley to the City. His guard had a wide spectrum of military experience: RAF Navigator; sailor from HMS *Ark Royal*; one had served in the Royal Welch Fusiliers; another with the Free French Forces; one was an ex B Special.

In Fermanagh A Company 4UDR carried out their first mobile patrol under an ex-Sergeant in the Specials, who was appointed Corporal for the night. A Landrover and driver/radio operator had been borrowed from the Regular Army and the five-man patrol carried out a series of road blocks. The patrol was about to set out when a small problem arose; each man had a .303 rifle, but no ammunition. Ten rounds per man were borrowed from the RUC.

The Newry Company Commander took a patrol out to Hilltown and the Spelga Dam, using a Landrover and a three-tonner, with a knife-rest and barbed wire coils to set up a roadblock, and hurricane lamps to signal motorists to stop. Waved in a circle to attract the driver's attention, they were liable to blow out at the vital moment.

Elsewhere companies carried on with the duties that many had carried out the night before as Specials, guarding key points.

Once the men had been formed into platoons, the NCOs had to be appointed on the spot. In Armagh the men of 2UDR assembled in the miniature range, with those officers who had already been selected.

"We had a battalion of private soldiers," the Adjutant recalled. "First we formed them into companies, then we asked them who their NCOs should be. After all they knew them better than anyone else. It was a long session, but by the end of it we had chosen the Sergeants and Corporals."

For the most part the NCOs selected had been Sergeants in the USC, or had held non-commissioned ranks in the regular forces or the Territorial

Army. For the Newry Company Commander the choice was easy. He was virtually reforming the old Newry Territorial Army Company of the Royal Irish Fusiliers, which had been disbanded some two years previously. In fact he had commanded the same TA company in the same modern drill hall that now became his UDR Company Centre. Many of the former TA volunteers had enlisted in the UDR, and he was able to select as his NCOs men who had been his NCOs in the TA, supplemented by ex-USC Sergeants. A high proportion of the Newry men were Catholics and the company had the highest Catholic percentage membership of any company in the UDR. He noticed that during the canteen break on the first training night, the two groups, ex-USC and ex-TA, kept apart, not on grounds of religion but because they did not know each other.

> "The next training night we ordered in some drink and opened up the bar in the canteen. I looked in at 10.30 and couldn't believe my eyes. The ex-Specials and ex-TA, including the Catholic blokes, were mixing. From there on we never looked back."

In some battalions, for the first weeks until there had been a chance to assess their worth, soldiers were appointed Lance Corporals for the night, the badge of rank being issued with the equipment for the patrol.

In later years new Commanding Officers would sometimes ask why some man had been selected for promotion. The answer was that at the time there was no one else. In fact few mistakes were made, though there was one problem not foreseen at the time. The filling of senior ranks with comparatively young men with years of service ahead of them was to cause a promotion block in the years to come.

There was an urgent need to train the companies. The first priority, as laid down by HQUDR, was to give refresher training to those who had served in the forces in the past; then to train the 25% who had no previous service experience, and finally the ex-Specials, who were already well used to handling the No.4 rifle and carrying out key point guards and patrols. The training teams in battalions were overstretched – the Training Major, a Regular Army Permanent Staff Instructor and a full-time PSI from the UDR in each company. Most of the last named had been Sergeant Instructors in the USC and, prior to that, had served in the Regular Army. Regular Army units provided instructors to help out with the training. The Parachute Battalion in Palace Barracks set up a small UDR training team. One member was a Greek Cypriot named Giorgio. Unfortunately Giorgio and two friends decided to rob Clandeboye Post Office, were caught and imprisoned. On his release he became a mercenary in Angola under the name of 'Colonel Callan', where he put to death a number of the white mercenaries under his command for alleged cowardice, and eventually was himself executed.

The annual training commitment for each soldier was twelve days and twelve two-hour training periods. Part of the twelve days included attendance at an annual camp. Provided the soldier fulfilled these commitments and was available for duty, he was entitled to an annual tax-free bounty of £25 a year.

In the early years the soldiers' lack of enthusiasm for training was a source of concern to commanders and Army staffs. Apart from days spent on the ranges, attendance at training sessions was poor. Instead of a day's pay the soldiers received a training expense allowance of 8s 6d (about 45p) a day for a Corporal and below, and 10s 3d (51p) for a Senior NCO. Travel allowance was not admissible. Though the bounty was welcome, it was initially substantially less than that paid to the TA. It was not that, in those early days, people had joined the UDR for the money, but when a man had been on duty once or twice a week and then given up his Sunday to train, the training expense allowance did seem very poor recompense.

In any case in the beginning the amount of military knowledge a soldier required was limited. Provided he knew how to handle his weapon safely, carry out a VCP and read a map, that was about the sum of it. Some men never did learn how to read a map reference. What was the point, they reasoned, when everyone knew the local area as well as their back yards? 'Willie John's farm,' or 'the loanins' or 'Fourmilecross' was a far more precise indication than an eight-figure reference, specially if you never could remember whether the Eastings or Northings came first. When companies began to be deployed outside their own areas, the need for the map reading instruction became more acute. A primary school head-master and commander of the Coleraine Company recounted the briefing of one of his patrols, tasked to carry out VCPs on the roads north of Belfast, well outside their accustomed area:

'"Right boys, there's about enough of you now for two VCPs so gather up all your kit and dump it in the back of that four-tonner over there as it's all we've got. Don't forget your flask and sand-wiches!'

'Now listen men the Training Major says we have to set up two VCPs at Grid—'

'What the hell's a grid, Sir?'

'Don't you know what a Map Reference is?'

'No Sarge, I don't know what that is either!'

"By now the poor PSI is beginning to realize that an Orders Group can have unforeseen difficulties. However, he has an inspiration.

'Gordon, aren't you a lorry driver? Good! Come here till I show you this map. I want one lot dropped here and the other there.'

'Ach! I know where that is. That one's the Horseshoe Bend and that's at the back of Hannahstown. Don't worry I'll get them there. If you make sure there's oil in the hurricane lamps I'll check the rest of the kit!'

"They found the Horseshoe Bend easily but the other VCP caused a bit more bother, including a stop outside the GOC's house, where of course the guard did not know where Hannahstown was either. Gordon and his boys did get there, however, just in time to be visited by the CO, who congratulated them on their map reading!"

The staff decreed that everyone must fire five rounds with their rifle before being allowed to go on operations. The only member of the Specials to enlist initially from the Garvagh platoon recalled:

"We were told to come forward to the 200 yard firing point where rifles and ammunition were waiting for us and told to fire ten rounds in our own time at four foot square targets. When we'd finished, the next detail came forward and got down and proceeded to fire the same rifles. I asked the sergeant in charge what I had scored. 'We're not keeping scores.' he said. 'All we're here for is to establish that you can handle a rifle safely. Now we know you can, so you've passed your recruit course and can go out on operations.' Apart from a course on radio procedures, that was all the training I ever did until I was promoted to Sergeant."

Training on voice procedure was a novelty to most people, including the ex-soldiers since the Army procedure had recently been radically changed and the USC had never had radios anyway. As soon as a suitable officer could be found, he was appointed Regimental Signals Officer (RSO). In 3UDR this was a producer in Ulster Television. Until he took a firm grip, the voice procedure was based on the remembrance of TV serials – 'Roger, over and out' or the Citizens' Band jargon that had recently arrived from America. A voice coming out of the night over a battalion net, "Are there any friendly bears out there?" Irate CO, "Get off the bloody air." Hurt pause, and plaintive voice comes back again, "You're not a friendly bear."

Initially there were no radios and the patrols made a point of carrying coins with them and setting up their VCPs close to a kiosk so that they could report back by telephone to battalion. When the radios did arrive, they were the C42 and A41 sets on issue to the Regular Army, the former carried in the back of a Landrover, the latter man-portable. Both were difficult to operate and, despite broadcasting on VHF, were limited in range, particularly in the rolling Ulster countryside. These were soon supplemented by Pye Bantams, a civilian-pattern short-range radio, suitable for a policeman on the beat to talk to a colleague down the street, but useless for enabling patrols or guards to keep in touch with their base. Before long the C42s were replaced by Pye Westminster sets. They were still single-frequency with a limited range but, by installing a larger set as a rebroadcast station on a prominent hill, the range could be greatly increased. In 1UDR the rebroadcast station was attached to a Post Office tower in the Antrim Hills. It gave the RSO some disturbed nights.

"A fault would develop in the land line and put the 'rebro' into permanent send. With 100 watts output it would completely black out communications across the whole of County Antrim, and by the time I could get up there with the GPO duty engineer the set would be so hot you could have fried eggs on it."

For the first weeks the Regiment's operational efficiency fell far below that of the USC's. After three weeks the total trained strength was less than a quarter of the Specials establishment of 8,600. A small number of military vehicles had been issued, but soldiers were still deploying to their key point guard locations in their private cars, and in some cases using them to send out mobile patrols. Knife-rests draped in barbed wire continued to be used for setting up road blocks, though some platoons had dispensed with hurricane lamps by purchasing their own hand torches. John Adams, headmaster of the primary school in Mountnorris, ex-SDC of the Hamiltonsbawn platoon and now commanding one of the Armagh companies of 2UDR, to use his own words,

> "nearly had a mutiny on my hands. There were a lot of complaints. We came to join the UDR, we were promised good clothing, we still had the old ammunition boots that you could have heard a mile off. We were promised vehicles to do VCPs, and we had none of these. After three weeks we were still carrying out the same old Seagahan guard. One of my Corporals came to me and said, 'Look, Major, I'm staying in this another fortnight. There has to be something done, or I'm out.' So I went and read the riot act, and something was done. We were taken off that guard."[1]

In Larne six men resigned because they were having to travel to their guard duties unarmed.

The MOD had instructed that, unlike the USC who had kept their rifles at home, the UDR weapons must be kept in centralized armouries, but the only available armouries were in TA centres or Army barracks. The soldiers of 4UDR were given special dispensation to keep their weapons, whilst in 6UDR Hill risked court martial by rescinding the order on his own authority until such time as the Battalion was given official permission to hold on to theirs. In other battalions some PSIs were collecting rifles from armouries, loading them into private cars to take them out to key point guards, returning in the early hours to withdraw the weapons and take them back to the armouries, travelling in the dark and unescorted. John Adams' company, now moved to Newry, would send a four-tonner each night to Tandragee transformer station, a journey of thirteen miles, picking up unarmed soldiers en route. At Tandragee, where there was an arms store, some of the men would be dropped off to guard the transformer and the rest would be issued with their arms and taken another thirteen miles to the water filtration plant at Castor Bay on the shores of Lough Neagh.[2] At the end of the night the process would be reversed. In Banbridge the men would report for duty at the company base, Finney's, a former greengrocery in the main street, travel unarmed down to Newry to collect their weapons, turn round and go back to

Banbridge to carry out patrols. It was not just that the arrangements were impractical and highly insecure, they added as much as an hour, or more, at either end of a night's duty, and men were having to leave home for their civilian jobs the following morning having been awake all night.

Those companies that did have an armoury were given authority to recruit twelve men to provide a full-time security guard force. They were known as 'conrates', from the fact that they received consolidated rates of pay, a pay scale adopted originally for the Territorial Army to cover the small number of soldiers employed full-time at TA Centres. Initially the CO, Adjutant, the PSI in each company and the members of these security guards were the only full-time members of the UDR; these few were the forerunners of the permanent cadre who in the final years composed half the strength of the Regiment. For the soldiers the rate of pay was so small that it was difficult to find volunteers for the security guards, and the standard was low.

In the early years few of the part-time soldiers who enlisted did so because of the pay they would receive, although it was more generous than the Specials' annual bounty of £12, for which they had to carry out at least one patrol a month, plus £1 for each additional patrol. The UDR's rates were the same as the Regular Army's. An unmarried Private 1st Class with less than six years' previous service received £2.19 a day, a Corporal £3.3s, a Sergeant £3.12s, a Captain on appointment £5.6s and a Major £7.2s.

A problem, never resolved, concerned the unemployed soldier. Aggravated by the troubles, the level of unemployment in Northern Ireland was rising. These men could have been, indeed were, a valuable source of manpower for the UDR, particularly because they were available to do duties by day and in the early hours. The problem was that for every day that an unemployed soldier did an operational duty with his company his unemployment benefit for that day would be deducted. To many it simply did not seem worth it, especially when one was putting one's life at risk, and the ruling was a disincentive to recruitment. Though representations were made to successive Under-Secretaries of State for the Army, nothing could be done; the same arrangement applied to members of the Territorial Army, the Ambulance Service and Fire Brigade, and any other unemployed person engaged in part-time public service.[3]

By the end of April the total number of duties carried out by the Regiment was 3,882; in July, the holiday month, it reached its peak with 14,056. By the end of the year the average for each month was 9,870. In every month the largest number of duties was carried out by 6UDR. They were the strongest battalion with the most trained men. In the beginning Tyrone was quiet, with few key points that needed to be guarded in the county. The main IRA threat was concentrated in Belfast and many of the major key points such as radio and television masts lay on the periphery of the city. Thus from the beginning 6UDR found themselves being tasked well outside their own county. For several months they provided the night guards on the BBC station at Lisnagarvey. On two or three occasions the Battalion deployed soldiers in double-decker buses as far as Belfast to carry out VCPs on the main routes into the city. It made for a long night, setting out about 7 pm and, for the companies in the west of the county, finally returning home at 6 am. In time other battalions too were allocated tasks well outside their own counties. Scott-Bowden encouraged such tasking. He was keen to ensure that the men could deploy where the need was greatest and to get away from the USC concept that men became Specials to protect only their own localities.

On 30 April 6UDR, along with 2UDR, took part in the first major operation involving the UDR. Mounted by 8 Infantry Brigade, it was designed to intercept movement of munitions from the South across the Fermanagh, Tyrone and Armagh borders. As well as the 400 from the UDR, 1,600 regular soldiers took part, the first operation on this scale to be carried out by the Regular Army along the Border.

It was not only the UDR that was finding its feet, but the Regular Army and the IRA as well. Although active in the Civil Rights movement, the IRA had been almost non-existent as a military force. In the August 1969 riots there were only some half a dozen gunmen and ten weapons to defend the Catholic areas.[4]

In December the organization split in two, Officials and Provisionals, over the issue of whether to give at least token recognition to the parliaments in London and Dublin.[5] The Official IRA (OIRA) adopted a policy of political action with Marxist undertones, while the Provisionals (PIRA) chose the traditional IRA policy of 'armed struggle'. The Officials did not eschew violence entirely, indeed they were responsible for some of the most notorious acts over the next two years, including the murder of a soldier in the Royal Irish Rangers whilst on leave at his home in the Bogside; but it was this deed that so enraged local opinion that the Officials declared a ceasefire, while retaining the right to act in self-defence. It was the Provisional policy of direct action that found favour with the people of West Belfast and it was there that they began to set up their organization.

In June the Labour Government lost the General Election. The change of government came at a sensitive time. Callaghan had taken a detailed personal interest in the decisions of the security forces, reckoning that "my political knowledge and instinct was of use in measuring the consequences of any proposed action by the Army or the police"[6]. Maudling, his Conservative successor at the Home Office, believed that decisions should be taken by the people on the spot. As a result Stormont's Joint Security Committee, under Chichester-Clark, was now free to decide tactics.

As the summer marching season approached, when the Orange Lodges commemorated the Battle of the Boyne, trouble flared up between the two communities. Shots were exchanged, leading to the death of five

Protestants and a member of the IRA, and the wounding of twenty-nine people, including three soldiers hit by gunfire.

As rioting spread and the regular battalions were drawn into the city, the GOC ordered the first call-out of the UDR from 28 June until 19 July. Some 2,037 soldiers, 80% of the total trained strength, answered the call. Key points were reinforced, additional guard duties taken on to relieve the Regular Army, road checks placed on roads leading into the city and along the Border. Within 30 minutes of receiving the call-out order 4UDR had manned the first vehicle check points along the Fermanagh border and by the next day 252 men were manning all nineteen VCPs.

On 3 July the fiercest rioting to date flared up in the Falls, following the search of a house by the Army and the police. Fifteen pistols, a rifle and a sub-machine gun were found. A hostile crowd gathered, the Army fired CS gas canisters to disperse them. Buses were hijacked to block the main roads. Grenades and petrol bombs were thrown. The rioting increased in ferocity and at 10pm, after reports had been received that the IRA intended to take on the Army that night, the GOC, for the first and only time, imposed a curfew on the Lower Falls. People were ordered to stay in their houses, apart from a two-hour shopping break. The Army secured the area and carried out searches for further weapons. The rioting continued, with the troops coming under fire, but by daylight on the 4th the worst was over and the curfew was lifted next day after 35 hours. Four civilians had been killed by the Army, thirteen soldiers wounded by gunfire and another five by a grenade. Over 100 assorted weapons, nearly 21,000 rounds of ammunition, 25lb of explosives and 100 incendiaries had been found. The security forces had fired 1,385 CS gas cartridges and some 1,500 rounds of ammunition.[7] The last remnants of the honeymoon period between the Catholic community and the Army had ended. The Provisionals had been seen by the local community to be taking effective action and had won valuable support. Belfast had entered a new and more deadly phase. No longer inter-communal riots, but gun battles between the security forces and armed terrorists.

One of the lessons of this first call-out was that the holding of weapons in centralized armouries greatly slowed down the response. 4UDR had been able to react so quickly only because they held their weapons at home. From then on the weapons policy was changed. In future soldiers outside the cities were permitted to keep their weapons. Orders for safe custody were strict. So long as the soldier was out of the house, the weapon must be broken down into its components – in the case of the No.4 rifle the body, the bolt and the ten rounds of ammunition – and each concealed in a separate hiding place.

After the Falls curfew the second half of the year was relatively quiet. In retrospect Brian Faulkner maintained that the ineffectiveness of the UDR over the period enabled the IRA to rearm and build up their strength unmolested and regretted that Stormont had allowed itself to be persuaded that the stand-down for the Specials could not be postponed.[8]

However, the period of quiet did enable the Regiment to get on with the urgent business of recruiting and training.

Recruitment was slow. In some weeks wastage exceeded enlistment. After six months the strength was 3,660. Five of the battalions had recruited an average 82% of their establishment, but 5UDR had little more than half and 3UDR substantially less. During the winter a recruiting campaign was mounted. Advertisements appeared in local and provincial papers and a new recruiting film was screened on television. The results were disappointing. By January the strength passed the 4,000 mark, but the wastage rate was worryingly high and the net increase over the next six months was under 200. Too many Catholics were leaving. For some the Falls Road curfew had sown the first seeds of doubt as to whether they wanted to be associated with the Army.

The establishment for officers was 248; by the end of July, 180 had been appointed, but only nine of these were Catholics.

The first commissioning course to appoint new officers from the ranks was held at Ballykinlar for two weeks in July 1970. The syllabus covered leadership at platoon level, tactics, fieldcraft, map reading, staff duties and first aid. One of the students, a member of the Kells Platoon recalled:

"It was great fun. I was 42 at the time, and I was one of the younger ones. There were some who were probably over sixty. The staff chased us about Ballykinlar and marched us from the huts to Abercorn Barracks every morning, and galloped us over the sand-dunes. The assault course was the worst part, but we were pretty good, we could stick it alright."

Another remembers practising laying ambushes and learning anti-ambush tactics:

"I felt a degree of horror when the instructor referred to the 'killing ground'. It was something outside my experience in the 'Bs'. I was greatly surprised when we were told that if we were fired on we should rush straight at the enemy; most of us would have thought of running in the opposite direction."

As a result of the course a further twenty-one officers were commissioned. A second course for thirty-six officers was run at Ballykinlar in the following April by Lieutenant Colonel Dion Beard, the first Commanding Officer from the Regular Army. With the assistance of four of the Training Majors as instructors, they drew up a syllabus and divided the students into four syndicates.

"The course went very well, but from the start it was apparent that some of the ex-Specials were there because of their length of service rather than their leadership qualities. I discussed this with the Training Majors who were aware of the problem and even suggested that if some of the older ones failed I would be doing the

Commanding Officers a favour. Naturally we kept a particular eye on the borderline cases, and at the end there were about five whose age and motivation in our opinion made them unsuitable for a commission.

"When I reported this to Brigadier Scott-Bowden he blew his top, as only he could. He took the view that we had been given the job of turning all the cadets into officers and that it was us, and particularly myself, who had failed. Having had the support of the Training Majors in the assessment, I said that we could not change our considered view, but that if he wished to award them a commission against our advice, it was up to him. The remark caused such a charge of colour that I feared for his health. However, as the cadets were already assembled for the commissioning ceremony, an instant compromise was needed. We agreed that the cadets in question should be told that they had not done very well on the course and that their commissions would be reviewed at the end of a year. In any case under UDR Regulations all new officers spent their first year on probation before their commissions were confirmed."[9]

The UDR ran one more Commissioning Course in October 1972. Thereafter all potential officers attended the two-week TA course held at Mons Officer Cadet School. When Mons closed down the course was run at the Royal Military Academy, Sandhurst. One cadet, who much later was to become one of the two Regimental Lieutenant Colonels, attended the third course at Sandhurst in March 1973. Of the twenty-nine students, a quarter came from the UDR. Though the course was physically taxing enough, it provided the unforeseen bonus of a fortnight's uninterrupted sleep.

"As would be expected the UDR contingent excelled at shooting and internal security matters but obviously knew little about defence against tanks or nuclear warfare. The Directing Staff regarded us with a manifest curiosity, coupled with a real desire to know what conditions were like in Northern Ireland at that time. In syndicate discussions the UDR's specialist role and practical knowledge was acknowledged, and our greater experience was self-evident on exercises. As we were able to talk from first hand about bombings and shootings and prison guards, our contributions were all the more interesting and relevant, both for the DS and for our fellow students from the Territorial Army. We were certainly not patronized, but we did feel we were viewed as having come down from the North-West Frontier."

By March 1971 the number of Catholic officers was eighteen and the total number of officers was just about sufficient for the battalions at their present strength.

Well before the first year was out the question of the future

Commanding Officers had to be resolved. The example set by the County Commandants in agreeing to form the UDR battalions had had the desired effect of encouraging many of their Specials to enlist in the new force. But several were already well past the retiring age for the Regular Army; they had agreed only to take on the job for a year and they were anxious to go. Torrens-Spence, who was by far the most senior lieutenant colonel in the Army list, had no army experience but had served for 33 years in the Royal Navy. He had had a distinguished career in the Fleet Air Arm, winning the DSO as the pilot of a Swordfish torpedo bomber during the raid that virtually wiped out the Italian fleet in the harbour at Taranto. In the post-war years he commanded the aircraft carrier *Albion* from '59 to '60. He once remarked to his Adjutant that he would have felt happier commanding a UDR battalion if he had had an aircraft carrier on Lough Neagh. Desmond Woods, who at one time had been the youngest holder of the Military Cross, had done a spell as General Montgomery's ADC in Kent in 1941, and won a second MC with 2nd London Irish Rifles in Italy, had been taken ill and stood down as CO 3UDR before his year was up. Two others were ready to retire.

The MOD agreed that these four should be replaced by four Regular Army officers and that the other three should be given extensions for a further two years.

Scott-Bowden never regretted his decision to accept USC County Commandants as the first COs. Nevertheless, according to French at HQUDR, there was from the outset some concern as to how they might react in an emergency.

"We regarded the Training Majors as sort of commissars. We had them half-watching their COs to ensure that they were behaving as military commanders and not as USC County Commandants might have done. If he did have a problem, the Training Major had direct access to HQUDR. They were all very carefully picked senior Majors, people who did not care whether they were liked or not, or if they were at loggerheads with their COs."[10]

Initially the decision to appoint Regular Army Commanding Officers was not universally popular. One of the four ex-County Commandants wrote in his account of his year in command of 5UDR that he

"whose home and family had long been established in Co Londonderry handed over command to Lieutenant Colonel Lys, an officer with no previous experience of Northern Ireland and, in accordance with MOD policy, a Roman Catholic. His religion did not affect in any way those who had already joined the battalion, but to the people of the county, from whom it was hoped to draw still more recruits, the appointment was attributed as a gesture to encourage the inherently disloyal section of the community to enlist, with the result that the Loyalists decided they would keep out."[11]

The first Regular Army CO, Dion Beard of the Royal Tank Regiment, took over command of 3UDR on 15 February 1971. A couple of weeks later a small bomb damaged a wooden hut close to Battalion Headquarters in Ballykinlar. It was thought to have been detonated by Loyalist extremists as a protest against his appointment, though there were some who said he had placed it himself as a means of injecting some urgency into the need for a security fence around the camp. At that time it was completely unprotected and open to the country road that ran alongside.

In later years some Unionist politicians maintained that the UDR should be commanded by Ulstermen and that Commanding Officers should be found from within the Regiment. The fact was that commanding a battalion was an intensely demanding job and no part-time officer could take it on unless he was prepared to give up his civilian employment for at least a couple of years, and none could be expected to do it for more than five years. Having commanded, there was no other UDR Lieutenant Colonel's appointment on the establishment. This meant that a UDR officer promoted to command was in effect accepting that in five years his time in the Regiment must end, and that at a comparatively early age he would be without a job. In any case the implied criticism of the Regular officers was wholly unjustified. By far the majority of COs, Training Majors and Quartermasters committed themselves to their battalion, to the Regiment and, it followed, to the cause of Northern Ireland whole-heartedly and unsparingly and without concern for their future careers. Even if at first they viewed their appointments with some apprehension, their battalions won them over. One cannot command a battalion on operations and not become committed to its cause. A very few failed. Most, looking back, would say that their time in the UDR was the best years of their lives.

There were in any case practical advantages to the system. It ensured that every two years there was an injection of new blood, men in their late 30s or early 40s, who, as time went on, had probably completed several tours around Northern Ireland. The COs of regular battalions and the staffs of brigade headquarters were their contemporaries and that helped to foster a better understanding of the UDR within the Regular Army, its capabilities, strengths and weaknesses. Some COs must have been irritated when, on introducing some new idea, they would be told by their Company Commanders that their predecessors three or more back had tried that and it did not work. A wise CO would bide his time and make no dramatic changes in his first six months. As the years went by a considerable number of regular officers – in the region of 400 – had served in the UDR and a very useful 'old boy' network grew up whereby, if one wanted a favour or to short-circuit the system, it was often possible to find in the right place someone with UDR experience and a great well of good-will on which one could draw existed throughout the Army. In the latter years a number of COs rose to General rank.

During the first year training was mainly concentrated on ensuring that every soldier had fired his rifle and passed his Annual Personal Weapons Test. During the summer four of the battalions held their first annual camps at Ballykinlar and Magilligan. Training on deployment of patrols by Wessex helicopter was introduced. For men who had never flown before and who, among the older men, had in their youth driven to market in horse and cart, the sight of their homes and farmsteads from a thousand feet up was a novel and exciting experience. The patrols practised 'roping down', climbing out of the side doors of the helicopter as it hovered 30 feet above ground and lowering themselves hand-over-hand down a rope; the method was soon abandoned since it was much slower than putting the men directly on the ground and made the aircraft more vulnerable to ground fire. For the individual it called for a certain amount of stamina and strong arms, climbing down hand-over-hand. In Fermanagh some slid straight down the rope, until the pilot complained that it was being damaged by farmers' hoary hands. One soldier, on being instructed by his Training Major to grip the rope with both hands, let go with the left, then let go with the right, did just that and hurtled down into a bog.

However, when Headquarters Northern Ireland produced a paper reviewing the progress of the UDR at the end of its first year the report was encouraging. The Regiment was now providing roughly 250 men per night to guard sixteen key points, including four Border police stations, plus on average seventeen nightly patrols. Battalions had made an important contribution to security by taking part in pre-planned contingency operations with the Regular Army. In July, when trouble had been expected in the gaol, 2UDR, reinforced by 3 and 6UDR, had co-ordinated the setting-up of twelve road blocks on the roads into Armagh, themselves providing six of the blocks and two heliborne patrols. On average soldiers in Belfast, Antrim and Down were carrying out at least one operational duty per week.

The main recommendation to come out of the review was that a full-time UDR battalion should be formed. A paper was submitted to the MOD proposing the creation of a battalion 600 strong, to consist of four companies, to be deployed in separate locations across the province. Operational tasks would be restricted to the Border and rural areas only and the battalion would continue to have no role in riot and crowd control duties. It would replace the paramilitary role that the RUC, reinforced by a USC reserve, had been unable to fulfil since the introduction of the Hunt Committee recommendations. The main advantage was that there would be one battalion able to carry out operations by day and night. It would reduce the number of Regular Army units required for emergency tours and take some of the heat out of demands for the creation of a 'Third Force'. It was foreseen that manpower would be drawn primarily from urban areas and, since experience had shown that Catholics living in urban areas were more ready to join the UDR then their rural counterparts, there was a fair chance that the battalion would include a reasonable percentage of Catholics.

Within the UDR the proposal was regarded with some trepidation. General Sir John Anderson believed strongly that a full-time battalion was not in accordance with the spirit of the Regiment as a part-time citizen force. He did accept the need for some daytime capability and agreed with HQUDR's alternative proposal for a full-time company in each part-time battalion, the solution favoured by Commanding Officers.

These tentative proposals were overtaken by an article published in the *Sunday Mirror* stating that "a new full-time, 600 to 800-strong armed force would be formed from the part-time UDR". The report concluded that the news would be welcome to "the hawks of Premier Brian Faulkner's government because the full-time force will be a mainly Protestant and Unionist body". This tendentious statement convinced the Nationalist Members of Parliament that the proposal for a full-time battalion had been forced on the MOD as a result of pressure from the Stormont government and that the new force would consist of ex-B Specials. One went so far as to declare that it might result in a force similar to the hated Black and Tans.

Some of the remarks made during the Stormont debate showed a greater degree of hostility towards the Regiment among Nationalist members than had been apparent before. Such remarks as that made by Paddy Devlin, MP for Falls, that the UDR had "drifted into a private sectarian type of force which the B Specials used to be" were depressing and an ill omen for the future. Whoever leaked the information to a journalist set back the project for years. Necessary though it was, it was put on the long finger, and six years were to pass before battalions were authorized to raise full-time platoons.

Scott-Bowden believed that initially there was a reluctance on the part of the MOD to commit funds to the UDR, until it was clear that the concept of the new Regiment was going to work. Gradually this attitude changed, starting with the appointment of a Deputy Commander, together with two staff captains at HQUDR. All were Regular Army officers. Within the first two months it had become apparent that the Headquarters was hopelessly under-staffed. In April 1971 authority was given to raise three new companies, in Coleraine, Newtownabbey and Saintfield.

A far greater degree of mobility was assured when an additional thirty-four ¾ ton Landrovers and twenty-six civilian motor coaches were authorized between the seven battalions, together with new VCP equipment. The dannert wire coils were replaced by the type of crush barriers used by police forces (and later discarded when it was found that two Landrovers parked to form a chicane made the most effective road block). Torches and Bardic lamps were issued, the latter the revolving, flashing orange light certain to reveal the presence of a VCP a mile off, for the benefit of friend and foe alike. Caltrops were introduced made from fiercely spiked chains which, when pulled across the road in front of a vehicle that had failed to stop, were guaranteed to puncture the tyres. They did, as the Colonel Commandant could testify. He was an early victim when he ran over a caltrop laid out ready for use on the grass verge.

In June, following trials carried out by 3UDR, fourteen Shorland armoured cars were taken over from the RUC. These were the vehicles whose use in West Belfast whilst fitted with Browning machine guns two years previously had been the subject of adverse criticism by the Scarman Tribunal. A bid was made for an additional twenty-six, sufficient for two per Border company and two for battalion headquarters. The Shorland was a three-man armoured car built on a long-wheelbased Landrover chassis fitted with a manually operated revolving turret on which a GPMG could be mounted. Built by Shorts, the aircraft and missile firm in Belfast, they were purchased by some forty-six countries for use by military and anti-terrorist police forces and have been employed in places as far apart as the Thai border against drug growers and at Amsterdam Airport in an anti-hijacker role. Though in time their usefulness was overtaken by the macrolon-fitted Landrovers, they proved to be exceptionally tough vehicles and on several occasions saved the lives of soldiers on patrol. A limited number of flak jackets were purchased in the United States and it was agreed that the No. 4 rifles should be replaced by the modern SLRs.[12]

Finally, too, the need for purpose-built accommodation had been recognized. MOD gave the go-ahead for the building of a new HQUDR in Lisburn, for a headquarters and one company of 3UDR at Ballykinlar, a headquarters and two companies for 4UDR at Enniskillen, two companies in Londonderry, a headquarters and one company at Palace Barracks, Holywood, and two companies also from 7UDR at Girdwood Park Camp in North Belfast.

In succession to Hattersley, Geoffrey Johnson Smith, Parliamentary Secretary (Army), was given special responsibility for the development of the UDR. He had become a well-known public figure in the fifties as a result of his four years as an interviewer on BBC television. He was a good listener and took to the task with enthusiasm, showing a ready sympathy and understanding of the needs of the Regiment. In particular his experience as a communicator meant that he was good at talking to the press, furthering the cause of the UDR. He was a fairly frequent visitor to the Province and became known and welcomed in the battalions. It was an unusual situation for a regiment to have its own official ministerial representative. His first visit to 3UDR was made memorable by the fact that, on landing at Ballykinlar, the escort, hearing a burst of firing on the ranges, thought they were under attack, leapt to the ground, stumbled and shot his own helicopter in the fuel tank, which caught fire. The fire was put out before it could take hold, but the Under-Secretary of State had to continue his journey by road whilst the Wessex drooped on the playing fields, looking like a poorly elephant.

After the relative calm of the winter, violent riots erupted in February 1971 in West Belfast and continued for a week, vehicles hijacked to make barricades, petrol, acid and nail bombs, and escalating gun battles. In the

New Lodge a Regular Army Gunner was killed, the first British soldier to be shot dead in Ireland since the Anglo-Irish War. Two unarmed policemen were gunned down.

From then on the RUC was rearmed; the Hunt Report recommendation that the Province could be served by a conventional unarmed police force had already proved to be unworkable. Chichester-Clark flew to London to demand that the Army should take control of the 'no go' areas and search them for munitions. Mindful of the violent reaction to the Falls curfew, the government would agree only to deploy another 1,300 troops. Chichester-Clark resigned and on 23 March Brian Faulkner was elected Prime Minister.

In July the situation deteriorated further, with ninety-four explosions in one night. By the end of the first week in August there had been 311 explosions and 320 shooting incidents since the beginning of the year, with ten soldiers, two policemen and thirteen civilians killed and over 600 people injured.

With the Regular Army drawn more and more into Belfast and Londonderry, UDR battalions were to find that they were the sole military presence in some rural police divisions. Greater use was made of their improved mobility. In January a set piece VCP operation was implemented, using some 400 soldiers, mainly from 7UDR but reinforced from time to time by 1 and 3UDR, deploying thirty-one road blocks in an outer ring on the main roads into Belfast, so preventing the movement of munitions into the city centre. It was usually mounted around a weekend so that the part-time soldiers could be used by day and night. To one part-time platoon commander, the call-out system seemed somewhat primitive:

> "The first intimation the soldier received of a call-out was when someone from his company knocked on his door and ordered him to report to his company location immediately, irrespective of what he might be doing at the time. The VCPs were so static that we used to ask people in adjacent houses if we could leave the knife rests in their gardens until the next time. Those were the days when the public were very generous to our men. I remember seeing one of our young soldiers acting as a cover sentry at the entrance to Roselawn cemetery surrounded by baskets of fruit, sweets, books, bottles of minerals that people turning into the cemetery had left for him. You would not be at a road block very long before some kind lady would come out with a tray of cups of tea. We had regular tea stops in Belfast."

All battalions were heavily committed over the Easter holiday. 5 and 6UDR mounted road blocks west of Londonderry, between the city and the Border, for over 60 hours. Commander 8 Brigade said their presence contributed to the prevention of any escalation of violence when rioting broke out in the city on Easter Sunday. For the first time 3UDR deployed a tactical headquarters and established a battalion radio net. On the Sunday they deployed VCPs on the Border roads to the south and west of Newry, supported by Ferret scout cars of the Scots Greys. On the Monday the battalion deployed mobile patrols along the Border from Carlingford Lough to Newtownhamilton, relieving the Guards Parachute Company who were providing cover for the Apprentice Boys gathering in Kilkeel. Tactical headquarters was in Crossmaglen. It was a beautiful day, nothing much happened, and in the quiet moments the Adjutant and Company Commander sat out on the low wall round the police station, admiring the good looks of the local girls. It was the year that 'hot pants' were fashionable.

On 8 May the Regiment suffered its first casualties from terrorist attack when a patrol from 5UDR travelling along a lonely Border road at Killea, south-west of Londonderry, in two Landrovers as yet unprotected by macrolon armour, was caught in a landmine explosion. The blast injured the driver of the leading vehicle, which crashed through a ditch and landed upside-down in a field. Two soldiers were injured. One, whose home was in the Waterside about four miles across country from the incident, lost an eye.

Despite the increased involvement in operations, looking back now these months seem a time of innocence, time when soldiers' photographs with names and even on occasion addresses were published in the local papers, time when luminous scotch tape was stuck on the front and side of soft-skin Landrovers and on traffic sentries' jackets so they could be seen in the dark. One night a platoon commander drove out in a Landrover to visit the guard on a rebroadcast station above Ardoyne.

> "At the turning off the main road through a gate I heard shooting down in Ardoyne and suddenly felt very alone. I drew my 9 mm pistol and got out of the vehicle to open the gate. What I did not know was that there was a cow lying behind it. The poor animal went 'moo' and frightened the life out of me and I nearly shot it. The guard commander who was waiting up the track for me said that between the gate and the rebro station the Landrover's wheels never touched ground, and I looked as white as a ghost."

In Dungannon the company administrative staff worked in a caravan parked at the top of the town square and the two four-ton vehicles were parked all day round the corner alongside the old Belfast Bank. Robin Chappell of 2UDR, the second Regular officer to be appointed to command a battalion, was living in a top-floor room in a hotel in the centre of Armagh. In June the newly appointed Adjutant of 3UDR was driving round Castlewellan looking for a house to buy, alone and wearing uniform. With nowhere else to live he set up a tent in the camp site at Tollymore Forest Park. When his family joined him for the summer holidays they moved into a more congenial site in the Forest Park at Castlewellan. In the evenings he would stand outside the tent using a

Bantam to do a radio check back to Ballykinlar. These were the times when soldiers would travel to duty wearing uniform, sometimes hitching a lift from passing motorists. In the Castlederg company a Catholic farmer used to come in to duty from his farm at Killeter, close to the Donegal border, in uniform, driving a tractor with his rifle over his shoulder. Others in the company travelled in on motorbikes and push bikes, in uniform, rifles slung across their backs. "It never entered your head that you might be fired on," their Company Commander recalled.

On the first evening of their annual camp at Magilligan the men of 3UDR, sheltering in a shed from the steady July rain, heard Dion Beard tell them that sooner or later they would come under fire and that the standard of training must improve. There was a lack of urgency in the battalion, he told them, a feeling among the soldiers that it could not happen to them. It was very hard, and took many months, to convince men who had known the streets and townlands, fields and lanes all their lives that from now on they must look at them in a different light – the likely ambush position, signs of fresh digging in a bank that might conceal a mine, the farm dog barking suddenly in the night.

Beard was right. In the early hours of 9 August Internment was implemented. The days of innocence were over.

CHAPTER FOUR

9 August – 31 December 1971
Internment

On 5 August 1971, the day that Parliament was due to rise for the summer recess, a debate was held in the Commons at the request of the Labour Opposition to discuss the worsening situation in Northern Ireland. "I do not think I ever approached a debate on Ireland with a deeper sense of impending tragedy as I did on that day," Callaghan wrote.[1] Aware that he had the full support of the Shadow Cabinet, he spoke out against the option of internment. He was not to know that Brian Faulkner, accompanied by Lieutenant General Sir Harry Tuzo, the GOC, and Sir Graham Shillington, the Chief Constable, had flown over to London secretly that morning to convince Heath, the Prime Minister, that internment was indeed the only remaining choice.

Faulkner described the situation in his autobiography:–

"Not only was the increased volume of violence causing alarm, but also the sheer audacity and provocative nature of many of the attacks, and the way in which they were preventing any kind of normal life in the Province. Simple things, like catching a bus or driving through the city to see a friend or going to the cinema, were becoming increasingly hazardous. Pedestrians and shoppers were being injured by wild gunfire, and by sudden explosions in shops, offices and business premises. Hotels, including the prestigious Europa Hotel in Belfast city centre, were being attacked; telephone exchanges, power stations and post offices were being blown up; buses were being hijacked and burned.

"I was holding long discussions with the GOC, the Chief Constable and my security advisers to see if we could improve our tactics in any way. But the message was beginning to come through that there was only one major unused weapon in the government's anti-terrorist arsenal – internment."[2]

Tuzo had found himself suddenly appointed GOC in early March when his predecessor, Erskine Crum, died of a heart attack four weeks after taking office. Internment, he said,

"was a most terrific decision. I probably never had to make a bigger one. A whole lot of people in Northern Ireland said there is only one solution to this, lock them up. It had worked in '56, but then there had been internment in the South as well. This time we had no such agreement. Without it, it became a still more difficult decision. I have always felt that it has been unfairly handled in accounts of those days, as if it had been some instant decision thrown out by Heath. In fact we all wrestled with the problem for ages. It was a matter of conscience and much heart-searching as to whether it is ever right to lock people up without trial. In the end it was decided only by a very narrow margin."[3]

The arrests began at 4.30 am on 9 August 1971.

Internment had been foreseen. The possibility had been discussed in Parliament and press, and advertisements had been published seeking additional recruits for the Prison Service. As the troops moved in to lift the 450 people on their arrest lists, women and children in their night clothes ran out into the streets, banging dustbin lids on the ground to warn of the approach of soldiers. The arrest parties were met with stones and petrol bombs and sporadic gunfire. Barricades were set up all over West Belfast and around the Short Strand in the east of the city. Families from both communities caught up in the violence abandoned their homes to move into safer areas where their own people were in the majority. Protestants living in the Ardoyne set their homes on fire before they moved, 200 houses, to prevent them being used by Catholic families. Some 7,000 people, the majority Catholics, were left homeless, and Catholic families, encouraged by the IRA, travelled on trains to the Republic where they were accommodated in camps set up by the Irish Army until they felt safe to return. There were reports of Protestant gunmen firing into Catholic areas. Violence spread to other centres. In Newry barricades were set up round the Catholic estates and Protestant shops were set on fire. In Belfast the OIRA engaged the Army in a prolonged gun battle. During the first three days twenty-one people were killed, most of them by the Army. Two soldiers were killed and a number wounded. By then of the 337 men initially arrested, ninety-seven had been released and detention orders had been served on the remainder. Over a hundred of those on the arrest list had managed to go into hiding or slip away across the Border. The arrested men were taken to one of three holding centres where they were screened prior to being detained in Crumlin Road prison or on board HMS *Maidstone* moored in Belfast docks. One of the holding centres was at Ballykinlar. That morning the Adjutant of 3UDR had begun the first day of his leave when he received a telephone call from the Battalion telling him to return. He found the camp had been transformed. All but a few huts belonging to the Battalion had been enclosed behind a perimeter of dannert wire, overlooked by guard towers. Beard had been woken in the early hours by the Second-in-Command of 42 Medium Regiment RA who had flown in overnight with the task of setting up the interrogation centre. It was the Regiment's third tour in Northern Ireland in a year. He wanted the key of the Battalion MT and accommodation stores and the Sergeants' Mess. Beard, who knew nothing about the operation, told him where he could go. The Gunners broke into the stores and took what was useful to them and enclosed the huts within the perimeter.

The announcement placing the UDR on call-out and instructing soldiers to contact their company headquarters was broadcast at 11.15 am. The response was gratifying. Out of a trained strength of 3,464, 87% answered the call. In 3UDR, the battalion with one third of its strength drawn from the Catholic community, only seventeen men failed to report on the first day and nine of those lived in Newry where some brave men – and a woman – were crossing the IRA barricades round their estates to report for duty at the company centre. The company's civilian clerical officer, a Catholic, lived in one of those estates, Barcroft Park.

> "When internment came it was hell for me, because my husband was away and not there to support me. I was going to work each day and getting verbal abuse from the men manning the barricades. I could not go down the town but people would be passing remarks as to where I worked, and when I went out I practically had to climb over the barricades pushing my son's pram."

Battalions were tasked to take over key point guards to relieve the Regular Army and to carry out road blocks and mobile patrols. In three weeks 5UDR carried out 196 VCPs in the area known as the Enclave, between the Foyle and the Border. Over a hundred thousand vehicles were stopped and over 40,000 searched. One of the tasks taken over by 3UDR was the 24-hour guard on the Prime Minister's house. The task was nick-named 'Admiral's Cup' to mark the fact that, despite the crisis at home, Heath was still sailing onwards aboard *Morning Cloud* in the Fastnet Race. The house was very vulnerable, set in a wood in fairly lonely country. It was ringed with flares and tin cans tied to trip wires, but, since badgers blundered into these and birds perched on the wires, there were frequent false alarms, with the reaction force being deployed from Ballykinlar. Beard met the Prime Minister on his return from Stormont that first night of internment:

> "He seemed quite relaxed, but we only talked about his personal security and that of the house. I discovered later that he always travelled in the same car in the same seat and always turned his bedroom light on before drawing the curtains. I gave him a short lesson on security over a glass of gin."[4]

Darkness was falling on that first night when the first UDR soldier was shot dead. A patrol of the Strabane Company was carrying out a VCP close to the Clady Bridge Border crossing. Winston Donnell was acting as traffic sentry. A car came up from Clady, turned round in the road and ran down the hill towards the patrol. Donnell stepped out into the road to signal the driver to stop. The occupants opened fire with Thompson sub-machine guns. Donnell died instantly. The GOC wrote to Commander UDR: "How can anyone doubt after this that the UDR is right in the front line with the rest of us?"

On the night of 12 August Rutherford Clarke, one of those who had attended the first commissioning course at Ballykinlar, was tasked to lead a patrol from the Newry Company along the road to Crossmaglen. On reaching the town they found the road blocked with a barricade of broken paving stones and a blazing Post Office van. Clarke sent the Shorland forward to push aside the van and then followed with the Landrover. In the square they came under a barrage of broken concrete thrown by a crowd who were using a railway sleeper as a battering ram to break down the door into the police station. It was about to give way when Clarke's patrol and a troop of 14/20th Hussars arrived on the scene. A Hussars Ferret Scout car pushed aside another Post Office van burning across the entrance and the patrol and the troop, arriving in the nick of time, drove into the station. The guard from 2UDR had been besieged inside the station for some hours and the guard commander had leant out of a window and warned the crowd, "Look, we have no gas, only steel bullets. If you don't disperse we'll have to use them." On the arrival of the patrol the crowd dispersed of their own accord.[5]

Six nights later Clarke was leading another combined Shorland and Landrover patrol from Newry to Castlewellan when they came under fire about two miles west of the latter town. Clarke reckoned that about ten rounds were fired at them from two weapons. They did not stop but returned fire on the move, expending twenty rounds from an SMG and one from a rifle. This is believed to be the first time that the UDR opened fire "in anger".

On 3 September a second soldier was shot dead, Private Francis Veitch of 4UDR, a 23-year-old single man who lived on a small farm with his widowed mother and sister. He was a member of the guard on Kinawley police station and at breakfast time had gone out of the front gate to a sand-bagged sentry post when three men opened fire from a passing car, then drove away in the direction of the Border.

By 13 September it was clear that the call-out could no longer continue. For five weeks civilian firms had been deprived of their employees. A few had begun to lose patience. Within the first four days Ulsterbus was reported to be warning their drivers that unless they returned to duty they risked losing seniority, or even their jobs. The UDR did their best to accommodate firms by arranging that men on the same factory shift were not all detailed for duty at the same time, but a prolonged call-out was disruptive, particularly for small firms. There was also the matter of pay. Some men did very well out of it, especially the conrates, since they were placed on Regular Army rates of pay during periods of call-out, a substantial increase for the ill-paid junior ranks. The part-time soldiers were paid daily so long as they made themselves available, whether or not they were on operational duty. This was little comfort for the self-employed man, the farmer forced to pay a neighbour to keep a farm going, the salesman working on commission. For many soldiers their Army pay was less than their civilian wages. Some firms and the Civil Service made up the difference. Others flatly refused to do so. Later discussions were held with the Engineering Employers' Association and representatives of Harland and Wolff's and Short Brothers and Harland to persuade them to encourage their members to make up the pay of their UDR employees on call-out, but this they refused to do, arguing that it was a government responsibility to make up the difference. Ultimately the loss of pay and disruption to industry resulted in a reluctance to call out the whole Regiment for extended periods and the UDR was never called out again for as long as five weeks. It is to the UDR's great credit that financial loss never diminished the response to a call-out.

For sixteen months the Regiment had been finding its feet. From now on the Regular Army's attitude towards the UDR began to change. The degree to which they had been able to take over static tasks and to reinforce overstretched units with mobile patrols secured a new-found respect for the Regiment.

Internment was a disastrous mistake. Although the Army and the police had drawn up a list of potential internees earlier in the year, the RUC intelligence records were out of date and new leaders had begun to emerge who were unknown to Special Branch. Many of those who were picked up were no longer active, while the real activists escaped the net. None of the original internees were Protestants. Internment of Protestants had been given careful consideration, but "we were able to arrest them through the normal legal processes, because the information came in from the law-abiding members of their own community," Shillington said.[6] But in Catholic eyes internment was seen as a measure directed solely against their own community. Within days rumours began to circulate that detainees had been subject to torture. Following a detailed article in a Sunday newspaper the Government set up an inquiry to investigate the allegations. Its report concluded that the in-depth interrogation methods involving hooding, forcing men to stand with their arms against walls for long periods, the use of continuous high-pitched noise, sleep and food deprivation did not amount to brutality, but that there had been ill-treatment in the case of eleven individuals.[7]

The Republican propagandists had a field day. Throughout Britain, Europe and particularly the United States, the belief was spread that large numbers of detainees had been tortured. The 'brutality of the Brits' became part of Republican mythology. Coogan, the historian of the Republican movement, wrote: 'Internment stimulated a far greater degree of support for the IRA than had existed at any time since the end of the Anglo-Irish War, and arguably even during it."[8]

For the UDR internment was a disaster of a different kind; it accelerated the loss of Catholic soldiers. Scott-Bowden had foreseen that would happen: "The UDR was as good a sounding board to test the reaction [to the introduction of internment] as any organization could have been," he said, but he was not there to see his forebodings borne out. Three weeks previously he had come to the end of his period of command and returned to India as Defence Attaché in New Delhi.

Catholic membership of the Regiment reached its highest percentage in July 1970, and its highest numbers, 593, in the following January. The degree of success in recruiting Catholics had varied with battalions. 3 and 7UDR had been markedly successful. The Londonderry Waterside Company was roughly half and half, amongst them men who lived in the Bogside and Creggan. All battalions had some Catholic members, including those with a predominately USC background. They were willingly accepted and respected for their courage. George Chambers, now commissioned into 3UDR, led his first patrol two days after internment:

"There I was, an ex-USC officer, commanding a patrol of eight men, of whom I was the only Protestant. We got along fine, both then and in the years ahead. Some time later a Catholic member of the company, who later became Regimental Quartermaster Sergeant, said to me one evening over a few drinks in the canteen after we had come back from a Border operation, 'Sir, I've just heard you were a Special. It's a remarkable thing that everyone I like best in this company seems to have been in the USC'."

The ex-USC section sergeant in Downpatrick was now commanding a section in which every man was Catholic.
In the Magherafelt Company:

"The majority were what one could describe as Loyalist, but there were some Catholics, including one who later became a Sergeant Major. He had no means of transport, and on a number of occasions he was seen thumbing a lift in uniform from Maghera to the drill hall in Tobermore. I heard two members of the company who were on the Orange side of the divide discussing his foolishness in standing out thumbing a lift in uniform. They agreed that if he was to survive they would have to make a detour to pick him up. So for the rest of the time while the drill hall was in Tobermore he was picked up and at the end of the night taken home by men who were the opposite of Nationalists. It gave me hope for the future that a man was being judged on his qualities rather than his religious or political views."

The CO of 7UDR had a Lance Corporal who lived in Andersonstown:

"One night I was sitting in my office when I got a phone call from him. There was coughing and shouting and screaming in the background and he said, 'Colonel, I'm sorry I'm not going to be able to make it tonight.' I asked him why, what was wrong? He said, 'There's tear gas all over the place. It's right through the road and

57

the houses and I just can't make it, sir.' I told him not to worry, just to look after himself."

Some of the Catholic recruits were ex-soldiers and were quickly promoted. Two of the Permanent Staff Instructors in 3UDR and one in 2UDR were Catholics, as was the CQMS of the Strabane Company and the CSM of the Newry Company. There were many more. If a man had previous experience he was earmarked for promotion. Religion did not enter into it. The fact that in some battalions the majority with previous experience were from the USC meant that it may have seemed that Protestants were being given an unfair advantage, but there was no question of their being favoured at the expense of Catholics. Indeed the chairman of the USC Association claimed that in 3UDR preference for promotion and allocation of appointments was being given to Catholics. In all twenty-three were commissioned in the Regiment. The Seconds-in-Command of 1 and 3UDR were Catholics with previous Army service. A Captain in 5UDR had been a prominent member of NICRA and had taken part in the October 1968 march. Like many others he was intimidated out, out of the UDR, out of his job and out of Londonderry.

Both Protestant and Catholic members of the Regiment were the victims of intimidation, but in the aftermath of internment it was mainly Catholic soldiers who were intimidated from within their own community.

It happened in every battalion area. In the Castlederg Company six Catholics received letters telling them to get out. A soldier from nearby Drumquin received two letters, crudely printed in capital letters

"Get out of that rotten force before you are shot. You are being watched very closely. What kind of Irishman are you anyway. Look at what you are supporting; brutality; murder and the worst kind of torture. Get out before it is too late."

The second was decorated with a sketch of a coffin marked 'RIP' and read:-

"Final warning. You have seven days to be out of the Orange UDR. If not we will take action against you without further warning."

A young teacher from a Catholic school, whom 7UDR had earmarked for a commission, came to see his CO almost in tears to say he was going to have to resign.

"He did not want to say why but he left me with the impression, deliberately, I believe, that it wasn't because of his family or friends but because of his colleagues at the school."

A corporal came to see the Adjutant of 2UDR. He broke down and cried. He said he had been told to resign or his mother would be burnt out. In the Newry Company the son of the guard Sergeant was burnt out of his home with his young family. Chambers' first Platoon Sergeant was an ex-regular born in Donegal. His wife was shopping in a greengrocers in Downpatrick when she was approached by two strangers. One took her by the arm and whispered that they knew who she was and where she lived, and that the IRA would get her husband if he did not get out of the UDR forthwith. The daughter of a PSI was so bullied at her Downpatrick convent school by fellow pupils, taunting her about her father being in the UDR, that he was forced to warn the staff that he would send her to a Protestant school unless the bullying ceased. In a letter to his Adjutant, saying he had come under pressure to resign, a Catholic from Castlewellan wrote:–

> "My experience in the UDR during the past seventeen months is one which I shall always cherish. I have learnt quite a lot of how people of different religions can live and work together, if only the rest outside the UDR could do the same. I intend to make my home in England. I do wish the UDR the very best of luck and health in the years to come."[9]

In Enniskillen one of the conrate guard was a Catholic. Some of his neighbours came knocking at his back door in the early hours, took him out and beat him and scraped his face with a scrubbing brush. He was a frail man and his company commander reported that his body was black and blue and his face badly damaged. He resigned the next day.

> "It was very, very soul-destroying," the Commander of the Waterside Company recalled, "when you were running a platoon and you lost good men, forced out, and you knew in your own heart that these men really enjoyed the UDR."

Intimidation took several forms: outright violence, direct threats of "get out or else", and more subtle threats; refusal to give service in a shop, or other shoppers falling silent when a wife came in to make her purchases. In Londonderry a pack of OMO washing powder would be left on a doorstep – O.M.O. for 'Odd Man Out'. A bullet posted through a letter box was a favourite ploy. A Catholic couple interviewed by the *Belfast Telegraph* described what it was like:

> "People, mostly of my own sort, stopped speaking to me. They regard me as a traitor to the cause. That only made me more determined. Then we started getting telephone calls. The usual stuff: 'You're a traitor, we'll get you'. I did not really worry about that. If you're going to get killed, you'll get killed."

The article continues:

> "His wife is afraid. 'When he goes out I have everything prepared in case I have to go to the hospital. Now and then I sit and wonder what we would do if he is killed.' His young daughter, who has been listening in, starts to cry."

Speaking of the attitude of the Protestants in his company towards him, this Catholic soldier went on:-

> "At first I didn't know who I would be going out with on any particular night. You'd maybe be alone with a boy from the Falls or the Shankill. You would get the odd fellow who would say, 'I wouldn't trust a mickey as far as I could throw him.' But that was just people not knowing enough about each other. I never came across anyone really bigoted."[10]

It was inevitable that in some instances there would have been remarks passed, sometimes in jest, some of them hurtful. But very few if any Catholics were forced to resign as a result of pressure from their fellow Protestants within their companies. Research has not revealed a single instance. Scott-Bowden never heard any suggestion that Catholics were being intimidated from within the Regiment. "If I had there would have been vigorous and explosive action!"

The ultimate intimidation was murder. The fourth member of the Regiment to be murdered and the first Catholic was Sean Russell, the 32-year-old father of five children. He lived in a predominantly Catholic estate at New Barnsley and was a committee member of a Republican club. He was also one of the original members of 7UDR. According to his brother, "He saw the Regiment as playing a part in the running of the community, and with Catholics taking a hand in it for the first time." It is likely that he had come under threat, for he had not reported for duty for six months, though, according to his CO, he was about to return. He was watching television with the children at his knee when the doorbell rang. One of the boys went to answer it. A man, masked and carrying a gun, pushed him aside, asked the father if he was Sean Russell, shot him in the head, then, turning the gun on the ten-year-old daughter, shot her in the thigh. Mrs Russell, preparing a supper in the kitchen a few feet away, saw it all happen. One son was playing out in the street and saw the murderer running past "with smoke still coming from the gun barrel".
Cardinal Conway issued a powerful statement:

> "The person who could shoot a man dead in his own sitting room in front of his wife and children is a monster. Nothing can cloud our cold, clear condemnation of these deeds. To condone them to the slightest degree, even in thought, would be to become morally soiled oneself."

In the fourteen months following internment seven Catholic soldiers were murdered. Over that period they averaged 7% of the total strength of the UDR, yet they totalled 28% of those killed by the IRA. According to Coogan it was IRA policy that their victims were not targeted on the grounds of their religion. Yet it is hard not to believe that those Catholics were murdered deliberately to persuade their co-religionists to resign from the Regiment.

In 1971 a quarter of the Catholics resigned, half of those in the five months following internment. Not all, of course, were intimidated out. There were those who were disillusioned by Government security policy, an impression that the main Army effort was being concentrated on the Catholic areas of Belfast and the one-sided application of internment. A Sergeant, who was a Catholic and a former Regular soldier, was serving with his son in 7UDR. They both resigned in April 1971, the father giving as his reason the increased pressure exerted on the Catholic community by the security forces. In their letters of resignation they made it clear that they had valued the help and friendship of the officers and men of their company and wished them success in the future. The CO called at the family home, but was unable to persuade them to change their minds.

In the aftermath of internment the Sergeant organized a meeting for all Catholic members and ex-members of the UDR. Some thirty-one attended and were addressed by Austin Currie, then Stormont MP for East Tyrone. He told his audience:-

> "I object to the role which the Army has played in interning people without trial and the role which the UDR has played in helping (Regular soldiers) to be available for this sort of activity. As a result of Army action and the policy of the British government, I am no longer obliged to say to Catholics that they should go into the UDR."

He made a point of emphasizing, however, that he was not encouraging Catholics already serving to resign, but at the end of the meeting seventeen said they would go, seven indicated they would serve on and five had already left. The *Belfast Telegraph* commented:

> "The threat of intimidation against members of the UDR is a serious matter. The UDR is more than an Army regiment. It is an experiment in cooperation between Protestant and Catholics. If the Catholics leave, the UDR will become a purely Protestant force by default."

The Sergeant went on to form the Catholic Ex-Serviceman's Association. Ostensibly intended as a vigilante force for the defence of Catholic areas in the event of a Protestant uprising and claiming a membership of 8,000, it was also vociferously anti-UDR, before sinking into oblivion.

The UDR tried to counteract the insidious effects of intimidation and to reverse the loss of Catholic members. Beard wrote a letter, a copy of which was given to every soldier in 3UDR, exhorting them to stand together against the threat and suggesting, for instance, that the soldiers meet socially at each other's houses in the evening "so the terrorists will never know when they may not find three or four members of the Battalion together in one home".[11] For a time the MOD's customary reluctance to allow relatively junior officers to make use of the media was set aside and individual Commanding Officers were permitted to appear on television and to write to the local press. A fortnight after internment Beard was interviewed on BBC television about the effects of intimidation, though a

Tyrone Catholic who had already resigned said he did not believe they were being intimidated. For two months the CO conducted a lively correspondence through the pages of the Newry *Reporter*, countering the accusations of the Newry Ex-Servicemen's Association. It did nothing to change the hostility of the members, but, as an on-going weekly correspondence, each side scoring points off the other, it was a valuable means of getting the UDR message across to the reasonable people of the town.

General Sir John Anderson had made every effort to keep open lines to the Catholic hierarchy. Back in October 1970 one of the Catholic members of the Advisory Council had had a long talk with Cardinal Conway on officer recruiting. The Cardinal had been helpful and asked for names of suitable candidates. It is not recorded whether anything came of this approach, but six months later Anderson and the Council member called on the Cardinal again. The discussion was described as "frank and clearly worthwhile".

Scott Bowden's successor as Commander UDR was a former Royal Irish Fusilier, Brigadier Denis Ormerod. He had gained experience of internal security operations in India prior to Independence in 1947, in Palestine and against the Communist guerrillas in Malaya. His mother's family came from the South of Ireland. He was a Catholic, as was his deputy, Kevin Hill. When Hill left he was replaced by another Catholic, Paddy Ryan, whose father had lived in Donaghadee in County Down. Whether it was a deliberate policy of the MOD to appoint Catholic officers to these senior posts Ormerod never knew. Certainly his religion did help him in establishing a friendly and understanding rapport with Cardinal Conway and Dr Philbin, the Catholic Bishop of Down and Connor. He and his wife visited the Cardinal on several occasions, latterly with the encouragement of the GOC, as Ormerod was the senior Catholic Army officer in the province. After one of these visits he wrote to the Cardinal:

> "to thank you for giving my wife and I so much of your time last week. We both enjoyed very much meeting you and we were most interested to hear your views on the subjects we discussed. From my point of view it was a very valuable afternoon and I greatly appreciate having been given the chance to have such a frank discussion with you"[12]

On the other side of the coin Ormerod found there was a degree of suspicion about him among some Protestants when he first assumed command:

> "Various people came to see me. One definitely got the message that they wanted to be assured about the attitude I was going to inject into the UDR. Dr Paisley was one of them. I think he came to search me out, to identify what I was like and what my approach was going to be."[13]

Whilst the number of Catholics was dwindling, the belief that the Government was at last taking resolute action against the IRA produced a dramatic upsurge in recruits from the Protestant community. In the first eighteen months applications had averaged about forty a week. In the week after internment they went up to seventy-two, then 169, then 376, and by the end of September there had been 1290 applications. As a result the existing battalions were in danger of becoming too large to command efficiently and on 15 September the Secretary of State for the Army announced that the Government had decided to form three additional battalions by allowing the strength of the Regiment to rise above the existing 6,000 ceiling. They would be formed by splitting responsibility for Counties Antrim and Tyrone, and Belfast.

8th (County Tyrone) Battalion was formed on 1 December 1971 out of the companies of 6UDR located in the east of the county. Battalion HQ was based in Killymeal House, an attractive period private house on the edge of Dungannon. As the staff moved in, the previous owners were moving out. Most of the house was used as a married quarter for the Commanding Officer and his family, the rest being taken over as offices, with an operations room in the stables. As prefabricated huts were erected in the grounds, the offices were moved out and half the house became an Officers' Mess. Although in time a perimeter fence was built round the whole complex, the house remained visible from the town and was very exposed.[14] For a series of Commanding Officers' wives living in the house was a strange experience. One said her small son was never short of a battery for his radio controlled toys; if one went flat he knocked at the Quartermaster's store for another. Lisa de Candole who lived in Killymeal from 1973 to 1975 remembered it as an ideal place for a five-year-old boy:

> "He could play soldiers all day long, and I didn't have to worry about him as he couldn't get out of the grounds because of the security fence. It was not long before Nicholas was kitted out in his own uniform, and many a visitor arriving at the gate was surprised to find one very small person on guard. We still have a cartoon showing the guard strength as $1 + 5 + \frac{1}{2} + \frac{1}{4}$, as everywhere Nicholas went so did our dog."[15]

The first CO was Lieutenant Colonel John Blackwell of the Royal Tank Regiment. There were five companies, two in an old primary school in Cookstown, two in Dungannon, in the TA centre and at Killymeal, and one in Aughnacloy in the old Clogher Valley railway station.

The Battalion had hardly formed when it suffered its first fatal casualty, Lance Corporal Wilson, a former Special, shot down whilst ill in bed at his home near Aughnacloy.

9th (County Antrim) Battalion was formed on 15 December 1971 out of the companies of 1 UDR based in the south of the county. Battalion headquarters and one company were established at Steeple Camp, a wartime camp beside the railway station, two companies in Lisburn and the fourth in Carrickfergus. The first Commanding Officer, Lieutenant Colonel 'Paddy' Liddle, had been a part-time Company Commander in

1UDR, had seen wartime service in the Royal Ulster Rifles and had attended the Army Staff College. Apart from the original conrate COs he was to be the only UDR officer to be given command of a UDR battalion.

10th (City of Belfast) Battalion was formed on 15 January 1972, taking over from 7UDR that part of the city lying west of the Lagan. Battalion headquarters and one company were based alongside the Police Vehicle and Radio Workshops at Lislea Drive. It had advantages and disadvantages. It had a clear but distant view of Milltown Cemetery and was used, though not by the UDR, for taking long-range photographs of mourners at Republican funerals; and it was overlooked by a footbridge over the railway. A gunman used the bridge to fire three rounds into the camp; all three penetrated the wall of a toilet, narrowly missing an officer closeted therein. Two other companies were based on the Antrim Road, but moved into the old TA camp at Girdwood Park as soon as accommodation had been built for them, whilst the company based in a disused factory at Carmoney on the outskirts of the city was divided into two. The first CO was Lieutenant Colonel Tony Hayes-Newington of the Cheshires.

From the end of July battalions were tasked to guard six of the most vulnerable police stations. By February 1972 these had been increased to ten stations with a 24-hour guard and thirty-five with a night guard only, a heavy drain on resources, though it was hoped that the raising of the age limits for enlistment from 40 to 50 for men with no previous service experience would make more older men available. It was not a popular task. It looked too like a reversion to one of the roles of the USC, a purely defensive measure that took the soldiers out of the public eye at a time when they should have been reassuring the public by their visible presence. One CO recalled an occasion when he had been told that there were no police officers available to accompany his patrol, only to find the television room in the police station packed with them. At such times, understandably, there was some feeling of resentment. This was aggravated by the substantial disparity between the soldiers' and the policemens' pay, with the latter receiving significant additional overtime payments and the former receiving no more than a day's pay whether he was on duty for eight hours or twenty-four. For the UDR there was never any overtime pay. The daytime guard would have been impossible had it not been for the men who volunteered to do duties by day on Voluntary Call-Out (VCOs), part-time soldiers on full-time duties, who could not be taken on as conrates as there was no place for them on the establishment. Many were smallholders who could combine the running of their holdings with their guard duties. They became an indispensable element within the Regiment. In the years before conrate operations platoons were authorized, it was they who gave the battalions a very limited daytime capability, and right to the end 'part-time/full-time' soldiers were still being employed. At first it seemed like a good arrangement for the volunteers, especially for those who could do other casual work in their off-duty periods. But there were major drawbacks. Since the soldier was paid only when he was on duty, when he went on holiday or, worse still, fell ill, his UDR pay ceased. Also service as a VCO did not count towards a pension. This led years later to a situation where VCOs who had transferred to conrate, completed 25 or more years' service and retired on reaching the maximum age were to find that, because their first years as a VCO were not reckonable, they had failed by a year or so, or even months, to qualify for an immediate 22-year Army pension.

On a night in September a patrol made up of a Shorland and a Landrover from the Rathfriland Company of 3UDR was approaching the Seven Sisters, where the road from Mayobridge to Hilltown climbs up round a series of blind corners, overlooked by high ground on both sides. The Battalion had already identified it as an ideal ambush position. As the Landrover entered the first bend a landmine made from a household gas container packed with gelignite, surrounded by lead pipes, rusty nuts and bolts and nails, and dug high up into the bank, exploded alongside the vehicle. Although the programme to fit macrolon protection kits was well under way, the Landrover was as yet unarmoured. The rear side was peppered with holes, the radio knocked out and the members of the patrol lacerated about the face and body. The young Second Lieutenant in command, though full of pieces of metal and bleeding badly, stopped a passing motorist who gave him a lift to a call box. Dion Beard, asleep in his room in a row of coastguard cottages down by the shore of Tyrella Bay, kept a radio by his bed.

> "I remember how much I dreaded the sound of it activating and of the duty officer starting to speak, because it could only be bad news. As soon as he told me a C Company patrol had been hit at the Seven Sisters, I didn't wait for the rest of the message but drove myself straight there in the staff car."

He arrived shortly after the injured had been taken away in ambulances. He described the scene as like a battlefield, the earth and scrap metal, blood and bandages strewn over the road and blood smeared on the front of the Shorland.

The soldier most badly injured was for a time on the very seriously ill list with a bolt lodged in his skull. He recovered, but had to be invalided out, and eighteen months later a second soldier was still receiving plastic surgery, having lost part of his nose and the roof of his mouth. Had the patrol not been wearing flak jackets some of them would probably have been killed. A piece of lead piping was embedded in one jacket and a nail had all but gone through another, the point sticking into the wearer's shoulder.

Sergeant Smyth was one of the many former Specials who had joined 6UDR at the outset. Like Winston Donnell, he belonged to the Strabane Company. Three months after his wedding day he and a friend, Daniel McCormick, a Catholic who had resigned from the Battalion, were parked on a small road 2 miles south of Clady and a quarter of a mile from the

Border, waiting to give a colleague a lift to work. Two gunmen hiding on the opposite side of the road opened fire on the vehicle, killing McCormick instantly. Smyth was hit in the side but tried to dive out and take cover. They moved in and shot him in the head. In four days three members of the Regiment had been murdered, Russell in Belfast, Wilson in Aughnacloy and now Smyth at Clady.

Ormerod issued a statement to the media:-

"If the IRA thinks these barbarous killings will frighten my men or stop recruitment they are badly mistaken. Men are still applying at a rate of 260 a week. I anticipate that more will join following these murders. Soldiers I have talked to have been shocked, but it has stiffened their resolve. After all this is what the UDR is all about, combating terrorism and murder. I think it is too early to say that there is a general war being waged by the IRA on the UDR. If there was, there would be no question of terrorism succeeding against the Regiment. Should that possibility ever exist what hope would there be for the men, women and children of Ulster?"

CHAPTER FIVE

1972

On Sunday 30 January NICRA organized a rally through the streets of Londonderry. As all parades had been banned since the previous August, the march was illegal. Units of the Regular Army were deployed to contain the march within the Bogside. Part of the crowd tried to cross the barricades and when youths began stoning the troops, soldiers of the Parachute Regiment moved into the Bogside to arrest them. Believing that they had heard shots directed at them, the Paras opened fire. Thirteen people were shot dead and a further seventeen wounded.

Controversy still continues as to the truth of what happened that day. What is certain is that Bloody Sunday was a disaster for Ireland. Britain stood condemned throughout the world, the Irish government and nationalist leaders maintained that the only solution left was a united Ireland, Catholic belief in the impartiality of the Army was further diminished and the Conservative government, who had already been considering the need to transfer responsibility for control of security from Stormont to Westminster, now pressed ahead with the imposition of direct rule for the Province.

The day was a tragedy too for the Regiment, and it had a lasting effect, for from then on it put paid to all hopes that the UDR would remain a balanced force, drawing its recruits from both communities. During 1972 another 108 Catholics resigned, reducing their numbers to 330, and, since the strength of the Regiment as a whole had increased, by the end of the year Catholics made up only 3.7% of the total. One of those to resign was the Sergeant Major of the Newry Company and himself an ex-paratrooper. His Company Commander noticed that he had bruises on his face. The 3UDR historical record records that:

"Seven Catholics had failed to report for duty with the Newry Company that night and a patrol had to be cancelled. On Tuesday two more from Castlewellan resigned and four from Downpatrick later in the week. Since then there has been a steady trickle of Catholic resignations, and perhaps as many as half of those that remain no longer do duties. Some resignations were a reaction to Bloody Sunday, but most were the result of intimidation. Not direct threats so much as pressure exerted by family and friends, and particularly wives. One Sergeant, who had to go round soldiers' homes a few nights later to tell them they were required for a call-out, was amazed by the emotional outbursts of wives persuading their husbands not to go."

The UDR never lost sight of the need to persuade Catholics to enlist. It was not just the case that, without Catholic participation, the Regiment would inevitably be labelled as a sectarian force and liable to suffer the same fate as the USC; it was the belief that the UDR could provide the proof that Protestant and Catholic could serve together in common cause.

Not long before he died General Sir John Anderson said that he had seen his task as Colonel Commandant as being something unique in the history of North-South Irish Relationships, namely to create a force for the defence of the North drawing its membership from both communities. In the early stages, assisted by the Advisory Council, he had seen that aim as being attainable. Now his goal was slipping out of sight. It was a matter of great regret not only to him but to all in the Regiment who shared his belief.[1]

In January 1973 HQUDR arranged for an open letter, signed by serving members of the Regiment drawn from all ranks and addressed to the Catholic community, to be published in the Northern Ireland papers. It was headlined on the front page of the Unionist *Newsletter* and Nationalist *Irish News*:

"We who are both Protestant and Catholic and represent every battalion in the Regiment are appealing now directly to Catholics – is it your wish to leave it largely to the rest of the community to create the peaceful and prosperous Northern Ireland that all of us so desperately want? . . . What better way than to join the UDR – give us a hand and feel that sense of satisfaction from an important job well done . . . We know from experience that Catholics and Protestants get on well together in the UDR."

Personal copies of the letter were sent to leading Catholics, including the Cardinal and Bishop Philbin. The Bishop wrote back:

"I have greatly regretted that the Catholic membership of the UDR, which had my encouragement from the beginning, has so greatly declined, and I hope that circumstances will lead to a healthier position which we originally obtained. I have read the open letter in the press. It was fortunate it was the *Irish News* that printed it in full."

But the Cardinal was less sanguine. "A growing minority of Catholics," he wrote to Ormerod after the Brigadier and his wife paid him a visit, "are no longer listening to their Bishops."[2]

There were always a few Catholics who continued to enlist, ex-regular soldiers and those living in areas where the two communities lived at peace with each other, but eventually it was apparent that, however much the Regiment might try, there was no hope of attracting back Catholic recruits in anything approaching the numbers that had enlisted in the first eighteen months without the support of the leaders of their community. At the beginning that support had been given, but, after internment and Bloody Sunday, it was never given again.

The atmosphere in Ireland in the week following Bloody Sunday had not been so tense since 1969. Yet the Civil Rights Association in Newry decided to go ahead with another illegal march through their town, already arranged for the following Sunday. On the Friday Faulkner flew to London to discuss the situation with Heath and Maudling in the light of the disaster in Londonderry:

> "Heath was quite candid about the situation," Faulkner wrote in his autobiography. "He referred to the march planned by the Civil Rights Association for Newry the next day. 'I am afraid there will be great pressure if things go wrong in Newry tomorrow, for a change of course,' he said."[3] "Newry was a crunch point," Tuzo recalled. "Bloody Sunday had occurred, the inquiry had not yet taken place, and nobody really knew the rights and wrongs of the thing. Those of us who by sheer mischance had not been present in Londonderry, of whom I was one, all went to Newry in force. I felt that if anything was going to happen I had to be there."[4]

There was a very real feeling that the country that weekend was on the brink of civil war. That feeling was not confined to Ireland; on the Sunday morning journalists and television crews from around the world descended on the town. With Newry being so close to the Border many hundreds of people were expected to come up from the South to take part in the march. At Daisy Hill hospital on the edge of the town an entire wing had been set aside and medical teams put on stand-by in case of a possible confrontation. At the Border a special train was waiting in readiness to convey casualties to Southern hospitals.[5]

5 Airportable Brigade was given the task of preventing the rally from reaching the town centre. Two regular battalions were to man road blocks in the town itself, whilst 2, 3 and 9UDR, supported by an armoured car squadron, were ordered to control access by deploying an outer ring of VCPs, covering every road, lane and track leading into the town. The UDR battalions took up their positions on the Friday evening. 3UDR opened an operations room upstairs in the Company Centre on Downshire Road, close to the Brigade operations room on the ground floor.

> "The situation was very tense," the battalion history records. "We received reports that Provisionals from Dundalk to Cork were moving into the town, a figure varying from 40 to 200, and billeting officers were said to be arranging accommodation for them in safe houses. Another report stated that they were planning to engineer a confrontation between the British and Irish army units, and on the strength of this report British troops were ordered to keep well back from the Border. In an extraordinary way the poor battered little

town of Newry had become the focus of world attention, and some 400 members of the international press corps together with fifty television teams were expected to cover the march. The Banbridge Company's road block was filmed by TV crews from Britain, Germany, Italy and Japan, and we encountered journalists from Canada (in a suspect car driven by Kilkeel Republicans), and from France a journalist who had left Paris that night. The commentator with a film crew from the Columbia Broadcasting Service said wryly that, if nothing happened in the town, there would be enough press corps to start a riot of their own. By Saturday evening townsfolk were moving out to stay with friends, and contractors were sending their lorries out to safe areas. Commander 5 Brigade signalled all units: 'Much rests on you. Good luck.' The Colonel Commandant, who had spent Saturday visiting the Battalion, determined not to miss anything, returned the following day and sat in the Battalion Tac HQ. He spoke for us all when he said, 'Can this really be happening in my own country?' Most of the men wore steel helmets and had blackened their faces, mainly to avoid recognition. In fact the VCPs experienced virtually no ill-feeling; all but four were supplied with tea and refreshments from local households, and a mother and daughter had walked down from the Republican-dominated Derrybeg estate to the gates of the Company Centre to hand over a large box of cakes and sandwiches.

"In the early morning mist, with the bells in the valley ringing for Mass and the armoured cars of the Queen's Own Hussars patrolling along the lanes, the VCPs awaited the arrival of the Civil Rights supporters. Many people, on coming to the diversions, parked their cars by the roadside and walked the remaining two or three miles. They were allowed to pass through the blocks after the men had been frisked. They were good-natured and caused no trouble. The atmosphere was more of a country walk on a pleasant premature Spring day, the bus parties queuing to pass through the VCPs, then forming up into small groups on the far side.

"At 3 pm a silence settled in the town. Light aircraft and helicopters carrying members of the Press Corps circled overhead. On the Brigade net a military helicopter pilot reported that the march had started. Shortly afterwards he reported that the head of the march had turned off its planned route and was moving into Rooney's Meadow, where a meeting was being held. The organizers had done what no one had dared hope they would do, turned the march away before it reached the inner cordon. Within an hour the VCPs were reporting groups of people moving out, away from the town, and soon there was a steady stream of supporters turning for home."[6]

As the patrols drove home through Banbridge the people stood in the streets and cheered them on their way. That the day did not end in disaster was mainly due to the effective stewarding of the rally and the wisdom and sense of responsibility of the organizers.

Responsibility for security in the Province still rested with ministers in Stormont. This division between London and Belfast was clearly unsatisfactory:

> "It was bad enough that British troops were involved," Maudling said, "but what was more difficult was that they were there to provide support for a Government to which they were not responsible, and in whose policies their own Government had no say. The Northern Ireland Government at Stormont made the laws and ran the administration; the British Army, which was responsible not to the Stormont but the Westminster Parliament, had to maintain law and order in appalling conditions on the basis of laws enacted and administration conducted on the authority of the Stormont parliament. I became convinced that this was a situation that could not indefinitely endure."[7]

Maudling persuaded the Cabinet that the time had come to prorogue Stormont, transferring responsibility for law and order to Westminster, appointing a Secretary of State for Northern Ireland and phasing out internment.

On 22 March Faulkner was invited to Downing Street to be told the Government's intentions. The one sticking point was control of security; but that was absolute. Without it, Faulkner maintained, the credibility of the Northern Ireland Government would be destroyed.[8]

The Government resigned the following day. A crowd of some 100,000 converged on Parliament buildings. Faulkner and Craig addressed them from the veranda, then went inside for the final session, half a century after the founding of the Northern state.

As Heath was informing Parliament of the decision to prorogue the Stormont Government, the Commanding Officers of the UDR battalions were summoned to Headquarters Northern Ireland to be briefed on the outcome of the Downing Street meeting. Major General Robert Ford, the Commander Land Forces, told them he recognized that they had a particularly difficult problem, but the position of the UDR was unchanged, and it was essential that the Regiment should hold together as an example to the rest of the country. The increasing reputation of the Regiment would be confirmed by its conduct over the next few days. Briefing notes were issued as a basis for every Company Commander to talk to his company that night, to ensure the men would hear the details from their own officers.

Rather than hold formal muster parades, with the risk that they might suggest to the soldiers that authority was worried about their reaction to the news, 3UDR put additional foot patrols into the towns in South Down. Morale was high; the men were glad to demonstrate to the people that, however much they felt betrayed by the British government, they could

71

continue to rely on the UDR. A report that a company in 10UDR had held a protest meeting and decided to resign en masse was without foundation.[9]

The UDR suffered its worst casualties in 1972, twenty-six dead and twenty-one wounded, almost twice the greatest numbers in any subsequent year. All but four were murdered off-duty, travelling to and from their civilian jobs, in their homes, about their farms. The first was a Sergeant in 9UDR, Maynard Crawford, shot from a passing car in Newtownabbey. In February the second Catholic was killed, 45 year old Tommy Callaghan, an Ulster bus driver who lived in Limavady. He was driving his bus at night through the Creggan estate when it was stopped by the Provisional IRA. They held him for two hours, then shot him through the head and dumped his body on waste ground. A colleague said of him, "A kinder, more gentle man you could not wish to meet." Bus services throughout the county were suspended for 24 hours as a mark of respect.

Four days later Captain Marcus McCausland was abducted and murdered on a lonely road between the Creggan estate and the Donegal border. The McCauslands, a Catholic family, owned a large estate on the outskirts of Limavady. Marcus had held a commission in the Irish Guards, had served as High Sheriff for the county and for four years had been a member of the Urban District Council. He had joined 5UDR at the outset, but had resigned in the previous January. He had been visiting his mother and friends across the Border and was on his way home in the early hours of the morning when he was abducted and interrogated for four hours before being shot and his body dumped in the snow. The Official IRA said they had had him under surveillance for some time and had killed him because he was working for British Intelligence, a claim that Army Headquarters dismissed as being without foundation.

To the Regular Army, accustomed to carrying out large-scale nuclear war exercises in West Germany, the red line of the Border highlighted on their operations rooms' maps had become as much a frontier as the Iron Curtain across Central Europe; but there were those in the UDR for whom it was the line of the hedge at the end of the farm or the road beyond the Customs Post where they had to go in the course of their daily lives. 5 Brigade had already issued a warning that IRA Active Service Units (ASUs) were being moved to the Border areas with orders to step up operations immediately, their primary targets to be individual members of the RUC and UDR. In March 3UDR suffered their first fatality when Lance Corporal Joseph Jardine, a Ministry of Agriculture livestock inspector, was shot whilst on duty at the Middletown Customs Post. A car came over from the South, three men got out and, whilst two held the Customs officers at gunpoint, the third shot Jardine with a prolonged burst from a TSMG.

Jim Elliott, a former Special and a Corporal in the Newry Company, lived with his wife and three children below the Bronte Church at

Drumballyroney. He worked as a lorry driver for a Newry firm, regularly transporting gypsum from a quarry in the South. On the late afternoon of Monday 17 April he had just crossed the Border travelling northwards on the main road from Dublin when he was abducted and, it was believed, taken by his captors back into the South. For 36 hours there was no word of him, whilst the police on both sides of the Border launched a full-scale hunt. His body was discovered on a lane at Altnamackan just off the Newtownhamilton-Castleblaney road. He had been shot eleven times. Six milk churns packed with a total of 500lb of explosives had been placed nearby, along with two claymore mines, wired to a firing point across the Border. It was feared that the body itself might be booby trapped and it took all day for the Army to clear the explosives whilst Gardai and an Irish army patrol located the firing point. Beard, Elliott's Commanding Officer, watching the clearance operation from the hillside, remembers a TV reporter asking him if it could not be hurried up a bit, otherwise she would miss the Six O'Clock news.[10]

The public revulsion caused by the murder and the use of the body to lure the Army on to the explosives was compounded by rumours that Elliott had been tortured. The rumours emanated from the fact that the relatives who had had the task of identifying the corpse had mistaken the damage caused by the bullets and by the body being dragged along the ground during the clearance operations as evidence of torture. A report in the local paper describing the injuries fuelled the rumours, particularly in Rathfriland, Elliott's home town, where a mob broke the windows of Catholic-owned shops. Paisley sought an emergency debate at Westminster, claiming that the Army and the police had made conflicting statements about the torture allegations, but when the inquest was held six weeks later the state pathologist confirmed that there was no evidence of torture. The Battalion history records: "An enduring memory of the funeral was the number of young male mourners who ought to have been in the UDR, yet Rathfriland remained a disappointing recruiting area. Their wrath stopped short at actually enlisting."

It was 4UDR who were to suffer most that year, with six soldiers murdered, four of them on their farms along the Border. Another ten were wounded. On 1 March Private 'Johnny' Fletcher set out from his home at Fervagh, a hundred metres from the Border on the minor road to Kiltyclogher in Leitrim to begin his day's work with the Forestry Commission. When he stopped to open the gate at the end of the track leading up to his house four gunmen were waiting for him. They took him back to the house and threatened to shoot him and his wife if they would not reveal where his SLR was hidden. Having found the rifle, they took Fletcher with them, promising that he would not be harmed, then shot him in a farm building on the Border.

Another soldier living in the area was believed to have been targeted. he lived 400 metres from the Border and was particularly vulnerable, as there was only the one road he could use to travel to and from work. The

Battalion decided that he and three other families living in the Garrison area must be moved at once:

> "We acquired houses for them in safer areas," Billy Dickson, the commander of the Monea Company explained, "and moved them by tractor, by Landrover and trailer and by car, lock, stock and barrel. Any cattle that had to go were brought to the local Thursday market and sold."

Most let out the land or hung on to it, farming it at a distance, others sold it at knock-down prices. For none of this did they receive any government compensation.

> "One of the saddest human stories to come out of the troubles," the *Belfast Telegraph* commented, "is the quitting of their farms by five UDR men on the Fermanagh border. They saw the writing on the wall after the particularly callous killing of Thomas Fletcher and are getting out. For farmers moving house is not as simple as it is for town dwellers. It means a whole new way of life in new surroundings for people who do not take readily to change. A family house has to be boarded up and livestock disposed of. The whole tragedy of Ireland is summed up in this scene. People are being driven further and further apart by events and after the mental separation – brought about by centuries of apartheid living – comes the physical separation."

A fortnight later a Private who farmed at the southern end of Upper Lough Erne came under fire from across the Border on the southern side of the lough. He was unharmed, but when he came under attack again in the same area in the following November he sold his cattle, moved out of the farm and was taken on by the Battalion on Voluntary Call Out. In July armed raiders called at the home of a family at Cooneen, a lonely hamlet south of Fivemiletown. Shortly after the two elder sons, both in the UDR, had set out from home for their civilian jobs, four men in two cars drove into the hamlet. Two went on to the post office and two came into the house:

> "They weren't masked, just beards on them," one of the sons said. "Black hair. Very respectable looking men. You'd think they would not have been at that sort of carry on. 'We're here for the guns,' they told my mother. 'There's no guns here,' she said. One of them stayed with her, held a gun to her head and said, 'You tell me where those guns are.' My mother said, 'There's no guns here.' The second fellow went to the kids upstairs. They were small at the time, twelve and eight. He got them out of bed and put them on the sofa downstairs, put the guns to their heads and told my mother, 'Now tell us where the guns are'. My mother said, 'There's no guns here'. They asked one of the boys. I think it was Ian says, 'There's no guns here'. They

went upstairs and pulled everything out, turned the beds up and all round the rooms looking for the guns, but could not find them. They came back down and one said to my mother, 'I'm going to shoot you if you don't tell us'."

Meanwhile the alarm sounding at the Post Office down the road had alerted the postmaster's son, who was sick in bed. He challenged the other two raiders with his shotgun, putting out the back window of their car as they made off, taking some cash with them. As they passed the house they fired two shots in the air to warn their companions and the four of them headed south for the Border, having failed to find the SLRs. They had been hidden on top of the wardrobe. 'If they had got them they wouldn't have been any use as the breech blocks were out of them."

On 21 September Private Tommy Bullock, 53 years old and a substantial farmer, was shot dead with his wife Emily in their farmhouse at the end of a lane a mile from Aghalane, the Border crossing point on the main Enniskillen – Belturbet road. A raiding party nine strong had driven across the Border in three cars. As the couple were sitting down to watch the early evening news three of the gunmen called at the back door of the house. Mrs Bullock answered and was shot down in the porch. They burst into the living room, firing wildly with a .303 rifle and an M1 carbine, smashing furniture and ornaments, and killing Bullock, who had been sitting in front of the television on the couch. The commander of the Lisnaskea Company went straight to the scene and had to step over the wife's body to enter the sitting room. He put his hand down the side of the couch where he knew Bullock kept his personal protection pistol; it was still there, he had had no chance to draw it. The house has lain empty to this day.

Meanwhile a second carload of gunmen had called at the home of a Lance Corporal close by. He was out, but his sister was in the house. She refused to open the door until she had hidden her brother's weapon, but when they threatened to shoot one of the children playing outside, she opened the door and ushered the child to safety. The men ransacked the house and took two uniforms but failed to find the weapon. Onlookers said that as the men drove away across the Border they were cheering and blowing the car horn.

Even this was not the end of the sorry catalogue of atrocities against the Border farmers of Fermanagh in that year. Early on the morning of 22 October the Bell family, father and two sons, had been checking their cattle at an outlying farm when gunmen opened fire on them from behind a hedge. The father and one son were slightly injured, but the other son, Robin, a member of 4UDR, was hit several times and died on the operating table. The assassins sped off in a car previously stolen in Clones in Co. Monaghan, abandoned it a mile down the road and used a boat to cross the River Erne into the South.

There were those who maintained that the Provisionals were following a deliberate policy of genocide and that they were targeting eldest sons so that the land would pass out of Protestant hands. Others believed that their aim was to remove Protestants who could observe their activities and put at risk their forays deeper into the county and beyond. It was also, of course, a fact that these farming families were the softest possible targets, in the sense that they could be attacked from the safety of the other side of the Border or that a safe haven lay only yards away. The Irish Government's denials that the IRA was operating across the Border from the Republic rang very hollow.

On the evening of the Bell murder two Catholics were stabbed to death on a farm not far away. One was a prominent Civil Rights activist. Locally it was assumed that the killings had been carried out by members of the UDR in retaliation for the death of their comrades. In fact the two men had been killed by members of a patrol of the Argyll and Sutherland Highlanders. Eight years later two of the soldiers were found guilty of murder, one of manslaughter and the platoon commander of withholding information. The UDR had had nothing to do with the killings, but in the seven years until the news of the arrests of the Argylls had broken only one more member of 4UDR was murdered in South Fermanagh.

Two more members of the Battalion were killed on patrol when a bomb exploded in a car they were checking out on a road into Enniskillen. The Battalion history records three car bombs in Enniskillen, others in four neighbouring towns, eight attacks on Customs caravans, several filling stations and two hotels destroyed. The list is not complete. There were twenty-five claymore incidents, four soldiers of the Royal Artillery were killed in separate ambushes, a Garda Inspector blown up by a bomb he was checking out on the Southern side of the Border, two policemen dead, one killed by a booby trap under his car, the other struck down in the first RPG7 rocket attack on the police station at Beleek.

In Fermanagh in particular 1972 was a terrible year. Of the fourteen other UDR soldiers murdered that year two more lived on or close to the Border. Colour Sergeant John Ruddy, Quartermaster Sergeant of the Newry Company by night and their Civil Service storeman by day, had served in the Regular and Territorial Army for 31 years and had joined the UDR at the outset. In his youth he had been a keen Gaelic footballer and had played soccer for Newry Town in the Irish League. He was now 50 years old and the father of twelve children. He had walked a short distance from his home on his way to the Company base when a gunman stepped out of the bushes and shot him eleven times. His wife was still standing on the doorstep with one of their daughters, waving her husband goodbye and two of the other children were following him on their way to school. All of them saw it happen. On the day of the funeral about 300 people followed the hearse from the house through the town to the Requiem Mass in St Mary's Church, a pathetic number compared to the processions at IRA funerals. The mourners included a large contingent from the

Battalion in civilian clothes and, it was believed, members of the Official IRA.

Willie Bogle lived with his wife and three small children at Gortnagross on the Tyrone-Donegal border. On the evening of 5 December the family drove to the nearby village of Killeter to shop. Mrs Bogle went into the post office whilst her husband and the children waited in the car. He must have noticed the gunman coming for him, for his wife described how she had seen him running towards the Post Office, crouching as he ran. As he made a grab for the door handle he was shot and fell into her arms. She told the inquest how she had pleaded, "Willie, don't die," and he had replied, "No, I never will," but he was dead before a doctor arrived. His assassin was believed to be a former member of the Castlederg Company. He was known for his Republican views and after a year he resigned from the UDR. Following the shooting he moved across the Border into Donegal and never returned.

The decision to allow companies without armouries to keep their service rifles and thirty rounds of ammunition at home had created an unforeseen problem; the homes became targets for terrorists hungry to acquire weapons. When early in 1972 the old No. 4 rifles were replaced by the modern self-loading rifles, the problem became acute.

One of the first weapons to be stolen was taken at gunpoint from a soldier who farmed near Rathfriland. On his return he had broken down his No. 4 rifle into its four parts, hiding the weapon itself in a wardrobe and the bolt, ammunition and magazine in a plastic bag underneath. He was watching television when a man and a youth came into the living room from the kitchen. The first intruder pointed his gun at the soldier's wife and children and threatened to shoot them if he would not reveal where his weapon was hidden. So the soldier told them it was in the wardrobe and the parts underneath; the youth fetched the rifle and a plastic bag, and the two went off into the night. Unfortunately for them it was the wrong plastic bag; it contained only some soap and talcum powder. Four months later gunmen again called at the farm. They locked the wife and young children in an outhouse, splashed the farmhouse with diesel and threatened to set it alight unless the soldier handed over his SLR, issued to replace the stolen rifle. Whilst this was going on, a son, also a soldier, called to see his parents. The intruders forced him to strip, put him against the wall beside the father and shot both men in the leg. Leaving the family still locked in the outhouse listening to the sounds of shooting and wondering if both men were dead, the gunmen made off with the son's SLR. Six years later it was found by the Gardai among a cache of seven IRA weapons.

Against men so cold-blooded and callous as to threaten the whole family, it was more than anyone could reasonably ask of a soldier that he should persist in his refusal to hand over his weapon. Yet not all the raiders had it their own way. The family at Cooneen and the Lance Corporal's sister at Aghalane had refused to give way to the gunmen's threats. In Downpatrick two men purporting to be telephone engineers and driving a Post Office van called at a home where the father and two sons were in the UDR. The mother was suspicious, since the home did not have a telephone, but she let them in when they explained that they had to locate a fault in the telephone system in the estate and produced what seemed to be a genuine authority. When one of the sons came downstairs, one of the men produced a gun, saying he was from the UVF and ordering him to lie on the floor. The mother struggled with the man, and the second son, who was at home recovering from pneumonia, went to her assistance. One of the intruders panicked and ran back to the van whilst the struggle with the second erupted into the hall and out onto the front step. One son had managed to grab the gun and, as the second man ran back to the van, he used it to fire three shots, one passing through the passenger window of the van. It was found abandoned outside the town, with blood inside it. After five instances had occurred of soldiers based in North Belfast having their pistols stolen by Loyalist paramilitaries, one of them being severely beaten in the process, their platoon commander took resolute action to ensure the weapons were returned.

Not all the weapons were stolen from homes; some, mainly pistols but including an SLR and two SMGs, 'went missing' from company armouries. A few were probably given away to paramilitaries of both hues, though it was seldom possible to prove that this was the case. If a soldier claimed that he had been 'forced' to hand over his PPW at a UDA barricade, it could have been true, but again it might not. In Castlewellan a SLR was stolen from the home of a soldier whilst he and his wife were out at bingo. There was a strong suspicion that he had arranged to be absent from the house that evening, a suspicion compounded when he became one of the founder members of a transitory and ineffectual organization in the town called The Irish Freedom Fighters (IFF). One of the members of the IFF was another ex-soldier from 3UDR who had resigned. (In their time in the Battalion both soldiers had been detailed regularly for the daytime guard on the Prime Minister's house!) Late one night the Battalion Training Warrant Officer was returning to his home, a lonely bungalow on the edge of the town. He parked the car badly, bumping the rear wheels against the kerb and rebounding forward. At that moment a gunman fired a shot which passed through the rear door and out the other side, missing the Sergeant Major by the distance the car had run forward. Next door neighbours reported that they had seen the former soldier apparently selecting a firing position in the field above the bungalow. Two spent SLR cases were found at the spot. The police took him in for questioning but had insufficient evidence to charge him. Next day he went on the run.

In all, between October 1971 and November 1973, ninety-six weapons were stolen from individuals in their homes, on their way to and from duty or in company locations, including forty-seven SLRs and thirty-seven handguns. About 70% were believed to have been stolen by Loyalist paramilitaries. After 1973 the number of thefts dwindled. By then the paramilitaries had found other sources for obtaining weapons more suitable for terrorist attacks.

Faced with these embarrassing losses, HQUDR reversed the Weapons Out policy, though, in some areas, particularly along the Border, soldiers were allowed to continue to keep their weapons at home. However, the murders of off-duty soldiers made it imperative that those who were most vulnerable had some means of defending themselves off duty less cumbersome than the SLR. Battalions were authorized to issue service .38 revolvers to such men. Alternatively the CO could recommend to the police that a soldier under specific threat should be granted a Firearms Certificate (FAC), authorizing him to purchase a handgun from a civilian gunsmith. Three thousand two hundred .38 revolvers were released from Ordnance stock along with 7,000 chains for securing front doors, and instructions were issued to every soldier detailing the security precautions that he and his family should observe.[11]

Soldiers were warned that so far as possible they should avoid sticking to a routine, but that was easier said than done. For many it was possible to choose at random alternative routes between home, civilian job and UDR base, but it was in the last half mile, the lane up to the farm, the turning into the home street, where there was no alternative, that the threat was greatest. Some routines were inescapable: the factory shift, the weekly market, the milking of the herd, the churn set out for collection at the end of the lane. Some had jobs that were tied to a fixed routine: the dustman, the postman, the bus driver, the driver of the Milk Marketing Board tanker.

The soldier must remain alert at all times, look out for strangers, the car that seemed to be following him, reluctant to overtake. He must drive with the doors locked on the inside, and when he pulled up at traffic lights he must leave room between himself and the car in front to manoeuvre out of harm's way. (When compulsory seat belt regulations were introduced, members of the security forces were initially exempt from wearing them.) Even at home he must not relax his guard. Outer doors must be kept locked – not easy when the farm kitchen door is the quickest way into the yard. Blinds must be lowered and curtains drawn at dusk, knocks at doors not answered until the caller had been identified; the doorstep should be illuminated by an exterior light; if the caller was a stranger the door should not be opened.

All the family must understand; there were instances where an assassin was let into a house by one of the children. Children must be taught an answer to give when school friends asked them what their father did; 'he works in town' or 'he has a business'. Wives must be told not to hang out items of military clothing on their washing line.

It was unnatural, but in time it became automatic, a way of life.

Unlike the RUC, where membership of the force was alone considered sufficient justification for the issue of a Personal Protection Weapon, in the UDR possession had to be justified in every single case. Some requests were turned down and letters from local politicians complaining that one of their constituents, a reliable citizen and a member of the UDR, had been refused a weapon to protect himself became commonplace. In time the police's attitude was that membership of the UDR was sufficient justification enough for the issue of a FAC. As a result, the strict rules that a soldier must be under specific threat before he could be issued with a service Personal Protection Weapon (PPW) were relaxed, with the headquarters taking the view that it was better for the soldier to hold a service weapon than a private one, as he was then subject to the strict rules of military discipline governing its holding and safe custody.

In due course most soldiers had a PPW or a private firearm. There were few instances where an off-duty soldier's life was saved by being able to fire back at his attackers. Arguably the fact that just one soldier's life was so saved justified their issue. On the other hand there were instances where the soldier did not have his personal weapon with him when he was shot, or, like Tommy Bullock of 4UDR, did not have time to draw it, for invariably it was the assassin who fired first. Sadly there were tragic cases of fatal accidents, with soldiers shooting themselves or members of their family, for constant possession of a weapon in the home led to careless handling and one mistake could lead to a needless death. Instant accessibility to a weapon also led to suicides that might never have happened if the means had not been ready to hand. Possession of a PPW was a reassurance as well as a deterrent, but they resulted in the deaths of many more soldiers and dependants than members of the IRA. Only one Provisional is known to have been shot dead by a soldier using his PPW in self-defence.

On the evening of 17 January seven internees escaped from the prison ship *Maidstone* moored in Belfast harbour. Sawing through the bars on a porthole, they swam across the channel, commandeered a passing bus and disappeared into the Markets. Headquarters 5 Brigade initiated an operation designed to close all the bridges over the old canal between Newry and Lough Neagh, thereby cutting off all direct land routes between the city and the Republic. 2 and 3UDR were called out for 48 hours. The following afternoon a fourteen-man foot patrol from the Kilkeel Company was moving along the main road from Warrenpoint to Newry. At that point where the Newry River flows into the north-west corner of Carlingford Lough about one and a quarter miles of the opposite bank lies in the Republic. A 17th century castle, Narrow Water, dominates this ancient route leading into the heartland of the North. The patrol saw about a dozen armed men dismount from cars on the other side of the Border, walk down through a wood and take up positions behind a wall above the river bank. The soldiers took cover behind the castellated wall of the more modern castle residence. The IRA fired first. The ensuing fire-fight lasted for some twenty minutes over the river and the main road, whilst traffic stopped and motorists dived for cover. The gunmen fired some 150 rounds and the patrol 101 SLR and 155 SMG, at that time the heaviest expenditure by a UDR patrol in any one incident. So far as was known, no one was hit on either side.

On the evening of 21 March a party from 4UDR had driven up to the ranges at Gortin in the Sperrins in the Battalion minibus to carry out a night firing practice. As they set out for home, an explosion at the side of the road blew the coach into the air and stripped off the back doors. One man was slightly injured, a piece of shrapnel lodging in his neck. A month later another party on the same range had a miraculous escape. They had intended to carry out the shoot from the 300 yard firing point, but the sun, shining into their eyes, made it impossible to see the targets. Instead they decided to use the 200 yard point, since at the shorter range the sun was less obtrusive. At the end of the day some of the men walked back over the grass to the transport. As they crossed the 300 yard point a soldier stepped on a pressure switch, setting off seven charges buried in the ground where the men would have been lying had it not been for the problem with the sun. He and four others were slightly injured. Had they used the further firing point, they would probably have been killed.

In June a patrol from the Castlederg Company came very close to being blown up by a bomb placed in the Derg Valley Hotel, as the Company Commander recalled:

"On walking around the back we discovered a sack up against the wall of the ballroom. It was dark at the back so I went to the Shorland to get a torch. When I came back one of the men in the patrol was kicking the sack and another was pulling out a coil of thin flex wire. At the end of the coil was a crocodile clip which was open at the end and there were two bright copper terminals staring us in the face. I can still remember them, shining in the light of the torch. I suddenly realized that this was a type of anti-handling device and that the other end of it was held open by a piece of soldering wire which gradually stretched until it snapped. In a matter of a very few seconds we were round at the front of the hotel and getting the men organized to evacuate the houses. Then we thought of the owner and his son upstairs in the hotel, asleep. I went upstairs and hauled him out of his bed and trailed him down the stairs, much against his will. When ATO arrived he declared it to be a bomb which he wouldn't touch with a '40 ft pole'. We all waited with bated breath out on the road. We heard a couple of shots from ATO's .22 rifle, and then an almighty explosion. Later we discovered that upstairs where the two men had been asleep, the pillows and bedclothes were completely cut to ribbons by the flying glass. It was only when we were going home that we realized how close we had been to blowing ourselves up with this device."

During 1972 the IRA had begun to change the pattern of its attacks. Street riots and urban gun battles became less frequent as they turned to a policy of planting bombs against 'economic targets', including pubs, restaurants and department stores in Belfast and in country towns across the Province.

In the first half of the year there were three horrific attacks in the centre of Belfast, with bombs exploding after inadequate warnings, killing eight and injuring over 300, many of them women and children. A decision was taken to seal off the city centre by erecting barriers, closing the streets to prohibit the passage of vehicles and to control the entry of pedestrians. In the beginning the barriers were manned by the Regular Army by day, with the UDR, mainly the city battalions, taking over by night and all day on Sundays. From time to time the battalions took over the whole Segment, as it was called, on a 24-hour basis to enable the Regulars to concentrate on other tasks of a higher priority. It was a heavy load, but it was a popular task; the UDR was operating more fully in the public eye.

One of the results of the riots in 1969 had been the emergence of un-official vigilante groups to protect the Catholic and Protestant working-class districts of the city. In September 1971 the Ulster Defence Association (UDA) was set up, organized on paramilitary lines, to co-ordinate the groups in Protestant areas. At its peak in 1972 it had some 40,000 members. Masked men armed with pick-helves began controlling the side roads leading into the Protestant neighbourhoods. They, and the more extreme Ulster Volunteer Force (UVF), also had access to arms. In May eight people were shot dead in a gun battle waged for 24 hours between the Catholic Ballymurphy and Protestant Springmartin estates. Another battle erupted in June. Loyalist assassination gangs made their first appearance. Unable to enter the Catholic estates, they selected their victims at random, mostly innocent men and women unconnected with terrorism. UDA influence began to spread to other Protestant centres, in Lisburn, Portadown, Lurgan, and barricades were set up to protect the estates. Initially they gained considerable support in some Protestant circles where they were regarded as legitimate defenders of the Unionist cause, threatened by the security policies of a weak government.

The barricades had a secondary purpose, to serve as a counter-action to those that the Republicans had set up, partly in West Belfast, but primarily enclosing the Bogside and Creggan districts of Londonderry, creating 'no-go' areas which neither the Army nor the police were allowed to enter. Within these areas, shut away from the normal processes of law and order, the IRA controlled the Catholic community and racketeering flourished. On Friday 30 June the UDA began establishing their own 'no-go' areas. They hijacked vehicles and, using pneumatic drills, worked through the weekend, setting up permanent barriers of metal bars and concrete blocks. By the Sunday evening they had established 'no-go' areas in the Shankill, Oldpark and Woodvale. The following evening they attempted to set up a further barricade in Ainsworth Avenue. This would have enclosed some fifty Catholic families and the Army ordered them to withdraw. They refused and a very ugly situation developed. The UDA called up reinforcements until some 1,200 of them were facing 250 soldiers. CLF, General Robert Ford, who had gone to the scene, contacted Whitelaw, the Secretary of State, by telephone, asking his permission to open fire, for otherwise the troops would be overwhelmed. Whitelaw said he must contact the Prime Minister and Defence Secretary. Ford warned him there wasn't time. Reluctantly the Secretary of State gave his permission. When the General told the UDA leaders he had authority to open fire, at first they were incredulous. Then, realizing that he was serious, they agreed to back down.[12]

On 26 June, following a concession by the British government that paramilitary prisoners being held for terrorist offences, of whom there were only eight Republicans and forty Loyalists at that time, should be granted 'special category' status and allowed to wear civilian clothes, the IRA called a temporary truce. On 7 July six of the Provisional leaders were flown over to London to hold talks with Whitelaw and other British ministers. "They simply made impossible demands which the government could never concede," Whitelaw recalled.[13]

Two days later the Provisionals staged an incident on the Lenadoon estate in West Belfast. When the Army intervened, gunmen opened fire on the troops. That night the Provisional Chief of Staff announced that the ceasefire was over.

On 21 July Belfast was busy as shoppers made the most of the last day of the Twelfth holiday. The first bomb exploded at ten minutes past two in Smithfield bus station. In the next hour eighteen more went off one after another right across the city, most of them with inadequate warning and some without warning at all. Seven civilians and two soldiers were killed and 130 injured, men, women and children. The *Guardian* reported that Belfast was reduced

> "to near total chaos and panic. Girls and men wept openly, hugging each other for safety, in the main streets as plumes of smoke rose around them and and dull thuds echoed from wall to wall. It was impossible for anyone to feel perfectly safe. As each bomb exploded there were cries of terror from people who thought they had found sanctuary but in fact were just as exposed as before."

The world was appalled by the scenes of carnage on television that night, showing ambulance men shovelling up into plastic body bags the scattered remains of the dead at the Oxford Street bus station.

July was the month of a heatwave, the month when a five-month-old baby was blown out of its pram and killed by a bomb in Strabane and a 71-year-old man was shot dead in Belfast whilst grappling with two bombers, the month of the abortive truce and Bloody Friday, the month that culminated in the largest operation mounted by the British Army in the last sixteen years, and in the destruction of an inoffensive village, the month that ninety-seven people met their deaths as a result of the violence.

Before Bloody Friday the decision had already been taken to mount Operation MOTORMAN. Its aim was to restore law and order by ensuring that there were no areas in which the security forces could not operate freely. Primarily that meant the Republican 'no-go' areas, but it was emphasized that the operation was not being mounted against the Catholic community. Rather it was designed to give them the chance to get the Provisionals off their backs. As for the Loyalist barricades it was foreseen that they would be dismantled voluntarily. If not, then they too would be removed by force. D Day was to be 31 July.

It was not expected to be a walk-over. The IRA in Londonderry was expected to resist. Seven additional battalions were brought in, bringing the total number of troops in the Province to 32,000, the highest number ever reached, before or since. For the first time armour was to be deployed; three Armoured Vehicle Royal Engineers (AVREs), converted Centurion tanks with bulldozer blades, were to be brought in by landing craft to remove the barricades in the Bogside.

In a small country in peacetime it was impossible to keep secret the fact that a major operation was under way. In 3 Brigade COs received the first intimation that it was being planned on 11 July, ten days before Bloody Friday. A warning order was passed on to the UDR Company Commanders the following day. It came at an opportune moment, for they were concerned about the adverse effect that the news of the Secretary of State's meeting with the IRA leaders had had on the morale of their soldiers.

5UDR was called out on 29 July, D-2, to impose a cordon round Londonderry, supported by armoured reconnaissance patrols. By H-24 the city was sealed off. The other UDR battalion commanders were given their tasks at a separate orders group on D-1.

At midnight on the 30th the BBC reported major troop movements round Londonderry. During the night Whitelaw announced on radio that the Army would be conducting substantial operations and warned people to stay off the streets. In the early hours he joined General Tuzo in Lisburn to await the first reports:

> "For some time Harry Tuzo and I sat in his office in considerable suspense. Was the Army being obstructed? Were civilians lying on the streets? These were the questions going through our minds. The Bogside and Creggan areas had been occupied and controlled by the IRA for so long that they had to be treated as enemy territory. We feared that the population as a whole would be instructed to obstruct the entry of troops by mass demonstrations and even by actually lying down on the streets in front of advancing vehicles."[14]

As the UDR Company Commanders drove into their battalion head-quarters to receive their orders, they listened to the first news reports on their car radios. It was probably the first time that anyone in the British Army had said goodbye to their family, shut their front door, taken the car from the garage and driven out along the road to keep an operational H Hour.

In Londonderry the advance of four battalions into Rosville and Creggan estates had met with little resistance. Two people had been shot dead. By 7 am the whole area had been secured and the dismantling of the barricades begun. By evening the last of them had been removed and the AVREs had been re-embarked on the landing craft. Searches had uncovered a considerable quantity of arms, including an anti-tank rifle and a .30 Browning machine gun. In Belfast all the barricades had come down. In some areas both communities had dismantled them of their own accord. There had been few significant arrests. Long before H Hour the Provisionals had slipped away across the Border. But, to show they were still in business, before the day's end they exploded three car bombs in the small County Londonderry village of Claudy. Nine of the villagers died, including a nine-year-old girl, and the main street was all but demolished. No warning had been given; it was said that the terrorists had gone to a call box to make a warning call, to find it was out of order.

The UDR's tasks during the call-out were the guarding of key points to relieve regular troops, including the provision of military back-up in the Armagh and Crumlin Road gaols, foot patrols in the city and town centres, including fifty men on duty at any one time in the centre of Belfast, mobile and foot patrols on the Border and in country areas. 7 and 10UDR implemented the preplanned VCP operation, deploying road blocks on the routes into Belfast. 5UDR had eleven officers and 580 soldiers patrolling east and west of the Foyle round Londonderry, with VCPs continuously on the main roads into the city. The VCP on the Culmore Road was provided with tea and sandwiches every night for three weeks by nuns from a nearby convent.

There were some notable successes. A 2UDR patrol searching along the old railway line at Portadown found a substantial quantity of bomb-making equipment. Another patrol from the Battalion uncovered explosives in a car at Camlough. Subsequent searches of the driver's house revealed three rifles, a pistol and ammunition. A 3UDR VCP on the road between Downpatrick and Killough stopped a car and found £900 in a pillow case, stolen a short while before from a Carryduff bank, together with four hand guns, all loaded. The five occupants, all PIRA, were suspected of having been involved in two other bank raids in East Belfast.

8UDR chased a car and arrested two men after they had thrown their revolvers out on the roadside. A 10UDR foot patrol came under fire from a passing car on the Shore Road. They returned fire. Later the car was found abandoned with blood on the floor. A wounded man, suspected of being a passenger, was admitted to hospital. On 13 August the battalions were stood down. Some 5,300 men and women had answered the call-out.

The GOC sent a signal to Commander UDR:–

"The Ulster Defence Regiment made an indispensable contribution to Operation MOTORMAN and subsequent security measures. Future security depends heavily upon part-time turn-out, and I know that the people of Northern Ireland can rely on an unselfish and disciplined response by members of the Regiment."

The MOD decided that those battalions with coast lines or major inland loughs within their operational areas should be given a waterborne capability by issuing them with Dell Quay dories, flat-bottomed, fibre glass boats powered by two 40 horsepower outboard engines. 3UDR had been given first priority because there was a strong suspicion that smuggling of munitions was taking place across Carlingford Lough, the whole length of the southern shore of which lay in the Republic.

The Boat Section was commanded by Dennis Faulkner. Beard had met him at his brother Brian's house, and, establishing that he was a Lieutenant Commander in the Royal Naval Reserve, suggested that he apply for a commission in the UDR with a view to setting up the anti-smuggling patrols. On the last day of annual camp the section put on a demonstration for the media on Strangford Lough. Journalists from three main national newspapers, the local press, and camera teams from the BBC, UTV and an American company came to watch and film from a fishing boat. The resultant publicity did much to show the public that the Regiment was being issued with varied and modern equipment. They were told about, but not shown, the battalion's 'secret weapon', a Decca marine radar mounted on a Landrover chassis. Initially it was operated by Gunner regiments on roulement tours and deployed at Killowen Point to keep watch over Carlingford Lough, backed up by a UDR mobile patrol. By the end of the year sufficient UDR operators had been trained to enable the Battalion to take it over.

During MOTORMAN the section, supported by the radar detachment, was deployed continuously for three weeks at a base camp in the grounds of the former Ballyedmond Hotel. During that time the dories, armed with Bren guns and a Karl Gustav anti-tank weapon, stopped, boarded and searched forty vessels ranging from pleasure craft to coal boats entering or crossing Carlingford Lough, including the passenger ferry running between Omeath and Warrenpoint. There were problems. The first was to establish which part of the waters were British and which Irish. A signal from the Foreign Secretary, Sir Alec Douglas-Home, gave the co-ordinates of a blue line down the centre of the lough which the dories should not normally cross. The Faulkners signalled a reply, "Have spent twenty hours patrolling the area and cannot find a blue line anywhere." The second problem was that the dories were underpowered. The 40 hp engines were old and could produce a speed of only eighteen knots. A single 120 hp engine in each dory with a top speed of 30 knots was essential. However the main problem was that there was only one site along the north, shore where the dories could be readily launched at low water. At Ballyedmond they were kept anchored offshore, and the crews boarded them by dinghy or by wading out to them. But all this meant that any reaction to a report from the radar of a suspect vessel was too slow. The crossing took only some four minutes at the southern end and by the time the boat patrol reached the scene the smugglers, if that was what they were, had turned back and gone ashore on the southern side.

It was clear that shore-based dories were not the answer. A paper by 3UDR was submitted to the MOD, recommending that a naval vessel be stationed in the centre of the lough. This was accepted and from early 1973 a small fleet tender took up station off Killowen with a crew of six and carrying a detachment of Royal Marines equipped with Rigid Raider dories. The marines would patrol the length of the lough and, for variety, carry out snap VCPs on the coast road running along the north shore. Whilst half lived on board, the other half was based in the UDR Company Centre at Kilkeel. The arrangement was intended to last a year. The ships subsequently were changed and upgraded, but 21 years on the Royal Navy was still there.

Meanwhile 3UDR continued to use the dories, supported by the radar, to mount occasional anti-smuggling patrols around other stretches of the coast, particularly the Mourne shore, with its history of smuggling stretching back two centuries.

There was talk of munitions for both Republican and Loyalist para-militaries being landed along the seaward side of the Ards peninsula, transported across the peninsula, then ferried across Strongford Lough and moved on by road into mid-Ulster. It made sense. The southern end of the Ards is a lonely place. The village of Portavogie is strongly Loyalist and it would have been an easy matter for the fishing fleet to keep a rendezvous at sea. Loyalist home-made weapon 'factories' were discovered on both sides of the lough. Since there were only three roads running north up the peninsula to the city, the probability of weapons moving by road being intercepted was high. So the lough was an obvious alternative route. 3UDR deployed the radar on several occasions at the southern end, scanning northwards, but the problem was the same as at Carlingford; by the time the dories were launched it was too late and a vehicle patrol sent to intercept a landfall alerted the boat crew by the sound of the Landrover tyres.

These anti-smuggling operations and patrols carried out by the Royal Navy, though showing no spectacular results, did put an end to any attempts to bring munitions ashore along the Northern coastline. As for the radar, it was withdrawn and despatched to the South Atlantic at the time of the Falklands War and, it is believed, was lost when the merchant ship *Atlantic Conveyor* was sunk by an Argentinian missile.

On 1 July the eleventh battalion was formed at Portadown, taking as its title 'Craigavon', the new town set up in the early '60s between Lurgan and Portadown. The Battalion was created from the Lurgan and Portadown Companies of 2UDR and the Banbridge Company of 3UDR, and was commanded by Robin Chappell, the first Regular CO of the Armagh Battalion and the only one ever to command two UDR battalions.

Three new companies were formed, in North Belfast, Carrickfergus and Magherafelt, and consideration was given to forming a twelfth battalion, east of the Sperrins and west of the Bann. If the rate of applications continued there was concern that the Regiment would exceed its new ceiling of 10,000 by the autumn and that it would be impossible to find sufficient experienced company commanders to command or instructors to train the influx of recruits. In the event the problem never materialized. In October the Regimental strength reached its peak of 9,176. Thereafter there was a decline, at first so rapid that it gave some cause for concern but then slowing down. It seemed that among those who enlisted in the aftermath of internment and MOTORMAN, there were men who acted on impulse and lacked real motivation. Half of those who joined after internment never completed their engagement.[15]

The upsurge in 1972 placed a heavy load on the ASVU and on the RUC. For a while the system was overburdened and that, it seemed in retrospect, led to a temporary deterioration in the standard of vetting. It was a lapse that was to cause the Regiment much harm.

CHAPTER SIX

The Regiment and the Loyalist Paramilitaries
1972 – 1973

There were two main Loyalist paramilitary organizations. The first was the Ulster Volunteer Force, (UVF), formed in 1966 with the stated aim of waging war against the IRA. By 1972 it was reckoned to have consisted of some 1,500 members, drawn largely from the Shankill district of Belfast, East Antrim and County Armagh. It was armed and organized on military lines, and by 1972 was heavily involved in sectarian murders.[1] Apart from an eighteen-month period in 1974–1975 it was always a proscribed organization.

The other and much larger paramilitary organization, the Ulster Defence Association (UDA), grew out of the Loyalist vigilante groups in Belfast. Initially there were in their ranks decent men, including ex-servicemen, who believed that they had an honourable role to play in defending their own neighbourhoods and providing leadership and advice for their beleaguered people. However, from an early stage there were instances of expropriation of funds accumulated through street collections, and an expanding involvement in criminal activities, extortion, racketeering and the establishment of illegal drinking clubs. Increasing militancy led to the creation of 'no-go' areas, building up to the confrontation with the Regular Army at Ainsworth Avenue in July 1972 and involvement in sectarian murder. From 1973 onwards acts of violence by the Association were carried out under the name of The Ulster Freedom Fighters (UFF). Though the latter was soon declared illegal, the UDA was not proscribed until 1992.[2]

One of the first indications that these paramilitary groups could pose a threat to the Regiment occurred in May 1972 when a soldier who worked in his father's bar in Newcastle reported that a customer from the Shankill Road had tried to recruit him into the UVF. He was told that he would be given the rank of sergeant and would be required to recruit other soldiers to form a UVF cell within his UDR battalion. To support his credentials, the stranger gave the soldier a UVF lapel badge.

An armoury storeman in 3UDR, a Catholic, reported that he had been approached by a soldier from 10UDR, asking if he would sell him weapons, saying he had £300 to buy them.

Despite the confrontation at Ainsworth Avenue the UDA was still considered to be mainly a vigilante organization and had not been proscribed, and this influenced Ormerod's guidelines to his Commanding Officers on how to handle the problem of involvement of members of their battalions in the Loyalist organization. If an officer belonged to the UDA he was to be required to resign. So far as the soldiers were concerned, membership was not necessarily to be considered as a bar to service in the Regiment. However, if a man's conduct arising from the UDA membership should constitute a military offence, then disciplinary action should be taken against him, and this could include dismissal.

On 14 October the first of a series of arms raids mounted by Loyalist paramilitaries was carried out on the guardroom of 10UDR at Lislea Drive in Belfast. In the early hours, shortly after the part-time night guard had handed over to the full-time conrates, a party of armed men overpowered the gate sentry, burst into the guardroom, disarming the other three soldiers, and made off with five SLRs. The Lance Corporal guard commander was discharged and was later found to be a member of the UDA. Two months later four of the rifles were among a cache of weapons and radios recovered during the search of a house in the Shankill Road.

On 16 October, following the death of a member of the UDA and a fifteen-year-old, hit by an armoured personnel carrier in East Belfast, Loyalist gunmen had opened fire on the Army in several areas of the city. During the removal of barricades an off-duty soldier serving in 10UDR was shot dead. Though it has never been established whether the fatal shot was fired by the Army or the gunmen, there is a suspicion that the soldier was one of those who had opened fire on the troops.

Four days later the UVF from East Belfast carried out a raid on the armoury at the Territorial Army Centre in Lurgan. Both the TA and 11UDR had arms stored there and the guard was shared between them. On that night it was the TA's turn. In the early hours fourteen armed men, some dressed in military style uniform, overpowered and tied up the guard and drove off in a battalion Landrover, having loaded it with twenty-two SLRs and thirteen SMGs. A military Landrover has two fuel tanks. The raiders did not know this and when the petrol gauge registered zero, instead of switching over to the reserve tank, they abandoned the vehicle, having hidden the weapons they could not carry in a patch of nettles, where they were found next day by a Regular Army patrol. Again there was a strong suspicion of collusion. The UDR conrate guard sergeant was a former Regular soldier who had won the Military Medal whilst serving with the Royal Ulster Rifles in Korea. He was later recognized on a television programme featuring Loyalist paramilitaries and was promptly discharged. In 1975 he was murdered by the UVF.[3]

By now COs were fully alert to the dangers posed by the Loyalist paramilitaries, through dual membership or subversion of their soldiers. In 3UDR Beard issued an unequivocal battalion order:

"I will not tolerate any active participation by members of this battalion in any organization which encourages violence . . . you cannot play in both teams. Either you believe in law and order applied equally to all men, or you believe in violence as a means of achieving political ends. In this respect the UDA is no better than the IRA. Not only should you take no part in UDA activities but you should actively discourage your fellow citizens (from doing so)."[4]

On 6 November the Brigadier in the course of a talk to Belfast Rotary Club spelt out the policy on dual membership.

This public explanation produced a widespread and highly critical reaction. "No ban on UDA – UDR chief," headlined the *Newsletter*.
In an editorial the *Belfast Telegraph* said:

"Membership of a British regiment should be totally incompatible with membership of a sectarian organization which has publicly defied at least one law on the wearing of paramilitary uniforms."

Ivan Cooper of the SDLP said the Regiment should be disbanded. Oliver Napier, chairman of the Alliance Party, issued a statement that the Commander's remarks

"only confirm that what many have suspected for a long time, namely that the UDR requires to be cleared of the minority of undesirable elements before it can gain the trust of the entire community." In a letter to a UDR officer he wrote:-
"The area in which I live in East Belfast is being completely terrorized by people in paramilitary uniforms who claim to be in the UDA. In that particular area there is not and has never been any IRA activity, so the only enemies of the Queen we have ever seen at first hand are the UDA.
"It appears to me just as irresponsible to suggest that there is no ban on UDA men being members of the UDR as it would be to suggest that there is no ban on Provos joining.
"I have also been informed by a number of Alliance members in the UDR that in their group there are men who make no secret of the fact that their joint loyalty is to the UDA, not to the United Kingdom. Some of these men boasted that they joined the UDR to receive arms training and also to get a licence for a side arm, allegedly for their own defence. These facts greatly disturb me. I am, however, convinced firstly that there are relatively few UDA sympathizers in the UDR except in the Western areas and in Belfast, and secondly that in the entire force unreliable elements form only a tiny minority of the whole. However, it is extremely important that the UDR should have the complete confidence of all the law-abiding population and that men serving in the Regiment should have full confidence in their colleagues. On that point in parts of the Western area of this Province moderates who are serving in the Regiment are afraid of some of their own comrades."[5]

The day after the Brigadier's talk to Rotary there was a third arms raid, the worst so far. 10UDR was responsible for providing a night guard at the Oldpark Telemetry Centre. Shortly before they were due to take over, the civilian watchman was overpowered by armed men. One of them took the watchman's place and, when the UDR guard arrived, the raiders first seized the three soldiers on duty at the gate and then captured the remaining eleven members of the guard. They escaped in the guard Landrover, taking with them fourteen rifles and ammunition. The vehicle was abandoned outside a UDA Club in the Shankill. One of the rifles was recovered two years later in a West Belfast Orange Hall. The raiders claimed to be members of the UVF. Though never proved, it was strongly suspected that there had been complicity between them and one or more members of the guard.

As many members of the Regiment, including Ormerod, realized at the time, the initial policy on dual membership was flawed. Apart from the obvious risks involved in having men within the ranks whose loyalty to their companies and comrades could not be assured, it led to a situation where battalions, though some were more robust than others, were reluctant to discharge men, even those who were well known to be helping to train the UDA.[6] These were quite open about their activities: so far as authority was concerned they were not committing an offence.

Obviously the policy had to be changed and changed quickly. On 27 November a Regimental Routine Order was published, to be repeated in Battalion Orders. It stated that if a soldier's sympathy for the UDA, CESA or any similar organization was strong enough to affect the performance of his duties or to call in question his future loyalty or his complete impartiality, he would be discharged.[7]

As subsequent events were to show, even that did not go far enough. What was needed was a simple, unequivocal ruling that in no circumstances could a member of a paramilitary organization, proscribed or not, serve in the UDR. A mistake had been made that was to have a lasting effect on the good name of the Regiment and the mistake was neither the Regiment's nor Ormerod's doing.

Chris Ryder was not overstating the case when he wrote:

"At a time of accelerating Catholic exodus from the force . . . and growing Catholic doubts about its impartiality, the Regiment and the Government lost a golden opportunity. If they had unambiguously asserted the incompatibility of dual membership, disowned and isolated the malignant influences that were to corrode the integrity of the force and mar the gallantry and sacrifice of the overwhelming majority of its members for years to come, the UDR story could well have been one of triumph.

"By failing to abide by the Regiment's self-proclaimed standards, the Government and Army extinguished all hope of meeting the impartial ideals which had been set for it. From that point on the UDR became irrevocably alienated from the Catholic minority. Everything that happened afterwards was merely a confirmation of Catholic suspicions and fears concerning the UDR, all now freshly aroused."[8]

Over the next three years the total number of discharges on grounds of suspected paramilitary connections amounted to well under 200, less than 2% of the Regimental strength.

Instructions were given to battalions to get rid of soldiers who persistently failed to attend for duty or training. As a result between November '72 and January '74 2,000 were discharged or left of their own accord. It was considered probable that some of these were UDA sympathizers. The majority of the discharges occurred in the city and the County Antrim battalions. Company commanders welcomed their going, maintaining that the quality of their companies had been improved as a result.

Ryder's generalization that there was a distinct lack of vigour in weeding out bad apples is overstated but does have some justification. Battalions were fully alive to the need to get rid of men whose loyalty was suspect, for if the situation was allowed to continue they presented a threat to the future existence of the Regiment. Indeed nowhere was their presence more resented than in their own battalions.

Nevertheless there were occasional failures to act with sufficient resolution to get rid of undesirable individuals. A member of Special Branch spoke of the embarrassment felt by some of his police officers on having to brief a patrol, one of whose members had recently been held in the station for questioning in connection with a murder and who was strongly suspected of paramilitary activities. The soldier's CO was made aware of police suspicions and in such an instance any scruples about taking punitive action against a man who had not been proved guilty of a crime should have been set aside. The man was discharged, but not until some time afterwards. On the other hand when three soldiers in another battalion were strongly suspected of a serious crime but the police could not establish sufficient proof to charge them, they were dismissed without further ado.

When Queen's Regulations and the Manual of Military Law were drawn up no one had foreseen the need to discharge soldiers on suspicion of paramilitary activity. Under the system a soldier could protest right up to the Army Board if he considered he was being wrongfully discharged. A few did. Suspicion or gossip were not enough. The application for discharge had to be substantiated by hard fact. But Special Branch was on occasion reluctant to provide factual evidence for fear of exposing a source, and the Army's security company was not entirely conversant with the nuances of life in the Protestant communities. What to them must have seemed hotbeds of UDA activity were to many of the soldiers in the City battalions their homes. They knew members of the UDA. Of course they did; they were neighbours, in some cases members of the same family. They drank in UDA clubs. So many public houses had been destroyed that they were about the only place locally where they could get a drink. It was difficult to distinguish between 'association' and 'involvement'.

As a result of the influx of recruits after MOTORMAN 10UDR was by now by far the largest infantry battalion in the whole Army, with 1,300 on strength. A third company was formed in the battalion base at Girdwood Park. An old TA Centre adjacent to Crumlin Road Prison, it was a difficult location. Snipers frequently fired into it (in eight months of 1972 there were seven such incidents); petrol bombs were lobbed over the gate and patrols entering or leaving the base were liable to be bottled or stoned. The three companies recruited from the nearby Protestant heartlands – the Shankill, Forth River and Tiger Bay. The CO, Tony Hayes-Newington, was so dissatisfied with the security information he was receiving through the Army and police that he instructed his Training Major to set up the Battalion's own vetting system:

"I set up what would better be described as an indexing system. We entered names for whatever reason, including association with incidents such as arms thefts and UDA activity reported in the daily Brigade SITREP, checking every name mentioned against the Battalion nominal roll. We investigated every potential 10UDR 'case'. I do not recall a single proven case nor one discharge up to the time of my departure in October 1978. Girdwood was always troublesome in my day. The people there came from the hotbed Loyalist areas and there were some hardliners among them. I believe the underlying reason was the type and calibre of leadership there, in Girdwood. It was only when we began to get in place young officers and new NCOs we had ourselves selected and seen through training that matters got better."[9]

It was greatly to their credit that most of the soldiers continued to do duties without becoming involved, despite the pressures put on them. Though initially soldiers from both communities had been the victims of intimidation, of the 288 cases reported between January 1972 and August 1973 all but a dozen were Protestant. Since the threat was usually anonymous it is not possible to allocate responsibility among the various terrorist organizations, but the numbers soared as the extreme Loyalist organizations became more active. In some cases the intimidation was directed against soldiers who had joined the UDA and, disillusioned by that organization, were anxious to get out of its clutches. Intimidation took the form of threatening letters and telephone calls, shots fired from a passing car, two abductions, the intimidation of a soldier's children and arson. Most of those intimidated continued to report for duty. There were fairly frequent incidents, particularly in 10UDR, of off-duty soldiers being beaten up by Loyalist thugs and forced to hand over their personal protection weapons. In the first half of the year there were six such incidents. In one the soldier was left locked up in the boot of his car. A soldier was driving in the Shankill Road area when two men, one of them armed, attempted to hijack his car. He opened fire with his personal protection weapon and killed one of the hijackers. Ten days later a pipe bomb was thrown into the soldier's house, damaging it so badly that the family had to be moved to a new home. After shots had been fired outside a community centre in Greenisland, a strongly Protestant area, a Corporal of 9UDR was tasked to lead a confidence patrol through the town. The Battalion received an anonymous telephone call, warning that the Corporal had better not patrol the town again. Next day three shots were fired at his home. A vehicle patrol of 7UDR in East Belfast came across two policemen trying to deal with a drunken brawl outside a public house. The patrol stopped to give help and several people were arrested. A few nights later a member of the patrol was drinking in another pub when he was accosted by one of the men he had helped to arrest. Thereafter the soldier's life and that of his family were made so intolerable that they emigrated to Australia.

A part-time soldier in one of the two Lisburn companies of 9UDR recalled an encounter with the local UDA:

"They used to carry out patrols in the town, masked, wander about with pick helves, and we had verbal clashes with them. There was no love lost between us. Our instructions were very specific, we had to stay clear of them, simply report on the radio and back off. That was very difficult. The ops room would inform the RUC, but they took no action either in those days. It was quite common to walk through Lisburn on a Saturday and have these fellows shaking a money box under your nose for the Loyalist prisoners. They were there in the streets quite openly with a pick helve, demanding money, and nothing was done about it. One night we stopped a van in Bow Street. The searcher noticed combat jackets in the back and ordered the three occupants out. I noticed one of them slipping something under his seat and found it was a grenade. We arrested the three of them and whilst we waited for the police to arrive one or two people urged us to let them go because they were, in their words, 'some of ours'. Subsequently a guy took the rap for it, said the hand grenade was his, and he was prosecuted and got two years. We had to go up to Crumlin Road Court to give evidence, which worried us a bit because we were told we could not be given any immunity and would have to give our names and addresses. In the event the guy pleaded guilty.

"I thought that would be the end of it, but about two months later the Corporal in charge of the patrol that night was drinking in a local pub. He went out back to the toilet and about six guys jumped him. Fortunately he managed to draw his PPW and fire one round into the ground. The police arrived and they were all taken to the RUC station. On the way there they made an arrangement with the

Corporal that if he did not press charges they would leave him alone. They confirmed they were out to get him. Their intention was to blind him for getting their man jailed. The Corporal had to live in the community, so he agreed not to press charges and nothing more came of it."

There were a number of UDR successes against the Loyalist paramilitaries during the first quarter of 1973. In January a patrol from 7UDR carrying out a routine patrol in the Braniel estate stopped a car carrying a number of men. One of them was Tommy Herron, the Vice Chairman of, and a leading spokesman for, the UDA. As all the occupants were abusive they were handed over to the RUC. In March a joint 1UDR/Regular Army patrol arrested four men who were suspected of having carried out a petrol bomb attack on a Catholic church in Larne. The next night a joint 10UDR/Royal Marine mobile patrol stopped a stolen car and arrested the four occupants. Earlier the four had thrown two bombs at the Christian Brothers' Club in the Antrim Road. A further bomb was found in the car along with a sub-machine gun and a pistol. The four were sentenced to imprisonment. The SMG was one of those stolen from the Lurgan armoury in October. In the following month, during an operation lasting over three nights, a hundred soldiers of 9UDR, using helicopters and backed by the police, played a leading part in the discovery of a UVF training area on a plateau surrounded by bushes at Fairhill near Ballynure. In the follow-up thirteen men were arrested and arms and ammunition seized.[10]

Three further arms raids were carried out by the Loyalist paramilitaries during 1973. On 6/7 March the Regiment had been called out to guard polling stations during the Border Referendum. In Dee Street in East Belfast the two sentries from 7UDR on duty outside the polling station were overpowered by six men. Having disarmed the sentries, the group then demanded that the other two members of the guard hand over their rifles, but the aggressive reaction of the guard commander and an RUC constable put the assailants to flight, albeit with the two SLRs. On the same day a ten-man guard from 10UDR was guarding a polling station at Berlin Street on the Shankill Road. A van drew up outside and a number of armed men dismounted and attacked the guard commander and two sentries standing outside. One sentry who resisted was pushed through a glass door and all three were overpowered. The raiders, who claimed to be from the UVF, then disarmed the remainder of the guard and made off with eight rifles.

A similar raid in April at Knockbracken reservoir on the southern outskirts of Belfast was foiled thanks to the determination and presence of mind of two members of 3UDR. A party of armed men, claiming to be from the UVF, drew up in a car on the main road, overpowered the Water Board security guard and marched him down to the guardroom at gun point, intending to set up an ambush for the guard when they came on duty. The two soldiers had arrived early. They took up fire positions and challenged the group, who turned and fled back to the car.

In October another raid took place, this time at the Battalion Head-quarters of 11UDR in Portadown. One man squeezed through a lavatory window that had been left open – probably intentionally – and held up the five-man guard, whilst about a dozen other armed men came in through the door. At that time, due to the lack of purpose-built armouries at many centres, weapons were kept secure in reinforced railway wagon containers. The guard commander refused to give up the key to the padlock and the raiders had to content themselves with the guards' weapons, four rifles and two sub-machine guns, five handguns, flak jackets and pocketphones.

Inevitably the weapon raids caused a loss of confidence in the UDR among Regular Army staffs and units, as well as an angry sense of betrayal among the members of the Regiment themselves. For all that, Tuzo took a fairly relaxed attitude towards the losses:

> "I remember how furious we were at HQNI, but I don't recall any suggestion at all that the whole Regiment was suspect. It is very sad that one or two people let them down, but after all the Regular Army had lost weapons before. You will always get bad elements. You were recruiting in the midst of a very volatile population, some with strong views, some open to bribes, and there was a lot of money about; undoubtedly the temptation was there."[11]

Why did the Loyalist paramilitaries join the UDR? According to a Loyalist source, they did so to obtain "free training, plus access to weapons, ammunition and intelligence". The same source's claim that "we always reckoned that in a doomsday situation, if the Brits were going to pull out or impose a solution we could seize Ulster with the UDR"[12] was rubbish. They never had any corporate influence in any battalion. Though UDA leaders encouraged some of their members to enlist, there is no evidence that they tried to pack sub-units with their members. Tuzo and the first three Commanders, and those first and second generation COs to whom the question has been put, all say that at no time did anyone from Army Intelligence and Security ever come to warn them that an organized attempt was being made to subvert the Regiment.

By the end of 1973 the process of weeding out the non-attenders had got rid of most of the soldiers involved with the paramilitaries. A few remained undetected, whilst others already in the Regiment became involved. Bearing in mind that over 40,000 men and women served over the 22 years, their numbers were small. The greatest harm they did was to provide support for the demands of politicians and others for the disband-ment of the Regiment. Greater significance was placed on their disloyalty than their numbers warranted. No doubt they regarded themselves as Loyalists, but they had no understanding of the true meaning of loyalty, to battalion, to company, to their platoon or the memory of their murdered comrades. They betrayed them. Apparently they had no problem in squaring their consciences with the fact that on the night they enlisted they had taken an oath on the Bible that they would obey the orders of the Queen, and the generals and officers set under her. They were contemptible.

CHAPTER SEVEN

1973

By 1973 the increasing experience and expertise of the security forces began to show results, with some Regular units returning for the third or fourth tour in the Province. Deaths, at 250, were almost half the previous year's, shooting incidents halved, and the number of people charged with terrorist offences nearly trebled. Nevertheless the Provisionals' campaign of bombings of commercial property, the use of landmines against security force patrols and the assassinations of members of the RUC and UDR continued. Despite the setting up of the Segment gates in the previous November, car bombs continued to cause great damage in Belfast, in towns across the country, and for the first time across the water in England. The number of bombs planted, though slightly down on the previous year, totalled 1,520. By night Belfast had become a dead city.

If there had been initial ministerial doubts about whether the concept of the UDR would work, by now all such doubts had been set aside. The Regular Army had come to realize that the Regiment had a vital role to play in the security of the Province and that whatever must be done would be done to further its development.

A major building programme had been launched and the first purpose-built accommodation, designed to house the Battalion headquarters and one company of 3UDR, was opened at Ballykinlar on 24 February. The £200,000 building consisted of a drill hall, offices, separate Officers' and Warrant Officers' and Sergeants' Messes, a Junior Ranks club, Stores, Armoury and Guardroom. A week later 4UDR's Battalion Headquarters was opened at Coleshill on the southern edge of Enniskillen, followed by a new HQUDR in Lisburn to replace the original, and by now hopelessly inadequate, bungalow. The new building was located opposite the entrance to Headquarters Northern Ireland in Thiepval Barracks, now rapidly expanding to house the increased staff and ancillary services required to command and maintain the army in the Province. Other permanent buildings were completed for 7UDR in Palace Barracks, Holywood, and for 5UDR in Duncreggan Camp, Londonderry, and one of the companies of 9UDR moved into Derryvolgie House in Lisburn. The Coleraine company had taken over Laurel Hill, a splendid Georgian house looking up the Bann, whilst the Clogher Company had occupied the historic Deanery after protracted negotiations to persuade the lady who lived in the old house with her Alsatian dog to move to a less spartan abode.

The Newry Company of 3UDR, based at the former TA Centre, had moved to a new base behind the RUC station in Rathfriland. They left behind a brave platoon of about a dozen local men who continued to carry out patrols in the town, on their own and jointly with the Regular Army who valued their advice and local knowledge. All but two of the Newry-based Catholics had resigned and it was hoped that the move to Rathfriland would encourage more men living in the country areas to enlist, a hope that was not realized.

The move from temporary accommodation, sometimes leaking war-time huts left over from the USC, into purpose-built, or at least properly adapted, accommodation played a significant part in fostering a greater sense of corporate identity within battalions and within the Regiment as a whole. From now on there were congenial centres where COs could hold regular conferences with their Company Commanders. Indoor training could take place in the drill halls and at the end of a training session the men could relax in a properly organized canteen. The drill halls served a secondary purpose as venues where occasional dances could be held. Though there was not much time for relaxation, at least soldiers could come together with wives and girl-friends and relax in the knowledge that they were in safe surroundings and need not worry about who might over-hear their conversations. Many a Regular Army officer and influential member of the county, invited to a guest night in an Officers' Mess, was surprised by the manner in which the traditions of the old Irish Regiments had been assimilated – the Loyal and Regimental toasts, the pipers playing round the table – and that despite the fact that there were some members who had never before owned a dinner jacket.

The posting in of Regimental Sergeant Majors from Regular units ensured that the Warrant Officers' and Sergeants' Messes became places where senior ranks, some of whom lived so far apart that they scarcely knew their opposite numbers in the other companies, could come together for an evening of good fellowship. As well as these social activities, battalions began to participate in most Army sports competitions, particularly football and orienteering. Pipe bands were being developed and 6UDR won the first inter-battalion competition. Henceforth the pipe band competition became an annual Regimental event. Regimental marches were adopted; "Sprig of Shillelagh" and "Garry Owen" and the slow march "Oft in the Stilly Night". A quarterly Regimental newspaper was introduced, and, most importantly, a Benevolent Fund was established to help serving and former soldiers and their families who were in need and to make immediate grants to the next of kin.

Thus a Regimental identity was developing and the Regular Army began to realize that the UDR was not, after all, so different from itself.

From the outset of his appointment as Deputy Commander Lieutenant Colonel Paddy Ryan had appreciated that:

"We were never going to change the thinking of any member of the Regiment. What we could change would be their attitudes, their reaction to events. Every step we took to bind them more closely to the Regular Army tended at the other end to loosen them a little from their natural affiliations to the Protestant majority. It was never going to be absolute but it was going to make them think before they did something. They would believe that what they were doing was the Army way of doing things. So every time there was an opportunity to create links with the Regular Army I took it, rather than keep the UDR as a totally separate force, an isolated force. We worked on such things as attendance on commissioning courses at Sandhurst, courses at the School of Infantry, attachments to Regular battalions, and a proper pay structure."[1]

It was certainly true that membership of the UDR did have a moderating influence, that moderate opinions expressed by instructors during recruit training and the even-handed example of junior officers and NCOs on patrols, though not always maintained, did have a beneficial effect, and that for many loyalty to the company and the platoon became greater than any loyalty they might have entertained to the extremes of Loyalist politics. As Ormerod said, "There were a lot of people who came into the UDR who changed their attitudes to life as a result of their joining. That was one of the most beneficial things we were doing in those early days."[2]

Battalions were achieving some excellent successes. Thanks to a reduction in static guards they were carrying out foot and mobile patrols each night, some of them jointly with the Regular Army. The regulars had come to appreciate the part-timers' local knowledge, a detailed knowledge that they could not hope to acquire in the space of a three-month tour. The UDR soldiers knew their way round their part of the country like the backs of their hands: they knew who had a questionable background; they could recognize strangers from other parts of the Province by their accents with remarkable accuracy.

January was an eventful month for 2UDR. On the 10th a mobile patrol from one of the Armagh Companies was driving down the main road from Moy towards the city when it ran into an ambush at Allistragh. The gunmen opened fire with an Armalite and a sub-machine gun from behind a hedgerow on high ground looking down on the road. The patrol dismounted, took such cover as there was in a very exposed position and returned vigorous fire. The ambush ended as suddenly as it had begun. There was one casualty; a ricochet had lodged in the wrist of the driver of the second vehicle, though he was unaware he had been hit until he found he could not cock his SLR. In the follow-up the next morning the sub-machine gun was recovered. In his haste to get away the owner had fired the weapon when the barrel was plugged with earth with the result that it had exploded. Apart from this the attackers escaped unharmed, the patrol's return fire having been too high, but, according to their subsequent report, "the farmer would have no need to trim the hedge that concealed the ambushers". The incident was described as "an admirable example of counter-ambush tactics".

A week later, on a night of hard frost and thick fog, a patrol from one of the Glenanne companies had mounted a VCP on a minor road in the same area. The commander had deployed part of his patrol in a long-stop position some 200 yards from the road check to catch any driver who tried to turn back. When a vehicle did stop and the occupants ran over the fields, the long-stop group gave chase and caught one of them. To make sure he did not escape again they removed his shoes and socks and brought him back to the car, where they found an Armalite, an M1 Carbine and two .303 rifles wrapped in sacking across the back seat. The arrested man, a prominent member of the Armagh Provisionals, was subsequently released on bail and absconded to the Republic.

The following week the Company that had been ambushed at Allistragh was carrying out a foot patrol in Armagh city centre when they noticed a man carrying a duffel bag and behaving in a suspicious manner. They followed him and, when he stopped to relieve himself against a wall, they searched him and found a dagger slipped inside his boot. He had abandoned the bag some way back. It contained a 25lb bomb, already assembled and only requiring the final connection. The man, who had recently arrived from Dublin, was subsequently sentenced to seven years.

February was particularly successful. It began with a search operation in the Castlewellan area carried out by the Kilkeel Company. By now active PIRA groups had grown up in the 3UDR area, based in Downpatrick and Castlewellan. The searchers' suspicions were aroused by a woman walking up and down outside a farm. When she hung out some washing that appeared to be already dry, they suspected she was trying to send someone a warning signal. A soldier was detailed to watch her and as he moved into position he noticed some dead gorse laid along a stone wall. He pulled it aside and discovered a cavity in the wall concealing a parcel wrapped in plastic sheeting containing two rifles and ammunition.

A car stopped short of a road block set up by the Lisnaskea Company and three men were seen to get out and throw something over the hedge. It proved to be a brand new RPG 7 rocket launcher of Soviet design, only the second one of its type to be captured by the security forces. The three men were arrested. Two nights later the Antrim Company was carrying out patrols in and around Randalstown when they stopped a car carrying a 25lb bomb. The three occupants admitted they were intending to place it beside the town's police station.

Ormerod, whose tenure of command came to an end in April, handed over the Regiment to Brigadier Harry Baxter. Baxter had served on the staff of the newly formed Joint Defence Staff under Lord Mountbatten and had spent the four years prior to coming to the UDR as Defence Attaché in Athens. Like his predecessor, and his Deputy Commander, he was a Catholic.

The Adjutant of 2UDR had a lucky escape when a bomb exploded at the Battalion Headquarters inside Gough Barracks, Armagh. A Catholic civilian, a well liked man, worked in the barracks as a fitter. Unbeknown to him the bomb had been hidden in the boot of his car while it was parked overnight in his garage at home. Next morning he drove into the barracks and parked the car, fortunately further away from the Headquarters building than was his usual custom. An hour and a half later it exploded. The Adjutant was on the telephone talking to the Second-in-Command:

> "All of a sudden the windows came in. A huge ventilator came down and dropped on my desk and the telephone flew out of my hand. I could hear the Second-in-Command shouting down the line, 'What's happened?' When I picked up the handset I found a big piece had been nicked out of it and a lump of metal was embedded in the office wall."

No one was hurt, but the CO's driver, who was standing outside, had the backside torn out of his trousers by a piece of flying metal. Some forty men drilling on the parade ground had marched off shortly before the explosion.

That night a single rocket was fired at Killymeal House, the residence of the CO 8UDR in the grounds of the Battalion Headquarters. The CO, his wife and infant son were asleep in the house at the time. The rocket passed over the roof and exploded beyond the base in open fields.

On 13 May a van drove through a VCP set up by the Cookstown Company of 8UDR near Ardboe in East Tyrone. It halted up the road, a flare was fired out of it and almost immediately four or five rounds were directed at the men manning the checkpoint, who returned fire. Later the van was found overturned, with a body slumped across the passenger seat. According to a death notice in the local paper, the dead man was OC of A Company of the East Tyrone PIRA battalion. He was one of the three members of the IRA confirmed as killed by the UDR over the 22 years.

In March the Regiment was called out to provide cover for the Border Referendum and again in May for the Local Government elections, guarding the polling stations and at the end of the day escorting the ballot boxes to counting centres. The companies were under operational control of Regular battalions and the fact that 3 UDR, for example, received orders from five different sources shows how difficult it was for a CO to keep himself informed as to what his companies had been tasked to do.

By now 10UDR was carrying out Segment duties around the city centre by night and on Saturdays on a regular basis, manning the gates and carrying out foot patrols. Though not the most interesting of tasks, it had its moments. A Corporal dealing with a traffic accident came under fire;

one round was returned at his attackers as they escaped into the fog. A patrol arrested two drunks in the process of raping a young girl, whilst another patrol saved the life of a man who came running down the street towards them, pursued by other men firing at him from a van. The commander of one of the Newtownabbey platoons and his Company Sergeant Major had their first experience of a car bomb, left in Castle Street, just off the city centre:

"A member of the public came up to say to us, 'You had better have a look in that black taxi'. It was parked outside the Castle Street entrance to Anderson and McAuley's large department store. So we had a look and here in the back was a bin full of explosives with a clock taped on the top of it. We were starting to get the area cleared when Joe said to me, 'Did you notice what time was on the clock?' I said, 'No I didn't,' and he said, 'Hang on a minute,' and we went back and had a look, which was a pretty daft thing to do. It was one of the old style alarm clocks, the type with the two bells on top, and we were looking at what time the alarm was set for. I can't remember the exact time, but we reckoned it was fairly close and we had a bit of difficulty clearing the area, because there was only our team. It was daylight and the shops were crowded on a Saturday afternoon so we had a job. We just got Castle Street cleared, the ATO turned up and the thing went off. Joe was with the ATO, trying to explain to him what was in the back of the taxi, when it went off and blew the both of them off their feet."

The 200lb bomb caused considerable glass damage but, thanks to the prompt action of the patrol, no one was injured.

During June 8UDR scored two more successes, the first when they stopped a car in Dungannon, discovered an M1 Carbine inside and arrested the two occupants. The next night a part-time Private was off duty at his parents' home when he saw a man and a woman place a bag at the entrance to the Electricity Board showrooms across the street. He drew his service pistol and ordered the man to stand still. Remaining in the shadows and making as much use as he could of the cover provided by the window sill, for the bomb was no more than 40 feet from where he stood, he banged on the floor to summon his mother and told her to call the police whilst the family took cover at the back of the house. He remained at the window, covering the two bombers until the police arrived and arrested them, and the bomb was defused. He was awarded the Military Medal, the first member of the Regiment to receive that award.

At Ballykinlar the Adjutant and Chief Clerk had been out visiting patrols in the battalion Austin Mini and were approaching the camp when they met two cars coming in the opposite direction, travelling very fast. A mile further on, in sight of the camp, they saw a vehicle parked at the road-side. Their suspicions aroused, they took its registration number. As they turned in at the camp gates a salvo of mortar bombs landed in the open field across the road. They phoned the number through to the police and gave chase in the Mini, but it was worn out with frequent use, and they arrived back on the road only in time to see the tail lights of the get-away vehicle disappearing over the brow of the hill. The police quickly established that the car had been hired that morning by a well-known member of PIRA. It was found outside his house, the engine still warm. He was arrested but not charged as there was no way of proving that he had been at the scene of the attack. All nine mortar bombs had fallen well short of their target and done no harm. If they had landed amongst the corrugated iron huts they would have caused serious casualties, for they were crowded with soldiers from 7UDR attending their annual camp. The Adjutant, taking cover behind some convenient sandbags whilst the bombs fell, was amazed to see the soldiers streaming out of the huts to see what all the noise was about.

During the year the RUC station at Belcoo in Fermanagh came under attack on five occasions. The station stands within yards of the Border where the main road from Enniskillen to Sligo crosses the bridge to Blacklion on the southern side. 4UDR provided a permanent guard for the station, and one Corporal was on duty during three of the five attacks. Looking back over twenty-one years he is not entirely sure which was which, but he remembers his first experience of coming under fire:

"We were attacked about two o'clock in the morning. There was quite a bit of gunfire from the bridge between Blacklion and Belcoo. They must have been firing on fixed lines, because the sandbags on one of the sangers was riddled just beneath where the sentry was standing. We were getting sand in our eyes. The police were running about looking for the loan of guns from us to have a shot at them. They brought out the twelve-bore shotgun, it was all they had, and started firing in the air like cowboys. The phone was ringing when all was over. The police answered the phone and the Gardai said there was nobody on their side of the border at all. The shooting was coming from elsewhere!"

The heaviest attack came on 12 December, when some forty rounds and six rockets were fired from the southern side of the Border. The Corporal was there again:

"Eight of us had just come in from a foot patrol. We were taking off our flak jackets when the boy in the sangar called that something was going to happen, things had got very quiet outside. I put on my flak jacket again, when there was a bang and the barracks shook. The first rocket was dead on target at the front gate, it blew it to bits. One of them went into the housing estate at the back, one landed through a telephone pole halfway between the barracks and Blacklion. Things settled down. We did a follow-up down through the fields in the front, could see nothing, went through the side gate to go round the town, back up, we came to the front gate and it wasn't there. It had just disintegrated. Actually, the rocket that went through the telegraph pole, the next morning it had disappeared. It was lying there and we hadn't touched it, but when ATO came, it had disappeared. Somebody took it as a souvenir."[3]

Other police stations came under attack during the year. Rosslea and Belleek in Fermanagh, Crossmaglen and Keady in Armagh and Benburb and Pomeroy in Tyrone.

At Pomeroy 8UDR was providing the guard, a task the Battalion had taken on in August 1971 and continued to fulfil for the next eleven years, using local men on voluntary call-out. It was a heavy commitment, three guards each of five men carrying out five twelve-hour shifts each week. There had already been two previous attacks on the station. The heaviest came on 16 August 1973. The Corporal of the Guard was fortunate to survive:

"I was up in the sangar on top of the water tower, it was sometimes round about half past ten at night. I was standing just nicely going round my sangar and the first thing I heard was the 'whist' going over the top of the roof. It didn't really strike me what it was at the time. Where it exploded I don't know, but then a minute or two after it, there was this unmerciful bang on the side of the sangar. An RPG 7 came straight through the sangar till it exploded on the outside. The tail fittings and all went straight through the sangar, just went past the side of my head, straight through her and blew the sangar in round me. I got up to my feet. We had the buzzer down to the boys down in the bottom and we told them to stand to. The three other boys came up onto the roof to me where there was another sangar. Then they started mortaring us. They were out a field length from us whenever the mortars started, then you could see them moving in, moving in all the time, but we didn't know at that time they had a man planted only about two hundred yards from us and he was radio controlling the mortar fire in on us. They were moving the mortar in closer and closer. Moving her in all the time and as they were moving in with the mortars there were at least three gun positions opened up on us. I tell you it was real bedlam. You couldn't see anybody, you could see the flashes out there in the dark. So we opened up into all likely positions you know and it was hectic for quite a while. It lasted, I would say, fifteen/twenty minutes. The mortar was on the back of a lorry. What actually happened the last mortar they fired exploded in the back yard of the station but the next explosion we heard she blew up with them. The mortar blew up and there was two Provos killed on the lorry. So the mortaring stopped, but they still continued to fire a lot of stuff at us. Eventually there were two red flares fired, and the attack was ended at that. I was firing a rifle, an SLR, and the rocket that came through the sangar to me had blown a lump off the end of the rifle. You know the flash eliminator on the end of the SLR? Well, the hot metal that came through the sangar had blown the end off the flash eliminator. I had gone on firing and didn't know at all."

In August a raiding party of eight gunmen crossed the Border intending to murder a part-time soldier, the owner of a garage. They lined up the staff and customers, among them women and children, and questioned them as to their identity. On learning which one was the owner, one of the gunmen aimed his revolver at him at point-blank range and pressed the trigger. The hammer had not been cocked. The soldier jumped to one side and ran to his bungalow. There he assembled his SMG, returned to the garage and opened fire on the raiders as they made off across the Border. Seconds later, as the women and children stood screaming in the street after their ordeal and some attended to a 13-year-old schoolboy shot in the arm, a bomb destroyed the garage and another the Customs post. A third had been left in the village Post Office. The ATO, a Staff Sergeant RAOC, tried to neutralize it with a controlled explosion. When that had no effect he went back into the building, the bomb exploded, and he was killed instantly.

The part-time soldier was awarded a Military Medal. A week after the attack, a message was received over the confidential telephone system that he was to be shot, and he and his family left Fermanagh to settle elsewhere.

There were four other incidents of note during the last week of August. When a car turned away from an 8UDR VCP three men armed with rifles were seen running away. The patrol gave chase, capturing two. On being questioned they revealed the name and address of the third. On the night of the 27th two car bombs exploded in the centre of Armagh, injuring four soldiers and sixteen civilians. 2UDR had deployed a patrol to stake out a suspect third car when they came under fire. Private Kenneth Hill was shot dead and a Corporal wounded. Two nights later a patrol of 8UDR found a rifle during a planned search west of Dungannon and a snap VCP set up by 5UDR east of Maghera arrested three Provisionals on the 'wanted' list.

September passed with little of interest to report from the battalions. Some were catching up on their annual camps, postponed from earlier in the summer because of the Assembly elections. Again the camps were held at Ballykinlar and Magilligan. They made a valuable contribution to the development of the Battalion. For eight days they could concentrate on training, making extensive use of the excellent ranges at both locations to complete the annual weapon classification that each soldier must pass to qualify for a higher rate of pay. But the camps were not well attended. The rate of pay was still low and some married men returned home at the end of the week with as little as £14, many having forfeited the wages they would have received from their civilian jobs. Unlike the

TA, the men were not paid their annual bounty on the last day, and in any case the UDR's bounty was still only £25, compared with the TA's £80 tax-free.

In the case of 3UDR, attendance was restricted by a spell of good weather for the harvesting and the arrival of the herring shoals off Kilkeel. For all that the Battalion mounted its first major search operation, concentrated on Thunders Hill Wood above Rostrevor.

The operation involved all three services; the Light Infantry provided a platoon and a search dog, the RAF, helicopters, and the Royal Navy tender moved up Carlingford Lough to intercept anyone trying to slip across to the southern side, and acted as relay station on the battalion net. The 3UDR tactical headquarters and cordon party were flown in from Ballykinlar in two Wessex and a Puma, the search parties following in two Pumas and by road. Lacking experience and training in search techniques, the Battalion had laid out corridors of white tape through the wood so that the searchers could move along them in line abreast through waist-high bracken and brambles, in the manner of policemen searching for clues in the aftermath of a murder. It was soon appreciated that anyone concealing a weapon must choose an easily identifiable landmark, otherwise he may not be able to locate it again. The search was shifted to tracks through the wood where some of the trees had been marked with white tape. Two hides were uncovered containing weapon-cleaning kits, but the weapons themselves had gone. Nevertheless it was a useful practical lesson in search technique and on the mounting of a helicopter-borne battalion operation, a significant step forward in the development of the Battalion.

In November the Royal engineers began sealing off roads along the lonely Donegal border whilst 6UDR helped to provide cover. The roads had already been cratered once, here and in South Armagh and Fermanagh, but some had been filled in again by locals, particularly farmers angered at having to make long detours to reach parts of their land. 4UDR provided similar cover along the east Fermanagh border in the following month in the remote Mullaghfad Forest, four miles from the UDR home in Cooneen, which had come under attack for the second time on 17 November. Seventeen months had passed since the previous attack and the family were expecting the attackers to return. An uncle, who was serving in the Clogher Company, had come visiting with his wife and children. They were all sitting talking when the twelve-year-old brother shouted, "There's a car at the back window, I think it's the IRA". One of the sons in the UDR described what happened:

"I told my mother and the visitors to get under the table and raced up the stairs as hard as I could belt it to get my rifle. We had no electricity at the time, only the gas. Upstairs you had to use a flashlight, and it took me the guts of a minute to get the weapon together in the dark. I went to the window and I could see a boy down at the car and some others at the back window lighting a fuse to a bomb. I fired at the car first, then at the boy at the bomb. When I opened up they started running and when they were running they fired a shot. A bullet ricochetted against the corner window and landed beside my mother. I told them downstairs, 'I'll cover yous till you get down the lane and head down the road towards Fivemiletown'. I got them out and covered them away down the lane, down the road to safety. I stayed in the house, me and my father, until the police came about an hour later."

Several of the soldier's rounds had hit the car and put it out of action. The raiders had abandoned it, along with an M1 carbine and full magazine and two petrol bombs. The bomb at the back window consisted of 160lb of ANFO packed into a creamery can.

"The window's a wee bit low to the road, and my father and mother were sitting there at the table, and it was just as well it didn't go off or they wouldn't be here the day. I wouldn't be here either, the toss you'd get. The boys were trying to light the fuse with a match. They should have lit it with a cigarette, because the match kept going out on them. They must have used eight to ten matches and never got her off."

3UDR had two successes before the year's end, one by accident. R. G. Hanna, Commander of the Kilkeel Company, his Second-in-Command and Company Sergeant Major were carrying out a recce in the old cemetery in the centre of the town to decide where to post sentries to cover the company Christmas party in a hotel across the road. They noticed tracks leading to an old tomb in a remote corner of the graveyard and, under the tomb, a lead box. They sent for the ATO who pulled the box clear. On being opened it was found to contain a Martini Henry rifle, a relic of the old UVF gun-running operation in April 1914, but still in good working order, a bayonet, three pistols and ammunition.

The other success was one of those rare occasions when there was something concrete to show for the VCPs carried out night after night. A patrol from the Rathfriland Company was in the process of setting up a VCP on the Rostrevor road east of Warrenpoint when a car raced through before it could be stopped. The next four cars halted, a man jumped out of the fourth, dropping a M1 carbine, and ran away, leaving behind a .303 rifle, ammunition and the three other occupants of the car. They were handed over to the police and came to court the following year. The three pleaded that they and the car had been hijacked by the one who had run away. That one man encumbered with two rifles could hijack a car containing three other men seemed beyond belief, but the judge gave them the benefit of the doubt and found them not guilty.

Two days before Christmas 6UDR was carrying out a foot patrol on a minor road running parallel to the Border South-east of Clogher. They had been tasked to check out a crossing frequently used by IRA raiding parties from the South. It was a large patrol, about two platoons, most of the soldiers very inexperienced. It was also very high-powered. Jack Reilly, the CO, was with them and the Deputy Commander, Ryan, had come down from Lisburn to join them. The Regimental Sergeant Major was manning the GPMG in the turret of the Shorland, covering the men on foot. The patrol took cover whilst they observed a group of houses and a bar across the Border. The bar was a well-known IRA haunt, and a group of people standing outside seemed to be observing the patrol. The driver was out relieving himself, the patrol getting to their feet to move on when there was an explosion almost directly under the Shorland. The armoured car was lifted a few inches into the air, but landed back on its wheels. The RSM was momentarily stunned and was about to open fire with the GPMG across the Border when Ryan shouted at him to wait as there seemed to be children amongst the group outside the bar. Some of the patrol were blown over and spattered with mud, debris and stones. One wheel of the armoured car was slightly buckled and the flash elim-inator on the GPMG dented, but otherwise there was no damage or casualties. It was a testimony to the Shorland's strength that it was driven away from the scene. The RSM's life was saved by the fact he was wearing his helmet.

A Garda inspector arrived on the scene and confirmed that the mine had been detonated from a small knoll on the southern side of the Border. It consisted of some 150lb of ANFO packed into three creamery cans, one of which had failed to detonate, hidden in a culvert under the road. Ryan's main concern was that Brigadier Baxter would find out that he had been there, as he was not supposed to go on Border patrols. Next morning he had his uniform dry-cleaned and kept quiet about his involvement. Months later, when he did tell the Brigadier, Baxter assured him that he had known all along.

In addition to Hill, seven other soldiers were murdered that year. James Hood, a 49-year-old Captain in 5UDR, was shot dead at his home, Straidarran, near Claudy. He and one of his twin sons had just returned home from duty with their company in Londonderry when a gunman hiding in the shrubbery at the back door fired one shot from a shotgun, hitting Hood in the back of the head, killing him instantly. Hood's brother was a Chief Superintendent in the RUC.

Twelve days later Corporal David Bingham, a part-time soldier and civilian clerical officer in the Lisburn Company of 9UDR, went missing on his way to attend a medical appointment at the Royal Victoria Hospital. By chance his car had been hijacked en route and used to plant a bomb near the city centre. His hijackers, discovering that Bingham was in the UDR, had shot him three times in the head and left his body in the boot of a stolen car.

David Deacon from Benenden in Kent had met his wife Sylvia in Londonderry whilst serving as a Petty Officer in the Fleet Air Arm. After nineteen years' service he retired from the Royal Navy in October '70 and the family settled into a house on the west bank of the Foyle, looking forward to a normal family life after the years of separation whilst David had been at sea. He joined 5UDR as a full-time Staff Sergeant. On the evening of 1 March Sylvia asked him to go out and buy her some shampoo. She never saw him again. She sat up most of the night waiting for him to return. Next morning she raised the alarm. Later the police came to tell her that his body had been found dumped near the Border. He had been gagged and bound hand and foot and a rope from his wrists attached round his neck in a noose to prevent him from struggling. He had been shot in the groin, then in the head. She was not allowed to see his body.

Every morning Corporal Franklin Caddoo of 8UDR drove his tractor down to the end of the lane from his farm to leave the milk churn for the Milk Board tanker to collect. The farm was near Aughnacloy, three miles from the Monaghan border. On 10 May his father heard shots and found his son's body lying in a fir copse near the tractor. He left a widow, who was expecting a second child, and a fourteen-month-old daughter. In September Private Mathew Lilly was shot at close range as he was collecting milk churns from a farm near Belcoo. The gunmen escaped in a hijacked car which Gardai found abandoned just across the Border.

There could have been others. In all battalions there were instances of soldiers coming under fire whilst off duty. One of these was a part-time Private in 2UDR. He and three other men were helping his brother, a member of the same battalion, to build a new silo at his farm close to the South Armagh border. A car drove into the farmyard, four gunmen dismounted and opened fire on the group with automatic weapons. One of the rounds shattered a concrete block as the Private was placing it in position on the wall. He immediately shouted to the others to run for it. Instead they jumped down into the septic tank. One of them managed to get out and away, but the other, an older man, tried to climb out but failed and eventually fainted. The Private jumped down into the tank and pushed this second man up over the wall into the field from where he was able to run off down towards the road. Then he saw that his brother had been hit and was lying by a barbed wire fence on the edge of the field. Under fire from the terrorists he ran across the field, rolled his brother into a ditch and dragged him about a hundred yards to the lane at the bottom of the valley, over the fence and up the next hill to the main road, where a motorist stopped and took the injured man to hospital. Satisfied that his brother was in good hands, he went back up the hill towards the farm to see what had happened to the others. When he was about 50 yards from the silo he saw one of them being marched into the pig house by two armed men. On seeing the soldier they fired forty shots at him as he ran back to take cover in the ditch. There he found one of the other men had collapsed and he began dragging him up the hill to the main road. The gunmen, who were driving out of the yard, stopped and opened fire again before driving off in the direction of the Border. For his courage in saving the life of his brother and his friends the part-time soldier was awarded the Queen's Gallantry Medal.

During the year the strength of the Regiment had dropped by some 1,400 to 7,500. Part of the reduction was due to the policy of dismissing soldiers who were failing to do duty. In fact the loss of manpower did not reduce operational effectiveness, with the men still doing on average more than two duties a week plus training periods. It was true that after three years on operations they were becoming tired and bored with static guards, but they continued to turn out with enthusiasm for patrols and for specific weekend operations.

However, the failure to recruit conrates was a major worry. By November only 272 out of 774 appointments for security guards had been filled across the Regiment. A significant pay increase in the annual pay review for the Armed Services, as much as 25% for a conrate Private Class 3, had failed to stimulate recruiting. Some of the guards at company bases in 3UDR were reduced to two shifts of two NCOs and two private soldiers, working for 24 hours day and day about. The problem was that civilian security organizations were offering much more. For instance the Water Commissioners paid about £10 a week more, plus generous overtime, to security guards at the Silent Valley reservoir. It was a worry, for the conrate guards were responsible for the protection of company bases, including the armouries, by day, covering in particular those dangerous hours after the part-time guard came off duty at 6am. Fortunately there were men willing to come forward to do duties on the Voluntary Call-Out (VCO) basis.

By the end of the year the MOD had agreed to the establishment of a recruiting team at HQUDR and a Sergeant in each battalion; it was hoped that this would reverse the downward recruiting trend.

In April a revised establishment had given each company a full-time Administrative Warrant Officer and each battalion headquarters a part-time Captain to fill the appointment of Intelligence Officer (IO). In each company a part-time officer or NCO was appointed Company IO, and thus the foundations were laid for collating low-level intelligence. The Captain selected for the post in 3UDR began to build up a filing system, maintaining a card for each person of interest:

"Authority was very wary of the word 'intelligence' in those days. They called us Battalion Information Officers. Meetings with the company representatives were always held on a Tuesday night. We would gather to talk about the situation, what had been gathered, what patrols had picked up. The idea was that if you had a six-hundred-strong battalion, that was twelve hundred eyes and twelve hundred ears out there in the community, living in it, working in it, bound to see things, and, given the right direction, they could add to the store of background information. We put out a weekly intelligence summary (Intsum) but we didn't seem to get an awful lot back from Regular units or Brigade. I can remember putting as a final comment at the end of one Intsum 'Is there anybody there? Say something, even if it's only "bollocks".' That stirred some people to respond to us."

Contact was made and trust gradually established with the Regular Army Field Intelligence Officers and the local RUC Sergeants, and through them Special Branch. It was a constant criticism by some Protestant politicians that the UDR lacked the local knowledge of the old B Specials. That may have been true to some extent in the early days, though experience showed that the B's information was so localized that they knew little or nothing about what was going on anywhere else. Now gradually the UDR was establishing a system that the B Specials had never developed, the ability to collate and pass on to the Regular Army and the police information gained at local level by the companies.

In March the Government had published a White Paper proposing a new Northern Ireland Constitutional Assembly, to consist of eighty members and a power-sharing Executive. The Executive would have limited powers, excluding for the time being any responsibility for security. Following an election, discussions would be held between the British and Irish Governments and members of the Assembly, with a view to establishing a Council of Ireland as a means of co-ordinating matters of mutual interest.

The prospect of sharing power with Nationalists and the threat of a Council of Ireland split the Unionist Party. When the elections for the Assembly were held in June, over half the successful Unionist candidates were opposed to the White Paper. By the year's end Faulkner's hold over his party was becoming increasingly tenuous. The anti-power-sharing faction had combined forces with Paisley's Democratic Unionist Party and Vanguard, the party formed by Craig, the former Minister of Home Affairs, to form the United Ulster Unionist Council.

Assembly members chosen from the Faulkner Unionists, SDLP and Alliance had been appointed to the ministerial posts within the Executive. They had attended the meeting at Sunningdale with the British and Irish government ministers. Despite his misgivings, Faulkner had reluctantly agreed to the setting-up of a Council of Ireland, on the understanding that the Irish Government would agree to the inclusion of a statement in the final communique that there could be no change in the status of Northern Ireland without the agreement of the majority in the Province. The trouble was that the two main parties within the Executive saw the Council in a different light; to the Faulkner Unionists it was to be purely consultative, to some within the SDLP a step on the road to a united Ireland.

The United Kingdom was facing its worst economic crisis since the war. As a result of the coal miners' overtime ban and a go-slow strike by the train drivers and electrical engineers, the Conservative Government had introduced a three-day week for industry and commerce. TV broadcasts were closed down at 10.30 pm each night. An OPEC embargo on oil supplies to the West was causing an acute shortage of petrol. Some garages would only sell £1's worth at a time, barely enough for the soldiers to report for duty and return home.

On 1 January the Stormont Executive took up office. On the 4th the Ulster Unionist Council decisively rejected the concept of the Council of Ireland; three days later Faulkner resigned from the leadership of the party. The outlook for 1974 was bleak.

1. A patrol of the Ulster Special Constabulary on the Donegal-Tyrone border, May 1922. *(Ulster Museum)*

2. British officers inspecting the defences of Belleek Fort after it had been recaptured from the IRA in June 1922. *(Ulster Museum)*

3. General Sir John Anderson, GBE, KCB, DSO, Colonel Commandant The Ulster Defence Regiment 1970-80.

4. General Sir Harry Tuzo, GCB, OBE, MC GOC Northern Ireland, on a visit to the UDR Company in Newry on 12 August 1971, three days after internment.

5. Enlisting the first recruits, Belfast, 18 February 1970. *(Pacemaker Press International)*

6. Recruits training on the No 4 rifle, June 1971. *(Crown Copyright: reproduced with the permission of the Controller HMSO)*

7. The Company base in the Old Deanery, Clogher, which came under IRA attack on 2 May 1974. It has since been demolished.

8. Private Eva Martin, who was killed in the IRA attack on the Company Base on the Old Deanery, Clogher, 2 May 1974.

9. 3 UDR VCP above Newry, 7 August 1974. The officer on the right is Major Ivan Toombs who was murdered at Warrenpoint in January 1981.

10. The destruction of the Sandes Home, Ballykinlar, as a result of an IRA van bomb, 28 October 1974. *(P. Ormerod)*

11. A Loyalist paramilitary cache consisting of a pistol, sawn-off shotgun and some 700 rounds of ammunition, found on waste ground in Larne by a 1UDR patrol on 2 February 1976.

12. The Queen inspecting the UDR Guard of Honour at Hillsborough during her Silver Jubilee visit in August 1977.

13. The first WUDR recruits. The two Greenfinches in the front row are wearing the old ATS wartime uniform.

14. A patrol at a road crossing the Fermanagh border, closed by the Royal Engineers.
    (Soldier Magazine)

15. Enoch Powell *(right)*, MP for South Down, about to go out on patrol with the Rathfriland Company. *(Outlook Press)*

16. Shorland armoured car at a VCP on the Antrim coast road.

17. Corporal Eric Glass, DCM, QGM, 4UDI and 4 Royal Irish, the most decorated UL soldier. *(Painting by Trevor Erskine)*

CHAPTER EIGHT

Formation of the Womens' UDR

From the beginning of the troubles Regular Army units had been able to call on the woman soldiers of the Royal Military Police to search female members of the public, but there were not enough of them to operate with the UDR on a regular basis. As a result patrols were unable to search females and, early in the life of the Regiment, a proposal was submitted for each battalion to be permitted to recruit a section of twenty woman soldiers to fulfil this role. However, there were problems; the company bases had no female accommodation or facilities; the idea of women becoming an integral part of an infantry battalion was a revolutionary one and any change in the structure of the UDR required the approval of Parliament. But by now there could be no doubt that women were being used to carry terrorist weapons, and in July 1973 a bill was passed authorizing the enlistment of women into the Regiment. Major Eileen Tye, a Regular Army officer from the Womens' Royal Army Corps, arrived at HQUDR to take over the post of Commander Women.[1] Recruitment opened officially on 16 August. Some 360 advanced enquiries had already been received and over the next five months 352 were enlisted, among them a small number of Catholics. The first enlistments were carried out by 2UDR at Gough Barracks on 16 September and the Womens' UDR (WUDR) came into being. In time the women soldiers became known as 'Greenfinches'.

To the storemen in the QM's departments the issue of female articles of clothing was an experience beyond their ken. Out of the dark recesses of some all but forgotten store across the water items of clothing left over from the days of the wartime ATS and smelling strongly of mothballs had been hastily packed together and despatched to battalions: battle-dress tops and khaki skirts, pleated and worn short as was the fashion at the time, khaki shirts and ties, green pullovers and the same berets as the men. For many months trousers were not permitted, on the improbable grounds that to a waiting gunman the trousered women would be indistinguishable from the men. In time a dispensation was given that they could be worn in helicopters, and Tye recalled the sight of a group of women being landed in a field and racing away to a hedgerow where, before the astonished gaze of the aircrew, they took down their trousers and pulled up their skirts before going on patrol. Wearing a skirt in the back of a Landrover on a mid-winter's night was a chilly experience, and the knee-length issue boots were a mixed blessing, unsuitable for leaping out the back in an emergency. One Greenfinch officer, the Assistant Adjutant of 10UDR, recounted how on night patrol she would wear two pairs of knickers, two pairs of tights, socks, the boots and bloomers. The bloomers were a source of ribald amusement, black and trimmed with white lace and so long that the lace showed under the skirts. 'Passion killers' the girls called them. The battledress jackets were unflattering to the female figure. The CO of 10UDR was inspecting an officers' drill parade. He stopped in front of his newly commissioned Assistant Adjutant. "'Come on shoulders back, chest out.' 'It's out as far as it will go,' she told him. Poor man, I can still see the expression on his face. He raced down the line, too embarrassed to inspect the rest!"

Initially a team from the WRAC Depot, led by a large, motherly WO2, Sergeant Major Brooker, an ideal choice for the task, was sent over from England to supervise the training. By the year's end the team had been released and the training in battalions had been taken over by UDR women with previous experience, assisted by male instructors. The course lasted a week and included drill, Army organization, map reading, searching of women and vehicles, radio procedure and a basic knowledge of first aid.

Many of the early recruits came from those executive and professional classes whose males were signally reluctant to enlist – Senior Civil Servants, a former barrister, school teachers, the headmistress of a primary school, laboratory technicians, an assistant air traffic controller. Many were married, with young children, and most of their pay went on wages for a baby-sitter. Women with infants were required to furnish a certificate stating that they had someone to look after their offspring while they were on duty. Some could rely on mothers to help out, provided they had not enlisted as well. The OIC Women of 7UDR has an abiding memory of her Sergeant, mother of a young baby. She and the Sergeant were about to accompany the men on what was to be their first Border patrol. "The helicopter was coming in to Palace Barracks to pick us up. My Sergeant had the baby with her. Her husband, who was ex-RAF, was just coming off duty. She ran over to him, gave him the baby and boarded the helicopter. That was the type of woman we had in the UDR." Many were married to members of the security forces. If their shifts did not coincide they could go for days without seeing each other, or if one was awake the other was catching up on lost sleep. The Assistant Adjutant of 10UDR and her husband, who was in the RUC, used to leave notes for each other.

An entry in 10UDR's history records that on the night of 28 October four women soldiers from the Girdwood Company accompanied a mobile patrol, the first recorded instance of WUDR being deployed on operations. Battalions had been instructed that the women must travel in pairs in the Landrovers and that in each patrol a male soldier must be detailed to look after them in the event of an ambush. The first standing order laid down that they should not be employed as radio operators on patrol, nor accompany foot patrols, nor patrol into areas of high risk without the authority of the CO. The orders were soon forgotten. Three days after completing her training a Greenfinch in 3UDR was acting as a searcher on patrol at Kilnasaggart Bridge just north of the Border on the road to Dublin. A Quartermaster who prided himself on anticipating every emergency had provided her and her fellow Greenfinch with a portaloo, loaded into the back of the Landrover. They declined the offer and, like all their number, managed well enough for the next twenty years.

Strangely enough, it was the men in the two city battalions who were slowest to accept the women, and the country battalions, who, with their USC experience might have been expected to be more conservative, were the first to appreciate their worth. They made good searchers. In the city they were soon employed in that role on the Segment gates, taking over by day from the WRAC members of the Military Police. It was a task that involved a good deal of abuse and the added hazard of razor blades and other sharp objects hidden under collars to cut the searchers' fingers. With their higher-pitched voices they made excellent signallers and, in time, as the UDR assumed greater responsibility, many of the operations rooms were manned by Greenfinches. By nature they were better than the men at First Aid. Before long some of the 10UDR girls were dealing with the aftermath of a shooting incident, a passenger on a bus hit by rifle fire, and in doing so finally won over their CSM, an old soldier who had deplored the incursion of women into a male preserve and had wanted nothing to do with them. Some of the Greenfinches in 3UDR filled a unique role. They were sent on a course at the rocket range in the Outer Hebrides to learn how to operate their Battalion's Seawatch radar.

Mostly the men were careful about moderating their traditional soldierly language in the presence of the girls. Sometimes they forgot, while abusive members of the public had no such inhibitions. The Assistant Adjutant, who had never heard some of the words before, used to memorize them so she could ask her husband what they meant.

Seven months after they had started undertaking operational duties the first woman was killed – Private Eva Martin, hit by rocket fragments in the attack on the base at Clogher. Three others were to die, two of them on patrol. A number were wounded. One Greenfinch, an assistant air traffic controller by day and a part-time Sergeant by night, described what it was like to come under fire:

"We had been very busy setting up vehicle checkpoints and doing spot checks on motorists. There was nothing unusual to report – until we approached the road junction. Gunfire! I heard a sound like a cracking whip behind my head.

"Thrown forward by the braking vehicle I struggled to my feet among a mass of people – no longer the friendly members of my patrol, but determined soldiers.

"I remember a split-second of reluctance to leave the Landrover.

It seemed to offer security when all around was thrown into confusion and danger. But I forced myself to follow the figures leaping to the ground in front of me.

"I dropped to my knees and crawled over the ground to the grass verge and pulled myself over towards the slope.

"Flares were exploding in the sky above me. They were intended to light up the enemy position, but they also made me feel uncomfortably larger than life as I tried to hide myself in the wet grass. My heart thumped madly as I put my face to the ground and silently asked God to be with us all.

"Sounds were still confusing, but after a few moments I dared to take a deep breath, opened my eyes and looked around.

"Another flare! I saw figures crouching and lying with weapons poised. I heard the anxious shouts from the men. Was I out of the Landrover? Was I all right? I realized thankfully that I was all in one piece and managed to shout a reply.

"There was no more gunfire. Indeed in the midst of the confusion of noise I had no recollection of how many shots had been fired.

"The sheer terror of the past few minutes kept me rooted to the spot some time. When I opened my eyes again I surveyed the scene – a deserted Landrover some yards away, figures crouched against a wall, an expanse of road and the grass slope and fence beside me.

"Friendly voices assured me that the gunman had gone, but I was reluctant to move since my mind could not be convinced that the shooting was over. As I scrambled those few long yards to the top and dragged myself under the fence I felt the sensation of bullets hitting the back of my flak jacket. I rolled across the ground towards the wall and realized that it was simply my pounding heart which had caused the terrible feeling.

"A member of the patrol assured me that injuries were confined to cuts and bruises and the other Greenfinch was also safe. The follow-up operation was now in progress and Regular Army and police were moving into the area to help us in the hunt for the gunmen.

"I looked around the trees and buildings, searching for a glint of metal, a flash of light or a moving body which might spell danger. The uneasy vigilance continued for nearly an hour before I thought of venturing from my cover. Then, feeling like a most unladylike Greenfinch, I stood up slowly. I was dirty, wet and smelt rather unpleasant. "Looking at my hiding place I could see piles of dirty sand and gravel and a large drain! I grabbed my battered beret from the sand, climbed over the fence and ran back to the Landrover.

"I stood in the darkness and gazed at the now peaceful scene. The first vehicle, which had carried our patrol commander, was involved in the follow-up operation. The men who had remained at the scene took turns at standing guard and finishing their flasks of cold tea. The police were busy conferring with the commander of my vehicle and a few hundred yards down the road the Regular Army were searching for the used rounds of ammunition and trying to find clues to the gunman's identity.

"As the sky began brightening in the east we set out on our interrupted journey home. Another patrol was over.

"Back in the familiar surroundings of my home I looked at my bruised knees, my scraped boots, my dirty wet uniform and my very muddy beret. I closed them out of sight in a case and fell asleep as soon as my head touched the pillow.

"The next morning I awoke tired but in an elated mood. I was tremendously aware of all the things around me which make life so wonderful, but which I normally took for granted. Suddenly I was very, very happy to be alive. My uniform washed easily. My beret dried out and I polished my boots just as I did after every patrol."

In each battalion a female part-time officer was appointed to command the women, though later they came under the command of their male Company Commanders who were responsible for their discipline. 7UDR's OIC was the first to attend the two weeks' commissioning course at the WRAC college in Surrey, followed by a Greenfinch in 3UDR who, as a wartime member of the WRNS, had served as a signaller on the troopship *Queen Mary*. A number were selected for the full-time officer post of Assistant Adjutant. One found that much of the course was concerned with teaching her how to behave in an Officers' Mess. It was not very relevant, she thought, to the life she had been leading on patrol. In later years a number of the officers were appointed Adjutants of their battalions. The first to command a company took over her battalion's Command Company in 1985. Others were posted to the staff of Brigade headquarters and to AIS in HQNI.

Accommodation was a problem, for the new bases had not been built with women in mind. They found themselves having to change into their uniforms in the civilian cleaners' stores, not much roomier than a brush cupboard, and queuing up for the single cubicle in the Ladies. As for the few companies still living in Nissen huts, there was no accommodation for them at all.

After four years when the establishment of full-time soldiers was increased under the 'Way Ahead' policy, the number of women had almost doubled, reaching their peak in 1986 with 216 permanent cadre and 530 part-time. Unlike the men, the total never varied to any significant extent, and from 1978 onwards never dropped below 700. Unlike the WRAC they were fully integrated into their battalions, sharing the same risks as the men, carrying out the same operational duties and receiving the same abuse. They were particularly good at chatting up the public at a checkpoint, for, however angry a motorist may be, some of the steam is taken out of his anger when he finds himself speaking to a woman. In the last years when they were authorized to wear full combat kit and helmets, it was difficult to tell man from woman until she began to speak.

The only difference from the men was that they were not armed, though a small number who came under high risk at home were authorized by the police to purchase PPWs. Most had no wish to carry a weapon. As they saw it, their role was to take on as many other tasks as possible and leave the men to get on with the fighting. They were allowed to fire the full range of weapons during annual camps, and HQUDR ran a WUDR .22 shooting competition, and in later years they were taught how to make safe a loaded weapon as part of their training on dealing with casualties. Though the rules are different now and women throughout the Army are trained and may be armed with the SA80, the change came into effect after the merger.

A study carried out in 1988 showed that half the women serving at that time were married and 42% of those were mothers, two-thirds with infants or children of school age. At that time pregnancy rules in all three Services were strict (some might say draconian). An expectant mother was discharged in the fourth month of pregnancy without maternity leave or pay. There was no guarantee that she would be allowed to return after the baby was born. If she did, her previous service did not count and she was expected to undergo a fresh recruits' course. Her previous service could not be taken into account in reckoning her seniority in the case of an NCO, nor towards the award of the UD Medal. Unofficially, battalions got round the previous service regulation by sending the girls on unpaid leave whilst keeping them on strength, but they were still far worse off than, for instance, women constables in the RUC who were entitled to paid maternity leave and reinstatement.

When Mrs Thatcher visited HQUDR in September '88 she reacted sympathetically when one of the women spoke to her about the inequality of the MOD regulations. In 1990 the European Court ruled that they contravened accepted European standards.

As a result the regulations were changed and servicewomen are now entitled to 14 weeks' paid and up to 48 weeks' unpaid maternity leave, at the end of which they may return to duty. Several thousand women from all three services have taken action against the MOD, amongst them seventy-eight members of the UDR who have received compensation totalling almost £370,000.

The policy of total integration of the women into battalions was an unqualified success. It helped to pave the way for the decision in 1992 to abolish the WRAC as a separate corps and absorb the Regular Army women into the new Adjutant General's Corps, though no other infantry regiment has achieved the same degree of integration as the Royal Irish.

Why Greenfinches? For many years the Army used a system of appointment titles as a convenient way of referring to individual officers and to other arms over the radio. 'Sunray' was a commander, 'Seagull' an adjutant, 'Sheldrake' the artillery, 'Foxhound' infantry. When the troubles began a whole list of new appointment titles had to be drawn up. The bomb-disposal organization became 'Felix', UDR male soldiers 'Greentops', the women 'Greenfinches'. With the exception of 'Felix' all the others have been forgotten now, but 'Greenfinch' has carried on and is still used by the Royal Irish, not so much for convenience but as a term of affection and respect for their years of service.

Once, on a bitterly cold night in the city, a Greenfinch was on duty on a windy corner near the City Hall. An officer visiting the patrol asked her how she was. "Well enough, sir," she told him, "but they gave us the wrong name. They should have called us Blue Tits."

CHAPTER NINE

1974. The Ulster Workers' Council Strike

During 1974 293 people were killed, forty-three more than in the previous year. Attacks on security force bases and patrols and bomb attacks on commercial premises, increasingly proxy car bombs, delivered to their targets by drivers under threat, and cassette incendiaries, continued unabated in the city centre and in towns right across the Province. Omagh suffered dearly with five bomb attacks in the town centre in the first two months of the year. In March two proxy bombs on separate days caused severe damage to the Army base in the Grand Central Hotel in Belfast's Royal Avenue. In Armagh ten shops in the commercial centre were destroyed by incendiaries. In June a car bomb caused massive damage in the main street in Dungannon. Towns that had escaped attention in the past now came under attack. On 23 July a car bomb was abandoned in Garvagh in County Londonderry. Vigilantes saw it and alerted the local UDR platoon. Corporal John Conley of 5UDR and his Lance Corporal tried to rescue an old man who delayed them by refusing to move out of his house. When the bomb exploded a piece of metal from the car penetrated Conley's body through the side of his flak jacket. He died in hospital an hour later. The old man was rescued unhurt from the rubble of his house which had been completely demolished. Border police stations regularly came under attack from small arms, mortars and rockets, and increasingly the Provisionals extended their bombing campaign to England, attacking civilian and military targets. The worst of these attacks occurred on 21 November when bombs exploded almost simultaneously in two pubs in the centre of Birmingham; twenty-one died and 162 were injured. It was a blatant and supremely callous attack on a purely civilian target.

In all some 700 explosions took place that year, 300 less than in 1973, but the security forces' failure to intercept the bombers was creating in the civilian population a deep sense of disillusion in the determination of government to take effective action against the IRA. The *Newsletter* leader writer declared that government security policy had led to the Army being regarded "not only as incompetent but with near contempt".[1]

The Regiment came under attack on over seventy occasions. These included proxy bombs at company bases at Rathfriland, Newtownstewart, Aughnacloy, Cookstown and Dungannon, a determined mortar and rocket attack on the Deanery at Clogher, eight landmine and twenty-seven shooting attacks on patrols and twenty-one armed assaults on off-duty soldiers, some of them perpetrated by the UDA.

Daylight patrolling and increased mobility led to increased successes. By the year's end the UDR battalions had apprehended fifty-four people caught whilst carrying out acts of terrorism and uncovered forty-three weapons, 1,419lb of explosives and fifty-six mortar and incendiary bombs.

Both the off-duty murders occurred in the first three weeks of the year. 22-year-old Private Robert Jameson of 6UDR was on his way home from work at the end of the day. He got down from the Omagh bus at Ballyard crossroads near Trillick and was walking up the lane to the family home when he was killed by a single shot in the back of the neck. He died in the laneway in his mother's arms. Cormac McCabe was headmaster of Aughnacloy Secondary School. For many people that job would have been responsibility enough, but in November 1971 he joined the UDR, was commissioned and appointed commander of the Aughnacloy Company. Two nights after the Jameson murder McCabe had taken his wife and two teenage daughters out to a meal at the Four Seasons Hotel, a favourite haunt of theirs, five miles away, across the Border in Monaghan. When he left the restaurant to go to the bar and did not return, his wife became alarmed. McCabe had been abducted. His body was found the following morning 500 yards on the northern side of the Border. He had been shot twice in the head. The pathologist reported that one bullet had been fired at a range measured in inches.

> "He was," said his Deputy Head, "the kind of man the community can ill afford to lose. He was one person to whom community relations were of great importance. People of all denominations were allowed to use the school for functions. Mr McCabe saw to that. All he wanted was to see peace between the two communities. Everyone in the village looked up to him."

At Westminster, with the government beleaguered by the continuing industrial unrest and the fuel crisis, Northern Ireland was no longer a major preoccupation. In November, following an overtime ban by the coal miners, a State of Emergency had been declared. On 7 February Heath announced that he had decided to go to the country; a general election would be held in three weeks' time. Inevitably in Northern Ireland the election was seen as a referendum on power-sharing and the Council of Ireland. The anti-Faulkner UUUC won eleven of the twelve Westminster seats. From now on, even amongst Faulkner's own colleagues, grave doubts began to emerge about the wisdom of trying to persist with the Council of Ireland.

In April an opinion poll was to suggest that 75% of the electorate was in favour of power-sharing [2], but it was apparent that Sunningdale was too much for the majority of the Protestant community to swallow. A minority Labour government took office and Merlyn Rees was appointed the new Secretary of State for Northern Ireland.

The election was the fourth time that the Northern Ireland voters had gone to the polls in less than a year. For the UDR the provision of security for elections had become almost a matter of routine. The problem was to vary operations and avoid setting a pattern which could be exploited by the paramilitaries on both sides.

The previous evening a patrol of the Lisnaskea Company, sent with a message to Rosslea police station, was ambushed on the return journey. The road to the north-east of Donagh, a strongly Republican area, runs along a valley overlooked by low hills. The Landrover was leading and the patrol commander, a Corporal, was following in his Shorland:

> "Just as we came to the lower side of Derrynawilt Cross there was an explosion and a mass of smoke." The explosion had blown a huge crater in the road and the armoured car had fallen forward into it. "Nobody knew really what was wrong, with the steam and the water. The crater was filling right up. We could feel the water was coming up round our legs. There were bullets singing on the road. Shooting was coming from the top of the hill, but we were below them, and the bullets were skittering on the road. At the angle the Shorland was lying we could just about get the GPMG around in the turret. I fired her, but she would have been firing very high. I told the other two to engage with rifles. The wee driver, he was a very good rifleman and a very stubborn fellow. We could see the gunmen's rifle flashes and we must have got very near them for they broke off the engagement. The Landrover had stopped about 200 metres further on. They had taken cover, but they wanted to come back to me. 'We're okay,' says I. 'One or two of you's come back but come the centre of the road. Creep or crawl, but stay in the centre of the road, stay away from the hedges'."

It was a wise order. When the area was cleared next day two other command wires were discovered leading to two smaller devices placed in the hedgerow. Thanks to the accurate fire of the Corporal's half-section the gunmen had not waited to detonate the secondary charges.

During March and April 8UDR was to come under repeated attack. On 3 March Private Roy Moffett lost his life when a landmine exploded under the second vehicle of a patrol on its way home from Gortin ranges. That same night a patrol from the Dungannon Company was ambushed at Eskragh Lough on the winding road that at that time was the main route from the town towards the west. A culvert bomb threw the leading Landrover into the air, turning it over on its back. This time the macrolon withstood the shock, but four soldiers were injured, two of them seriously. The patrol came under fire as they dismounted and the half-section in the second vehicle returned thirteen rounds. Two nights later a landmine exploded under a culvert on the Donaghmore – Castlecaulfield road just after a patrol from the Cookstown Company had passed over it. This time no one was hurt and the vehicles were undamaged.

On 8 April a considerable gun battle ensued when some forty rounds were fired by two gunmen at a foot patrol in the centre of Dungannon.

The patrol returned fire, as bullets shattered windows and people at home watching television took cover, lying on their floors. That night incendiaries started fires in three drapers' shops in the town. Next night another culvert mine exploded just after a patrol had passed over it on the road past Eskragh Lough. The next night, the 11th, the Battalion mounted a VCP operation to close off all the roads into Dungannon. The Company Sergeant Major, WO2 Harold Sinnamon, was going round the town with a five-man foot patrol. Despite the torrential rain he was glad to be out with his soldiers, for he had been pressing for some time to be allowed to play a fuller part in his company's operations. The patrol was passing along John Street when the Sergeant Major went into a derelict house. A member of the patrol was standing outside on the step when he saw a blue flash and the next thing he knew he had been blown through the wall of the house next door and dropped into the cellar. The Battalion Second-in-Command was first at the scene. He found Sinnamon lying in the basement where he had fallen when the floor collapsed. He was alive and did not appear to be wounded. An ambulance was summoned, but he died before it reached the hospital. A piece of metal had gone through his flak jacket and penetrated his lung. He was buried on Easter Sunday following the funeral service in the parish church at Pomeroy where he had been a church-warden, glebe warden and secretary to the vestry. Thousands of people lined the streets of the village to watch the cortège pass by, the coffin carried by his fellow Sergeant Majors from the Battalion.

By early April, faced with the escalation in PIRA violence across the country, the alarming numbers of successful arson attacks using the new cassette incendiaries and worried that these attacks were a deliberate attempt to increase the public's disillusion with government security policy and thereby to destroy the Executive and the Assembly, Headquarters Northern Ireland implemented a week-long, Province-wide co-ordinated VCP operation. The UDR was placed on selective call-out, with 100 extra men per battalion to be deployed each day. Despite the fact that the Regiment carried out nearly 19,000 duties during the seven days, the operation did not deter the Provisionals. On 9 April there were two car bombs and ten incendiary attacks in Belfast City Centre. The main shopping streets were closed and evacuated and people took refuge in the grounds of the City Hall. Some fifty vehicles were hijacked and used to block the main roads out of the city; three of the vehicles were booby-trapped.

In Fermanagh a particularly senseless murder took place that week. The road running south from Derrylin passes through quiet countryside, small fields scarcely touched by the passing of time. Once it was the main road from Enniskillen to Belturbet in the Republic. Now it was little used, except by the farming families who lived along its length, people such as the Bullocks murdered in 1972, for where it crossed the river into the Republic the bridge had been blown by Protestants.

For the visitor it seems an improbable battleground, for there is a deep sense of peace. There is just one small village between Derrylin and the Border, Teemore, a few houses clustered round a cross roads, a church and a small modern red-brick primary school in a grove of conifers. The headmaster, George Saunderson, had been until the previous year Second-in-Command of 4UDR but had now retired. Before that he had commanded the Lisnaskea Company and held rank of Lieutenant-Colonel in the Army Cadet Force. He had served in the Royal Inniskilling and Royal Irish Fusiliers and the Parachute Regiment as a Captain throughout the war.

It was the last day of term before breaking up for the Easter holidays. The children were gathered in one classroom. Saunderson had gone to the kitchen for a cup of coffee. A car turned into the school yard. The cook in charge of the kitchen told the coroner what happened next:

"A man got out of the passenger seat beside the driver," she said. "He had a gun with him. He walked past me and never spoke a word. The other men got out of the car and one stood on the outside of the kitchen. I watched the first man go into the kitchen and I heard him speak to Master Saunderson.

"I heard him say, 'What's your name? What's your name?' The master put his hands up and said, 'Saunderson'. I knew what was going to happen and could not look."

Saunderson was shot in the back with ten rounds and died instantly. He was at that time the fourth ex-member of the Regiment to be killed. The killers hijacked a car and a lorry, using them to block the Border crossing, crashed through a Garda road block and hijacked another car which was found burnt out in Cavan. Towards the end of the decade the murder weapon, an AK47 Kalashnikov said to have been used in at least twenty other killings, was sold at an auction in America to raise funds for the Provisionals. The bidding was so brisk that, so it was said, "the sale price soared beyond the IRA's wildest dreams".

Just before midnight on 2 May PIRA carried out what was to be their most determined attack ever against a UDR base. A training night was drawing to a close at the Clogher Company in the Deanery, the Georgian house on high ground on the edge of the village. The Company Commander was in the company operations room: "I was just chatting when I heard the crump, crump, crump, and recognized it from my TA days as the sound of mortars. I shouted, 'Mortars! stand to'!" The IRA raiding party had taken up position north and south of the Deanery, most of them on a small hill about 800 yards to the north, and opened fire with RPG7 rockets, mortars and small arms. The part-time guard stood to and returned fire. Members of the troop of 1 Royal Tank Regiment based at the Deanery ran to their Ferret scout cars and opened fire with their Browning machine guns, while the troop commander drove out of the base to the south to cut off escape routes to the Border. A total of fifteen mortar bombs and two or three rockets were fired at the base, plus a

126

considerable number of small arms rounds. The Company Commander, who had gone to the front door to make sure that everyone had stood to, saw one rocket come through the heavy wire protective fence, bounce in the forecourt about ten yards in front of him, skip up and explode against the inside of the opposite fence. The mortars were being fired off-line and the bombs falling short, and did little damage. But one of the rockets hit a tree and exploded outside the landing window at the moment that a Lieutenant, Private Martin, the company clerical officer and his wife Eva, head of the modern languages department at Fivemiletown High School and part-time Greenfinch, were running down the stairs to take shelter. She was struck by a metal fragment and killed instantly. The Lieutenant was wounded in the head, leg and stomach. "The lights had gone out, we were having to feel our way, and Alan, the Lieutenant, was trying to crawl out of the way of people going up and down the stairs." The Company Commander is not sure how long the attack lasted, any time between five and twenty minutes, while "all hell broke loose". Then the noise died down and in the sudden silence he heard the drip, drip of blood down the stairs. It was to be an abiding memory. As news came through of the attack, patrols from the Battalion and from 4 and 8UDR, arrived to see if they could help. Two of Martin's fellow Greenfinches took over the running of the operations room for the remainder of the night. Ambush and cut-off parties were organized and the Garda alerted, but the follow-up was hampered by cars and lorries blocking the roads, hijacked by the raiders to cover their escape to the south. A Garrand rifle and twenty-seven mortar bombs were found beyond the perimeter fence.[3] Baxter visited the base the next morning. He was worried about how the Greenfinches would have reacted in the aftermath:

"I thought, is this going to be the crunch moment? Am I going to have tears? But all I got was, 'It's not going to affect us. We'll turn out just as much and we'll get more people to join, so don't worry'."[4]

The Provisional Volunteer in charge of the mortars was Sean O'Callaghan, from Tralee in Co Kerry. In 1996 he wrote an account of the attack on the UDR base for the *Sunday Times*:

"About forty people were involved; I had trained some of them. I set up my home-made mortar tube on a road while some of the others clambered up a bank overlooking the base with an RPG-7 rocket launcher, a heavy machine gun, an AK-47, Armalites and other weapons. The Brigade commander fired a rocket as a signal to start the attack. There was heavy return fire from inside the base; a foot patrol came out and armoured cars joined in with machine guns. I felt very exposed in the road and I could see tracers, like a hail of small bright lights, pouring towards me.
"I concentrated on my mortars and tried to ignore what was going on around me. We had walkie-talkies but they did not work very

well; I could not hear the guy guiding my fire from the bank. The man who was supposed to be getting my mortar shells for me vanished. The battle lasted about 25 minutes. When we were given the order to withdraw, there was pandemonium in the back of the lorry. Somebody fired a Sten gun from inside as we were driven away and then tried to use the rocket launcher, which would have fried all of us in its backblast.

"We were dropped near the Border and escaped into the Irish Republic on foot. Back at a safe house in the early morning, I found two bullet holes in my jacket and heard on the radio that a woman UDR officer, Eva Martin, aged 28, had been killed.

"Looking back I think it was a stinking, shameful thing to have been involved in. But when you are wrapped up in a cause you do not take much of normal life into account. I think I was slightly upset that it was a woman who was killed, but this may just be retrospective. I did not find out the full, harrowing story until long afterwards: that her husband, who also served on the base, had found her body in the dark on a rubble-strewn staircase during the attack and recognized her by touch."[5]

The Lieutenant recovered and returned to duty but later was attacked in his own home and decided to leave for the sake of his family.

Two nights later a patrol from the same battalion stopped a car containing four men. One tried to throw a pistol over a hedge, a second was found to have a pistol in his pocket. They admitted that they were on their way to collect a car bomb to be exploded in Enniskillen. As a result a joint Army/police team went straight to a farm near Tempo where they found a 500lb bomb packed into the boot of a car, ready for use, more explosives in a milk churn, bomb-making equipment and five assorted weapons. Five men were arrested and charged.

The overwhelming success of the anti-Faulkner Unionists in the February general election had ensured that the days of the Assembly were numbered. A group of Loyalist Trade Unionists realized that the surest way to bring pressure to bear on the British Government to dissolve the Assembly and halt what they saw as the drift into a united Ireland was to call a general strike. They held the trump card, control of Bally-lumford power station which provided nearly 70% of the Province's power. Appreciating that they would need the heavy hand of the para-militaries to enforce the strike and the co-operation of the anti-Faulkner Unionists to win the support of the Protestant community, the Ulster Workers Council, as they called themselves, set up a co-ordinating committee to include West, the new leader of the Ulster Unionist Party, Paisley, Craig and the leaders of the UDA and UVF, as well as represen-tatives of the less militant 'doomsday' bodies. The strike began on 15 May.

On the first morning there was little public reaction, but then the heavies stepped in. Workers who went home for lunch were 'advised' not to return in the afternoon. Groups of thugs from the UDA began roaming the city centre, telling shops and businesses to close. In Harland and Wolff's the shipyard workers were warned that any cars left in the car park after lunch would be set alight. During the day the output from Ballylumford was reduced by 40%. Buses and lorries were hijacked to block roads and the ferry port of Larne was cut off by UDA road blocks. It was the first night of many to follow that families cooked their meals by candlelight over camping stoves and wondered what they used to do in the days before television:

> "What worried us," Faulkner wrote, "was that virtually nothing had been done all day to stop the intimidation and thuggery. We could see the value of a low Army and police profile when it was hoped the strike was simply a damp squib which would fizzle out, but we could not see the virtue of making them stand by and watch whilst this massive intimidation and disruption went on."[6]

In a newspaper article written twenty years later Rees said:

> "Much nonsense had been written about the role of the Army in that strike. It is for Northern Ireland to deal with the paramilitaries. The Army's role is not to put down civil insurrection."[7]

That was all very well, but, if not the Army, who else was left to face up to the thugs? The RUC, its morale badly damaged by the events of 1969–1970, was in no position to take resolute action and was given no clear orders. The UDR was never called out. Two battalions carried on with their week-long annual camps at Magilligan and Ballykinlar. On the Sunday 3UDR deployed from Magilligan by road and air along the Fermanagh and Tyrone border, with companies in the UDR base in Clogher and the police stations at Rosslea and Kinawley. Two days before, three car bombs had exploded in the centre of Dublin at rush hour and a fourth in Monaghan. In Dublin twenty-six people died and over a hundred more were injured, and another seven killed and twenty injured in Monaghan, the greatest number of dead in any one day of the troubles. The bombs were believed to be the work of Loyalist paramilitaries and 3UDR had been deployed as reinforcements along the Border in case the Provisionals carried out a retaliatory attack.

By the second day UDA barricades, some consisting of women and children standing in the middle of the road but no less effective for that, had closed all the main roads into the city and the entrances into Loyalist estates. Out in the country roads were closed with bomb hoaxes in hijacked tractors, felled trees and telegraph poles. The output from Ballylumford was further cut back, seriously reducing the power to factories. Seeing that the authorities were not going to take resolute action, unwilling to face the hassle at the barricades, and with a large part of the Protestant community in sympathy with the aims of the UWC, if not the methods of the UDA, the people stopped trying to go to work. Those who did found that the city was deserted, their offices and work benches without light and power, and staff afraid to answer phones in case the caller was a member of the UDA checking to see if they were still at work. Milk and bread supplies began to dry up and there was concern that food would run short.

Despite the absence of any call-out of the UDR the soldiers flocked in to do duty. It was not just a matter of having nothing else to do, there was a growing feeling of frustration that they were not allowed to take more positive action. "Stand back and observe" were the orders. Where possible, and it was usually possible, since the people manning the barricades regarded them as 'their' soldiers, they talked their way through. On occasion, when talking did not work, the patrols pushed the barricades aside, regardless of orders. 'Talking through' led to accusations of the UDR fraternizing with the strikers. That was unjust. It was surely better to persuade than to use the heavy hand and, in any case, how could one use the heavy hand against the mothers pushing prams that 7UDR encountered blocking the main Bangor – Belfast road? Better to find another way round, though in this instance the patrol commander informed the ladies that he was on his way to patrol the Short Strand, the Nationalist enclave within East Belfast, and was waved on his way. On another occasion a part-time company from the same battalion was despatched to Ballybeen estate in Dundonald, where a Regular Army company had been stoned and bottled. The Company Commander was in the process of trying to summon another two companies when the 7UDR operations officer arrived with the part-time soldiers. One of them said he knew the local UDA commander. They made contact with him and the rioting stopped forthwith. Across the lough, the soldiers belonging to the Newtownabbey Company of 10UDR who lived in Monkstown were finding it impossible to report for duty as the whole estate was sealed off with UDA road blocks. The Platoon Commander and his Sergeant went down to the estate where they found a man the Sergeant recognized, despite the mask. The Sergeant

"stated to him very clearly that he knew him well, and that this strike would not last for ever and if he didn't let our blokes come out of Monkstown to do duty, then he would have severe problems."

Next night all the Monkstown soldiers were allowed through the barricades to join their platoon.

Naturally there were soldiers who supported the aims of the UWC and there were reports that some had been seen helping to man the barricades. For those who lived in the UDA-dominated estates, in East Belfast for instance, the only way they could get out to do duties was to agree to take a turn on the barricades.

"If a soldier decided that he did not want to play his part, then the tyres of his car were slashed and brake fluid poured over it. If they felt really vicious the UDA would then break windows and even go so far that wives would be refused service in the neighbourhood shops."

Considering the difficulties, the number reporting for duties each day during the two weeks that the strike lasted was very satisfactory. There were just two instances of attempts being made to subvert the loyalty of the soldiers, a platoon in 8UDR and a company in 3UDR. Both failed.

7UDR mounted guards on the Goliath crane in the shipyard, on the oil refinery at Sydenham and the electricity sub-station up on the Castlereagh hills. Some forty drivers from 1, 9 and 10UDR were drafted into Lisburn to help out the Royal Corps of Transport. In nine days they logged over 15,000 miles delivering supplies, including rations, to units all round the Province as well as meeting troop reinforcements at the docks and taking them to their temporary camps. All over the Province the part-time soldiers, patrolling alongside the Regulars in the city or acting on their own out in the country, did their best to keep roads open.

The senior Company Commander in Newtownabbey warned his CO that the failure of the security forces to take more positive action against the illegal barricades was having an adverse effect on the morale of the two local UDR companies. Eventually, in the last days of the strike, it was agreed they should be used to support the Regular Army in an operation to remove the barricades around Monkstown. The Operations Officer of 10UDR was there:

"I travelled in with the leading troops at first light on that final morning and it was a significant moment for all of us. For local men who previously had been obstructed in going to and from duty by men known to them – in some cases petty criminals and certainly hoodlums – operating under the UDA flag, there was the supreme satisfaction in that they were carrying out their duties properly and acting in the best interests of law and order."

The part-time soldiers led the Regulars into the estate by back ways. There was no resistance; the barricades were still in place but the UDA had melted away.

Across the country filling stations had been closed down or taken over by the UDA. To enable them to continue to report for duty the UDR soldiers were allowed to buy Army petrol at 50p a gallon. Then, at last, the government decided to use the Army for the specific purpose of manning the petrol stations to supply fuel to a limited number of essential users. The troops moved in during the early hours of Monday, 27 May, taking over twenty-one stations. It was far too late. In effect the Strike Co-ordinating Committee controlled the country. The barricades were no longer required and were being dismantled. The Committee was issuing passes to commercial firms to enable them to continue delivering essential supplies. George Chambers went personally to the strike headquarters on Hawthornden Road to obtain passes authorizing the Milk Marketing Board to collect, process and deliver milk supplies. Employers, the Ulster Farmers Union and Unionist members of the Executive were trying to persuade Faulkner that negotiations must be opened with the strike leaders. Rees refused to countenance it. And, indeed, what was there to negotiate about? On the afternoon of the Tuesday Faulkner resigned as Chief Executive and the Executive collapsed. The UWC had won hands down; the strike was called off the following day.

For the UDR the UWC strike was to prove a turning point. Before it began the GOC had discussed with the Commander, Baxter, the possibility that in some battalions significant numbers of soldiers might not report for duty.[8] In Londonderry a Regular Army company had been brought into Duncreggan camp as reinforcements. "I think the Army was afraid we weren't going to do duties," the Londonderry Company Commander recalled. "But we had a 99% turnout, and for two weeks the Regulars lay on their beds in the drill hall with nothing to do. We did it all."

"During the strike the UDR came of age," Baxter said. "After that there was a great all-round improvement in the attitude of the Army and the Police." He received a congratulatory signal from Major General Peter Leng, Commander Land Forces:

> "My profound and sincere thanks for the extra hard work and long hours which the UDR have put in so willingly on behalf of law and order in the recent troubled days. I congratulate all ranks on their very high standards which is now so much the pattern of UDR affairs. Well done indeed."

It was a just reward for the loyalty of the soldiers to their battalions and their steadfastness under the most difficult conditions. Any doubts that remained about the Regiment's essential role in the security of the Province were resolved. From now on the question was how greater use could be made of its proven reliability.

It was coincidental but fitting that when the Forces Pay Review Body published its annual report at the end of May, it recommended substantial increases, an average of 15% for all the Armed Services, including the UDR. The basic rate for conrate junior ranks, about £40 a week, now compared favourably with the wages of civilian security guards. As a result there was an upsurge in applications, particularly from part-timers keen to transfer to full time and by the end of the year conrate strength had increased by a third to 1,234. Battalions were able to recruit up to their establishment of three guards at each base, selecting younger, more active men, and, on one of the days they were not on guard duty, used them to provide limited daytime patrols. By the end of the year most battalions were able to mount several daylight patrols each week, whilst increasing use was made of part-time soldiers at weekends, with the non-Border battalions sending platoons and sometimes companies into Fermanagh,

Tyrone and South Armagh to carry out operations under command of the Regulars or the local UDR battalion.

In September 45 Commando Royal Marines had invited 2 and 3UDR to provide an NCO and four men at their observation post at Drumuckavall at weekends to relieve their people for other tasks. The OP was built along a hedge on the forward edge of a low ridge overlooking the road from Dundalk to Crossmaglen, close to the southernmost tip of South Armagh and about a hundred yards from the Border. The ridge had come under fire frequently and a month previously a Corporal and a Marine had been killed in a mine explosion. The OP was built into the crater and roofed with sandbags. On the morning of 28 September three NCOs and two privates from A Company 3UDR were flown into the OP, the Puma helicopter touching down for a moment out of sight on the reverse slope of the feature:

"The area was relatively quiet," one of the NCOs recalled in his incident report. "The only movements were the occasional car on the Dundalk road and a farmer operating a combine harvester a few hundred yards behind us on the north side of the Border. Although we did not take much notice at the time, thinking back it seemed rather strange that in the middle of the afternoon the farmer stopped his work and took the machine from the field, and simultaneously the occupant of the red farm sent his dog to move the cows from the field directly in front of us. About 7pm we heard an explosion and at first thought it had come from Crossmaglen. Then there was a second explosion, this time no more than 50 yards behind the observation post. Ted, the Sergeant of the Royal Marine Commandos in charge of the observation post, realized we were under mortar attack. As he radioed an attack was taking place more mortars were exploding around us. The next one blew away part of the wall of the post and the next exploded on the roof leaving a large hole. During this time we had been returning fire under Ted's orders, along the hedgerows directly in front of us and along the Dundalk road. Obviously this fire had some effect, as the mortars ceased firing for approximately ten minutes. When the attack restarted the mortar was no longer on target and it was apparent that it had been moved. After firing approximately six more bombs, it was getting back on target, but by this time reinforcements had arrived from Crossmaglen and we were given orders over the radio to cease fire. Then there was a burst of automatic fire directed at the back of the observation post. At the time we thought it was the reinforcements returning fire at the enemy. It was not until an officer arrived to find out how we were and told us that none of his men had fired a shot that we realized there must have been more terrorists waiting for us to leave the observation post. The officer left, and then started one of the longest nights I have ever spent. Next morning we could see how intense the attack had been, as the fields around were littered with large craters left by the mortars."[9]

The detachment, under the command of the Marine Sergeant, had reacted well, firing 107 rounds in return.

3UDR's particular forte was the mounting of large-scale battalion search operations, controlled from a tactical operations cell set up in the back of a Landrover. The operations were mounted on a Sunday when the part-timers were available. Usually there was a find of some sort – a weapon, ammunition. Even when there was not, the operations provided valuable experience in working together as a battalion, planning a search and allocating areas from aerial photographs, giving out orders at Battalion Orders Groups, company commanders passing on the orders to their companies, platoon commanders to their platoons, radio communications over a busy battalion net – all part of the business of learning to be more efficient soldiers.

Initially the searches were mounted in the local area around Castlewellan. The Provisionals were still active in South Down, led by a man who lived in that town. On 28 April one company deployed by helicopter to place VCPs round the town, sealing the roads in and out without warning, while the remainder cordoned off twelve suspect houses. One of the UDR patrols searching the area around one of the houses found three incendiaries, too far away to attribute to the occupants, though there was little doubt they were responsible. The following day the local SDLP member complained to the CO and the Secretary of State that soldiers had prevented people going to Mass. His complaint was published on the front page of the *Irish News*. Three days later, acting on the information acquired by the UDR during the search, the Regular battalion carried out a search of the parochial hall in Kilcoo, the village next to Castlewellan on the main road to Newry. Under the floor boards lay two rifles, ammunition and bomb-making equipment. With permission from HQNI, 3UDR wrote and distributed a thousand copies of a leaflet with a letter from the CO on one side apologizing to anyone who had been delayed on their way to Mass but pointing out why the search had been necessary, with photographs of the finds in the parochial hall on the reverse.[10]

Later in the year searches became more wide-ranging. In August 226 men and women searched the open ground on the hills south-east of Newry and found some 400 rounds. The following month the battalion joined 45 Commando RM in a search in Crossmaglen.

Such operations were an ambitious undertaking for a part-time force with only limited training, especially in a high-risk area such as South Armagh. Sometimes there were hitches. The Irish, be they Planter or Celt, share two characteristics that made the mounting of an operation a headache for the Battalion Operations Officer, especially if an exactly timed programme of helicopter lifts was involved – a relaxed attitude towards punctuality and a refusal to be hurried. Also one could never be sure how many would turn up on the day. Although volunteer soldiers, they could be detailed for a duty, and those who persistently failed to turn up were disciplined or discharged, but there were always unforeseen hazards that could prevent a man coming in – a car broken down, sickness in the family, an emergency at work, sheer fatigue even, and possibly a party that had gone on too long and too liberally on the previous night. It was the last that was the cause of a situation Brian Scott never forgot. On this occasion the company had held a farewell party for the Royal Scots Dragoon Guards. A battalion search operation was scheduled for the following morning.

"I was there at 7am – boots tied somehow, puttees stuffed in the pockets of my combat jacket, beret feeling like a medieval torture instrument. But I was there along with the assembled Company – the OC, CSM, six other officers, eleven Greenfinches . . . and three soldiers. The OC paced up and down before the milling few. 'I'm ruined! The CO will have my scalp . . . Ach! I was getting too old for this game anyhow!' But nobody else came. He had the CSM assemble the 'company' in the briefing room and made his dispositions. The large wooded area in South Down that was A Company's responsibility was broken into sectors, a search team assigned to each, every search team to travel in its own Landrover. I found myself the driver and part of a team that consisted of one other officer, and a Greenfinch. Each 'search team' had been instructed to send frequent sitreps to give the impression of intense A company activity on the battalion net. The Colonel arrived with his Rover Group. 'Cordon Troops?' he asked. 'High Ground, Sir', muttered the OC. The CO gazed around the horizon. 'Well concealed . . . well done,' he said and moved on to visit the other companies. Meanwhile, our two man/one woman search team moved along the forest tracks, searching only around likely 'markers'. At one point the OC stormed past us, entirely alone, rifle in hand and one of the old Bantam radios slung from a shoulder. 'Get a grip on your section, Ken,' he growled without stopping. 'Get a grip on yourself, Brian,' said Ken, 'and I had to repress a fit of giggles. Not too long after that we were searching around a widening in the track, where a car had space to reverse, when the Greenfinch's head popped out of the undergrowth. 'Ah . . . Sir?' she said meekly. We went to look and, bless her, she had found three sacks that contained about 200lb of explosives. It was the only find of the entire day."

One search in the early years produced an unexpected result. A patrol was working up a mountain lane when it was met by a strong chemical smell. "Sheep dip," the patrol commander pronounced, but he was an Englishman and could not be expected to know any better. The soldiers, noses quivering like excited bloodhounds, went straight to the poteen still, hidden amongst trees behind an isolated bungalow on the mountainside. The police were called and took away the illicit distiller, whilst the distiller's wife stood at the doorstep, baby in arms. It looked like a scene from the bad old days of the evictions and everyone felt sorry. They need not have worried. When the case came to court, the distiller received a fairly nominal fine and within weeks was rumoured to be back in business. As for the still, finely fashioned from a copper boiler, it somehow found its way into the Quartermaster's store and from there later disappeared, though no one admitted to knowing where it had gone.

On seven occasions that summer patrols prevented proxy bomb attacks. Late on a June night a patrol of 5UDR stopped a car on the Coleraine – Limavady road and found inside it a battery and an alarm clock with two wires attached to it. The two occupants were handed over to the RUC and subsequently they led them to Ringsend to show the police the bomb they had been making. A week later it was 4UDR's turn. A patrol flagged down a car travelling towards Newtownbutler on the road from Clones, driven by a local man. As he slowed down he switched on his left indicator, signalling to a following car which stopped back down the road, and two men were seen to run away across the fields. The second car had been stolen from a house in the South by five armed men an hour previously. When the patrol searched it they found two bombs. In July 9UDR stopped a car containing a 100lb bomb on the outskirts of Randalstown. The driver had been ordered to leave it outside an electrical shop in the town and his family had been threatened to ensure that he complied. The patrol instructed him to drive out of town to an open area where the bomb exploded harmlessly an hour later.

Next month a 3UDR patrol intercepted a proxy bomb bound for Newcastle. The circumstances were the same, the driver had been ordered to leave the bomb outside the Arlington Hotel whilst his girlfriend was held hostage in an estate in Castlewellan. In September the Castlederg Company, acting on information, discovered a bomb-making site south of Strabane, with 150lb of HME already filled into two beer kegs, detonators, cordtex and empty milk churns.

On 1 September a Donegal man was driving his wife and two small children into the North when he was stopped by gunmen just across the Border at Clady. They forced him to turn back into Donegal to a cottage where they loaded a bomb into the car and instructed him to leave it outside the Newtownstewart Company base, a converted farmhouse a couple of miles outside the village. Meanwhile, they told him, they would hold his family at the cottage to make sure he carried out their instructions. He left the car, with the 150lb bomb ticking away inside, outside the base and shouted a warning to the UDR guard. One of them, a local farmer, leapt in behind the wheel and drove the car to a field where the bomb exploded harmlessly twenty minutes later. When asked why he had taken such a fearsome risk he explained that the company centre had just been repainted after an accidental fire and he had not the heart to start repainting it all over again. "What did it feel like driving a car with a bomb in the back?" the Brigadier asked him. "Sir," he said, "I could feel the devil reaching out for me."

On 7 November a proxy bomb was delivered at the company base in Dungannon, the third such attack that year against the companies of 8UDR. That day one of the Sergeants, an ex-Regular soldier in the Royal Ulster Rifles and a postman in civilian life, had been sent out to Stewartstown where there had been a tragic incident at an electricity transformer. The IRA had cut a hole in the perimeter wire and planted a bomb. A bomb disposal team had gone to the scene and made the mistake of going in through the same hole. One of them stepped on a pressure plate, initiating an explosion which killed the ATO and a Sergeant in the Royal Hussars, whilst a police constable had both his eyes blown out. The UDR Sergeant knew the ATO and had heard him give a lecture on bomb disposal only the night before. The top half of his body was lying over the overhead cables. Another bomb disposal team was flown in and the Sergeant and his patrol returned to their company base in Dungannon. He was putting his SMG back in the armoury when he heard someone falling down the stairs, shouting that there was a bomb at the gate. It was a familiar story, a van hijacked, a bomb loaded on board and the owner forced to drive it into the base. The Sergeant grabbed his SMG, got into the van and forced the unfortunate driver at gun-point to drive into the 'critpit', a reinforced pit that had been built at the entrance to most Army bases to counteract the menace of the proxy bomb. For a heart-stopping moment they found they couldn't get in; one of the Corporals had parked his own car across the entrance to the pit. With minutes to spare they got the van inside and the bomb exploded. The pit worked perfectly, cutting down the effects of the blast, and only minimal damage was done to the base.[11]

It was not the first time, nor the last, that the UDR Sergeant was involved in a fearful incident. Earlier in the year he had been on the late postal shift, collecting mail from the centre of the town, inside the barriers that had been erected to protect Dungannon from the bomb attacks:

"There was the three letter boxes down inside the barrier had to be collected. The town was full of people walking about. To open the box you had to get down on your knees to get the letters out into the bag. I was taking them out when I saw a pair of feet standing by the side of me. I looked up and I was looking down the barrel of a .38 revolver. I looked the other road and I was looking into the same thing. I just got up nice and easy. I could only see two people and they weren't masked. Says I, 'What's wrong?' One says, 'We want that van'. As soon as I saw the gun I thought I had had it. I was just waiting on the bang, but says I, 'There, take the van there, she's there for you'. I was hoping they would make a move to take the van and I would get a chance of getting my PPW out. 'No,' he says 'you'll drive the van.' I got into the van, he was standing at the door and I just put her in gear and made to drive to get away. He just jumped right onto my knee and hit me up the mouth with the pistol barrel and told me he would blow my head off if I would do that again. Suddenly all these heads appeared up with masks and armalites leaning across the barrier – it consisted of concrete 'dragons' teeth'. They had this other van just on the other side of it and the doors opened. They loaded these fertiliser bags into my van, inside the barrier. One of the fellows got in beside me and the other boy got into the back of the van and started wiring up the bomb. When it was done the fellow beside me kept his pistol at my ear and told me to drive on up the street. They wanted to leave the bomb at the foot of the steps up the police barracks beside the Post Office on one side of the square. He had a thing in his hand like a radio and he warned me, 'If you don't turn right into the square, I'll press this and you, van and all will go up'. I maintain to this day that they intended me to go up with the van. They knew I was in the UDR and they must have felt my pistol when they gave me a shove. So as soon as he got out his side, I just pulled on the handbrake and rolled out and rolled until I was at the back of the War memorial, thinking it would give me a bit of shelter. Nothing happened and I ran like billy-o into the police barracks. There was an Inspector and a Constable on duty. 'Hit the alarm,' I said, 'there's a bomb out there.' I knew it was an awful big one because the weight in the van was desperate."

Between them they cleared the area and the Bomb Disposal team was summoned. For some reason the bomb had failed to function, but the ATO set off a 'controlled' explosion, causing extensive damage. Three days later the Sergeant remembered that when the gunman had been getting out and he had let out the clutch, the bomb had moved and there had been a blue flash. Evidently the sudden movement had disconnected the detonator. Despite the fact that the town was busy, no one saw anything. A pensioner leant against a wall watching the whole incident but he was well known as a man who went round the town collecting for the IRA.

Not a week went past in this eventful year but one or more of the battalions was involved in an incident of some kind. It would take too long to record them all. One of the few occasions on which the UDR became involved in a gun battle in Belfast occurred on the evening of 22 June. An eight-man guard from 10UDR had set out for Ballygomartin Radio Relay Station above the city. At the junction of the Antrim and New Lodge roads they ran into an ambush, a burst of automatic fire hitting the windscreen of one of the vehicles. The men carried out their anti-ambush drill, taking cover in the grounds of Duncairn Presbyterian Church and returning fire. Two patrols from 4 Light Regiment RA heard the shots and deployed on the north side of the gunmen's fire position. A hostile crowd gathered outside the bar, preventing the UDR soldiers from carrying out an immediate follow-up. They fired three rounds into the air when the crowd became threatening, and, believing they had heard more shots directed at them from across the Antrim Road, they opened fire again. In all the guard had fired twenty-five rounds from their SLRs. None of them were hurt, but one of the gunners was killed.

The leader of the Castlewellan PIRA was running almost a one-man war, mounting shooting, arson and bombing attacks in the local area and hiding up in safe houses or taking refuge across the Border. The IO of 3UDR had learnt that he was in the habit of going to the Sunday night dance in the parochial hall at a small, isolated village out in the country and set up an operation in an attempt to catch him. Young couples, each consisting of a soldier and a Greenfinch, dressed in party clothes and unarmed, drove to the dance in their private cars. Outside in the car park the IO and another Greenfinch, posing as a courting couple, were in contact by radio with patrols hiding up whilst they waited for the order to mount blocks on the five roads into the village. When one of the couples slipped out of the dance and told the IO that their man was there the patrols moved in and everyone leaving the hall was checked. He was not amongst them; it seemed that, elusive as ever, he had slipped away across the fields. But later in that year, masked and carrying a rifle, he bumped into a Regular Army patrol in the woods above Castlewellan and was shot dead.

A patrol from the Ballykinlar Company was setting up a VCP on the western edge of Castlewellan when the CSM, ex-platoon Sergeant in the USC and a Bisley shot, saw a figure whom he thought to be a soldier a short way up the lane. The figure brought a weapon into the aim and the Sergeant Major heard the sound of a bolt being cocked. He shouted a warning to the rest of the patrol to take cover, but before he could open fire the gunman had run away across a building site. It was only a small, routine incident, but significant as an example of how the initiative lay with the IRA. To the gunman his target was in uniform, he had no 'rules of engagement' other than the tacit one, 'Shoot your victim before he has time to defend himself', and if he did make a mistake his organization would publish an 'apology' to his victim's grieving family. To the soldier the gunman could be dressed as any other civilian; he had to make sure that if he opened fire he would be governed by the rules of engagement, which every soldier carried, that the man was not only armed but about to endanger the lives of himself or his comrades. Inevitably there was a moment of hesitancy before he made up his mind. Not only that, there was the certainty that if he opened fire and killed a man, he would have to justify his actions afterwards, possibly appear in public at an inquest, and, if he had got it wrong, even face a civil charge. If in these circumstances some soldiers 'shot to miss', who could blame them?[12]

Two weeks later the CO of 3UDR was holding his usual Monday morning conference when there was a heavy explosion and the sound of falling glass. Someone shouted along the corridor, "My God it's Sandes!" A 300lb bomb loaded into a van stolen in Andersonstown had exploded at the front of Sandes Soldiers' Home just across the road from the UDR Battalion Headquarters. The bombers had chosen their time well for in the canteen some forty soldiers were having their morning break. The blast spilt a pan of fat over the fire in the kitchen and in moments the corrugated iron and wood building, built in the late 1920s, was an inferno, the ribs of a skeleton full of flame, a column of black smoke hundreds of feet high drifting out over the sea. Soldiers from the 1st Battalion The Duke of Edinburgh's Regiment (1 DERR) rushed from their barracks to carry their comrades out of the building and laid them out on the grass. One of them, his face covered in blood, still grasped his billiard cue. 3UDR Operations Room alerted Brigade Headquarters and requested helicopters for casualty evacuation whilst fire engines converged on the camp from Downpatrick, Newcastle and Ballynahinch and ambulances from the county hospital in Downpatrick, followed by the media. In the primary school 100 yards away the staff comforted the pupils, many of them children of 1 DERR families. Glass from broken windows covered the floors of their classrooms. In the 3UDR building the roof had been lifted off a few inches and settled back in place, walls had cracked, door frames splintered and all the windows broken along the front of the building, including the Junior Ranks Club. Two soldiers from 1 DERR were killed and thirty people injured.

The media was critical of security:

> "There must be considerable anxiety," the *Daily Telegraph* correspondent wrote. "that terrorists were able to drive past the headquarters of a local unit of the Ulster Defence Regiment to within 50 yards of the Army's main gate, park a van containing a bomb, and drive off again through narrow country roads without being detected."

In fact 3UDR had pointed out several times, most recently in March, that the main gates should be moved, but nothing was done on the grounds that over the years it had become the custom to allow the general public to make use of the Home.

The last weeks of the year were full of incidents for a Sergeant of 4UDR. On the night of 13 November he was in command of a mobile patrol unit on the Kinawley – Swanlinbar road when an explosion occurred beside the leading Landrover, throwing it on its side. He fired off a couple of rounds from the GPMG in the Shorland turret of the second vehicle and dismounted to see whether anyone was alive, whilst the remainder of his crew gave him cover. None had been hurt, though they were badly shocked, including the two Greenfinches.[13]

A month later, on the afternoon of 16 December, the same Sergeant had been carrying out a mobile patrol in the Gortineddan area about half a mile from the Border on the road to Ballyconnell in the South. He turned northwards to carry out VCPs around Derrylin, leaving a small foot patrol to lie up observing the Border road. It was a useful ploy, for any gunmen seeing the mobile patrol move away would assume that the coast was clear. He had completed a road check when the other half of the patrol reported that they were under fire. In those days of single frequency radios, communications in that area of the Border were always unreliable, and the Lisnaskea Company Commander, who farmed near Newtownbutler, some ten miles to the east, kept an Army issue radio at home in case he was needed in an emergency. His wife had learnt to use the radio when he was out and played a useful if somewhat unconventional role by relaying messages between patrols. This was one such occasion; but for her, the two patrols would have been out of touch with the Operations Room. The Sergeant hurried back to Gortineddan where he dismounted under cover and took a foot patrol forward to join up with the others. They came under rifle fire as they moved forward and shot back at two gunmen up on high ground. The light was fading when the Shorland commander saw men on top of Church Hill and fired a burst; the men took cover in a ditch and lay up until darkness fell. It transpired later that they were Gardai who had come up from the Southern side to support the patrol. The UDR stayed on the ground long into the night whilst a helicopter with Nitesun checked out the high ground and the Gardai searched on their side.

Three nights before Christmas the same Sergeant was spending a rare quiet evening at home when he received a telephone message to turn out at once as there had been another attack on Kinawley police station. 4UDR still occasionally used the highly effective USC call-out system whereby in the immediate aftermath of an incident individuals would go from their homes to pre-arranged cut off positions close at hand, in the hope of intercepting the attackers before they could slip away. The Sergeant and one of his Lance Corporals went to Cassidy's Cross on the main Enniskillen – Swanlinbar road. He found a number of people there already, Regular Army and police, and a car parked up near a telephone kiosk. He learnt that a police car had been passing the crossroads when the mortar attack began and had seen the car in the roadway and a figure in the kiosk. Suspecting that the caller was organizing the get-away, they threw open the door and put a gun to his head. It was a dummy. At that moment they came under fire and in an exchange of shots they immobilized the car. Unknown to them at that stage there was a bomb in the boot. The gunmen had been about to wire it up, guessing that in the follow up a patrol would see the figure in the kiosk, stop to check him out and be caught in the blast from the car. The fortuitous arrival of the police car had interrupted them before the bomb was armed. The sergeant joined the others in carrying out the search of the surrounding area. He was particularly impressed by the gung ho enthusiasm of a civilian armed with an SMG. "He was into all the derelicts and places where you would expect terrorists to hide, calling on them to come out with their hands up

– in a Southern accent!" He found out later that the stranger was a Sergeant from the Garda; the RUC patrol car had been taking him back to his station across the Border when they came across the car and the dummy at Cassidy's Cross.[14]

The seventh and last member of the Regiment to be killed in 1974 was Private John McCready, a 34-year-old farmer serving in the Rathfriland Company. On the night of 16 November he was a member of a joint patrol made up of three members of his company and a driver and radio operator from the company of 1 DERR responsible for security in the town. They were travelling in one of the Regular company's open-topped Landrovers. The Rathfriland Company Commander had joined them. They had passed along the brightly lit dual carriageway on the east side of the town and were about to turn into the High Street when they came under fire from a balcony in the North Street Flats. The Company Commander

"turned to tell the radio operator to make a contact report, but discovered there was no one in the back of the vehicle. I then found that the driver had also taken cover and the vehicle was travelling along on its own momentum.

"I went round to the other side of the vehicle and found a member of 1 DERR taking shelter alongside the front wheel. I asked him if he was a radio operator, and when he said he was not, I called out for the operator. I then told the driver to get the set and send a contact report. I was told he could not man the set, so I ordered my Corporal to do so. He told me that he thought that Private McCready had been hit about the head. I went round the corner into the alleyway and found the Lance Corporal trying to revive McCready. There was no trace of wounds of any description on his face. We stripped his jacket off, opened his shirt to see if there was any body wounds. The Sergeant from 1 DERR arrived with his foot patrol and took over the radio but had some difficulty in making it work, possibly because the operator when he jumped over the side had dragged the headset and microphone with him. Eventually he made contact by using his pocket phone and requested an ambulance for McCready and two civilians who were lying about twenty yards to the rear of the Landrover, screaming that they had been hit."

McCready had been hit in the armpit by a single round, entering his body behind his flak jacket and causing a wound from which he died in hospital an hour later. The two unfortunate passers-by, a pregnant 21-year-old girl and her 15 year-old sister, were not seriously hurt. The rest of the patrol, pinned down in a brightly lit road, were fortunate not to suffer further casualties. The basic rule, "In the event of an ambush, drive out of the killing ground," had gone by the board when the Regular Army driver baled out of the vehicle without waiting for orders. "It should not be assumed by the UDR that Regular soldiers always know how to react quickly in any situation," the CO wrote in his comments on the incident.

McCready was to have been married a fortnight later to a Rathfriland girl. She had been his girlfriend since he was fourteen. A few hours after the news had been broken to her, her wedding dress and bridesmaids' dresses were delivered to her home.[15] The funeral took place from the family farm, deep in the country behind the Mournes. Although their land bordered the strongly Nationalist parish of Kilcoo, the McCreadys were much respected and lived at peace with their neighbours. The cortège, some 2,000 strong and packed shoulder to shoulder, walked the one and a half miles along the narrow country lane through the winter sunshine to the Presbyterian church at Drumlee, a lone piper at the head and McCready's comrades from the Kilkeel and Rathfriland companies escorting the coffin. In accordance with family tradition the coffin was carried the whole way. It took one and a half hours for the cortège to reach the graveyard,

"Friends meeting and talking animatedly, breaking away to 'disappear' behind the hedge, discussing the quality of a herd of bullocks that had come to the gate to watch us pass. At times when we went through a dip in the lane we caught a glimpse of the Landrover away ahead piled with wreaths, and could hear the faint skirl of the pipes. Eventually we came to the squat little church and the men of McCready's section, including those who had been with him on the patrol, carried the coffin past the 1 DERR firing party lining the road with arms reversed. Hundreds of people had to stand outside in the evening chill, listening to the sermon over the public address system. The Moderator, Dr Temple Lundy, gave the address. The brothers carried the coffin to the grave, past the ranks of our men, whilst the women of the family stood in a sad little group on the slope above. The firing party was drawn up on a hillock with a piper, and a bugler, dressed in the black helmet and red jacket of the 1 DERR ceremonial dress, the group silhouetted against the setting sun. They fired a volley and as the bugle sounded the Last Post, an echelon of birds flew high overhead. The piper played the lament and the official mourners, including a representative from the Secretary of State's staff and the RUC Divisional Commander, stepped forward one by one to lay their wreaths and salute the grave."

The morning after the shooting 1 DERR carried out a search of North Street Flats and found a loaded rifle, a shotgun, two Spanish revolvers and a large quantity of ammunition, the largest find made in the town up to that time. An 18-year-old girl, two youths and two young men were imprisoned in connection with the murder, the men being jailed for life.

McCready was the 46th member of the Regiment to be killed. By now the staff had drawn up standing procedures for the conduct of funerals. In theory the procedures were fine, in practice they were extremely difficult to implement, particularly when the family had requested a full military funeral. Trying to assure it *was* military without seeming to usurp the family, exercise some discreet control over the arrangements without appearing officious when the mourners could be numbered in thousands, and still ensure that the official mourners, the Secretary of State's representative, the Brigade Commander, COs and senior police officers had their proper place in the cortège and at the graveside for the wreath-laying, required firmness applied with tact, detailed pre-planning, rehearsals for firing and bearer parties, and discussion with the clergy, and all to be achieved in at the most a couple of days. There was also a problem of exercising some measure of control over the media, lest soldiers could be identified on the TV news that night and in the papers the following day. In time photographers came to understand that their photographs could be a danger to life.

Ryan, the UDR Deputy Commander, who drew up the standing procedures for funerals, said:

> "They were not overtly political, but in a deep way every funeral was a political statement. In the Border counties when a man was buried in those little Protestant churches, it was like a frontier burial. These were a beleaguered people burying one of their own and determined to stay put. They were terribly moving examples of grief and determination to stay."

Sometimes (though not at the McCready funeral) the preacher in his address did attack the perceived deficiencies in the Government's security policy. The Secretary of State was represented at a funeral by a senior member of the NIO and no one could object to a preacher taking the opportunity to express the fears and frustrations of his parishioners. It was when sermons developed into political harangues that they became objectionable, both to the military mourners and certainly on occasions to the bereaved families, whose spirit of forgiveness seemed stronger than that of their clergy.

By coincidence it had already been agreed that 3UDR's annual fitness for role inspection by Commander UDR, due to take place on the Sunday following McCready's murder, should be based on a search operation covering the environs of Newry. It was to be a major operation consisting of the four companies of 3UDR with a platoon of 1 DERR under command in case of a riot developing, elements of 2UDR and the Banbridge Company of 11UDR.

It was planned meticulously, with the companies moving on separate routes from their home bases, to converge at the rendezvous near Bessbrook, keeping well away from Newry and observing radio silence until the last minute, since surprise was essential if the Provisionals were to be prevented from moving munitions from outside hides into their houses. Precisely on time the companies drove into their search areas, each to a separate road, whilst E Company secured a landing zone and four Wessex and Puma helicopters brought A Company for Carryduff. Tac Headquarters was set up in the grounds of the ruined Barcroft House, concealed under camouflage nets. Search areas were secured, OPs deployed to observe any suspicious movement out of the estates, and the searches begun, working from the backs of the estates over the fields up into the high ground and the embankment of the main line to Dublin. Before long the Banbridge Company reported finding 56lb of Frangex, hidden under the sports pavillion, wrapped in newspapers three days old. Later the same Company reported an even more impressive find, two Armalites, a No 4 rifle and ammunition, hidden in a canvas bag dug into a bank in the grounds of St John of God Hospital. To round off the day E Company found fifty rounds of carbine ammunition buried at the edge of a wood. Dusk was falling as the helicopters returned, navigation lights flashing, to collect A Company, and the road parties withdrew, following different routes well out into the country, in case PIRA had time to set up an ambush on the roads that had been used on the inward journeys. The operation, which had been a notable success, was front-page news the following morning, especially the discovery of the Armalites, one of Japanese and the other of American manufacture, the first of that type to be discovered, suggesting that the Provisionals had found a new source of weapons.

In mid-December a significant operation took place in Tyrone unnoticed by the rest of the Regiment. For four days 8UDR assumed full responsibility for the permanent VCP at Aughnacloy on the main Londonderry – Monaghan road, together with the stretch of the Border within the Battalion area. Other battalions had been operating on the Border all year, but always under the command of the Regulars. This time the UDR was on its own. 8UDR had already managed to raise a full-time Operations Platoon and, supported by part-time soldiers, fed by the Greenfinches and commanded by the Lieutenant Albert Turner, they took over the check point on the edge of the village. At that time it consisted of a wooden hut where drivers and their passengers crossing the Border were interviewed and their details recorded, a thatched cottage for sleeping quarters and a soggy OP in a ditch covered with camouflage netting overlooking the approach road from the Republic. "We had lots of visitors from senior officers, the Brigade Commander, Commander UDR and the Regular CO, to see how we were managing. We came out of it with flying colours." From then on 8UDR and other battalions began taking over the PVCPs on a regular basis. The success of Aughnacloy cleared the way for major developments in the role of the UDR over the next two years.[16]

CHAPTER TEN

1975

The Cease-Fire

In December 1974 Provisional Sinn Fein agreed to declare a cease-fire over Christmas and then extend it for a further fortnight. In Belfast some 20,000 people took part in a peace demonstration, coming down from the Falls and the Shankill to converge at St Anne's Cathedral and walk together to the front of the City Hall for an ecumenical service. After five and a half years of violence and the blessed respite of a bomb-free Christmas, there was no doubt of the overwhelming desire for peace. The cease-fire ran out the following day, 20 January. That evening a UDR patrol was returning to Kinawley from an observation task down on the Border, travelling in a civilianized van driven by a Captain from a Regular unit. As they approached the old customs post at Mullan on the Enniskillen–Swanlinbar road they came across four gunmen in the act of hijacking a CIE bus. One of the men came towards the van, carrying a rifle. The Captain reversed back down the road and ordered the patrol to dismount and take up fire positions. When the gunman knelt down and brought his weapon into the aim, the patrol opened fire and shot him dead. The other three escaped by car back across the Border whilst the patrol continued to fire, hitting one of them. The dead man was identified as Kevin Cohen. Like most of the active gunmen in the Fermanagh area, he was not a local man but came from Sligo. An M1 Carbine was found at the scene.[1]

In the same week a mobile patrol from one of the Glenanne companies of 2UDR was in the process of packing up a VCP on the southern side of Whitecross when a rocket struck the Landrover, penetrating the driver's door and breaking up inside the vehicle. The patrol had not yet remounted and the vehicle was empty, but the commander and several soldiers, standing between the two vehicles at the time, suffered minor blast injuries.

Despite this and other incidents discussions continued between Provisional Sinn Fein and the officials at the NIO, leading to the declaration of an open-ended cease-fire on 10 February. Rees, the Secretary of State, ceased to sign interim custody orders authorizing the detention of suspects without trial and began a gradual release of the remaining internees. By the end of the year the last of them had been released and internment had been phased out.

Whilst the uncertain cease-fire continued, the UDR battalions were improving their methods of operation. 3UDR had been experimenting for the past year with co-ordinated battalion VCP operations. About three times a month multiple patrols would be tasked to provide VCPs to seal off a town or a known area of terrorist activity; patrol on parallel routes across the battalion operational area or seal off a river line by placing road checks on all the bridges. Deployment was controlled by codewords: a codeword for the order to move, another to report the patrol in place, others to impose or break radio silence. In any one night there would be several phases involving as many as forty-eight VCPs carried out in a relatively small area. Orders were minimal. Before the operation each patrol commander was given a task table listing the grid references of his VCPs in each phase and the appropriate codewords.

The operation had four advantages – for a limited time the battalion could dominate an area of terrorist activity; the public was reassured by the intensity of patrolling; the terrorist was put off balance, and it was a simple matter to draw in neighbouring battalions, deploying across inter-battalion boundaries. On occasions RUC patrols would join in.

The successful use of the system depended on a high standard of radio communication. It was not until mid-1976 that battalions were issued with double frequency radios working through relay stations, enabling operations rooms to maintain contact with patrols in all parts of the battalion area. Until then, in order to communicate across the mountainous area of South Down for co-ordinated VCP operations, it was necessary to deploy a Tactical HQ vehicle on top of high ground in the centre of the general area selected for the night's operation. The Operations Officer remembers a night spent parked by the highest road over the Mournes with frost sparkling under a full moon and on another watching from the summit of Slieve Croob the dawn break over the Irish Sea on midsummer's morn. Such occasions made up for the nights of wind and rain, huddling in the back of the Landrover with a Signals NCO and two Greenfinch operators, relaying messages between the patrols and the terminal back in Ballykinlar, sending out the codewords to implement the phases and in the quiet moments playing a game of 'Mastermind'. Subsequently a number of other battalions adopted 3UDR's multiple VCP operations.

On occasion daylight patrols from the off-duty conrate guards would be sent out on foot on 'Farmer's Daughter' patrols, chatting up the occupants of isolated farms and, if the householder was willing to do so, filling up a proforma with such details as the description of the car, whether legal weapons were held in the house, and if there was a dog, did it bark? In particular had they seen strangers in the area or heard unexplained movements at night? Civilized vans were brought into use to deploy foot patrols, thereby avoiding the telltale sound of Landrover tyres. There were strict instructions about such deployments; the driver and escort could wear civilian clothes, but the patrol, out of sight in the back, must be in uniform and the vehicles could not be used for VCPs.[2]

Co-operation between the police sub-divisions and battalions was improved by holding weekly joint tasking conferences to co-ordinate patrol activity. Though these placed an additional burden on the small number of full-time officers in the battalion, for there was still no place on the establishment for an Operations Officer and some battalion areas covered as many as three different sub-divisions, these conferences, which were to continue for many years, played a valuable part in building up confidence and mutual respect between the two organizations. Where possible a police constable accompanied a patrol (a decade before this became a political issue with the Irish government), but this was not always possible as there were simply not enough policemen to go round. The UDR welcomed the general principle, for it was appreciated that policemen were more experienced in dealing face to face with the public and if, by chance, there was an altercation, better that a police constable deal with it than a soldier. In practice the arrangement was not entirely a happy one. Relations between Commanding Officers and Divisional Commanders were excellent, operationally and socially. They understood each other's difficulties. They were friends. There were some difficulties at constable/soldier level. From the soldier's point of view the constables, both regular and reserve, were substantially better paid, including over-time. They had to be taken back to their stations at the end of their shift at midnight whilst the soldiers went back on patrol for another two hours or more. There were accusations of policemen sitting in the backs of Landrovers, taking no useful part in a VCP. From the policeman's point of view there was some reluctance to be seen in the company of the UDR who, they claimed, concentrated their checks on cars belonging to Catholics. Some claimed too that, by associating with the UDR, they would no longer be acceptable in Nationalist areas. However, none of this was a serious problem. Constables and soldiers soon got to know each other; some came from the same neighbourhood, even the same family.

The main development in extending the UDR's operational role came with the introduction in December 1975 of PRUDR, the Province Reserve UDR. Each of the fifty-six companies would take it in turns to provide at the weekend a reserve force to operate anywhere in the Province, in practice mainly in South Armagh, under the operational command of the Regular battalion.

Companies found themselves on operations more rugged and physically demanding than anything they had experienced before, including living and eating (and delivering hot meals) out in the field by day and night. One subaltern reported how 40 Commando RM had deployed his platoon in three sections based on Forkhill, Crossmaglen and Bessbrook, and also assigned them to sections of Marines. In Forkhill one section carried out a 27-hour rural patrol, whilst in Crossmaglen the men had gone out on three six-hour patrols, one rural and the other two centred on the town.

"We were made aware of the need for physical fitness," he wrote in his after-action report. "To patrol in this type of countryside, and not to use the easy way from field to field certainly put us to the test. Few of the men had experience of foot patrols of such long duration, coupled with constant alertness at all times, and by 5 pm on Sunday every man felt that this had been real soldiering."

PRUDR gave part-time Company Commanders a chance to command their men in the field without anyone looking over their shoulder. It dispelled any last lingering USC prejudices against UDR companies being used not necessarily in their own local areas, but where the threat was greatest and so long as they were given a worthwhile task, PRUDR was popular with the soldiers who felt they were operating right up at 'the sharp end'. Brigadier Peter Morton, then a Lieutenant Colonel commanding his battalion, 3 PARA, in South Armagh in the summer of 1976, described a PRUDR weekend:

"It was a Saturday and, as frequently happened at the weekends, a company of UDR soldiers from Belfast had been sent to me for use over the two days. This company went by the rather grand title of Province Reserve UDR but what it meant was a bunch of largely part-time and barely trained soldiers transported to the countryside for a weekend. The difficulty was making use of their talents (they were quite good at searching buildings, stone walls, hedgerows and the like for weapons or explosives) whilst not putting them at risk nor placing them where they could come into much contact with the public. On this occasion we had asked them to search an un-populated area between Camlough and Silverbridge and took the opportunity to fly out to visit them. It was a rotten day, wet and windy, yet they seemed very content but hopelessly at sea in that unfamiliar rural environment and I did not rate their chances very high if they were attacked by terrorists. Most importantly, however, they felt that they were deep in 'bandit country', so I knew that on this occasion at least I would not be pilloried on Monday for failing to provide a sufficient challenge for them."[3]

It was true that there were risks involved, but there was no way a UDR battalion could be taken off duties for three months, as Regular units were, to concentrate on training for a Northern Ireland tour. South Armagh required a very high degree of soldiering skill. Mistakes could lead to disaster, as some Regular units were to learn at tragic cost. By the time PRUDR was phased out early in 1978, each company had carried out the commitment not more than twice, but the lessons they had learnt helped to prepare battalions for the time when they would take over their own Tactical Areas Of Responsibility (TAOR).

The relatively few attacks carried out by the Provisionals in the first three months of the cease-fire were attributed mainly to a group in South

Armagh, who, according to Rees, appeared to be out of control. They styled themselves the South Armagh Republican Action Force. One of these attacks on 14 March involved the landmining of a mobile patrol from one of the Glenanne companies of 2UDR. The command wire device, buried under a pile of stones where a drain had recently been laid, exploded as the third vehicle was driving past, badly damaging it and injuring five soldiers. A Sergeant received head injuries and a broken leg and a Private, who had only enlisted six weeks earlier, suffered a fractured skull. It was the third time that particular vehicle had been through a landmine attack.[4]

Although thirty members of the security forces were murdered during the year, the majority of the 257 deaths arose from intercine assassinations carried out between the various rival paramilitary organizations and from an orgy of random sectarian killings, for which both sides were responsible. In an attempt to end the political stalemate and to find an agreed solution for the future government of the province, Rees called a Constitutional Convention, involving representatives of all parties. It was a forlorn hope. The Unionists refused to accept power-sharing, the other parties would settle for nothing less and after nine months the Convention was disbanded. The harsh fact was that at that time the divisions between the political parties were too irreconcilable to enable the Ulster people to govern themselves.

There was an uneasiness in the Protestant community about government plans, an unease that was reflected in the Regiment, suspicion that the NIO was secretly pursuing a policy of withdrawal from Northern Ireland. Paddy Devlin of the SDLP suspected that the intention was "to encourage the Provisionals to call a permanent cease fire and to lure them into mainstream politics with a view to arranging a comprehensive political settlement that would allow Britain finally to get out of Ireland."[5]

It was this loss of faith in the intentions of the British Government that led to an incident that was to harm the reputation of the Regiment. The Magherafelt Company's base consisted of a collection of huts and one of the adapted railway goods wagon armouries, all inside a perimeter fence without a gate. In the early hours of the morning of 16 June a vehicle of the same pattern as an Army staff car drove up to the entrance. The occupants were wearing uniform. The lone sentry, assuming they were a visiting Regular Army patrol, walked over to talk to them. He confirmed that the last patrol of the night had dispersed and the duty officer had gone home. As he was talking to the driver the front seat passenger got out and struck the sentry over the head with a pistol. The raiders frog-marched him up to the guardroom, overpowered the guard, ripped out the telephone wires, broke open the blister lock steel box containing the key and proceeded to remove the entire contents of the armoury: 149 SLRs, thirty-seven SMGs, three .22 rifles, thirty pistols, a General Purpose Machine Gun (GPMG) and a considerable quantity of ammunition. The raid had been well planned, but now the twelve raiders made their mistake. There were more weapons and ammunition than they could fit into the two cars. Instead of taking a selection and leaving the rest, they loaded the lot into the company Landrovers and drove off to a rendezvous. Afterwards it was assumed that their companions, seeing the Landrovers approaching the RV, mistook them for an Army patrol and drove off in panic; the raiders, stuck with more weapons than they knew what to do with, hid them in a slurry pit and set the two vehicles on fire.

By morning the raid was international news.

"Huge arms theft. Dramatic haul from UDR," the *Belfast Telegraph* headlines reported. "It is more than disgraceful," the leader writer commented. "It is terrifying that raiders of whatever hue can force their way into a regimental depot and steal more weapons than the security forces have captured this year – including a weapon of such awesome proportions as the General Purpose Machine Gun. Either there was some collusion – if only to the extent of providing the raiders with inside information – or security precautions were totally inadequate."[6]

The only small consolation in a sorry story was that it was a search party from the Magherafelt Company that found the weapons on the evening of the following day. They had been searching all morning and had returned to base for lunch when the Intelligence Sergeant received an anonymous telephone call saying that they were hidden in a slurry pit. They resumed the search in the afternoon and around teatime they saw polystyrene packaging from the ammunition boxes floating on top of the slurry at an outlying pig farm three miles to the north of Magherafelt. All the military weapons were there, plus a few more of their own that the raiders had abandoned.

A Board of Inquiry found that the Company had been negligent in performing its guard duties. As soon as a soldier had completed his turn as a sentry he was allowed to go home, with the result that the strength of the guard dwindled as the night passed and was at its weakest in the early hours, the time when the raiders chose to strike. The Company Commander was fined £100 and disciplinary action was taken against two other officers and two soldiers.

There was never any proof that there had been collusion from within the Company, though some years later a man who had served in the company for three months in 1972/73 was sentenced along with two other local men to ten years for a number of UDA-related offences, including the Magherafelt raid. The raid was thought to have been carried out by Loyalists from Londonderry who, concerned about the government's future intentions for Northern Ireland, sought to acquire weapons for a 'doomsday situation'.

HQUDR sent out a flurry of signals and instructions to battalions to tighten up security measures. A member of battalion headquarters permanent staff was to visit each company guard during the 'grey hours' between 2 am and 8 am when the last patrols were home and centres were at their most vulnerable (a task that could take four hours in a dispersed battalion). Holdings of weapons in company bases were to be reduced to 85% of strength, LMGs withdrawn[7] and GPMGs for the Shorlands kept in Regular Army armouries. In particular, whilst rifles were to remain in company armouries, soldiers were to keep the breech blocks at home, an arrangement that was found before long to be too impractical to sustain.

Six weeks later intruders broke in under the perimeter wire at Coolkeeragh power station outside Londonderry, surprised the guard, also from 5UDR but in a different company, and made off with their six rifles. Later three members of the guard were found to have paramilitary connections.

How could these raids have been allowed to happen? Fatigue was one reason. A fair proportion of the UDR had now served continuously for five years; despite the cease-fire, duties were averaging nine a month, which meant some men were doing well in excess of that number. Perhaps it was inevitable that guard duties had become regarded as an opportunity to catch up on a night's sleep. Boredom was another. Constant repetition of the same duty had led to guard commanders no longer reading their orders, believing they knew them by heart, nor to brief their sentries. Rumours of government policy and the continuing cease-fire had resulted in a loss of sense of purpose. The cease-fire had induced a false sense of security, and units, not just UDR battalions, had become complacent and lowered their guard.

There was worse to follow.

The Miami Showband was one of the leading groups in Ireland, playing at Protestant and Catholic venues across the country. On the night of 31 July they were returning in their van to Dublin after an engagement in Banbridge when they were stopped by what appeared to be a routine UDR patrol on the main Dublin road. Though the men were dressed in military style uniform and carrying what appeared to be service weapons and some wore UDR berets and badges, they were in fact a bogus patrol consisting of members of the Mid–Ulster UVF. Whilst they lined the group up and questioned them, two of the men, later identified by the UVF as 'Major' Boyle and 'Lieutenant' Somerville, were in the act of concealing a bomb under the front seat of the van when it exploded. Both men were killed instantly. The rest of the bogus patrol panicked and opened fire on the group, killing three and wounding a fourth. The fifth managed to escape and raised the alarm. Police investigations led to the arrest of two men, the first a Lance Corporal, the second a Sergeant in the Lurgan Company of 11UDR. Both men were dismissed and in October of the following year they were found guilty of murder. It seems that the UVF had planned that the bomb should explode once the van had crossed the Border, killing the group and implicating them in the smuggling of explosives, though what they were supposed to be doing taking a bomb into the Republic is not clear.[8] Coming in the wake of Magherafelt and Coolkeeragh, the revelation that two of the suspects were members of the UDR came as a bitter blow to the Regiment. Baxter on his visits to battalions was conscious of

"a feeling of shame on the part of our own soldiers that this could have happened, a realization that there were rotten apples in the barrel and couldn't something be done about it?"[9]

The three disgraceful events, following hard on the heels of each other, confirmed in the minds of Nationalist politicians and their people that the UDR was not to be trusted and from then on they never missed an opportunity to cast doubts on the reliability of the Regiment.

Six and a half months had passed since the last member of the Regiment had been murdered. Then in the early hours of 3 June, eight weeks before the Showband murders, three friends, returning from the Munster Dog Show at Fermoy, were shot dead by gunmen near the Border at Killeen on the main road to Dublin. One of them was Sergeant Alfred Doyle, a Platoon Sergeant in the Portadown Company of 11UDR. He had a great love of dogs and recently had taken to entering his Golden Labradors at shows. He had joined the Regiment within three months of its formation and had been promoted to Sergeant at the early age of 21.

By mid-July the cease-fire was beginning to fall apart with the killing of four members of the Green Howards as they were moving in to clear a suspect device near Forkhill. In August, following peaceful marches to mark the fourth anniversary of internment, the worst violence for months erupted in Belfast as security force bases came under attack and the troops were drawn into prolonged gun battles. During the month thirty-one people died. Among them were two Catholics shot dead near Newtownhamilton as they were returning from a Gaelic football match in Dublin. The UVF claimed that the killings had been carried out by a patrol from the Protestant Action Force in retaliation for the murder of a local grocer and former RUC Reservist in the same area in the previous week. They went on to claim that a number of their patrols had been operating in the South Armagh and South Down areas over the weekend. A police patrol car had seen the illegal VCP shortly before the shooting, but, since the men wore uniform, they had assumed it was a routine military patrol. 2UDR operations room overheard the report on the police radio. The duty officer phoned the commander of the Newtownhamilton Platoon to check whether he had a patrol out, since he knew nothing about it. When the Sergeant confirmed they were not his men, the operations room realized it must be an illegal VCP, but it was too late.

With the Miami Showband murders fresh in everyone's mind and the revelation that at least one of those arrested in the aftermath was a soldier in the UDR, there was a storm of accusations that rogue members of the Regiment were setting up illegal road checks in South Armagh. Seamus Mallon, Convention member for the area and deputy leader of the SDLP, demanded that all UDR weapons be called in and ballistically checked. The Newtownhamilton Platoon replied publicly that they would be only too glad to have their weapons checked and the slur disproved, but Mallon maintained that was not enough, all weapons must be withdrawn for checking.[10] A deputation from the SDLP met the Secretary of State and gave him a list of members of the UDR whose association with paramilitary groups, so they alleged, "was so obvious as to merit their immediate dismissal", and told him that unless the Regiment was brought under strict control "its credibility as a force would be so questionable as to raise the matter of its continued existence". Mallon demanded immediate action against "those in UDR centres in Lurgan, Portadown and Dungannon and 9UDR in Antrim who had inserted condolence notices in the press after the death of the two men killed in the Miami 'own goal'."[11]

Rees said in a statement after the meeting that he had full confidence in the competence and integrity of the UDR, but if the SDLP or anyone else had evidence to support their allegations it was important to bring this to the notice of the police. There was never at any time any proof that the UDR had set up illegal VCPs in the area. Mallon's accusations were allegations, not proof.

> "If he had come forward with proof," the RUC Divisional Commander said, "of course we would have investigated. Most of the illegal VCPs in the South Armagh area were carried out by the Provos, and in a lot of cases they were not reported. If the local people thought they were PIRA they did not report them."

PIRA retaliation was swift. Three days after the murder of the two Catholics a full-time soldier in 8UDR was shot and seriously injured whilst watching television at his parents' home near Dungannon. It was the second attempt on his life in two years.

The next day Corporal Bertie Frazer, a member of the Newtownhamilton Platoon, was returning home from helping a friend take in his harvest when he was ambushed and shot dead within sight of his home in the village of Whitecross. He had served his country voluntarily for the past thirty years, starting as a boy of eighteen in the Ulster Home Guard, followed by the USC, and was one of the first to join the UDR. Lance Corporal Joe Reid spent the next day out with his company on operations in the Whitecross area in the follow up to Frazer's murder and had returned to his home near Keady when there was a knock at the door. His daughter answered. A young man asked her if Joe was in. She called her father, who came down the stairs holding his pistol behind his back. As he opened the door shots rang out and he fell dying in the hall. Reid was an agricultural contractor by profession and a highly respected fellow councillor with Seamus Mallon on the Armagh District Council.

On the evening of 1 September a gang of men burst into Tullyvallen Orange Hall, where a meeting was drawing to a close, and opened fire, killing four men and injuring seven. A fifth died three days later. The South Armagh Republican Action Force admitted the murders. The Platoon Sergeant of the Newtownhamilton Platoon had a patrol down by the County Bridge about a mile away on the Monaghan border when he heard about the shooting over the radio and hurried back to the hall:

"It was the first time I had ever seen anyone shot, and it was a sight to behold. There was a guy sitting on the stage, I think he had been hit seven times, but he was still sitting there in shock. The next guy I went to, he must have been hit in the back for his whole chest was just lying. There was money lying all over the floor. The treasurer had had some in his hands when he was shot dead and he was still holding it. I phoned for ambulances, and the police came. We gave a hand with first aid, though at that time we weren't really into first aid like the soldiers are now. We talked to them, got them settled. I sat and talked to the man who had been hit seven times for a good while, and it was days after before I even realized he had been hit. We were trying to patch up one fellow and a doctor came over and told us, 'You can forget about him'. Some of my patrol were outside, going down the road, down the side of the hedge, and they found blood on a fence. We got the tracker dog, but it couldn't find them. We got a helicopter with a searchlight, we crawled around for a good while, but there was nothing there. I took a patrol down the road, towards the County Bridge which we presumed was the way they went. It was hard at this time of the morning when you are up around that part of the country, to rap doors. I went to a farmhouse and did rap the door and shouted, 'UDR! Have you seen anything suspicious?' I was told to get out the road or I would be shot. People had heard the shooting and were up to high doh. That sight inside the hall was awful."

The same day the wife of a Corporal in Fermanagh had a lucky escape when she picked up a booby-trapped milk churn and a device underneath it, 15lb of ANFO, failed to explode.

The persistent maligning of the UDR was causing concern in the NIO where discussions were taking place about a possible extension of the role of the Regiment. The Advisory Council, worried that the morale of battalions could be damaged, discussed what could be done to counter the hostile propaganda and to educate the public in the role of the Regiment as an essential part of the security forces. It was agreed, not without some trepidation, that a request from one of the television companies for facilities to make a film on the Regiment for a weekly local current affairs programme should be accepted. It had already been arranged that the *Guardian* would produce a feature article. COs should be sent on courses in television interview techniques; the hard-pressed PRO at HQUDR should be given an assistant. Battalions should be encouraged to hold lunch parties for influential local people, politicians, councillors, clergy. The trouble was that the people battalions most needed to win over would seldom accept an invitation. The *Guardian* article was sympathetic and perceptive:-

"In the last couple of years and more particularly in the so-called cease-fire period, the UDR has become a fundamentally important unit of the British Army. Its 7,835 members account for more than one-third of the Army's total man-power in Northern Ireland and, although it is a part-time force, it is extraordinarily cost-effective with a tiny administrative 'tail'. In some areas, notably the Army's 3 Brigade patch, which stretches from Fermanagh to South Down, in which the UDR provides 57% of Army strength the Regiment could not be withdrawn without a total collapse of security policy. The role of the Regiment has changed out of recognition since the early days. It is still kept clear of riots and provocative sectarian situations, but otherwise it does precisely the same work as the Regulars. The most startling aspect of the gradual transformation is that it has been achieved with no additional stiffening from the Regulars. In fact the UDR is the nearest thing Britain has ever had to a citizen army with a thin veneer of top brass presiding over farmers, shops assistants, teachers, the odd peer of the realm and so on. In the women's section, there has been a similar radical break from tradition with the 650 or so coyly named 'Greenfinches' performing every military task alongside the men, apart from bearing arms. The overall impression of the modern UDR for this observer is of efficiency, undeniable courage and a strange brand of loyalty rarely seen in other branches of the security forces."[12]

The television programme, largely made in 3UDR, was shown in March of the following year. The battalion took considerable trouble to give the film crew all the help they needed, launching the dories in Dundrum Bay and laying on a search operation which took place in heavy rain. As a result the film material was good, but it seemed that the makers were prejudiced against the Regiment even before filming began. The producer never visited the Battalion and the commentary was generally hostile. It was some consolation that in the aftermath of the programme most of the criticism was directed against the television company, not the Regiment.

A film made by an Irish company shown in the Republic a year later was worse. Again 3UDR was chosen for part of the filming, going to great trouble to stage a waterborne intercept and search operation on Strangford Lough. Relations with the film crew were excellent. Perhaps it was naive to suppose that the resultant film would be favourable to the Regiment. In the event the commentary included such phrases as "the UDR was created as a successor to the B Specials and a sop to the Loyalists", claiming that it was sectarian in composition. It included an interview with Andy Tyrie, the then commander of the UDA, who said he encouraged his members to join the UDR to gain military training. He pointed out that the Army kept UDA members in the Regiment under surveillance for a long period and never allowed them to form a complete platoon or section. He agreed that, in a doomsday situation, they might refuse to go on duty against the loyalist population. (Later, in an interview in the *Daily Mirror*, he described the Regiment as an impartial force with a good disciplinary record. "They proved it when they wrecked our Action Council Stoppage this year.") In a classic example of how a skilled commentator can prompt someone untrained in interview technique into making a remark on the spur of the moment, which, given time to reflect, he would realize was foolish and damaging, the Magherafelt Company Commander said he mistrusted half the Catholics in his area. It was a generalization, a figure quoted without prior consideration or qualification, but it was regarded as evidence of a sectarian attitude amongst senior ranks in the Regiment. The fact that one former member of the UDR claimed that he had served simultaneously in the Regiment and the UDA for three years proved nothing, not even that he had ever been in the UDR. However, both films did have one beneficial effect; they showed the UDR as a versatile, efficient, well-equipped organization and once and for all dispelled the 'Dad's Army' taunt.

Whether or not there was an orchestrated campaign against the Regiment, it is certain that some SDLP politicians, principally Seamus Mallon and Michael Canavan, the party's security spokesman, and some clergy, notably Father Faul, the Dungannon priest, came to be regarded as conduits for complaints against the security forces, and, albeit unwittingly, allowed themselves to be used by mischief-makers. Though this is not to question the good faith of those who passed on the complaints to the authorities, some of the complainants at worst invented and at best exaggerated their complaints to denigrate the security forces and waste the time of the police. Some came to court, some were proved and the soldiers punished; in some one side was as much to blame as the other.[13] If a member of the public complained directly to the UDR, he was asked to report the details at the local RUC station. The police, if satisfied that there were grounds for the allegation, would task the Military Police Special Investigation Branch (SIB) to carry out an investigation. The Irishman is a very convincing spinner of stories; it was difficult, sometimes impossible, to tell which was truth and which fiction. In time the police were able to judge pretty well in advance whether a complaint was likely to be genuine by the reliability and background of the complainant. If someone had never complained before and was unlikely to do so without good reason, there had to be some substance in the complaint.

It must be said that courtesy is not the Ulsterman's strong point. He is apt to sound abrasive, even though that is not the intention. Soldiers are not policemen. Unlike them, they are not trained in dealing with the public, though years later – far too late, some would say – courtesy training was included in recruits' courses. Yet Coogan, the chronicler of the IRA, who could be expected to be critical of the UDR, wrote that he never encountered anything but courtesy from its patrols. But, he added, he noticed that Catholic friends were more fearful of being stopped at a UDR road check than by the Regular Army.[14] If that was true, it was because they had come to believe the extremes of Republican propaganda. So far as soldiers at road checks were concerned, the public fell roughly into three categories. The great majority, who, despite the fact that they were having to put up with something unknown anywhere else in Western Europe, being stopped as they went about their lawful business by armed soldiers, remained extraordinarily polite and long-suffering. Then there were those, often men who considered themselves important, who thought that security measures were fine for everyone except themselves and were the first to criticize if they thought security lax, but who would be brusque, impatient and sometimes downright rude when stopped. Indeed who could really blame them, if they were late for an important engagement and had already been stopped more than once? Then there were those who deliberately went out of their way to cause trouble, those who refused to open their boot or get out of the car until the police were present. The wise soldier came to realize that, at best, they were only trying to waste police time, and at worst delaying a patrol whilst a colleague was moving a weapon along another route. Of course there were times when patience snapped and courtesy was overridden by anger. It required a very high standard of discipline to keep one's temper with an abrasive driver on a foul night of wind and rain, knowing full well that the great majority of Ulstermen were long abed, contributing nothing to the security of their country other than carping about the inadequacy of the government's security measures. One night in the hills above the city a motorist stubbornly refused to open his boot. Losing patience, the patrol commander, within the motorist's earshot, asked over the radio for a jemmy to be delivered to his location. The response was immediate. The motorist found he had the key after all, the boot was unlocked and the contents proved to be nothing more sinister than a stack of pornographic literature. Frequently patrols would stop men they knew were in the IRA, including those suspected of being responsible for murdering their comrades but who could not be arrested for lack of evidence. There was an occasion when a Corporal questioning the occupants of a car at a road check found that one of them was a man who had recently completed a prison sentence. That man had been found guilty of driving a car involved in a murder. The murdered man had been the Corporal's father. Being a soldier at a road check required not just a high standard of discipline but sometimes an almost super-human measure of patience and even-handedness. Bearing in mind the thousands upon thousands of vehicles stopped at road checks each year, the wonder is not that there were complaints but that so few of them were sustained.

The Provisional Army Council never terminated their cease-fire with a public announcement, but when seventeen bombs exploded across the country on 22 September to all intents and purposes it came to an end. The UVF retaliated by killing eight Catholics in the first week of October. When they dropped off a bomb outside a bar in Killyleagh, among the injured were a Sergeant in 3UDR and his wife, and the 15-year-old daughter of a Corporal. Both families were Catholic.

During that month and on through the remainder of the year the momentum of the attacks on the UDR increased. In Londonderry a Lance Corporal in 5UDR became the first of the UDR's victims of an under-vehicle booby-trap (UVBT). A device exploded under his car as he was driving away from home to his job at a local bakery and he lost a leg. Four nights later a culvert bomb exploded between the two vehicles of a patrol from the Cookstown Company near Ardboe on the west side of Lough Neagh, the third such ambush in that area. The leading Landrover was badly damaged and a soldier and two policemen had to be evacuated to Magherafelt hospital, but were not seriously hurt. The hidden bombers opened fire immediately after the explosion and the patrol replied with sustained fire, but in the dark were unable to see whether they had hit anyone. Nine days later it was the turn of 2UDR. A patrol from the Loughgall Company had a fortunate escape when a land-mine was detonated under the road as they were driving from Charlemont back to base. Fortunately the main force of the explosion was on the other side of the road and there were no casualties and only superficial damage to the vehicle. South of Dungannon the macrolon armour on a Landrover saved a patrol of 8UDR from injury when gunmen opened fire with thirty high velocity rounds, some of them striking the vehicle.

The killings continued in South Armagh, with the shooting of Lance Corporal Johnny Bell of the Glenanne Company, the 50th member of the Regiment to be murdered. He had been over to the village to buy the Sunday papers and was turning down the lane to his farm on the edge of the National Trust's Ballymoyer Wood when gunmen opened fire and went on their way, leaving him to die. His father had been murdered in the Troubles of the 1920s and his brother-in-law in the previous August.

Two nights later fifty-six members of the Regiment's massed Pipes and Drums, drawn from all battalions, played at the British Legion Festival of Remembrance at the Royal Albert Hall before the Queen and members of the Royal Family, a packed hall and a nationwide audience of millions of television viewers. Not only for them but for every member and every family of the Regiment it was a moment of particular satisfaction when the commentator announced their entry into the arena "with pride and admiration". Thanks in large measure to the enthusiasm and dedication of the Quartermaster of 3UDR, Major Don Langdon of the Parachute Regiment, the band gave a professional display. Earlier in the performance a detachment of three soldiers and a Greenfinch from 11UDR had taken part in the muster of representatives of all the armed services. The pro-vision of this muster party was an annual event and each year its appearance down the steps into the great arena, marching as a separate detachment, was greeted with sustained applause.[15] The Director of Personnel Services wrote that the appearance of the Pipes and Drums and the staff and patients of the Medical Rehabilitation Unit

> "updated the symbolic relevance of the Festival and will have brought home to the many millions of BBC viewers that self-sacrifice is still required in the defence of freedom."[16]

The sacrifice went on. Two days later Colour Sergeant Joe Nesbitt, Company Quartermaster Sergeant of one of the Armagh companies, was shot dead as he drove from his home in Darkley to Gough Barracks in Armagh to carry out his nightly task of issuing arms and equipment to patrols. He had served in the RAF through the war years, then joined the USC and, when that was disbanded, the UDR. Having lived in the Border area for eighteen years he was well known and had come under threat on several occasions. So far as he could he varied his route to Armagh, but he could not vary the time as he had to be in barracks ready for the patrols.

In the second half of November three police officers were killed in two separate incidents in Tyrone. In reaction to these attacks and to counter the threat of retaliation by the UVF, the GOC ordered 8UDR to be called out for a week. They kept the peace, with only one incident in the area, but the call-out emphasized that without more full-time soldiers a wholly part-time battalion could barely sustain an effective call-out for a longer period. As it was, over 90% of the men and women had reported for duty. The call-out was significant for two reasons. Firstly it introduced a new flexibility in the employment of the UDR by deploying a single battalion as a reaction to an upsurge of violence in its area, an arrangement that was to be implemented on three more occasions in the next five weeks. Secondly the UDR CO had taken under his command for that week all the troops, including the Regulars, deployed into his area.

December was a seasonable month for 3UDR. The Battalion again mounted a search operation for the annual Fitness for Role inspection, carried out by the Chief of Staff from HQNI. One company was flown in two Pumas to Narrow Water Woods and a second into Thunders Hill Wood above Rostrevor, whilst the other two moved in by road. The teams had no sooner begun to search along the southern edge of the wood when they found 771 rounds of assorted ammunition and twenty-one detonators packed in sweet jars and biscuit tins, and later in the day a further 117 rounds. The Chief of Staff had just flown in to be briefed and the Operations Officer had the satisfaction of telling him that the first find, and a large one, had already been made. There were those that maintained it was a put-up job, too good to be true. In fact both finds were a classic example of the effectiveness of the systematic system of searching, the first marked by the broken branch of a prominent tree lying over the hide built into a stone wall, the second by a yellow-tipped post. A find in the following week was more convivial, though unfortunately the battalion did not reap the benefits. Two members of a patrol searching a derelict found sixty-one bottles of Irish and Scotch whisky under bales of straw.

A week before Christmas the Battalion was warned that the Secretary of State would be paying a visit the following day, along with seventeen colleagues. It seemed a large number, but it was explained that it was the Secretary of State's birthday, a kind of mobile birthday party. Mr Rees had already visited the Battalion twice, the second occasion only a fortnight earlier, but his easy manner and his obvious sincerity and commitment to Northern Ireland made him a welcome visitor. In the event it turned out that one member of the party was the Prime Minister himself. Harold Wilson met a group of soldiers, Greenfinches and civilian staff, talking to them all between re-lightings of his pipe, and was briefed on the systematic search system, Thunder's Hill Wood, and the whisky find.

Right up to the last day of the year the violence continued in South Armagh. The Provisionals hijacked a CIE goods train close to the Border and blew up the engine seconds before a Dublin-bound express was due. The driver and guard of the goods train managed to flag down the express 300 yards short of the wreck. In Dundalk a car bomb exploded outside a bar, killing one man. Three more died, one a 14-year-old boy, and six were injured in a gun and bomb attack on a bar at Silverbridge on the Crossmaglen–Newry road. The Loyalist Red Hand Commando admitted to carrying out both attacks. When, in the face of these attacks, 2UDR was called out for three days to take over the area north of Newtownhamilton and thereby relieve the newly arrived battalion, 1 Royal Scots, to concentrate on the Border, there was an immediate political outcry. Seamus Mallon called the deployment "the most ill-advised decision taken by the NIO", whilst a DUP Convention member claimed that the use of the UDR to protect Republican enclaves was a desperate bid to "placate the implacable". It was small thanks for the soldiers who, with three days to go until Christmas, gave up the opportunity to go shopping with their families and carried out over a thousand duties in the three days. Small thanks too for the fact that on the second day, on a road near Whitecross, a 200lb landmine was detonated under one of the battalion Landrovers, turning the vehicle on its side and slightly injuring three members of the patrol.

The Provisionals chose New Year's Eve and a bar in Gilford, a quiet Protestant village where nothing ever happened, to obtain their revenge. The bar was crowded as the villagers celebrated the year's end when the bomb exploded. Three patrons died, two instantaneously, the third after midnight, thereby becoming the first terrorist victim of 1976.

CHAPTER ELEVEN

1976 – 'The Way Ahead'

The New Year began with the killings and counter-killings in County Armagh rising to a crescendo. On the night of 4 January Loyalist gunmen burst into two homes and shot dead five innocent Catholics, seriously wounding two others, one of whom subsequently died. The South Armagh Provisionals reacted swiftly and brutally. Each weekday a minibus ran between Bessbrook and Glenanne carrying some of the workforce to the textile factory at the latter place. The workers at the factory were drawn from both communities, Catholic Whitecross and Quaker Bessbrook, and got along well together. On the evening of the 6th the minibus stopped as usual in Whitecross to let off three of the Catholics. Two miles beyond the village, at the top of the brae by the manse in Kingsmills, some dozen gunmen halted the bus, lined up the twelve occupants, found out which one was the Catholic and told him to make himself scarce and then mowed down the rest in a hail of fire from five different weapons. Ten men died at the scene, one of them a former Private in 2UDR; only one, though grievously injured, survived.

It was one of those moments when the Province seemed to teeter on the brink of disaster. Urgent and obvious action was needed to calm the fears of both communities. The Spearhead Battalion began flying in the following evening and the Government announced that a sub-unit of the SAS would be deployed into South Armagh.

3 and 11UDR were placed on selective call-out; the BBC news bulletins the following morning included instructions to the soldiers to report in to their companies by midday. In effect the call-out had begun the previous evening as soldiers, hearing of the Kingsmills massacre, came in to their company bases without orders to ask what they could do to help. Brigade Headquarters had ordered the two battalions to mount the maximum number of patrols immediately and within two hours the four patrols already detailed for duty that night in 3UDR had been increased to ten. The following day the Battalion deployed a composite force of 100 men and women drawn from all the companies into the Newry area, under operational control of the Royal Scots, setting up a VCP on the main road to Dublin and the road to Bessbrook and carrying out reassurance patrols on the roads into the town from the north and east. By mid-morning the patrols were in position, working in eight-hour shifts and being relieved

at their posts by fresh patrols despatched from the company centres. To keep a force of 100 soldiers continuously deployed and maintained in the field involved the whole battalion and by the time the call-out ended four days later over 71% of the men and women had carried out three or more duties.

The Regular reinforcements and the call-out of the UDR had the desired effect; a temporary peace settled on South Armagh and for the moment there were no terrorist incidents. The call-out had gone well; the system of mustering selected battalions at short notice when an escalation of violence occurred in their general area had proved effective. Yet the Regiment was at a watershed. There was a limit to the extent to which a wholly part-time force could be used in this way. It could cope with the routine of night-time and weekend operations, but for most battalions their day-time capability was still limited to one or two patrols, and sudden call-outs for several days on end were placing demands on men and women that they could not be expected to sustain indefinitely.

Disruption of family life was an accepted part of the job, but, with rising unemployment, soldiers were concerned that employers would discriminate against them in favour of those who did not ask permission to take time off from work unexpectedly and with little warning. Some, especially those belonging to a workforce drawn from both communities and concerned about their personal safety, did not admit to their employers that they were in the UDR; but if they disappeared for several days on end whenever there was a call-out there was no way of keeping their UDR membership a secret. And there was still the problem that, for some, particularly the self-employed, a call-out meant they would be out of pocket.

After six years on operations the Regiment was becoming more professional. The early years of learning as they went along and profiting from their mistakes were passing. A significant number of soldiers, particularly among the officers and senor NCOs, had served from the beginning, averaging two duties a week and two weekends a month since 1970. By Regular Army standards they were undertrained. The pressure of operations had left little time for training. But within the limited scope of their task, mobile patrols, foot patrols in rural areas except South Armagh, helicopter and dory patrols and Segment duties in the city, they were by now as experienced if not more experienced than the soldiers in roulement battalions.

They lacked the military discipline gained by the Regular soldier on a long recruits' course at his depot, on the drill square and the assault course, and refined by service in his battalion. But the UDR soldiers were more mature, the maturity of men who had made their own place in life, set up homes and brought up a family. They belonged to close-knit communities. If they went wrong, their family circle would know and they would lose respect. Charges were rare; many years were to pass before the first UDR court martial. Discipline in the Regiment was different, but it was there. The RSM of 6UDR, the first conrate soldier to be given that appointment, recalled that

"The biggest problem for me was adapting from the very high standards of discipline in the Irish Guards and at the Military Academy at Sandhurst. I found if you asked a UDR man to do something, he would jump off his tractor and come and assist you, but if you said, 'You will,' he would put his two fingers up at you. You had to have a different approach to the UDR. Nevertheless the discipline was there and I was very proud when I led a patrol to have those men behind me. If you came under fire they would support you, they would not back down. Under fire they were very highly disciplined; it was self-discipline."

This was no small praise from an exceptional soldier, who was an ex-regular, had years of great experience and who had seen combat elsewhere.

The building programme had progressed rapidly. By the end of the year the majority of the new battalion headquarters had been completed and many of the original and inadequate prefabricated company huts had been replaced by spacious purpose-built brick buildings. 2UDR had moved from Gough Barracks, the old Royal Irish Fusiliers depot in Armagh, out to a large new barracks, Drumadd, built on a hillside on the edge of the town to house both a Regular battalion and the UDR Battalion Headquarters and Armagh Company. The barracks was always very vulnerable, overlooked from the hill on the opposite side, but was never directly attacked. HQ 9UDR, along with one company, took up residence in new accommodation built on the original site beside Antrim railway station and two of the other companies had been rehoused in a newly built centre in Carrickfergus. In September the Headquarters and two companies of 10UDR took over a newly constructed building in Windsor Park, located, somewhat surprisingly, in the centre of the most desirable and up-market residential area of Belfast, off the Malone Road. Probably because of the expense of real estate in that area, it was always very cramped and parking space was inadequate, and it was only by good fortune that casualties were not greater on the two occasions it was attacked. All this new building and the enthusiasm with which MOD had carried out the programme gave a comforting assurance of the long-term future of the Regiment.

The Regiment's strength had remained more or less static. Thanks to an intensive recruiting campaign on TV, on the newly opened commercial radio station, Downtown, and with full-page advertisements in the national press, new recruits came forward to replace those who decided they had served long enough. The average age of the Regiment was dropping, with 40% under 40 and 75% under 50, and increasingly recruits were being drawn from the 19–24 age bracket. There was some concern about the drain of trained men to the RUC, attracted by the higher rates of pay.

It was always to be so. Understandably the police accepted the best. On the other hand it was a sign of the growing competence of the soldiers that by August the Champion Recruits on the last six Regular Army recruits' courses at the Royal Irish Rangers Depot at Ballymena had all transferred from the UDR.

The problem of finding experienced officers to replace the original Company Commanders remained, but at last a number of potential officers was coming forward. By January 1977 there were twelve attending the TA commissioning course at Sandhurst and another six waiting to go. Younger men, under 30, were appearing before the UDR Commissioning Board and the standard was reasonably high, though the response from some sectors remained disappointing. There was still a feeling of some resentment that those who ought to be giving a lead by taking a commission, the young men from professional and executive classes, were failing in their duty to their country by refusing to do so.

The criticism was not entirely fair. Young men studying for their exams and establishing themselves in their professions would enlist as private soldiers but could not afford to take on the additional commitments of being an officer. One private soldier, managing director of a large city firm, pointed out that he employed a mixed workforce and must not jeopardize good relations by letting it become known that he was in the UDR. A Chief Executive on a Roads Services Division of the Department of Environment was another private. He took in good part derogatory remarks from his patrol about the state of the roads whenever the Landrover hit a particularly vicious pothole. By 1976 the Regiment had developed about as far as it could go so long as it was entirely a part-time force. The time had come to consider how it should go on from here.

Four weeks after taking over as Secretary of State in March 1974, Rees, in his first major speech to the Commons, told the members that "the cornerstone of my security policy is a progressive increase in the role of the civilian law enforcement agencies in Northern Ireland".[1] Enoch Powell, now MP for South Down agreed: "The whole operation has to be seen less as a military operation than as a police operation, and increasingly the UDR and the Army must be part of a strategy which is a police strategy."[2] Three months later the UWC strike had underlined, Rees recorded, "how much we depended on the Army for basic security and the inability of the RUC to react quickly to events".[3] From then on the Secretary of State was determined that the police, not the Army, must take the lead in security. In January 1976 he set up a Working Party under John Bourn, the Under Secretary at the NIO, with as the principal members, Jack Hermon, then an Assistant Chief Constable, and the Chief of Staff at HQNI. They completed their report, *The Way Ahead*, by the end of June. The principal recommendations were an increase in the establishment of the RUC and full-time reserve, the creation of Mobile Support Units in each police division, and an increase in the conrate establishment of the UDR to enable battalions to take over operational tasks from the Regular

Army. The MOD, worried about the effect of the continuing over-stretch on the Regular Army, welcomed the proposals.

Resident battalions serving in Northern Ireland were too heavily involved in security tasks to enable them to keep up their General War training. Too many were leaving the Army, due in part to family separation and low job satisfaction. The UDR must become something more than a means of enabling local people to play their parts in opposing terrorism. From now on it was to assume an essential role in enabling the Regular Army to continue to fulfil its worldwide commitments. To do so battalions must be able to provide operational cover 24 hours a day and every day of the week.

By December the conrate establishment had been increased by nearly 300, not as much as had been hoped, but enough to raise a full-time Operations Platoon in the four Border battalions and 8UDR.

Despite their limited daytime capability, some battalions began taking over their own Tactical Areas of Responsibility (TAORs) in quiet areas from the Regular Army, before the Bourn Committee completed its deliberations. 7UDR had been running its own TAOR in East Belfast for the past two years with the Military Police under operational control to look after the Nationalist Short Strand. In May 9UDR assumed responsibility for South Antrim, 11UDR the Portadown area, whilst 3UDR's TAOR covered Police Division G, stretching from Ardglass to the southern edge of Belfast and including all the Ards peninsula. It was not easy. From now on battalions with their own TAORs had to man their own operations rooms continuously. They had been authorized to recruit conrate Captains as Operations Officers, if they could find anyone with sufficient experience, but four months were to pass before an establishment for a small operations room staff was agreed and then only enough for one shift. The CO, Training Major, Adjutant and Operations Officer had to draw up a roster to ensure that one of them was always immediately contactable. At night a part-time duty officer would be responsible for running the TAOR; it was asking much of someone unaware of the day's developments and whose thoughts and energies all day had been devoted to a civilian job. Between 5 and 8 am the TAOR was left in charge of a Corporal guard commander and at weekends and holidays the conrate officers and senior NCOs gave up more of their scant spare time to take a turn as watchkeepers.

Responsibility for a TAOR meant that every occasion on which the police required military support had to be handled by the battalion. The command and control arrangements for 3UDR were a nightmare, but typical of what was happening elsewhere. In its own TAOR in East Down and the Ards the battalion had its part-time company based at Carryduff along with two Newtownards part-time companies of 7UDR under operational control, plus the patrols of the RAF Regiment at Bishops' Court to cover Lecale; in the Newcastle–Castlewellan area, a different police division, one or two part-time companies patrolled under the direction of the Regular battalion in Ballykinlar and in the west, the Warrenpoint–Newry area, one and sometimes two companies came under 3 PARA. Somehow it did work. Each week the CO attended two different Divisional Action Committees (DACs) to be briefed on the operational situation, now chaired by the RUC Divisional Commander, and the Operations Officer attended three separate tasking meetings to agree the tasks for his patrols for the following week with the Sub-divisional Commander. With no full-time officers in the companies, and part-time company commanders involved by day in demanding civilian jobs, be it running a business or a farm, tasking had to be carried out on a central-ized basis, with the Operations Officer issuing a weekly task table, co-ordinating the operations of all the companies as well as, in most weeks, planning and controlling a battalion multiple VCP operation. In 3UDR the Operations Officer, who was also the Adjutant, was working on average 70–77 hours a week. In other battalions, unable for the time being to recruit an Operations Officer, the Training Majors combined operational planning with their primary task of training their soldiers. The desire to press ahead with the new arrangements for the police and UDR was understandable, but for months the pressures on the small full-time staff of battalions became almost insupportable.

The media referred to the new policy as 'Ulsterization'. Hermon had often said that "Ulstermen had to learn to live together and be policed by Ulstermen. If they had to kill, let them kill each other, not English soldiers."[4] In 1976 that is what happened. Twenty-four members of the RUC and fifteen UDR soldiers were killed, all but two of the latter whilst off-duty. A further three ex-members of the Regiment were murdered, bringing the total killing of members of the local security forces to forty-two, three times the total suffered by the Regular Army in that year. In addition four officers and fourteen soldiers were wounded, some of them very seriously, seven whilst on patrol. There were thirty-three attacks on off-duty soldiers at their homes or places of work or travelling between the two, including three instances of petrol bombing. Patrols were attacked on thirty-one occasions, including four culvert mines and the booby-trapping of a rifle range. Apart from 1972, it was the year that the Regiment suffered its heaviest casualties.

In February another member of the Newtownhamilton Platoon was murdered down near the border, 57-year-old Private Joe McCullough. A single man, he farmed at Altnamackan, just up the road from the Orange hall at Tullyvallen. Since the massacre of the Lodge members in the previous September he had been living with neighbours and visiting his farm daily to feed his animals. On the evening of 25 February he went to the farm as usual. When his neighbours discovered the following morning that he had not returned they went in search of him and found his body at the end of his lane, stabbed in the throat and stomach. A pig appeared to have been injured by a booby-trap in the sty.

At the Commander's annual study weekend the audience was in a critical mood. The message was coming back loud and clear – the Regiment had reached breaking point and could not contribute any more without at least a greater daytime capability than the one or two patrols that battalions were raising from their conrate guards, and a larger administrative staff. The Operations Officer of 3UDR recorded:

"'Commander expects maximum turn out by the UDR battalions' is becoming a frequent phrase in signals ordering some new VCP operation at 24 hours' notice.

"The staff have forgotten that the UDR is a part-time force; that we have been on operations continuously for over six years; that an increasing tiredness is setting in; that we still have family ties and homes to run; that Operations Officers coming back into barracks to open Immediate signals and give out fresh orders may have to undertake, as I do, a 36-mile journey; and that retasking of patrols at short notice means making telephone calls round the country, with little hope of finding anyone of sufficient authority to take a message in the middle of a Sunday afternoon. This is the danger of 'Ulsterization', that the UDR will be given more and more to do at a time when battalions have reached the point that they have nothing more to give."

Among the audience at the study weekend was Brigadier Mervyn McCord, due to take over command of the UDR from Baxter in ten days' time. Having served all his life with the Royal Ulster Rifles and the Royal Irish Rangers, including combat service in Korea where he had won a Military Cross, he was attuned to the ways of the Irish soldier. In 1970–71 he had been a Lieutenant Colonel on the operations staff in HQNI and had been much involved in the formation of the UDR. Now, listening to the comments at the conference and joining in the conversation in the mess in the evening, he was dismayed by what he called

"an undercurrent of unease. All the enthusiasm of the first years had gone, to be replaced by a feeling of frustration and bitterness. It was clear that the Company Commanders felt they were not trusted, that they were kept in the dark about operations in their area, and that nobody in HQNI was interested in their problems, particularly on the question of personal security. Four of them had been at school with me in Coleraine, and they told me privately with great sincerity and sadness that they felt that the Regiment had reached a crossroads. Unless they were used properly it would die and many of the easily led would fall under the influence of the extremists in such organizations as the UDA."[5]

Over the next few weeks McCord spent long hours travelling round all the companies talking to the soldiers. He concluded that they were very tired, that something must be done to counter media criticism and that operational tasks must be made more worthwhile.

A full-time Sergeant in 2UDR had been selected to command a trial Operations Platoon in 2UDR, a pilot scheme for the Regiment to test the feasibility of full-time platoons. Two or three times a week he would take a combined Regular Army/UDR patrol down into South Armagh, deploying by helicopter. Sometimes when the fog came down and the helicopters were grounded, they would stay overnight in Crossmaglen. He knew the local people and they knew him and, before they became frightened of being seen talking to members of the security forces, they would sometimes pass on snippets of information.

> "On one occasion a local farmer, a Catholic, came up from the Border and stopped in his tractor and started to fiddle with the engine. As we were passing he urged us in a low voice not to go down near the Border crossing point as he thought there was a bomb there."

The ATO found a bomb at the point where the patrol would have gone.

On 22 March, shortly after midday, the full-time platoon was carrying out a foot patrol in South Armagh, three miles north-east of Crossmaglen. It was a mixed patrol, ten from the battalion plus a Sergeant and a Corporal from a Regular battalion. Though no one had thought to warn them, a Post Office van had just been hijacked from the nearby village of Cullyhanna. Some of the patrol had set up a VCP on the road by Drummill Bridge whilst the remainder brewed up a meal in the shelter of a bank. Unknown to them the four gunmen who had stolen the van had taken up fire positions in a farm on a hilltop, overlooking the VCP. Suddenly the patrol came under heavy, accurate fire. They could hear the crack of the rounds passing overhead, two rounds striking the ground at the heels of one of the Sergeants. From behind the protection of the bank they returned ninety-nine rounds. The UDR Sergeant was all for sending a group round to cut off the gunmen's withdrawal but the Regular Sergeant decided that if they did so they might be walking into a trap. For a brief moment he saw the gunmen moving out of their positions to return to the van. When one crossed the gable end of the farmhouse he fired four rounds, two of them striking the edge of a window but fortunately missing the 90-year-old farmer sitting at his fireside in the room. Moments after the gunmen had sped away in the hijacked van, the pilot of a Scout helicopter who had been due to collect the patrol asked over the radio if he could be of any help. The UDR Sergeant asked him to give chase to a red Escort that had passed through the VCP three times, the third occasion moments before the firing began. The pilot landed, the Sergeant and three of his patrol scrambled aboard and they chased after the Escort down the Dundalk road towards the Border. The pilot brought his helicopter down so low that the driver came to a halt and the Sergeant and his escort jumped out and arrested him. He was handed over to the police at Crossmaglen but later released as there was no proof that he had been involved. It had been a spirited action, with nobody hurt on either side, though one of the soldiers had

169

had a narrow escape when a bullet passed through the mess-tin he was carrying at the brew-up.[6]

In April five UDR soldiers died, four in the first six days. On the 1st, the sixth anniversary of the formation of the Regiment, Private Jack McCutcheon of the Magherafelt Company was murdered. Next day another member of the same company, Staff Sergeant Bobby Lennox, died. He was a postman and was on his daily delivery round at Gulladuff, to the north of Castledawson. The IRA used a ploy they were to repeat on several occasions to lure a postman to his death – a bogus letter addressed to a remote house, the house taken over by gunmen lying in wait for their unsuspecting victim, bound by his employment to go to that address, however remote, however dangerous the area. As he lay dying, the three gunmen came in close and pumped some further twenty rounds into his body.

Three days later Corporal Robert McConnell was killed near his home in the Tullyvallen area. Like Joe McCullough, his neighbour, he was another member of the sorely pressed Newtownhamilton platoon. A bachelor, he lived with his sister, Rebecca. She suffered from multiple sclerosis and each night he would go over the fields to his cousin's house and bring her back with him so she could help put Rebecca to bed. He was shot as he and his cousin were walking across the fields.

On the night of the 6th, an hour before midnight, a 2UDR patrol was travelling back from the Border post at Middletown to Armagh in two vehicles. A short way outside the village the road runs along a hillside, tree-lined at the top and enclosed by a low stone wall at the base. As the vehicles rounded the hill they came under heavy fire from three positions up among the trees. The driver of the second vehicle was hit several times in the leg and lost control, the Landrover swerving across the road, hitting the stone wall and turning over on its side. The leading vehicle stopped up the road and flares were sent up, but the gunmen had already melted away. One of the Greenfinches, Lance Corporal Gillian Leggett, was lying unconscious, bleeding from a head wound, and died in the ambulance. The assassins had left behind a booby-trap in a gateway in the expectation of inflicting further casualties on any troops following up the ambush. Next day the bomb exploded as a farmer was opening the gate and he lost both legs.

Gillian Leggett, the second Greenfinch to be killed, was the wife of a Staff Sergeant in the Irish Guards, seconded to the battalion as a PSI. She was 33 years old, a former member of the WRAC and the mother of two young children.

"The soldiers and Greenfinches found her death very difficult to cope with," the CO, Richard Elliot said, "and so did I. I never ever thought of it happening. An officer is brought up to believe that one day he must give orders which he knows will lead to his men being killed, but not women soldiers."[7]

"The battalion was stunned," McCord recalled. He made a point of going out on patrol with the same company on the following night. The simple drumhead memorial service held in Gough Barracks with a piper playing a lament from the ramparts made a lasting impression on him and his wife. The senior Greenfinch in the battalion, talking later to an English provincial reporter, said,

"Many of the girls in the battalion were friends of Gillian. When she was killed they went on patrol as usual the night after. Some were frightened. But they went out just the same because it made them more determined than ever to keep fighting."[8]

Private Edmund Stewart was murdered just a week after enlisting in 8UDR, having previously served for nine years as a Regular in the Inniskilling Dragoon Guards. He was staying with his brother-in-law at Dunamoney near Dungannon. Two men called at the farm to tell them their cattle were straying. When they went out to round them up, they were both shot. Stewart died at the scene, his brother-in-law four days later.

Throughout the spring and into the summer Republicans and Loyalists escalated their attacks across the Province. In Belfast the Segments were joined in one continuous area enclosing the whole of the city centre behind barriers and gates. PIRA retaliated by making greater use of their cassette incendiaries, a mixture of sugar and chemicals packed with a wrist watch inside a plastic cassette tape box. They could be smuggled through the Segment barriers, hidden, for instance, inside a box of tissues and slipped into the pocket of a line of coats in a department store to cause a major fire. The crescendo came on the four days 13–17 May, after the Provisionals had announced they would be concentrating their attacks on the RUC. Fifteen people died, five of them policemen. At 3 am on the Saturday the UDR guard was leaving the police station at Belcoo at the end of their tour of duty when they came under fire from the direction of a housing estate in the town. A joint Army/police team carried out a search behind the estate and located the firing point. Two dogs were sent in to check the area. When they did not react, the police moved in and began collecting empty cases. It was a classic 'come on'. There was an explosion, a Sergeant and two reserve constables died instantly and a third constable was blinded. Later the same day a police patrol car was ambushed in Warrenpoint – another Sergeant dead and two constables injured. By the end of May twenty-four people had died in one month alone.

However, all was not gloom. Patrols were achieving significant successes in recovering terrorist munitions. In the first half of the year they found ten weapons, over 5,000 rounds of ammunition and some 3,000lbs of explosives, including bomb-making equipment belonging to Loyalists on the Ards peninsula. 3UDR, on their first search operation using amateur frogmen along the Bann north of Hilltown, found over 700 rounds of ammunition on the river bottom. There was still more to retrieve, but daylight was fading and the search was called off until the morrow. The Brigade Major was furious and insisted that the river bank should be staked out overnight. The battalion could not understand the fuss. The ammunition had undoubtedly been jettisoned by ex-B Specials on their disbandment to avoid embarrassment and no one was likely to want to incur the further embarrassment of taking it back again. It was one of those occasions when the UDR had a better understanding of a local problem. A Sapper diving team took up the search the following day and the total haul amounted to 2,000 rounds. Though the find had no terrorist implications, the figures were a useful statistic in the NIO weekly security report. The angry Brigade Major was 'H' Jones who was later to win a posthumous Victoria Cross leading his battalion, 2 PARA, against the Argentinian position at Goose Green during the Falklands action in 1982.

The last week in April saw an innovation that did much to boost morale as well as improving the standard of training over the years. The MOD had agreed that UDR battalions could hold their annual camps in Great Britain, a welcome change from the limited attractions of Ballykinlar and Magilligan. Across the water there would be not only more extensive and challenging range facilities but the opportunity to train outside the confines of barracks and to relax off-duty in the local pubs and neighbouring towns. The Regiment chose Warcop for the first camp, a battalion-sized hutted camp on the edge of an attractive Cumbrian village: an Elizabethan manor house, stone houses alongside a beck of clear water, a humped-back bridge, the ranges on the hills above, and, happily, a village pub practically at the camp gates. There was only one potential snag. Since the UDR Act had laid down that members of the Regiment could be required to train only within Northern Ireland, only volunteers could be taken to camp across the water. However, that proved no problem; the four battalions who went to camp for a week each in this first year took with them over 1,600 men and women. They travelled by coach to Larne, ferry to Stranraer and special train to Warcop, which had its own military siding, and, in the case of 4UDR, from Belfast to Liverpool on the Royal Fleet Auxilary *Sir Percivale*.

Since these were the first UDR battalions to appear on the mainland, they attracted considerable attention from members of the Army Council, including the CGS and VCGS, as well as the GOC Northern Ireland, the Directors of Infantry and Army Training, and from the media, both national and local Northern Ireland press, with radio and television, including ITN's 'News at Ten'. The nationwide coverage "did much to make the UDR better known and understood." Training consisted mainly of weapon firing on the excellent ranges and patrol exercises over the open countryside, not unlike parts of rural Ulster. The Saturday was a free day and coach parties departed for the Lancashire coastal towns, Blackpool and Morecambe. The Greenfinches from 4UDR were invited to visit Eaton Hall outside Chester by the owner, the Duke of Westminster, their neighbour back in Fermanagh. The pipes and drums gave a display in Appleby, the local town. Local people came to welcome this annual influx of the Ulstermen; they fitted in and their behaviour, bearing in mind that they were relaxing from long hours of intensive operations, was generally impeccable.

The attacks on off-duty members of the Regiment continued through the summer and three officers survived assassination attempts in the space of five weeks. On 8 June a Corporal from the Rathfriland Company was at his usual place of work in Fishers' coal yard in Newry when two gunmen walked in and opened fire on him. He dived for cover, but was hit five times. The gunmen escaped across the Border in a car stolen earlier that morning in Forkhill. As a result of quick action by the RUC and excellent co-operation with the Garda, an unarmed Garda patrol stopped the car. The gunmen opened fire, wounding one of the Gardai in the knee, then drove back towards the North and were lost. One of them was recognized as a man wanted for the murder of Colour Sergeant Ruddy, now living in Dundalk. When Gardai raided the house, they found a plan of Fishers' coal yard. Meanwhile the Corporal had remained very cool, giving instructions for a message to be sent to 3 PARA at the Downshire Road base and to his Sergeant Major in Rathfriland. Despite the number of his wounds, he was not seriously hurt and was able to leave hospital three weeks later. His wife was expecting a baby at the time. Later in mid-August he went to see his doctor, complaining of a headache and while he was being examined a fragment of bullet fell out of his head![9]

The Major commanding the UDR company in Kilkeel was working in his office in Fishers' builders supply yard, 100 yards from where the corporal had been shot. Unbeknown to him, a quarter of a mile away two armed men were stealing a bread van that made a daily delivery to a nearby shop. One held up the two delivery men whilst the other emptied the bread from two of the drawers and ordered the two to lie down inside, one to each drawer. With the two hapless men locked inside, they drove to Fishers' yard where one kept watch whilst the other knocked at the shop door. When the unarmed doorman let him in, the gunman pistol-whipped him, knocking him unconscious. The Major, whose office was behind a glass screen at the far end of the building, heard shouting in the outer shop. Looking up he saw the gunman coming towards him, holding a 9mm pistol aimed at him, ten feet away. He pushed back his chair, turned and dived head first through the glass of the ground floor window, landed on his hands and knees and crawled under a parked trailer. The gunman, thwarted of his intended target, turned to leave just as a 17-year-old clerk was trying to take refuge in the lavatory. The gunman shot him in the leg and fired another nine rounds as he lay on the floor. He survived but never fully recovered. The Major sustained cuts to his head, hands and back and a deep gash in a thigh muscle, but he had returned to duty with the Kilkeel Company within a few weeks.

In those days a fair number of members of the security forces, UDR and police reservists, lived or worked in Newry and had done so happily for years, for it had not been a bitter town. Some of them worked for Fishers. Two members of the Rathfriland Company, one of them later to become the Company Commander, were in the same building at the time of the attempted assassination of the Major. Over the years at least four members of the security forces employed by the firm were murdered and another four wounded. The Major reckoned that one of the employees was passing information to the Provisionals. For the sake of all his family he must move out of the town, though his people had lived in South Armagh for three centuries. When he was offered the chance to set up a new branch of the same group in the quiet North Down town of Bangor he did not hesitate to accept. But after he had worked there for nine years, the group was taken over and the new owners, an English firm, put in its own manager, telling him he could either return to the Newry office or resign. It was a Hobson's choice; to return to Newry would have been the equivalent of accepting a death warrant. So after twenty-eight years' service with the firm he resigned with a small redundancy payment but losing, as well as a good salary, his share option and pension rights, and the use of a company car. For the next eight years he worked for 3UDR as Battalion Welfare Officer at a reduced salary and, being part-time, without any entitlement to pension or leave and sickness pay. In all he reckoned the threat to his life had cost him some £40,000. He was just one example of how a soldier coming under dire threat and forced to leave home and civilian job suffered not only the stress of the threat and the disturbance of uprooting home and family, but on occasion considerable financial loss. Eventually, very late in the day, around 1990, the MOD agreed to a scheme of compensation for loss of earnings (CLOE). His experience was used as an example in arguing the case for CLOE, but when it was introduced, the scheme was back-dated only to the beginning of the year and the Major received nothing. It was not only to the soldiers who laid down their lives that Northern Ireland owes a lasting debt of gratitude.

On 30 July Private Robert Scott was killed near Moneymore. He worked on his father's farm but found time to help out an 86-year-old widow who lived in a cottage on their land. He had decided that morning to call on her to chop some wood and make her a cup of tea. Getting down from his tractor to open the gate he triggered off a concealed device attached by a fishing line and a drawing pin to the bottom of the gate. He died instantly, the fourth member of the Magherafelt Company to die that year. The same morning, not far from the Scott farm, another member of the company was severely wounded when a bomb exploded under his car.

The Cookstown Company Commander had already been shot once, back in October 1972 when he was hit in the head by nine bullets from a Thompson sub-machine gun fired from a passing car. He survived and returned to duty. On 11 August he had gone down to the factory:

"It was a beautiful morning and I had my youngest son with me. He was thirteen at the time. I was standing in the doorway talking to the foreman and a couple of charge hands. The foreman, who was sitting in a chair, stood up to get cigarettes, I stepped back, and as I did so the sniper fired. The bullet took a groove out of my head, and if the foreman had not stood up and I had not stepped back, I would not be here today. I was armed at the time and took off after him, but the factory was completely surrounded by a chain link fence, which meant I had to go right round to the gate, and by that time he had gone."

The fifth anniversary of the introduction of internment was a particularly violent time in Belfast, with the first intense gun battles for months. Young, the CLF, received a message from Commander 39 Brigade, warning him that it was going to be a bad night in the city. He had talked to Newman, the Chief Constable, who told him he had been getting the same message.

"By God it was a bad night. I had every reserve I could get from 8 Brigade as Belfast was absolutely hot, then Ken [Newman] and I were eventually down on the ground, taking over an office in one of the battalion bases, where he could talk on the phone to his people, and I to mine. Merlyn Rees was on the phone from London asking what was going on.

"I had no more troops to bring in. The whole of 7 and 10UDR were out. They weren't called out, they simply turned up. That was one of the greatest strengths of the Regiment. They were all volunteers, they did not have to come, but, if there was a crisis, they just turned up, and you'd find a whole company waiting for orders. They weren't just interested in defence of their neighbourhoods, but of the whole community."[10]

An official call-out was implemented the following morning for 1 and 5UDR and a company of 6UDR to take over the tasks of the Regular units from 8 Brigade sent to help out in Belfast, followed that evening by 7, 9 and 10UDR. All five battalions, plus the one company, remained on call-out for the next six days. *Visor*, the weekly newspaper for the Army in Northern Ireland, reported that: "Perhaps the most significant feature of the call-out was the patent evidence that the UDR can take such operations in its stride and that there is now a high degree of confidence between the Regular Army, the RUC and the resident UDR battalions."[11]

In the second half of the year the Provisionals turned their attention to County Antrim with multiple arson attacks on Portrush and Ballymena. On 27 September a company of 5UDR was firing on the isolated ranges on the cliff top above Port Ballintrae, along the coast from Portrush. They had completed one practice at 100 metres and moved back to the 200 metres firing point when there was an explosion in the shingle bed. A Corporal and a Private soldier were seriously injured. A clearance operation the following day revealed that a milk churn containing 70lb of home-made explosive had been buried in the shingle, presumably some weeks previously as the range had been in use the previous day. Evidently during the night the terrorists had returned under cover of darkness and connected up two pressure plates, made out of boot polish tins concealed under the surface of the shingle.[12]

In three weeks in the autumn seven members of the Regiment were murdered. HQ UDR had sent a signal to COs reminding them of the ever-present threat to their soldiers, and particularly at that time, to officers and senior NCOs. Within hours another postman had died, Lance Corporal Stanley Adams of 8UDR, shot and killed as he delivered mail to a lonely farm near Pomeroy. On the same day Captain Ronnie Bond, Second-in-Command of the West Foyle Company of 5UDR, was shot outside his home in Londonderry; he died ten days later. On 9 November Lance Corporal Jimmy Speers of the Maghera Company was working at his garage in Desertmartin. Three men drove into the forecourt and asked him to check a leak in the car's radiator. As he did so they killed him. Two days later Lance Corporal Winston McCaughey was shot down outside his home at Boveedy, the third member of 5UDR to die in the space of a week. Lieutenant Colonel Ian McBain, who had been born in Belfast and had taken over command of the battalion in March of the previous year, has never forgotten that

"dreadful week. I was home on leave in Scotland and I got the message that Ronnie Bond had been shot. I then came home to the Battalion and he died on the Sunday. We buried him on the Tuesday. I got back to my house on the Tuesday evening having buried Ronnie Bond, the phone went, another one murdered, Lance Corporal Speers in Desertmartin, so I went rushing off down there. We were having a dinner party on the Wednesday; Commander 8 Brigade was coming. I had just hopped out of the bath, the telephone rang, one of my soldiers had accidentally shot and killed a Royal Hampshire in Maghera. I went rushing off down there, leaving my wife to cope with the dinner party. That was the Wednesday night. The Thursday we buried Speers. Got home on Thursday night, telephone, another one, McCaughey. It was the most extraordinary week I have ever had. I got into some sort of state on that Thursday night. I went back into the room, having taken the telephone call, and June, my wife, said, 'Another one?' and I said, 'Yes,' and we laughed. That's not the sort of thing you would normally laugh about but it had got to the stage where it was incredible. We didn't laugh for long. I then started getting calls from the CLF and GOC saying, 'How are you coping?' Well, you just cope. It just goes on, there's nothing you can do about it. But that was a really black week."[13]

Four days later a foot patrol of 11UDR in Lurgan came under Armalite fire at close range. One member of the patrol, Private George Lutton, was killed and another wounded. In admitting his murder the Provisionals confirmed that they intended to step up their campaign against the UDR. Paisley led a UUUC delegation to demand from the Under–Secretary for the Army greater security for members of the Regiment. Harold McCusker, Unionist MP for County Armagh, wondered whether too much was being asked of the soldiers. "Is it too much to expect men to serve as soldiers at night and by day to become unarmed and vulnerable artisans, with SLRs and other sophisticated weapons at one moment and a spanner, a spade, a pen the next?' All the Unionist parties urged that the government must do more to provide protection for the individual soldiers. Oliver Napier, the Alliance leader, said, "You cannot expect men to take a stand and go out every night to protect the community if the community, through its government, does nothing to protect them."[14]

The spate of murders came at a time when the Regiment was under mounting criticism from the SDLP. Too many soldiers, their politicians claimed, had been guilty of serious offences, including involvement in terrorism. John Hume, in a hard-hitting article in the *Sunday Independent* in June, recalled the arms raids and weapon losses, made unsubstantiated accusations of UDR involvement in murders committed at illegal VCPs and included a list of twenty people who he claimed had been convicted of serious offences whilst serving in the Regiment over the past six years. The Miami Showband murder trial had taken place in October and it was the fact that the two accused were now known to be members of the Regiment that was so damaging. In a Commons written reply the Under–Secretary for the Army stated that thirteen members of the Regiment had been convicted of serious offences in the previous four years, six for murder and manslaughter, two of them being the result of negligent handling of loaded weapons; another six had been found guilty of bombing offences and one of a charge of intimidation. Another four soldiers were facing separate charges of murder, manslaughter, assault and armed robbery.

Between April '75 and April '76, out of 2,700 applicants to join the Regiment, 1,200 were rejected on various grounds. In the same period 1,439 soldiers had been discharged, either because they had completed their three-year engagement or they had failed to report for duties or training, and some on disciplinary grounds. On balance the strength fell by thirty-eight during that period. The statement in Ryder's book that 1,000 were dismissed and 10,000 applicants were rejected, implying that all the dismissals and rejections were on paramilitary or disciplinary grounds, was a misrepresentation of the facts. That of the 18,000 people who had served since the Regiment was formed only twenty had been convicted of serious offences, less than a quarter of one percent, was a matter of great credit to the disciplinary standards of the UDR.

McCord had been dismayed to find how little the general public knew about the UDR. The Regiment had been at fault in failing to tell its story. One of his first tasks was to instruct his Chief Of Staff and the two UDR press officers to prepare a list of the main criticisms and the replies, together with a list of vital statistics. When he had studied these, he produced a series of tape-recorded interviews, listening to the results and refining the answers until he could answer them naturally and almost without thinking. He set up a Regimental public relations committee composed of the press officers and battalion PROs, and arranged to conduct a number of influential people on visits to battalion operations. These included

> "The Lord Mayor of Belfast, representatives from Chambers of Commerce, headmasters from leading schools, senior Civil Servants, Members of Parliament representing constituencies in Northern Ireland and across the water, and senior staff from the Army and the police. One of the most successful of these was by Airey Neave, the Shadow Secretary of State, who, following a briefing in HQUDR, gave an excellent broadcast interview from the steps of the head-quarters."

In November McCord made a forthright speech in the defence of the Regiment at the opening of 10UDR's new battalion base:

> "Members of the Regiment cannot ignore the very tiny percentage of those who have betrayed the trust given to them. The fact remains that like the Regular Army and the RUC they are subject to the law of the land. It is right and proper that those who have betrayed their trust should be punished. There is nowhere that they are more wholeheartedly condemned than by the vast majority of the Regiment."

He told the audience how at the funeral of Captain Bond someone had come up to him and said, "You will need someone to replace Ronnie. Here's my application."

The address was given widespread coverage and broke the logjam, he recalled. Thereafter he was allowed to give interviews and take part in world-wide broadcasts. A company commander told him that he had heard him being interviewed on radio whilst he was on holiday in Norway.

In the following months public relations endeavours included a 26-minute documentary on the Regiment produced by the MOD which it was hoped would be shown on television in North America; an eight-minute film made by the Central Office of Information on the WUDR, part of a package of films being made by the government film agency in an attempt to counter Irish Republican propaganda in the United States in the run-up to the Presidential election; a 30-minute sound documentary broadcast by Radio Medway, a local station covering South-East England; a feature film on Australian TV; an interview with McCord on RTE which the British Ambassador in Dublin declared had been 'highly effective'; an article in the US published international journal *Newsweek* and articles published in local papers as a result of battalion press days.

Thus for a while the Northern Ireland Office and the Army Information Services fought back on behalf of the UDR and the battalions came to realize that they had to make the effort to sell themselves to an indifferent public. All these efforts had little effect.

A member of the public approached a UDR patrol on the outskirts of Belfast. He told them he had seen men carrying boxes from a house in the city and loading them into a car. The patrol commander radioed the information back to the Battalion Operations Room who passed it on to Brigade. As a result a car bomb was intercepted and four men were arrested and charged with murder. The man had driven out of town to find a patrol in an area where he would not be recognized. As a result of his courage he prevented more deaths being added to the year's total of 297.

CHAPTER TWELVE

1977 – 'The Way Ahead' Implemented and the UUAC Strike

'The Way Ahead' directive was issued in January laying down the future role of the Army as "operating in support of the RUC in the establishment of law and order throughout the Province." It looked to the co-ordination of intelligence effort, the rationalization of Army and police boundaries and, where possible, the setting up of joint RUC/Army operations rooms. In practical terms it meant that from now on all battalions' operations, patrols and searches would have to be cleared with the local RUC sub-division. In June the Secretary of State announced that the police would be increased by 1,200 and the UDR permanent cadre to 2,500 full-time soldiers, sufficient to form a Command Company headquarters and Operations Platoon of forty men in each Battalion.

To encourage the part-timers to transfer to full-time, new terms of service were introduced to replace the former conrate terms. From the soldiers' point of view the new terms were an improvement. Although they already received the same basic pay as their Regular equivalent ranks, from now on they would qualify for the Regular Army's triennial increments for length of service, and, like the Regulars, a pension after twenty-two years.

For the majority of officers the new terms were also welcome. For years their rate of pay had been calculated at 75%, later increased to 85%, of their equivalent rank in the Regular Army. From now on they would receive 95% of their Regular equivalents. The term "conrate" was dropped and the full-time element became known as the permanent cadre.

Plans were agreed for the longer term development of the Regiment. These were to be implemented gradually as circumstances permitted. They included a path to promotion to Lieutenant Colonel and above for part-time officers, the possibility of appointing two or more Colonels Commandant and a means of giving serving officers more say in the non-operational running of the Regiment by the creation of the Seconds-in-Command Committee.

Another innovation was that serving soldiers in the Regular Army could transfer directly into the permanent cadre without loss of pension rights. It made good sense. The many Regular soldiers who had met and married a local girl on a previous Northern Ireland tour could go on soldiering whilst living at home. Many proved a valuable asset, with their higher standard of training and their experience of service in parts of the Province where the UDR did not go. Others were not welcome – men with debt and welfare problems recommended for transfer by Regular units glad to see the back of them. Some, as future events were to show, were unsuitable on security grounds.

As well as the Operations Platoons, battalions were given manpower cover to set up full-time intelligence cells, including a senior NCO from the Regular Army to assist the part-time UDR IO. The Regular Army Training Majors were retitled Training Intelligence and Security Officers (TISOs) and given, in theory, a supervisory responsibility for the management of intelligence and security in their battalions. In fact the UDR IOs were far more experienced and fully capable of running their own cells, and the Adjutants had always held the additional appointment of Unit Security officer, attending courses at the School of Intelligence in Kent, and there was a feeling that the renaming of the Training Majors had been more to do with politics than practicalities. In any case they were now even more fully occupied in improving the knowledge and capabilities of the new Operations Platoons.

The part-time IOs had already established good working relations with their local Special Branch officers. Naturally Special Branch passed on to them only information they needed to know; the same principle was applied in the Branch's dealings with the Regular Army at any rank and, indeed, within the RUC.

> "In some cases the relationships with the Branch built up slowly," explained the IO of 3UDR, who held the post for eighteen years, "with others we hit it off right away. It was very much a matter of personalities. If you hit it off with another person they learnt to trust you. No doubt we were tested, fed a bit of information to see who we would tell and whether it would come back to the Branch through some other channel. Once we passed those tests, trust built up fairly quickly. In time there were some SB officers who told me damn near as much as they had, on the proviso that the information stayed with me. These were things I knew that I could not tell the CO, not because he was not to be trusted, but because it would have made no sense to tell him; it did not affect the running of the Battalion or the conduct of operations. But I had the information at the back of my mind, and with it I could quietly guide our operations."

For the most part the information produced within UDR battalions was low level and unspectacular, the small pieces that helped to build up the jigsaw of suspects. It came from patrol debriefings and the daily analysis of car check sheets maintained in each patrol, recording the registration numbers and particulars of cars passing through a VCP. It came also from the soldiers themselves, information picked up within their own communities or gleaned in the course of their civilian jobs. The staff had to be careful to sift hard fact from local gossip. Information came in from both communities. One battalion had as a useful contact a priest and, until it became too dangerous to be seen talking to the security forces, Catholic farmers, particularly the older generation, in country areas, along the Armagh border and in East and West Tyrone, would pass on information to people they knew were in the UDR. Nor was information confined to Republican terrorists; information about the activities of Loyalist groups was received and passed on up the intelligence chain. The card index 'P Files' in the intelligence cells were not confined to Republican suspects.

The UDR was not normally allowed to operate in civilian clothes. However, it was accepted that in certain circumstances some elements of the battalion staff could not operate effectively if there was an absolute ban, and in these circumstances the ruling could be waived, but only on the authority of the CO and with the knowledge of the police. The battalions did not mount long-term covert operations, nor did they deploy observation posts as such, though they would lie up in the country for a few hours keeping watch on a suspect farm. Military covert operations were highly skilled and required specialist training, and were left to the Regular Army.

One such plain-clothes patrol from the Magherafelt Company produced a useful success. A Corporal described what happened:

"We were travelling about the wee roads around Bellaghy when we saw these two cars parked at the side of the road by a house. We went past and parked the car in a field and we walked back again towards the house. There were three boys down in the back garden and they were burying what we thought was maybe explosives. Willis shouted down at the boys, 'Put your hands up, come up with your hands up'. While this was happening there was a boy at the back door and when he heard Willis shouting for the other boys to come up the field he went back into the house. We didn't know, but what he was doing was stuffing a Thompson sub-machine gun up the chimney in the kitchen. Willis told me to cover these three boys. I had nothing to cover them with so I put my hand in my pocket and let on I had a gun and they didn't know any different. While I was questioning these boys, one of them ran away down the field. I ran after him and he stuck in a wee sheugh that ran across the bottom of the field, for he was a wee small man. I jumped over on his back. He turned round to me and said, 'I know you, don't I? Let me go'. I knew the man nearly all my life so I let him bloody go but it didn't do any harm anyway like, for I don't think he ever did anything again. I went back up to the house and I told the other boys that he had escaped. We used the telephone in the house to ring up for a mobile patrol and for the police to come and they found the Thompson up the chimney and these other three .303s down the field."

Valuable information came from soldiers who lived in Republican areas and in some instances had notorious Republican activists as their neighbours. Those who lived in South Armagh were a particularly fruitful source of information, men like 'Jim', as a member of the intelligence staff recalled:

"I remember as well this night, old 'Jim' ringing to come quickly up, that he needed to speak to me. When I went up to the company he was there awful excited, he had word that there was a lot of stuff going to be moved through to the other side of Armagh and it was to happen that night, and it was going to be moved in compost lorries. I got on to the Ops Officer and told him the information was good, and he put patrols out on the ground. But at 2 o'clock the patrols were called in. The next morning old 'Jim' wanted to know what we had got. I had to tell him that nothing had come through. 'It did,' he said, 'cause they rang and told me it had left,' but it must have happened after 2 o'clock."

In all six members of 2UDR working with the battalion intelligence cell, including 'Jim', were murdered and two wounded, one permanently disabled. The IRA may not have known that they were passing on information, for it is improbable that there was any leak from the intelligence cell, but they must have realized that members of the battalion living in South Armagh were a potential source of information for the security forces, as well as being easy targets, and should be eliminated.

All soldiers, both Regular and UDR, were given low-level intelligence briefings before going out on patrol. Photographs, supplied by Brigades, of people suspected of being involved in terrorist activities were displayed on the walls of briefing rooms and were included in patrol briefing packs. Training was given in terrorist recognition, and the soldiers were tested on their ability to recognize local suspects. Patrol commanders kept notebooks giving their addresses and car registration numbers. 'Know your enemy' is an old adage for a soldier.

Photographs did fall into Loyalist hands – lost, stolen, inadequately destroyed when no longer required, or deliberately handed over. Information was passed on, deliberately or through careless talk. A soldier might tell a workmate where he had been last night with the UDR and what had happened, not with any ill intent but because it was still uppermost in his mind. Those living in solid Loyalist districts still drank in UDA-controlled clubs; there was nowhere else locally to go.

Casual conversation could lead to information being passed on. On occasions soldiers were brought before the courts for holding or passing on documents likely to be of use to a terrorist organization. But the small number of such cases only showed that information was passed on, not that the practice was prevalent, nor was it confined to the UDR.[1]

Detailed information on Republican and Loyalist terrorists, the kind of information that the paramilitaries needed to plan their assassinations, was tightly controlled, kept in locked cabinets in the intelligence cells, available only to the specially vetted staff working behind security grilles in offices manned night and day. The detailed intelligence that some critics have accused the UDR of passing on to the Loyalists was not available to the soldiers.

Each year Commander UDR held a Study Weekend at Ballykinlar, attended by the COs, Company Commanders and Adjutants. Senior guest speakers were invited and part of the time was devoted to syndicate discussions followed by a general discussion on a specific subject. They were convivial occasions, enabling the UDR officers from different battalions to meet and exchange ideas and experiences, especially in the Officers' Mess on the Saturday night. In 1977 the study was devoted to 'The Way Ahead' directive. The audience was heartened by an upbeat talk by the officers from the staff at HQNI, leaving no doubt that they welcomed the formation of the UDR intelligence cells.

The GOC spoke and then invited questions. The Second-in-Command of 5UDR pointed out that a quarter of the soldiers murdered so far had come from his battalion (sixteen out of sixty-eight), that he himself felt 'old and tired', and that he believed authority failed to appreciate the weariness and near despair of members of the Regiment. Another speaker supported him, saying that the room was full of men who were 'old and tired'. Others agreed, for these Study Weekends were always marked by more blunt and outspoken comment than would have normally been heard – or allowed – in any other similar military gathering. It was fair comment, for the problem of ageing Company Commanders had still not been resolved.

The Second-in-Command had a particular reason for being depressed. One of his fellow commanders, Peter Hill, who had commanded the company now based in Duncreggan Camp since 1972, had been murdered three days previously, shot down by two men in a car parked outside his house as he drove home from work. Hill was the head of one of Londonderry's largest businesses. He was at that time the fourth prominent Derry businessman to be murdered, but when it was suggested that his death had been due to the Provisionals' newly adopted policy of targeting senior men in commerce across the Province, the Provisional spokesman reacted angrily, saying Hill had been targeted because he was "a serving member of the forces of occupation and, as such, classified as a target, the same as any other member of the occupation forces of the British Army or RUC, Protestant or Catholic."[2]

Hill had been on the point of resigning. In fact he had a letter of resignation in his hand when he was shot. His UDR company in Duncreggan was the only one located in the city west of the Foyle. Since Bloody Sunday the intake of recruits had virtually dried up, the company could do little more than guard itself, and Hill, trying to cope with the near impossible task of commanding a UDR company inside Londonderry city and at the same time keep a business going despite the bombs, was on the verge of a nervous breakdown.

After his forthright intervention at the Study Weekend the Second-in-Command received an understanding letter from McCord saying that he and the GOC were already aware of the strength of feeling in the Battalion as a result of the run of murders. There were more to come.

In the first five months of the year there were twenty-six attacks on off-duty soldiers. Seven men were murdered, eight wounded, two of them seriously, and there were three instances of under-car booby-traps, though none of the drivers were injured. A Company Commander in 9UDR had a very lucky escape. He was reversing out of his garage when he heard a scraping noise. Thinking that he had brushed against one of the childrens' bicycles, he got out to check and found he had been dragging along the ground a 9lb device that had fallen off the bottom of the car.

Private John Reid of the Aughnacloy Company, a 52-year-old farmer, owned extensive land on both sides of the Border. He was shot whilst feeding his cattle at Emyvale in County Monaghan, and his body dumped a yard inside Northern Ireland. Six days later two more were murdered, Corporal David Graham as he arrived at his workplace in Coalisland, and Private David McQuillan, standing at a roadside in Bellaghy, waiting for one of his UDR comrades to give him a lift to work. McQuillan's 14-year-old son, waiting across the road for the school bus, saw it happen. "It was horrible," he said, "I saw them kill my daddy. He tried to run away, but he didn't have a chance. I ran across and turned him over but he was dead."[3]

Eric Shiells had served in the Royal Navy during the war and was now a Captain in 8UDR, director of a Dungannon building company, one of the town's most prominent businessmen and father of six children. He was leaving his home to return to work after lunch when a car drew up beside him and gunmen pumped rounds into him at point blank range. Some 2,000 people attended the funeral at the town's Presbyterian church, including representatives of the Irish Rugby Football Union. He was a past president of the Dungannon Club.[4]

McQuillan was the fifth member of the Magherafelt Company to be murdered in fifteen months. Another six had survived attacks since the beginning of the year. The persistence of these attacks had an adverse effect on the morale of the company:

"They did not want to go out on patrol," McCord recalled. "I went to Magherafelt on three successive nights and eventually persuaded them that what they were doing was not in the best interests of the Regiment or themselves, and that they were denying all that their murdered comrades had stood for. They felt that not enough was being done to track down the murderers. I knew that intelligence and undercover forces were making a major effort against these

185

people. In the end after three nights of talking I persuaded them that this was the case, and they resumed their normal duties."[5]

5UDR was a difficult battalion to command, being spread over such a wide area. From battalion headquarters at Ballykelly on the shores of Lough Foyle it was sixteen miles in one direction to the companies in Londonderry, the same distance in the opposite direction to the company in Coleraine, 22 miles southwards over the mountains to Maghera and a further nine miles on beyond that to Magherafelt, the most distant company of all. McBain used to visit the companies once a week at night:

> "Monday was the Derry companies; Tuesday Maghera, Thursday Magherafelt and Coleraine, so I had Wednesday and Friday evenings at home. Inevitably there was something at the weekend. I could not have any completely free weekends. Very little family life. I used to drive round during the day, but to cover these sort of distances you could only spend an hour or two with each company, talking to the Company Commander about his problems. It was very difficult to get a feel for what was happening."[6]

With only three Regular Army officers in each battalion, the role of the Commanding Officer was in a sense a lonely one, and it was essential that COs were supported by reliable TISOs and QMs. It was in part because of the need to improve the overall standard that McCord pioneered the affiliation of each UDR battalion to a Division of Infantry. There were many advantages to the arrangement. It meant that Divisions took a personal interest in 'their' UDR battalions and ensured that the officers, warrant officers and senior NCOs selected from the Division for attachment were of a high calibre; if they proved not to be the staff at HQUDR could go directly to the Division to have them changed. The arrangement did not extend to the selection of Commanding Officers; so far as possible they came from their affiliated Divisions, but, in order to ensure equality of opportunity among officers selected for command across the Army, some continued to be drawn from the combatant corps, cavalry, gunners and sappers. McCord made a point of insisting that among the TISOs selected by the Divisions there would be some who had already been recommended for promotion at a later stage. In this way attachment to a UDR battalion came to be regarded as a step on the way to promotion and, in the case of Warrant Officers, a step on the way to becoming RSMs of their Regular battalions and later to gain commissions. In time several RSMs came back to their old UDR battalions a few years later as commissioned quartermasters. From now on divisional staffs paid regular visits to 'their' battalions. But the greatest advantage of all was that the affiliations brought the UDR more closely into the Regular Army.

During the period between the announcement in the previous July of the 'Ulsterization' of the security forces and the end of the following April, thirty-one members of the RUC and the UDR had been murdered by the

Provisionals. Among Loyalists there was increased disillusionment with the Labour government's security policy; it seemed that 'Ulsterization' meant only that more of the Ulster security forces were being killed. A new vigilante organization, the Ulster Service Corps (USC), had begun to carry out unauthorized VCPs. It was formed mainly of ex-Specials and was answerable to the United Unionist Action Council (UUAC), formed by Paisley of the DUP and Baird of the United Ulster Unionist Movement in the aftermath of the Government's rejection of the Convention's final report. The USC patrols were unarmed, or armed with legally held weapons, served little purpose to anyone other than as a political gesture and soon went home when the weather turned bad. From time to time UDR patrols would encounter them, take the leaders' names and tell them to go on home. In time the authorities lost patience with them and five members of an Armagh USC patrol were charged and brought before a court in Portadown. The UUAC staged a protest march through the town to coincide with the hearing and Paisley called on Loyalists to be prepared to make sacrifices. This was the first conformation of rumours already circulating that the UUAC was planning another general strike.

In April the Action Council issued an ultimatum to the Government. If it did not take powerful and effective action against the IRA and implement the Convention's recommendation for a return of majority rule at Stormont, the Council would call a strike.

This time, unlike in 1974, support was lukewarm. The Ulster Unionists and the Orange Order wanted nothing to do with it; the majority of the workforce at Shorts aircraft factory and in Harland and Wolff, and most significantly, the power workers at Ballylumford were against the strike action. Above all there was little enthusiasm amongst the general public; the fears of earlier years that the Government was planning a withdrawal had evaporated and for the moment most of the country was content enough with the direct rule from Westminster and weary of the interminable squabbles among local politicians in the now defunct Convention.

A new, tougher Secretary of State, Roy Mason, had taken over at the NIO, determined that this strike would not succeed. Under a new Chief Constable, Newman, RUC morale had been restored. The police would take the lead, with the Army in support. The Army too had learnt lessons. Procedures for providing Military Assistance to Civil Ministries (MACM) had been drawn up for the United Kingdom. Reinforcement battalions were flown into the Province and military technicians with their vehicles moved in by sea to maintain the electricity, water, sewage and fuel supplies.

On 29 April orders were issued to all units. All eleven UDR battalions were to be placed on selective call out for at least a week. In the event it was extended for a further week, the longest call-out since 'MOTORMAN'. Initially the GOC had decided not to call out the Regiment. McCord was dismayed. If it was not called out, it would look as if the Army did not

187

trust the soldiers' loyalty to respond. The GOC was adamant. McCord felt so strongly that he was prepared to resign if the decision was not rescinded. It was, he recalled, the most unpleasant interlude in his whole military career, but his stand was fully vindicated. The GOC relented and the Regiment, unaware that there had been any doubt, responded magnificently.[7] Only in 3UDR did six hardline Loyalists who had not reported for duty for some months try to persuade their fellow members of the Kilkeel Company to refuse to do duties. They failed and were persuaded to resign, an insignificant six out of 7,660.

The strike began on 3 May. In the early hours the first reports began coming in to the UDR Operations Rooms of obstacles on rural roads, trees felled, milk churns and oil drums placed across roads with batteries on top and wires coming out of them. By the time the morning rush hour had begun the police and Army had cleared the main roads and, though traffic was lighter than usual, it was apparent that the majority of people were reporting to work. During the day UDA gangs roamed the streets of the main Protestant towns, forcing factories and shops to close down. By the day's end the police had received 400 complaints of intimidation. On the second day the intimidation was stepped up and by the third the number of reports to the police had risen to 1,000, as commercial life in the Protestant towns came to a standstill. There was a worrying lack of resolution among factory managers and shop keepers; the failure of the security forces to take resolute action against the 'heavies' in 1974 had not been forgotten.

But the workers at Harland and Wolff were still coming to work and the shipyards remained open. On the third day of the strike the UDA began blocking roads in East Belfast to prevent the workers from reaching the yards. Hermon, then Deputy Chief Constable (Operations), described what followed:

> "The Inspector had been told by his Superintendent to act as he thought best. He warned the UDA fellows two or three times that he would have to disperse them, but they didn't desist. So he ordered his men to draw their batons and charge them and chase them right off the Newtownards Road, to the cheers of an awful lot of people. It was the first time the RUC had raised its profile in that sense. The media and the TV cameras were there and had recorded it all, and the news reported that the RUC had taken control and driven the UDA off the streets of East Belfast."[8]

From then on there was no hesitation about removing road blocks, if possible by persuasion, if necessary by force.

Within hours of the strike, Michael Campbell–Lamerton, commanding 9UDR, had appreciated that the main activity in his area would be around Carrickfergus and Larne, where on the second day the strikers had blocked off the town and closed down the cross-channel ferry service. He set up his tactical headquarters in Carrickfergus, and for the next few days "the battalion was working non-stop removing road blocks in Carrickfergus, Larne, Larne docks and the roads to Ballylumford power station on Island Magee. All these incidents were dealt with directly by 9UDR officers and soldiers showing outstanding restraint, loyalty and professionalism. Many of the road blocks were manned by workmates and friends, but that did not deter our soldiers from doing their duty."[9]

Charley McCartney had been promoted Major and taken over command of one of the two Ballymena companies on the morning the strike began. Ballymena was the heartland of Paisley's country. Although McCartney's soldiers were under extreme pressure, being questioned by neighbours as to whether or not they supported the strike, all but one had turned up for duty on the first morning. The company's task was to keep open the main road into the town and up to St Patrick's Barracks. They deployed a patrol at the main roundabout on the by-pass round the town on the road to Larne and stayed there until the strike collapsed, stopping and talking to every motorist, trying to dissuade them from joining the strike. Some called them disloyal, but their brief was to remain polite and good humoured and to avoid being drawn into arguments. Though later the rest of the town was closed off by farmers on their tractors, the main road remained open. McCartney overheard one of his soldiers telling a farmer who had come on his tractor to join the blocks that he wouldn't do that if he was him as four tractors had already been burnt that day. It was quite untrue but effective; the farmer wheeled round the roundabout and went away home.

As in 1974, everything depended on the reaction of the staff at the power station at Ballylumford, across the harbour from the cross-channel ferry terminal at Larne. The largest power station in Ireland, at that time it provided two-thirds of the power for the Province. Though technicians from the three services had been brought in to keep the station running if the workers downed tools, it is very doubtful whether they could have done so, any more than they could have done three years before, for every power station has its idiosyncrasies. There were in any case other ways of forcing the shut-down of the power, such as cutting off the fresh water supply. There was a hard core of workers who could be influenced by the paramilitaries. In fact, a senior member of the security staff was OC of the East Antrim UVF. However, the majority of the workers had had their fill of industrial unrest since the UWC strike and felt they were now being used for political ends. Despite intimidation they refused to join in.

"After 48 hours it became apparent that Ballylumford was the key to the strike's success and that we must ensure at all costs that those workers wanting to get to work could get to work," Campbell–Lamerton recorded. "This required an extremely high level of VCPs, observation posts and quick reaction forces in the Larne, Ballylumford and Carrickfergus areas. For the next few days, I set up a mobile advanced tactical headquarters on Island Magee to ensure we could support the workers going to and from the power station. We had check points dotted all around to deter groups of workers sealing the approaches to Ballylumford, including the small ferry that brought the workers over from Larne.[10]

Commander 39 Brigade, realizing that 9UDR could not maintain the pressure of activity for much longer, placed 1 RWF under the UDR battalion's operational command, with the two battalions' tactical head-quarters co-located. Campbell–Lamerton was a Scots rugby International blue and the CO of the Welch Fusiliers a rugby comrade, which helped to ensure that what might have been a difficult situation worked well, the Regulars and the UDR vying with each other to produce the smartest and quickest reaction forces.

On the 5th, to stiffen the resolve of the power station work-force, the Secretary of State invited the shop stewards up to Stormont Castle and explained the future security measures the Government was planning to introduce, including an increase in the UDR permanent cadre. Mason gave each of the shop stewards a written copy of the proposals. Next day the workers voted by a large majority against strike action.

By Monday morning it was apparent that the strike was beginning to peter out. Shops were re-opening, people who had stayed away from work were going back. In Belfast the Pipes and Drums of 10UDR played in the city centre to show the public that all was well. In an attempt to keep the strike going by causing fresh disruption farmers used their tractors to block the main roads out of the city into County Down, and around Tandragee and Portadown, but particularly around Ballymena. From the outset it had been foreseen that the town would play a key role in the strike. Ballymena was Paisley's town; he had lived there since he was two years old; if he failed there he would be discredited and the strike would collapse. Bulldozers and other heavy plant manned by the Royal Engineers were standing by in St Patrick's Barracks to move road blocks including the farmers' tractors. An area had been allocated for their disposal on the town dump. A section of Military Police was ready to back up the RUC with additional arrest teams and a detention compound had been erected on the tennis court inside the barracks. From about 9 o'clock onwards tractors, slurry tankers and lorries began converging from the surrounding countryside and by 10.30, apart from the 9UDR patrol on the road in from Larne, the town was sealed off. In his operations room the UDR Operations Officer and the Sub-Divisional Commander watched the tractors over the 'heli-tele' system, the pictures relayed to their television set from the helicopter hovering overhead. The town was out of control, large numbers of strikers roaming the streets and forcing shops and businesses to close. Hermon flew in to St Patrick's Barracks to take control.

His instructions from the Chief Constable were specific. If the blocks could not be moved by peaceful means, then they must be removed by force, for if the blocking of Ballymena succeeded other towns would follow and the resources of the police and the Army would be stretched beyond the limit. He had several meetings with Paisley, the last in the UDR company office on the Tuesday morning. Hermon warned him that he intended to remove the barricades, by force if necessary, and that anyone who attempted to obstruct the police would be arrested. By mid-morning the police contingents were in position and closing in on the barricades. Paisley and eight of his supporters were lined up across the road. When they refused to move they were arrested and taken to the UDR headquarters where they were held for a short period in the tennis court compound, warned that legal action would be taken against them and released. Paisley instructed his followers to remove the barricades and disperse in peace. The seige of Ballymena was over.

Ten miles away across country at Toomebridge other farmers had decided to close the main road from Belfast to Londonderry by using tractors and farm machinery to block the bridge over the Bann. It was a foolish choice, for Toome is a strongly Republican town. When a farmer fired two shots in the air the locals retaliated. A lorry load of 'Toome pebbles', stones as big as a man's fist, was dumped in the middle of the bridge and used as ammunition. The farmers retreated, abandoning their tractors, two of which were set on fire and others pushed into the river. Meanwhile the Regular Army guard was marooned in the nearby police station, watching it all happen but too few to intervene. Their Company Commander in Magherafelt reported that he was unable to get through to them. 9UDR sent out three patrols and they got through without difficulty, though the foot patrol heard two shots pass overhead, fired from the notorious estate in Trea Gardens. They reflected wryly that if they were falling foul of both sides they must be doing their job rightly. The farmers refused their offer of tow ropes to salvage their tractors from the river and they remained there for the next two days, sinking deeper into the mud.

Elsewhere in the Province it was the events of that day, Tuesday 10 May, that finally ensured the failure of the UUAC's plans. Loyalist paramilitaries shot dead a 46-year-old bus driver when he stopped to pick up passengers on the Crumlin Road; evidently he had been chosen at random because the Ulster bus drivers had voted unanimously to work through the strike. In the same area a car bomb blew up at a filling station that had remained open, killing John Geddis, a Corporal in 10UDR, who had just driven in to fill up his car. His wife, who was sitting beside him, was taken to hospital suffering from severe shock. He was one of three members of the Regiment to be killed by Protestant paramilitaries during the twenty-two years. Ironically he was the son of the Independent Orange Order spokesman on the UUAC. His father blamed his death on the people who failed to support the strike, for if they had done so, he claimed, the garage would have been closed.

In Larne Campbell–Lamerton decided to make a last attempt to remove the blocks round the docks by peaceful means. With his signaller and two escorts he set off alone to speak to the dockers, warning them that he would mount a full-scale operation to break through the blocks if they would not remove them. When they called him 'an English bastard', he momentarily lost his cool, saying he might be a bastard but he had played rugby for Scotland. They cheered and let him through, and a crane operator, one of the Battalion's part-time soldiers, still in uniform, started up the machine and by Thursday the port was back in action.[11]

Shortly after midnight the UUAC announced that their strike was over. Paisley, resilient as a rubber ball, claimed that it had been a success, that without it the Government would not have been prepared to introduce the new security measures announced by the Secretary of State, and as a result he would continue in politics. A week later his brazen optimism was justified; at the district council elections, when the UDR again provided security but this time was not called out, the DUP gained control of Ballymena, their first council, and held the balance of power in seven others. Ulster Unionists lost thirty-five seats, most of them to the DUP. The strike had caused an abiding rift between the two strands of Unionism.

The stand-down came just in time for the Pipes and Drums to lead the Lord Mayor's Show through Belfast, with 7UDR providing the Regimental float. There was no doubt that the Regiment had come out with its reputation enhanced. The fact that several battalions, notably 9UDR, had taken Regular Army sub-units under command was particularly significant. Most of the work of keeping routes open had fallen to the battalions in the east of the Province. One of 7UDR's tasks had been to provide escorts on the Belfast to Bangor trains to protect the drivers from attack.

10UDR, during a routine search, had found two handguns, leading to the arrest of six Loyalist paramilitaries. But it was 4UDR in the west who made the most spectacular find, a RPG7 rocket launcher, the first to be recovered for three years, then followed it up with three more finds of explosives, detonators and ammunition. 9UDR celebrated the strike's end with a rugby match, the Battalion and Carrickfergus against the RWF, refereed by Campbell–Lamerton, and followed by a joint dinner. The Welch Fusiliers won. The Chamber of Commerce and Industry sent a message on behalf of its members "and the working men and women of Ulster" thanking the Army for its "unconditional tact and support in allowing the Ulster people to exercise their democratic right to work".

As the strike was drawing to a close a patrol found one of the wild goats at Scrabo stuck on a ledge on the quarry face, unable to go up or down. Whilst they waited for a vet to put it out of its misery, they christened it 'Paisley'.

Three months later all eleven battalions were called out again for four days to help cover the Queen's visit to Northern Ireland in this her Silver Jubilee year. The dates chosen for the visit could scarcely have been worse – 10 and 11 August. The day before was the anniversary of internment when it had become traditional in the Republican areas for the women to bang dustbin lids and, to the intense annoyance of the decent people of the areas, for the hooligans to hijack vehicles and set them on fire. The day after was the annual Apprentice Boys parade in Londonderry.

The programme for the visit was that the Queen and the Duke of Edinburgh would sail into Belfast Lough on the Royal Yacht, fly by helicopter to Hillsborough to attend a garden party, sail up the coast overnight to Portrush and visit the new University of Ulster at Coleraine the following day. The international media would be arriving in force. The worry was that, with so much of the Army and the police deployed to cover the Royal visit, the Provisionals would have a free run to cause mayhem elsewhere and any incident would have world-wide press coverage. Some 32,000 members of the security forces, including the Spearhead Battalion, were deployed. 7UDR was given the task of securing the south side of the Lough from Holywood to Bangor and, together with 3UDR, staking out the road the helicopter would follow between Bangor and Hillsborough, patrolling out on either side and checking all buildings out to surface-to-air missile range. The two battalions deployed the previous day, 7UDR setting up a tactical headquarters in the Holywood Hills and 3UDR in the police Divisional Headquarters in Newtownards. Some of the companies camped overnight in the fields.

At 11 o'clock on a fine summer's morning the Royal Yacht *Britannia* sailed into the Lough, accompanied by the missile destroyer HMS *Fife* and the minesweeper *Gavington* and escorted by six rigid raider craft manned by the Royal Marines. Other rigid raiders, some of them provided by the UDR, with coxswains from the battalions and an RUC constable on board, secured the anchorage off Cultra, preventing civilian craft from entering the restricted area. Her Majesty transferred to *Fife*, boarded the Wessex of the Queen's Flight and flew as planned along the patrolled routes to Hillsborough. In the forecourt of the Castle she inspected a guard of honour drawn from all eleven UDR battalions. The Regimental Pipes and Drums, together with the band of The Royal Irish Rangers, provided the music. Afterwards the GOC told McCord it had been outstanding. "I have not seen better. Drill, turnout and bearing were all of a very high order."

Before going out into the garden for the reception she held an investiture in the Castle, the first time an investiture has been televised. She presented the GOC, Sir David House, with the Knight's Cross of the Bath and a British Empire Medal to a Private in 4UDR who lived alone in a traditional Irish cottage so close to the Border that Donegal began on the other side of his yard. Her Majesty and the Prince walked down the line of white tapes laid out between the marquees and the giant rhododendron, meeting the guests, amongst them representative officers and soldiers from all the UDR battalions and their wives.

That evening there was a reception on *Britannia*, now anchored in Bangor Bay. Among the guests were UDR soldiers who had distinguished themselves on operations, accompanied by their wives. McCord introduced them all to Her Majesty.

"She spent a long time talking to them, so much so that eventually I was standing on the outside of the group, thinking, 'God, what have I let her in for now?' The Captain saw I was looking worried. I told him I was concerned that I had dropped Her Majesty in at the deep end, because the soldiers had no inhibitions about talking to her. He told me not to worry, that she was a past master at deciding when she had had enough, but she talked to them so much that the reception went on for about an hour longer than scheduled."[12]

One of the soldiers told Her Majesty how one night whilst off duty he had come across an armed man robbing a filling station. Drawing his PPW he kept the raider covered until the police arrived. When a patrol did come, they mistook him for the gunman, opened fire and slightly wounded him. The police officer who had shot him was also a guest on *Britannia* that night.

When the last guests had gone ashore, *Britannia* sailed up along the Antrim coast to Portrush, the rigid raiders hitching a lift on one of the escort warships and providing the same security screen off Portrush harbour the following day whilst the royal couple, now joined by Princes Andrew and Edward, visited the university outside Coleraine.

The 'Way Ahead' policy had given the RUC a renewed sense of purpose and, as a result, by 1977 they had become increasingly effective against the paramilitaries. Regular Army battalions had been instructed to raise Close Observation Platoons (COP), composed of soldiers trained in covert observation. Permission was given to deploy the SAS throughout the country, no longer confining them to South Armagh. Improved intelligence was enabling the security forces together to make new inroads into the terrorist ranks.

The Provisionals were at their lowest ebb. They had failed to exploit the unrest during the UUAC strike and had been unable to achieve the spectacular incident that would have caught world headlines during the royal visit. In December a large consignment of munitions packed into two electrical transformers for shipment from Cyprus to Ireland was intercepted by Belgian customs, and in Dublin Seamus Twomey, the chief of staff, who had organized the resupply, was arrested by the Garda. The flow of funds from the United States was dwindling as even the Irish–American community came to appreciate the evil and indiscriminate nature of IRA violence. The ceasefire had achieved nothing.

The fortunes of the Loyalist paramilitaries were also in decline. In March, twenty-six members of the East Antrim UVF were sentenced to a total of 700 years imprisonment on a variety of charges, including murder. In June nine members of the organization in Coleraine were gaoled for a total of 108 years. In May the police had finally acquired sufficient evidence to enable them to round up and charge the depraved Shankill Butcher gang who since October 1975 had committed nineteen particularly sadistic, random sectarian murders.

194

The marked drop in civilian deaths that year, 112 compared to 297 in 1976, was largely due to the decline in sectarian murder. September was the first month since the troubles had begun that no civilians had been killed.

For the next two years the Provisionals switched from car bombs to incendiary attacks, particularly larger blast incendiaries, hung from a meat hook outside windows to produce a more devastating effect. Whilst the number of explosive bombs planted during the year dropped by 657, the number of incendiary attacks increased by 369. Few towns escaped their attentions. One Saturday night in Downpatrick, after the shops had closed, eleven devices were found in premises along the main street. Fortunately only one ignited. If they had all gone off the town's main shopping area would have been destroyed. On that occasion 3UDR struck lucky. To prevent a repetition, the battalion mounted one of its multiple VCP operations five days later, closing in on the town. A car stopped short of a VCP and the occupants ran off into the marshes. The patrols deployed to cordon and search the area, firing off flares over the marshes in the dark. After one and a half hours two bedraggled youths were apprehended trying to slip across the main road. They admitted to placing incendiaries in the town in the past and, as a result, ten teenagers, both boys and girls, all under eighteen and the youngest fifteen, were arrested and charged, variously with planting incendiaries and membership of Fianna Eireann. Unfortunately there was insufficient evidence to charge the 'godfather' who led these youngsters into terrorism.[13]

In October devices were left in seven cinemas, three in Belfast, where there were only four cinemas still open, and one, the largest, the ABC, was destroyed. During Christmas week, in a further attempt to destroy the simple pleasures of ordinary people, the bombers focused their attention on hotels, with co-ordinated attacks on seven hotels across the province, three in Fermanagh and one on the outskirts of Belfast. All escaped serious damage but on the last night of the year the beautiful old Great Southern Hotel on the shore of Carlingford Lough at Rostrevor was burnt out and never rebuilt.

Although the number of civilian casualties was considerably reduced, forty-four members of the security forces were killed in 1977, only ten less than in the previous year. After Corporal Geddis died in the bomb explosion at the filling station during the UUAC strike, another seven members of the Regiment were murdered before the year was out, all of them off-duty, three in succession from 10UDR. Corporal Hugh Rogers, a Catholic, was still a member of the Battalion, though he had not done duties for the past year. He was shot as he was leaving his home to go on night shift. His funeral was at the Roman Catholic church in Derryvolgie Avenue. He had been a Scout master there for five years and his four daughters sang in the choir. The Requiem Mass was attended by Dr Philbin, Bishop of Down and Connor. Five days later Second Lieutenant Robin Smyrl of 8UDR was killed by gunmen as he slowed down to negotiate a narrow bridge on the outskirts of Gortin on his way to his work as manager of a clothing factory in Plumbridge. Robert Bloomer, a 29-year-old Private in 8UDR, was ambushed at the end of the lane leading down to his home at Eglish near Dungannon. Despite being hit five times he rolled out of his car and returned two rounds at his attackers. His wife heard the shooting, ran up the lane, helped her husband into the car and drove him the two miles to his parents' house. On seeing his condition, his father suffered a heart attack. He recovered, but his son died of his wounds a week later.

For the past four years 24-year-old Margaret Hearst had been the Civil Servant clerical officer in one of the Armagh companies. She was also a part-time Greenfinch. An unmarried mother, she lived with her 3-year-old daughter in a mobile home in the grounds of her parents' cottage, three miles from Middletown. On the Saturday evening of 8 October her parents were away from home, visiting a friend who had been shot a fortnight earlier and was still in hospital. Her aunt and two young brothers were in the cottage. Suddenly a milk churn shattered the window of the room. A man standing outside pointed a gun at them through the broken glass and demanded to know where the UDR girl was. Margaret, who had been in bed, heard the noise and went to the door of the caravan. The gunman saw her, smashed open the door with the butt and fired two bursts at the Greenfinch as she cowered on the bed. She died instantly, hit by ten rounds at close range. One round passed through a partition into the next room where her child lay in bed, asleep through the whole terrifying incident. The bullet struck the toy lying in bed beside her, the Kermit frog character from the television 'Muppet Show'. The killers then crossed the Border to attend a dance in Monaghan.

Margaret Hearst's death caused a wave of revulsion throughout the United Kingdom in a public that was becoming immune to the killings. The national press published detailed accounts of the murder, illustrated with photographs of mother and child and the toy pierced by a bullet. Archbishop O'Fiaich, newly appointed Catholic Primate of All Ireland in succession to the late Cardinal Conway, issued a statement:

> "It is saddening and sickening that, within a week of my ordination at Armagh, when representatives of all sections of the community were linked in brotherly affection round the altar, this harmony should be shattered by the brutal murder of this young woman."

Some 1,500 people, Catholic and Protestant from both sides of the Border, attended the funeral. Greenfinches escorted the coffin on the three-mile walk from the Hearst home to the Church of Ireland church in Middletown, whilst others lined the path from the gate to the church door. The Provisionals admitted they had selected her because of her "involvement in the British war machine". The RUC and Garda mounted an intensive search on both sides of the Border. The murder weapon, an Armalite, was found hidden in a hedgerow and three local youths were arrested and charged and subsequently admitted their guilt. One who was 16 years old at the time of the shooting was sentenced to indefinite detention, a 17-year-old was found guilty of manslaughter and sent to gaol for ten years, another 16-year-old for five years.

One of her fellow Greenfinches believed that Margaret Hearst had had a strong premonition of her death. She had taken out life insurance under ADAT, the Army Dependents Assurance Trust, and had written her will, including instructions for the care of her child. In her Bible she had underlined passages referring to life after death. Between her death on the Saturday night and the opening of her company office on the Monday morning, her desk was forced open and her diary stolen. It has never been recovered. Her fellow Greenfinch doubted whether there was anything incriminating in it, but evidently someone thought there might be.

At one time the Hearst family had lived in Monaghan and the father still belonged to an Orange Lodge on the southern side. Three years later he too was murdered. Happily the child has grown up to be a bright, intelligent young woman, who has obtained a degree.

The fourteenth member of the Regiment to be killed that year was Lieutenant Walter Kerr, an assistant bank manager, fatally injured in Magherafelt when a booby-trap exploded under his car as he was reversing out of his garage to take his two children to school. A Private in the same company escaped injury when a booby-trap exploded as he was moving a wheelbarrow at the piggery at Bellaghy belonging to his father, a former UUUP convention member. A Lance Corporal, who in later years was to become mayor of Ballymoney, lost a leg when a bomb exploded under his tractor. In October gunmen ambushed a school bus outside Ballygawley in Tyrone, shot dead the relief driver, a Catholic, and slightly wounded the only passenger, a 15-year-old school girl. The Provisionals admitted they had made a mistake; they had meant to kill the regular driver, a part-time Sergeant who had taken the day off sick for the first time in fourteen years.

CHAPTER THIRTEEN

1978–1979

In his New Year message Mason claimed that the tide had turned against the IRA and that 1978 would be a year of hope. His optimism, as usual, was premature. During the previous year the Provisionals had been undertaking a major reorganization. The nature of that reorganization was confirmed when the Garda arrested Twomey and found in his possession a paper which said in part:-

> "We are burdened with an inefficient infrastructure of commands, brigades, battalions and companies. We recommend reorganization and remotivation, the building of a new IRA. We emphasize a return to secrecy and strict discipline . . . We must gear ourselves towards Long Term Armed Struggle, based on putting unknown men and new recruits into a new structure. This new structure should be a cellular system."[1]

The reorganization involved the formation of Active Service Units (ASUs) consisted of a few volunteers, brought together for a specific operation. They worked on a 'need to know' basis, the members of one ASU knowing only the minimum necessary about the membership and operational plans of other ASUs, and the volunteers were thoroughly trained in resistance to interrogation. With the arrest of Twomey direction of operations in the North passed from Dublin to Northern Command, to new leaders, younger activists.

At the annual Regimental study weekend at the end of February the GOC, Creasey, told the UDR Company Commanders of the feeling of euphoria he had found in the country on assuming command in the previous November, based on the belief that the Provisionals were almost beaten. Now, he said, there were sufficient PIRA units to pose a very real threat into the foreseeable future. The Chief Constable confirmed the General's assessment. In 1977 the police had been so successful in interrogating suspects that they had begun to make significant inroads into PIRA strength, but in September they had reacted by making a flood of complaints about ill-treatment during interrogation. This ploy had proved so successful that by the end of the year they had slowed down the rate of police investigations. Now three factors had helped the Provisionals to recoup – training in resistance to interrogation and the cellular reorganization had reduced the flow of intelligence to the security forces; ASUs had been issued with new weapons, and at the end of 1977 a shortage of explosives had forced the bombers to use mortar bombs as the explosive content for large incendiaries and this had led them, almost by chance, to discover the napalm effect of a cased charge device.

Meanwhile the UDR was assuming an increasing operational responsibility and by October 1979 the Regiment was providing the first line military support to the police in two-thirds of the country. On 1 January 1978 3UDR assumed responsibility for virtually the whole of East and South Down, one of the largest TAORs of any battalion in the province, Regular or UDR. Further increases in the permanent cadre establishment allowed for a full-time IO, assistant operations officer, and sufficient men and women to provide three shifts in the battalion operations room. In some operations rooms the staff were manning as many as five radios on separate nets. New huts were built to accommodate this additional full-time manpower, but for the time being there were no baths or showers, kitchens or dining halls.

Between April 1977 and April 1980 the permanent cadre increased by more than 900, including 138 WUDR, and by December 1979 the Regiment had reached its full-time ceiling. The part-time numbers, however, were falling, as soldiers transferred to the permanent cadre, and in the same three-year period the part-time strength dropped by over 1,100. It was a trend that was to continue through the remaining years of the UDR, until in the final year the male permanent cadre strength was greater than the part-time; but the part-time soldiers always remained an essential part of the operational capacity of their battalions.

Increased operational responsibility demanded an extended training syllabus. All battalions had received their search equipment to bring them up to Regular Army scales including explosives detectors, and search teams had been trained at the Royal Military School of Engineering at Chatham. Training of intelligence staffs was completed and thirty-nine officers and senior NCOs attended an advance intelligence course at the School of Service Intelligence. From 1979 annual camp for all battalions was held across the water every year. In that first year five went to Warcop and six to a new location, Barry Buddon, a hutted camp situated on a triangle of dunes on the north side of the Tay estuary, not far from Dundee. The facilities were somewhat limited, but that was offset by the hospitality of the local people – that is, apart from the local MP, who wrote to the Defence Minister complaining that it was insensitive to allow the UDR to train at the camp, bearing in mind the large Catholic population in the neighbourhood. His objections rebounded on him, with a flood of letters to the *Courier*, the Dundee newspaper, the majority welcoming the presence of the Regiment. One wrote: "My sensitivities as a Catholic resident of Monifieth are moved to such an extent that I would like to extend an unqualified welcome to the UDR and my whole-hearted support for their efforts . . . to defeat the politics of murder and terrorism in Northern Ireland."[2]

In the winter of 1978 300 permanent cadre soldiers from the Operations

Platoons attended a week's training at the Cinque Ports Training Area, (CPTA), advanced ranges located on the great shingle beaches of Lydd and Hythe on the Channel coast, used by Regular units for their pre-Northern Ireland training. From 1979 a newly constructed training range in Ballykinlar was allocated to part-time companies at weekends to enable them to practice more realistic shooting.

The most significant advance in training facilities came at the end of the first decade with the creation of the UDR Training Camp, based in the old Weekend Training Centre at Ballykinlar. The camp opened on 2 July 1979 with the first four-week course for permanent cadre recruits, covering basic infantry training, including physical training, drill, assault course, range firing, foot and mobile patrols, VCP procedures, map reading, signals, first aid and a grounding in legal responsibilities. On 28 July the forty-seven successful recruits took part in a passing out parade taken by Brigadier David Miller who had taken over command of the Regiment from McCord in March '78. Courses were not limited to permanent cadre; others were run for platoon commanders, potential NCOs, and platoon sergeants, as well as skill-at-arms, surveillance, intelligence photography and search up-dating courses.

For its first nine years the Regiment had been regarded as a separate entity in Army sporting competitions. UDR teams that won a competition for units in Northern Ireland, such as 11 and 3UDR tug-of-war teams, who came first and second in the Northern Ireland Championships in 1978, were debarred from competing outside the Province and the Regular Army units they had beaten took their place in the UKLF Championships. The main reason behind what seemed a very unfair restriction was that part-time soldiers taking part in sports were deemed not to be on duty and therefore not entitled to pay, and, more seriously, were not insured if they were injured on the field, nor entitled to travel at public expense to compete across the water. In 1979 the restriction was dropped and the 3UDR tug-of-war team, made up of members of the Kilkeel Company, became the first UDR team to compete in an Army competition outside Northern Ireland. They scored an immediate success, securing second place in the 640kilo class of the Army Championships. Their results the following year were remarkable. Having won the Northern Ireland and Army Championships, they went on to represent the Army in the Inter-Service contest, held during the Royal Tournament at Earl's Court. They beat teams representing the Royal Navy, Royal Air Force and the United States Navy, each in two straight pulls, and so became the Inter-Service Champions, receiving the cup from the Prince of Wales. The 3UDR team then lost three of its leading members, passing the torch to 4UDR who went on to win the Army Outdoor Championship seven times, the Indoor three times, the Inter-Service six times, and the Princess Royal's Cup at Royal Windsor Horse show four times in succession. In the '79–'80 football season 10UDR won the UK Infantry and Army Football Challenge Cups, and won the former again in '83 and '84. When 7 and 10UDR were amalgamated in '84 the new battalion won the Northern Ireland Cup year after year and carried off the UK Infantry Cup in '85 and '89, finally losing their dominance to a team from 3UDR who won it in '91 and '92. 3UDR was also highly successful in golf, winning the Northern Ireland Cup in every year from '82 to '90, and the Army Inter-Unit Cup in '83 and '90. The Greenfinches too played no small part in bringing credit to the Regiment on the sports field, particularly in orienteering and hockey. In the former they won the Northern Ireland Women's Services Championships on five occasions, the UKLF Championships in '82, and were runners-up in '85, '86, '88 and '89. Indeed there were few Army championships where the UDR, men and women, did not make their mark, with individual successes in athletics, tennis, canoeing, swimming and skiing.

Since the first team had gone to Bisley when the Regiment was only four months old, battalion teams had returned each July to compete against the Regular Army in the Army Rifle Association Major Units Championship, firing with rifles, pistols, light and sub-machine guns, each year improving their placing. In 1979 for the first time the Regiment scored a major success when the team returned with the enormous silver Henry Whitehead cup, one of the most coveted trophies since it had been presented to the ARA in 1903. Five members of the Regiment gained places in the Army Hundred out of 720 competitors. In all the UDR soldiers collected two gold, two silver and eighteen bronze medals at Bisley that year.[3] In the World Pipe Band championships at Nottingham, the Pipes and Drums of 5UDR, competing against 260 bands, amongst them Canadian, Dutch and Belgian, won both the Piping and Marching and Discipline trophies, improving their placing on the previous year when they had been 2nd and 1st.[4] In July teams from 1 and 2UDR successfully completed the 100-mile Nijmegen March organized annually by the Royal Netherland League of Physical Culture. Some 17,000 people took part, drawn from all over Europe and further afield. The UDR teams were considered to be so well turned out and so enthusiastic that they were invited to form a Northern Ireland contingent to lead the 1,400-strong British Army contingent through Nijmegen on the final day.[5] Thereafter in every year the Regiment was represented by a team drawn from one of the battalions.

In September teams from 2 and 5UDR took part for the first time in the Cambrian Marches, held over two days across the rugged hills of the Brecon Beacons in Central Wales. During the two days foot patrols from eighteen army units, carrying full equipment and weapons, covered some 25 miles, living rough and competing in tests of military skills en route, including day and night shoots, navigation, communications and water-manship, ending with a tactical river crossing and a race against time in an assault boat along the Brecon Canal. The 5UDR team came in fifth, winning the falling plate shoot and beaten into second place in the night shoot by 2UDR. "It was a hard slog," *Visor* commented, "for the Ulstermen to leave their homes in Northern Ireland on the Thursday and to be finding their way across Welsh hillsides in the dead of night 24 hours later."[6]

All these stories, well covered in the press, showed to the public the growing competence and, indeed, the improved physical fitness of the UDR.[7] That was the good side; unfortunately there were still stories that showed the Regiment in an unfavourable light.

In May a permanent cadre Private named Davis, who had served in 5UDR from 1971 until his run-out date in the previous November, pleaded guilty to a particularly gruesome murder as well as armed robbery of a bank and a post office, and was sentenced to life imprisonment. All three crimes had been committed whilst he was still a member of the UDR. His victim was a 71-year-old farmer who had happened to see three men, one of them known to Davis, changing the number plates on a car that had just been used in a post office robbery. Davis and a friend called on the farmer to ask him to change his evidence; when he refused to do so, they bludgeoned him to death and buried him in a shallow grave. Someone in the Provisional IRA witnessed the burial and informed the police and, when they did not follow it up, PIRA issued a public statement. Davis and his colleague then dug up the body and dumped it in a water-filled quarry, tied to a concrete post. Months later the colleague underwent a religious conversion and informed the police. Davis admitted the murder and took detectives to the quarry where the badly decomposed, battered body was recovered by a Sapper diving team. At the trial the judge recommended that Davis serve a minimum of 15 years in gaol. In the same week three UDA members were gaoled for their part in the arms raid on the Magherafelt Company base.[8]

In the winter of 1979 five men and two women from South Derry were awarded a total of £9,400 compensation for criminal assault, allegedly carried out by the members of a UDR patrol from the Magherafelt Company. The seven were on their way home from a function at the GAA Club in Bellaghy in the early hours of the morning when they were stopped by the patrol at Gulladuff, close to the spot where the postman, Colour Sergeant Bobby Lennox of the same company, had been murdered two days previously. Two of the men were taken away up the road and beaten with rifle butts and a baton. Whilst the others waited by the car, they heard firing and, remembering the Miami Showband incident, feared that their companions had been shot. However, at that moment another car came on the scene and the seven were sent on their way. The judge said he had no hesitation in coming to the conclusion that their stories were true and strongly condemned the UDR for their refusal to co-operate with the police or to serve summons on members of the company.

Seven more members of the Regiment were murdered during 1978, all but one off-duty. Corporal Cecil Grills of the Rathfriland Company was one of those who worked in Fishers' Yard in Newry. On 12 January 1978 he was driving home at the end of the day. Since he lived in a modern estate on the edge of town, there was little he could do to vary his route, apart from the random use of the short stretch of Arthur Street. He was driving up that street when a gunman opened fire from behind a wall. He was killed instantly; it was the third attempt on his life. The company clerical officer was a near neighbour, and on most days Grills would give her son a lift to or from school. On this occasion she had collected the boy from her mother's and was driving home to tea when she came on the scene moments after the shooting, Grills' body lying in the middle of the road and the assassins running away. The murder weapon had been used in a number of other killings, including the Kingsmill bus massacre. The Battalion historical record commented bleakly: "His death underlines the fact that, despite PPWs and armoured vests, once the name of a soldier from the UDR has come to the top of the PIRA target list, he has very little chance."

Four weeks later Sergeant Jock Eaglesham, a postman and a platoon sergeant in 8UDR, had just delivered mail at the primary school in Rock, a remote village east of Pomeroy, on his daily delivery run when gunmen opened fire on his van. He was hit several times and died moments after the headmaster ran to his aid. Jock, as he was known by both communities, was a 59-year-old Scotsman who married a local girl whilst he was stationed in Tyrone during the war. He had spent virtually his entire adult life in uniform – Regular Army, TA and, since 1970, the UDR. He was a member of St John Ambulance and his experience with that voluntary organization made him a gifted battalion first aid instructor. In the Battalion his combined duties of CQMS and a Platoon Sergeant involved such long hours of duty that on many occasions he would go out on his postal rounds having not been to sleep all night. His CO described him as "a true Christian, whose modesty, humility, gentleness and courage are a lasting inspiration to all who came in contact with him".

The following morning Corporal William Gordon, a schools attendance officer in Maghera, was setting out to take his two children, Lesley aged 10 and his son, 8, to their primary school, as he did every morning. The family lived in a neat modern estate within sight of one of the sangars at the company base. Before driving off Gordon opened the boot and checked under the car which had been parked in a lay-by overnight, for only the day before a warning had gone out to battalions to be on the alert for booby traps. He had driven forward a few feet, Lesley beside him in the front seat, his son in the back, when an explosion tore the car apart, blowing off the roof. Gordon and Lesley lay dead in their seats, the boy had been blown six feet out into the road, seriously injured. His mother cradled him in her arms as horrified neighbours rushed to her aid. The murders caused nationwide revulsion. Virtually the whole town turned out to line the streets on the day of the funeral, the two coffins carried through the crowd. In some towns across the province shops closed down as a mark of respect.

The Maghera and Magherafelt companies were called out for four days to assist the police and Army carry out an intensive search over a

120-square-mile area of South Derry and North Tyrone, supported by helicopters and search dogs. Extra detectives were drafted into the area and an incident centre set up to co-ordinate the operation. The RUC informed the media that they were looking for six known terrorists, particularly Francis Hughes, whom they had described on a previous occasion as highly dangerous. Like his friend and equally committed terrorist, Dominic McGlinchey, he came from Bellaghy. For Hughes time was fast running out. A month later he was severely wounded in an encounter with a patrol during which one of the soldiers was killed. Hughes was sentenced to life imprisonment and was the second H–block hunger striker to die, after refusing food for fifty-nine days.

The system for initiating the device had consisted of a length of nylon so fine that at a cursory glance it was difficult to see, attached to the valve cap on the off side front wheel. As the car moved forward the line tightened, pulling out a dowel separating the claws of an ordinary domestic clothes peg, the peg closed, two drawing pins completed a circuit, detonating a booby trap fixed on the underside of the vehicle by the driver's legs. It only required a small quantity of explosives; the effect of the blast inside the enclosed confines of a vehicle was devastating. Instructions were issued to all soldiers on the paramount need to check their vehicles on every occasion before driving off. They were advised to carry a piece of matting so they could get under the car to inspect it. That was all very well, but to anyone passing by in the street or a public car park it was immediately apparent that the driver was a member of the security forces. A favoured alternative was to drop the keys and look under the car as one bent down to pick them up. After checking, soldiers were advised to drive forward a few yards with a window wound down to minimise the effect of an explosion in an enclosed space. Passengers should not be allowed in or near the car until it had been moved a short distance. Despite the frequency of the Under Vehicle Booby-Traps (UVBTs) some soldiers failed to look thoroughly enough, or not at all. On a wet dark night there was a temptation to take a risk. Sometimes the risk proved fatal. In all, thirteen serving and four former members of the Regiment were killed in such attacks, one by a booby-trap at a farm gate, all the others in vehicles. Another twelve were injured, ten of them losing one or both legs.

The day after the Gordon murder the Provisionals issued a statement saying they were investigating the incident. "The Republican Movement and the Republican people, our friends and sympathizers could not and would not countenance an operation in which the lives of innocent civilians were placed in jeopardy."

But there was no excuse. If the PIRA had targeted Gordon so well they must have known that the children were likely to be in the car.

That same morning, before the statement was released, one of their volunteers placed another such device under a school bus, driven each day from Ballymoney to Rasharkin by a Corporal of 1UDR. For some reason the device failed to work when he drove off, but after he had travelled some four miles along the road to the village, with eight children from the Catholic primary school as his passengers, the bomb fell off onto the road and exploded, showering the bus with debris. Miraculously none of the children was hurt.

A week later PIRA carried out one of their most horrific attacks against a purely civilian target. La Mon was a popular hotel and restaurant in quiet countryside convenient to Belfast in the mainly Protestant area of North Down. Friday was invariably a busy night, people holding parties at the end of the working week. On 17 February there were two functions taking place in the restaurant, the Northern Ireland Junior Motor Cycle Club's annual dinner dance and a dinner organized by the Irish Collie Club. Outside on the window sill the bombers placed a cased charge incendiary, one-gallon petrol cans packed round a mortar bomb to give a napalm effect. At 8.57 pm they phoned through a warning. When the police rang the hotel a man in an extremely agitated state said that the bomb had already gone off and the hotel was ablaze. A young woman attending the Collie Club dinner described how the burning fuel flowed down the centre of the function room, trapping the guests. A photographer, arriving at that moment to take photographs at the motor cycle function, said he would remember the screams of the people being burnt alive for as long as he lived. The Company Commander was on duty in his Company operations room in Carryduff when the sangar sentry reported a red glow in the sky to the south, followed by a radio report from one of his patrols that there had been a major incident at the hotel. He and one of his fellow officers, Brian Scott, went to the scene. The building was an inferno and there was little they or the patrol could do, except stake out the area. He had been a Royal Marine Commando during the war and the sight reminded him of scenes he had witnessed in Yugoslavia:

> "My main impression was all the bodies being brought out. I said to one of the firemen it was tragic that there seemed to be a lot of children amongst them. He said they weren't children but grown-ups, and I realized then that they had been so incinerated that they were reduced to half their size, laid out in charred heaps waiting for the ambulances." Scott described how the firemen came out of the flames carrying "black steaming lumps like bits of log, unrecognizable as human beings and threw them into the back of an ambulance with an awful 'clunk'. We stood beside a tree that was glowing like amber, every branch and twig against the night sky, glowing and pulsing in the wind, a tree from hell."

Twelve people died, three from one family, two from another, and twenty-one were injured.

3UDR was about to mount a multiple VCP Operation on the roads leading to Castlewellan. Instead nine patrols were diverted to other hotels in North and East Down, hampered in their efforts to co-ordinate follow-up action by the fact that as yet the RUC had not established a divisional operations room. The attack was not unexpected. Patrols had been visiting hotels since the PIRA attacks of the previous year, including La Mon, but it was impossible to cover all of them every night. Early in January two devices had been defused at the Four Winds Hotel in Carryduff, a few miles away.

The RUC issued thousands of leaflets showing the trunk of a blackened body, limbless apart from the remains of one leg, designed to shock. They picked up twenty leading Republicans, but only one, Gerry Adams, was detained. He was charged with membership of the IRA, held on remand for seven months and then released by the Lord Chief Justice on the grounds that the evidence against him was insufficient to sustain a conviction. It made little difference. On his release he became Vice President of Provisional Sinn Fein (PSF) and encouraged that organization to become more actively involved in political activity, the policy of a ballot paper in one hand and an armalite in the other.[9]

The Provisionals were dismayed by the universal condemnation, even from their customary supporters. They held another inquiry, which claimed that their volunteers, having planted the bomb, were delayed in telephoning through a warning by being held up by a UDR patrol. It may have been true, but no record could be found of any likely suspects having passed through a VCP. In any case there was no excuse. If the aim was to destroy the hotel without causing civilian casualties, why chose the busiest time of the busiest evening of the week and place the bomb on the sill of a function room? There is only one conclusion; there were among them those who had become indifferent as to whom they killed.

In the months following the disaster of La Mon PIRA observed a policy of avoiding bomb attacks which could cause civilian casualties. By the end of the year only two more civilians had been killed by bombs. Attacks on the security forces, including the UDR, continued unabated, particularly in Fermanagh where the cross-border ASUs, after a relatively quiet period, stepped up their operations.

On Sunday afternoon 25 June a Corporal and his section from 4UDR were nearing the end of a day-long mobile patrol in south-west Fermanagh on the road that runs parallel with and close to the Border from Garrison to Belcoo.

"We were just coming down to Scribbagh Post Office. I can remember seeing people – it was a nice sunny Sunday afternoon – standing out taking the air. Suddenly there was the sound of gunfire. It takes a second or two to realize that it's you that they're shooting at. 'Put down the foot.' The driver put down his foot. It's a bit of straight road, the Post Office was up on a height on our right-hand side as we went down. On the left-hand side there's what we call a stone dip, a big lay-by. There's be about 200 yards of a straight road there. The driver put down his foot and we went down the straight as fast as the Landrover could go and the gunfire all the time. The only thing I could liken it to was doing the butts, doing the targets for weapon practice; when the guns fire you can hear the clip of the bullet into the targets above your head. It was a strange thing because there was no panic, no great excitement, racing down this road and them firing at us like hell. About half-way down, we were just about opposite the lay-by when there was an explosion. Fortunately for us that bomb was on the back of the bank, it blew clay and stones out between the Landrover and the Shorland but it didn't do any harm. Around that time one of the boys in the back said, 'I'm hit'. I screwed round in the seat and asked them to watch he didn't fall out because the back of the Landrover was open. The Shorland was hareing after us. Some of the boys said the bullets beat the road after us like hail, between the two vehicles. There were two M60s. It was one of the only, if not the only, time in Northern Ireland that two M60s were used. Luckily enough for us the M60 isn't easy to fire, they were up on a height firing down on us and they were firing over our heads for part of the time. I said to myself we're not going to get stopped here, get the hell out of it. I grabbed the radio and called 'One One Bravo, Contact, wait out'. We turned off at Cashel Cross and stopped there. When we stopped the wounded soldier wasn't too bad, his left arm was smashed, but Alan Ferguson, who had never said a word, was dead. We didn't know at the time but there was a sniper up on the hill and it transpired afterwards he had a Woodmaster, an American sniper rifle. He must have fired in through the back doors of the Landrover as we drove down. There was just one strike mark on the Landrover beside the back door, he must have put in a couple of shots. One of them hit Alan Ferguson. The wounded man was very lucky – the bullet had nicked him on the chest, tripped the arm, turned on the bone, went down the arm and carried through the elbow. When we stopped he was stable and conscious. Alan Ferguson was dead, without a word, it just happened as quietly and as quickly as that."[10]

In all there were ten attacks on off-duty soldiers during the year. Time and again postmen, milkmen and school bus drivers were singled out by PIRA. They were the easiest of targets, for the nature of their jobs meant that they had to keep to a routine, be at the same place at the same time, day in, day out. They were obvious targets for those who planned to murder with the minimum risk to themselves.

Corporal Jimmy McKee of 6UDR was shot whilst at the wheel of his empty school bus in the country between Omagh and Cookstown. Though wounded in the arm, he drove on for another mile and a half, then stopped, probably to get help. The assassins, a man and two women, the latter armed with pistols, hijacked a car, caught up with him and killed him with a blast from a shotgun.[11] In October Captain Charles Henning of 2UDR had just delivered his sheep to the market in Newry when he saw two gunmen in a car. He ran back into the market, but one of the men followed him and shot him in the head. He died a week later. Only a small proportion of the huge crowd of mourners could find a place in the small Presbyterian Church at Jerretspass, deep in the farmland of East Armagh. The Moderator told them: "You people are living in an area where your life is cheap. You love the area, you were born here, your parents were born here, but because of your deep convictions your life is in jeopardy."[12]

On the morning of 21 August Lance Corporal Glass of 4UDR was driving seven of his fellow workers along the Belcoo–Garrison road in a Fermanagh District Council van, on their way to Lough Melvin to clear a stretch of the shore for a fishing contest. A mile short of Scribbagh Post Office, where the patrol had been ambushed in June, the van came under fire. The front-seat passenger, Patrick Fee, a 64-year-old Catholic, fell forward, mortally hit, collapsing against Glass as he wrestled to keep control of the van. Glass turned round to shout a warning to the others in the back to keep down and saw two other men hit. Despite the cries to stop, a shattered windscreen, and not realizing that he had been hit twice in the arm, Glass kept driving as fast as he could out of the killing ground. He stopped the van about two miles up the road and ran to a house that he knew had a telephone, but the owner refused to let him in for fear her daughter should see the carnage outside. He ran on to a shop nearby and was able to contact the police and ambulance. Whilst he waited for help to arrive, despite his own wounds, he did what he could to treat the other three wounded men. When a Regular Army patrol arrived on the scene, the NCO patrol commander said Glass was the only one who could tell him what had happened and assist him in preparing the wounded for evacuation. It was apparent to the NCO that, but for Glass's presence of mind, more would have been killed. He was awarded the Queen's Gallantry Medal.

Battalions could seldom know how many lives had been saved by the presence of their patrols. The only assessable measures of their success were the number of munitions found and the number of suspects arrested, the unspectacular but steady attrition against the paramilitaries. In January 1UDR found two handguns, a rifle and 660 rounds of ammunition in Ferris Park in Larne, probably Loyalist paramilitary munitions. In February the same battalion was carrying out a planned search in fields in the Dunloy area, when the search dog indicated at three large boulders. In a plastic bag hidden beneath them they found all the ingredients needed to make up a device.

In April word reached 3UDR that a device had been left at the Horseshoe Bend, a notorious corner where the main road from Banbridge climbs up over the hill and down to Castlewellan. The bend, overlooked by a derelict farmhouse set back up the hillside, was acute and traffic had to negotiate it in low gear; it was an obvious ambush position and had been used for that purpose on a previous occasion. The Battalion despatched the standard signal to all units across the Province placing the road out of bounds to military traffic and arranged for the Army Air Corps to carry out a photographic reconnaissance flight early the next morning. When the aerial photographs showed no sign of a device, the Operations Officer and search adviser used one of the civilian vehicles to drive over the bend. A caravan that happened to be going the same way gave them an additional measure of protection and a reason for travelling slowly enough for them to see a length of white wire on top of the rocks piled in a ditch at the entrance to a culvert under the road. It seemed suspiciously obvious, suggesting a come-on. It was one of those occasions when one had to try and reach into the mind of a terrorist. Could the coil of wire be a come-on and the derelict booby-trapped? Arrangements were made for the AAC to carry out further photo reconnaissance over the weekend. Nothing further could be seen, so a search team was sent in on the Monday morning; it discovered a command wire, a length of cordtex, threaded through the culvert. Clearly it had been put in place recently, and somewhere in the area there must be explosives waiting to be connected up. A week later a farmer told police he had found three milk churns among the straw in his barn. As a Minister of State from the NIO was due to be in that area the next day the Battalion deployed troops overlooking the barn during the night and the next morning, after another RIC flight, the ATO, a young Captain, carried out his first clearance operation for real. He managed to pull one churn out of the barn, containing 100lbs of ANFO and 5lbs of Co-op. In trying to blow a hole in the other two churns to release the explosive he set fire to the straw and burnt out the barn, the churns and his 'wheelbarrow'. Thanks in no small measure to the timely warning from local people in a strongly Republican area, at least one and possibly three land-mine attacks had been aborted.

10UDR had another notable success in May. As a result of a tip-off from the police they carried out a search of Balmoral Golf Club and uncovered four sub-machine guns, three of them home-made, a large quantity of spare parts and some 600 rounds of ammunition for the guns, some of it packed inside a garden gnome. Again it was probably a Loyalist cache. Up on the North coast, a patrol from 5UDR, carrying out snap VCPs in the Ballykelly area, following attacks on bridges on the main Belfast–Londonderry line, arrested three suspects who were subsequently charged. In July 8UDR had two good successes. When a part-time patrol from the Cookstown Company stopped a car outside Coalisland the driver ran away over the fields, leaving behind a rifle and ammunition. The police called at his house, but he had already gone on the run. In the same month the Operations Platoon found a rifle during a planned search in Moy. In August it was 6UDR's turn, two IEDs discovered in two weeks, the second, near Carrickmore, consisting of three milk churns packed with explosives. A week later 10UDR, who, since they had acquired trained search teams, had been carrying out frequent random searches of derelict houses around the city, found a rifle in good condition hidden in an attic. In September 1UDR found a SMG and a Sten gun at a farm outside Ballymena; the latter had been stolen in an IRA raid on the Royal Irish Fusiliers Depot in Armagh in 1954.

1978 saw a succession of visits to the Regiment by politicians from Westminster, and one Royal visitor, the Duchess of Kent, though she came to Ballykinlar in February not to visit the UDR but to open the new Sandes Home. She had her first encounter with the UDR (but by no means her last) when she met some of the Greenfinches at a tea party in the new canteen. In April Airey Neave, the Shadow Spokesman on Northern Ireland, and his wife visited the Headquarters and six of the battalions, followed days later by six members of the Conservative Northern Ireland Committee, among them Michael Mates and Ian Gow. Gow and Neave were both to die as a result of bombs placed under their cars by Republican terrorists based in England.

On 18 June Margaret Thatcher, who had taken over as Leader of the Conservative Party from Heath in 1975, paid her third visit to the Province and her first to the UDR, accompanied by her husband and the Neaves. They spent the afternoon with 3UDR, flying out in a Puma over Strangford Lough to watch a search team from the operations platoon roping down to search the small island of Dunnyneill (to the consternation of a family party caught in the down draught as they were setting up their picnic), then landing on Pawle where others of the operations platoon and Roamer, the labrador, were searching a derelict. Back across the Lough the party landed on the coast just north of Killyleagh where the Battalion radar was being used to direct the dories practising interceptions of other craft. She was fascinated by the radar and, despite a very hot day, spent five minutes shut inside until her husband Dennis knocked on the door and told her it was time to fly back to Ballykinlar for tea. She told him to go away, she was enjoying herself.

Such visits, and there were many more, including the Chief of the Defence Staff, all the members of the Army Council and senior staff officers and civil servants from the MOD, and the Labour Defence Group did much to foster an understanding of the way of life of the men and women, and of the Regiment as an integral, different, but essential part of the Regular Army in Northern Ireland.

During the comparative lull in attacks on civilian targets since La Mon a surprising transformation had taken place. In most towns and villages the ugly barriers and bollards made out of concrete-filled oil drums had been removed and streets re-opened, though some remained pedestrianized and in others control zones were imposed where no unattended cars might be parked. A new mood had taken the country, a sense that people were determined to get on with living their lives as enjoyably as possible, a refusal to be intimidated any longer by the terrorists. Gradually life was returning to Belfast. At the Arts Theatre in Botanic Avenue, about half a

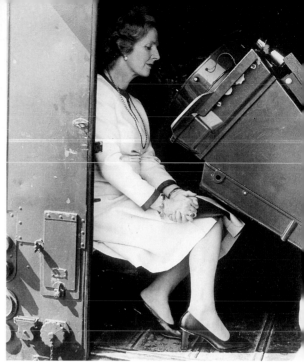

8. Airey Neave, Conservative Shadow Secretary of State for Northern Ireland, with Mrs Thatcher, talking to the 3UDR dog handler, Corporal Brian Brown. Neave was killed by a UVBT in March 1979, Brown in Kilkeel in May 1986.

19. Mrs Thatcher, then Leader of the Opposition, inside the 3UDR Landrover equipped with a Decca Marine Radar during her visit to the Battalion in June 1978.

0. A search team landing from a Royal Navy minesweeper on an island in Strangford Lough.

21. Firemen searching the crater after a landmine attack in which three members of 3UDR were killed on 6 January 1980. *(Down Recorder)*

22. The military funeral of a UDR soldier.

23. The Remembrance Sunday bomb explosion, Enniskillen, 8 November 1987. Soldiers of 4UDR searching through the rubble. *(Gordon Miller)*

24. The aftermath of the bomb in Enniskillen. *(Pacemaker Press International)*

25. The after-effect of an Under-Vehicle Booby Trap. The driver was killed. *(Mourne Observer)*

26. Two tons of home-made explosive found by a search team from 6 UDR concealed in a specially constructed concrete bunker near Sixmilecross, Tyrone, on 21 May 1984.

27. Eight beer kegs, connected to a command wire, found in a culvert north of Ballygawley by a Regular Army patrol under command 8UDR on 28 September 1985.

28. Abortive IRA mortar attack on 3UDR base at Kilkeel in March 1986. Of the eight tubes, only two fired, both bombs missing the base.

29. 2UDR patrol dug in on the Border during the joint British-Irish operation to close all crossing points to prevent the munitions landed from *Eksund* in November 1987 being moved into the North.

30. Patrol taking cover from flying debris, Smithfield, Belfast 1987. *(Pacemaker Press International)*

1. UDR team in the Northern Ireland Army First Aid competition.

2. Prime Minister Margaret Thatcher talking to soldiers of 6UDR, September 1989. *(Pacemaker Press International)*

33. Explosion on Ballydugan Road killing four soldiers of 3UDR on 9 April 1990. The remains of their Landrover can be seen on the left. *(Pacemaker Press International)*

34. Remains of the Company Centre at Glenanne after the explosion on 31 May 1991 which resulted in the death of three soldiers in 2UDR. *(Pacemaker Press International)*

mile from the city centre, a musical had opened, Tim Rice and Andrew Lloyd–Webber's *Joseph and his Technicolor Dreamcoat*. It was young, light-hearted, irreverent, tuneful, colourful – everything that Belfast needed at that moment. Word went round, people flocked back into the city to see it, sitting in the aisles and on the stairs of the small theatre. At the end of the opening night the audience "stood up and cheered and cheered. It seemed as if they cheered not just the cast but the fact that suddenly Belfast had come back to life again."[13]

From then on life did return to Belfast, as new eating places opened around Bradbury Place and down Great Victoria Street towards the city centre. In the last years of the decade violence had become a way of life. The politicians had been marginalized and had nothing positive to contribute, violence was not acceptable but at least it was endurable, time was passing and there was no visible end, but meanwhile life went on and one might as well keep one's head down and make the best of it.

Now, suddenly, on the morning of 14 November, PIRA reintroduced the car bombs. At 11.32 a car bomb exploded in the centre of Armagh, causing widespread damage; three minutes later another explosion in the centre of Dungannon; the damage was severe and thirty people slightly injured; at 11.42 a third partially detonated in Cookstown; between 11.44 and 11.47 five blast incendiaries went off in Londonderry and another three were neutralized; at 12.16 a car bomb badly damaged the new library in Enniskillen; at 14.33 three bombs went off in the docks area of Belfast; 18.03 two bombs in Newry; 19.27 five in Castlederg; at 03.00 a bomb was neutralized in Strabane. The attacks had been well planned and co-ordinated right across the country. Such tactics were hard to counter, concerted attacks followed by days of comparative quiet; PIRA chose their days, the security forces had to be out on the ground day after day and all day to thwart the next round of bombs.

On Christmas Eve, in a wide-ranging and highly political interview on RTE, Cardinal O'Fiaich said he believed the Catholic community had very little support for the UDR, regarding the Regiment as the B Specials reconstituted in a new form. A month earlier Dennis Faulkner, in his role as Chairman of the Industrial Development Board, had called on the Cardinal at the latter's invitation to discuss development projects in the Province. As he was leaving O'Fiaich had mentioned that he had heard he was in the UDR and did he not find it difficult to square his conscience with his membership of the Regiment? Faulkner had then stayed on for another hour, trying without success to convince the Cardinal that his opinion of the UDR was ill-judged.

Baxter, who on retiring from the Regular Army had become representative Colonel Commandant to take some of the load off the shoulders of Sir John Anderson, was no more successful despite being a Catholic himself. He called twice on the Cardinal, seeking his help to encourage Catholics to enlist and his people as a whole to support the Regiment. "It was disastrous," Baxter recalled. "He showed absolutely no interest in the

UDR and certainly was not prepared to help in any way at all. When I asked him what responsibility he felt he had as Cardinal for Roman Catholic servicemen in the province, he said absolutely none."

Christmas passed quietly, but on the morning of the 27th as 3UDR returned to duty an easterly gale was raging along the County Down coast, accompanied by exceptionally heavy rain. In the afternoon the first reports of serious flooding were coming in. Over the next three days the Battalion called off all normal operations and concentrated its resources on flood relief with the assistance of the Regular battalion in Ballykinlar, the 2nd Battalion The Light Infantry whose reserve company, working in the teeth of the gale, filled some 7,000 sandbags. UDR patrols laid the sandbags as the flood waters rose, in Newcastle, in villages along the coast, in Annsborough, Downpatrick and Comber where the river was flowing over the main street and the Carryduff Company was rescuing stranded motorists. In Annsborough too the river burst its banks and flooded into a housing estate. The CO, driving round the area, was dismayed to find that the local authorities were still enjoying their prolonged Christmas break and had done nothing to help the unfortunate residents. He despatched the Operations Platoon with blankets, heaters and hot food, and the soldiers spent the rest of that day helping the families to mop up. On the third day they provided the same assistance to householders in parts of Downpatrick where the Quoile marshes had risen and overflowed into the town. The Rathfriland police reported that two farmers were stranded on top of their tractor surrounded by flood water where the Bann had overflowed over acres of fields and that all attempts to rescue them had failed. The Platoon Commander and a section of the Operations Platoon who had just returned from relief work at Annsborough were sent back again in the gathering darkness to Cabra with the Gemini. They reported back over the radio that they had launched the dinghy, but the water was so rough they could not get near the men or even see the tractor in the dark. The police were becoming anxious, the men had been stranded since four o'clock, and it seemed possible they would die of exposure if they did not drown. Brigade Headquarters could not help; the storm was too great to risk a helicopter and there were no amphibious vehicles available in the Province. The Platoon Commander reported back that he would try again. A tractor towed the Gemini through the first flood and he waded the rest of the way, pulling the dinghy by a rope looped over his shoulder while the coxswain guided the stern. It was an anxious time for those listening in the Operations Room, unable to offer any further help, wondering whether all four would be lost, and a great relief when his voice came faintly over the air, saying he had reached the two men, put them in the dinghy and was on his way back to dry land. The CO went out to meet them with blankets and a bottle of whiskey. One of the rescued men was the son of a publican from Kilcoo, a strongly Republican village. They all went back to the bar, the CO, rescuers and rescued and the rest of the section and celebrated the success of the operation – an event akin to the Christmas truce on the Western Front in 1914. The Platoon Commander told how he had given the publican his pistol to keep safe whilst he waded out to the tractor. He was subsequently awarded a Queen's Commendation for Brave Conduct.

3UDR's efforts, supported by the Regulars, brought great credit to the Battalion. A SDLP councillor from Castlewellan was quoted as saying, "On Thursday when danger threatened once more it was the UDR on whom the burden fell. Despite the fact that they carried out emergency relief work in an excellent and exemplary manner, there were no emergency services in evidence." Four weeks earlier he had held a meeting with the Commanding Officer to complain about the Battalion carrying out house searches.

A 20-year-old private in 11UDR, Bobbie McNally, was the first member of the Regiment to die in 1979 when, in March, a UVBT exploded under his car as he was driving out of a car park in Portadown. Grievously injured, his leg had to be amputated, and a week later he succumbed to his injuries. He was the first UDR soldier to be murdered by the Irish National Liberation Army (INLA), an illegal Republican terrorist organization set up in 1975, drawing recruits from the Official and Provisional IRA. The organization had developed a new and highly effective initiation system for an under vehicle booby-trap, the mercury tilt switch. A tube containing mercury was wired up to a few ounces of explosives attached magnetically to the underside of a car. So long as it was on a level plane the device was safe, but when the vehicle went up or down an incline, a hill or a bump in the road, such as a 'sleeping policeman' ramp, the mercury flowing along the tube touched two contacts, thereby closing an electrical circuit which set off the explosives. The device, unlike the Provisionals' system of thread attached to a tyre valve, could be placed in seconds and was used frequently thereafter, notably in the killing of Airey Neave twenty-four days later as he was driving up the ramp from the House of Commons underground car park.

As a result of the widespread industrial unrest at the beginning of the year, the Labour Government had been defeated in a no confidence motion and a General Election called for 3 May. The Regiment was called out from midnight to cover the polling on the following day. 3UDR's particular concern was the safety of Enoch Powell who was standing for re-election in South Down. He was living in Spa at that time and had been a good friend to the Battalion, on one occasion going out at night with a foot patrol through the streets of Newry, wearing combat kit and with face blackened. After the murder of Neave, the killing of another Member of Parliament, a controversial man and a household name, would have been a major coup for the INLA. He was a courageous man, but he maintained that he could not canvass effectively unless he published the venues for his election meetings in advance, and he was unwilling to give the Battalion his itinerary on polling day. Though accompanied by a plain

213

clothes escort, in order to keep an additional eye on him as best they could, 3UDR patrols were instructed to report his progress using the code name 'Mighty Mouse'. He won the seat handsomely, doubling his majority, the Conservatives gained a comfortable majority and the country had its first woman Prime Minister.

In June, as the UDR was preparing to provide cover for the first elections to the European Parliament on the following day, PIRA carried out a daring attack on the 10UDR base in Malone Road. As they drove along the main road into the city in the middle of the morning gunmen opened fire from the back of a hijacked tipper lorry and lobbed two home-made hand grenades over the wooden fence into the base. Two soldiers standing talking outside the headquarters building were both hit, one superficially, but the other, Private Eric Gore, was killed by a bullet wound to the heart. Thereafter a more substantial perimeter wall was built, incorporating a sangar designed like a modest medieval tower to merge into the environment of that highly respectable neighbourhood of town.

There were three attacks on patrols during the summer. On the morning of 17 July a 400lb bomb packed into a trailer exploded beside a 4UDR mobile patrol travelling along the main Lisnaskea road, three miles west of Rosslea. The second Landrover was blown down the road, landing on its side minus its roof. The four soldiers were taken to Erne hospital and one, 22-year-old Private Grant Weir, was later evacuated by helicopter to the RVH, very seriously injured.[14] The trailer had been left ten yards from a bus stop where three women were waiting for the Enniskillen bus. One, a 32-year-old mission worker, was killed instantly in the blast and her mother and another young woman injured.

On 2 August a patrol from 2UDR had escorted an ATO party out to Drumsallan crossroads, six miles north-west of Armagh to check out a burnt-out car that had been used in the INLA shooting of a RUC constable outside the courthouse two days earlier. On their way home a 300lb land-mine exploded beside the ATO's soft-skinned van, blowing it off the road into the crater and killing two of the bomb disposal party. They were the Regular Army's 300th and 301st deaths by terrorist action. The explosion was followed by gunfire from two or three locations and the UDR escort dismounted and returned twelve rounds. Thanks to the prompt, precise contact report sent out by the patrol commander, another UDR patrol was able to cut off the bombers' escape route, causing them to panic and ditch their motor cycle, helmets, anoraks and a loaded revolver. The finds led to the positive identification of one of the two and he was subsequently charged with murder. Two days later three members of 6UDR were lucky to escape when a large landmine demolished a bridge on the Omagh road outside Fintona just as they were about to drive over it. The first vehicle had already crossed, the other was about 100 yards behind when the explosion occurred. The front wheels of the Landrover fell forward into the crater, but the soldiers and two civilians sustained only minor injuries.[15]

214

Attacks on the security forces were routine events in the terror of those days and for all but the victims families, soon forgotten by the public as they were overtaken by the next killings, but the events of the Bank Holiday on 27 August combined to form one of those peaks of disaster along with Bloody Sunday, McGurk's Bar, Kingmills, La Mon and horrors still to come, that at the time induced a national sense of hopelessness and despair that the killings would never end.

So far as the Commander of 3 Brigade, David Thorne, was concerned, the Warrenpoint massacre, as it came to be called, was a disaster waiting to happen. For over a year he had been warning that the situation in his Brigade area was deteriorating, especially in South Armagh. Of the thirty members of the security forces killed in 1978, eighteen had been murdered in his area; by August 1979, the total was nineteen out of twenty-eight. By the end of that year more soldiers had been killed on operations in 3 Brigade than in any previous year of the troubles. The growing effectiveness of the Provisional ASUs and their ability to mount co-ordinated Province-wide operations were, he believed, being under-estimated. Despite the fact that some province-wide attacks had involved as many as six ASUs acting simultaneously, the security forces had had no prior warning from their fragmented intelligence organization.

Thorne submitted a paper to HQNI and HQRUC, the main conclusion of which was that there must be a more effective method of coordinating the intelligence effort, and that the manner in which 'The Way Ahead' policy was meant to be implemented must be clarified. The RUC, lacking any experience of military operations, their planning, command and control, seemed increasingly to be trying to assume what were essentially the Army's tasks. Thorne had expressed his views openly, logically and frequently, and he knew that the GOC, Creasey, and the CLF, Trant, agreed with him. He believed that Creasey, who had a difficult relationship with Newman, the Chief Constable, favoured the appointment of a Director of Operations over the top of the Army and the police.[16] All this rivalry, misunderstanding, lack of trust, whatever it was, came to a head in the week following that August Bank Holiday.

For many years the Mountbatten family had spent part of the summer holidays at Classiebawn, a gaunt castle on the cliff edge looking down on the small fishing village of Mullaghmore on the Atlantic coast of Sligo. On Bank Holiday morning the Earl and members of his family had taken their launch out of the harbour and sailed a short way out into the ocean when a bomb exploded on board, shattering the wooden boat. Mountbatten, one of his 14-year-old twin grandsons and a 15-year-old schoolboy from the public school, Portora, in Enniskillen, were killed instantly. His daughter, Lady Brabourne, her husband, mother-in-law, the Dowager Lady Brabourne and the second twin were seriously injured; the Dowager Lady Brabourne died in hospital. The Provisionals admitted responsibility for the murders.

As the news of the killing of Prince Philip's uncle was flashed round

215

the world, a convoy consisting of two Landrovers and two soft-skinned four-ton vehicles was setting out from Ballykinlar, delivering a party from the 2nd Battalion, The Parachute Battalion, to the company base in Newry. At the last minute the decision was taken to go the long way round by the coastal route. The dual carriageway from Warrenpoint to Newry runs along the eastern side of the Newry River; for the first mile the river marks the Border and the wooded western bank lies in the Republic. Half-way along there is a 16th century tower house, Narrow Water Castle, and on the other side of the dual carriageway a gate lodge stood at the entrance to the drive up to the modern castle. It was well known as a dangerous route; it was here in January 1972 that a patrol from 3UDR engaged PIRA gunmen in a firefight across the river, followed a few days later by a prolonged battle between the Marines and gunmen on the west bank. On another occasion a landmine had been discovered in a culvert nearby under the road. It was a route that the UDR, with their greater knowledge of the country and of past events, would have had severe reservations about using with soft-skinned vehicles.[17]

A trailer loaded with straw bales was parked in a lay-by on the river side of the road. At harvest time it seemed an innocent enough sight, though just the week previously 3UDR had warned its companies of the potential dangers posed by trailers and horse boxes after the attack on the 4UDR patrol on the Rosslea road. As the second four-tonner was passing the trailer, watchers on the other side of the river sent a radio signal to detonate the device hidden under the straw. The vehicle, caught in the full force of the explosion, disintegrated, leaving six dead and two injured. A Royal Marine detachment on patrol in Warrenpoint heard the blast and sent a contact report. The Newry company sent a platoon to the scene, followed by the Company Commander and his relief, Major Peter Fursman. A Wessex with a doctor and two medical orderlies and a reaction force from the Queen's Own Highlanders, the South Armagh battalion based at Bessbrook, landed on the central reservation. The CO of the Highlanders, Lieutenant Colonel David Blair, landed in a Gazelle in the field behind the gate lodge and ran over to talk to Fursman whose vehicle was parked beside the lodge. At that moment, as the Wessex was taking off with the wounded twenty minutes after the first explosion, a second radio-controlled device made up of in excess of 1,000lb of explosive, went off in the lodge, totally demolishing it and killing another twelve soldiers, including Fursman, Blair and his signaller. The Wessex was damaged but escaped the full force of the blast. From across the river a gunman or gunmen fired several bursts; the troops replied and, in the exchange of fire, an English visitor was shot dead and his cousin wounded.[18]

With eighteen soldiers dead, sixteen of them members of the Parachute Regiment, the casualties were the worst suffered by the Army in any one incident since the Korean war. There was immediate and international revulsion. Messages of sympathy came from, among many others, the

216

Queen and the Duke of Edinburgh, the Pope, even the Russians. 3UDR felt a personal sense of loss. The Battalion had shared the barracks at Ballykinlar with the PARAs and since their arrival a month earlier had formed a close and happy association, helped by the fact that the two Adjutants were cousins by marriage. Blair and Gordon–Duff, the UDR CO, were contemparies in the Queen's Own Highlanders, and command of their respective battalions could have fallen on either's shoulders, whilst until recently Blair's RSM had been RSM of 3UDR. For the PARAs it was a terrible blow, creating a unique situation in peacetime – a battalion living, not a peaceful life but at least not an unduly abnormal one, accompanied by their families, now faced with sixteen dead, sixteen funerals to arrange, eight widows living in the married quarters. Thorne flew in to visit them and stopped by to talk to Gordon–Duff, suggesting that it would be wise if the UDR soldiers stayed out of the PARA canteen for a while. In fact the paratroopers' reaction was admirably disciplined and restrained, tempered by shock and sadness rather than anger. Gordon–Duff flew to Edinburgh to attend Blair's funeral and representatives from each of the companies of 3UDR were present at Roselawn cemetery outside Belfast for the burial of one of the soldiers whose family lived in Finaghy.

Two days later Mrs Thatcher flew into the province to be briefed, first at Brigade Headquarters in Portadown and then by the RUC in Gough Barracks, Armagh. There had been no prior discussion with the GOC or CLF as to what Thorne should say in his brief. In any case they knew well enough what line he would take, for he had been repeating it time and again for months past. He recalled:

"I began my briefing by describing the scene that confronted me as I came down the road at Warrenpoint on the afternoon of the 29th, past the bodies, the smoking vehicle, the crater, and Barry Rogan the Para Company Commander in Newry telling me that there were seventeen dead and handing me David Blair's epaulette. I had kept it in my pocket as I had intended to give it to Anne, his widow, for their son. Now I put it on the table beside Mrs Thatcher and told her it was all I had left of the CO of the Queen's Own Highlanders.

"I went on to explain to her exactly what the situation was, using factual evidence, comparing 1977 with 1978/79, illustrating the deterioration of the situation, the level of casualties, the amount of explosives used, the number of incidents. I told her there was nothing new in what I was saying. In the past I had briefed the Secretary of State and his Permanent Under-Secretary, as well as the GOC and CLF. They all knew my views. I went on to tell her what we were doing to try and create proper co-ordination of the police and Army effort in a way that would allow our resources to be used to the best effect and to minimize the chances of loss of life and success for the IRA. I said we had set up a joint Army/police operations room in Bessbrook and a joint Army/UDR operations and intelligence centre at St Angelo in Fermanagh, and that we were working on setting up others in Omagh and Dungannon. But more needed to be done."

A general discussion followed, with the GOC putting the case for the appointment of a Director or Co-ordinator of Operations. The discussion was inconclusive, but Thorne was satisfied that the Prime Minister was in no doubt that something had to be done to improve Army/police co-operation. However, at Gough Barracks the Chief Constable presented a more sanguine picture of the overall situation. He pointed out that it would be wrong to shape policy on the sole basis of South Armagh. Elsewhere 'The Way Ahead' was beginning to work. Mrs Thatcher listened in silence, agreed that the establishment of the RUC should be increased by 1,000 and then left without further comment to fly back to London that evening.[19]

In her memoirs she wrote:

"Back in London, we continued our urgent discussions on security. There were two major questions. How were we to improve the direction and co-ordination of our security operations in the Province? And how were we to get more co-operation in security matters from the Irish Republic? On the first, we decided that the difficulties of co-ordinating intelligence gathered by the RUC and the Army would be best overcome by instituting a new high-level security directorate. On the second, we agreed that I would tackle the Irish Prime Minister, Jack Lynch, when he arrived shortly for Lord Mountbatten's funeral."

The discussion with the Taoiseach got nowhere. To all the requests that RUC officers should be allowed to attend the interrogation of terrorists in the Republic, that helicopters should be allowed to overfly the Border, more effective liaison between the RUC and the Garda and the British and Irish Armies, she received the same reply, that the Irish side would 'study' it. "I knew what that meant," she wrote. "Nothing doing. I got so exasperated that I asked whether the Irish Government was willing to do anything at all."[20]

In Whitehall the decision had been taken to appoint not a Director of Operations but a 'Co-ordinator', together with a small Army and RUC staff. Sir Maurice Oldfield, former head of MI6, was called out of retirement to fill the appointment. So far as Thorne was concerned the creation of the appointment was all that he had looked for, but his time as Brigade Commander was drawing to a close and he left the Province two months after Oldfield's arrival. He took him on a tour of his Brigade area in South Armagh and invited him home for supper. His impression was that Oldfield was "a charming, highly intelligent, able man who understood politics and political manoeuvring, but that he was probably not a tough enough personality, a man who could be ridden around."[21]

According to Hermon, Oldfield's appointment made little difference. Creasey's time as GOC ended at the beginning of December, he returned to the Oman and sadly died, too young, in 1986, remembered with affection by the UDR. He was replaced by Lieutenant General Sir Richard Lawson and a month later Hermon, after spending the previous year on secondment to the Metropolitan Police, took over from Newman as Chief Constable.

Hermon and Lawson hit it off from their first meeting. Both were determined that 'The Way Ahead' policy would be made to work, and so it did. That is not to say that all irritations between the Army and the police suddenly evaporated, but at least there was no longer a major problem at the head.

On 28 September Pope John Paul arrived in Dublin on his historic three-day visit to Ireland. Vast crowds attended open air masses in Phoenix Park and at Drogheda. The majority of the Catholic community in the North travelled south and south-west to Dublin, Drogheda, Galway or to the shrine at Knock. Orders were given to Army units, including the UDR battalions, to carry out constant patrols on all roads leading to the south to ensure that they were not blocked by Loyalists. VCPs were to be kept to a minimum, though it was accepted that the Provisionals might take the opportunity of heavy traffic to bring munitions into the North. In his address to an audience of a quarter of a million at Drogheda, His Holiness made an impassioned plea for an end to violence.

The Provisionals rejected the appeal. In the next four weeks they murdered one former member of the UDR and three serving members.

One of the places that Corporal Herbie Kernoghan of 4UDR had on his Monday morning delivery run of fruit and vegetables was St Tibiney's Primary School at Rosslea, a mile from the Border. On 15 October, just as the school was opening and the first children arriving, two gunmen pulled in and held up the headmaster and four of his staff at gunpoint. Colm Toibin, who talked to the headmaster during his 'walk along the border', described the headmaster's account of what happened:

"He had come to work one morning and walked into the school kitchen, to find the caretaker and the kitchen staff sitting at a table. He had asked what was going on, but was met with silence. Then he saw a hooded man beside the door who asked him who he was. Another hooded man appeared in the room as well. It was clear that they were waiting to kill someone, but the staff had no idea who. Names went through all their minds; they didn't even know which side the hooded men were on – they might have come to shoot a teacher with Republican sympathies. He asked them to let him go and get the children out of the way. 'None of the children will be harmed,' they said, and told him to shut up. Soon the staff discovered that the two hooded men were waiting for Herbie, who came on certain days in a delivery van. He was a part-time UDR man.

"They waited in the school for the sound of a van to approach, knowing that if Herbie was there, as he always was, then he was going to be killed. The two hooded men told them to lie down on the floor, and not to raise the alarm for ten minutes. Then the van came. The staff heard the sharp, piercing sound of the gunfire. Herbie hadn't got a chance. They pumped twenty-one bullets into him, having got up close to him. Some of the children would have seen it. Their teacher sat opposite me in his living room, and asked me to imagine the effect it had on them. 'There was,' he said, 'screaming and hysterics.' The killers escaped over the border."[22]

Two weeks later his widow gave birth to a son, the couple's fourth child. She named him 'Herbert'. The Secretary of State condemned the killers as "the enemies of peace whose shadow is cast across every desk and cradle in the country".

By the end of 1979 seventy-six serving and ex-serving members of the security forces including ten members of the Prison Service had been murdered out of a total of 120 killings during the year. The security forces had killed one member of the IRA.

CHAPTER FOURTEEN

1980–1981 Tenth Anniversary

By the end of the 1970s the building of the Regiment had been completed. Now at the beginning of a new decade it was a matter of honing the professionalism of the battalions. Old soldiers, as old soldiers will, look back upon the first ten years as a time when life in their companies was 'more fun'. It must seem a strange term to use of a decade in which ninety-nine serving and eighteen ex-members had been murdered. Battalions had been under intense pressure, success and tragedy had gone hand in hand. Yet there was a great sense of achievement for those who had served through the first ten years, a sense of having built out of nothing a force that was now able to take over the role of the Regular Army in a large part of the Province, a sense too of having helped to contain the violence of the IRA. The majority of men and women had had no previous service in the armed forces. They were, as they would have been the first to admit, amateur soldiers, able to stand back and find a quiet amusement in the traditional ways of the Regular Army, able to laugh at their own mistakes whilst determined to do better next time. There were more characters in their ranks and most of the light-hearted stories come from that first decade.

As the older men, many of them ex-B Specials, had begun to resign, the average age of the battalions decreased. By March 1981 the average in 3UDR was 31, the average length of service 5 years.

A change of emphasis had been adopted in recruiting advertising – the attraction of good wages rather than a call to serve one's country, using, among others, the slogan "Can you think of a more rewarding part-time job?" It did not mean that the men and women who joined now did so only for the money, which, though improved, was still substantially less than the pay of the Police and Prison Service, but it did mark the difference between the soldiers of the 1980s and those who in the 1970s had enlisted out of a sense of duty without much regard to financial reward.

Unemployment was soaring in the Province, as one after another the big multi-national companies pared down their work force or closed down their plants altogether. Full-time service in the UDR permanent cadre had become an attractive alternative to being on the dole and battalions opened waiting lists of part-time soldiers anxious to transfer to full-time service. But the Defence budget was overspent, a moratorium had been imposed on further expenditure and for the time being any increase in the establishment of the full-time Operations Platoons, still just forty soldiers in each battalion, was out of the question.

On the other hand the total strength of the Regular Army in the Province was being run down and the UDR battalions tasked to take on a number of static duties. One of these was the guard on Cloona House, the GOC's residence, where the situation was becoming precarious as a new housing estate, being built to relieve pressure on West Belfast, was spreading out to the perimeter fence round the house. In November one of the four Regular battalions responsible for Belfast was withdrawn, vacating the Grand Central Hotel building. Responsibility for military support in the city centre passed to the two UDR city battalions and a small increase in the full-time establishment was authorized for the two battalions to enable them to assume these additional duties.

For the remaining battalions the only way to find additional manpower was to close down some bases and amalgamate companies, releasing full-time guards and administrative staff for operational tasks. Over the next three years ten bases were closed. The closures involved longer journeys, and therefore longer nights, for some of the soldiers and marked the final break from the B Special concept of platoon huts set up convenient to the men's homes.

On a quiet Sunday evening, 6 January 1980, a seven-man section from 3UDR's Operations Platoon had gone out on a routine patrol west of Castlewellan. For most of the way the road from there to Hilltown lies along a winding country road, except for the first three miles to the reservoir at Loughislandreavy, where it runs broad and straight. As the patrol was heading back to Ballykinlar along this stretch of road 600lb of home-made explosive packed into a narrow pipe culvert beneath the road detonated under the leading vehicle. The second vehicle, unable to stop in time, crashed into the crater. It was a huge explosion, leaving the first Landrover a shattered wreck bent into the shape of a letter L, water rapidly filling up the crater from a broken water main.

Of the four soldiers in the leading vehicle, three died at the scene. Private Rickie Wilson of Newcastle was still in the vehicle, the other two, Jim Cochrane of Downpatrick and Robert Smyth of Comber, were trapped under water by the wreckage, their bodies recovered by firemen. Two had died from skull fractures, one may have drowned. The other four members of the patrol were injured, but not seriously. A scratch patrol sent to secure the area reported finding a command wire. Other patrols accompanied by the police spent the night visiting the houses of suspects, looking for strangers to the area, in the belief that an incident on this scale was beyond the capability of the local ASU, but they found no one, and no one has ever been held responsible for the attack. The following day 2 PARA continued to secure the area whilst a Sapper search team followed the command wire to a disused farmstead on the hillside above. The first fifty yards had been dug in alongside the road and then built into a stone wall. A motorist reported seeing a group of men and two vehicles on the road at the scene in the early hours of the Sunday morning. The location had been well chosen – a clear view over a long straight road, telegraph poles to act as markers, and on a still Sunday night the unmistakable sound of the Landrover tyres audible from far off. It was the first time a culvert mine had been used in County Down.

The tragedy was national and international news. Up to that time the casualties were the worst suffered by the UDR in any one incident, and in the moment of the explosion the total of UDR murders passed 100 and the total deaths in the Province since the troubles began exceeded the 2,000 mark.

Jim Cochrane was a member of a Catholic family. His was the first funeral, held in St Patrick's Roman Catholic church in Downpatrick. The parish priest conducted the Requiem Mass. About half the mourners were in uniform, members of the battalion and from other battalions. The Deputy Chief Constable and Mrs McAtamney were there and local councillors from all the parties, including the SDLP. Gordon–Duff read the lesson. As the congregation sang 'Abide with me' the family carried the coffin out of the church and down to the road where it was draped with the Union flag and Cochrane's belt and beret placed on top. The bearer party from the Operations Platoon carried the coffin for the first quarter mile, then took their places on either side of the hearse and, led by a piper, the cortège wound its way up the hill to the cemetery in pouring rain, watched by a few spectators. It was the last of the funerals attended by the Colonel Commandant, General Sir John Anderson. He was already suffering from the Parkinson's Disease that was to be the cause of his death eight years later. A frail, sad figure, it was typical of that good man that, though he was wearing a coat, he set it aside when he saw his soldiers marching uncovered in the rain. The funeral, the *Down Recorder* commented, had "set a dignified example to the whole Province of cemented community understanding and tolerance."[1]

The military mourners returned to Ballykinlar to dry out their uniforms on the radiators, clean the mud of the graveyard from their shoes and, an hour later, went out again to Newcastle for the funeral of Wilson. Smyth was buried in Comber the following day. The service was to have been taken by the Reverend Robert Bradford, an ultra right-wing Unionist politician and a Methodist minister. But on the previous day he made a public statement saying among other things that the tragedy had damaged the morale of the Regiment and that all IRA members should be shot out of hand. The battalion told Bradford quietly that his attendance at the funeral would no longer be appropriate.

Mrs Cochrane told an American reporter:

"I am proud that my son fought for his country, the country he loved, and I am proud that he died with two Protestant friends. It goes to show that they can enjoy life, make entertainment together and even die together in a common cause." Wilson's mother agreed, "I have no bitterness with my neighbours. It is definitely not religion, it was never religion . . . I can't blame all Roman Catholics for the IRA."[2]

For months afterwards, opposite the estate at Annsborough where exactly two years before the battalion had gone to the help of the residents when the river broke its banks and flooded into their homes, a sign was daubed on a wall pointing the way to the 'UDR graveyard'. In 1996 the Cochrane family placed a small unobtrusive memorial recording the names of the victims at the site of the landmine. Within days it had been smashed to pieces. There were those for whom hatred must be carried beyond the grave.

PIRAs tactic of using a culvert mine in a relatively quiet area where none had been used before had proved so successful that there was an ever-present concern that they would try it again. The Battalion's reaction was not to be deterred by the threat, but to put into effect more unpredictable patterns of patrolling, making greater use of foot patrols deployed into the country north of the Mournes. Throughout the Brigade, areas of greatest threat were placed out of bounds to 'green vehicles' and patrols deployed by helicopter or by other means, but helicopter flying hours were limited, money was short and the moratorium was in force.

The aim of operations was to keep the members of the ASU off balance, to make them realize that there was no time of day or night and no corner of their neighbourhood where they could rest assured that they would not encounter a UDR patrol. With the improved training standards of the full-time soldiers the Operations Platoon began undertaking extended patrols, going out for 48 hours, walking across the country to carry out VCPs on the roads, then disappearing again, bivouacking by night in the forests, keeping some outlying farmstead under observation. Before moving on, they would enter the farmyard to leave footprints in the mud or to set the dog barking, so that the farmer would know a patrol had passed by. In time the part-time soldiers also were able to undertake these extended patrols at weekends. By midsummer word came back to 3UDR that these tactics were succeeding and the local ASU had indeed been knocked off balance, and for months thereafter there were no more culvert mines in South Down.

The new pattern of operations demanded higher standards of training. Greater use of foot patrols required improved physical fitness. Cross-country movement called for better map reading and instruction on how to cross obstacles avoiding the obvious route, for gateways could be booby-trapped. Extended patrols involved living out in the open, posting tactical sentries, setting up bivouacs, the cooking of army ration packs, the performance of limited observation of suspect dwellings. As always there was a continuing need for improved terrorist recognition, total under-standing and instantaneous recall of the provisions of the Yellow Card, describing the circumstances in which the individual soldier could open fire, weapon skills, confident use of the increasingly sophisticated search equipment, how to react in an ambush and carry out a follow-up, action to be taken on locating the terrorists' command wire and firing point, personal security, and an understanding of the organization and methods of working of the police.

The announcement of the Annual Services Pay Review gave the part-time soldiers an added incentive to train. As well as an average increase in basic pay of sixteen and a half percent, at last the parsimonious annual bounty, which had always lagged far behind the Territorial Army rate, was increased from £25/£35 to £150 for the first year, £250 for the second, £350 for the third and subsequent years. It continued to be tax-free. In addition the arrangement whereby a soldier on training was paid only a nominal sum, which had long acted as a disincentive to take part in training days and evenings was cancelled and from then on each soldier received the same rate of pay for training and operations.

Brigadier Pat Hargrave, who had taken over from Miller in March, already had experience of the UDR while commanding his battalion at Ballykelly in 1974. His impression then had been that the staff and Regular Army battalions failed to appreciate the worth of the Regiment. On returning to the Province he found that attitude still existed. If it was to be dispelled, training must be improved.[3] The number of courses at the UDR Training Centre in Ballykinlar was extended. The centralized course for permanent cadre recruits was increased from four to six weeks, then eight, eventually to ten. In eleven months of 1979/80 over 1,000 soldiers had attended courses at Ballykinlar, with thirty–forty permanent cadre recruits under training at any one time. Since the formation of the Regiment the training of part-time recruits had been a battalion responsibility and usually took place over three weekends. Now the battalions were encouraged to run these courses over a continuous eight-day period, and if at the end the recruits failed to pass an efficiency test they were not allowed to go out on patrol. As well as Warcop and Barry Buddon the locations for the annual camps were extended to include Lydd and Hythe where the ranges provided a degree of realism not available on the conventional butts and firing points of Ballykinlar (though improvements had begun there, including the building of a mock Belfast street). At Hythe a similar street scene had been laid out inside the circular walls of one of the old 18th century coastal fortifications. Another range consisted of gunmen moving through a street crowded with pedestrians, the firer's ability being tested by the number of gunmen he could shoot without hitting an innocent pedestrian. (The range warden showed a marked degree of trust in the firers; he kept pet rabbits and goldfish between the firing point and the targets.) For the men it was an interesting week and for everyone there was the attraction that on their day off London and France were in reasonable reach. In fact it was possible at the end of a day's training to take the ferry across the Channel, dine in Calais and catch the boat home at midnight.

Hargrave introduced other measures to improve the image of the

225

Regiment – stricter enforcement of the upper age limit and that problem that no Commander so far had been able to eradicate entirely, the wearing of long hair and the occasional beard. That was resolved once and for all two years on when the Falklands Campaign and the image of the lean, mean warriors of the Commandos and Parachute battalions, close-cropped and clean shaven, put hirsute man out of fashion.

To mark the tenth anniversary of the Regiment the officers held a dinner in the banqueting hall of the City Hall, attended by the Secretary of State, the Lord Mayor, General Sir John Anderson, making his last appearance in his Regiment and greeted with a standing ovation, and all the previous Commanders. The Chief of the General Staff, General Sir Edwin Bramall, told the officers:

> "I have come here quite simply with one important purpose and that is, as the professional head of the British Army, to bring the Army's warmest best wishes and to pay its greatest respect to you, our youngest regiment." He concluded, "The United Kingdom as a whole is proud of you, and it is a privilege for me to be the instrument by which this respect, admiration and gratitude is passed on to you."

In May the Council granted the Freedom of the City to the Regiment. A representative guard of honour, selected from all the battalions, with a detachment of Greenfinches at its centre, was drawn up in front of the City Hall under the stony gaze of Queen Victoria's statue and inspected by the Lord Mayor. The guests were invited into the Council chamber to watch the conferral of the Freedom, Alderman Bell handing over the scroll contained in a silver casket. He pointed out that the roll of Honorary Burgesses was a long and illustrious one, including the names of members of the Royal family, Sir Winston Churchill and the Ulster Field Marshals. "On no occasion," he told the guests, "has the Freedom of our City been more dearly won, more richly deserved, or more gladly given than the honour we confer today on The Ulster Defence Regiment."[4] It was the first of eleven Freedoms to be conferred on the Regiment during its life-time. In June the Duke and Duchess of Kent attended a Regimental garden party in the gardens of Hillsborough Castle.

Another nine serving soldiers and four former members of the Regiment were murdered in 1980. Off-duty soldiers were attacked on over fifteen occasions. Eight were wounded, including two Greenfinches. Patrols came under attack on six occasions. Half the killings occurred along the Border.

A Corporal in the Lisnaskea Company, a former member of the Irish Guards, was ambushed as he was driving up to his house. He was hit several times. After months of slow and painful recovery he returned to duty. His wife, who was eight months pregnant, lost her baby; it was thought that shock had brought on her miscarriage. Three days later Corporal Aubrey Abercrombie, also from 4UDR, was found shot dead at the wheel of his tractor on his farm north of Kinawley. In the same month a Greenfinch was wounded outside her parents' home. A car had stopped down the road, three men got out and one lifted up the bonnet. Along with her mother she went out to see if they could help. Two of the men opened fire and shot the Greenfinch in the thigh. They had probably been waiting for her father. She had joined the UDR after her boyfriend, Alan Ferguson, had been killed in the ambush of the patrol on the Garrison–Belcoo road two years previously.[5]

In June Private Richard Latimer of the Lisnaskea Company was murdered as he was serving two customers in his hardware shop in Newtownbutler. He was the third member of the parish church to be murdered since the beginning of the year.

Anger was escalating among the Protestant community over these repeated murders along the Fermanagh Border and, as the people saw it, the failure of the Government's security measures. Fermanagh families are closely knit. If one is hurt, there are many to grieve; the hurt spreads through the community, among relatives, in-laws, cousins. Some have farmed the land for generations; it is their land. When the Archbishop of Canterbury visited the Province, the Reverend Kille, Rector of Rosslea, told him that it was the heirs in the families with one son who were being targeted in order to end the inheritance.[6]

Until the troubles began the two communities had lived for years in quiet harmony with each other. Now the IRA had destroyed that. Protestants could not but be aware that information about their daily lives was being fed to the IRA based across the Border by their Catholic neighbours. Not all, but which? Whom could one trust? There were acts of courage when Catholics warned their Protestant neighbours of an impending attack. There were also acts of betrayal when they failed to do so, as Roy Kells was to experience a few months later.

Kells is well known and respected by both communities in Fermanagh. He owns a Ladies and Gentlemen's Fashion business, set up by his father in the 1920s, with three branches across the county. The Lisnaskea shop has been destroyed twice by bombs and rebuilt each time. Lisnaskea is a pleasant town, one long main street on the road from Enniskillen to the Cavan border. Like Castlederg in Tyrone it is one of the frontier towns that has suffered grievously from bombs and shooting attacks. When a car bomb had wrecked the town centre in 1972, it was Kells and five of his men on their way home from patrol in the early hours who had seen the lights of the car parked in the main street, realized what it was and evacuated the town centre.

In 1980 Kells was commanding the Newtownbutler platoon. Latimer was one of his soldiers. He was determined that something must be done to persuade the Government to take more resolute action to protect his people. Together with some other senior members of his platoon he set up the rather grandiosely named Fermanagh Committee for the Defence of British Democracy. It was, he insisted, no more than a pressure group. It did not make use of vigilantes, it had no connection with Paisley's Third

Force, and when the UDA announced it would send down some of its people to sort out the IRA, it was told they were not wanted. The committee did nothing unlawful and, by persuading the people that something was being done to fight their case, it prevented them, if they were considering doing so, from taking the law into their own hands.

Once it had been set up, Kells handed over the running of the committee to local leaders of the community, people who had no direct involvement in the UDR. A protest rally in Newtownbutler, attended by several thousand people, was addressed by the two Unionist party leaders, Paisley and Molyneaux, and drew the attention of the media to the plight of the people. In July Paisley arranged for four of the widows to meet the Prime Minister. Kells flew over with them and sat in an outer room at 10 Downing Street whilst Mrs Thatcher saw the four women alone, "and cried with them," he said.[7] Mrs Latimer told reporters that the Prime Minister had been very kind and listened very attentively. "She gave the definite impression that she did not realize things were quite so bad."[8] In the House Mrs Thatcher told MPs, "I think I learnt more from seeing them than I ever could have by reading any number of papers or letters."[9]

One of those attacked while going about his civilian job was a Sergeant in 8UDR who had already undergone two terrifying experiences – being forced to drive his van with a bomb on board and dealing with a proxy bomb delivered to his company base. On this Saturday in July he had a letter to deliver to a house where an old couple lived "away up an awful old lane". His suspicions had been alerted by a car moving around in the area with three people in it, two of them girls, though they could have been men wearing wigs. He took a 9mm pistol from its hiding place between the front seats of the van and slipped it into the waist band of his trousers:

"The only mistake I made, I didn't put one up the spout. So I went on out and across the road, over to another place and just the same car went past with the same people in it. Says I, 'there's something wrong'. I went to this house. The door was closed. I got the letter ready in my hand as I was driving up and before the van stopped, I pulled the brake on her and was out like lightning. Just as I was going to put the letter under the door, the door opened, two boys came out masked to there, one fired one round and it went past my face. You know a bullet would suck the wind. It was that close to me I thought I was hit but I couldn't feel nothing, so I rolled and he fired another one at me on the ground and he missed again and just at that I rolled and got a shot off into the air. I didn't aim, for I couldn't. I didn't have time to look. So I took a run down this lane. It was an old isolated place, there could have been thirty men, I didn't know how many, and I didn't know which way to run really, but I saw a bunch of nettles and says I, 'There's a sheugh there'. I had a good few rounds loose in my pocket. Says I, 'If I could get in there and get a bit of cover I could hold them off.' Jesus, I jumped in, there was a big stump of a tree, there was no sheugh at all. I just hit my backside on the tree and bounced out in the middle of the lane again. By that time they were standing behind the wall and I could hear them cursing and swearing. So I went down the lane a bit, nice and quiet, for I didn't know if somebody else would step out with an Armalite or something. The next thing I heard was thump, thump, and I saw the two boys coming running down the field. They were sixty yards off me in this field of hay cut. So I lined up on the first boy and I called him but he didn't stop, and I got blazing. He went to ground so I moved to the second boy, who did the same. Says I, 'God I have got them.' Then I looked round and the first boy, he was running again and the second boy got up and I shot again. I had only seven rounds in the magazine, that's all she held. That was my last episode."

By now search teams within the Operations Platoons were carrying out frequent searches, some speculative, some based on information supplied by Special Branch, others the result of detailed search analysis, taking into account such factors as the location of suspect houses, reports of suspects passing through road checks, previous finds and attacks, the remoteness of an area and likely supply routes. Their persistence paid off and battalions marked up an impressive record of finds in the first five months of the year. In February a search team from 1UDR, acting on a report that a civilian had stumbled upon weapons and ammunition near Ballymena, uncovered two home-made sub-machine guns, a zip gun, pistol, safety fuse, detonators and ammunition, almost certainly belonging to Loyalist paramilitaries. In March the Dungannon Company of 8UDR found two weapons on the wartime airfield at Ardboe. In April 2UDR, 8UDR and the RUC carried out a highly successful search operation south of Blackwatertown, discovering two hand guns, one of them brand new, followed the next day by two .303 rifles, an SLR and some 4,000 rounds, hidden in a plastic pipe built into a bank. Four days later a routine patrol from the Cookstown Company came upon a massive 900lb landmine, packed into nine milk churns, already wired up and emplaced in a culvert under a road a mile from Cappagh. It was the biggest bomb found so far that year.

John Turnly was a member of a Protestant family established in the Glens of Antrim for over two centuries and a leading figure in the Irish Independence Party. He was shot in front of his Japanese wife and children, as he arrived at a hall to address a meeting in Carnlough, twelve miles along the Antrim Coast Road from Larne. Larne was a hotbed of Loyalist paramilitaries, some of whom had served, and regrettably two who still served, in the local UDR company. It is hard to believe that suspicions did not exist, not least because the Company IO, a man of absolute integrity, had a close and trusted working relationship with the local Special Branch.

The police acted resolutely in the aftermath of the murder, rounding up some thirty to forty people representing all the Loyalist paramilitary organizations. Among those taken in and subsequently charged with para-military-related offences were two permanent cadre soldiers, one of them a Sergeant. One of the three UFF members eventually found guilty of the killing and sentenced to life imprisonment had served in the company as both a permanent cadre and a part-time soldier and had been allowed to continue to use the company canteen after he resigned from the Regiment.[10]

There was a positive side to what was otherwise deplorable publicity for the UDR. At the murder trial it was revealed that it was as a result of the suspicions of a Corporal in 5UDR who stopped the getaway van on the Ballymena road two and a half hours after the shooting that the three were identified and subsequently arrested. And, though this could not be revealed at the time, the Larne Company intelligence cell had submitted a report some ten days before the murder giving positive evidence, provided by soldiers living along the coast, that Turnly was under surveillance by Loyalist paramilitaries.[11]

For the first two years of the decade events in Ireland were dominated by the hunger strike conducted by the Republican prisoners in the H–Blocks in the Maze. In the first instance they refused to wear prison clothes, wrapping themselves in blankets. When the authorities refused to concede their demands to be allowed to wear their own clothes, they escalated their protest, smearing their cells with their own excrement. That too failed to move the authorities and on 1 March 1981 the leader of the Provisional prisoners, Bobby Sands, began his fast to the death.

The National H–Block Committee showed great skill in publicizing the plight of the prisoners, albeit self-inflicted, organizing street protests throughout Ireland. At first the marches were orderly, but, as the strikers weakened, the protests grew more angry, with demonstrations in towns and villages across the Province regularly ending in hooligan violence, supplemented by hoax bombs to cause further disruption. It was a time when the RUC came into their own, handling the demonstrations virtually without military intervention, though there were many nights when UDR patrols deployed to protect them against the threat of gunmen while they policed the parades. As Sands weakened the tension grew and the rioting escalated, hyped up by the international media who had returned in force to their usual watering hole in the Europa Hotel. UDR battalions were instructed to advise those soldiers whose circumstances put them at high risk to move into barracks for the time being. Few accepted the offer; it was not a time to leave one's family on their own. Annual camps across the water were postponed until later in the year.

Sands died on 5 May 1981. The huge funeral passed off peacefully and the press corps switched their attention to Londonderry to await the imminent death of the next prisoner, Francie Hughes of Bellaghy, former OC of the South Derry ASU.

While they waited a journalist from RTE suggested they should cover the other side of the story by interviewing the widows of the victims of terrorism. A local man, Alistair Wilson, gathered together a group of local widows and brought them to the hotel. Among them was Sylvia Deacon, whose husband, Colour Sergeant David Deacon, had been murdered in 1973. They gave a number of interviews and were filmed for the American Broadcasting Company television network. Encouraged by the media interest that their interviews had generated, and with the help of Wilson and Marlene Jefferson, who had just completed her term of office as the city's first woman Mayor, they formed a small group, calling it "The Widow's Mite". They took David Deacon's wedding ring, engraved with the names of his wife and children, and had it melted down and refashioned in the shape of a biblical mite, stamped with a candle to represent the Light of Truth. The mite was passed to groups of widows across the Province, shown to the local press and to District Councils to persuade them not to provide financial support to the H–Block Committee Campaign. In three cases they were able to reverse a council's decision. They travelled to Scotland where they addressed meetings, appeared again on television and raised enough money to finance a trip to America. Sylvia Deacon was invited to address the Monday Club at the Conservative conference at Blackpool and afterwards talked with Mrs Thatcher in her hotel room. As a result the British Embassy arranged for Mrs Jefferson and three of the widows to carry out a lightning speaking tour of the United States. The three were Sylvia Deacon, Marlene Wilson, who had lost a husband and a brother in the RUC, and Georgie Gordon, whose UDR husband and 11-year-old daughter had been killed by the under-car booby trap. In five days they travelled to six centres across the country, Cleveland, Minneapolis, St Louis, where, among others, they addressed an audience at the University's centre for International Studies, San Francisco, Los Angeles and Washington. They gave talks, were interviewed on television, including the Walter Cronkite Show, and took part in radio phone-ins, during one of which they talked to Father Sean McManus, head of the Irish National Caucus, and were a match for him. It was an exhausting schedule, repeating time and again the stories of their bereavement. By the time they came home they were worn out. It had been a courageous campaign by women, who, apart from Marlene Jefferson, had no experience of public speaking. "I'm glad we did it," Sylvia said. "We got a good reception from the American people. They had no idea what was going on. They heard only one side of the story – the IRA propaganda machine."[12]

When Francie Hughes died, a week after Sands, another prisoner came forward to take his place. All through the summer that pattern continued. As one died another took over, until in time the world lost interest, the press corps departed, the deaths were no longer news, their names forgotten by all but the grieving families. The Dungannon priest, Father Faul, played a leading role in advising relatives to persuade their menfolk to abandon their protest, until at last, on 3 October, the last five agreed to give up their fast. The hunger strike was over. By then ten had died of starvation. Three days later the Government agreed that prisoners should be allowed to wear their own clothes.

Ireland had a new generation of martyrs. From a position of weakness Sinn Fein had gained the support of the Irish people at home and abroad, including many who had no truck with violence of the IRA. For a while there was a very real concern that Sinn Fein would take over from the SDLP as the principal political party of the Nationalist community.

As 1980 drew to a close morale in the Province was low. Soaring unemployment and the failure of the political parties to agree on the formation of a new Assembly and Executive, as proposed in a Government Green Paper published in July, affected both communities. Protestants had no faith in Government security policy. They saw the Army strength being run down and bases closed, and the killings went on. The success of the protests by the H–Block Committee and the start of the hunger strike in October were creating international sympathy for men who had been involved in the murder of their people.

The UDR, being drawn in the main from that community, shared its feelings. There were other factors. In accordance with the policy of police primacy, the public profile of the Army, including the UDR, had been lowered "until it just about disappeared from sight".[13] The fact that advertising for recruits on television, radio and in the national press had been stopped and the annual camp at Lydd/Hythe for the permanent cadre cancelled, officially because of the need to cut back on defence expenditure, had raised doubts about the Government's commitment to the future of the Regiment.

As the hunger strike moved on its tragic course through 1981, the level of violence increased, fuelling Protestant disillusionment. Excluding the ten hunger strikers, 100 people died; half of them were members or ex-members of the security forces, twenty-two RUC, eighteen UDR and ten Regular Army. The combined total of serving and former members of the Regiment was the highest since 1976 and exceeded only in 1972. There were ten attacks on patrols resulting in the death of one soldier and the wounding of six others. In addition to the fatalities there were twenty other assassination bids against off-duty soldiers in which ten were wounded, among them another postman and three school bus drivers. The attacks included four under-vehicle booby-traps. Three of them failed to detonate properly, one under the car belonging to the Operations Officer of 10UDR; the fourth killed the 17-year-old son of a soldier from Lisnadill in Co Armagh as he was putting his father's car away in the garage for the night.

Ivan Toombs was an officer in Customs and Excise and commanded the UDR company in Rathfriland. In 1976 as a part-time Captain he had been shot and seriously wounded on his way to work at the Customs post on the Dublin road south of Newry. On recovering from his wounds he had been transferred for his own safety to the VAT office in the Customs and Excise headquarters in Belfast. However, Warrenpoint, his home town, was rapidly increasing in importance as a container port, and Toombs applied to become the senior Customs Officer there. On 16 January he was working at his desk when two gunmen rode into the dock area on a motorcycle. While one of them covered the Customs Officer on duty at the door, the other burst into Toombs' office, weapon in hand, took up a firing position and pulled the trigger. The gun jammed. Toombs tried to reach his pistol in his briefcase. The gunman lunged at him. Toombs grappled with him and, being the stronger, would have overcome his assailant, but the second man, hearing the first calling for him, ran down the corridor, told his companion to stand aside and opened fire. As Toombs lay dying, the first man calmly cleared his weapon and pumped further rounds into his body to make sure he was dead. His wife Mary, who was in Daisy Hill hospital in Newry recovering from a serious operation, was brought the news by her rector. She got up from her bed and returned home to look after the five children. She and Ivan had talked about the arrangements for his funeral. With typical modesty he had asked that it should take place without military honours. Bishop Eames gave the address, recalling a conversation with Ivan at a lunch in the Battalion Officers Mess at Ballykinlar two months earlier:

> "We talked of many things, not least the difficulties of the present time in our Province. How well I recall his words, 'Surely some day people will come to see that there are some things that are so good that they will endure.' What a memorial those words provide.
>
> "As Christians we believe there are certain 'things so good that they will endure', – love, so much stronger than hatred; unity of purpose so much more lasting than division; charity and understanding which outlive suspicion and violence; faith which endures and outlives smallness and meanness."

News of the murder reached 10 Downing Street as an Alliance deputation was meeting with the Prime Minister. Oliver Napier, the Party leader, who had attended the same lunch in Ballykinlar, recalled that Mrs Thatcher was horrified. "The message came through as we were discussing the security situation. It reinforced the kind of thing we live with."[14]

Ivan Toombs was a thoroughly good man, father of a charming, attractive family, assistant Scout master, keen sports player, a moderate man who had joined the UDR at the beginning after ten years in the USC, a man who believed he had a duty to help protect the whole community. He was typical of the best type of UDR officer. Talking to him one would never have known he was a man living under constant threat; his calm acceptance that he would be killed sooner or later was extraordinary. "I'm not bitter," his wife said. "We both knew this would happen sometime, and now I must pick up the pieces and keep our family together in the town we grew up in."[15]

Toombs was set up for murder by a fellow Customs Officer, Eamon Collins, who in his youth had worked as a clerical officer in the MOD in London. In 1978 he joined Customs and Excise and was stationed at the post on the main road to Dublin in his home town of Newry. Already an angry and embittered man, he soon discovered that his work gave him access to information about members of the security forces. He began passing this information on to the IRA in Dundalk. He arranged to be attached to the Customs Office in Warrenpoint where he spent most of his time "working out ways to kill Ivan Toombs. The more I found out about him, the more admirable I found him. He was a man of simple tastes who behaved decently towards all, the sort of man who would have rebuked anyone who made an anti-Catholic comment. I liked him and felt that in other circumstances we might have been friends."[16]

Collins provided the IRA with detailed drawings of the layout of Warrenpoint Customs Office and official papers to enable the assassins to persuade the officer on duty to let them in. After two years of planning, the killing took place. Collins attended the funeral, to show the respect of one soldier to another, or so he claimed in a 1995 television programme, though in his book he records that he did so to target other members of the security forces among the mourners; the probable reason is that suspicions would have fallen on him if he had stayed away. He went on to become an effective and dedicated member of the IRA, reconstituting the ineffectual local Newry ASU and acting as its intelligence officer. In 1985 he was arrested. He turned supergrass, but under pressure from his family and on the basis of an assurance from the IRA, delivered to him in prison, that no action would be taken against him so long as he did so, he retracted his evidence. He was taken to court charged with five murders and forty-five terrorist-related offences. Though he had provided the evidence against himself in the first instance, the judge was concerned that the confessions might have been obtained under duress and Collins was released. In 1997 he was seriously injured when the IRA tried to kill him in a hit-and-run accident. In January 1999, after he had given evidence on behalf of the *Sunday Times* in a libel case involving a senior South Armagh Provisional, he was brutally murdered outside his home in Newry. There is little doubt that his assassins belonged to one of the Republican groups.

His book is a disturbingly honest account of how after four years as an IRA activist he "no longer existed as a human being".[17] It answers the question that many have asked, "How could they do it?" They could because they hated with a deep, corrosive hatred, the unforgetting, unforgiving legacy of centuries. In Collins' case he began to hate, he claims, because of the harsh treatment of his family by a Regular Army patrol, but the sum of the evil he generated far outweighed any wrong that may have been done to him and his people. "The IRA always approved attacks on the UDR with a special enthusiasm," he wrote, "and within the wider nationalist community the killing of a member of the UDR is always more popular than the killing of a policeman."[18]

In February a second attempt was made to murder Roy Kells as he was working in the shop window in Lisnaskea with two assistants, changing the seasonal display.

> "I was facing the front out on to the main street when I heard two shots fired. I immediately turned to my right and my eyes met a gunman standing four feet away from me and pointing a gun directly at me. Our eyes actually locked together. He fired a third shot which hit me, grazing my temple and drawing some blood. I fell to the ground and he fired two more shots over my head. There was a semi-circle of five shots in the hoarding behind the back of the shop window."

The gunman hid his weapon under his coat and ran. A fellow member of Kells' platoon from up the street had heard the shots, handed him a gun and together they rushed into the bar next door. A customer told them the man had run through the bar and out the back by a door that was always kept locked but on that day had been left open.[19]

Private John Smith of 7UDR worked in a garage in Ormeau Avenue. Each day he walked there from his home in East Belfast. His route took him through the Markets district, the home ground of an INLA unit. In March two INLA gunmen, wearing white painters' coats and carrying a tin of paint, followed him along the street and shot him in the back of the head. On the following Sunday the priest in nearby St Malachy's Church challenged any member of the congregation to get up and leave if they supported the killers. No one moved.[20]

Three members of the Regiment were killed in April. On 28 April Lance Corporal Richard McKee was killed outright when the civilianized minibus he was travelling in on an administrative run from the base at Rathfriland to Ballykinlar came under fire. His funeral took place in Clonallan churchyard where Toombs had been buried three months earlier. The night before, Cardinal O'Fiaich called on the family in Warrenpoint and prayed at the coffin, accompanied by Monsignor John Magee, a Newry man and the Pope's personal emissary in the Vatican. He had come from Rome in the last fruitless attempt to persuade Sands to call off his hunger strike.

In May Private Alan Richie was killed when gunmen stepped out into a quiet country road at Gulladuff after a two-vehicle patrol from 5UDR had passed by and fired through the open door into the back of the rear Landrover. Two days later the CO of 7UDR, Lieutenant Colonel Edward Cowan, who had only taken over the Battalion a fortnight earlier, came within inches of being killed when a high velocity round fired by a sniper overlooking the Short Strand bus depot grazed his neck. Apart from the graze he was unhurt and joined in the hot pursuit to locate the firing point and empty cases. Over the next six weeks there were other sniper attacks in the same area, a run-down Catholic enclave in the predominantly Protestant East Belfast, and two policemen were wounded. When later in the year in the same area a member of a 7UDR patrol was shot and wounded in the arm, the Battalion mounted a major follow-up operation carrying out a systematic house-to-house search lasting over two days, assisted by the police and Regular Army search teams. One of the companies cordoned off the area. Angry residents told the media that the UDR had placed them under virtual curfew. Unfortunately, when terrorists base themselves on a network of small streets it is the innocent inhabitants who suffer. The searches uncovered, as well as various items of bomb-making equipment, the sniper rifle and ammunition. An 18-year-old girl was arrested at the scene and charged with attempted murder.[21]

In June three armed masked men took over a house in the country south of Lisnaskea. When Lance Corporal Ronald Graham arrived to deliver groceries they shot him dead. A Sergeant in 8UDR was shot as he was delivering mail to an isolated farm near Ballygawley. Although wounded he returned fire with his PPW, hitting one of his attackers in the chest. A man, said to be a heavily traced member of PIRA from the Dungannon area, was admitted to a Monaghan hospital. He had not been taken into custody and two weeks later he slipped away, leaving a relative in his place in the hospital bed.

In July another Sergeant in 8UDR had a lucky escape from death. He had driven down to Cookstown from his home out in the country. As he was going through the gates of the company centre the sentry shouted at him, "Get away from that car."

> "I thought they're taking a bloody hand out of me, so I drove on down and parked. Someone came running down after me, saying, 'Get away from the car, get away from the car.' I didn't know whether to take him seriously or not but by God when I went back a bit I saw this white lunch box underneath the car. The ATO was sent for, and the Commanding Officer arrived down. My whole fear was the Commanding Officer lighting on me and giving me a bloody dressing down for not checking my car. He was very nice about it, he never said a word."

Two years later the Sergeant was to suffer a greater tragedy. In July 1983 he had gone to Bisley with the Battalion shooting team. On the last day an announcement was made over the tannoy that a member of 8UDR should report to Range control.

> "I went and was told there had been a bomb attack on a UDR man's home. It's funny the way you get a feeling like, I just knew that it was my house. I had the key left for my sister in a wee shed at the back. She was that type of a woman, she liked to make sure when

I was coming home that the house was right. She went to get the key, opened the door of the wee shed – Boom! The bomb was in behind the door and she was just plastered up against a wall. Her legs was an awful mess."

She died of her injuries two months later.

"I had my ups and downs, but that was the worst," her brother said. "It is something you never get over because I know she died because of me. It was hard to take. I left the wee house and went to live in Cookstown then."[22]

Faced with the continuing attacks on off-duty members of the UDR, the Scientific Adviser at HQNI had drawn up in 1978 a fairly rudimentary method of assessing the extent to which each soldier was at risk of attack. This system of Risk Assessment was now being refined in each battalion and within each intelligence office a Risk Assessment cell was established. The core of the system was the soldier's risk assessment file, covering such questions as where he lived and worked, whether his job meant that he had to maintain a fixed daily schedule, whether he had been attacked in the past or attacks on other people had taken place in his neighbourhood. The answers to these questions enabled the Risk Assessment Officer to calculate a 'score'; anyone scoring twenty was at High Risk, over that figure, Very High Risk. These were supplemented by individual interview sheets, giving the address and grid reference of the soldier's home and work place, details of the family, the car, where it was parked during working hours and so on. The file was continuously updated with any reports the soldier might make about cars he believed had followed him home, suspect persons that he believed had been observing his movements, or anything he felt might indicate he was under risk.

Completing the details involved a great deal of work by the companies. The problem was to convince the soldiers that they must keep the information up to date. Information might be received that a soldier driving a red car was under threat; a warning would be sent out to all red car owners, only to discover later that several others had sold their cars and bought others which happened to be red, but had never told their company office so that their record could be updated. It was a matter of dispelling the 'it-won't-happen-to-me' syndrome; but in time, as lives were saved, soldiers came to realize that the Risk Assessment System was not just another facet of military bureaucracy.

By 1983 the system was computerized, with a computer in each Risk Assessment cell and all members of the intelligence staff trained how to operate it. If a warning was received, it was passed on by the duty watch-keeper to the company operations room; the company informed the Company Commander who would warn his platoon commanders and so on down the line to the individual soldiers. There were times when the warning had to be passed on immediately, for a life could be at imminent

237

risk. Sometimes it was vague – "a UVBT under a soldier's car in County Down tonight" – at other times specific. When Special Branch obtained information that a man possibly working for a certain firm in a certain area who rode a small red motorcycle and wore a green jacket and a blue helmet with a distinctive badge was under threat, the computer printed out his name in minutes, the soldier was brought into barracks, resigned from his civilian job and was taken on the permanent cadre.

On other occasions the information left vital questions unanswered, such as "a man who leaves his daughter to college will be shot at 8 am on 9 June". What man? What college? The information was received at midnight on the 8th. The first trawl showed that no one had recorded on their risk assessment proforma information about leaving a daughter to college. The trawl was narrowed down to married soldiers with daughters of college age who could be pupils at the two colleges in the area from which the information had originated. When this still produced no results attention was turned to former soldiers. With two hours to go a man was identified who fitted the information – a former soldier whose brother was a Member of Parliament. An hour later the polling stations were due to open for the Westminster General Election.

At times the information was so precise and the threat so imminent that the soldier and his family would be moved out overnight into a mobile home or an empty married quarter in the nearest military barracks and stay there, sometimes for months, until such time as the Housing Executive could allocate him a house in a safe area.

Sometimes the system was not enough to save a soldier's life but the information he had provided for his file could contribute to the arrest of his killers. When a Corporal was shot dead in Kilkeel it was found from his file that he had repeatedly reported a local man watching his movements. The name was passed to the police who confronted the man with this evidence. He admitted passing the information to PIRA and was sentenced to life imprisonment.

Soldiers graded as being at Very High Risk were issued with 9mm service pistols in place of the smaller calibre .22 Walther. Individual anti-ambush drill became a regular feature of annual camp, with soldiers being taught how to tumble out of a moving car, roll into a fire position and open fire against a figure target with a PPW.

On 5 August a series of bomb attacks took place across the Province, the worst for over a year – a car showroom in Armagh, a hotel wrecked in Dunmurry, twelve shops destroyed in the centre of Lisburn, widespread blast damage behind the City Hall, two bombs in Newry and the railway line to Dublin cut again near the Border. On the 22nd a car bomb exploded in the main street of Bangor. Fifteen minutes later another exploded in Fisherwick Place near the City Centre, wrecking a newly completed office block and causing extensive damage to the Presbyterian Assembly Building.

In September two more members of the Regiment were murdered, in

October another, plus a former member who had resigned a month earlier. At the beginning of November the Chief Constable warned that the Provisionals, having regrouped during the hunger strike, were about to step up their attacks. The recruits who had flocked to join the organization during the H–Block campaign had now been trained and the success of that campaign in the United States had ensured that ample funds and munitions were available.

The Chief Constable's warning proved all too accurate. Within 24 hours a part-time soldier in 5UDR was shot six times and was very seriously injured while he was up a ladder, painting premises in the centre of Londonderry. In the early hours of the morning of the 10th Private Cecil Graham, brother of Ronald who had been murdered in June, was shot as he was leaving his in-laws' home after visiting his wife, a Catholic, and their six-week-old baby. The child had been born prematurely with a heart murmur and, in order to help the mother to nurse him, she and their infant son had moved temporarily into her parents' home. Wounded, Graham tried to crawl back into the house but the gunmen closed in and pumped ten rounds into him. His father-in-law, who had served in the Army in France during the war, helped him into the house. It was said that none of the neighbours dared to go to his aid. He died the following day. Eight hours later a Corporal in the same company was ambushed as he drove down the lane to his farm. Despite being hit he was able to drive on but crashed the car further down the lane. He took to the fields, lay low for a while and then walked one and a half miles cross-country to a safe farmhouse. That same day Charles Neville, a former Sergeant in 2UDR, was murdered as he left his place of work in Armagh.

The killings built up to a crescendo on 14 November when three gunmen walked into a community centre in Finaghy and shot dead the Reverend Robert Bradford and the caretaker. Bradford, a Unionist MP, was an ultra-Loyalist, the man whose immoderate public statements had prompted 3UDR to ask him not to officiate at the funeral of one of the three soldiers killed in the landmine at Castlewellan. Loyalist anger was near boiling point. Next day two Catholics were shot and one of them died. Even moderate men were voicing their dissatisfaction over Government security policy. There had been too much talk of reductions in force levels and the closing down of bases and of looking ahead to a time when the police could take over sole responsibility for security. As a result of the policy of maintaining a low public profile in the media and of conducting more operations covertly, the impression had been created that military operations had been run down and the close accord between the Army and the Protestant community had suffered as a result. Distrust of Government intentions had been heightened by a meeting that had taken place at 10 Downing Street a week before Bradford died between the Prime Minister and the new Taoiseach, Garret Fitzgerald, when the two had agreed to set up, as Thatcher recorded, "the rather grand sounding Anglo–Irish Inter-Governmental Council which really continued the existing ministerial and official contacts under a new name'.[23]

The Official Unionists and the DUP, Molyneaux and Paisley, reacted with anger, but separately. When the former said that, unless security was improved, he would advocate the setting up of a citizens' force, the latter said he already had a Third Force in existence and could put between 25,000 and 50,000 men on the streets. Some 600 men, some masked and wearing combat jackets, paraded for Paisley in Enniskillen. The Unionist stoppage next day was marked by dignified gatherings at war memorials across the Province, but the Secretary of State was jostled and booed when he attended the Bradford funeral. That same day another member of the Lisnaskea Company, Corporal Albert Beacom, was murdered on his isolated farm near Maguiresbridge. His wife was feeding their ten-month-old daughter when she heard the shots and ran out into the yard. He died in her arms. A Catholic was killed in Lurgan by the UVF. In the evening the Third Force paraded again, at New Buildings in Co Londonderry. Press photographers were taken aside to a lonely place nearby where a line of masked men on a given signal raised handguns into the air. It was the first time that members of the Force had appeared with weapons in public. Next day James McClintock, formerly a Corporal in 5UDR, was murdered at New Buildings on his way home from work; the day after, Lance Corporal John McKeegan of 6UDR was shot dead while delivering wood in the Ballycolman estate in Strabane. McKeegan was a cousin of McClintock's widow.

On the Wednesday the *Newsletter* published a page-high notice, signed by Paisley and the other two DUP MPs, headed "The Crisis of our Generation now upon us," listing the attacks on members of the UDR and RUC that had taken place in the previous week, culminating in the murder of Bradford and declaring an "Ulster Day of Action" on the following Monday. It would involve a total stoppage of work from midday, tractor and car cavalcades converging on major towns and a massive demonstration in Newtownards that evening. "Units of the Third Force – which already exists – will parade," the announcement concluded.

Security arrangements for the Day of Action were in the hands of the police and UDR battalions received their instructions from RUC divisions. A call-out was not considered necessary, but part-time soldiers patrolled the main roads overnight and all the permanent cadre were called in to supplement the patrols, act as a reserve and carry on patrolling the following day. In the event the day passed peacefully. The UDA, who had little use for Paisley since the UWC strike, refused to have any part in the demonstrations and instead held their own protest meeting in the shipyards. Molyneaux addressed a smallish crowd at the Cenotaph beside the City Hall. The police estimated that some 10,000 men and a few women paraded in Newtownards, three-quarters of them wearing some form of paramilitary dress, some with official armbands. The man leading the parade wore a combat jacket, UDR beret and cap badge and was thought to be a UDR 'company commander'. Afterwards several battalion adjutants were summoned to HQUDR to see if they could identify him, but police had failed to photograph the ringleaders and the only photograph of the man, reproduced from television, was so blurred as to make positive identification impossible. The adjutants had little doubt that the man was not and never had been a 'company commander' in the UDR.

When, later in the week, a group of about 100 men paraded in a Loyalist estate in Londonderry and their anonymous leader claimed that there were UDR soldiers and RUC reservists in their ranks, SDLP and Alliance politicians demanded that the RUC should carry out an investigation. Father Faul claimed that the police and UDR had failed to take any action against the armed men in the parade at New Buildings and repeated the allegation that there were members of the security forces amongst them. These accusations of UDR involvement in the Third Force were to be repeated on numerous occasions. There may have been a few serving soldiers in these publicity demonstrations, but it is unlikely that men who were carrying out regular operational duties with their companies would be willing to give up any more nights out of bed for the sake of Paisley's self-aggrandisement. There was little Paisleyite involvement in the Regiment. The media reported that the CO of 11UDR in Portadown had issued an order to his battalion that any soldiers who became involved in the Third Force would be dismissed. It was the kind of unequivocal state-ment that should have been issued by Headquarters Northern Ireland, both then and even more so in the early 1970s in regard to UDR/UDA dual membership, but, when asked if the order was official policy, an Army spokesman stated only that it was not the custom for a Headquarters to comment on orders given by a Commanding Officer to his soldiers. During his two years in command Hargrave never heard of a single case of a serving member of the Regiment being identified with the Third Force. Within HQNI it was not considered a matter for serious concern.[24]

Major General Peter Chiswell, the new CLF, a former PARA CO who had commanded his battalion in Belfast, a man with a reputation for standing no nonsense, issued unequivocal orders on how the Army should react on encountering a Third Force patrol. If the members were armed or acting illegally (and the carriage of clubs or wearing of face masks was now illegal) they were to be arrested. 3UDR expanded the orders into a directive for patrol commanders. On encountering an illegal patrol the UDR patrol commander was to deploy half his men in fire posi-tion and block off the road. He was then to go forward on foot with the other half of his patrol, block off the road on the far side of the illegal VCP and tell the men they were under arrest. The situation never arose. From then on the Third Force faded into obscurity.

After the violence of the previous two months December passed peace-fully. The future looked hopeful. Information provided by supergrasses was making inroads into the leadership of the paramilitaries. There were signs of a high-level leadership struggle in the INLA, with two leading members shot. Members of the Mid–Ulster UVF had been rounded up and in general the Third Force rallies had been poorly attended. For the first time in three years a month had passed without anyone being murdered; the Segment gates were opened for late-night shopping and Christmas was a peaceful time.

CHAPTER FIFTEEN

1982–1984

In every year but two between 1978 and 1990 the IRA's first target of the year was a member of the UDR. In 1982 their victim was a soldier in 3UDR who lost most of his foot when a bomb exploded under his car in Newcastle on the evening of New Year's Day. A companion, who was not a member of the Regiment, was killed. There were thirty-one attacks against serving and ex-serving members of the Regiment in that year, including seven UVBTs. Seven serving and eight ex-members were killed; two lost both legs, one an arm and a leg.

One of the dead was Sergeant Tommy Cochrane, knocked from his motorcycle and abducted as he was on his way to work at a fabrics factory in Glenanne. For an agonizing week the family waited for news of him, until his body was found dumped at the side of a road. In Belfast the day after his disappearance Lenny Murphy, leader of the Shankill Butcher gang, abducted a passing Catholic in retaliation and asked the local SDLP councillor to tell the Provisionals that he would set his hapless hostage, Donegan, free when they released Cochrane. In fact Donegan had already been put to death in Murphy's customary sadistic manner. When Cochrane's son, by now aware that his father was dead, heard of Donegan's murder, he phoned the widow to express his sympathy and placed a condolence notice in the press. Murphy was murdered three weeks later, probably by the IRA, though the Loyalist paramilitaries, sickened by his atrocities, were glad to be rid of him.

Jay Nethercott's father had been a policeman at Coalisland at the time of the IRA's abortive campaign in the Fifties. The family had lived for several generations in the strongly Republican area of East Tyrone. They were well known and respected by their Catholic neighbours. Jay knew their sons, had socialized with them in their school days and some had been his classmates at the technical college. He knew them by their Christian names and inevitably, when the latest troubles developed, he came to know which had been recruited into the IRA. He was nineteen and still at college when he joined the UDR as a part-time soldier and was shot in the hand on his first patrol. In due course he was commissioned and commanded the Dungannon-based permanent cadre company, one of the most successful companies in the Regiment. In December 1982 James Gibson, a former member of the Battalion, was murdered while driving a school bus at Annaghmore near Coalisland. At the time patrols from the company were operating in the area.

Jay had gone out in a civilianized car to visit his men, taking with him a subaltern and a Staff Sergeant from the Regular Army, for the Regulars could learn much from the UDR's intimate knowledge of the district. They were driving back into town when they saw four armed, masked men tumbling into a car which sped past them in the opposite direction. They made a U-turn and gave chase. The gunmen stopped outside a Catholic primary school; lessons were over for the day, the children coming out, mothers waiting in cars to pick them up. The gunmen abandoned the car there, first attempting to set it on fire by firing shots into it and sped off in a second vehicle. Jay's party continued the chase, racing along back roads at high speed. The car stopped at a fork in the road, the four men still masked and armed, one with an Armalite. A fifth was waiting in the hedge to collect the weapons. The Staff Sergeant swung the car round and stopped the width of the road from the gunmen. Jay wound down his window and opened fire with his 9mm. They had had enough. They sped away, throwing their gloves, masks and articles of clothing out of the windows as they went. The man in the hedge ran off across the fields, leaving the Armalite at the roadside. Jay ordered up one of the patrols, a major search was mounted, the Armalite recovered and the man who had run away over the fields arrested. The other four got away. Jay was awarded a Queen's Gallantry Medal.

Within their own areas the soldiers and the terrorist families were not strangers to each other; they were not to either side an abstract 'enemy'. Some were neighbours. Some, like Nethercott, had socialized in their youth before the troubles began. Kevin Toolis asked a Sinn Fein councillor if "he had ever had a casual conversation with his enemy, his neighbour. 'No,' he said, 'I have never spoken to them. You bump into them in Cookstown on Saturday if you are out shopping with the wife and kids. They could be standing next to you in a supermarket queue. I have been that close to them but they would not say anything. You look at them and they look at you'."[1]

It was the business of the full-time platoons in particular to know all about the suspects in their operational area. In time an uneasy relationship developed between soldier and suspect. "We would pass the time of day with them," a platoon commander explained.

"I remember once I was searching this car that belonged to an IRA fellow that I knew well, when I found a £5 note under the back seat. I gave it to him and he said, 'Thanks very much'. He was one of the 'godfathers'. One time I was sitting on the wall of this house that belonged to a well known Republican family, waiting for the son to come home. I saw him coming down the lane, and he jumped up beside me and said, 'How are you doing, pal?' I gave him a cigarette and we were sitting having a smoke when his mother came out; she was a real bad woman, she didn't like us at all. The son was a real up and coming gunman. He's doing time now. He had killed people.

And there I was sitting beside him, giving him a cigarette. I like to think we gained a little respect when we talked to them like that, but I am not sure. It made you aware certainly. They got to know us, probably knew our names rightly. But there's no doubt about it, they would have shot you if they got the chance."

As a further measure to protect UDR soldiers who came under particular threat, arrangements were made for NCOs from the Security Section to carry out a survey of the home, recommending what should be done to make the house more secure. Funds were available for the installation of devices such as bolts on outer doors, external lighting and blinds. Those with telephones were advised to make sure their numbers were 'ex-directory'.[2]

At times these security surveys showed a lack of understanding of life in Northern Ireland. It was not that individuals were careless about their own safety, but what they were not prepared to do was to change the whole pattern of their lives. The same sense of responsibility that had persuaded them to enlist in the Regiment meant that many were leaders within their own community, farmer's co-operative, political party, church, lodge, councils, villages committees, and as such they lived public lives. To have given up these responsibilities and adopt a lower profile would, they believed, have been another kind of surrender to terrorism.

Despite the inroads being made into their organizations as a result of the supergrass system, both PIRA and INLA remained in business. The Provisionals continued to mount simultaneous multiple Province-wide car-bomb attacks. In July an ASU operating in London carried out two attacks that caused particular revulsion. The detachment of the Household Cavalry was making its daily ride from the barracks to Knightsbridge to take over the guard in Whitehall. At Hyde Park a radio-controlled bomb made up of gelignite packed around with nails exploded at the side of the road. The results were devastating. Three soldiers died, including the subaltern of the guard and the standard bearer. Seven of the horses were killed and others, people and horses, injured. Two hours later another bomb exploded under the bandstand in Regent's Park as the band of the Royal Green Jackets, stationed at Aldergrove, was playing selections from 'Oliver' whilst the audience sat around in deck chairs. Eight more soldiers died. In all fifty-one soldiers and civilians had been injured in the two attacks. In December two members of the INLA carried a bomb into the Drop-in-Well Inn outside the gates of the base at Ballykelly. It exploded beside a pillar, bringing the concrete floor of a supermarket on the first floor crashing down on the crowded disco. Another eleven soldiers died, with four girls and a youth; of the sixty-six injured, twenty-five were soldiers.

In April 3UDR mounted the first of its joint operations with the minesweeper HMS *Cygnet*. The search teams embarked in Dundrum Bay and were ferried out in the Battalion's dories to the warship lying off shore. *Cygnet* then sailed through the Narrows into Strangford Lough and put the search teams ashore on Castle Island. From there they were lifted from island to island in a Royal Navy Wessex, their deployment controlled from a tactical headquarters established on the ship's bridge, manned by members of the Battalion operations room staff. The complicated operation went without a hitch, the sea calm and the day bright, and by the end of it twenty-one of the islands along the western shore of the lough had been searched.

It had gone so well that the Battalion decided to mount a second operation in June and invited the Brigade Commander, Brigadier Michael Hobbs, to join in. This time the plan was to put teams ashore to search the abandoned village at Sheepland, north of Ardglass, and Guns Island off Ballyhornan. Nothing went right. The plan was as before, to embark the search teams in the inner bay at Dundrum and ferry them out to *Cygnet* lying off shore. A force four wind was blowing, the dories had a rough ride and the transfer to the decks of the ship as she rolled in the heavy swell was not easy. After the tactical headquarters, along with the CO, Charles Ritchie, the Brigade Commander and two search teams had been embarked, the ship's Gemini broke down and had to be towed back to *Cygnet* behind one of the dories, Ritchie making pointed remarks to the Captain about the Army having to rescue the Navy at sea. The weather was deteriorating, the swell turning to white caps, whilst the RAF Regiment patrols tasked to cover the landings from the shore had been diverted to intercept an armed gang who had rammed a car belonging to the manager of a Ballynahinch bank and made off with the money he was taking to a branch in Saintfield. After one more lift had been completed the decision was taken to send the remaining search teams round by road and *Cygnet* set sail, the dories lashed to the stern and all but swamped in her wake. The Brigade Major was huddled in a corner of the deck, looking ill, and below deck a soldier had been so sick that he had sat on a fire extinguisher, setting it off, vomit and foam slopping over the floor. A steward served soup; the First Lieutenant poured wine; the glass shot off the end of the table. As the sea was now too rough to put the teams ashore under the black rocks of Sheepland Harbour, *Cygnet* hove to in the relatively calm waters between Gun's Island and Ballyhornan village. The engine of one of the dories refused to start, then became detached from its mounting and would have sunk to the bottom if the coxswain had not hung on to it. One engine in the second dory failed, leaving just one engine between the two to ferry the search teams across to the island. The Brigade Major was finally sick over the rail. Before *Cygnet* went on her way, her task done, the Captain asked if the Battalion had any more operations planned. He was too polite to say so, but the implication was that, if there were, he would make sure his ship was in other waters. The search teams were landed on shore and then ferried across to the island, where there was a final, unseen complication. It was the height of the nesting season. The huge gull colony took flight, wheeling and screeching overhead, leaving their eggs to go cold and the fledglings floundering pathetically in the grass, so many that it was hard to avoid stepping on them. The search was brought to a rapid conclusion.

Throughout the Brigadier remained remarkably good humoured.

> "'Let it be clearly understood,' he wrote to Ritchie, 'that I thoroughly enjoyed my day, and my only sadness was that my enjoyment was not shared by all my staff and most of your Battalion. It was great fun and I would love to come again (whatever the weather). Incidentally it was a pleasure to see someone as competent as your coxswain trying to negate the inexorable progress of Murphy's Law'."[3]

Swatragh is a village on the main road south from Coleraine, halfway between Garvagh and Maghera. For many years back it has had the reputation of being a troublesome place and there had been several occasions in the present troubles when patrols driving through had come under fire. On the night of 8 November a multiple mobile patrol composed of two vehicles from the Coleraine Company commanded by a Sergeant and four from the Garvagh Platoon were being briefed in the platoon base in Garvagh before setting out to patrol the Draperstown area. It was an important night, as the CLF, General Chiswell, accompanied by the new UDR Commander, Brigadier Peter Graham, was visiting the Battalion. The officer in charge of the Garvagh base had looked in to make sure all was well before going on to Magherafelt for duty in the South Derry operations room. Chiswell and Graham sat in on the briefing. The General warned the patrols that the senior South Derry Provisional, Seamus Kearney, a Swatragh man on the run and wanted for at least two murders, was believed to be back in the area. The General and the Brigadier went on ahead down the road to Magherafelt whilst the patrol prepared to follow, the two Coleraine vehicles leading, the Garvagh four following a few minutes later, and their officer, accompanied by the Battalion second-in-command, bringing up the rear in a civilian car, with boiler suits over their uniforms and their SLRs in the boot.

The Coleraine group had passed through Swatragh village and was about to cross the bridge on the southern side when it came under fire. The patrol took cover, put up flares and engaged the gunmen. The second group was just entering the north side of the village when the Sergeant in the leading vehicle saw the flares. Hurriedly he deployed his men to cover the other entrance to the village. The firing had died down and all was quiet. Then suddenly the members of the patrol, observing through their night sights, saw a figure cross the road in front of them and disappear into the yard of the 'Rafters' Bar'. The two officers, following up behind the patrols, had also seen the flares. They pulled up behind the Coleraine group, checked that no one had been hurt, though a round had blown off the end of a soldier's rifle, and sent back a Landrover to block off the front entrance into the bar and prevent the customers leaving. The

Garvagh men had cordoned off the back. Some of them went into the yard to search for this lone man but failed to find him. One stayed behind in the yard to keep watch. He was standing up on a shed, having a quiet smoke, when he noticed an open door into a narrow passage between two buildings, which he was sure had been closed when they had searched the yard. He called the Sergeant and together they pulled out a man hiding inside. He gave a false name and address, but a member of a police patrol that had now arrived on the scene recognized him as Seamus Kearney. Thanks to the resolute action of the whole patrol, and to the fact that the vehicles had travelled in two separate supporting tactical groups, leading Kearney to assume the coast was clear when he slipped away from the firing point and crossed the road into the yard, they had captured one of the most wanted men in the country.

Meanwhile Chiswell and Graham had just arrived at Magherafelt when they heard the contact report and doubled back on the road towards Swatragh. On the way they met two vehicles coming towards them, travelling fast. Convinced they contained the gunmen making good their escape, the General ordered his driver to turn round and take up the chase. They caught up and overtook, forcing the cars to stop, only to find it was the police taking Kearney away. Not to be done out of a slice of the action, they returned to Swatragh where Graham helped the patrols to locate the firing point. It had been quite a night.[4]

Each new Commander UDR during his two-year tour carried the Regiment further along the road to greater professionalism. Peter Graham, who took over command in May 1982, was no stranger to Northern Ireland. From October 1970 to September 1972 he had served as Brigade Major, the senior staff appointment, in 39 Brigade. He returned to the Province the following year as Second-in-Command of his battalion, 1 Gordons, on a four-month tour in Andersonstown and Turf Lodge. In 1976 he was back again for a further two years, commanding 1 Gordons, the resident battalion in Palace Barracks, which they shared with 7UDR.

Graham is remembered as the Commander with the Six Points. Soon after his arrival he gave the battalions a list of six principles that all soldiers were to learn by heart. To make sure they had done so, when he visited companies he would ask the men and women to repeat them. One battalion had them printed on labels for the soldiers to stick inside their berets. Once when visiting a patrol he saw a figure silhouetted against the night sky repeatedly taking off his beret and holding it over his head. "It's your six points, sir," the soldier explained. "I knew you'd be asking me what they were. I have them here in my beret, but it's too bloody dark to read them."

There are still old soldiers who remember them:

Pride, in the Regiment and in the appearance and bearing of the individual.
Alertness, on operations and off duty.

Discipline, acting within the law, and having the self-discipline to keep going when cold, wet and tired.

Fitness. "Fit people recover more quickly from injuries."

Shooting, including the ability to engage a fleeting target. "If you fail on the few occasions when you are asked to do that, then all your training has been a waste of time."

Cooperation, with the Regular Army, the police and the civilian population.

Cooperation was also about improving the image of the Regiment.

It became apparent that INLA based in Newry were planning to assassinate a member of the security forces living in the Mourne area. To counter the threat 3UDR mounted an operation to deploy VCPs for up to eighteen hours a day on at least two of the three roads into Mourne. They maintained the operation for six months. Frustrated in their efforts to mount an attack, the INLA members began deliberate harassment of the patrols in the hope that the soldiers would lose their patience, leading to a fracas and eventually to the withdrawals of the VCPs. "It is to the absolute credit of the Mourne men," Williams, the CO, wrote, "who do not take harassment easily, that they maintained their cool, behaved impeccably and, with the RUC, dealt with many awkward incidents." In the end it was one of the trouble-makers who lost her temper and was charged and found guilty of assaulting a UDR Sergeant and a Greenfinch. Thereafter this particular harassment ceased.[5]

Graham believed there was a need to make a greater effort to sell the image of the Regiment through the media. The policy of restricting publicity about the Army, including the UDR, in favour of the RUC had gone too far. It may have made sense for the rest of the Army, but there was a feeling within the Regiment that the efforts of the soldiers, the extremely long hours of duty and their hazardous way of life, constantly at risk, were not receiving the recognition they deserved from the public. When Charles Moore, then a correspondent and now editor of the *Daily Telegraph*, asked permission to visit the UDR as the basis for one of a series of articles he was writing on life in the Province, it seemed like an ideal opportunity to publicize the Regiment in one of the most prestigious national papers. Moore's visit was sanctioned by the staff at Lisburn only after several days' delay and with seeming reluctance. Naturally Moore became aware of this and he ended his article by saying, "The UDR is an organization that any politician should be proud to foster; a force of law deeply rooted in the people. Yet it is no thanks to the politicians that it is a success."[6]

In 1984 the Central Office of Information, acting on behalf of the UDR, commissioned a commercial consumer research organization to carry out a survey of attitudes to the Regiment among members of the public, with a view to establishing what type of advertisement would be most effective in attracting recruits. The results of the survey showed that

Graham was right to be concerned. They made depressing reading. The UDR, the survey concluded, was not held in the highest esteem among the general public; they could not see whether, or how, it contributed to the security of the Province; the officers were believed to be predominantly Englishmen drawn from the Regular Army and the soldiers from lower grade, unskilled members of the working class with poor educational attainments. Clearly the UDR was failing to sell itself and the policy of minimizing publicity in the media and of failing to accredit their successes was harming the image of the Regiment.[7]

Another problem Graham had identified, as had his predecessors, was the need to improve the standard of training. He found that the soldiers were well trained in the basic skills, but constant repetition of the same tasks had led to a degree of sloppiness. A further increase in the part-timers' bounty, bringing it up to £500 for third-year soldiers, provided an opportunity to apply more rigorous qualifications. In future the soldiers must complete twenty-two days training each year, fire their weapons test and an alternative weapons test and pass one or the other, pass an internal security test and, in the case of WUDR, a first aid test, complete a basic fitness test and attend four lectures given by an RUC officer. From now on annual camps would include a 24-hour battalion exercise incorporating the kind of situations that patrols could expect to encounter on operations back home.

The compulsory attendance at RUC lectures was a recognition by Graham of the need to improve understanding between the police and the UDR. The lectures carried out by a RUC training team were well received, but it was unfortunate that there was no reciprocal arrangement, for the failure of the police to understand the UDR was more marked than the reverse.

The difficult relationship between the Chief Constable and the GOC that had existed at the end of the '70s was now all in the past, but lower down relationships between some sub-divisions and their supporting battalions were not always as harmonious as they should have been. There was a feeling that the police were over-estimating their ability to cope alone. Policemen were not like soldiers. They did not think like soldiers. They were not and never could be substitutes for soldiers. By taking the lead in security they did not become the Army in a different uniform. They had their own way of working; it was not the Army way. As a first principle the concept of command was entirely different.

The RUC could carry out road checks, though they had a much softer approach than the Army's VCP. To the Army they seemed almost too casual, committing the kind of mistakes that would have resulted in a patrol commander being disciplined – inadequate warning signs, cover sentries standing in the open instead of deploying in a fire position to protect the other members of the patrol. Some things the police could not do, except for the highly trained members of E4. They could not carry out cross-country patrols or lurks or live out on the ground. Hours of duty were dictated by the need to be back at the station at fixed times for the change over of shifts. Officers at sub-divisional level had little appreciation of the staff work involved in laying on a military operation. Battalions, instead of being given a general aim and being left to task their patrols to achieve that aim, would find the police tasking individual patrols. Such tasking tended to be unimaginative, not deeply thought out on the basis of a military intelligence appreciation, defensive rather than offensive. There was little understanding of the need for detailed planning and a slow, deliberate approach in carrying out an operation to clear a suspected device. There was on occasions a lack of clear demarcation between the two forces. On occupied house searches an experienced UDR search team, trained at RSME to carry out very specific procedures, would find themselves detailed to provide the cordon whilst an untrained DMSU carried out the search.

If soldiers are to search thoroughly they need to be encouraged by the enthusiasm of the briefer, by being given as much information as possible and by an assurance that there is a good chance of success. 3UDR historical record describes a search operation that illustrates the irritations involved in working with the police when police officers tried to assume the role of the military. It was to be a joint search with the police, directed by an Inspector. The Battalion provided four patrols, the DMSU three. The account goes on:

"The Inspector in charge never turned up, nor ever explained why. The DMSUs arrived under-strength by one patrol, without maps, air photographs or lunch. A Sergeant of Special Branch gave an uninspiring intelligence brief. In the absence of the Inspector the Battalion had to take over the operation, with the RSM, who had attended a Search Adviser's course, controlling it on the ground. He returned late in the afternoon, fuming. Whilst our soldiers had searched as thoroughly as possible an area that was far too large for them to cover in detail, and in the process found a sack containing silver stolen from the Parochial House, he reported that the DMSUs had not even tried. Most of them, including the Inspector and the Sergeants, had never received any such training. At one stage the sole policewoman had had to be taken in a patrol car some two miles back to the RUC station to go to the toilet, declining the offer of one of the Greenfinches to show her how they managed by going behind a bush. At 2 pm the Inspector declared they had done enough and they all went home. Our teams searched for another two hours until they had finished their sectors."[8]

Fortunately the friendships that had been forged over the years between the Battalion officers and Divisional and Sub-Divisional Commanders and their Inspectors were strong enough to keep these irritations within bounds, and with time the problem was largely resolved. Invitations for parties of four police officers, both men and women, to accompany their local battalion to annual camp, live in the messes and take part in the training and social activities proved particularly successful. Joint study days were organized and increasingly DMSU's took part in the multiple VCP operations.

With this increasing confidence in the RUC that in some areas they could cope on their own, it was time to tackle the perennial problem, that the UDR recruited best in the mainly Protestant areas where the need for them was least. Large companies in these quiet areas were told to go easy on recruiting more part-time soldiers. Conversely companies in dangerous areas, who needed all the men they could get, had to be advised to be careful about accepting recruits who would be at unacceptable risk. Though part-time platoons from quiet areas continued to reinforce the hard-pressed battalions at weekends, it was not possible to move individual part-time soldiers from one side of the Province to the other, but permanent cadre soldiers could be moved. By April 1982 there were 455 permanent cadre soldiers in the two Antrim battalions covering the most peaceful area of the Province. Yet 8UDR, the weakest battalion, responsible for the area of highest terrorist activity in East Tyrone, had only 164 permanent cadre, and 2UDR, the second weakest and always under pressure in Armagh, 184. Accordingly during 1983 the decision was taken to increase the permanent cadre establishment of the battalions in the areas of greatest threat and to fill these posts with full-time soldiers from the quiet battalions. There were problems in doing so. Regular soldiers could have been posted without further ado, but UDR soldiers lived at home and many, particularly the NCOs, owned their own houses. For those who opted to live in barracks in their new battalions rather than commute, in some cases from one side of the country to the other, there was only limited barrackroom accommodation. For all that, the moves were effected with little fuss. By August the new arrangements had come into effect and ninety soldiers had been transferred, including a complete formed platoon from 9UDR to 2UDR.

However, the MOD considered that more drastic measures could be taken in addition to this redistribution of manpower. In the light of the reducing terrorist threat and the increased confidence of the police, there was, the Ministry considered, no longer a need for all eleven battalions of the UDR. Soon after taking up command, Graham was summoned to HQNI to be told by the GOC that he was under pressure from London to reduce the size of the Regiment by at least two and possibly three battalions. Graham was to carry out a review in great secrecy, consulting only with Baxter, the Colonel Commandant, and Faulkner, who by then had been promoted into the newly created post of Regimental Colonel. He produced a paper in his own hand, giving their recommendations. The first was obvious enough – clearly there was no need for two battalions in County Antrim. 1 and 9UDR could be amalgamated without any loss of efficiency, indeed it would lead to greater operational effectiveness as the boundaries of the new battalion would coincide with the new boundaries of RUC divisions due to come into effect in the autumn. By taking over the Ballymoney Company from 1UDR, 5UDR's TAOR would extend east of the Bann to cover North Antrim, coinciding with the new RUC K Division and bridging the intelligence gap across the river.

The second amalgamation, the two city battalions, 7 and 10UDR, was not so straightforward. An amalgamated battalion would be the largest in the whole of the Army, and not only its size but the role of military commander for Greater Belfast, (excluding the west and a small part of the north of the city that were to remain the responsibility of Regular battalions) would place a heavy burden on the Commanding Officer.

The amalgamation of 1 and 9UDR took place on 20 May 1984 with a parade in Ballymena and the salute taken by the GOC. Battalion headquarters of 9UDR in Antrim became the headquarters of the new battalion, with companies based at Antrim, Ballymena, Larne and Carrickfergus. The companies at Ballymoney and Lisburn were transferred to 5 and 11UDR respectively, and the 5UDR platoon base at Garvagh was handed over to the RUC. 7 and 10UDR's amalgamation parade took place at Palace Barracks on 14 October of the same year. Battalion Headquarters remained at Windsor Park on the Malone Road, with two companies based there, three remaining in Holywood, and others at Girdwood Park and Ladas Drive. In all 7/10UDR had on that day, 1,425 all ranks on its strength, including 475 permanent cadre and 156 Greenfinches.

The amalgamations made available about a hundred permanent cadre posts and these were redistributed to other battalions to enable them to fill their new establishments, approved that spring, regularizing the creation of permanent cadre companies of three platoons and at last giving all battalions an adequate daytime capacity.

Increased daytime patrolling called for increased administrative back-up. The days when soldiers came on duty with a packet of sandwiches and a thermos of tea made up by their spouses were past. From now on battalions that did not have access to a Regular Army dining hall had to feed their soldiers, and a special course was set up at the Army School of Catering to train UDR cooks. Despite these increases, the administrative staff of a UDR battalion remained substantially smaller than in a Regular battalion. Though this was another reason why the UDR was so cost-effective, the problem of lack of staff became acute as Regular sub-units were taken under command. Had it not been for the dedication of quarter-masters, administrative officers, cooks, mechanics, storemen and clerical staff, the administrative back-up for the soldiers deployed on operations would have broken down.

In July 1982 the Prime Minister announced in the House of Commons that the Queen had approved the introduction of two new awards for the Ulster Defence Regiment, the Long Service and Good Conduct Medal (UDR) for permanent cadre soldiers and the Ulster Defence (UD) Medal for all part-timers, both officers and soldiers. The former was based on the LSGC awarded to the Regular soldiers, and the qualifications were the same, fifteen years full-time service and a clean Regimental conduct sheet. The qualifications for the UD Medal were more controversial, for they were tied closely to the long service medals awarded to the Territorial Army, though there was little similarity between the life of the peacetime Territorial and that of the UDR on operations, apart from the fact that both were volunteers. In fact the qualifications for the UD Medal as they were originally drafted had nothing to do with conditions of service in Northern Ireland. The officer or soldier was required to have served part-time for twelve years, passed his annual range course in the case of the men, and attended annual camp or a course in lieu.

Although a number of people had already completed the requisite service by the time the awards were announced, it was soon apparent that few filled all the qualifications. There were several anomalies. For instance, permanent cadre service could not count towards the qualifying period. As a result a part-time soldier who transferred to permanent cadre – and many of the soldiers who did so transferred because they had come under threat in their civilian jobs – would have to serve a further fifteen years before becoming eligible for the LSGC. It was therefore possible for a soldier to serve the full twenty-two years of the UDR's existence, eleven part-time and eleven on the permanent cadre, and at the end have nothing to show that he had served in the Regiment at all. The main stumbling block was attendance at annual camp. It was understandable that a member of the TA should be required to attend to qualify for the Territorial Medal, for camp was the high point of the Territorials' training year, but there were good security reasons why part-time soldiers of the UDR were unable to do so, at least not every year – reluctance to leave his family on their own under threat, for example, or to ask an employer for time off. Eventually it was recognized that the requirement to attend annual camp at that time was impractical and 'emergency' conditions were introduced whereby the part-timer had only to complete fifty operational or administrative duties each year. For each additional six years the part-timer qualified for a clasp.

The most unfortunate anomaly was that whilst the part-time officers and soldiers could qualify for the UD Medal and the permanent cadre soldiers for the LSGC(UDR), the permanent cadre officer received nothing to show he had ever served in the Regiment. Attempts to change the qualifications so that they would be eligible and for permanent cadre service to count towards either award were continued for the next eight years. Discussions in the MOD took place up to Defence Secretary level and the Prime Minister was asked privately to intervene. It was accepted that the original decision to tie the UD Medal to voluntary service on the lines of the TA without taking into account the operational service of the UDR in Northern Ireland had been a mistake. But in the end the qualifications remained unchanged, mainly on the grounds that the part-timers were at far greater risk than the permanent cadre. So far as the casualty figures were concerned this was irrefutable. All of the officers and 80% of the soldiers killed by terrorists action were part-time. In all 429 permanent cadre soldiers received the LSGC(UDR), making it an unusually rare medal which one day will be eagerly sought after by collectors. Up to February 1996 1226 UD Medals had been awarded, though this is not the final figure as a few ex-soldiers are still coming forward who resigned without applying for the medal.

In 1983 ten members of the Regiment were murdered, twice as many as the Regular Army, but only half the number of fatalities sustained by the RUC. There were seven attacks on patrols, resulting in four dead and five wounded, and twenty-one attacks on off-duty soldiers, leaving six dead and ten wounded. Under-vehicle booby traps killed two serving and one ex-serving member, and seriously wounded a third.

Early on the morning of 13 July a convoy of five Landrovers from 6UDR was preparing to set out for Ballykinlar to spend a day on the ranges. The soldiers were late and in a hurry to get away. There was a last-minute problem with radios. There had to be one at each end of the convoy, but the rear vehicle had been issued without one. It was moved up to the middle of the convoy and Corporal Harron's Landrover took its place. In such chance circumstances are some men's fate sealed whilst others are spared. In London that day the Commons was due to debate a motion proposing the reintroduction of the death penalty for six categories of murder including terrorist killings.

The convoy was about to begin the long descent of the hill down to Ballygawley when there was a massive explosion.

"It was awful. We did not know what had happened," one soldier recalled. "We stopped and saw it was the rear vehicle that had been hit. We took up cover positions and some of us went back to the vehicle to see what way we could help them. We could see three bodies in the vehicle, Neely with his elbow stuck out of the window. He always drove that way. The two tanks of petrol under the front seats had caught fire and the rounds of ammunition had begun to explode in the heat. We knew there was nothing we could do."

One of the soldiers, John Roxborough, had been standing up in the hatch. The explosion had blown him out of the vehicle onto the roadside. A doctor from the Republic who happened to be passing stopped to treat him. He was still conscious, but died in the helicopter on the way to hospital.

In all four soldiers had been killed – Corporal Tom Harron, Privates Oswald Neely, Ron Alexander and John Roxborough. Harron was 25 years old, married with a two-and-a-half-year-old daughter; Neely, 20, married with a daughter of four months; Alexander and Roxborough both single and 19. Fortunately all four were members of ADAT, the Army Dependents Assurance Trust, a military life insurance scheme by which for a small monthly premium the next of kin of any soldier who died in service would receive a monthly income until such time as he would have reached his 55th birthday. Most members of the UDR were persuaded to join the scheme.

The Commons sat late that evening and rejected, by a substantial majority, the death penalty for any form of murder. It was a wise decision; all through its history Ireland has cherished its martyrs.

Five weeks after the landmine 6UDR lost another soldier. Corporal Ronnie Finlay of Sion Mills was leaving his place of work in Strabane when two men on a motorcycle came up from behind his car and opened fire at him at very close range as other employees from the factory dived for cover. Finlay was one of five brothers who had served in the Castlederg Company. Two of them were still serving. One, the Company Sergeant Major, organized his brother's funeral.

On 9 March a Captain and his two sons, a Sergeant and a Corporal, all three serving in 3UDR, were driving home from work along the Annsborough–Spa road in the Corporal's car. He had stopped at the T-junction at Drumnaquoile when he noticed two hooded men across the hedge on the other side of the road, about ten yards away. Shouting a warning to his father and brother, he ducked down under the dashboard. Almost simultaneously the vehicle was struck by automatic fire and the windscreen and rear windows disintegrated. The car stalled on the opposite verge, a few feet from the gunmen, who continued to pump a whole magazine of twenty rounds into the vehicle whilst the three men lay helpless inside. Miraculously their injuries were not severe. The father was hit twice in each hand and arm, the Corporal once in the hand. The Sergeant in the back seat was unharmed. When the firing ceased the two sons managed to get their father out of the car and help him across the road into the shelter of a bank. Meanwhile the two gunmen ran down the road towards a get-away car, stolen from a nearby farm a few minutes before the ambush. The Corporal ran out into the road to identify the car, and then, although he was unarmed, ran shouting towards the gunmen, hoping to scare them off. He had almost reached them when the man with the Armalite knelt down and took aim at him. The Corporal dived into the garden of a cottage. The gunman, evidently unnerved by this unexpected reaction, sped away up the road. Their car was found abandoned up in the hills. For some reason, probably to give them a field of fire, the gunmen had broken the back window and fragments of glass were found in another car belonging to a leading member of Castlewellan PIRA. He was charged with attempted murder and possession of firearms. The evidence proved too flimsy to sustain a conviction, but a dangerous terrorist had meanwhile been put out of circulation for several months.

The Corporal was awarded the Queen's Gallantry Medal. None of the three was carrying their PPWs at the time, a particular irony, for all three were members of the Battalion shooting team and the two brothers had won several prizes at Bisley the previous year. Three weeks after the ambush the Sergeant had an accident with his pistol, causing severe injury to his thigh. It was the final irony; the only member of the family to escape the ambush uninjured ended up with more serious injuries than the gunmen had been able to inflict on the other two.[9]

Three weeks after the ambush three men took over a house opposite the police station in Castlewellan. While one guarded the occupants of the house, a woman and four children, the other two took up fire positions at an upstairs window and waited for the reserve constable who was due to give evidence at the trial. One man fired at his car while the other engaged the sangar sentry, but neither policeman was hit. In the following week 3UDR carried out intensive searches in and around the town, including houses belonging to the family of the arrested man, while the family's private warning signal sounded on the roof of their establishment along the main street. A revolver was found down the back of a chair in a bar, but it was impossible to say who owned it. Of the Castlewellan Armalite which had first been used in the town five years ago there was no sign.

Down on the Fermanagh border a patrol from the Lisnaskea company received a report of suspicious activity on the Inishfendra Island opposite Crom Castle, the isolated home of the Earl of Erne. On crossing over to the island they discovered a party of German tourists in the act of loading a 300-year-old cannon onto a specially constructed trolley before hauling it down to their cabin cruiser. When asked what they were doing, none of the party understood English. The patrol sent for the Earl. When he arrived at the scene they asked him what they should do. "Shoot them," the Earl suggested. Suddenly the visitors could speak English. They explained that they had found the cannon on a holiday the previous year and, thinking it had been abandoned, had returned with their home-made trolley to collect it. The Earl persuaded them to move the cannon across to the castle where it is now displayed in the Visitors' Centre. In 1689 James II's forces advancing into the North had attempted to lay seige to Crom as a preliminary to clearing the way to Enniskillen, but the Jacobite cavalry lost their way amongst the loughs and islands and were defeated. The cannon had probably belonged to the defenders of Crom.[10]

On 10 May three foot patrols of 2UDR were patrolling in the general area of St Patrick's Catholic Cathedral in Armagh when a grenade was thrown at one of the patrols from the cathedral grounds. The commander saw it coming and shouted a warning. It exploded between him and the leading man. Though wounded in the legs the Corporal radioed a contact report before running across to his injured comrade and dragging him to safety. The other patrols had been able to react swiftly, cordoning off the cathedral grounds. One of the soldiers had seen a man running into the cathedral itself. The police were called and, with the ready agreement of the cathedral authorities, carried out a search, but found no one. The patrol was adamant that they had seen a man run inside and that he must still be there. The police looked again and did find a man, hiding in a confessional. He was arrested but remained silent and, since there was no proof that he had thrown the grenade, he had to be released.

On 21 September 7UDR received a report from the RUC that an armed robbery had just taken place at the Bank of Ireland on the Ballygowan Road. Two men had escaped on a stolen motorcycle which they had abandoned in a nearby estate. A patrol was sent to the estate, commanded by a Private. He questioned people in the area and learnt that two men had been seen to run into a particular house. The patrol put out a cordon and sent for the police, who entered the house and found the two men, along with a loaded shotgun and revolver. The latter had been used in the murder of two Catholics and a member of the UDA in East Belfast. A Battalion search team arrived to carry out a detailed search and recovered £7,000 in notes. As a result the two men were charged with the bank robbery that day, two others with an earlier robbery at a different bank and a fifth with an attack on the house of the sister of a Protestant supergrass. The patrol's prompt reaction and persistence had resulted in the rounding up of a complete UVF cell. Four days later during a major search operation covering some 8 square miles of quarry country south of the Cookstown to Omagh road, set up by 8UDR and involving permanent cadre and part-time companies and Regulars from the attached company of the Cheshires, the part-time soldiers found 1950lbs of home-made explosives, packed in fifty-four bags.

The 25th of September was a typically quiet Sunday at the end of a relatively quiet summer. Many of the battalion officers were returning home from a Regimental dinner held in the Royal Artillery Officers' Mess at Woolwich on the Friday night. At five minutes past four the Brigade ordered the implementation of two of the preplanned VCP operations, followed a few minutes later by a phone message to the effect that a major break-out had taken place at the Maze. The escape had been meticulously planned under the direction of Brendan McFarlane who had taken over as prisoners' leader from Bobby Sands. Part of the plan was to persuade a number of relatively unimportant prisoners to join the escape without briefing them on the details, knowing that they would distract the pursuers while they milled around outside the prison, allowing the hard-core Provisionals to get clean away. Six handguns had been smuggled in, fitted with silencers. Armed with these and home-made knives, the escapees climbed into a lorry that had brought supplies to the prison and passed safely through the first two security gates, but then encountered a group of prison officers coming on duty. One of the officers drove his car across the main gate, blocking the lorry's escape. Fierce fighting broke out, shots were exchanged and six officers were stabbed, one of whom died, though subsequent diagnosis showed that he probably died from a heart attack. In all thirty-eight prisoners escaped, the largest break-out in British prison history, some on foot across country, others by hijacking cars. By nightfall sixteen had been recaptured. The remainder had gone. Particulars of six vehicles were radioed to battalions. In 3UDR four patrols immediately available were tasked to man the preplanned VCPs. Four hours later the RUC activated for the first time their new Province-wide VCP operation.

From the first, attention was focused on 3UDR's TAOR. The VCPs remained in position all night, hampered by fog. By first light the following morning arrangements had been made to close the escape route round the southern side of the Mournes by deploying five more road blocks in a line from the Banbridge–Castlewellan road to Newcastle, three from 3UDR, one from the RUC and one jointly manned. They remained in position continuously for the next nine days while the Royal Navy guard ship kept a radar and dory patrol watch over Carlingford Lough and later a second ship took up station off Kilkeel. By mid-morning the police reported that they had picked up two of the escapees walking along a lonely road to the north of Castlewellan. Within an hour a car, one of those hijacked by the escapees, was found abandoned at the entrance to Castlewellan Forest Park. From then until last light 3UDR searched the forest with a company of the Devons and Dorsets (D and D) under command, four RUC tracker dogs and an airborne reaction force from the Duke of Edinburgh's Royal Regiment (1DERR) overhead, while two DMSUs searched traced houses north and west of the town and deployed an outer cordon. By the third day it was reckoned that any escapees who had failed to slip through the net would have gone to ground and the decision was taken to check all the holiday homes and caravan parks from Ardglass to Annalong. This was a mammoth task, lasting for several days and involving 3UDR with the D and D company still under command, and one DMSU. On the afternoon of the third day it was learnt that two men had taken over an isolated farmhouse on the Leitrim Road north of Castlewellan and were holding the owners hostage, a widow and her daughter. A major operation was immediately mounted to close off the area and surround the house, 3UDR, the D and D company and a DMSU providing the outer cordon and a second DMSU and RUC Special Support Unit the inner. At first the two men refused to surrender, but after the RUC had sent for a local parish priest they agreed to come out. One had been the OC of Londonderry PIRA and both had been sentenced for the murder of members of the UDR.

Of the twenty-two who had got clean away in the initial panic, only the four around Castlewellan were picked up. Eighteen had made good their escape. Some left the organization and began a new life abroad under assumed names. Others resumed their activities and subsequently three were killed. Others were extradited, among them McFarlane from Holland. The escape was a huge boost to Republican morale at a time when the Provisionals were reeling from the supergrass arrests.

Throughout, 3UDR had continued to meet its routine operational tasks, protecting the Lord Chief Justice, who was involved in a supergrass trial at the time, clearing the routes into Ballykinlar, guarding the ammunition sub-depot and company bases, and still found time to win the Army Golf Championship.[11]

Such a level of operations could never have been maintained if the part-time soldiers had not been available by night and at weekends to relieve the permanent cadre patrols. Over the eleven-day period the part-time soldiers had carried out on average between three and four duties by every man and woman in the Battalion. For all ranks it was a time of long hours spent out on the ground.

Another ten UDR soldiers were killed in 1984, bringing the total to 147 by the end of the year. 6UDR had suffered particularly heavily. By July, of the seventeen murdered in the previous twelve months, ten had belonged to that Battalion. Once again the first person to be killed by the Provisionals, the first death in the Province in the New Year, was a member of the Regiment, Private Robert Elliott of 6UDR, shot outside his house in Castlederg.

The commander of one of the Ballykinlar companies worked in the headquarters of the Blood Transfusion Service in Durham Street, close to the Westlink and overlooked by the high-rise Divis flats. On the morning of 19 March he was parking his car in the back yard when he saw men crouched down in a firing position. They fired three shots at him and missed. He ran towards the back entrance into the Blood Transfusion building, while one of the men ran across to cut him off. They jostled in the doorway, and the man fired two shots, hitting him twice. The company commander struck the man a heavy blow in the chest and ran up the corridor. The second man followed him, firing as he went, and shot him twice more. He realized that one of the rounds had passed right through his body and saw it shatter a telephone on the opposite wall. He collapsed in the office, still conscious, and told a member of the staff to call a doctor and ambulance. An ambulance driver, who was transporting two elderly patients, heard the emergency call over the radio, went straight to the headquarters, put the wounded officer in the back beside the alarmed old people and took him to the RVH. Gerry Adams, wounded in an ambush in the city the week previously (and treated with blood from the Blood Transfusion Unit), was just leaving the RVH with his bodyguard. The police grabbed the Sinn Fein men by the collars and hauled them out of the way. The company commander was placed in the Intensive Care Unit and operated on that afternoon. Although he remained very seriously ill for nearly a week, with four .38 rounds through his chest and a further wound in his left hand, he made a rapid recovery. In less than three weeks he had been discharged from the Royal and visited the Battalion three weeks to the day after the shooting. By July he reassumed command of his company.[12]

On the Western boundary of Tyrone a salient ten miles deep reaches into Donegal. It is a country of poor land, bog and rushy fields and extensive forest. There are no villages after Killeter at the base of the salient. The Corgary Road, the only road going anywhere, runs the length of the salient from Killeter into Donegal, though the crossing had long been sealed, and on down to Ballybofey. For most of the way it runs a field's length away from the Border. The road was out of bounds to military vehicles, for, overlooked by the high ground on the Republic's side, it was a very vulnerable place. It was also an ideal approach for terrorists crossing over from Donegal to carry out attacks around hard-pressed Castlederg. From time to time foot patrols were landed by helicopter to check out vehicle movements and call at the farmsteads.

On 14 July, a year and a day after the four soldiers from the same battalion had been killed in the Ballygawley landmine, two sections from the Castlederg Company were put down by a Lynx helicopter about half-way along the road. Most of the men and women were unemployed and were being used on part-time/full-time duties. Three were from the same family. A car came up the road and the patrol was checking it out. The Lance Corporal described what happened next.

"I went back to Heather who was reading the map at the time. We were to check a house just opposite and we were looking at the map to make sure that was the house. Heather was sitting behind me. As the car drove away I got up and walked on to start up the foot patrol again. Just as I moved away the explosion went off. All I can remember is this loud explosion. I thought it was never going to stop. I felt stuff against my back. A few seconds passed, the other brick shouted at us. They thought the bombers were in a small planting and they wanted to run down into it but I shouted them back for I thought it was too dangerous, it was so close to the Border [in fact it was just on the other side]. I didn't see anybody, but the others said they had seen someone with a dark jacket at the edge of the planting. The other half of our section ran up towards me and found Heather in the field. They shouted she was still alive. They tried to give her first aid, but I think she was maybe dead at that time. Within minutes the helicopter was there. It took me and Heather to Omagh hospital. Her foot was blew off, and I could see the blood over the floor of the chopper. By chance our clergyman was in the hospital and he came and told me Heather was dead. My lungs had collapsed as a result of the blast. I was in intensive care for, I think, three days and then I was moved to Musgrave Park. I didn't know that Norman McKinley had been killed. He was on the other side of the road from where Heather was sitting, on the side that the bomb was in. They didn't find him at first, he was blew down the field a hundred yards or more. The bomb was dug into the side of the road and the command wire was underground and running into the South. Up to that time it had been quite normal for members of the same family to be on the same patrol. After that it all changed; it's like everything else, everything changes when something happens."

Thereafter instructions were issued that, whenever possible, members of the same family would not be involved in the same patrol and must not travel in the same vehicle or be part of the same half-section on foot patrol.

Lance Corporal Heather Kerrigan was the fourth and last Greenfinch to be killed. Her brother-in-law, Lance Corporal Thomas Loughlin, had been killed four months earlier when a device blew up under his van. Heather had been the bridesmaid at the wedding, Norman McKinley the best man. There is a group wedding photograph. Now all but the bride had been murdered.

Max Arthur, in his book *Northern Ireland Soldiers Talking*, records a conversation with a Greenfinch Corporal, Heather's friend:

"I had just come off stag [duty] one morning at 1000 hours and Heather and I passed each other on the road. We had planned to go out that night with all the other Greenfinches in the company. Their unit was short of one person and Heather had asked me if I would do a double shift and go with them. I said I couldn't as I had been on stag all night. She asked me to go to a shop and get her an outfit for the evening. By the time I got it and arrived home, the word had come over the news that a Greenfinch had been blown up. I knew it was Heather. She was killed instantly. It changed my life completely. Before that, Heather and myself used to go to a lot of car rallies and travel a lot with Catholic and Protestant fellas, but when Heather was killed I saw a different light. I just couldn't understand how people could be so biased. What was the difference between Catholic and Protestant? The day she was killed I blamed every Catholic in the town. It is only now, two years later, that I've come to my senses again, and I don't think everybody is exactly the same. It's the one bunch that is doing it.

"The actual hurting side is gone, but in my mind Heather is always there. If I'm in trouble or if I have a problem, I go out to Heather's grave and sit for ages talking to myself; the comfort of knowing she's there helps. It was an awful blow to me. The night Thomas Loughlin was killed it was the first time Heather and I ever discussed anything about death. We suddenly realized how easy a target you can be in the UDR. The two of us sat that night and talked about what we would do, what we would wear. She wanted Number 2 dress if she ever got killed. I took it down to the morgue the next day."[13]

Fourteen past pupils of Castlederg High School were killed in terrorist attacks – one a Regular soldier, another a policeman, the other twelve members of the UDR.

A permanent cadre solder in 8UDR was one of several who lived close to the border in the neighbourhood of Aughnacloy. On 25 August he and his young wife had gone out to celebrate the birth of their three-week-old daughter, leaving the baby with neighbours. In the early hours they collected the infant, placed her in her carrycot on the back seat and set off for home, three hundred yards up a lonely lane, negotiating a steep hill and a sharp bend. On the far side gunmen opened fire at them, seriously wounding the husband in the back of the head. He fought to keep the car under control, driving on out of the ambush for another 60 yards before he hit a ditch and the car toppled over on its side. Shocked and dazed, Helen, his wife, feeling the blood flowing in the dark and realizing her husband was critically injured managed to get out of the car, leaving the baby on the back seat, and ran quarter of a mile down the road to the nearest house to summon help. She had to pass the ambush site and the gunmen paused in their escape to fire two more shots after her. A part-time Private had been returning home from a patrol when he heard the shots. He warned the RUC and company operations rooms and, waking his brother, the two men, armed with a shotgun and their PPWs, visited other UDR houses in the neighbourhood to establish the location of the shooting. They arrived at the house just after the police. They rendered first aid and saved the soldier's life. Despite the severity of his wounds, he made a complete recovery.

The Stevensons were a well-known Tyrone family who had owned the mill at Moygashel until it was taken over by Courtaulds in the late sixties. In 1974 Harry Stevenson enlisted in 8UDR. His wife, Paddy, was in charge of the Greenfinches and his son had been a Private in the battalion until he was invalided out after he had sustained serious injuries during a land-mine attack on a patrol. In 1977 Harry was asked by the Northern Ireland Development Agency to take over management of the ailing Tyrone Crystal Company in Dungannon and put it on a sound footing. He accepted the task, having received an assurance from East Tyrone PIRA that he would be safe so long as he worked for the company and no longer served in the UDR. By 1980, by which time his assignment to Tyrone Crystal had been successfully completed, he rejoined the Battalion as Second-in-Command. He had come under specific threat in the past and for a few months had been escorted to and from his home. In October '84 he was warned by Special Branch that an attempt was to be made on his life as he was driving to work along the Old Dungannon Road. An SAS team was assigned to his protection. Two members of the team, Corporal Frank Collins and Trooper Al Slater, took up residence in the Stevenson home. For the next two mornings he drove to work in his armour-plated Saab with one of the two escorts lying across the back seat. On the second occasion they were followed by a senior member of East Tyrone PIRA and it seemed probable that the ambush would take place next morning. Stevenson stayed at home while Slater took over the wheel of the Saab and Collins hid under a blanket in the back. The rest of the troop was mounted in a Lancia and a Renault. The plan was for the Lancia to precede the Saab and for the Renault to follow on behind. Two soldiers in uniform concealed themselves on the Tamnamore roundabout where the Coalisland road crosses the motorway, their task to report on any suspicious movement and act as a cut off. The driver of the Renault was 'Andy McNab'. Both he and Collins have included accounts of the operation in their autobiographies describing their experiences in the SAS.[14] The fact that the accounts differ illustrates the confusion that now reigned. The team leader in the Lancia radioed that there was a yellow van behaving suspiciously and that he was going to stop on the far side of the roundabout to cut it off. The Saab continued down the Old Dungannon Road, shadowed by the Renault. The yellow van came suddenly out of a side road and drove on in front of the Saab. Collins described what happened next:

> "The van crawls along. We keep our distance. We have strict instructions not to get closer than 200 metres. My gun is over Al's left shoulder. We expect the lads to respond to our call any minute, but so far we are on our own. The rear windows of the van are blackened and suddenly they move. Plates are dropped down. Inside are the hunched bodies of men holding weapons. We know that this is it. Everything in our bodies, our eyes, our ears, our arms, our toes, every cell is focused on the van in front. Finally the van stops in the middle of the road, indicating that it will turn right into a junction. There is no on-coming traffic and nothing to stop it from turning but it stays in the middle of the road. It is waiting for us to get closer. I imagine what the men inside are saying. They are swearing at us, willing us to approach. We do. We have no choice. We know that we have passed the 200 metres safety zone, and slowly, very slowly, we near the van. Al is angry. Where are the boys? Why aren't we going for it? Somewhere there is a car full of lads, fully tooled, who should have swung past us, but for some reason, perhaps because of the earlier false alarm, they aren't there. The men in the back of the van are getting bigger. Then surprisingly the van turns right. We move past it, but it turns round and comes straight back up behind us. This manoeuvre has, finally, alerted the team leader in one of the cars. As the van accelerates to overtake us – it has to fire from its rear windows – our boys emerge in hot pursuit. At last."

According to McNab the van turned back towards the roundabout, saw the Lancia and opened fire. The three SAS rolled out and returned fire. By the time the Renault closed up the gunmen were speeding away from the scene. McNabb and his team joined in the firefight, following the van, but lost it in the maze of small roads north of the motorway. By then Slater in the Saab was safely away down the Dungannon road; the gunmen had sprung their ambush too late. They escaped along the small roads running towards Lough Neagh, abandoning the van up a lane and hijacking two other cars on their way.

In the crossfire a 48-year-old plant hire contractor had been killed as he was driving out of a yard, hit by a stray round. The 8UDR Operations Platoon had been standing by as quick reaction force. They hurried to the scene and found the abandoned van. It had been struck by just one round. A witness who saw the incident said, "I don't want to denigrate the SAS, but they made a real bitch of it that day."[15] Collins agreed. "The number of bullets fired was remarkable. Whole magazines of Armalite were flying around but none of us died." Their cars were shot to pieces.

In later weeks Special Branch received information that a known Provo had been seen digging in a bog drain near Coalisland. 8UDR arranged for the Sappers to dam the drain and search the bank and the bed, using a digger. They came up with an Armalite, covered in mud and water but still in good condition. It had been abandoned there in the flight from Tamnamore. Eleven days before that it had been used in the murder of Simpson, a former member of 2UDR, and in September to kill Private Robert Bennett and a civilian in a shooting at Dungannon timber yard.

Stevenson served in the battalion for a further year until he reached retirement age. He was provided with an armoured saloon car, a radio and a direct alarm system to the RUC station, and the doors and windows of his home were protected with macrolon. In the end he and Paddy concluded that never again would they be allowed to live a normal life in Ulster. Their friends shunned them, counting them too dangerous to visit. Their son and his family and their daughter had already moved to England and they decided to follow them.

Many UDR families suffered heavily, both psychologically and financially, for their loyalty to their country and their determination not to be cowed, but perhaps none more than the Stevensons. They received some financial compensation, but it could never cover all they had lost.

Slater, the SAS trooper who drove Stevenson's Saab, was awarded a Military Medal. Two months later he was shot dead in an encounter with the IRA at Drumrush in North Fermanagh. He was one of two members of the SAS recorded as killed by terrorists during operations in the Province. The UDR owes a debt of gratitude to that regiment and other undercover elements for the unnumbered occasions on which by their presence they protected the lives of off-duty soldiers. Five days after Drumrush two PIRA volunteers riding a motorcycle were waiting for a victim in the grounds of a hospital in Derry when they were surprised by a patrol and killed. Fifteen members of the UDR worked in the hospital.

Battalions continued to add to the list of successes, particularly in the recovery of large quantities of explosives – 1UDR 854lbs in a quarry near Tyrone; 11UDR a 700lb device designed to catch a cordon party during a search operation following the find of two petrol bomb factories in Lurgan; 6UDR a massive 3,800lbs, already made up into sixty-six separate bombs, concealed in a concrete pit near Sixmilecross; 8UDR 1,200lbs, divided between eight milk churns bombs, leading to the arrest and charging of two men, one a member of PSF.

In May most of 3UDR had gone to annual camp at Warcop, leaving the Operations and Intelligence officers to run the TAOR, with a company of the Devons and Dorsets under command, when orders were received from Brigade Headquarters to mount a major search operation. The operation was to be controlled by the Battalion Operations Room with at one point some 400 members of the security forces under its control, including three companies and a platoon from three different Regular Army battalions, an RAF Regiment search team, three platoons of 3UDR which had not gone to the annual camp, five helicopters to overfly the area by night and two DMSUs.

Over the past eight months the IO's attention had been drawn to a lonely farm north of Castlewellan. From sightings of vehicles from the Republic and movements of the local ASU he suspected that the farm was being used to store munitions in transit. The search operation was concentrated on the farm and derelict buildings in the neighbourhood. The fact that a large number of police would be arriving to provide security cover for a Loyalist parade in Castlewellan within the next 36 hours added urgency to the search.

At first a search of the farm revealed nothing, but on the second day a team from the Royal Highland Fusiliers, not realizing it had already been searched, returned to search it again. Inside a barn, with no attempt at concealment and evidently unloaded in a hurry, the team found ten beer kegs containing some 2,000lb of explosive, a sack containing another 1000lb, cortex fuse, detonators and a van with false plates, stolen in Dundalk three weeks earlier. It seemed probable that the farmer, knowing the farm had been searched once, had thought it safe to store the bomb-making equipment there. He had disappeared, explaining that he was going out to check his sheep, and was not seen again. The operation illustrated triumphantly the ability of the UDR staff in an operations room and intelligence cell to plan and execute an operation involving many Regular soldiers, and all done in the absence of the CO and half the battalion at Warcop.[16]

Two weeks after being involved in the rescue of a mother and her five children from a car that had crashed and burst into flames at one of his road checks an officer in the Magherafelt Company was shot and seriously wounded:

"I was late that night because the CO was coming, and I should have been earlier. I was driving up towards Castledawson over the top of the wee brow of a hill, a place that you should only be doing 40 at the maximum, but I was doing maybe 70 or maybe 80. I was going as fast as the wee car would go. They opened fire on me at the top of the hill. I suppose they were hoping like that they would have knocked me out and I would crash the car at the bottom of the hill. Luckily enough they just wounded me. I lost the nerve in the right leg so I drove on with the left leg as far as I could and I managed to get round the corner. The speed kept going like, although it dropped off a bit, but it kept me going on, so I got away. I wasn't thinking clearly like but I remember thinking I was coming up near the hill head where the man who used to be my SDC in the B men lived, so I attempted to stop there with him, but I had too much momentum going, and I couldn't judge the braking with the left foot to get the damn car stopped. So I went maybe 50 or 60 yards down past. There was no way I could get the car turned to come back up again with only one leg. I tried to start the car but she wouldn't bloody start for me, so I had to wait there just for anybody to come to me. There was a young boy, he was a family friend. He saw the car sitting with the flashers on and I was waiting all this time like with the gun in my hand just in case the boys [the gunmen] would come up behind me. As soon as he came over to me he asked what was wrong. Was the car broke down? No, I said, I was shot. The cub started to shake like. I knew he was going to be no good to me so I sent him down into Bellaghy Police Station to tell them what had happened. But that was still taking too long. A girl who was in our Company at that time saw me sitting and stopped. All this time there was cars going past me, not a bloody one stopped with me except her. Whenever she knew what had happened, she went into Castledawson to a pub to phone for an ambulance. While she was in there, a chap, I think he was a reporter, overheard her making the telephone call and he followed her out the road to where I was and, good enough, the chap he got things organized, got me lifted into his car and took me up to the hospital."

The officer is permanently disabled, unable to work in his father's construction business. He was not the first member of the family to suffer at the hands of the Republican terrorists. His brother, a reserve constable, had been shot dead while on mobile patrol near Castledawson; it had been the second attempt on his life.

On 14 March Adams, by now President of Provisional Sinn Fein, had been attending the Belfast Magistrate's court answering a charge of obstruction and was being driven back to West Belfast, accompanied by three of his bodyguards. As they were driving along Howard Street, just off the city centre, a car drew alongside them and twelve shots were fired into the Cortina, wounding Adams and two of his colleagues. An off-duty permanent cadre NCO of 10UDR happened to be driving down the street at the time and heard firing immediately behind him. He assumed that he had been the target and, when the car overtook him, weaving in and out of the lunchtime traffic, he gave chase. In Wellington Place, on the approach to the City Hall, the car was trapped behind a bus waiting at a bus stop. The soldier drew up behind it, leapt out, drew his PPW and told the two men who were trying to escape on foot to stand still. A third man remained in the car; it transpired he had shot himself in the hand. One of the men addressed the soldier by name and he recognized them as residents of the Protestant community in his part of Belfast. By chance an off-duty police officer who knew the soldier by sight was nearby and helped him to detain them until a police patrol could arrest them. The three were members of the UFF: two were sentenced to eighteen years, the third to twelve.

Adams' party meanwhile had driven straight to the Royal Victoria Hospital. Sinn Fein claimed that the SAS had been following his car and there were suggestions that there had been more to the assassination attempt than was apparent, but there is no doubt that the NCO's presence was pure coincidence. Only a brave man could have reacted as he did and his Queen's Gallantry Medal was well deserved. Now a marked man to both Republican and Loyalist terrorists, he was forced to leave home and eventually to leave the Regiment. It was a strange irony that the men who attempted to murder Adams should have been arrested and imprisoned as the direct result of the bravery and swift reaction of a UDR solder.[17]

CHAPTER SIXTEEN

1985–1986 The Regiment Under Pressure

In 1982, in an attempt to stimulate some positive political movement, the Government set up a new Northern Ireland Assembly. Initially it was to be a consultative body to discuss how devolved powers could be transferred from Westminster to Stormont. As agreement was reached on each subject between the parties: power would be devolved at the discretion of the Secretary of State, 'rolling devolution', as it was called. From the outset the idea never had much chance of success once the SDLP and Sinn Fein had decided to have no part in it. However, both parties did put up candidates to stand in the election for the new body in October. Sinn Fein polled well, taking 10% of the vote and winning four seats, while the SDLP results, 18.8% and fourteen seats, were comparatively poor. The British were worried. If the trend continued, Sinn Fein might in due course take over from the SDLP as the majority party representing the Nationalist people.

The Irish Government shared that concern and in 1983 set up the New Ireland Forum, a consultative body to consider "the manner in which lasting peace and stability could be achieved in a new Ireland through the democratic process and to report on possible new structures and processes through which this might be achieved."[1] Since out of the parties from the North only the SDLP participated, it was hardly surprising that when the report was published in May of the following year the three possible solutions had a strongly Nationalist bias. The Prime Minister rejected all three proposals in her usual forthright manner. The Unionists were delighted and lulled into a false sense of security, believing that Thatcher's response marked the end of attempts to reach a political accommodation with Dublin.

Nevertheless intergovernment discussions continued over the next two years, leading to the signing of the Anglo–Irish Agreement in November 1985. One of the frequent topics of these discussions was the future of the Ulster Defence Regiment.

Since the 1974 Assembly the SDLP had looked to the Irish Government to represent its views in discussions with the British. The party had become increasingly insistent that the UDR was beyond reform and must be disbanded. In the aftermath of the Forum report an unofficial committee had been set up by the British–Irish Association under the chairmanship of Lord Kilbrandon to comment on the report's recommendations. The findings of the committee were made public in November 1984. The fact that the members considered that the three all–Ireland solutions proposed by the Forum were impractical was largely overlooked. The one point on which the SDLP and the media concentrated was the recommendation that the UDR should be gradually run down, its role taken over by an expanded RUC and the full-time soldiers absorbed into the Regular Army. The Committee had made the mistake of believing that policemen could be an alternative to soldiers. There was no indication that it had studied the operational problems involved in implementing its recommendation, nor had the members received an authorative briefing from the military on the role of the Regiment.

From now on the UDR came under relentless pressure. Every adverse incident, whether true or false, was grist for the mill of the SDLP's and the Irish Government's case for disbandment.

A former member of the Press Office at Headquarters Northern Ireland wrote of this time that

"a clear pattern began to emerge. It is well recognized that the most effective and damaging propaganda campaign should have at least some element of fact or truth in it. The more truth, the more effective it will be.

"It would begin with an incident of some kind. Let's say a UDR patrol stops a car on a lonely country road around midnight one dark night. The three male occupants are recognized as Republicans (possibly a couple of them were on the fringe of the IRA). Perhaps they are abusive; in any event they refuse to identify themselves or to say where they are coming from or going to. The vehicle is searched but nothing suspicious comes to light. The men are obstructive, maybe arrogant. The patrol commander has to make a decision. Does he detain them or let them go? After 15 minutes he decides to let them drive on and duly logs the incident.

"Next day the *Irish News* carries a front-page report of the incident. But things have changed. According to the report, three young Catholic men from the South Armagh area had been stopped at a UDR roadblock and detained for over an hour. One of them, the driver, had received medical attention for a black eye and swollen cheekbone, allegedly from a blow with the butt of an SLR. The side window of the car had been smashed in and the paintwork of the driver's door dented and scratched. All three men had been subjected to verbal abuse and had been literally in fear of their lives.

"Later in the day the *Irish News* phones AIS and asks for a comment. They are told that a car with three men in it was stopped for 15 minutes before being allowed to proceed. There had been no complaint about the incident, but if one were received it would be fully investigated by the police.

"The story runs again the following day and has been picked up by two Dublin papers. A priest is quoted as saying that the entire

270

Catholic community is in fear of the UDR. A local SDLP councillor says he is raising the matter with the Irish Government. In an interview on RTE midday news an Irish Government minister says he will be pressing the Northern Ireland Office to hold a full inquiry. Later in the interview, speaking on behalf of the 'entire Nationalist community' he calls for the UDR 'which clearly is a sectarian force' to be disbanded.

"On the BBC Northern Ireland television news that evening a DUP MP speaks out angrily at what he describes as 'a plot, orchestrated by Dublin, to do away with the UDR'. He suggests it's high time the Government told Dublin where to get off.

"Two days after that a junior minister at Westminster, without directly mentioning the controversy, expresses the Government's confidence in the Regiment and of the tremendous job it is doing.

"Who can judge what actually happened that dark night in South Armagh? Did the patrol go too far – or were they the victims of a skilful propaganda coup? Was it based on the whole truth, a half-truth or a downright lie? We will never know, but the record shows that no official complaint about the 'incident' was ever received.

"This pattern was repeated many times, so much so that, in their training, soldiers were warned to look out for and guard against it."

Unfortunately in recent years events had occurred, and others were now to occur, which provided ammunition for the Regiment's critics.

In January 1982, following an incendiary attack on a timber yard in Armagh, a patrol from 2UDR was tasked to investigate suspicious activity at a supermarket in that city. As the patrol was cordoning off the area two men broke away, were challenged but failed to stop. One of them turned towards the soldiers and, believing that he was armed, they fired two shots, killing the man almost instantly. In the follow-up the police found another man on the roof who confirmed that the patrol had given a challenge.[2] The inquest was adjourned eight times because of discrepancies in evidence and concluded by recording an open verdict.

In July of the following year a foot patrol from the same battalion became involved in an altercation with a group of young people in Armagh in the course of which a youth, Martin Malone, was shot dead. The Cardinal officiated at the Requiem Mass. In his address he reminded the mourners of his recent condemnation of the murder of the four members of 6UDR in the Ballygawley landmine and went on, "How can one pronounce the deliberate killing of a member of this force [the UDR] as murder and the deliberate killing of an unarmed bystander by a member of that force less than murder?" To many people it seemed that the Cardinal's statement had prejudged the outcome of the trial.

The patrol commander, Corporal Baird, was charged with murder. In his evidence he described how late at night his patrol had stopped to question three youths and girls outside the Republican Callan Estate. The girls refused to give their personal details and Baird requested RUC assistance. While waiting for the police to arrive a crowd of some twenty people had come down from the estate and surrounded the patrol. Baird was struck and, fearing that he would be knocked to the ground and his rifle stolen, he had cocked his weapon and pointed it at the crowd. He was certain that the safety catch was applied, but the rifle went off and Malone was hit in the chest at a range of a few feet.

At the trial in November 1984 Baird was found not guilty firstly of murder and then of manslaughter. The judge said that the prosecution case had been handicapped by the unreliable evidence of the civilian witnesses and that it had failed to prove that Baird did not fear for his safety. In such a situation the cocking of a weapon had been a reasonable step to take. From the Regiment's point of view it was a satisfactory outcome, but the incident followed by the trial had proved further adverse publicity, compounded when it was revealed that Baird had previous convictions for assault and disorderly behaviour. The offences had taken place before he joined the UDR and had been decreed by the Army vetters not sufficiently serious to debar him from enlistment.

On 8 November 1983 Adrian Carroll, a member of a well-known Republican family, whose brother had been killed in a controversial RUC shooting eleven months previously, was shot dead as he was walking home through the streets of Armagh. The Protestant Action Force claimed to have killed him. Three weeks later the RUC took in for questioning fifteen members of 2UDR. The news was headlined, nationally and internationally. The reaction in the Regiment was one of dismay.

In March 1986, some two and a half years later, six of the soldiers, all permanent cadre, were brought to trial, five for murder and a sixth for withholding information. According to the prosecution case a multiple patrol had been sent out around lunchtime to carry out a search on the Moy road. This search completed, they moved to a second area close by to carry out a further speculative search. During this second search three of the accused had allegedly driven back to the Technical College in the city and dropped off one of their number, Latimer. There, while the other two returned to the search area, Latimer pulled civilian clothes over his combat kit, put on glasses and a cap, and waited for the patrol's return. The search over, five of the men in two vehicles returned to the college and enacted a charade of 'arresting' Latimer in his civilian clothes and bundling him into one of the vehicles.

While the second vehicle returned to the RUC station, the first dropped Latimer off close to the route that Carroll was known to follow on his way home from his place of work. They drove around while he followed and shot Carroll, then picked him up again, and the three drove back to the station, Latimer taking off his outer layer of civilian clothing in the back of the vehicle.

After a trial lasting over sixty days the four were found guilty and sentenced to life imprisonment. They appealed, but in 1987 their appeal was rejected.

Much has been written about the alleged inconsistencies in the evidence of witnesses. In 1991 Ken Maginnis was instrumental in drawing up a dossier containing new evidence, calling for a retrial. Ian Paisley Jr, the DUP leader's son, wrote a book *Reasonable Doubt. The case for the UDR Four*, published in 1992 with a foreword by Robert Kee, the respected broadcaster who had recently presented a programme on the history of Ireland for the BBC. Kee wrote that, long before reading Paisley's book or becoming acquainted with him, he had become convinced that the Four were innocent of the crime for which they had been committed.[3] Other people of influence publicly declared their disquiet about the verdict.

These two documents did make a strong case for concern as to whether the guilt of the four men had been established beyond reasonable doubt, reinforced by the opinion of an authority on syntax analysis, who declared on a BBC 'Newsnight' documentary that none of the confessions signed by the Four were genuine. When electronic tests carried out on the instructions of the Chief Constable on the original confessions signed by the accused showed that they had been amended at some stage, the case was put up for appeal for a second time and in 1992 the convictions of three of the Four were quashed. Latimer, who had committed the actual murder, remained in prison on the strength of other evidence against him. From the point of view of the Regiment's reputation it was the worst possible result, for, bearing in mind the manner in which the crime had been committed, if one was guilty then all were involved to some degree, while the drawing out of the case over nine years had kept alive in the minds of the public the disgraceful fact that one member of the UDR while on duty had committed a coldly calculated murder.

When the Prime Minister paid her Christmas visit to the Province shortly after the arrest of the soldiers she dropped in to Drumadd Barracks where she met the resident battalion, the Grenadier Guards, and some members of 2UDR. The Cardinal complained that the Prime Minister's action in talking to the UDR had been 'insulting' and Hume raised the visit with her in the Commons, telling her that it had caused a deep feeling of outrage among the Nationalists of Armagh. In February the Duke of Edinburgh, Colonel of the Grenadiers, flew into Drumadd to visit his battalion. The UDR was not involved in the visit. That did not prevent Mallon from making a vitriolic attack on the UDR during a BBC interview, calling the visit a calculated insult. HQNI was about to issue a statement in support of the Regiment when Barry, the Irish Foreign Minister, protested to the British Ambassador. As a result the Headquarters statement had to be put on hold and the opportunity to make a prompt reply to Mallon's criticisms was lost. Responding quickly and effectively to such allegations was always a problem. There were arguments in favour both of issuing a full and powerful defence, and of maintaining a dignified silence, but, as one member of the Advisory Council pointed out, a policy of silence meant that "sections of the community interpreted it as acquiescence, and it left the case for the Regiment to be made by certain extreme politicians on the other side with whom the Regiment would not necessarily wish to be associated."

The NIO was not unsympathetic. John Bourn, the Assistant Under–Secretary, recalled that ministers and their staff spent a great deal of time rebutting unfounded accusations against the UDR. "Looking back over newspaper records of the time, and what was said on radio and television, there was too great a tendency on the part of the media to represent the UDR as the B Specials in another guise and to describe them as a Protestant force given licence to go out and deal with terrorism in a pretty rough and ready way."[4] The NIO view was that there would always be those who would use every opportunity to criticize the Regiment; the UDR's aim should be to win over moderate opinion by ensuring all ranks appreciated and observed the need for impeccable standards of behaviour, whatever the provocation.

From the beginning of 1985 there was a spate of hostile publicity arising from the coincidence of a series of incidents occurring within weeks of each other. In the early hours of 15 January a patrol of 7/10UDR had set up a road block at the roundabout under the motorway at the beginning of Kennedy Way, a route favoured by terrorists going on a mission out of West Belfast. The soldiers recognized a stolen car; five youths had taken it for a joyride. Joyriders were the curse of the decent people of the city. Realizing that the car had been recognized, the driver rammed the car in front, reversed into the car behind, knocking over three of the soldiers and sped away. The soldiers opened fire with some thirty rounds and the car crashed into a ditch. Two of the occupants were injured in the crash and the three others had sustained bullet wounds; one, a 17-year-old youth, Paul Kelly, who had already been before the courts on a previous occasion for joyriding, had been killed by a single round. Contrary to some press reports he was not shot as he was running away. He was the twelfth joyrider to die in six years.

Before the day was out Barry, without waiting for the results of the RUC investigation, had delivered another protest to the British Embassy in Dublin, referring to the UDR as "a dangerous source of division" and demanding that the soldiers involved should be suspended from duty and their weapons removed. The *Irish News* declared: "The very real fear is that the patrol was intent on murder . . . No wonder many fear for their lives when stopped by the UDR . . . No wonder the word 'defence' in the title is regarded as a sick joke . . . No wonder many feel it should be 'attack' instead."[5]

Barry's remarks and those of the leader writer of the *Irish News* were but an example of the hatred that was being directed against the UDR by some Nationalist politicians and sections of the press, not only in Ireland. There were other accusations that the UDR was implementing a shoot-to-kill policy. That the accusation was totally untrue is proved by the statistics. Over twenty-two years UDR patrols shot dead seven people – a 16-year-old Protestant in Newtownstewart who failed to halt in the aftermath of a bomb incident and was found afterwards to be deaf, an IRA volunteer who opened fire on a patrol as he broke through a road block, a second armed IRA volunteer who was attempting to hijack a bus on the border, Paul Kelly, the young joyrider, and another who failed to stop at a road block in Belfast and who, the soldiers said, threatened them with a gun, the shooting of the man outside the Armagh supermarket and Malone, accidentally shot in the altercation in Armagh.

In a speech at the SDLP annual convention in 1988 the party leader, Hume, told the delegates:

> "If I were to lead a civil rights campaign in Northern Ireland today the major target of that campaign would be the IRA.
>
> "Let the record speak. Up till last Saturday 2,705 people have died in the twenty-year period of the current troubles. 31% of these were members of the security forces. 14% were members of paramilitary organizations. 55% were ordinary civilian men and women from both sections of our community, 69% of whom were from the Catholic community and 31% from the Protestant community. And who killed all those people? The statistics are devastating. 44% were killed by the Provisional IRA and 18% by their fellow-travelling 'republican' paramilitaries. 27% were killed by Loyalists. 10% were killed by the British Army. 2% were killed by the RUC and 0.28% by the UDR. In short people describing themselves as Irish Republicans have killed six times as many human beings as the British Army, thirty times as many as the RUC and 250 times as many as the UDR."

That the figures were not higher was due to the discipline and experience of patrol commanders. To take but one example. A foot patrol of 7UDR was carrying out snap VCPs in the Border area near Newtownhamilton when, ignoring a signal to stop, a car accelerated through the checkpoint, brushing the patrol commander's legs and forcing the other soldiers to jump out of the way. The men cocked their weapons but held their fire. The car drove into a field, turned and stalled; a man got out and dropped into a crouching position. It looked as if he was about to fire on the patrol, but no weapon could be seen. Again the NCO told his patrol to hold their fire and physically stopped a police constable who had come up into the aim. The man was arrested after a struggle, during which he tried to grab the rifle and caused one shot to be fired. A hand grenade was found in the car. In a difficult situation in a dangerous area the patrol commander had shown great coolness and his soldiers an admirable standard of discipline.

On 26 January Private Geoffrey Edwards, who had been arrested in December 1983, pleaded guilty to the murder of Peter Corrigan, a Sinn Fein election worker, shot down as he was walking in Armagh, and a further eighteen charges, including six of attempted murder. One of his intended victims had been Seamus Grew; he had escaped unhurt but was shot dead by the RUC with Roddy Carroll three months later. In another attack two men and a 5-year-old child were injured by a booby-trap Edwards had placed under a car. He was jailed for life, as well as being awarded seven twenty-year concurrent sentences. He had been a permanent cadre soldier in the same company as the UDR Four.

On the weekend after the conclusion of the Edwards trial the SDLP held its annual convention in Belfast. The agenda included five motions calling for the disbandment of the UDR. In his speech Mallon pulled out all the stops. He told the conference that he appreciated that he had to tread softly because he was treading on the graves of the soldiers and the grief of their families. He and others in the hall had walked in the funerals of UDR men killed in sectarian assassinations. But, he went on, "This regiment encapsulates all of the ugly facets of political life in Northern Ireland and by its behaviour has brought not just its own regiment into disrepute but has tarnished the very name of law and order and justice." By passing the motion the conference would make it clear to the Government the extent to which the continuing existence of the UDR was a bar to political progress. Another delegate claimed that the sole purpose of the UDR was to be an armed wing of the British establishment designed to enable the Unionist population to dominate the Nationalists. Another described the Regiment as "loyalist mercenaries funded by public money to keep the croppies down". The shooting of the teenage joyrider was condemned as 'summary execution'. The convention passed an unanimous resolution calling for the disbandment of the Regiment as a matter of urgency.[6]

No doubt there was not a delegate there who would have condoned murder from whatever source, but was there not a danger that such intemperate remarks could reassure a Republican terrorist with murder in his heart that in choosing a UDR soldier as his next victim he was acting on behalf of his people?

Roger Preston had taken over as Commander UDR from Brigadier Peter Graham in July 1984. A Light Infantryman, he had commanded his battalion in Ballykinlar and already knew the UDR well. He was a fortunate choice to lead the Regiment through two difficult years – the campaign to have it disbanded, followed by the violent Loyalist reaction to the Anglo–Irish Agreement and the pressures that that placed on the soldiers. He succeeded because he was a man everyone liked. When he defended the Regiment's reputation in public he did so all the more effectively because he came across as a sincere, thoroughly decent man with a warm affection for his soldiers and a sympathetic understanding of the difficulties and risks they faced. At the same time he fought with a robust determination to improve the UDR's image. In February in an interview on RTE he put up a vigorous defence of the Regiment's reputation. Some 32,000 men and women had served in its ranks. Nine had been convicted of murder, six of manslaughter. The UDR regretted the crimes committed by its members and was bitterly ashamed of them.

> "But let us get this into perspective. It is not a question of the whole Regiment being thugs and bullyboys, as some people have described. One or two bad soldiers ruin the name of the Regiment. 99% are decent, hard-working, good, efficient soldiers. To suggest that because nine have been committed for murder the rest are potential murderers is disgraceful."[7]

The Labour spokesman on Northern Ireland took up the call to the Government to consider phasing out the Regiment. In the Commons the Secretary of State, Douglas Hurd, replied that the UDR was indispensable to the security of the Province and that it was "quite wrong and misleading for generalized accusations to be built on the basis of particular cases".[8]

Some accusations were unfounded. A member of the public picked up a list of suspected Republican terrorists, evidently dropped by a soldier in South Down. It was titled 'Stop/Hit List'. He sent it to Father Faul who forwarded it to the Irish Government as proof that the security forces were operating a shoot-to-kill policy. The implication was that the list had been compiled by the UDR. In fact it had been made out and annotated by a foolish soldier from another unit.[9]

A week later Barry was at it again, demanding an explanation for the action of soldiers at a UDR PVCP on the Fermanagh border who had been instrumental in delaying a Sligo man for five hours. According to the story told by this man, he had been escorted away by two men in plain clothes in an unmarked car, blindfolded, taken into a building and interviewed three times in an attempt to persuade him to become an informer. In fact the PVCP was not manned by the UDR, but by another Regular unit that wore the green beret. The UDR had nothing to do with the incident. The NIO could not say so, as that would have been to accept the rest of the allegations. So the UDR case went by default, the media had their headlines, 'Curb UDR bullies, Barry tells London', the leader writer of the *Irish Press* wrote of an innocent man being invited to 'spy for the UDR' and more ammunition had been provided for the disbandment of the Regiment, never mind whether or not it was true.

Unfortunately there were two more damaging events in the following months.

The 15th anniversary on 1 April passed quietly; for the moment it was deemed wiser for the Regiment to keep its head down and not draw further attention to itself.[10] On Easter Monday of the following week Martin Love was walking home from an Enniskillen hotel in the early hours when he was shot dead by a lone gunman. He was the son of a member of the Alliance Party. The UFF admitted killing him, on the grounds that he was involved with PIRA. His father vehemently denied the claim and the RUC said they had no reason to think that he had been involved in any paramilitary activity. He was, it seemed, another victim of unfounded gossip. Within hours a part-time soldier from 4UDR was arrested and charged with the murder. In September 1986 he and a Regular soldier were found guilty of Love's murder. Both were jailed for life and the UDR soldier was given additional concurrent terms of imprisonment for collecting information and for armed robbery, which he admitted along with his involvement in the killing.[11]

In May a part-time soldier from 1/9UDR pleaded guilty to being a member of the UVF and of supplying weapons used in an armed robbery and was jailed for five years. Another soldier in the same platoon received a suspended sentence for possession of a weapon and ammunition. The two had been among thirteen men from the Ballymena area rounded up by police on suspicion of being involved in Loyalist paramilitary activity. The arrests led to the discovery of a cache of twenty-seven weapons.

Were there some reasons why, after a relatively trouble-free period since the Miami Showband murders of 1975, there were so many occurrences in the six months between December 1984 and May 1985 that showed the UDR in a bad light? Possibly there were three contributory factors.

There was around this time a worrying shortage of officers, nine permanent cadre and no less than eighty-eight part-time. In addition, the average age was too high. By early 1987 nineteen out of the total of ninety-four permanent cadre officers were over 45 years of age; the youngest was 24 and only eight were under 28. Unless young men could be encouraged to take a commission, in ten years time there would be a chronic shortage of Company Commanders. A recruiting campaign was mounted, directed at potential officers. By April 1986 150 replies had been received, but the standard was generally disappointing.

The new CLF, Major General Jeapes, may have touched on another contributory factor when speaking of his impressions of the Regiment in August 1985, following his initial visits to the battalions. On the whole he had been greatly impressed by the morale and determination of the soldiers, but he had sensed "a certain war-weariness and uneasiness among some of the older and longest serving men".

Defence counsel at the Edwards trial had underscored the reasons for this war weariness and unease. He had pointed out, not as a defence but as "an inadequate explanation as to how a law-abiding citizen can find himself in the dock", that Edwards in his seven years' service had seen at least fifteen of his friends and associates murdered and believed, "rightly or wrongly, that not enough was being done to combat the violence of terrorism".[12]

By the beginning of 1985 159 serving and former soldiers had been killed in terrorist attacks.

In the same period the RUC had lost 206 members. Bearing in mind that they were the larger force, the police were suffering proportionately roughly the same fatal casualties. There were some cases of policemen taking the law into their own hands, but less so than in the UDR. Was there any reason for this disparity? Bruce suggests three – the RUC was more selective in whom it enlisted; only a small proportion were part-time reservists, whereas the greater part of the UDR were still part-timers; and the UDR was more likely to be deployed into areas that brought them into frustrating contact with known Republicans, "manning vehicle check points in 'bandit country' and experiencing the situation of being sure who the IRA operators are but being unable to do anything about it".[13]

The criminal involvement of a few UDR soldiers was a disgrace, but critics need to think back and be eternally grateful that never once in the quarter century of the troubles did the Army, the police or the UDR become involved in the deliberate, organized reprisals practised in the 1920s by the Auxiliaries and the Black and Tans and tacitly sanctioned by the British Government. And this despite the fact that the Provisionals killed eight times as many members of the Army, the police and the prison service as the security forces killed members of PIRA.

So far as the SDLP was concerned the UDR was an unreformable sectarian force and must be disbanded. The party was unable to appreciate the operational problem of finding nine battalions from elsewhere if the UDR was disbanded and, however much its politicians impressed their views on the Irish Government, that problem was, quite simply, insoluble. Gradually the Irish appreciated that this was so. From the outset of the inter-governmental discussions running up to the Anglo–Irish Agreement the Prime Minister had emphasized that there could be no changes in the structure of the RUC and the UDR; any such changes would be strongly opposed by the majority community. For his part, the Taoiseach, FitzGerald, pointed out that "so difficult was the relationship between the UDR and the nationalist population that no prospect existed of the police winning the confidence of the minority so long as the UDR played a role in the security system".[14] However, by the time of their April meeting Fitzgerald had accepted the disbandment of the Regiment was simply not possible. Instead they were advocating that it should "conduct operations only in support of the RUC, under the operational control of Regular units giving military support to the RUC, and mount checkpoints only in the presence of and in support of the RUC, who alone should have powers of arrest." When Thatcher and FitzGerald met at a European Council in Milan in June the Irish side was generally satisfied with progress on drawing up the Agreement, but disappointed that there had been a lack of firm commitment by the British regarding the confidence-building measures, including action on the RUC and the UDR. Thatcher argued that any such measures must not be announced as part of the Agreement for fear that they would exacerbate the Unionist reaction. FitzGerald countered that, unless there were simultaneous changes in the RUC and UDR, the whole effect of the Agreement would evaporate. The Taoiseach decided that unless he spoke out bluntly the talks were in danger of breaking down.

"We were not saying 'Abolish the UDR', I told her. We were saying that it should be used in support of the police, with a number of improvements in its training and organization. We hoped that we could get such an arrangement accepted by the minority in Northern Ireland, but without knowing if we could do so."

Encouraged by the Prime Minister's response, he went on to tell her that what was needed in the UDR was a corps of competent and professional military officers down to company level, as well as adequate numbers of experienced NCOs. The part-time membership of the UDR should be disbanded and better control of UDR operations should be ensured.

Thatcher "intervened to say that she admired their courage. Many of them had been shot. They were a remarkable group of men. I acknowledged that men had been murdered in the most appalling circumstances; but the fact was that the UDR and RUC had come to be seen as representing one section of the community. In some areas the UDR harassed local Catholic boys, many of them their neighbours with whom they had grown up. This harassment went on and on and had become a problem that in Northern Ireland tended to have the sort of end that we all knew. The UDR were seen by the minority as a hostile force. There must be visible changes. We were not suggesting anything that would make them less effective; we were making concrete suggestions so that they could act more effectively in support of the police and attract community support."[15]

The two sides, led by Thatcher and FitzGerald, gathered at Hillsborough on 15 November for the signing of the Agreement. The first article confirmed that there could be no change in the status of Northern Ireland without the consent of the majority. An Inter-Governmental Conference was to be established with a permanent joint secretariat based next door to the battalion location at Palace Barracks, on the main road from Belfast to Holywood. The Conference would meet at regular intervals and would consider, among other subjects, political matters put forward by the Irish side on behalf of the minority, security, including the relationship of the security forces to the communities, and cross-border security co-operation.

Preston, the Commander, had written to the battalion COs telling them of the measures that were about to be implemented in regard to the Regiment and in some cases had already been implemented, all of them to the UDR's advantage. COs were to brief their soldiers, reminding them at the same time that they had no right to refuse duties or to take part in any action that would bring the Regiment into disrepute; they had the right to vote and to resign, and nothing else. The warning proved unnecessary; in the days that followed there were only two resignations that could be attributed to the Agreement. "No one's going to act the bloody hero and lose their pay cheque in order to help the DUP," an officer was quoted as saying.[16]

On 4 December, a week before the first meeting of the Inter-Governmental Conference, Preston held a press conference to announce the measures affecting the UDR. He emphasized that none of them had been brought about by political pressure as a result of the Agreement. That was true, but the fact that the talks had taken place and that the Irish side had repeatedly criticized the UDR had doubtless encouraged the MOD to agree to measures which it might otherwise have said it could not afford. Only a year previously, despite objections from the Headquarters, the post of Deputy Commander UDR, held by a regular Lieutenant Colonel, had been written out of the establishment. This was to be reintroduced, though the role of the Lieutenant Colonel would now be the planning and organization of training. Ten additional Regular Army Senior NCOs were to be posted to the Regiment, one to each battalion and the tenth to the UDR Training Centre; permanent cadre officer cadets would attend the Regular Army six-month commissioning course at Sandhurst and part-time recruit training would be increased from eight to fourteen days, the extra days to be completed within the recruits first three months of service.

On the weekend following Hillsborough the Taoiseach said during an interview on RTE that as part of the Agreement there would be a police presence with Army, including UDR, patrols, "so that in future people would be stopped by a RUC man, guarded by the UDR and the Army, and that it is the police who will have direct contact with the public". Barry amplified his leader's remarks by saying that the Irish government was pressing for the scaling down of the UDR acting alone. The objective was that "the UDR should act only in support of the RUC and should not be in a position of stopping people at checkpoints and questioning them". They were unfortunate and misleading statements, for they gave the impression that there had been a change in the legal powers of the UDR and could have led to members of the public refusing to be searched or questioned unless a policeman was present, or, more dangerously, refusing to stop at all.

FitzGerald seems to have been under a genuine misapprehension. He records that in July the British had assured him that it was intended that progressively, as circumstances permitted, the number of patrols with a RUC presence would be increased.[17] He had failed to appreciate that to provide a policeman with every patrol would have involved either scaling down Army routine operations or increasing the RUC strength, by an extra 1,000 officers, Hermon had calculated.[18]

So far as the UDR was concerned the need for a RUC presence with a patrol whenever possible had long been accepted. There was no feeling that the police officer was there to check up on the behaviour of the patrol, simply an appreciation that policemen were more suitable for dealing with the public, and that in any normal society it was a policeman's, not a soldier's, job.

FitzGerald felt he had been let down by the British. "Six years after the signing of the Agreement, and despite constant pressure from the Irish side, one third of patrols continued to be unaccompanied by a police presence," he records in his autobiography. "Nothing in the negotiations could have given reason to the Irish side to expect such an outcome."[19] Nevertheless, he continues, one of the outcomes of the Agreement was that by 1986 there had been "a notable reduction in complaints of harassment of the nationalist community by the security forces".[20] Could that have been because in the run-up to Hillsborough the Nationalist politicians had been looking for complaints to support their demands for the disbandment of the UDR? A similar reduction occurred six years later after the UDR became the Royal Irish Regiment, yet the same soldiers were doing the same job in the same way and only the name had been changed.

By chance the weekend after Hillsborough – the same weekend that the Taoiseach was speaking on RTE – the UDR's annual study period for all COs and Company Commanders was being held in Ballykinlar. The first day was given over to discussions on how to improve the UDR's image and encourage members of the minority community to join the Regiment. The second day wound up with an address by the Secretary of State, Tom King. The UDR Chief of Staff, Major Johnnie Dallow, was detailed to meet him in the Mess and provide him with coffee until it was his turn to speak. King was worried. How would the audience receive him, he asked. Dallow admitted that he did not know. He need not have worried. He told his audience that he welcomed the opportunity to speak to "the leaders of a key element of the security forces who are also influential members of the community". He pointed out that the Agreement was a two-way arrangement and that the British could equally raise matters with the Irish side. "But power rests exclusively with me, and not a jot has left my hands by the signing of the Agreement." It was, he went on, "a recognition of the Unionist position and a recognition by the minority that Irish unity is abandoned for the time being, and that their position is recognised. Northern Ireland is not for sale." It was a courageous address, given without notes, lasting some fifteen minutes, followed by questions, and was rewarded with prolonged applause that went on longer and was more enthusiastic than the dictates of courtesy demanded. "I remember I was glad it wasn't a standing ovation," Dallow recalled. "Otherwise I would have had to note the names of those who did not stand!"[21]

The previous weekend had seen the SDLP convention repeat its call for disbandment of the UDR. Mallon told the delegates that he had in his possession a confidential document prepared for the security committee of the SDP – Liberal Alliance by Lord Hunt, whose report in 1969 had led to the formation of the Regiment. In preparing the Alliance report, Mallon alleged, Hunt had interviewed the former Chief Constable, Sir Kenneth Newman, and Field Marshal Sir Edwin Bramall, who had just retired as Chief of the Defence Staff, and that both had said they would like to see the Regiment phased out – "abolished" was the word Mallon said the Chief Constable used.[22] Newman promptly denied Mallon's claim, but it took a little time to contact Bramall who was in the Far East. His reply was read out at the study weekend; the Field Marshal wished the GOC to tell the assembled audience that the claim that he had advocated the abolition of the Regiment was absolute nonsense and that he hoped that that would put an end to "these extraordinary rumours".

The main focus of the Provisionals' attacks during 1985 was directed at the RUC. In February during a mortar attack on the cramped police station in Newry one bomb fell on a crowded portacabin, killing nine officers, including a Chief Inspector and two women constables, the worst casualties suffered by the force in any one incident since its formation. The success of the attack encouraged the Provisionals to concentrate their efforts on police stations, using vehicle bombs or mortars fired from the back of a lorry; Newry again, Newcastle, Plumbridge destroyed by a lorry bomb; in September eighteen mortar bombs landed on the Training Centre in Enniskillen; three other attacks that month, five in December, the most successful at Ballygawley, a highly professional raid resulting in the death of two constables and the destruction of the station. By November there had been seventeen incidents involving remote-control devices, in one of which an Inspector, two constables and a woman constable lost their lives. In June a 1,000lb bomb exploded near the centre of Belfast, causing extensive damage, with the facades of some building collapsing into the street; in the following month another bomb exploded a short way up the street causing further extensive damage. Other bombs exploded in the main streets of country towns – Ballynahinch, Antrim, Omagh, Strabane.

The other elements of the security forces escaped relatively lightly that year – two Regular soldiers and a principal officer in the Prison Service killed, and four serving and one ex-member of the UDR, for the Regiment the lowest fatalities in any year since 1970.

The murder of Private Jimmy Graham of the Lisnaskea Company attracted national and international media attention, for it epitomized the courage and suffering of the UDR soldiers and their families. Jimmy was another school bus driver. He and other members of his family had joined the UDR at the beginning. One brother, Ronnie, had been murdered in June 1981, Cecil five months later. Jimmy had already come under attack twice.

On 1 February he was parked outside the primary school at Derrylin, four miles from the Border, waiting to take the senior pupils to the baths at Enniskillen for their weekly swim when two gunmen approached and fired at him through the windscreen. He tried to escape by running down between the seats, but was killed before he could return fire. People gathering in the village for the St Brigid's Day Mass heard the killers cheering as they drove away towards the Border.

Some 2,000 people attended the funeral; the Bishop of Clogher, the

Right Reverend Gordon McMullan, who had buried Ronnie and Cecil, cut short a visit to New York to give the address. Two local priests, Fathers Gaffney and Harding, issued a statement saying that "the people who did this are not worthy to be called Christians or indeed men, for after accomplishing their bloody task they left the scene with howls and cheers."

A 21-year-old soldier in the same company was courting Ronnie's daughter. Two weeks before Jimmy's murder he had just called at his girlfriend's house when two gunmen fired at him. He was hit several times, but managed to take cover behind the car and return fire. His attackers fled, having fired about forty rounds. Although he survived, the sight of him crawling up the path to the door followed by the killing of her brother-in-law a fortnight later was too much for Ronnie's widow who suffered a nervous breakdown.

A week before Jimmy was murdered a teenager had been charged with the killing of Ronnie. He told the police that he had been recruited into the Fianna, the junior wing of the IRA, by a woman teacher at his school when he was only thirteen years old. A month later he had received written instructions to collect two rifles from a barn and hide them in the hedge opposite Ronnie Graham's house. He pleaded guilty to that charge and to collecting information about the movements of members of the security forces which he passed on to the teacher. He was jailed for seven years.[23]

Some years earlier Hilary, the Grahams' Greenfinch sister, had been hit by a car while on duty at a VCP and seriously injured. Later she was to die of cancer.

Except possibly during the two World Wars, there can hardly have been another British Army family who suffered so dearly for their service to their country. Why them? They were well liked and respected; two of the brothers were married to Catholics. They were an outspoken family, maybe too outspoken in a situation where some reticence would have been a wiser course. "They were hard men," Kells, their Company Commander said, "and whatever they did they put their best into it. Whether it was working in the factory, in the UDR, driving a van or a school bus, whatever they did, they were quite determined they were not going to be put out of their work. I spoke to Ronnie a short time before his death and suggested to him that he should retire, but he was quite determined to carry on."[24]

Four weeks after Jimmy Graham's murder Private Trevor Harkness was killed when a bomb exploded beside his foot patrol in Pomeroy. Thereafter for the next eight and a half months no member of the Regiment was killed by the IRA. Possibly they reckoned that the murders gained sympathy for the UDR and detracted from the demands to have the Regiment disbanded.

Three days after the signing of the Agreement the killings began again with the shooting of Sergeant Robert Boyd. Boyd was the permanent cadre transport NCO in 5UDR. He was one of the longest-serving members of the Regiment, having enlisted in March 1970, three weeks before Vesting Day. He was also a Catholic. At the end of his day's duty he had returned to his home in Prehen Park in Derry when a man armed with a rifle got out of a car parked across the road opposite the house and opened fire. Boyd ran to the front door, hammering to gain entry, then, still under fire, ran round to the side of the house where he collapsed. The gunman followed and fired a further burst. PIRA admitted responsibility and within days a neighbour had been charged with the murder. Boyd was buried after a non-military funeral. His widow had to remove the cards from wreaths sent by members of the security forces for fear of retaliation against the family. Before the month was out, on the day after the Commons had approved the Agreement by a huge majority of 426, Gordon Hanna, a part-time Captain in the Kilkeel Company, was killed when a device exploded under his car.

By the end of the year the Regiment, and the Regular battalions, were heavily committed to the protection of police stations in country areas. By day the guards were carried out by full-time companies, assisted by the part-timers at night; and part-timers were used to increase the level of daylight patrols. The number of nights that the soldiers spent out of bed increased and companies and platoons from Regular battalions already in the Province, supplemented by the Spearhead Battalion, were placed under command of UDR battalions to relieve some of the pressure by taking over the guards.

Despite these measures the Provisionals continued to attack police stations across the country. Twice they mounted mortar attacks on UDR bases. In February bombs landed inside the perimeter of 8UDR's battalion headquarters at Killymeal, demolishing three portacabins. The occupants, members of an attached Regular company, heard the launching and the flight of the bombs and took cover under the beds, suffering only minor injuries, though everything in the building above waist height was shredded by shrapnel. A fifth bomb landed in the grounds of the next door school.[25]

In March an attempt to mortar the company base at Kilkeel failed when bombs sailed over the top and landed in a field beyond. The mortars had been mounted on a flatbed lorry disguised and given false registration plates to match another lorry which made deliveries each weekend to the cul-de-sac used as the baseplate position for the attack. Bags of logs had been used to hide the tubes. It was a fortunate escape; an hour later the Saturday night dance attended by some 100 people would have been in full swing in the drill hall.[26]

In 1986 it was again the RUC who took the brunt of the casualties, with twelve dead. The Army suffered four fatalities during that year, the UDR eight, plus one ex-member, Herbie McConville, shot dead as he was delivering meat in Newry. He had been the Company Sergeant Major in the Rathfriland Company.

Victor Foster was eighteen years old and had served in the Castlederg Company for the past six months. On the night of 15 January he and his fiancée set out in his car from the house at Spamount, a small mill community. They had driven a few hundred yards when a device, activated by a mercury tilt switch and attached underneath on the driver's side, exploded, killing Foster outright and blinding his fiancée in one eye. The young couple had put down a deposit on their house that morning. The funeral took place from the church where they had planned to get married.

On 3 February a section of 4UDR was carrying out a foot patrol outside the Border town of Belcoo when a RCIED was detonated in a stone wall. The lead man, Private John Earley, took the full force of the explosion and was killed outright.

Three months after the killing of Foster, Private William Pollock from the same battalion died at Glasagh, near Castlederg, when a device fixed to a farm trailer exploded as he was hooking it up to his car. Pollock had been married six months and he and his wife had moved into their new bungalow just five weeks before he was killed. At the funeral the coffin was draped in an Ulster flag because, a local DUP councillor claimed, "the Union flag really meant nothing to them any more". Pollock had been a friend of Victor Foster and had attended his funeral. According to this councillor, he told friends that if he was killed he did not want "any of those big boys with medals to attend his funeral".[27] The widow tore up the condolence letter from Tom King and returned it to the NIO and for the first time a Secretary of State's representative did not attend the funeral. Months later Mrs Pollock told the Battalion that she regretted that she had allowed herself to be persuaded to destroy the letter and arrangements were made for her to receive another copy. Thereafter on rare occasions other bereaved UDR families followed her example and arrangements were made to ensure that they were always asked in advance whether they wished to receive a condolence letter and for a NIO representative to attend the funeral. Almost all of them did.

Early in the morning of 28 May the police received three telephone warnings to the effect that there was a device in a filling station belonging to a prominent South Down GAA player on the Newry road outside Kilkeel. A police patrol carried out a search of the premises with the owner and found nothing untoward. When a further warning was received a patrol from the local company carried out a further search and still nothing was found. In the afternoon a male caller, speaking on behalf of the IRA, rang RUC Newry to confirm that there was a device in the filling station. A permanent cadre patrol was sent to the scene and Corporal Brian Brown with his dog Oliver arrived from Ballykinlar. Brown was briefed that during the morning employees at the garage had found two oil cans which had not been there the previous day. They had picked one up and rocked the other, but then set them down as there was no sign of a device. Possibly Oliver touched one of them, for it exploded, killing Brown and the labrador. The fact that the container had already been moved once by the member of the garage staff suggested that the device might have been fitted with a double initiation system; such a system had been found in a car stopped at a checkpoint in Newry earlier in the year.[28]

Brian Brown had been a search dog handler since 1976 and was a veteran of numerous clearance operations in South Down and along the Border, one of the most experienced dog handlers in the Province. In the aftermath there were suggestions that he had advised against carrying out the clearance that day as his dog had been working in the morning and was tired; but, it was said, he came under pressure to clear the filling station and went ahead against his better judgement. If so, it was a fatal mistake and an uneasy feeling lingered that Brown suffered an unnecessary death. He was awarded a posthumous Queen's Gallantry Medal.

Martin Blaney was the tenth member of the Aughnacloy Company to be murdered. Gunmen had taken over a house belonging to two women beside the lane leading back to Blaney's farm. As he drove home from working at the little parish church of Brantry they opened fire, killing him and his dog lying across the back seat.[29] At the funeral in Caledon the Archbishop of Armagh, Dr Robin Eames, participating in his thirty-seventh funeral for a victim of terrorism, told the congregation:

"The individual courage of men and women who live in isolated areas and are prepared to give their free time to the community through membership of the UDR is beyond praise. The UDR must be at the frontier of a community's resistance to terrorism. While I do not condone for one moment, but utterly condemn individual incidents when the good name of the Regiment in the past has suffered through the actions of a few, I feel society does not always fully appreciate the role of the UDR. The Regiment has been asked to carry an immense burden. It has paid a heavy price in loss of life. It has received criticism, often from those far-removed from the dangers it faces, which has been far from fair or objective. In its increasingly professional approach to its work, its members must never forget their duty to all members of the community, irrespective of political or religious outlooks. But the community must never forget what the UDR is doing day and night for it."

Four days earlier a Sergeant who was a part-time member of the Magherafelt Company had had an extraordinary escape when he had gone out to his farm to check on his cattle. A lane led up to the meadow with a stone wall on one side and an orchard on the other. The trees overhung the lane and the Sergeant was in the habit of gathering the fallen fruit to feed his herd. As he bent down to pick up an apple he touched a piece of fishing line, a trip wire running into the dry stone wall and connected to a box containing 2lb of commercial explosive. The fruit was ripe and the fact that children regularly raided the orchard and might well have set off the device could have been used as a valuable source of propaganda against the IRA in a strongly Republican area, but the police ruled that no publicity should be given. As a result locals were able to convince themselves that there never had been a device and that the UDR had fabricated the whole story.[30]

The entire Protestant community had been incensed by the Anglo–Irish Agreement. Not only had it been drawn up without their representatives being consulted, but for the first time since the creation of the state the Republic had been given a say in the affairs of Northern Ireland through the joint ministerial conference, enshrined in an international document lodged with the United Nations. Furthermore the joint secretariat was to be set up on Ulster soil, a constant reminder of the Republic's involvement in Northern Ireland's affairs.

A week after Hillsborough the Unionist leaders held a massive demonstration in front of the City Hall. The 'Ulster says No' campaign was launched and every Protestant town and village erected its banner proclaiming that the community said 'no' to the Agreement.

Both Unionist parties resigned their seats at Westminster to force by-elections, confident that the results would show the extent of united Protestant opposition to the Agreement. The SDLP contested only four seats. In one, Newry and Armagh, the sitting Unionist member was beaten by the SDLP deputy leader, Seamus Mallon, indicating, to the considerable relief of both governments, a swing away from Sinn Fein to the constitutional Nationalists in the IRA heartland.

Unable to do anything to change, let alone cancel, the Agreement, the Loyalist hooligan element took over, venting their anger against members of the Catholic community and the RUC, but mainly the latter, assaulting them in street disturbances and in their homes. By the end of 1986 there had been 564 incidents involving police families and 120 had had to abandon their homes.[31] Apart from isolated incidents the UDR escaped the hooligans' attentions. When a 1/9UDR patrol arrested a leading member of the UDA during a riot in an estate in Ballymena, the soldier carrying out the arrest subsequently came under threat.[32]

11UDR patrols were heavily committed in Lisburn, where the petrol bombing of Catholic homes had become a nightly occurrence. On three occasions patrols arrested stone throwers or petrol bombers, only to release them when an aggressive crowd had gathered. The experience of the patrol that had allowed itself to become involved in a confrontation in Armagh, leading to the accidental death of the youth Malone, had not been forgotten.

In March the Unionist leaders called for a Day of Action. A DUP demonstration in the city centre degenerated into a riot, the violence growing more serious after dark, with shots being fired in Loyalist areas, cars and buildings set on fire on the Shankill and Newtownards roads. Inevitably there were accusations that off-duty soldiers had been involved in disturbances and a major effort was made in battalions to establish the names of any soldiers who had been involved. They amounted to twenty. Those who were charged by the RUC and found guilty were discharged from service; others were dealt with under military discipline, which tended to be more severe than the courts in the scale of punishment awarded.[33]

Another eleven involved in the disturbances in the summer were dealt with in the same manner. Critics would say that soldiers as servants of the Crown should not become involved in political protests, even out of uniform, and the critics would be right. But that was all very well for members of the Regular Army. They were not living within their own neighbourhoods, hearing day in day out, from their families, in their clubs, and reading in their newspapers that their community had been unjustly treated and was under threat. The wonder is not that thirty-one out of 6,500 allowed themselves to become involved in Loyalist protests, rather that the number was so few. It was a tribute to the high standards of command and control and to the qualities of the soldiers, the GOC said, adding that the UDR was subjected to detailed critical examination and that both the Chief of the General Staff and ministers were well satisfied with its performance.

On 15 November 1986 the Unionist leaders addressed another vast crowd in front of the City Hall to mark the first anniversary of the Agreement. It had been an ugly night. In Ballysillan a crowd of fifty youths began petrol bombing a police patrol; a Hotspur, trying to get away, ran over a Protestant and killed him. Another patrol came under fire in Carlisle Circus. Petrol bombs were thrown at Catholic houses in Lisburn, and in Omagh the home of a Greenfinch was attacked. Paisley had started to address the multitude when a small gang of hooligans at the back of the crowd began breaking shop windows and looting the contents. In a sports shop they discovered a store of golf balls and used them to pelt the police, who replied with baton rounds. Paisley appealed for order and was barracked by the mob. Ken Maginnis went down to try and reason with them and was verbally abused by drunken teenagers. After two and a half hours forty-seven shops had been damaged and fourteen looted. The vast majority of the crowd had been orderly, but viewers watching the news that evening, in the Province and further afield, would remember chiefly the remarkable sight of police Landrovers being bombarded from all directions with a barrage of golf balls.

It was the climax of the Loyalist demonstrations against the Anglo–Irish Agreement. Responsible leaders realized that the country was in danger of drifting into anarchy at the mercy of the hooligans, and that such scenes as the City Hall riot, seen by the world on their television sets, did incalculable harm to efforts to restore the economy of the country. A more realistic mood began to predominate. Ulster could go on saying 'no' until the cows came home, but in fact there were only two choices – accept the will of parliament or declare independence. Though the Protestant community continued to resent that part of the Agreement that had given the Republic a say in the government of Northern Ireland, most people felt that after a year it had not made much difference to their lives, a view shared by Mrs Thatcher who was disappointed that insufficient practical measures had been taken by the Republic to help in the defeat of the IRA. "Our concessions alienated the Unionists without giving the level of security co-operation we had a right to expect," she wrote.[34] Overall the Loyalists protests against the Agreement were causing more problems than the Agreement itself.

Despite the unrest amongst the Protestant community, the soldiers had remained steadfast, enlistments had gone up and the number of soldiers leaving the Regiment had gone down. As a result, in the first five months after Hillsborough, the overall strength had increased by ninety-nine and between April 1985 and April 1986 the regimental total had gone up by 130, the first such increase for five years. Furthermore Catholic numbers had increased by twenty compared with a year ago. By the end of the year the first six officer cadets to undergo the full six-month Regular Army commissioning course had passed out of Sandhurst, three within the top thirty out of a course of 150 Regular Army cadets.

In the wake of Hillsborough the Nationalist criticisms abated somewhat and it was mainly the DUP who seemed intent on damaging the morale of the Regiment and undermining the faith of the soldiers in their officers by circulating malicious and unfounded rumours. The RUC suffered the same treatment. It is difficult to understand what motivated the members of Paisley's party, except that it had plans afoot for the formation of a new Loyalist paramilitary force, Ulster Resistance, and it suited that purpose to undermine public faith in the effectiveness of the security forces. On the morning the Agreement was signed Paisley had informed the media that UDR soldiers in Ballymena were being ordered to report to their bases to be disarmed prior to the part-time being phased out, a distortion of the facts that seemed designed to sow seeds of doubt at a sensitive time. Commenting on the Commander's statement on the implications of the Agreement for the Regiment, the DUP press officer claimed that "the injection of the Englishmen overseers in each battalion is nothing more than London and Dublin insisting that the UDR is not to be trusted," whilst the extension to recruit training was "a deliberate policy to make part-timer membership even more difficult". A DUP councillor claimed that there were to be "mass resignations" after, he alleged, soldiers had been warned that they would have to resign if they belonged to any of the Loyal Orders.[35] The *Newsletter* published this groundless story under the heading "UDR about to fold up". A journalist in North Antrim, Paisley's constituency, asked if it was true that soldiers were to be required to reaffirm their oath of allegiance. Robinson, the party deputy leader, advised Protestants to refuse to co-operate with police officers accompanying UDR patrols as they were there on the directions of the Anglo–Irish Council.[36]

To many in the Regiment it seemed that the DUP's concern was not the good of the UDR but an attempt by the party to win a place as the main voice of the Protestant people.

In June the Regiment held its one and only Tattoo, a two-day event in the Ravenhill rugby grounds. It was an enormous success. The weather was hot and 12,000 people came to see the free-fall drop by the Red Devils, the Greenfinches abseiling from the roof of the stands, the UDR dogs, the mock encounter with a terrorist ambush, and Beating Retreat with the Regimental pipes and drums and the bands of the Duke of Edinburgh's Royal Regiment and the RUC. As the crowd joined in the humming of the evening hymn, 'The day Thou gavest', it was a deeply moving and satisfying moment. It was Brigadier Roger Preston's last moment of command. At the end of the display he and his wife Polly were piped out of the arena to drive to the ferry, to retirement and a walking holiday in Kashmir. He told a *Belfast Telegraph* reporter that his time in command had been "interesting and at times frustrating".[37] In the Regiment's eyes he had shared their frustrations with sympathy and understanding and met the challenge admirably.

The Advisory Council decided it might help to foster a better understanding of the Regiment and discourage unfounded rumours if the four main Northern Ireland political parties were to be given briefings at HQUDR. The NIO havered, saying that the time was not ripe, but eventually agreed. On the morning of Ravenhill four members of the Alliance Party came to the Headquarters to be briefed, including the party leader, John Cushnahan. They were followed by the Official Unionists, Ken Maginnis and two others, all three former members of the UDR. John Hume, accompanied by Mallon, came from the SDLP, listened but made little comment. Only the DUP failed to answer the first, followed by a second invitation, and never came for a briefing.

1986 had been an exceedingly busy year for the Regiment. Most battalions had taken under operational control one or more Regular companies on police station protection duties, placing a heavy load on the administrative staffs, whose establishment was still woefully inadequate. Over the year 11UDR acted as a firm base and operational headquarters for a total of some twenty-eight Regular rifle companies, tasked into the TAOR to support the RUC during the Loyalist disorders in Portadown and neighbouring towns.

As the Commander LandForces pointed out in his review of the year, the UDR had had to face pressures in 1986 that it had not had to face before. The soldiers' steadfastness and common sense in the face of all manner of rumour and provocation had brought the Regiment great credit.

CHAPTER SEVENTEEN

1987–1989

Michael Bray commanded the UDR for twenty-seven months, longer than anyone else, and never ceased in his efforts, despite setbacks, to improve the image of the Regiment. Two years earlier he had obtained a degree in International Studies at Cambridge and had written as his thesis a paper on relations between the government and the media, principally in times of war. Now he had the opportunity to put his theories into practice. Although the RUC Press Office still took the lead in dealing with the media on operational matters, the policy of playing down the role of the Army in Northern Ireland had been relaxed. With the support of Pascoe, the GOC, and Hermon, the Chief Constable, Bray obtained permission from the NIO to

> "address the issues of the day in public so far as they concerned the UDR, and to challenge those who sought to discredit or undermine the Regiment.
>
> "It was an uphill struggle at times. If I wanted to speak, a prepared piece as opposed to something impromptu, the text had to be cleared with the NIO, as well as HQNI and with the Ministry of Defence. Trying to get two separate Ministries to agree on some text, especially the MOD who did not really understand the issues, was like trying to push a boulder up Snowdon."[1]

Five months after taking over command he held his first media briefing at Ballykinlar. He took Mallon to task for continuing to demand the disbandment of the Regiment, saying: "he should realize that the SDLP and the UDR have one thing in common – seeking to bring about peace by peaceful means. If they did more to support the Regiment instead of seeking to undermine it, it would be better for both of us."[2]

In the next two years he spoke out several times in the same forceful manner. He was very good at it and many in the Regiment were glad that they had a Commander ready and willing to challenge their critics. But each appearance on television or in the press was liable to spark off a controversy of counter-criticism and Bray was to experience the problem to which there is no one answer – is it better to speak out and risk becoming involved in a slanging match, prompting one's opponents to give their contrary views, or better as a serving soldier to stay silent when your men and women are unjustly criticized and leave it to the politicians, to whom controversy is a way of life, to do battle on their behalf? Bray had no such doubts. As their Commander it was his responsibility to stand up for his people. King, the Secretary of State, was a constant ally and a good friend to the Regiment, but the Brigadier was the man on the ground and, he maintained, there was no one else who could answer effectively the repeated criticisms and allegations, all too often ill-informed.

Unfortunately two events in 1987 gave fresh ammunition to the UDR's critics.

The Coleraine Company of 5UDR was based at Laurel Hill, the mid-17th century house overlooking the town and the Bann. In 1986 two junior NCOs in the company, one of them an armoury storeman, had joined the local UDA. During the night of 22 February 1987 the storeman smuggled three members of the paramilitary organization into the base in the boot of his car. In the dead of the night they came out from their hiding place, overpowered the guard and played out a charade of forcing the storeman to hand over the keys of the company armoury. They loaded the entire company weapon holdings into the van, including 144 SLRs, two LMGs, twenty-eight pistols and over a thousand rounds of ammunition. An hour after the raid began they departed, leaving the guard gagged and bound. Ten minutes after they had gone on their way a soldier coming on duty and unable to get into the base looked through the guardroom window, saw the guard and raised the alarm. An hour later the police intercepted the van on the motorway heading for Belfast, arrested the driver and recovered all the weapons. Within days four members of the UDA had been arrested and charged, including the two soldiers who admitted their part in the raid.[3]

Six months later a Colour Sergeant in 7/10UDR drew the keys to the armoury in Palace Barracks, removed a number of weapons, including thirteen pistols and two LMGs, loaded them into the company minibus and took them to a Shankill Road social club where he sold them to the UDA for £3,000. He then absconded to the Republic, was arrested by the Garda in Dundalk acting on a tip-off from the RUC, was extradited back to the North and sentenced to five years' imprisonment. He had been able to draw the armoury key without arousing suspicion because, as an instructor, he was on the list of persons authorized to have access to the weapons. Yet he had an appalling record, dating back to the early '70s. He had lost two personal protection weapons, one stolen when he was in a drinking club and used within hours in the murder of a Catholic. He had family connections with the Loyalist paramilitaries. He was drinking heavily and in financial difficulties. All this was known to the security service, but previous attempts to have him discharged had come to nought. His present Commanding Officer knew nothing about his record, though other members of the Battalion told him after the event that they had known the Colour Sergeant was a liability.

Commander Land Forces expressed his views in no uncertain terms. The Minister for the Armed Forces and the Secretary of State had taken a very serious view. The UDR could not afford a repeat of such an incident and action must be taken to ensure that any soldier who was liable to do harm to the Regiment was discharged. Bray had already put measures in hand following the Coleraine raid. These were now formalized. With immediate effect COs, accompanied by their TISOs, were to discuss with Company Commanders anyone in their companies who might be a security risk, including those whose drink or financial problems might make them liable to subversion. Company Commanders were to draw up lists after discussions with their platoon commanders and Senior NCOs. Battalions were to maintain confidential records of anyone whose reliability was cause for concern. The first lists were to be completed by the end of October and thereafter were to be formally reviewed every six months by the CO, TISO and Company Commander. Depending on the degree of security risk, a soldier could be put up for discharge, moved to a less sensitive post or kept on the list for reassessment in six months' time. All paramilitary social clubs were to be placed out of bounds to members of the Regiment. Lists of the clubs were to be displayed on notice boards, together with an unequivocal order stating that any soldier who was a member of a paramilitary organization or associated with such an organization or was found drinking in one of the out-of-bounds clubs would be discharged.

Bray was well pleased with the results of the first vetting review. The reaction of the Company Commanders had been positive, except for one, and he had been removed from command. There were very few cases where there was concern about possible paramilitary association. Only one soldier had to be removed on those grounds and a second because of mental instability. In most cases where paramilitary association was suspected, the suspicions were tenuous and out of date. In the few problem cases that had arisen most were of a welfare nature – drink, debt or matrimonial.

When reports of the new code of conduct appeared in the press, coupled with an interview Bray had given on RTE, Mallon's comments on behalf of the SDLP were predictably sour: a code of conduct would not change the fundamental problem of the Regiment which he described as a sectarian force which had been responsible for State-funded sectarian murders.[4] Bray and Mallon had already crossed swords after the Brigadier had given an interview in October to the Londonderry *Sentinel*. To most people what he said was unexceptional, but his remarks, that the UDR would "welcome any indication from the minority community that they are prepared to work for reconciliation as opposed to widening the gap between the Regiment and the minority community" and that it was "because of the opposition that we find from most of the leaders of the minority community, which encourages an unjust and unbalanced view of the UDR, that we have too few Catholics in our ranks", were taken by Mallon as an attack on the SDLP. He accused the Brigadier of making a highly political statement attacking a specific political party, that it was "unethical and unprofessional" and that he would be making his views known at "the highest level".[5]

Bray came to realize that these confrontational episodes were achieving nothing for the UDR and that nothing he or anyone else said would alter the SDLP's party policy that the Regiment should be disbanded. Attempts by Commanding Officers to make contact with their local SDLP representatives had not proved successful, least of all in those districts where their councillors were vying with Sinn Fein for support. Instead Bray decided that efforts should be concentrated on reaching out to the ordinary moderate members of the public. Central briefings would be held at HQ UDR for people nominated by the battalions, as many as seventy at a time, including clergy from all denominations, followed by a question and answer session. These briefings were to prove so popular that, after three had been held, people were asking for invitations. Others were held for headmasters and career masters, with the additional aim of improving recruiting among school-leavers in the hope of overcoming the chronic shortage of officers. At the first of these briefings fifteen out of fifty-five masters who attended were from Catholic schools. Other briefings were held for members of the British and, later, separately the Irish members, of the Anglo-Irish Secretariat at Maryfield. Bray was encouraged when a guest from South Armagh told him: "The best way I can describe the progress made by the UDR is to say that five years ago, when I was driving along in the dark and I came to a road block, I used to say to myself, 'I hope it's not the UDR'. Now when I am driving along and I come to a road block, I say to myself, 'I hope it is the UDR'."

A rewarding way of getting across to ordinary people in both communities was through an energetic policy of Community Relations, the raising of funds and the provision of practical help and equipment for charitable groups. By this means people who had never met and talked to UDR soldiers found that they were men and women much like themselves, not, as some politicians would have them believe, people to be feared. Despite all the demands of operational duties battalions made remarkable efforts in the Community Relations field. In 1988 7/10UDR undertook eighty projects, many of them aimed at broaching the sectarian divide, providing both practical assistance and funds, raising nearly £15,000 for a wide variety of charitable causes, a large part of it by the companies. In 3UDR a Greenfinch Sergeant and a group of helpers from the companies arranged for twenty handicapped children from a Special Care School to come to Ballykinlar each week to play indoor games in the gymnasium, and when the weather permitted took them for nature walks into the forest parks and along the nearby beach. In 1989 alone the battalions raised a total of £56,700 for a wide range of charities.

Though many of the charities could never publicly acknowledge the help they had received, the pleasure of bringing some enjoyment to the sick and handicapped, the elderly and the children, or of helping an institution to buy some piece of medical equipment that it could not otherwise afford was reward enough in itself.

In October 1987 the Province was swept by torrential rain, the heaviest rainfall ever recorded in some areas. The north and west were worst hit, particularly Omagh and Strabane. By mid-afternoon 6UDR had been authorized by Brigade Headquarters to provide whatever assistance was necessary. A platoon of the Light Infantry was despatched to Gortin ranges to fill sandbags with sand from the butts, whilst the UDR began laying thousands of sandbags in the centre of Omagh and at the married quarters at Campsie where the river soon burst its banks. A thousand bags were laid round the Nestlés factory to replace the sacks of powdered milk the manager had used in an attempt to keep back the rising waters. By early morning the floods were out of control. After an emergency conference with the police, held in knee-deep water, the decision was taken to close the bridges connecting the two halves of the town as they were in danger of collapse. Residents were being evacuated by boat, in vehicles and carried on shoulders from the town centre and some of the married quarters. At 2am in Strabane the Gunners of the battery of 22 Air Defence Regiment under command 6UDR, hearing an explosion and believing that a bomb had gone off, ran to investigate and were met by a four-foot wall of water sweeping down the main street as the flood defences collapsed, washing away cars and goods from broken shop windows. The soldiers, working waist-deep in the fast-flowing current, began evacuating the centre of the town.

Rescue operations continued across the TAOR through the night and into the following day. At the RUC's request the UDR cookhouse provided 500 hot breakfasts. As the full extent of the damage became clear to the civil authorities requests for assistance multiplied – food for people trapped in their homes, pumps, sandbags, heaters and the rescue of stranded householders. By evening, thirty hours after the rain had begun, 500 soldiers from the UDR and the Regular units, employed continuously, without sleep, under the direction of the RUC and 6UDR, rescued some 750 people, though the exact number would never be known, filled 7–8,000 sandbags, put out fires caused by electrical short circuits, rescued livestock and delivered food supplies.[6]

Around 9pm the watchkeeper in 11UDR received a message that six horses were marooned on a small piece of high ground near Moira where the Lagan had burst its banks. A Captain set out with one of the battalion assault boats, his wetsuit and lifejackets, and six soldiers. Arriving at the location they had to manhandle the boat for some 500 metres over the fields in the dark to reach the water's edge, and then paddle round hedgerows to the horses. The UDR Captain picks up the story:

"Unfortunately the outline of the boat kept frightening them so I had no option but to get out and swim and wade to the horses, then wait for them to calm down and proceed to get a head collar on one after managing to catch it – a slow process. It was equally as slow and difficult to get the captured animal out of the flooded area and to safe ground, mainly because the area was littered with barbed wire fences which were below water level. Indeed, while swimming the first horse to safety it looked as though I might well lose it as it became trapped by its hindquarters over a wire fence and a fencing post pushing against its stomach. This required my going under, breaking away the post and wire while the horse tried to break itself free at the same time. One had to alternate between this task and lifting the horse's head above the water to keep it breathing.

"The next task was now to find a new route out and this could only be done by breaking down what one could of the hedgerow and by twisting and breaking the usual four strands of barbed wire, again a slow process under water. With this done and the horse coaxed and pulled through the hedge it was then a simple swim of 50 metres to safe ground."[7]

One by one all the horses were brought to safety. Their owner told the local paper: "I can never thank the UDR enough for their kindness especially the man in the wetsuit whose stamina was unbelievable. The whole thing was a miracle. I did not think it was possible."[8]

In December three people were drowned when their car drove into the Bann near Toomebridge. A nearby UDR VCP heard the crash and a soldier and a policeman dived into the river to rescue a girl who had managed to escape from the vehicle. The other three were trapped and, though the two rescuers dived underwater in an attempt to release them, they were driven back by the cold. The woman's boyfriend who died in the accident was, according to the Provisionals, one of their active volunteers.[9]

Public Relations remained an unresolved problem, as much for the Regular Army in Ulster as for the UDR. At battalion level relations with the local press were good. Young reporters would be taken to annual camps where for a week they would be absorbed into the battalion, taking part in exercises and range practice, and on their return publishing double-page accounts of their experiences. Bray was particularly good at dealing with the media, persuasive in his arguments and quick-witted in dealing with interviewers' 'fast balls'. The problem arose in countering unjustified and inaccurate criticism. All too often complaints against the Regiment were publicized in the press, aired on radio or television or passed to the Irish Government before the battalion, yet alone Regimental Headquarters, knew anything about them. No doubt the complainants would have argued that by doing so they ensured that their complaints were taken seriously by the authorities. To the Regiment it looked all too like a policy of deliberate denigration; once the complaint was publicized, whether it was true or false and subsequently denied, the harm had been done. There were those so anxious to find fault that they made no attempt to check the details or the validity of the complaint and were so vague about the time and place that it was difficult to follow them up.

When an Armagh priest referred a complaint about members of 2UDR direct to the Irish Government and the CO, David Strudley, asked him why he had not raised it with him in the first place, the priest said it had not occurred to him to do so. Thereafter Strudley gave the priest his office and home telephone numbers and encouraged him to pass on directly any further complaints.

As a result a valuable understanding grew up between soldier and priest, and Strudley felt a sense of achievement when he received a message back from the Sisters of Mercy that his soldiers were more polite than they used to be. He had called on the Mother Superior. He was, she told him, the first British soldier she had ever spoken to. His experiences in Armagh showed what could be achieved to improve relationships, provided it was done in a quiet, unpublicized way, but sadly in the CO's last months the relationship tailed off. Strudley never knew why, but suspected that the priest had been 'leant on' by those who disapproved of any sort of contact between the military and the church.[10]

In fact formal complaints against individual patrols were remarkably few. When Bray pointed out to Mallon that after the UDR had manned the Middletown PVCP for a year, dealing with a steady stream of traffic between Armagh and Monaghan, and there had not been even one complaint, the MP had nothing to say. CO 1/9UDR in his annual summary for the historical record reported that in 1987/88, a year when his patrols had searched 51,000 vehicles, the Battalion had received six complaints, one of which had been substantiated; in the following year eight, five of which had been groundless, in two there had been faults on both sides arising from mutual irritation, and the eighth had arisen from the rudeness of a soldier who had been disciplined.[11] Where soldiers on duty were the targets for physical assaults, battalions were encouraged to ask the police to charge the assailants.

Bray devoted the greater part of his Study Weekend in February 1988 to a discussion on means of improving relations with the minority community. Each of the Majors attending the conference was required to submit in writing his suggestions. Though some pointed out that in their part of the Province Protestants were the minority community, the vast majority of the sixty-two replies were devoid of bias, moderate in tone and sympathetic to the problem. But there were few proposals that were not being tried already. All agreed that the greatest need was to ensure that soldiers behaved courteously at check points and that this depended on good leadership. Some suggested that vehicles should be selected for search before the drivers had been asked for names and addresses, to avoid the assumption that the vehicle had been picked out because the name was a Catholic one and the address in a Nationalist area. Training must be given in chatting-up techniques, Greenfinches should be used rather than male soldiers and care should be taken to avoid siting VCPs where they would interfere with worshippers going to Mass. "The very character of our patrolling," one wrote, "is sometimes too aggressive and inconsiderate. Hard targeting is often insensitive in quiet housing estates, and insisting on walking on the pavement, diverting pedestrians onto the road, is inconsiderate. It is all too easy for a soldier who is being conscientious to be seen by the public as being arrogant and bad-mannered, due to the fact that he is in uniform and has a weapon in his hand."

By now most of the COs had served in the province with their parent Regular battalions at least once and many more often as platoon and company commanders. They had had time between tours to assimilate and reflect on the lessons they had learnt and now returned to put them into practice in their UDR battalions. Operations became more sophisticated and less stereotype; no longer the two-vehicle patrols widely dispersed over the whole TAOR but frequent coordinated VCP operations at battalion and company level, concentrated on one area, often planned and executed by part-time company commanders, seeking new methods of deployment to keep the terrorists off balance, using foot patrols backed up by mobile patrols in reserve. Cooperation with the RUC was now excellent, though the UDR found it necessary to take the lead in persuading Sub-Divisional Commanders not to expend the resources of the battalion on routine tasks of limited operational value or to spread them too thinly over the whole sub-division. The police's attitude to the conduct of operations tended to be different to the Army's – defensive, preventing attacks taking place rather than going out to look for the terrorists, seizing the initiative and interdicting their movement. The problem of finding sufficient constables to accompany every patrol remained unresolved. In most areas less than half had a policeman.

From the beginning of 1987 the Regular company in Keady-Middletown under operational control of 2UDR had been withdrawn and its place taken by a permanent cadre company drawn in turn from 1/9, 7/10 and 11UDR. The experiment of tasking the UDR to control twelve miles of the South Armagh border proved a great success, for it showed that the full-time companies were now well able to operate independently in most areas of the province. But the arrangements placed a heavy load on 2UDR, maintaining with an inadequate administrative staff an attached company on the Border and keeping it supplied along roads liable to landmine and ambush, and, because of restrictions on flying hours, without the benefit of helicopter support. The regular fortnightly change-over between companies was a nightmare – the security of convoys, the alternating of routes from a limited choice of roads, approaching the two bases from unpredictable directions. It was a strain too on the three battalions who were providing the roulement companies as well as continuing to take turns to find the guard force at Crumlin Road prison and provide reinforcements from part-time platoons to help out the Border battalions at weekends.

When a car bomb exploded outside the vehicle tax office in Queen Street at the end of January '87, injuring eleven people, it was the first major attack in the city centre for over a year. Mortar attacks on police stations continued. Between the last week of March and the end of April eighteen people were killed, including seven RUC officers, a Regular soldier and two members of the UDR. On 25 April, the same day that one of the UDR soldiers was murdered, Judge Gibson, the second senior member of the judiciary, and his wife were returning by road from a holiday in France. Gardai escorted them through the Republic as far as the Border and an RUC escort was waiting for them a mile into the North. In that mile gap the Provisionals had left a van parked at the side of the road containing a remote-controlled bomb. It exploded as the Gibsons drove past, killing the judge and his wife.

As a result of the upsurge in killings the UDR was placed on a limited call-out. In effect this meant that the 400 part-time/full-time soldiers, instead of being limited to twenty duties a month, would be available for duties all day and every day, whilst all part-timers were encouraged to volunteer for extra duties. It was more a gesture than a major increase in security cover. It was a long time since there had been a total call-out of the part-time element. Such blanket call-outs had become unrealistic unless the situation was exceptionally grave.

In May the IRA suffered their heaviest casualties in any one incident since 1921 when the Black and Tans in Cork had killed twelve volunteers. Two ASUs, under the leadership of James Lynagh and Patrick Kelly, came together to mount an attack on the RUC station at Loughgall, a quiet village in the relatively peaceful orchard country of Co Armagh. The operation was to be a carbon copy of the successful attack on the police station at the Birches nine months earlier – a bomb loaded into the bucket of a digger, driven through the perimeter wire to detonate beside the station. It should have been an easy target, for, like the Birches, the station was only manned by day. The movements of the eight-man team, especially Lynagh who lived across the Border, and the bringing together and storing of the explosives in a farm building in the neighbourhood had been observed and the security forces were aware that an attack was being planned. On the evening of 8 May four men stole a digger from a house two miles from the village. Earlier in the afternoon a van had been hijacked in Coalisland. About 7.30pm the digger and the van arrived outside the police station. Some of the gunmen leapt out of the van and opened fire while the digger was driven at the gates through the perimeter wire and the bomb exploded, demolishing one end of the building. Soldiers deployed in and around the building opened fire, killing all eight attackers. Sadly two brothers drove into the village as the firefight was taking place, both wearing overalls similar to the Provisionals; one was shot dead, the other seriously injured. A total of eight weapons were recovered from the bodies. They had been used in at least seven assassinations in the previous sixteen months, including the murder of four members of the UDR. Lynagh, a Sinn Fein councillor in Monaghan, was believed to have been involved in thirty murders. In 1980 he had been charged with the murder of Harry Livingstone, a former member of 2UDR, but was acquitted by a Dublin court.[12]

Although, by coincidence, the part-time companies of 2UDR were away at annual camp in England, Strudley had been warned that something was brewing and had stayed behind in Armagh. Since the operation was being mounted from his barracks at Drumadd and was taking place in his TAOR, he had a measure of operational responsibility. The permanent cadre company was standing by and on a prearranged codeword moved into position to set up an outer cordon of road blocks around the village, one of them deployed in the main street through the night. The Battalion's task was peripheral, but, as Strudley pointed out, it was "a very good example of how, without any difficulty whatsoever, full-time soldiers could work with some very specialized people."[13]

Loughgall marked a low point in the fortunes of the Provisional IRA. The operation had been a blunder, the security and planning poor, the attack badly executed. The very active East Tyrone group had suffered a damaging blow and over a year was to elapse before PIRA mounted another coordinated operation on the same scale. Instead they turned to soft targets, off-duty members of the security forces where the risk to the attackers was minimal.

During 1987 there were thirty-three attacks against off-duty serving soldiers and another six against ex-members of the Regiment. Eight of the serving personnel and three of the ex-soldiers died. Eight of the attacks were under-vehicle booby traps. Seven were discovered in time or detonated prematurely. The need to look under a vehicle before driving off had been well learnt at last.

Once again the first attack of the year in the Province was made against a UDR family, though in this case the attackers were INLA. Desmond Farley, a member of the UDR from the beginning and before that a B Special, farmed in the hill country south-west of Markethill about ten miles from the Armagh border. His 70-year-old mother lived with the family. His brother George had come over to visit them on New Year's Day. After dark, as the family were standing at the door saying goodnight to their visitor, gunmen opened fire on them. Desmond and his mother were hit. The two sons tried to drag her into the house but came under fire again. Desmond's wife fired the alarm rockets installed on the roof of the farm since a previous attack. The air-bursts were seen at the Company base at Glenanne and patrols and a helicopter were rushed to the scene. Desmond and his mother were taken to hospital. He survived, but Mrs Farley died five weeks later. The attackers were believed to be from the maverick INLA group operating on the Armagh border, led by Dessie O'Hare, described as "a limited unstable man – a seething angry man, ready to kill and maim for little cause".[14] O'Hare's family lived within a mile of the Farley farm.[15]

A Corporal serving in 8UDR had survived an assassination attempt in 1978. Nine years on, by which time he had been promoted to Sergeant, gunmen had taken over a house close to his home out in the country and held the owner and his family hostage overnight. As he was driving down the lane from his house a car belonging to the hostage family drew out across the road in front of him, blocking his way. A gunman got out of the car and opened fire with a rifle at a range of a few feet, hitting the Sergeant's vehicle several times. He rolled out of the driver's door and ran round the back of his car. Though wounded in the left arm, he opened fire with his PPW. His assailants got back into their car and drove past the soldier who had taken cover in the ditch and continued to fire back. At that moment a school bus came along the road. The driver, realizing what was happening, told the children to get under the seats. The attackers reversed back towards the bus. The Sergeant ran towards them and fired one more round from the shelter of the bus, driving off the gunmen who were in some confusion, realizing that this was no soft target. Five shots from his magazine of nine rounds had hit the car.[16]

Corporal James Oldman was manager of a furniture and hardware store in the quiet village of Ederny on the north side of Lower Lough Erne. A bachelor, he lived with his mother in nearby Lack and had been in 4UDR for seventeen years and three days. On the morning of 3 April he drew up at the door of his shop, along with his 13-year-old cousin. He had given her a lift to catch the school bus. Two men approached the car from the rear and opened fire. One of them ordered the girl to get out and then the two fired a further forty-seven rounds into the dying man.

The ripples caused by the casual brutality of the terrorists spread wide – a good man dead, a widowed mother bereaved for the second time, a schoolgirl left with a terrifying memory to haunt her for the rest of her days, and a family knocked up in the middle of the night and held prisoner at gunpoint in their own home, knowing they were being used as unwilling accessories in the murder of a decent man, a man well known to them, and powerless to prevent these armed strangers as they waited by the window over the street for James Oldman to park his car.

There were four other attacks on UDR personnel in and around the city in June, three of them against soldiers from the same company of 7/10UDR. Private Joe Tracey was shot dead as he was installing new electric wiring in a group of flats being renovated off the Lisburn road. The *Newsletter* published a story that the Provisionals had infiltrated the Battalion, a wild rumour promptly denied by HQ UDR.[17] Nevertheless someone must have informed on him. It was the first day that he had worked at the flats and, until he reported that morning, he would not have known where he would be working.

That evening the officers of the Regiment were due to hold a party for a hundred guests, culminating with the regimental pipes and drums beating retreat in the garden of Lord Dunleath's house, Ballywalter Park. Rain had fallen all evening, a mist had settled on the gardens and the light was fading prematurely as the pipes and drums emerged from among the trees at the sound of a bugle call and marched down the sloping lawns.

302

The UDR flag flew at half-mast from the roof of the great house. At the end of the display the twenty-two pipers, fourteen drummers and four drum majors formed up to play the Evening Hymn 'The Day Thou Gavest', followed by the Sunset Call, and a lone piper played 'Oft in the Stilly Night', the lament fading into the distance as he marched away through the garden. The Colonel Commandant, General Sir David Young, stepped forward to tell the officers and wives and their guests that it had been the widow's wish that the retreat should go ahead. He asked that everyone should stand in silence in memory of Tracey and the other 165 men and women who had died in the ranks of the Regiment. It was a deeply moving moment, one that those who were there have never forgotten – the rain, the white mist and in the silence the birds singing their evening chorus in the trees round the lawn.

In July Private William Megrath was shot dead as he drove through the Twinbrook area of West Belfast on his way from work. A member of 11UDR, he was the last Catholic soldier in the UDR to be murdered.

Tragedy was simple to quantify. All too often the headlines in the Belfast evening paper reported the murder of another soldier. A member of the Regiment on his way home at the end of a day's work would see the bill-board 'UDR man murdered' and wonder which battalion and whether he had lost another friend. In the English dailies the news, now almost routine, would be reduced to a paragraph on an inside page. Success was less obvious to measure – by the extent to which the level of violence had been contained rather than by specific successes. Over the year the number of deaths and explosions increased by over a third compared with 1986. On the other hand, thanks to sustained patrolling, to more imaginative tasking, improved RUC liaison and pooling of intelligence, additional helicopter flying hours and, in the case of the Regular units, increasingly successful covert operations, the number of incidents in some areas had gone down dramatically, particularly in 6UDR's TAOR in West Tyrone and 11UDR around Portadown, while 5UDR was able to record that several terrorist operations had been aborted as a result of the Battalion's patrol activities.

In July the Provisionals issued a statement through the Republican press saying that, because of security forces' presence in the area, they had had to abandon a landmine near Baxter's Cross. The same morning a part-time patrol from the Castlederg Company were searching a suspect's car when they came across a trace. When placed on a map it appeared to show the line of a command wire at a place called Baxter's Corner. A clearance operation lasting over two days led to the neutralizing of a 600lb landmine.[18] In August during a series of search operations in their extended TAOR in North Antrim 5UDR found two caches of home-made explosives in the Dunloy area. In all it amounted to 5,400lbs.[19] In October 6UDR became involved in an operation to clear a huge device, 3,500lb of home-made explosives packed into fifty-eight bags, wired up and hidden in a stolen slurry tanker. It was one of the largest assembled devices ever recovered by the security forces and would have caused widespread death and destruction had it been set off in a built-up area.[20]

The IRA always showed great ingenuity in developing improvised weapons. One of these appeared for the first time in 1987, the anti-armour grenade, and was soon being used all over the Province against police stations and patrols. In two separate attacks in the following January they caused the death of police officers. In December a patrol from the part-time company of 5UDR was carrying out a VCP outside Limavady, when they stopped a car containing two people known to them as suspected terrorists. They gave the car a thorough search, but, finding nothing untoward, allowed the driver to proceed. The next car stopped short of the checkpoint, probably intending to turn back, but the junior NCO patrol commander had deployed two of his men in hidden positions further down the road, cutting off any attempt to escape. The Greenfinch Corporal carried out a thorough search of the vehicle, uncovering an arsenal of munitions, including two of the grenade launchers, eleven grenades, 450 rounds of ammunition, 40lb of explosives, two detonator cords, detonators and timers. The two men in the car and the two who had already passed through the checkpoint were arrested and charged. It had been a particularly successful year for 5UDR.[21]

Remembrance Sunday fell on 8 November. Across the Province UDR detachments paraded at their local war memorials, laying wreaths of poppies inset with the Regimental crest, remembering the dead of two World Wars and, more immediately, their own men and women killed in terrorist attacks. Two battalions held parades in their county cathedrals. 3UDR attended the Cathedral of the Holy Trinity in Downpatrick, whilst 4UDR, after a ceremony at the town War Memorial, would march through the streets of Enniskillen to Saint Macartan's. Sergeant Gordon Miller went along each year with his camera; it was one of the few occasions when he could take photographs of the soldiers wearing Number 2 dress and medals. He took a number of pictures of the 115 men and women from the two local companies forming up in the car park and then walked down to the War Memorial. There he met his old friend Sam Gault standing on the pavement between the railings and the wall of St Michael's reading room, a large, old three-storey building at the rear of the memorial. Gault had retired recently from the RUC as a Sergeant following a heart attack. His wife was a senior NCO in the Battalion and had sustained minor injuries in a landmine explosion during a patrol near Kinawley some years back. His younger son was standing beside him. They talked for a while, then Miller remembered he had left his spare film in the car and went back to fetch it. It was a quarter to eleven. In the car park the parade had been fallen in and the Second-in-Command, Roy Kells, was about to hand over to the Commanding Officer, Jeremy Broad. Miller was walking back down Belmore Street towards the memorial. Suddenly there was an explosion down at the far end of the street, not loud, more a dull thud, and as he watched in horror the gable end of the reading room

304

began to bulge out and collapsed on the people standing below it. For a moment there was silence, and then the air was full of screaming. The parade, ignoring the possibility of a second device, broke ranks and ran, meeting people flying in panic out of the thick brown cloud of choking dust, some clutching children, others helping elderly relatives, people dressed in their Sunday best, red poppies in their lapels. The soldiers, the members of the Ballyreagh band who always played at the parade, and bowler-hatted members of the Royal British Legion, but mainly the soldiers, began tearing at the rubble. Miller saw men lifting lumps of masonry that at other times they would have thought beyond their strength. Some searched with a particular dread, fearing that members of their own family would have been standing there. Enniskillen is a small community; those they did not know by name they would know by sight.

Captain Iain McDonald of the RAMC was a qualified nurse, nearing the end of a six-month attachment to the Battalion. He too had come in civilian clothes to watch the parade and take photographs. Whether on or off duty he always carried in his pocket a few plastic airways in case of an emergency. He ran to the scene and began treating the serious casualties. A man had been crushed by a section of the wall, the roof of his skull lifted off and lying beside him. He was obviously dead. As well as being trapped under the rubble of the fallen building, some of the casualties were pinned against the metal railing along the edge of the pavement. A couple were caught from the waist down, lying face down in the wreckage and pushed against the rails. The woman had been crushed, the man unconscious and breathing heavily. McDonald inserted an airway and, leaving the man in the arms of a soldier with instructions to keep the airway clear, he moved on to look for others, stopping several times to insert airways for people unable to breathe under the weight of the masonry. A trapped man screamed for the weight to be taken off his legs. Two others lay unconscious beside him.[22]

Some of the Greenfinches had run to the scene with the men. One of them had been selected to lay the Battalion wreath at the War Memorial. She was nervous about it and had asked a Sergeant to show her the procedure in the drill hall. As they drove down to the town she had said to him, "Norman, there's an awful funny feeling in the air today. The shivers are running through me." Now, kneeling in the dust and debris, she helped the casualties as best she could. Like all the Greenfinches and many of the men, she had been soundly trained in First Aid and the 4UDR team had won the Northern Ireland First Aid competition that year against all comers, Regular, UDR and TA. But now they had no First Aid equipment with them. She talked to those who were conscious and helped the men to lift the seriously injured on to stretchers. The nuns from the convent had brought down blankets and they used them to cover the living and the dead laid out on the footpath. Nine years on she wept as she described the scene. "It's something I'll never forget. Every time I go round there, I just imagine I can see people laid out on the footpath."

After an hour the last casualties had been extricated. Some had been hit by flying glass and masonry, but the seriously injured had been struck by the broken wall. Eleven died and over sixty were injured, among them thirteen children, the youngest two years old. Six of the injured were in intensive care. The dead included three married couples. Sam Gault was among the dead, his younger son slightly injured. The elder boy and his wife should have been standing beside him, but so many people stopped them on their way to admire their new baby that they had been delayed. There were many such stories – the woman who was standing by the railing when she realized she was still wearing her driving shoes and went back to the car to change into her good pair; the Sergeant whose family was delayed by a puncture; the Broads' nanny had arranged to take their small son to see the parade; for an agonising time the CO feared that they might be amongst the dead. Two of the injured were the parents of the Second-in-Command of one of the companies on parade. His mother was in a critical condition and it was vital that she was flown at once to the RVH in Belfast. The pilot of the Army Air Corps Lynx agreed to take her, though thick, low cloud would make the flight hazardous. As far as Aldergrove he was able to navigate by radio beacon, but from there on he had to fly by dead reckoning. As he hovered over the city a hole appeared in the thick blanket directly over the hospital and he was able to land. She survived.

As the soldiers reported in, unbidden, for duty Broad mounted a major Battalion operation, with foot, mobile and heliborne patrols. The Greenfinch who had tended the casualties and then gone to the hospital volunteered to go out with the patrols.

As soon as the bomb had gone off messages had been flashed to all units and police headquarters, warning them to recheck the routes of their parades and around their War Memorials. That evening a caller from the Provisionals 'West Fermanagh Brigade' rang Downtown radio to say that a 200lb landmine had been abandoned on the road to Pettigo, the village astride the Border. It had failed to explode that morning while two members of the security forces were standing on it. The Garda and the Irish Army located the firing point on their side of the Border. From it a command wire led to a device placed at the point where, according to the RUC, "up to fifty young people were getting ready to march and up to a hundred of their parents and friends were milling around the scene,"[23] as they formed up for the Pettigo Remembrance Parade. It was four times larger than the Enniskillen device.

The slaughter in Enniskillen generated worldwide condemnation. There had been no attempt to give a warning. It was suggested that the device had gone off prematurely, quarter of an hour too early, a claim that failed to explain why the bomb had been put there in the first place. If it had detonated any later it would have killed more civilians, for more would have gathered by then, but still it would have not killed members of the UDR. Each year the soldiers led the parade, circled round the back of the memorial and took up positions furthest away from where the bomb had been placed. The British Legion and the youth services, the Boys' Brigade, Scouts and Guides, would have been closer, but any casualties among their ranks were likely to have been relatively minor, caused by flying glass. The men who selected the location for the 40lb of Semtex on the upper floor of the reading rooms must have known it was likely that the wall would collapse and civilians standing below, where they always stood, would be killed. It seems they did not care.

The Queen, President Reagan, the Pope and the Taoiseach sent messages of condolence. Even the Soviet news agency 'Tass', in a rare condemnation of the IRA, described the bombing as a barbarous act. The TV news bulletins repeated again and again the film taken by a spectator with his video camcorder showing the soldiers in their best uniforms searching through the rubble, but little reference was made to the UDR. Mrs Thatcher, clearly very angry, was interviewed outside 10 Downing Street on her return from the Cenotaph. Archbishop Eames, who had been due to preach at St Macartan's, had gone instead to the Erne Hospital, shaken and appalled by the scenes he had witnessed.

Out of the disaster, the horror and anger, came one voice of extraordinary courage, dignity and compassion. On the news programme on the morning after the bomb Gordon Wilson, who owned a store in the town, described how he had held hands with his daughter, Mairie, a 21-year-old nurse at the RVH, as they lay side-by-side, trapped by the rubble. Each time he spoke to her she assured him she was all right, but still screamed in pain. Finally she said, "Daddy I love you" and fell silent. She died that evening. Wilson told the world that he forgave her killers. His simple words spoken in a quiet voice made a universal impression and seemed to summarize the futility of all the killing over the past eighteen years. Bray and Faulkner visited the Battalion and talked to the assembled officers and Senior NCOs. They listened for an hour and heard not a word of antagonism towards the Catholic community, not one word of desire for vengeance or retribution:

> "It was the most remarkable display of Christian response," Bray recalled. "What I was seeing was what the world saw in Gordon Wilson, What I was doing was sitting in front of fifty Gordon Wilsons, and I thought they were a totally admirable people."

There were no reprisals, but there was anger, though not anger against the Catholic people as a whole. Many Protestants had Catholic friends. In the past the two communities in Fermanagh had not been deeply divided. Out in the countryside they lived as neighbours. That evening one of Gordon Miller's Catholic neighbours telephoned him to apologize in tears on behalf of his people. But there was anger that within the Catholic community there were people ready to pass on information to the IRA gangs operating on the other side of the Border. Over the years almost 200 people had been killed in Fermanagh. No one has ever been prosecuted for the Remembrance Day bomb.

In the days that followed Prince Charles and Princess Diana flew into St Angelo, visiting the Erne Hospital to talk to the survivors and the medical staff, and at Battalion Headquarters the officers, men and women who had taken part in the rescue. Among the many letters received by the Commanding Officer was one from the Chief of the General Staff, General Sir Nigel Bagnall.

"We have all watched with horror and sympathy the events of Remembrance Sunday in Fermanagh, but at the same time saw the splendid work being done by the men and women of 4UDR and those Regular soldiers attached to you, in the immediate rescue operations. How fortunate it was that we had immediately available a Regiment so well trained at administering first aid. In the days that followed the courage and dedication shown by the Battalion, both collectively on operations and individually in their conduct in the community, have been outstanding. We will do all in our power to see that this tragedy is not forgotten and that it strengthens everyone's resolve to defeat terrorism. I know many of you have lost friends and relations and I would like you to know you have the Army's sympathy and gratitude for the outstanding performance of your Battalion."

Amongst many others was one from the Senior Surgeon at the Erne Hospital: "The efficiency and professionalism with which your men and women carried out their task is only what I would expect. However, in the chaos of that morning they were nothing short of superb."

Two Sundays later the act of remembrance that had been so cruelly postponed was held in front of a very large gathering – politicians, senior police and military, and people who had come from across the country. Most of the soldiers who had been there on the day paraded again, but the Greenfinch who was to have laid the wreath on the day, the awful scenes too fresh in her mind, arranged for her daughter who was also a Greenfinch to lay it in her stead. At 10.45, the moment the bomb had exploded, the Prime Minister stepped forward to lay a wreath on behalf of the nation at the foot of the War Memorial. The pipes and drums of 4 and 6UDR led the parade to the cathedral where the Archbishop told the congregation that only time would tell whether the tragedy of Enniskillen would mark a turning point in Northern Ireland's violent history.

In the immediate aftermath of the greater tragedy few knew that another tragedy had involved the UDR. On the day following the Enniskillen bomb a 20-year-old student was obtaining work experience on a landscaping project in the Protestant Highfield Estate of West Belfast when he was shot dead. Two local men were arrested and charged, both Protestants. For whatever reason, possibly because he came from Ballygawley, they had assumed he was a Catholic and had killed him in retribution for the

Enniskillen bomb. In fact he was a Protestant. Both his parents had served in the UDR, his father until recently a part-time Company Commander in the Tyrone Battalion, his mother still serving as the Battalion Welfare Officer. Like Gordon Wilson, they said they could feel nothing but sorrow for their son's assassin.

The Prime Minister ordered a review of security. One of the most significant outcomes was the decision to return to the Province a third Brigade Headquarters to control operations in the Border Zone from Armagh to South Derry. More effective use would be made of the Regular battalions already in the Province by allocating them TAORs along the border, whilst within the Zone the Chief Constable would delegate to the Army the lead in counter-terrorist operations. The decision was greeted with some dismay by senior police officers who feared that this was a reversal of 'The Way Ahead' policy, but in time the police came to accept, and even welcome, the new arrangement. Apart from improved control of the Border, it had one major beneficial result. At last, years late, studies were put in hand to ensure that the boundaries of military and police operations at battalion/division and company/sub-division coincided and that the police, Special Branch and the CID operated within the same boundaries.

The Headquarters of 3 Infantry Brigade moved into Drumadd Barracks, Armagh, alongside 2UDR, in February 1988 and took operational control of the BZ on 1 July. 4UDR was the only one of the UDR battalions to be included in the new organization and the only one to retain a TAOR that included a stretch of the Border, taking in the western boundaries of Fermanagh. The CO of 4UDR welcomed the change. Rather than reacting to the tasking of the police, which was in the main defensive, he now had far greater flexibility in initiating and carrying out offensive counter-terrorist operations. No longer were the part-time companies confined to the inner areas of the county, where the threat was relatively low and operations tended to be unimaginative, the routine mounting of foot and mobile road checks at section level. Now they could participate in the full range of operations from section to company level throughout the new TAOR, extending right down to the border. As a result over the following months, though the number of PIRA operations was the highest for five years and included five murders, most of the attacks were confined to the immediate Border area; they could no longer penetrate the more heavily patrolled Border Zone.[24]

Other UDR battalions had mixed feelings about the change, for in some instances it meant that they lost one or more companies as they were placed under the operational control of the new Brigade. The greatest change affected 6UDR; though the Commanding Officer continued to be responsible for his whole battalion, he was left with operational control of only two of his companies.

A week before Enniskillen the French intercepted a Panamanian registered ship with an Irish captain, the *Eksund*. She was carrying 150 tons of weapons and explosives, including AK47s, twenty surface to air missiles and two tons of Semtex, a highly efficient, compact Czech-made explosive. During the trial of the captain in Dublin, a Garda officer claimed that the ship had brought in 242 tons of material from Libya in the two years before its seizure. The information caused alarm on both sides of the border. If true, the Provisionals now had at their disposal an arsenal of weapons sufficient to last them for years to come.

On 23 November the British and Irish security forces deployed on a coordinated cordon and search operation. Whilst the Garda, supported by the Irish army, mounted 'Mallard', searching across the Republic for arms caches hidden in previously prepared underground bunkers, the British troops dug in along the Border to cover all crossing points for the next ten days. 2UDR was responsible for sealing off that part of the Border that lay within the Middletown-Keady TAOR, using one of the UDR roulement companies from 1/9UDR at Middletown, another from 7/10UDR at Keady and, in addition, a Gunner battery, and all the permanent cadre they could redirect from other tasks. The battalion borrowed Pigs, armoured personnel carriers, to cover the crossings, while the soldiers off duty lived in bunkers dug into the fields, with sheets of corrugated iron or gates borrowed for the time being and later returned, covered with groundsheets to give some overhead shelter. It was bitterly cold, the temperature well below zero, and they had no heat. Under the cover of darkness local people brought them hot water and saucepans of potatoes. But the results were disappointing.

'Mallard' continued for several months on into 1988. In January Gardai uncovered oil drums dug into the sand dunes near Malin Head, the most northerly part of Ireland and within easy reach of Derry. They contained amongst other munitions, ninety Kalashnikov AK47s and five general purpose machine guns. In February the RUC stopped a lorry at Sprucefield on the road from Dublin to Belfast loaded with fifteen AK47 rifles, a GPMG, two rocket launchers, twenty grenades and 3,000 rounds of ammunition. Three weeks later a still larger cache was found in North Dublin; thirty rifles, twelve rocket launchers, ninety-one 7lb blocks of Semtex, sixty-four grenades and 32,000 rounds. In May 1992 fifty-one AK47s, two GPMGs and 20,000 rounds were discovered in a bunker at a farm in County Cork.

Around the same time the Loyalist paramilitaries had also established a supply line for munitions from the Middle East, purchased with the help of South African agents. But because the great majority of the Protestant people rejected terrorists of whatever hue, it was easier for the RUC to obtain information about their intentions. At the beginning of January a pre-planned police roadblock outside 11UDR's headquarters at Mahon Road on the outskirts of Portadown stopped three cars driven by members of the UDA, packed with sixty-one rifles, thirty pistols, 150 handgrenades and 11,500 rounds of ammunition. Next month the police found another Loyalist cache at a farm in the hills above Belfast – thirty-eight more rifles, fifteen pistols, a rocket launcher, grenades and 40,000 rounds.

The main find of weapons, belonging to Ulster Resistance, a Loyalist paramilitary group believed to have associations with Paisley's Democratic Unionist Party, resulted from an arrest made by a part-time patrol of 2UDR. The patrol from the Glenanne Company was carrying out road checks when they received a message that there had been a robbery in Markethill and that they should look out for a car driven by the son of one of their own company Senior NCOs. They found the car outside the local hotel and handed over the driver to the police. The son was not a member of the UDR, but battalion intelligence indicated that he was involved in criminal activities on behalf of a Loyalist paramilitary organization. Next day the police found an assault rifle in a hay barn outside the village. That night four teams from 2UDR moved in to cordon the area during the hours of darkness, with orders to start searching at first light. Within the first hour the teams had found grenades, magazines and ammunition. The searches continued over a wide range of East Armagh for the next five days, conducted mainly by the UDR and RUC, reinforced by search teams from the Regular Army. At the end the RUC put the haul on display for the media. It included a rocket launcher and rockets, seven rifles, two shotguns, three handguns, a considerable quantity of ammunition, military clothing and equipment, including maroon berets with the Ulster Resistance badge, radios and maps. 2UDR was never given credit publicly for a highly successful operation against a Loyalist paramilitary organization, an example of why the UDR felt that too often the RUC failed to give public acknowledgement of its successes.

In addition to improving the image of the Regiment, Bray was concerned to improve the quality of life of the permanent cadre soldiers. The Regiment had been given an increase in the permanent cadre establishment to enable it to take over Keady-Middletown, but recruitment had been disappointing and by the summer less than half the posts had been filled. As a result the workload on the existing soldiers was increased and time for training reduced. Most of the battalions were failing to meet CLF's target of four training days a month, but 2UDR, heavily committed to supporting Middletown-Keady, was achieving only two. It was not just a matter of finding more recruits to fill the new posts; trained soldiers were leaving at an alarming rate to join the RUC, who were looking for 500 more full-time reservists. The police had been given a 7½% pay increase as well as an increase in accommodation allowance, an allowance to which the UDR was never entitled, although they too lived in their own homes. By the end of 1987 fifty-six soldiers had been accepted for transfer to the RUC and inevitably the police took the best.

One major attraction that the Army could offer that was not available to the police was service overseas. For Regular soldiers life consists of periods of operations, often in unpleasant and sometimes dangerous conditions, but in between there are periods that offer variety, a good deal of fun and a chance to see the world. For the UDR soldier life was a continual round of operations, constantly under threat, on or off duty, and all in his own country.

In April Bray launched 'Break 88' at a media briefing in Lisburn. The aim, as he explained, was to ensure that every permanent cadre soldier spent at least a week out of the country during the summer. Battalions showed ingenuity in arranging ventures that provided a welcome break from the daily routine of operations. 2UDR organized a 125-mile trek crossing glaciers in Norway in weather varying from bad to atrocious. A party from 6UDR took part in a Brigade exercise on Salisbury Plain; others from 5UDR joined a NATO exercise in Denmark. 4UDR sent a group on attachment to a Regular battalion in Hong Kong, 11UDR to Gibraltar. Others organized adventure training expeditions. The idea of such attachments was not new; in 1986 they had been even more widespread, including the Falklands, Cyprus, Kenya and Belize, but 'Break 88' was a catchy title that caught the attention of the media. By April 1989, while the rest of the Army was worrying about its falling intake of recruits, the UDR had reached its new permanent cadre ceiling and had had to open waiting lists for volunteers.

Much of the limited time available for training in 1988 was taken up with the conversion from the SLR to the new, smaller 5.56 SA80. At the same time the machine guns were replaced by the Light Support Weapon, the SA80 mounted on a bipod. The new weapon was light and highly accurate, and 3UDR reported an immediate increase in the number of soldiers passing their Annual Weapons Test at the first attempt. Training involved not just weapon handling on operations but an entirely new arms drill on parade. On 9 July 1988 the first recruits' passing-out parade with the new weapons was held at Ballykinlar. During the parade four soldiers marched off carrying SLRs to mark ceremonially the last appearance of the old rifles, though conversion was not complete in 5UDR until the spring of the following year. The introduction of SA80 marked the end of the Weapons Out policy under which, since the early days of the UDR, soldiers at high risk had been allowed to keep their service weapons at home. The last few had been held by members of 6UDR.

Once again the first person to be murdered by the IRA in 1988 was a member of the UDR. On 16 January Private John Stewart, a 23-year-old part-time soldier, was going on duty from his parents' house. His father guided him out onto the road and watched him drive away. He was turning back into the house when he heard a burst of automatic fire. Sadie, his wife, heard it too and remarked that Killymeal seemed to be getting it again. "No, it's John," her husband shouted and ran to the bedroom to unlock the wardrobe where he kept his shotgun. Sadie ran out to the front gate. She saw John's car on the pavement a hundred yards down the road, another car on the opposite side, a man walking across to the smashed car, to finish off her son, she supposed. She yelled at him, he took fright, jumped into the get-away car and the three gunmen raced down the road past the gate. Sadie threw stones at them as they sped past, hoping that might cause them to crash, as her husband rushed out with his shotgun, but he was just too late. "I ran up the road to John," he recalled. "He says, 'The IRA shot me, daddy; get me out of here'. Well I was helpless, I couldn't get him out. This car pulled up, and there's a doctor from Dungannon going on call. He and I lifted John out and put him in the car and took him to hospital. John would say now and then, 'Keep her going, keep her going'."

At the hospital they told him that as far as they could ascertain no vital organs had been hit and John should be all right. A helicopter flew him to Musgrave Park Military Wing. His father went with him and was allowed to talk to him before he went into the operating theatre. "Tell Mummy I'll be all right," he said. His father never spoke to him again. He flew back to Dungannon to fetch Sadie and return to the hospital, but there was fog on the motorway and they were delayed in reaching Belfast. By then John's condition had deteriorated and he had been moved to the Royal. When his parents arrived, they were told their son had died on the operating table.[25]

As Stewart lay in hospital fighting for his life, another member of the same battalion, Tim Armstrong, a Captain in the permanent cadre who had served in the Falklands with the Royal Irish Rangers, had taken his fiancée out for a meal in Belfast. Two days before they had been to see the minister to discuss the arrangements for their wedding. Unable to obtain a taxi in the early hours of the morning, they set off to walk back to his parents' house in Upper Malone. As they were walking down the Ormeau road a man came up behind them and shot Armstrong in the back of the neck. PIRA denied responsibility and the inquest heard that he had probably been shot by a Protestant gunman in the belief that he was a Catholic. Some years later the man suspected of being responsible, a leading local Loyalist, was killed by the IRA.

Any hope that the losses in the attack on Loughgall or the disaster of Enniskillen would have a lasting effect on the Provisionals' resolution to continue the armed struggle was soon dispelled. There was no shortage of volunteers to take the places of those who had been killed and by the beginning of 1988 the East Tyrone group was back in business.

Of the 104 people who died as a result of the troubles in 1988, sixty-seven were murdered by the IRA. Of these twenty-two were Regular soldiers and twelve soldiers in the UDR. Most of the Regulars lost their lives in two particularly murderous incidents. In June a party of Regular soldiers from 8 Infantry Brigade drove down from Derry to Lisburn to take part in the town's annual charity 'fun run'. While their minibus was parked unattended in a public car park, a member of PIRA placed a Semtex booby trap underneath it. The run over, the six men set off for home, driving along Market Street into the centre of the town, crowded with spectators drifting away after the run. As the minibus drew up at the traffic lights the movement activated the tilt switch and the vehicle exploded in a ball of fire, killing all the occupants and injuring eleven bystanders.

Two months later a party of Light Infantry soldiers returning from leave were travelling in a civilianized military bus from the airport at Aldergrove to their base at Omagh. On the main road north of Ballygawley, not far from where the four soldiers from 6UDR had been killed in the landmine five years earlier, a 200lb bomb exploded, blowing the bus fifty yards into the hedge, killing eight of the soldiers, none of them over 21, and injuring twenty-eight others.

Ten days after the Ballygawley bomb three leading members of Central Tyrone PIRA believed to have been responsible for the blowing up of the bus were killed in an ambush at Drumnakilly, five miles east of Omagh on the road to Carrickmore. Three members of the *Sunday Times* have described the incident in detail in their book *Ambush. The War between the SAS and the IRA*.[26] According to their account, the Security Forces believed that the three men were preparing to commit another murder and had chosen a lorry driver, a former part-time soldier who had resigned from 6UDR a few months earlier, as the next victim in the "sustained campaign of assassinations, which the terrorist leaders hoped would inexorably drain the lifeblood of commitment, loyalty and, not least, the recruiting ability of the RUC and the UDR".

The PIRA arms cache was put under covert surveillance and when the three terrorists were seen collecting weapons from the cache it was assessed that the killing was likely to take place the following morning. A substitute soldier took over the ex-UDR soldier's lorry. At a spot already selected beside a derelict farm the driver drew into the side of the road, ostensibly to change a punctured tyre. For six hours, an agonising wait for the substitute driver, nothing happened. At last the Provisional gunmen drove down the road, saw the lorry and opened fire on the soldier, who, realizing what was about to happen, was running for cover behind a brick gatepost. The car stopped and, as the three terrorists prepared to finish off their target, they were confronted by the soldiers. All three terrorists were killed.

During the year the IRA carried out a series of bomb attacks in and around the city centre. A prime target was the new Castle Court shopping complex, being built on the site of the old General Post Office and the grand Central Hotel which had ended its days as the Regular Army's base on Royal Avenue. It was the task of a patrol from 7/10UDR to check each night that the Segment gates beside the building site had been closed. When the patrol drew up on the night of 24 February two soldiers, Privates Fred Starrett and James Cummings, got out to check the barrier. As they did so a 250lb bomb, hidden behind a hoarding, was detonated by a command wire run out through the Castle Court site to a firing point in a parallel street. It was the largest device to explode in the city centre for several years. The results were devastating – shop windows blown out, their contents destroyed, roofs lifted, a water main punctured, the streets littered with glass, the top blown off the Landrover, one of the soldiers dead, the other dying. The driver of the vehicle described how his body armour had been so badly damaged that it had to be written off as scrap.

Corporal William Burleigh of 4UDR was killed by a booby trap placed under his car parked in a field while he was attending a sale of agricultural equipment near Derrylin. His daughter Catherine had helped tend the dead and wounded at the Remembrance Sunday bomb. It was the third tragedy in her young life; in the previous summer she had been talking to a Regular soldier over the radio as he was on patrol in Beleek when he was shot dead. By chance Colonel Richard Neal of the United States Air Force, one of the Defence Attachés at the American Embassy in London, was visiting 4UDR with his wife Doreen and three teenage children. He had already arranged two holidays in Tennessee for the children of bereaved UDR families, financed by the UDR Benevolent Fund, and was now paying a private visit to say goodbye to the many friends he had made and to introduce his successor. The Neal family had spent a glorious day on the Lower Lough visiting Devenish Island with Vera Harron, the Greenfinch Battalion Welfare Officer, as their guide. When they returned to the pier a messenger was waiting to tell Vera of Burleigh's death. That evening the Second-in-Command took Rich and Doreen out to meet the bereaved family. It must have seemed to them a sad contrast, a beautiful day in a glorious setting ending in a murder. "It was more than that," Neal said. "The people are all so kind, so out-going and friendly, and yet they kill each other."

In August Lance Corporal Roy Butler, a full-time soldier in 7/10UDR had gone shopping with his wife Marie and their 2-year-old daughter at the newly opened complex, the Park Centre, close to the Falls Road. The previous evening he had been a member of his company football team playing against a representative side from Glentoran football club, the league champions, in an exhibition game to raise funds for twin baby girls, born blind, the daughters of a soldier in 5UDR. The shopping centre was an unwise place for a member of the UDR to go – indeed it was out of bounds to them – but Butler's wife was a Catholic and her old home was on the Falls Road. The centre was crowded with people when a boy about ten years old walked up to the Lance Corporal and touched him on the arm. At that point two gunmen dragged Butler out of the store, away from his wife and child, and shot him eight times in the head and chest. "Women and children screamed and panic-stricken shoppers ran from the scene as the two gunmen raced through the shopping centre, guns held above their heads," the *Irish News* reported. A leading article, under a heading 'Murder Most Foul', in the same Nationalist paper said in part:

"No one now even begins to justify these latest killings, and it is to be hoped that the usual nauseating pap about the armed struggle will not be heard from the supporters of violence. Even in a community hardened by the violence of twenty years, yesterday's murders

315

carry a special charge of revulsion and horror. Every murder places in greater emphasis the sheer futility and the sheer blindness of this campaign that can promise nothing but more and more of the blood-stained same. As a consequence of these continued atrocities Sinn Fein must now see itself at a crucial point in its development. By now the protagonists of the political process have accepted that their original slogan of ballot-box and Armalite was a piece of glib nonsense that had nothing to do with democracy and everything to do with a virulent totalitarianism."[27]

Shortly after midnight on 25 September Private Stephen McKinney drew up in the driveway of his parents' neat modern bungalow. He had just finished his last UDR duty; later that day he was to go over to England to start a business studies course at a polytechnic. As he pulled up at the front door three gunmen concealed around the garden opened fire at a range of a few feet. Stephen fell mortally wounded; his brother who came to the door to save him was shot in the face. Seamus Mallon, the McKinneys' MP, said that the IRA would try to justify the murder by describing the victim as a member of the British occupying forces:

"On the contrary Mr McKinney was a fellow Irishman who was killed in what was nothing more than a cowardly sectarian murder, carried out by those seeking vengeance. There can be no hiding place," he went on, "for those who seek to hold the community at ransom by cynically killing people because of their religion or political beliefs."[28]

Finally, nine days before Christmas, Private John Moreland of 3UDR was murdered as he was delivering coal to an estate on the outskirts of Downpatrick.

It had been a grim year. There were fifteen other reported attacks against serving and former members of the Regiment, including four UVBTs, none of them successful. In most of the attacks the soldiers escaped serious injury, but a Private in 8UDR lost his lower leg and three fingers when a booby-trap exploded in the goat-milking machine on his farm. The device, fitted with a mercury tilt switch, had been attached to the handle.

In the aftermath of Enniskillen the South Donegal ASU had been stood down and reorganized. Martin McGuinness of Sinn Fein said the disbandment was a clear message that killing civilians was wrong. "We must not, in challenging British rule, be the initiators of further injustice."[29] Words were cheap. What mattered was a determination that such 'mistakes' should never happen again They did – five more times in 1988, another eleven killed by accident, eight of them Catholics.

Each morning a school bus driver and part-time soldier in 4UDR would collect teenage children from south-east Fermanagh and take them to the Protestant and Catholic secondary schools in Enniskillen. Overnight his bus was parked in the grounds of a primary school in nearby Maguiresbridge. Some time during the night of 27 June a booby-trap with a mercury tilt switch and timer was placed under the vehicle, armed to detonate as soon as the bus was moved; but something went wrong. The bus was passing through Lisnaskea with twelve children aboard when the device exploded, blowing off its front. A 14-year-old girl, whose father was serving in the Battalion, sustained critical injuries to her chest and lungs. The soldier driver had undergone a First Aid course and, despite injuries to his eye, was able to give her mouth-to-mouth resuscitation. The other eleven schoolgirls were treated for shock and minor injuries. One mother told how she had been sitting at home when she heard the explosion. Her 14-year-old daughter had just left the house to catch the bus. "By the time I got there the children were being brought out. I saw Sinead, and all she said was, 'Mummy, I'm frightened.' She was very quiet, and I thought she was all right, but when she got home she started to scream, and I saw that she had a piece of metal stuck in her side through her cardigan."[30]

Two other deaths that summer, neither as a result of terrorist action, caused much sadness in the Regiment. Vera Harron, 4UDR's Assistant Adjutant and Welfare Officer, who had taken the American Attaché's family out to Devenish in the spring, an attractive 33-year-old, had gone to Portugal for a holiday with her sister Sandra, a Sergeant in the RUC. They both died as they slept, overcome by a gas leak from a water heater in their apartment. A month earlier, on 16 April, the Regiment's much-loved first Colonel Commandant, General Sir John Anderson, died in London, sixteen days after the eighteenth anniversary of the formation of the Regiment he had helped to raise. The *Times* obituarist wrote of his appointment: "No better choice could have been made. He threw himself with all his ardour and vigour into the task of raising the new force and ensuring that it got off to the best possible start."[31] The Regiment held a memorial service at the cathedral in Downpatrick, attended by some 400 people. Eight clergy from the four main churches officiated, among them the General's old friend Canon Maguire, the parish priest.

Around this time PIRA turned their attention to a new target – car bomb attacks on Army married quarters and on estates where a preponderance of the residents were members of the security forces. Most of the Regulars' married quarters were outside the perimeter wire, unprotected and integrated with the civilian community. They were the softest of targets.

In November the wife of an RSM out walking her dog in the married quarters estate at Campsie in Derry saw a man park a car and hurry away. The car appeared to be heavily laden, the boot tied down with cord. Her suspicions aroused, she telephoned her husband who had the registration number checked out, but the check revealed nothing untoward. A few minutes later the Samaritans and Radio Foyle received calls warning that a bomb had been left in the estate. It exploded half an hour later, causing extensive damage to the quarters in the immediate vicinity.[32] Four weeks later, just as it was getting dark, another Army wife saw a man park and walk away from a car in the Pond Park married quarters estate on the northern edge of Lisburn. She rang the Military Police who sent a patrol to the estate where they found the car with a package on the back seat. They had already begun evacuating the estate when warnings were received by the BBC, Downtown Radio and the *Irish News* that the bomb would go off in half an hour. In fact it exploded twenty-five minutes later, as the last house was being evacuated. The Provisionals announced that they now regarded Army families as legitimate targets.

Four days later, in the early hours of the morning of 15 December, the RUC stopped and searched a local man on the edge of Antrim town. When the patrol found a loaded revolver and a firing pack for a remote control device in his possession, the man admitted that a bomb had been hidden in a culvert at the entrance to Springfarm Estate and led the police to the place. The estate included a number of married quarters. The device had been intended to blow up the van which took the husbands to duty each morning. The whole estate had to be evacuated whilst the area was cleared and the bomb defused. Patrols from 1/9UDR cordoned off the estate and evacuated the families, 139 military dependants to the barracks at Steeple Camp, the civilians to a church hall. The evacuation plan, drawn up by the Battalion after the Campsie attack, worked well, though there were unforeseen lessons to be learnt – the care of pregnant mothers and sick children, the collection of cats and dogs and other sundry pets, the provision of nappies, videos, toys and games to keep the children amused, and food for the pets. After eleven hours the device, consisting of 100lb of Semtex, had been neutralized and the area cleared, and the families were allowed to return to their homes. The whole operation was a considerable success for the security forces; what could have been a disaster on the scale of the Ballygawley coach had been averted and in the process twelve men had been arrested and were charged with various offences.[33]

Four days later, a week before Christmas, the Provisionals left a car bomb in Blenheim Drive, an estate of modern £30,000 bungalows on the edge of Richhill in Armagh. About half the people living there were members of the security forces and their families. Among them was a former Regular soldier and his young wife. He had served in the Royal Artillery, had completed two tours in the Falklands and, after six years' Regular Army service, had transferred to 11UDR. The couple and his mother were about to sit down to tea when there was an urgent ringing at their door. A neighbour, panic-stricken and hysterical, explained that she had received a telephone call to the effect that a car bomb had been left in the estate. He calmed her down sufficiently to obtain the precise details of the warning. He phoned the RUC and told his mother to phone the 2UDR Operations Room. He walked through the estate until he found what he thought was the car, though it was difficult to be sure because the street lighting distorted the colour. He set in motion the evacuation of the houses, by telling neighbours to warn their neighbours, and returned to the car to confirm his identification. By the light of a torch he saw a box on the back seat. Despite the fact that he knew time must be fast running out, he double-checked that all the houses had been evacuated. A police patrol arrived and cordoned off the area. Seconds later the bomb exploded with devastating effect. All sixty-odd bungalows were damaged, four so badly that they had to be demolished. Roofs were blown off, tiles scattered, a gable-end cracked from top to bottom, upholstery, curtains and carpets impregnated with pulverised glass, doors and ceilings ripped away, Christmas trees and presents smashed and strewn across living room floors. The Battalion Welfare Officer spent all night comforting UDR families, all of whom were paying off mortgages. Some whose homes were no longer habitable had to move out at once to stay with family and friends. Loans to tide the families over Christmas were arranged from the UDR Benevolent Fund.[34]

These attacks were cause for considerable concern. How could a man go on duty to protect the public at large whilst knowing that meanwhile his own family was at risk? 1/9UDR stepped up patrols round the Antrim estates and in the north of the Province the part-time soldiers of 5UDR were put on voluntary call-out to provide 24-hour guards to cover the married quarter estates in Derry, Campsie and Eglinton. By the time they stood down on 3 January they had performed some 25,000 man-hours.

The Lisburn estates were a particular worry, for they were on the edge of the town, five minutes' driving by fast roads from West Belfast, while HQNI at Thiepval Barracks and the affluent commercial centre of the town presented additional attractive targets. An extra company was formed in 11UDR, X Company, based at Thiepval and reinforced with part-time soldiers on voluntary call-out, drawn from 1/9, 3 and 7/10UDR to carry out operations in the new Lisburn TAOR. The arrangements lasted for seven months, placing a considerable strain on the Battalion, to the extent that the great majority of sporting and adventure training activities had to be cancelled and the CO reported a deterioration in the quality of life of his soldiers.[35] By July 1989 the ad hoc company had been replaced by additional permanent cadre within 11UDR, G Company, based at Thiepval. Though the Regular Army was facing an alarming shortage of recruits at the time, the UDR had more applicants than vacancies for the permanent cadre. The sensible course would have been to allow the UDR to increase its full-time establishment against the Regular Army short-fall. The MOD thought otherwise. It had agreed at last that 170 additional permanent cadre soldiers could be taken on to make up the very serious shortage of administrative posts in all battalions. Now this would change; the UDR could still have its increase, but the posts would be used to form the new company to protect Lisburn and the battalions would have to continue to manage as best they could with inadequate administrative staffs. This failure to solve the problem of the administrative staffs, resulting in the misemployment of trained soldiers and thereby a reduction in men and women available for operations, was one of the factors that led three years later to the demise of the UDR.

CHAPTER EIGHTEEN

The Stevens Inquiry. 1989–1990

Two members of the Regiment were killed in 1989, the lowest number of casualties to occur in any one year. One of the dead was Private John Hardy. Hardy called most days at a meat factory on the edge of Dungannon to collect offal. On 14 March he was loading his lorry when two gunmen approached him and shot him several times. At the subsequent trial the court heard a statement made to the police by one of the gunmen. He described how he had taken up a position behind the lorry:

> "I saw John Hardy come out, and he saw me at the same time. I fired two or three bursts of automatic fire and saw him fall." He followed the wounded man into a room behind the loading bay. "I saw his feet sticking out of the door. I heard him moaning. I knew he wasn't dead so I fired at his head to make sure I killed him."[1]

He worked in the factory and knew Hardy well and had asked permission to take the afternoon off so he would be free to join the murder team.

The gunmen escaped in a stolen car but ran off the road and bogged down in a field. They fled across country, discarding two rifles, masks and clothing, whilst one jumped into a lough in an attempt to wash off any forensic evidence. Meanwhile the three-man back-up team, who had been guarding the household whose car had been stolen, had crashed and abandoned their get-away car. Within five minutes of the shooting the Battalion had flown patrols into the area, backed up by the police. All six men were arrested. More patrols, divers to search the lough, search and tracker dogs were deployed round the locations of each stage of the incident and cordons were kept in place overnight to secure the evidence, including the two rifles found by the 8UDR search dog. It was a textbook follow-up operation with CID in overall control. As a result the evidence was so incontrovertible that at their trial two of the men pleaded guilty; they and two of the others were found guilty of murder and all four men were sentenced to life imprisonment. One of them told the police how they identified and selected their victims. When stopped at a VCP they would fix their full attention on one member of the patrol and memorize his features. They would then look for him around the town when he was off duty and follow him to his home which they would keep under surveillance until they had put together a detailed dossier on the soldier's habits and movements. In Hardy's case they had targeted two members of the security forces working at the meat factory. They tossed a coin to decide which one they would kill.

Taking out of circulation four murderers was one of a number of successes during the year. A patrol from 2UDR in the country between Moy and Armagh watched a car being driven in a suspicious manner. Since several members of the security forces lived in the area, they set up a VCP and stopped the car. The driver had not come to notice before, but the three passengers were known Provisionals. They were dressed in military-style parkas, heavy trousers and boots, and looked as if they had been intending to lie out in the open. All four were arrested. The driver confessed to the murder of two Catholics, one of them a 14-year-old girl, both killed when a bomb detonated outside Benburb police station as they were driving past. The three Provisionals were released without charge. In subsequent operations RUC and UDR search teams uncovered several hides containing two AK47s, two shotguns, two grenade launchers, ammunition, timing devices and Semtex.[2]

In the city a patrol from 7/10UDR stopped a stolen taxi, found two home-made sub-machine guns inside and arrested the three occupants, Loyalists returning from shooting up a Republican Club in the Markets area of the city. A week later the RUC requested the Battalion to carry out a house search in the Markets, an operation that was accomplished without any friction with the locals and resulted in the recovery of two rifles and 200 rounds, Republican this time. Later in the month the Battalion returned to the same area with some fifty soldiers taking part in a cordon and search operation lasting over three days, ending with a find by a DMSU of 600lb of home-made explosives concealed in a coal bunker in a garden.

8UDR celebrated St Patrick's Day by finding in the hilly country near Cappagh a rifle, hand grenade and a considerable quantity of bomb-making equipment, including a device made up and ready for use. In June a routine patrol from the same permanent cadre company found an improvised grenade launcher and ammunition under a cattle trough a couple of miles from the previous find. To round off a good year, the company, while on patrol in Coalisland, saw two members of PIRA standing beside a car in an alleyway. The constable accompanying the patrol noticed two drogue bombs on the back seat. The two men were arrested, later followed by a third. During the follow-up searches over the next six days the company search dog indicated at a manure heap; dug into it was a barrel containing two rifles and a pump-action shotgun. The same company had other, lesser successes. Seldom a week passed without them being involved in some incident.

In June the *Irish News* reported that the UDR was to be issued with federal riot guns (FRG), the weapons used by the Regular Army and the police to fire plastic baton rounds against a riotous crowd. HQNI confirmed that their issue to the Regiment on a strictly limited basis was being 'actively considered', but emphasized that the policy that the UDR was not to be deployed in riot control situations remained unchanged. The decision was widely condemned; the Irish government and the British Labour Shadow Northern Ireland Minister, Kevin McNamara, expressed their concern. Seamus Mallon said he had no doubt that if the guns were issued to the UDR they would be used at the earliest opportunity. One of the few balanced comments came from the *Belfast Telegraph*:

> "Reaction to the announcement . . . has been unusually hostile, even for Northern Ireland . . . There has been almost universal condemnation from all shades of nationalist opinion, suggesting that the opposition is directed not only against the use of the plastic bullets, but against the UDR itself."[3]

The decision had been taken on the strength of those few occasions when UDR patrols had become involved in riotous situations, usually at a rural road checkpoint, and, having no other means of handling the situation, had been forced to withdraw or, more humiliatingly, send for the police to rescue them. Detailed instructions were drawn up for the issue of the weapons and their use. Patrols would carry them only when authorized to do so by the CO. Nevertheless the decision was a mistake. A situation in which a patrol was in danger of being overwhelmed by a crowd was likely to occur at less than the twenty-metre permitted minimum range; there was a real danger that a patrol would be set up by the IRA to precipitate an incident, and, since the guns would not always be carried, the chances were that none would be available when needed. In due course the weapons were issued to battalions. They were never used, but the controversy ran for months, repeated by politicians as another excuse for castigating the UDR.

The reaction of the media and Nationalist leaders showed that in the aftermath of the Anglo-Irish Agreement the Regiment continued to be a sensitive issue and that there were those who would never miss an opportunity to denigrate it. The issue of the FRG was still making news when Mallon asked the Secretary of State for Defence whether he was aware that the UDR was using a public relations promotional video which was "explicitly critical" of the SDLP. Neither HQNI or HQUDR knew what he was talking about. It transpired that a Member of Parliament, who had attended a briefing at HQUDR, had told Mallon that a slide of a soldier and a boy holding a football had been shown to illustrate that the Regiment felt that it was used as a political football. No political party in particular was mentioned, indeed, so far as the members of the Regiment saw it, all political parties were apt to become involved in the game. And of course the ridiculous aspect of Mallon's complaint was that he was proving the Regiment's point; the UDR was being used as a political football and some MPs were so keen to join in that they made their public statements before they were certain of their facts. The offending slide was removed on instructions from the MOD, but the game went on.

There now occurred a sequence of events that were to cause more harm to the reputation of the Regiment than anything that had gone before. The fact that many of the accusations were to prove unjust made no difference, the harm had been done and the stigma remains.

Since the arrival of Headquarters 3 Brigade the roulement companies from 1/9, 7/10 and 11UDR had been redirected to Rathfriland, working out of the 3UDR company base behind the police station. Sets of montages of local terrorist suspects, held in plastic folders, were issued to each company by the 3UDR Intelligence staff at the beginning of its tour of duty and checked back at the end. Not being local men, it was important that the patrols had some means of recognizing terrorist suspects, some of whom were based across the Border in Dundalk. In February, when C Company 7/10UDR had completed a tour, it was found that six photographs were missing. The Special Investigation Branch (SIB) was called in but could not identify the individual who had been responsible for removing them. One of the photographs was of a Rathfriland man, Laughlin Maginn. On several occasions patrols had encountered Maginn in company with members of Castlewellan PIRA. In the previous August he and a well-known Provisional had been stopped near Hilltown; the latter was carrying wet overalls, gloves, balaclava and radio. Maginn had a radio and tried to evade the patrol. Subsequently his family was to deny that he was involved in the organization, but there was no doubt that Maginn was associating with the IRA.[4]

A year later, on 25 August '89, Maginn was shot dead in the living room of his home. The UFF admitted responsibility. Over the past year there had been an upsurge in murders carried out by the Protestant para-militaries, five of them by the UFF. Most, including Maginn's, were regarded as random sectarian killings. Four days after the murder a BBC reporter, following an anonymous telephone call, was conducted by armed, masked men to a house where he was shown montages and a video of IRA suspects, among them Laughlin Maginn. Stung by the allegations that they were carrying out random sectarian killings, the UFF's intention was to show that in fact they targeted people suspected by the Army and the police of being involved in Republican terrorism. There was little doubt that the montages and the film had originated from security force sources. Suspicion focused immediately on the UDR, and 3UDR specifically. Special Branch and the SIB carried out a thorough check of the arrangements for the safe custody of montages in the Battalion and were dismayed on being shown a filing cabinet with its drawer full of photographs of suspects issued by Brigade Headquarters. When the IO had asked the Brigade staff what he was supposed to do with them, he had been told to pin them on notice boards and wherever they could be studied by the soldiers. The IO ignored the instructions and continued to issue the photographs on a strictly limited basis and pinned them up for display only in locked patrol briefing rooms. The inspecting officers were satisfied with the arrangements, indeed, they went as far as to say that they were a model for the rest of the Army. The photograph of Maginn had been produced by the RUC and was not one of those stolen from Rathfriland earlier in the year, but the video, focusing on photographs of suspects on a briefing room wall, could have been filmed in the Battalion.

The team was still carrying out its investigation at Ballykinlar when a Company Sergeant Major discovered that six montages had been taken overnight from a locked drawer in his office. Ten days after the loss had been discovered the *Sunday Times* reported that the montages had gone missing. The BBC took up the story and repeated it in all its news bulletins. The RUC announced that a senior police officer would be carrying out an investigation into the missing photographs. Eddie McGrady, the local MP, said the UDR should be confined to barracks pending a full-scale inquiry by outside, impartial investigators. Other members of the SDLP repeated their demand for the Regiment to be disbanded. McGrady's remark that 3UDR was the battalion that had been considered to be "the most open and the most representative of both communities", and the *Down Recorder*'s leader that "there appears to be at very least a serious flaw in the administration of Ballykinlar"[5] showed what harm could be done by an ambitious journalist in his rush to submit an exclusive story before he was in possession of all the facts. In fact the lost Ballykinlar photographs had nothing to do with the leaking of information to the Loyalist paramilitaries. Subsequent investigation, involving interviews by the police of fifty-one soldiers, showed that they had almost certainly been removed and immediately destroyed by a fellow senior NCO with a grudge against the CSM, an explanation that was to be accepted by the Stevens Enquiry.

Charles Ritchie, who had commanded 3UDR from 1981 to 1983, had returned to the province in October 1988 to take over command of the Regiment from Michael Bray. He had received no forewarning of the RUC investigation and the first he heard about it was when a member of his staff told him it had just been announced on the lunchtime news bulletin. That same day the media reported that two members of C Company 7/10UDR, the company that had been at Rathfriland when the montages had been stolen back in February, had been arrested, together with a third man, a civilian, and charged with the murder of Maginn, and the civilian and one of the soldiers with a second murder, a Catholic barman shot in Lisburn in June. Both soldiers were former Regulars, one from an English infantry battalion, the other a Scottish. Both had transferred directly into the UDR and no doubt their former battalions were glad to see the back of them. For it had soon become apparent that both were thoroughly undesirable and 7/10UDR was in the process of discharging them when their part in Maginn's murder came to light. But a serious flaw in the system, not appreciated until then, allowed Regular soldiers to transfer to the UDR without first being put through the same vetting as civilians applying to join the Regiment.

On the day following the arrests Ritchie was told that the Defence Secretary, Tom King, wished to see him at six o'clock that evening in the

MOD. King sat at his desk, flanked by the CGS, Sir John Chapple, and the Private Secretary:

"It was pretty frosty," Ritchie recalled. "I was quite literally on the mat, standing in front of the desk until I was motioned to a chair.

"'How was it possible,' King asked, 'for two serving soldiers to carry out a murder without anyone being aware in the Regiment that they were active members of a Protestant paramilitary organization?'

"I started by explaining that the permanent cadre soldiers lived at home. We had no idea how they spent their spare time, nor whom their friends were. Surely their platoon commander should have known, I was asked? I pointed out that, because of the shortage of permanent cadre officers, the platoon commander was a sergeant. Why was there a shortage of officers? I had hoped he would ask me that question. I remember saying to him, 'Would you, sir, if you were a member of one of those Ulster families who have produced generations of officers for the Regular Army, have been happy for your son to go to Sandhurst, knowing that once he was commissioned into the UDR he would be ineligible to attend Staff College and could never rise beyond the rank of Major? That is why we are not getting enough officers. They are being denied the same career opportunities as the rest of the Army. King asked the CGS if that was true. Chapple confirmed that it was."[6]

They agreed that in future all the officer cadets for the UDR would be selected in the same way and to the same standards as applicants for commissions in the Regular Army and that action must be taken to ensure that permanent cadre officers had the same career opportunities as their Regular counterparts. The new measures would take time to implement. Was there anything that could be done immediately to overcome the shortage of officers? Ritchie proposed that junior officers from the Regular Army should be seconded to the UDR to fill vacant platoon commander slots, an arrangement that was implemented forthwith and proved an unqualified success.

However, if permanent cadre officers were to gain command, they must have acquired, so far as possible in their limited Northern Ireland role, the same background experience and must compete for promotion to Lieutenant Colonel on the same footing as their Regular contemporaries. Measures were now taken to give them the opportunity to widen their experience – attendance at the Platoon Commanders' Battle Courses and the Junior Division Staff Course at the School of Infantry; attachments to Regular battalions and postings to the staff at HQNI and Brigade headquarters. One officer who attended the Joint Services Defence College for officers from all three services at Greenwich went on to command one of the Royal Irish Regiment Home Service battalions, the first officer whose entire military service had been in the UDR to be given command of a battalion. He was a Catholic.

For two months the UDR came under intense scrutiny, with hardly a day passing without some article in the UK and Irish press, hostile or supportive, depending on the politics of the paper. The Regimental scrapbook contains a representative selection of some two hundred articles. In the *Daily Telegraph*, Ryder, who a week earlier had published a groundless report that the recruitment of part-time soldiers was to be phased out, with the Regiment becoming a wholly full-time force,[7] now wrote a disgraceful article under the heading "A loyal or a Loyalist Regiment?", saying among other things that it was no wonder that IRA propagandists referred to the UDR as "Ulster's Disreputable Rogues". Mrs Thatcher, on a visit to 6UDR, told the press, "The UDR has done remarkable work and suffered greatly. They are a very, very brave group of men."[8] That evening when she met Ritchie at Hillsborough she told Peter Brooke, the new Secretary of State, "Come with me to the Festival of Remembrance at the Albert Hall, Peter, and listen to the audience cheer when the UDR march down the steps." She assured Ritchie that she was not contemplating any changes to the Regiment. Turning back to Brooke she told him, "You just tell that to Haughey, Peter." She had gripped Ritchie's arm so tightly that he bore the mark of the Prime Minister's thumb. "She could not have been more supportive," Ritchie said.

August saw the twentieth anniversary of the commitment of the first Army units to the troubles. The Provisionals had threatened to mark the anniversary by ensuring that it would be a month the British would never forget, but the threat failed to materialize. The GOC sent a signal to his Brigade Commanders, congratulating their soldiers on their vigilance. Now, days later, the General told the Advisory Council that the murder charges against the two soldiers, the theft of the Ballykinlar montages and the resultant adverse publicity had been a severe set-back, not just to the UDR, but to the whole of the Army in the Province. There was a crucial need, he said, to regain the moral high ground. Until all ranks of the UDR accepted the need to operate to the same high standards as the Regular Army there was little hope of implementing the major improvements that were currently under consideration. Some members of the Regiment had a misplaced sense of loyalty; the numbers were small but sufficient to provide a target for its opponents. Leadership was crucial; currently this was inadequate, mainly because of the shortage of junior officers.

On 14 September the RUC reported that another montage of twelve suspects had disappeared from a locked cabinet in Dunmurry police station. Since the police must now come under suspicion, Annesley, who had taken over as Chief Constable from Hermon in June, decided that the time had come to set up an outside investigation to cover this latest loss, along with the disappearance of the Ballykinlar montages, the claims by the UFF to be in possession of photographs of suspects and any associated matters which came to light during the course of the Enquiry. John Stevens, Deputy Chief Constable of Cambridgeshire, who had served as a detective with the Metropolitan Police, was appointed to head the

Enquiry, assisted by a team of senior detectives personally selected by him from ten police forces in England. Within days the team had begun its investigations. In the following week a spate of montages began to appear from various anonymous sources. The *Sun* printed on its front page photographs of eight men and women with their faces obscured, claiming that "it is now believed that more than seventy IRA suspects have been identified to the Loyalists by the UDR". The montages were traced to a Regular soldier who, like many others, had kept them as a souvenir of a tour of duty in Northern Ireland. Someone sent Mallon photographs of ten Newry men. Four photocopied pages of Republican suspects were delivered anonymously to the Belfast offices of the *Independent*; another forty-odd photographs of people living in Tyrone and Armagh were sent to the *Western Daily Press* in Bristol. There were others.

The media was giving the impression that the main source of the leaks was the UDR. The Chief Constable issued a statement, printed large in the Belfast papers and the *Irish Times*, saying:

> "While some commentators have been quick to apportion blame in a general manner, this aspect must await the outcome of Mr Stevens' enquiry." He went on, "I would be failing in my duty if I did not allude here to a serious and ongoing feature of life in the Province. In the past eighteen months and not least during the summer of 1989 the RUC, supported in full measure by the Army, including the UDR, has faced a potential level of terrorist violence and public disorder unprecedented in recent years. As a result of hundreds of security forces operations, complemented by a significant level of public support for our stand against violence, many lives were saved and massive disorder averted."

The *Sunday World* held a telephone vote. Readers were asked to ring one of two numbers to register a 'yes' or 'no' to the question "Would you disband the UDR?" Over the next four days many members of the Regiment and their families rang the 'no' number several times over; no doubt Republicans were dialling and redialling the 'yes'. The paper published the results in the following edition; 7,398 calls had been received in favour of keeping the Regiment, while 5,738 had called for its disbandment. Burke, the Republic's Justice Minister, said in a RTE interview that, in view of the almost daily revelations about leaks, the Irish government was calling into question the very existence of the UDR. Collins, the Foreign Minister, had gone to the States to brief Congress on the leaks and the Chairman of the Friends of Ireland Group in Congress had called for the disbandment of the Regiment, comparing it to death squads in San Salvador.

On 17 September all company commanders were summoned to HQUDR to hear an address by the Colonel Commandant, General Sir David Young. He spoke bluntly. The Regiment had been brought into disgrace and its magnificent record tarnished by the actions of a tiny fraction of its members. It was up to the company commanders to ensure that any of their soldiers suspected of divided loyalties were removed from the UDR.

The Anglo-Irish Intergovernmental Council, which had already spent seven and a half hours in September discussing the issue of the UDR and collusion between the security forces and Loyalist paramilitaries, met again in London on 5 October for a further eight hours. The Irish side was reported to be asking for:

- confinement of the UDR to static duties, excluding contact with the Nationalist community.
- cancellation of the plan to issue the FRG.
- accompaniment of all UDR patrols by police officers.
- changes in vetting procedures.
- stricter monitoring of sensitive documents.[9]

In the early hours of that morning Paisley, accompanied by leading members of the DUP, launched the party's 'Hands off the UDR' petition by pasting up posters on the columns of the GPO in Dublin and the gates of Leinster House, while his daughter and a group of supporters staged a protest outside the NIO in London. Posters were stuck up in Protestant areas across the Province and signatures collected for a petition to the Prime Minister. In London the Council's discussions were inconclusive, with the British side apparently giving nothing away.

On 8 October, three days after the Council meeting, twenty-eight members of the Regiment were arrested by the police in 'dawn swoops' reminiscent of the introduction of internment in August 1971. That same morning, while the police were questioning the arrested soldiers, Superintendent Alwyn Harris set out with his wife to attend Harvest Festival in Lisburn Presbyterian Church. He had driven a few yards from his bungalow, within sound and almost within sight of HQUDR, when a booby trap exploded under his car. His wife escaped with superficial injuries, but Harris, who had been due to retire, was dead.

Twenty-six of the soldiers belonged to the same company of 7/10UDR as the two members charged with Maggin's murder. That the arrests had been carried out at all was bad enough, but it was the overt manner in which the whole operation had been mounted that caused intense anger at all levels in the Regiment. Most of the soldiers had been picked up at their homes, with RUC Landrovers blocking off their streets and armed policemen surrounding and searching their houses. All the precautions they had taken over time to ensure that their neighbours were not aware that they were members of the UDR were undone at a stroke and their lives put at risk as a result. The gratuitous statement released by the RUC Press Office stating that some 300 police officers had taken part in the arrests revealed the scale of the operation. Initially Stevens had intended to order the arrest of the entire company, about a hundred soldiers. Senior officers of the RUC had dissuaded him, doubting whether he had sufficient grounds to justify arrests on this scale.

Notwithstanding the fact that the UDR had offered Stevens whatever assistance he required from the outset of the Enquiry, and despite an understanding made between the UDR and the RUC three years previously that whenever possible the Commanding Officer would be informed before one of his soldiers was arrested, neither the Commander nor the CO, nor anyone else in the UDR, had any forewarning that the arrests were about to take place. Most of the soldiers had returned from a training exercise the previous evening. If the RUC had taken the Regular Army staff officers at HQUDR into their confidence they could have arranged for the soldiers to be arrested in barracks that evening and their homes searched the following morning by officers in plain clothes.

"What were they expecting?" the soldiers were asking. "Armed resistance?"; and "Can anyone remember 300 police being used in a single operation against the IRA?"

It was apparent that the police had little appreciation of the fact that objects found in some of the homes were legitimate tools of a soldier's trade. There was nothing sinister about maps or training pamphlets, nor odd pieces of equipment. One soldier was arrested for being in possession of a slide for a SLR, with which he had been issued, a piece of metal for an obsolete weapon that was no longer on issue and that to all intents and purposes was a piece of scrap. A soldier should not acquire a rifle magazine, any more than a carpenter should keep a chisel belonging to his employee, but it was hardly a criminal offence. There could be few people in the Army, officers or soldiers, (or policemen for that matter) who did not have a few rounds of ammunition somewhere around their homes, accumulated over the years. Anyone with a licensed firearm was allowed to purchase a small quantity of ammunition each year for range practice; often there was no opportunity to use it all and the rounds accumulated.

Ritchie was furious when he first heard about the arrests later that morning. Accompanied by General Hodges, the CLF, he drove across to HQ RUC to complain to the Chief Constable. On the way the General tried to calm him down, pointing out the harm that would be done if there was a rift between the Army and the RUC, particularly if the rift became public knowledge. Only the paramilitaries would benefit. Ritchie got little satisfaction out of what was an angry interview.

"Annesley was frightfully defensive about the whole thing, but gave me no comfort whatsoever. I did point out to him that it was an extraordinary misuse of police time to have diverted such a large number against fellow members of the security forces when it would have been better directed against terrorism. I think he appreciated then the enormity of what he had done, how wrong it was and how unnecessary."[10]

330

Later Ritchie had a meeting with Stevens. It was a cold, unfriendly encounter.

"He made a half-hearted attempt to justify the arrests by pointing out what had been recovered, but that amounted to next-to-nothing of significance. He seemed to be completely out of his depth in Northern Ireland. I pointed out to him that we were living in a terrorist situation, not in some cosy suburb in Cambridge. The people he had ordered to be arrested were professional soldiers, not members of some paramilitary organization. If his officers had come round to my house, they could probably have found a couple of handfuls of ammunition I had lying around the place. Essentially we agreed to disagree, but his attempts to placate me failed miserably."

Stevens did agree that, if there were to be any further arrests, they would be carried out with greater discretion, a tacit admission that the manner of the earlier arrests had been over the top. Later two full-time soldiers of 7/10UDR were arrested and charged with the theft of the montages from Dunmurry police station. Again both were arrested at home, one discreetly by a plain clothes officer, but in the second case RUC Landrovers were deployed to surround the soldier's house. Stevens rang Ritchie to apologize. It was the last time that they spoke to each other.

Within a week most of the arrested men had been released, only two facing more serious charges remaining in custody. Six months later eight were brought to court. The magistrate agreed that the offences were largely of a technical nature. The cases against two were dismissed. Six were found guilty; five were fined £50, the sixth £100. Amounts of ammunition found in their possession ranged from eleven rounds of .22 to seventy-eight rounds of 9mm. Later one man was found guilty of repairing hand guns for the UDA. The two who had removed the montages from Dunmurry police station pleaded guilty and were sentenced to twelve months. In their defence one claimed that a suspected terrorist dressed as a postman had been seen in his neighbourhood and he had taken the photographs to show to his mother in case the man came to her door looking for him. Though no excuse for the theft, it was a reasonable explanation and the judge accepted that neither soldier had taken the montages to pass them on to the paramilitaries.

Out of all the soldiers arrested not one was found guilty of passing on montages to the Loyalist paramilitaries and only the one, the repairer of arms for the UDA, guilty of collusion.

With Ritchie under orders to remain silent, it was left to the Unionist politicians and councillors to speak out in support of the Regiment. At the Ulster Unionist annual conference Mrs Edith Elliott, whose ex-UDR husband had been murdered at Ballybay cattle market in the South in 1980 and whose brother, also a member of the Regiment, had been murdered a year later, received a standing ovation when she made an impassioned speech in defence of the UDR.[11] At a Regimental dinner in

Woolwich Archie Hamilton, the Minister for the Armed Forces, told the officers that the UDR was indispensable and that it had his full support. When he said that all 'rotten apples' must be weeded out he was roundly applauded.

For four nights after the arrests protest riots broke out in East Belfast, with petrol bombs being thrown at the police, and in one case a patrol came under fire. The situation was defused by 7/10UDR, the Battalion of the arrested soldiers, providing escorts for the police patrols.

There was widespread concern in both forces that the manner of the arrest operation would cause lasting damage to relationships between the UDR and the RUC, but for the most part, due to the good sense of both sides, no lasting harm was done. Many police officers let it be known privately to their UDR counterparts that they had every sympathy with them and had had little stomach for what they had been ordered to do, especially in a month in which seven people were murdered by the PIRA, including Superintendent Harris and a second police officer:

> "I can think of no one in the RUC that I ever spoke to who thought that the arrests were properly carried out," Ritchie said. "Many, many people came up to me and apologized or rang me up and said how awful they thought it was."

Shortly after the Stevens Report had been released Chief Superintendent Paddy McCullough, in his Presidential address to the Superintendents' Association, told the members:

> "In view of the often appalling and frequently malicious libels and slanders heaped upon our colleagues in the Ulster Defence Regiment, we would wish, on this occasion, to confirm our admiration for the sterling service rendered to the community by its members and, of course, to the members of this Association in its operational tasks.
>
> "It has been the subject of the cruellest criticism and malicious speculation from a wide spectrum of sources which, we feel, has not been replied to as aggressively and sure-footedly as its bearing and reputation warrant.
>
> "Those of us who have had the privilege of serving with members of the Regiment have long since recognized their integrity and commitment and their contribution, at very great personal cost, to community peace. No other body of men and women have, within our knowledge, been subjected to such sustained calumny over such a long period of time. This Association is pleased to record its appreciation of the Regiment and is glad of this opportunity to do so."[12]

The arrests were a disgraceful episode that should never have happened, and probably never would if the Chief Constable had had more time to play himself in. Association with two soldiers suspected of murder was

332

insufficient grounds for arresting twenty-six other members of the same platoon. Two years later six of the soldiers sued the RUC for wrongful arrest. The cases were settled out of court without admission of liability by the police, each soldier receiving a five figure sum in compensation. Others would have sued if they had not been worried about the security implications of going to court and having their names published as a result. Eleven soldiers gave up their homes and moved their families to areas where they would not be known. Security reviews were carried out on eighteen other houses and additional security measures installed at a cost of some £25,000. The arrests caused great embarrassment to the Government, police and Army. They caused enormous and lasting harm to the reputation of the Regiment.

Over the years a whole library of books has been published on the troubles. The majority of them are critical of the UDR, recording the arrest of the twenty-eight as a result of the investigations by Stevens. With the passage of time the triviality of all but one of the offences brought to court has been forgotten. In some accounts the arrests and charges are linked with the arrests of Loyalist paramilitaries. The authoritative and admirable *Political Directory* states that "fifty-eight people were arrested as a result of the enquiry; thirty-four charges of having information likely to be of use to terrorists were brought against ten members of the UDR and thirty-two members of paramilitary groups."[13] So far as the UDR is concerned this impression left for posterity, that collusion between the UDR and the Loyalists was widespread, is untrue and an unwarranted slur on the loyal service of 40,000 men and women.

While the Enquiry was still under way and the charges against the soldiers had still not been heard, HQUDR learnt that the BBC intended to make a film about the UDR for its weekly "Panorama" programme. The regimental PRO and the Chief Information Officer from HQNI met a senior member of the production team at the Europa Hotel. They were provided with a broad range of the subjects that the programme would cover. To the PRO it was apparent from the outset that it would be biased against the Regiment, pre-empting the publication of the Stevens Enquiry. The title, 'The UDR, a Question of Loyalty', said it all. She advised Ritchie to have nothing to do with it.

Ritchie agreed and suggested a compromise. The BBC should make the programme, then show it to the Secretary of State, the GOC and Ritchie himself, and give them an opportunity to comment on any allegations. The "Panorama" team refused to accept such an arrangement and, on the basis that if the Regiment did not cooperate it would seem to be a tacit admission that it had something to hide, the decision was made between the NIO, the MOD and HQNI that Ritchie must agree to take part. He was briefed by the Director of Public Relations in London, by the NIO press office and the GOC, and rehearsed several times on how he should deal with the sort of questions he was likely to be asked. Clearly it was going to be a politically sensitive programme. Afterwards he regretted the

333

rehearsals; when it came to the interview he was so busy trying to remember what he had been told he should and should not say that he felt it would have been easier to go into it with his mind uncluttered by advice.[14]

At an early stage the Headquarters learnt that the production team had been calling at the homes of soldiers, sometimes after dark, without warning, armed with information about them and asking pertinent questions. One of those visited had already been warned that he had been targeted by the IRA. When the Headquarters pointed out that the team was in danger of drawing attention to the soldiers and putting them at risk the BBC apologized, but the visits continued, with the soldiers reporting back to their battalions, and the battalions to the Headquarters, that the team had tried to interview them.

Three weeks before the programme was due to go out the team filmed a long interview between John Ware and the Commander. Ware was an experienced investigative journalist with a formidable reputation, Ritchie a transparently honest, decent man, but lacking that ability to parry the awkward question that had made Bray, his predecessor, adept at handling the media. Ritchie was tired and nervous, and it showed. He was all too well aware that the interview had gone badly and three days before the programme was due to be screened he sent out to battalions a letter he had received from Peter Brooke, reiterating his support for the Regiment, with instructions that it should be displayed on all company notice boards.

The programme went out on 19 February 1990, three days after an off-duty soldier had been shot in the head as he was driving his tractor along a country road in Tyrone. Brooke and Cope, his Minister of State, watched it with Ritchie in his married quarter. It was the first time any of them had seen it. As had been apparent from the outset, the BBC team had decided in advance to denigrate the Regiment and, having decided on their editorial policy, had put together a programme that would provide the justification for their prejudices. It was a programme almost completely lacking in objective balance. It included an interview with a man convicted of the murder of a policeman who claimed that harassment by UDR patrols had driven him to join the IRA, a former soldier who claimed that he had served simultaneously in the UDR and the UVF, a man who would no doubt have regarded himself as a true blue Loyalist but had so little understanding of the meaning of loyalty that he would betray his Regiment and his comrades before an audience of five million; the mother of the murdered Laughlin Maginn and Father Faul, the Dungannon priest, who, after describing the harassment of a family who had no terrorist connections, went on to repudiate any suggestions that most UDR patrols behaved in that way. "I have said it again and again. Most of them are very decent men, good law-abiding men, well disciplined. It is a minority who do this." Coming from a man who was known as a conduit for complaints against the security forces, it was the most convincing, if partial, defence of the Regiment in the entire programme.

Collins, the Irish Foreign Minister, commented on the failure of the British Government to honour its assurance under the Anglo-Irish Agreement to provide a policeman with every UDR patrol. The Irish side had observed the Agreement diligently and at very great cost, he claimed, but the British had lacked the political will to live up to their solemn assurances. If the Prime Minister was watching she must have nearly hit the Downing Street ceiling, bearing in mind her conviction that the Irish had failed to live up to their undertaking to improve Border security and had in recent days refused to extradite two of the Maze escapees.

The programme contained a number of inaccuracies, but by far the most damaging part arose from Ware's query about the briefing of UDR soldiers on Loyalist paramilitaries. He claimed that of ten soldiers he had interviewed, all of whom had spent several thousand hours on patrol, half had said that they had never been shown photographs of Loyalist paramilitaries and only two said they had been shown them on a regular basis. Ritchie, caught unawares, replied that the RUC was well able to deal with Protestant terrorism and for that reason it was not a role specifically given to the UDR, and that 'as a matter of course' patrols were not briefed on the identity of suspect paramilitaries on the Protestant side. How, Ware went on, were the Catholic community to interpret the Brigadier's comment that effectively the UDR sought only Republican terrorists? The implication was that the UDR operated only against Republicans, an implication that most of the critical press and Nationalists politicians seized on the following day. It was untrue. Ironically the PRO, who sat in on the interview, could have pointed out that Ritchie's answer gave a misleading impression. In areas where Loyalist paramilitaries were likely to operate, patrols were briefed about them. As a Greenfinch in 7/10UDR she had been briefed regularly for years on the identity of suspect Protestants and shown photographs of them before going out on patrol. "I could have named the paramilitaries in the Shankill Road just as I could have named the PIRA in West Belfast," she recalled. Fatally a decision had been taken in advance that the whole interview with the Brigadier should be conducted without interruption.

The fact that Ritchie's reply was then shown to the Irish Foreign Minister without the Brigadier's knowledge seemed to many in the Regiment to be motivated not by a desire for objective reporting but by malice. For had not Ware shown more courtesy to Collins by letting him comment on Ritchie's reply than he had to Ritchie by failing to let him have forewarning of his loaded questions?

It was left to Collins and Brooke to wind up the programme. The former said that he could not see that the UDR had a role as it was presently constituted. "People do not regard it as a force they can depend on, as a force they can have respect for, a force whose credibility is questioned now more than ever before." Brooke, who had appeared hesitant in the interview with Ware, said forcefully that the Regiment was "an integral part of the British army and will continue to be so, so the idea that it is going to be disbanded (for which the Irish Government have not themselves asked) is not a working part of anyone's scenario."

Out of the 78-minute interview with Ritchie, the BBC had used about two minutes.

The following day the newspapers published full accounts of the programme. The BBC in Belfast reported that it had received some 200 telephone calls. A deputation from the DUP led by Paisley handed in their 'Hands off the UDR' petition at Downing Street and then went on to a meeting with the Vice Chairman of the BBC, who maintained that the programme had been "fair, accurate and impartial".[15] Lord Hunt wrote to the *Independent*, recalling that a commission set up in 1985 by the Liberal and Social Democratic Alliance, of which he had been a member, had recommended that the role of the UDR should be taken over by the RUC, "given that the RUC is under direct rule accountable to the British Government," and that the "Panorama" programme had reinforced his opinion that the Regiment should be phased out.[16] It was a damaging letter, for it was as a result of Hunt's report on policing in Northern Ireland in 1969 that the UDR had been set up. It was also surprising to find that a former senior Army officer with a distinguished career, including Deputy Commandant at the Staff College, should make the same mistake as the politicians and the journalists, that the Army and the police were wholly interchangeable. Young, as Colonel Commandant, wrote to Hunt inviting him to enlarge on his opinion as to how an increased RUC could be organized and trained to carry out the current military role of the UDR, reminding him that the UDR was part of the British Army and therefore, like the police, under the control of the British Government. Hunt did not reply.

Most commentators concentrated on Ritchie's remark that as a matter of course patrols were not given briefings on Loyalist paramilitaries. An article in the *Guardian*, the general tone of which was set by the crass comment that

> "we also know, or think we do, that Ulster is a pretty terrible place where only a reckless bonehead would join the Army or the police, in which task he must surely expect to live by different rules from the gentlemen of other regiments of the British Army," went on to say that "what it [the "Panorama" programme] exposed for the first time was the official policy ordaining that the UDR should concern itself exclusively with the IRA and not Protestant suspects. Although this has often been assumed to be the case, the Regiment has not previously admitted it."[17]

The leader of the Alliance Party, Alderdice, who in September had had a helpful private meeting with Ritchie and received a full briefing on the Regiment, was quoted as saying that he should consider his position as Commander, and that he had given the impression that his soldiers "should not trouble themselves about Loyalist paramilitaries. Such a position strips him of any credibility in the Nationalist community and also in the law-abiding Unionist community where people want the Loyalist paramilitaries dealt with just as much as they want to see the Republicans dealt with too."[18] The *Belfast Telegraph*, consistently the most moderate member of the Irish press, pointed out in its leader

"To those with an open mind the main criticism of the programme is by highlighting the misconduct of a few members there is a danger of creating the impression that the entire regiment is corrupt. This is not the case, nor was that assertion made. Father Denis Faul, who has been tireless in documenting the alleged transgressions of UDR members, stressed that the vast majority of soldiers perform their duties in a manner above reproach. For the Brigadier to admit that its operations were directed almost exclusively against Republican terrorist groups, with the fight against Protestant extremists the domain of the RUC, only adds to the fear of many nationalists that the UDR exists only to operate against their section of the community and is not even-handed in its approach to security."[19]

Some of the criticism was unpleasantly personal. Alderdice's remark that Ritchie should consider his position as Commander was at least courteously expressed; the *Guardian*'s comment that "his performance was depressing proof that it is not the moral faculties of the terrorists alone that are blunted by their crimes" was vituperative, while a review of the programme by a TV critic in a Sunday paper included a personal attack so disgraceful that Ritchie considered taking legal action. As a Scotsman who had spent most of his military career in a Scottish Regiment, Ritchie had a ready empathy with his Ulster soldiers and they in turn welcomed his irrepressible sense of humour. Visiting patrols long after midnight he would go up to some cold, wet cover sentry, who was probably wishing he was tucked up in his warm bed like any other sensible person, and enquire, "What mean, lean killer have we here?" Now he felt that he had failed the Regiment and was hurt by these criticisms. Sadly there were many who could not believe that he had had no forewarning of the Stevens arrests and felt that he had failed to speak up in the UDR's defence then, and now in the wake of the "Panorama" programme he had failed to do so again. The criticism was unjust. He was anxious to make some kind of public rebuttal, but he was under orders to remain silent, in the first instance because nothing must be said that could damage Army-police relations and in the second because, in the view of the NIO and HQNI, any official comment on the BBC programme would only give it a higher profile and a greater credence than it deserved.

Faulkner, who was a member of the local BBC advisory body, complained to Marmaduke Hussey, the Chairman of the BBC Board of Governors, while he was on a visit to the Province. In the summer he and Young attended an angry meeting in London with John Birt, the Deputy

Director General, and Ware to air their complaints about the programme and the manner in which it had been put together. Shortly before that meeting one of the soldiers mentioned in the programme, anonymously but inaccurately, had lost his leg in an under-car booby trap. He was one of those who had warned his battalion that the BBC team had been to see him in January and he had spoken personally to Ritchie about his fears that the visit had jeopardized his safety. The *Daily Mirror* ran the story on its front page under the headline "BBC sets up soldier for murder"[20]. Hussey, who had lost a leg at Anzio whilst serving as a subaltern in the Grenadier Guards, was very concerned and expressed a wish to visit the soldier when he was next in the Province, but the Corporation denied the accusation absolutely. Of course there was no proof that the visit or Ware's inaccurate assertions about the soldier had caused the IRA to target him, but, as Faulkner pointed out at the London meeting, could they be sure?

A summary of the Stevens Enquiry report was published on 17 May and debated in the Commons on the same day, three months after Ware had said that the Enquiry was expected to show that many of the leaks of information to the Protestant paramilitaries had come from within the UDR. Annesley and Stevens held a joint press conference to present the report. The Chief Constable made a point of referring to the UDR:

> "Throughout the Enquiry the UDR has been subjected to a level of wholesale denigration that is simply not justified. I think that the UDR does an exceptional job in the Province, and the RUC simply could not operate effectively without them. It is, I think, particularly poignant that, whilst the whole Regiment is being criticized in a catch-all way, their members, like my officers, are being murdered by terrorists as they perform their duty on behalf of the whole population of Northern Ireland."[21]

The Enquiry was the most extensive of its type ever undertaken in the United Kingdom. In all Stevens' team had taken written statements from 1,900 witnesses; 2,000 investigations had been undertaken, and 2,600 documents of all types had been recovered from Loyalist paramilitary organizations, principally from the UDA. Some were original security forces documents, many were photocopies. All the documents were classified under the lowest security grading.

The report included a summary of eighty-three recommendations, thirty-one of which referred to the RUC and thirty-four to the Army. Of the latter seventeen referred principally to the UDR and fourteen of those were recommendations for improving the system for vetting of recruits and serving soldiers. Stevens pointed out that individuals adversely reported on by the RUC Vetting Section had nevertheless been enlisted, a small number of whom had gone on to commit terrorist-related or criminal offences whilst in the Regiment.[22]

However, a review carried out in the aftermath of the report showed that the situation was not as bad as Stevens had implied. It was true that the RUC had reported adversely on a fair number of applicants, mainly on the grounds of civil convictions, but a few because they had connections with other persons involved in paramilitary activities. In most instances the police had not made a specific recommendation against enlistment. Many of the convictions were of a minor nature – traffic offences such as speeding. A few were of a sufficiently serious nature to warrant a review as to whether they should be retained, but in only one instance was it decided that a soldier should not be allowed to re-engage after his current contract ran out. As for the small number who Stevens claimed had been enlisted and then gone on to commit terrorist-related offences, there were only three, and they were awaiting discharge. Nevertheless Stevens' general recommendation on the need to tighten up vetting was accepted and measures were introduced to ensure the system was more stringent.

From the UDR's point of view the most significant conclusion of the report was that "the passing of information to paramilitaries by members of the security forces is neither widespread nor institutionalized". The police investigation had not been limited to 7/10UDR. Around thirty soldiers in 11UDR, the battalion based in the strongly Loyalist Portadown/Lurgan area, had been questioned, their lockers and homes searched, but anything that was found – maps, pamphlets, patrol commanders' notebooks, small quantities of ammunition – were legitimate tools of their trade. None was charged and no evidence was found of collusion. It would be wrong to deny that there were a few men in most battalions who probably were in touch with Loyalist paramilitaries. Nevertheless the fact that such a thorough investigation carried out by a highly experienced and completely impartial team of outside detectives under the direction of a Deputy Chief Constable from an English force had reached the conclusion that passage of information to the paramilitaries was neither 'widespread nor institutionalized' and that out of all the men arrested and charged only one was found guilty of an act of collusion was a vindication rather than a criticism of the reputation of the UDR.

Stevens had pointed out that, because some of the matters covered by his investigation involved the security of the State and others were still *sub judice*, some aspects of the report must remain confidential. Rumours at that time and since have suggested that some of these matters concerned the UDR. A very senior police officer who has recently re-read this classified annex has confirmed that there were no such conclusions in so far as they referred to the UDR.

There remained a suspicion, in wider circles than the UDR, that the Regiment had been used as a whipping boy to divert attention from the RUC. The *Times* Irish correspondent commented that it was hard to avoid the conclusion that Stevens "had either taken a formal decision or just drifted away from an investigation of the RUC, mindful perhaps of the explosive consequences" and went on to suggest that "perhaps policemen were more skilful at covering their tracks than, for example, members of the UDR."[23] Stevens rejected any such accusation. No evidence had been found to justify any charges against a member of the force. He pointed out that 213 police officers had been interviewed about the disappearance of the Dunmurry montages. Nevertheless the doubt remained. Was there really no evidence after some 2,000 investigations that not a single member of the RUC, not even a part-time reservist, had been involved in collusion with the paramilitaries?

If the Regiment had been used as a scapegoat, it was for understandable reasons, for while the RUC had begun to receive grudging acceptance from the Nationalist community, it was all too apparent that acceptance of the UDR was already a lost cause.

In the concluding sentence of his "Panorama" programme Ware had said, "Unless this regiment of Protestants can earn the trust of Catholics it will remain for ever part of the problem that it was intended to solve." It was in recognition of this that in the summer of 1990 a select few members of the staff in HQNI and HQUDR began to consider whether there might be a revolutionary way of solving the problem while still meeting the essential military role of the Regiment.

At the Commander UDR's Study weekend in November 1989 the senior Intelligence staff officer from HQNI had told the audience that the Provisionals had some 300 activists to call on and about another thousand prepared to give them active support. Only some 20% of the Libyan munitions consignments had been recovered and for the next two years the violence was likely to continue at its present level. It was a depressing message for hard-pressed company commanders.

The Intelligence staff officers' assessment proved to be all too accurate. Nine serving and three ex-members of the Regiment were among the eighty-one people killed in 1990. Another thirteen were injured in varying degrees, one losing one leg and two others both legs in UVBT explosions. The first to die was Olven Kilpatrick, a part-time Private in 6UDR, shot down as he was serving in his shoe shop in Castlederg. He was the seventeenth soldier from the Battalion to be murdered in the Border reaches of West Tyrone.

On 9 April a two-vehicle patrol had set out from 3UDR's base at Ballykinlar for Downpatrick. As they drove along the Ballydugan road towards the race course, a police patrol was discovering overalls and a boot on the parallel Vianstown road. There had been a warning that PIRA was preparing to mount a major attack in the area, the overalls were wet though there had been no rain, and, suspecting that that might indicate a landmine had been placed in a ditch, the station in Downpatrick rang the Battalion Operations Room, advising that the Ballydugan road should be placed out of bounds. As the duty operator answered the telephone a contact report came over the radio from the patrol; one of the vehicles had just been blown up.

Half a mile beyond the Georgian manor house at Ballydugan the road crosses the old marshes. A culvert spans a flood ditch. The first Landrover had crossed the culvert when there was a huge explosion, blowing the second vehicle some 30 yards over the hedge into a field, setting it on fire. A woman motorist travelling in the opposite direction stopped short of the crater. At the inquest she told how she had been 200 yards from the first vehicle when she heard a massive bang.

"Everything seemed to light up. Everything seemed to fall down on top of the car. I realized a bomb had exploded." She ran to the wreckage and saw two soldiers lying underneath. "I realized immediately that both were dead. I tried to pull the bodies out, but had to stop for fear of being burnt. Everything was deadly quiet. I saw a soldier crying and asked him if they were his friends. He replied, 'Yes there were four of them'."[24]

They were all members of the permanent cadre company – Lance Corporal John Bradley the patrol commander, and Privates John Birch, Steven Smart, and Michael Adams. Other people stopped to help, but the fire was setting off the ammunition in the wrecked vehicle and there was nothing they could do. One of the first to arrive was a Corporal from the same company on his way to duty at Ballykinlar. He found the surviving members of the patrol disoriented and suffering from shock. He took a radio from one of them and sent the contact report, set up an incident control post and secured a helicopter landing zone. He tried to pull the bodies clear of the vehicle, despite the danger from the exploding ammunition, but realized there was no point; they were all dead. He deployed the airborne reinforcements as they arrived and coordinated the operations of the police, fire and ambulance services until a more senior officer could take over. After two hours he drove on into camp, his clothes dirty and covered in blood, changed into uniform and returned to the scene. The casualties, dead and wounded, were the worst suffered by the Regiment in any one incident. The funerals took place during the week in East Belfast, Bangor, Newtownards and the small fishing village of Ballywalter – Methodist, Mormon, Presbyterian and Church of Ireland. Three of the four were former Regular soldiers. John Birch had been a fisherman. His brother had been drowned while trying to rescue his first mate in Dover Harbour on the night of the hurricane in 1987. John's widow Angela gave birth to their son five months after the landmine.

The following Sunday was Easter. Eddie McGrady, the SDLP MP for South Down, referred to the attack as "the Holocaust of Holy Week." The Cardinal-elect, Dr Cathal Daly, said that the murders were a horrifying reminder of how far some members of the community had departed from Christian teaching.[25] Baron Crespo, President of the European Parliament, sent a message to the Commander expressing the "deep outrage" of his members and asking that their sympathy be passed on to the families. The Prime Minister, linking the murders to the refusal of the judiciary in the Republic to extradite three leading IRA members, was quoted as saying, "I am very, very depressed". Two days later the Taoiseach, Haughey, was due to come to Belfast to address a conference of the Institute of Directors. Despite a move in some quarters to cancel the invitation, the visit went ahead and a protest demonstration organized by Paisley outside the Europa Hotel passed off peacefully. On the last Sunday of the month the principal clergy of all the churches in Downpatrick led a peace march from the centre of the town out to the site of the explosion, some 2,000 people, old and young and children in prams.

Today four cherry trees mark for posterity the place where the lives of four young men were suddenly wiped out.

Such was the intensity of operations in that year that half the permanent cadre companies were failing to meet the GOC's guidelines of not more than 60 hours' duty in each week and one night in four out of bed, while duty for the part-timers was coming round one night in three. Compared with the hours worked by the Regular Army the targets might seem low, but the Regular reinforcement battalions were in Province for four and a half months (later increased to six) and it is not difficult to work long hours if the soldiers have an end point in view; the UDR soldiers had no such end point. In July the average weekly working hours for the permanent cadre were 65½, but for some the figure was substantially higher, with soldiers in 7/10UDR working in some weeks as much as 96 hours. Few of the IRA's attacks within the city at that time caused serious damage, but they were frequent, with the same targets being selected again and again.

Between April 1990 and March 1991 there were three bombing and eight shooting attacks on the Royal Courts of Justice, with gunfire being directed from the Markets against workmen renovating the building and at sangars manned by the 7/10UDR guards. In the same period there were three explosive and two incendiary attacks against the newly built Castle Court shopping complex in Royal Avenue, a prestigious target, a symbol that a greater measure of normality was returning to Belfast, attracting to the city mainland department stores. Shorts, the aircraft and missile firm, came under attack twice; in February a small bomb damaged a hangar and a light aircraft, and a month later fourteen devices planted simultaneously at the works at Sydenham and Castlereagh and within the area of the Harbour Airport caused minor damage and casualties. The task of patrolling the long security fence enclosing the airport increased the Battalion's workload, as did the mounting of lurk patrols on the main Belfast–Dublin railway line. In May and again in June patrols from 11UDR gave cover to ATO and Sapper search teams while they dealt with devices on the line at Lurgan. On the first occasion the ATO's vehicles were moved to the seat of the explosion on a flatbed wagon pulled by a diesel engine of CIE, the Irish public transport company.

Two attacks on UDR bases failed. On the morning of 26 April a flat-bed lorry fitted with sixteen mortar tubes was parked in the middle of a bungalow estate just across the road from Mahon Barracks, Headquarters of 11UDR and RUC J Division, on the outskirts of Portadown. Two minutes later the lorry exploded, scattering tubes and bombs in all directions, some falling within the camp perimeter, all of them blinds. Every one of the twenty houses in the recently completed estate was damaged, some so badly that they would have to be demolished, and two residents were injured. Within the camp there was little damage and no one was hurt.

Two days later the police in Dungannon received a telephone call to the effect that there had been a small explosion in a van parked in an estate in the town. When a call was made to the Parochial House by a member of the IRA stating there was a bomb in the van 8UDR mounted a clearance operation. There was indeed a bomb, 1,200lb of high grade HME, and the remains of a detonator that had evidently exploded prematurely while the device was being armed. The intended target had probably been Killymeal House. The van was an exact replica of one belonging to the construction firm that came daily into 8UDR's base.

After their success against the 3UDR patrol outside Downpatrick PIRA continued to use landmines detonated by command wire. Two such attacks were foiled on two days in May when patrols from 8 and 11UDR found a total of 1,000lbs of explosive deployed ready for use.

On 24 July three police officers were killed when a 500lb CWIED exploded as they were driving along the Armagh-Killylea road. So far as the rest of the world was concerned it might have passed off as just one more violent incident out of Northern Ireland, except that a 37-year-old nun who was driving past at the time was also caught in the blast and killed, and the murders became international news. The watchers at the firing point never knew it, but by chance they had missed a more lucrative target. The same day Ritchie had been to 2UDR with his successor Angus Ramsay, who was on a preliminary visit to the province before taking over command of the UDR in the autumn. Shortly before the explosion the two Brigadiers, wearing uniform, had driven along the road. They noticed a car pulled into the side and, as they passed, the passenger's head went down and he appeared to be talking into a microphone. "I think when they realized who we were, they just weren't quick enough to detonate the bomb," Ritchie recalled. He was able to give the police a fairly detailed description of the bomber. In the follow-up a patrol from 2UDR found two AKM rifles and magazines hidden among the bushes, both identified as having been used in numerous murders, and as a result two terrorists were arrested.

Between late September and the end of the year another two serving and three ex-members of the Regiment were murdered. Colin McCullough, a 22-year-old Private in 11UDR, had been to the pictures in Belfast with his fiancée. On their way home they parked at a favourite place for young couples, the car park in a local nature reserve on the shore of Lough Neagh. As they sat talking three gunmen approached the car and fired fifteen rounds, killing McCullough by his fiancée's side. Two weeks later a young Catholic sitting with his girlfriend in the same place was murdered in retaliation by Loyalist paramilitaries. It was a tragic time for the Battalion. In the space of five weeks four other soldiers died, three as a result of heart attacks and the fourth by his own hand.

WO2 Albert Cooper was the manager of a Cookstown exhaust fitting garage and part-time Sergeant Major of the company based in the town. In October 1988 he had come under fire while turning into the driveway of his bungalow out in the country, but had escaped with a minor head wound. He moved his wife and three young children to a less remote house in an estate in the town, and continued to serve in the Battalion while running the garage. Two years later a woman telephoned asking if an exhaust could be fitted to her car; Cooper told her to bring it in right away. A young woman drove the car into the yard, held a brief conversation with the Sergeant Major, turned and walked away. He had just got into the car to drive it into the workshop when there was an explosion, killing him instantly. Witnesses said the woman looked back and smiled before running to a car waiting out in the road. Within days a local man and a young woman, a 19-year-old nurse, had been charged with the murder, and in her case membership of the IRA.[26]

"Evil lady dressed in black delivers death bomb" reported the headline in the local paper. But the greater evil belonged to the faceless men who could persuade a woman not yet out of her teens, in an honourable profession devoted to saving life, to commit a murder in the name of their cause. Cooper's brother made a public appeal that no one should be killed in retaliation. "As far as I am concerned taking bodies to graves is no way to answer any problem. Killing people will never bring peace." The appeal was in vain. Over the previous two years tit-for-tat killings had escalated in the Murder Triangle covering North Armagh and East Tyrone. A week before Cooper's death a Cookstown member of Sinn Fein had been murdered; a week after, Loyalist paramilitaries killed a Catholic working at a farm near Stewartstown.

In December a former member of 5UDR, Bertie Gilmore, had driven with his wife half a mile down the Maghera road outside Kilrea to visit a site where they were building their retirement bungalow. As they sat in the car gunmen fired at them, killing the husband and leaving the wife very seriously injured with wounds to her head and stomach. Before driving away, the assassins rammed the car of a nurse who had stopped to render first aid.[27] A few days later a known Provisional was stopped at a VCP. "I hear we got one of yours on Saturday," he taunted the patrol commander. "I hope the old bitch dies as well. We'll get more of you before Christmas is out."

An INLA gang opened fire on a bungalow at Victoria Bridge belonging to a member of 6UDR. The soldier was known to be under imminent threat and a detachment from the Regular Army had taken over the bungalow. They returned fire, killing one of the gunmen and capturing the other two. Afterwards it was alleged that the dead man had been a double agent who had warned the security forces of the impending attack.[28] In the aftermath it was imperative that the UDR soldier sell up and move his family elsewhere. Although by now a government scheme had been introduced to compensate people intimidated out of their homes by offering them a fair market price for the house they must now leave, the compensation did not allow for the fact that a house of the same standard in a safe area would be substantially more expensive. As a result the UDR family found themselves in an impossible situation.

Two significant innovations took place during the year. In March the UDR Depot at Ballykinlar became responsible for all military training in the Province, under the command of a Regular Army Lieutenant Colonel on the strength of the UDR. From now on, as well as running UDR courses, including the permanent cadre recruits, the Regiment would be responsible for courses for the Regular Army and RAF Regiment individual reinforcements on first posting to the Province, for unit search teams and combat medics, skill-at-arms and NCO command training and for the management of the various weapon ranges spread across the sand dunes.

Then the study on the harmonization of police and military operational boundaries was finally completed and the new boundaries came into effect on 1 November. HQ 3 Brigade at Armagh assumed responsibility for 3, 8 and 11UDR (2UDR had already passed under its control in June), whilst 4UDR was now placed under 8 Brigade in Derry. As a result of the changes there were some adjustment of companies within battalions. 11UDR's companies based in Lisburn passed to 1/9UDR, reducing the Portadown battalion by 220 at a time when the activities of the Loyalist paramilitaries and the emergent Lurgan PIRA were making heavy demands on the Battalion. 4UDR assumed command of the Clogher Company of 6UDR, and two weak part-time companies in Enniskillen were amalgamated at Grosvenor Barracks. The new barrack block, built alongside the original Battalion Headquarters at Coleshill, partially underground and designed to withstand mortar attack, had been officially opened a year earlier by the Duke of Westminster. Grosvenor was the family name.

In October the *Belfast Telegraph* and *Newsletter* reported that a soldier in 8UDR had rung their offices, claiming that thirty members of the permanent cadre company had gone on sick leave as a protest against their officers' alleged failure to support them in the face of malicious complaints by Sinn Fein.[29] It was a ridiculous reason and his comrades resented the fact that he had told the press, for the story, picked up by other papers, could only encourage Sinn Fein by showing that complaints were affecting the company's morale. The report was an attempt to provide a spurious reason for the fact that some twenty-six soldiers, reluctant to leave their families alone and under threat, were intending to report sick rather than attend a week's intensive training in Kent. Since under their terms of service they could not be compelled to serve outside the Province, some twenty were left behind. The whole rather silly affair had blown over in a couple of days and was dismissed as a storm in a tea-cup. But there was more to it than that. To some it was a symptom of unease within the Regiment. It had been a difficult two years – the accusations of collusion, the Stevens Enquiry, the "Panorama" programme, the long hours of duty with no end in sight. There was a great need for something good to happen to lighten what seemed unrelenting gloom. That came in the following year.

CHAPTER NINETEEN

1991–1992: The Final Months

In 1987 the Regiment submitted a case to the MOD, asking that the Queen be approached with a view to approving the award of Colours to the nine battalions and suggesting that they might be presented in 1991, the 21st anniversary of the formation of the UDR. By June 1988 the Queen had given her consent[1] and designs for a Royal and Regimental Colour for each battalion, the latter incorporating the Arms of the appropriate county, the City of Belfast or Craigavon Borough, were submitted to the College of Arms. There Garter Principal King of Arms checked that they were correct heraldically and obtained the Sovereign's signature of approval on each design. By May 1990 her approval had been received and the Royal School of Needlework tasked to embroider the nine sets. Time was short, but the MOD agreed to give the UDR precedence over other infantry battalions. By early 1991 the first five were completed and the decision was taken to hold the presentation to four of the five battalions at the end of June.[2] With just two months to go, and after several other locations had been considered and discarded on security grounds, the playing fields inside Thiepval Barracks were chosen for the parade. A planning date had been agreed, but was not finally confirmed until mid-May, leaving just six weeks to send out invitations and receive replies. These gave only the date; the place was not revealed to the guests until a fortnight beforehand.

The Queen had decided that she herself would present the Colours. Only the Sovereign has the prerogative to decide whether Colours should be awarded and the decision to present them personally was her's and her's alone. It was an unusual decision and a great honour for the UDR, for normally the Sovereign presents Colours in person only to those regiments of which she is Colonel-in-Chief.

Some months in advance a select few were let into the secret that the Queen would be coming. It was made clear to them that if the news leaked out the presentation would be cancelled. Great care had to be taken at the planning conferences not to refer to the 'personage' as feminine. In the printing of the programme the word 'royal' had to be deleted from the Royal Salute and the Queen was described as 'principal guest'. A deliberate false trail was laid by letting battalions know that the Secretary of State would be taking the parade, but that produced such a groundswell of disappointment that the COs had to be told in the strictest confidence that in fact the Queen would be making the presentation. The secret was well kept. Few of the men and women on parade knew that Her Majesty was about to present them with their Colours until she stepped out on the dais. "You could almost hear the gasp of the soldiers on parade suddenly realizing who was there," Ramsay recalled.

Three days before the parade the guards and a representative detachment of 150 Greenfinches from the four battalions assembled at the Maze for their first joint rehearsals. The day chosen for the presentation, 29 June, was the 75th anniversary of the day that the men of the 36th Ulster Division formed up in Thiepval Wood in preparation for the great attack on the Schwaben Redoubt, the opening of the Battle of the Somme. Her Majesty was returning to Northern Ireland for the first time since her Silver Jubilee visit in 1977. She landed in the barracks in a Wessex helicopter and was escorted to the saluting dais by the two Colonels Commandant. The four battalion guards, the Greenfinches at their centre, were drawn up on the playing fields, the families on one side, a large contingent from the media on the other, the invited guests and VIPs in the stands. As the Queen inspected the guards, accompanied by the parade commander, the Regimental Colonel, Isaac Clarke, a part-time officer, the four stands of Colours were laid on the piled drums set up in front of the parade.

The Queen took up position facing the drums. A persistent soft rain began to fall. A lady-in-waiting produced a plastic umbrella. The Chaplain General to the Forces, the Reverend James Harkness, accompanied by Chaplains from all the main Churches, consecrated each stand of Colours in turn. Eight Ensigns marched forward and knelt on the hassocks bearing the regimental crest in tapestry, resting on wooden bases made by a soldier from 4UDR who lived alone within yards of the Border. The Senior and Junior Major from each guard placed the Queen's and Regimental Colours in the Ensigns' belts, presented to the battalions in the proceeding weeks by the Lord Lieutenants of Counties Antrim, Down, Fermanagh and Londonderry. The Queen moved along the line, touching each Colour and bowing her head in salute. Taking her place on the dais she addressed the parade:

"The UDR stands for those who are not prepared to stand by and let evil prosper. It provides for everyone in Northern Ireland – regardless of faith or background – the opportunity to make a contribution to the defeat of terrorism. That contribution needs courage and a sense of duty, together with a determination, which I share, that terrorism cannot be allowed to win. I salute your courage, your sense of duty and your resolve. And I would like to say that I know how much you rely on the devoted loyalty of your wives, husbands and families in helping you in your task. Without them you would find the challenge you face that much harder; with them you can meet it with confidence. They are right to be proud of you.

"I congratulate you on your turnout and bearing, and a parade of the highest order. I now entrust these Colours to your keeping, confident that you will guard them with the same indomitable spirit which you show in the daily round of soldiering. I hope that they will encourage you as you strive for the objective to which you devote your lives, and which we all share with you – peace and safety for the people of Northern Ireland."[3]

Clarke replied on behalf of the Regiment, word-perfect in a brief speech that he had learnt by heart, ignoring suggestions that he should stick a crib on the blade of his sword. The Colours were marched back to their guards as the National Anthem was played and the whole parade marched past their Sovereign with Colours flying, while the Pipes and Drums played the regimental marches, 'Sprig of Shillelagh' and 'Garryowen'.

It had stopped raining.

The Queen walked down the line of stands to talk with a group of widows, disabled soldiers and others who had been forced to move their families out of their homes. She posed for formal group photographs with the officers and Senior NCOs of the guards, then walked on to the GOC's house nearby where, in a private ceremony, witnessed only by Lady Faulkner and their daughters, she conferred on Sir Dennis the knighthood he had received in the New Year's Honours. It was another unusual occurrence on that day; Lady Faulkner was not well enough to travel to Buckingham Palace to attend an investiture.

A lunch was held for the selected guests in the Air Hall, an indoor tennis court converted into a passable dining room for the occasion. At the conclusion Sir David Young presented the Queen with a silver statuette of a UDR soldier mounted on a granite plinth fashioned by a stonemason from Mourne – the 'Little Ulsterman', the General called it. Her Majesty returned to her helicopter to fly to Hillsborough for a garden party and thence to return to Edinburgh.

The day had been an enormous success.

Considering that the UDR had little time for arms drill and seldom wore parade dress, and there had been only three full rehearsals, the standard of the parade had been highly professional. The Regiment had come a long way from those early years when the men marched with the rolling gait of the Orangemen following their Lodge banner and the farmers walking over pasture and plough.

Back in Edinburgh the Queen instructed her Private Secretary, Sir Robert Fellowes, to write to Sir David Young:

"When the Queen was back at Holyrood House last night, and talking about the visit, Her Majesty asked me to be sure to write to you to express her congratulations, through you, to the men and women of the UDR on a magnificent parade.

"The Queen's experience in these matters means that she is well aware of the vast amount of staff work and preparation which goes into a parade of this sort. The fact that in the UDR's circumstances these had to be conducted largely in secret laid extra demands on all those involved. If it is any consolation to them, the result, as The Queen said in her speech, was a parade of the highest order, and you must as Colonel Commandant have been deeply proud."

The Colours parade was Sir David's last act as Colonel Commandant before handing over to his successor, General Sir Charles Huxtable.

The following Sunday and Monday the press carried front-page pictures and reports of the parade. Inevitably the comments in the Nationalist press were hostile.

"Considering the dubious history of the UDR," one journalist wrote, "the continual harassment in nationalist areas and allegations of links with the paramilitaries, the Queen's short speech of endorsement represented a political *démarche* that can only be regarded as untimely and hamfisted."[4]

But such comments could not mar the success of the occasion. It had been an enormous boost to the morale of the Regiment, royal recognition richly deserved.

Angus Ramsay, who took over from Ritchie as Commander UDR in November 1990, had first served in Northern Ireland in the early '70s when, as a platoon commander in the Royal Highland Fusiliers, he had survived an explosion while guarding Unity Flats in North Belfast, protecting the occupants from the Protestant crowds, who were apt to vent their spleen against the Catholic families living in the tower block. He came to the UDR after attending the US Army War College in Pennsylvania.[5]

The Provisionals had developed another new device, the Mark 12 mortar. A shaped charge weapon fired horizontally from a mortar-type tube, it could penetrate armour on a vehicle or a sangar up to a range of 70 yards. The first successful attack was carried out on the evening of 1 March against a 2UDR mobile patrol as it approached the outskirts of Armagh. The two vehicles were held up by roadworks. When the temporary traffic lights turned to green and the first Landrover began to move forward, a bomb fired from the mortar hit the bodywork, blowing off the sides and the roof. One soldier, Private Paul Sutcliffe, was killed instantly. A second, Roger Love, a 20-year-old single man who lived with his parents and three sisters, was kept alive for three days on a life-support machine. When his family knew there was no hope, they agreed that the machine should be switched off and his kidneys be donated to save some other life. Of the other two soldiers in the vehicle one had severe chest injuries and never regained the use of one arm; the other had one leg amputated below the knee. Sutcliffe, an Englishman who had served in the Duke of Wellington's Regiment before joining 2UDR, came from a small Lancashire village, Barrowford. A party from the Battalion attended the military funeral in the parish church, the only UDR funeral held outside Northern Ireland. His remains were cremated and his ashes scattered on the Mournes.

In November Private Michael Boxall died and another soldier lost an eye in another mortar attack on a 5UDR patrol outside Bellaghy.

The IRA continued to use their customary weapons, the car bomb and the conventional mortar. On the evening of 3 February a PIRA gang forced their way into the home of a man in Tobermore, tied him to the front seat of a van containing a 1000lb bomb and told him to drive it to the UDR base at Magherafelt. To make sure he did so they blindfolded his wife and took her at gunpoint in a following car. A part-time soldier was on guard duty in the front gate sangar when the van crashed into the security bollards a few yards from his post. The driver struggled to untie his bonds, screaming that the van contained a bomb. The soldier sounded the alarm and, leaving the relative safety of the armoured sangar, ran out to release the driver and dragged him to safety. As they crouched down behind cover the bomb exploded just two minutes after the van had hit the bollards. Thanks to the soldier's courage and instant reaction, for which he was awarded the Queen's Gallantry Medal, the driver's life was saved and no one was seriously hurt.

Over the next two months a van bomb outside the Court House in Banbridge caused extensive damage and a soldier in 3UDR had a remarkable escape from severe injury when a UVBT blew him out of his van in the centre of the town. In Belfast there was another attack on Shorts, the sixth, and in Trillick in Tyrone another part-time soldier escaped with his life when two gunmen fired on his tanker lorry. A foot patrol from 8UDR carrying out a VCP on the Lurgylea road, just north of Cappagh, came under heavy automatic fire from at least one GPMG at 800 yards range. The firing was accurate, the rounds passing over the heads of the soldiers as they took up fire positions along the hedgerow. One of the men, seeing that a woman motorist had been caught in the line of fire, broke cover, pulled her from the driving seat and shielded her with his body until the firing ceased, then led her away to the shelter of a nearby house. The fact that he had risked his life to save her perhaps made some impression in a neighbourhood where the UDR was hated.

The UDR base at Glenanne had been built in 1972 to house two companies of 2UDR. It formed an outpost out in the country ten miles south of Armagh, on the dividing line between the mainly Catholic and the mainly Protestant areas. On the one hand it was a visible security presence for a beleaguered people; on the other it was very vulnerable, out on a limb. Seven of the soldiers had been murdered and most of those who lived along the Border, the gallant Newtownhamilton Platoon, had resigned. Politically it served a purpose; operationally it was no longer viable and a decision had already been taken to close it down.

On the night of 31 May the base was unusually crowded. About forty people had gathered for a social evening. One of the Sergeants was duty officer; his wife Jill, a Lance Corporal Greenfinch, was running the bar up on the first floor. Half an hour to midnight a man who lived along a lane on the sloping ground a field's distance above the base heard a heavy

351

vehicle entering the driveway. Looking out of the window he saw a tipper lorry being manoeuvred into the field while four armed and masked men provided cover. Believing that the base was about to come under mortar attack he rang the Battalion Operations Room. But it was already too late. Having supervised the closure of the bar the Sergeant had gone to the Sergeant's mess to change out of his uniform. Something heavy crashed down on the roof, a mortar bomb, he guessed. He shouted to two off-duty members of the guard, Lance Corporal Crozier and Private Blakely, to follow him and raced down the stairs to the guardroom to sound the stand-to alarm. The guard commander told him there had been a phone call from Armagh, relaying the man's message about the lorry outside his house. The Sergeant turned to the wall to press the alarm button. At that moment there was an almighty explosion – not a mortar but 2000lb of a new home-made explosive, packed into the lorry, which had been despatched driverless down the slope of the field. Gathering momentum it had crashed through the steel screen and chain-link fence, throwing fragments up onto the roof and coming to rest against the corner of the main building. Seconds later the device exploded. It was one of the largest bombs ever detonated by the IRA. So great was the sound of it that it was heard in Balbriggan outside Dublin some 60 miles away. The blast tore the building apart.

The Sergeant looked up and saw the wall of the guardroom toppling down towards him.

"I felt a thump on the back of my neck. It knocked me down to my knees. The next thing I remember is somebody shouting my name. 'Are you alive? Are you there?' I stood up, and I saw that the reinforced wall had come down. The bench of the guardroom stopped it. The guard commander was lying there with reinforced concrete up on his chest, and he said, 'Fuck me. I thought I was going to lose my life.' I could see that his whole chest was trapped under this slab of concrete. The place was a mass of rubble. There was a big raging fire that was creeping towards him. It was only a matter of feet from him. The oil tank at the back of the building had ruptured and was just a big ball of fire. The ammunition in the back of the guard house was starting to explode with the heat. I got between him and the fire. I put my arms under his armpits and pulled him out. I went to see if there was anybody hurt up the stairs. I waded through the rubble and couldn't see the stairs. There was a mass of twisted wire. The stairs had gone. It was just like a rubbish tip. I heard the wife shouting. She didn't know where I was. She thought I was still caught upstairs, changing in the Sergeants' mess."

The Sergeant's wife had been upstairs in the bar talking to friends when they heard the crash as the fencing fell on the roof. They had taken cover under a table and then the bomb exploded.

"The place just went into complete darkness. The wires came down from the ceiling, bits and pieces of wood were hitting our legs. It was like a slow-motion picture, watching the glass smash, and then the window frame came in. We lay there a long long time. We thought it was a mortar attack. It was an awful feeling, just lying waiting and waiting. It seemed like an eternity. One of my colleagues said, 'Right. We'll make our way out of here.' We were all helping each other, shoving things out of the road and climbing over things. We were banging into electric wires, and eventually got to the top of the stairs, and there were no stairs. The stairs had just completely disappeared. It was at that stage I said to one of my colleagues, 'Oh my goodness, Phillip's over there changing.' So he crawled over as far as he could go to the Sergeants' Mess. He came back and said, 'Jill, I'm sorry. I can't get any further.' At that time the fire was coming up the other side of the building, and I said to him, 'Oh my God, Phillip is dead.' We all helped each other down over the rubble in the pitch darkness down to the bottom of the stairs to get out. Somebody shouted at me, 'Phillip's here, Jill. He's OK'."

The Sergeant assembled the survivors at the main gate and carried out a quick head count. Three of the men were missing.

"We went on up in case they were maybe trapped and still alive. Went up to the guardroom and the stores. The fire was still raging. Of course the water was off. Climbed up the rubble to the Other Ranks' accommodation. Checked the toilets. Shouted their names. No sign. Bits of reinforced concrete falling everywhere. By this time the police had arrived at the main gate. I got into the police car and used their radio to tell battalion what had happened. A friend came up and said, 'Is there anything I can do?' I said, 'There is. You can follow me. There are three missing.' At that time the fire brigade had arrived. They followed us in, but this time we went in through the bottom corridor, where the drill hall was. Went up the corridor to the bottom of the stairs. That's where we found the bodies of Paul Blakely and Bobby Crozier. There were lying face down. I turned them over. Their faces had gone, no eyes, no noses, just black holes. They had followed me down and must have been caught in the blast coming down the corridor."

There was still a man missing, Sydney Hamilton. The firemen used detector equipment to locate his body under the rubble. He had been standing behind the Sergeant when the bomb went off and had been blown through the wall into the car park.

The three who died, Lance Corporal Bobby Crozier and Privates Paul Blakely and Sydney Hamilton, were members of the permanent cadre guard, two of them middle-aged. Between the three of them they had eight children, the youngest Karen Blakely, three months old. Eighteen

353

months earlier the family had had to move out of their bungalow in Richhill when it was wrecked by the car bomb in their estate. Of the twelve injured, three were detained in hospital. One was the Sergeant, his neck damaged when the guard room wall fell on top of him. His wife went to see him next day. The car taking her to hospital called first at the base. When she saw the devastation for the first time in daylight, the company's home destroyed, the cattle lying dead in the fields, one animal blown into the next field, the scorched grass, she realized how lucky she was to be alive and her husband not badly hurt. The blast and debris had caused serious damage to the private houses across the road from the base – windows and tiles broken, ceilings brought down, every window smashed in the little primary school. Of the lorry which had been stolen in Kingscourt in the Republic on the previous day only pieces were found; even the engine block had disappeared.

One of those who came to Glenanne to commiserate with the survivors was the newly appointed Catholic Primate of All Ireland, Archbishop Cahal Daly. The Church of Ireland primate, Archbishop Eames, gave the address at all three funerals.

Glenanne was never rebuilt. All that remains now to show that the base was ever there is the lines of trees running along the old entrance road and a memorial stone by the main road, carved with the names of all the soldiers who were killed over the years while serving there. John Adams, their former company commander, retrieved the Roll of Honour book and brass plates from the rubble and presented them to the Presbyterian Church in nearby Mount Norris, where they were dedicated in 1993. Every year since it was built a Service of Remembrance had been held in the Glenanne base on the evening of Remembrance Sunday; the tradition continues now in Mount Norris.

A member of the congregation wrote of one of the services:

"People have gathered from all across the county, from Armagh City down to the Border. John Adams reads out the names of all those soldiers who were murdered whilst serving or having served in the Armagh Battalion. There are forty-seven names. To the visitor, and even to those who have heard them read year after year and can put faces to names and remember friendships lost, it still seems an appalling number. The minister takes as his text 'Blessed are the Peacemakers'. Out in the dark night one can sense how for 25 years men with murder in their hearts roamed like wolves through this quiet countryside, waiting to pounce on unsuspecting prey. And yet, if there was bitterness at the time, there is no sense of it now. Bitterness is self-destructive. Instead there is a palpable sense of comradeship, of a community bound together both by a shared tragedy and the satisfaction of a job well done. One feels they will come here on this second Sunday of November year after year until they too have all gone on their way."[6]

On the morning that the three Glenanne funerals took place, one after another, a Corporal from 4UDR was at his place of work as foreman of Ballycassidy sawmill, next door to the military base at St Angelo, when a large tipper lorry drove into the yard, the driver hurrying away in a waiting car. Using a forklift truck the Corporal looked into the back of the lorry and saw a row of mortar tubes. He shouted a warning to his work-mates to clear the mill, jumped into a car and raced round to the gate of St Angelo to warn the company that they were about to come under attack. The guard sounded the alarm and, while the soldiers took cover, the Corporal rushed back to the mill to ensure that the area had been cleared. A few minutes later all the bombs exploded simultaneously on the lorry, causing extensive damage to the mill building. St Angelo was notorious as one of the most cramped, overcrowded bases in the Province; a mortar bomb landing in it was certain to cause much damage and possibly many casualties.

In July a planned search of Cappagh village mounted by 8UDR led to the discovery of a number of items, including a video of armed, masked men. It was apparent that the film had been shot in the hilly country outside the village. The search was extended to that area the following day. A member of the cordon party noticed what seemed to be a hide dug into a pile of quarry rubble. Instead of drawing attention to his find, he reported it quietly to the patrol commander and the place was left undisturbed until a planned search could be mounted. The results were spectacular – a GPMG, AKM rifle and loaded magazine, Heckler and Koch with two loaded magazines, some 825 rounds of ammunition for the machine-gun and 2lb of Semtex. Seven local men were arrested.

In August two former members of the Regiment were shot down. One, Ronnie Finlay, who had served eighteen years in 6UDR, was the third member of the family to die by terrorist hand. His wife had driven him to a farm about three miles from the Border where he had worked for the past thirty years. They had their two sons with them, one ten years old, the other a baby. As Finlay got out of the car, gunmen who had taken over the farm and were holding the owner and his family gagged and bound, opened fire from an upstairs window, killing him instantly. They shot out the tyres on the Finlays' car before escaping in the farmer's car and abandoning it at the Border.

In five days in November Loyalists murdered four Catholics and a Protestant, the IRA four Protestants. In the face of this escalation of tit-for-tat killings the GOC on 15 November ordered the call-out of 1,400 soldiers from 1/9, 2/11 and 7/10UDR. As always the part-time soldiers, all volunteers, responded splendidly. "Thank God for the UDR!" Paisley said, adding that the call-out "demonstrates the need to retain the UDR, for in this hour of crisis it is only large military presence that in a short time of an emergency can be brought in to assist in this terrible situation."[7] Predictably the SDLP and Sinn Fein complained that the action would only heighten tension. By 27 November the Spearhead Battalion had been flown into the Province and on 2 December the three UDR battalions were stood down.

The Provisionals stepped up their car bomb attacks. On 4 December a 1200lb bomb in Glengall Street severely damaged the Europa Hotel, the Unionist Party Headquarters and the Grand Opera House, completely restored ten years ago after lying derelict for years as the result of an arson attack. A symbol of Belfast's resurgence, it had to close its doors once again for nine months.

On 26 November a part-time Private set out from Omagh on his regular delivery run. At the last moment Ken Newell, a Lance Corporal in the Battalion, agreed to go with him. Both had been on the 6UDR Colour parade two days earlier. On every fourth Tuesday the run took in South Armagh. One of the delivery points was a filling station on the Concession Road, the road from Dundalk to Castleblayney that runs through Northern Ireland for about a mile before re-entering the Republic. The filling station was a hundred yards from the Border. The two part-time soldiers had begun to unload when the proprietor said there was a mistake in the order and he would have to ring the depot. They sat in the lorry waiting for him to sort out the error. The Private took up the story:

"I suddenly noticed that everybody had disappeared. All the cars from the petrol pumps had gone. Two minutes later I heard a screech of brakes from behind us and looked up to see four masked men getting out of a car. Two were armed with Armalites and the other two seemed to have pistols. Two terrorists went to each side of the lorry and pulled us out. They put me down on the ground and gave me a body search and started to tie my hands behind my back. I was put in the car boot and I think that Ken Newell was put in the back seat. I could feel that the car had been turned round and was going back over the Border. I thought we were driven for about twenty minutes, much of the time along country roads, judging by the bumping I felt in the boot. We were taken to a farm building where they questioned Ken. I was kept in the boot where I could hear Ken being questioned about the UDR and the police. Until then I had thought they were just going to hijack the lorry. After about half an hour I was moved again to another farm building where they put a hood over my head. They made me stand in a corner and began to question me. They knew all about me, my nickname, where I lived, my car registration number. They took my driving licence. They still have it. They said they had been watching me for the past four months but they did not seem to know that I was still in the UDR. Every half hour or so they put me back in the car and moved some-where else, where somebody else questioned me. Once there seemed to be about a dozen of them. They questioned me about the UDR. Did I know anybody in the Regiment or the RUC? Did I know what time patrols went out and where they went? Sometimes they would punch me in the stomach or on the side of the head. I just kept denying that I was in the UDR, although they seemed to know I had joined in 1983. They asked if I would agree to drive a bomb into the barracks. I knew about the 'human bombs' they were using and that they would probably tie me in, but I said that I would do it, as I thought it would give me a chance to get away. They then said that it was my last chance to tell them the truth, or they would shoot me. They told me that they had killed Ken and that they would kill me unless I talked. They made me kneel down and put a rifle to my head and started to count down from ten to zero. I braced myself and then there was a click as they took the safety catch off and I waited for the trigger to be pulled. They then laughed and joked with each other about what they had almost done and said that they were fighting amongst themselves to see whose turn it was to shoot me."

The soldier was held captive for fourteen hours, moved from place to place and questioned again and again, whilst Seamus Mallon made a public appeal for his release.

"I knew that I was going to be killed," he continued, "but the longer it went on the more determined I became not to give in. I was only too aware that nobody in my situation had ever survived and I knew that if I told them who I was they would certainly shoot me."

Eventually in the early hours of the morning his captors took him back over the Border and dropped him off, still hooded, near Crossmaglen. He managed to remove the hood and dialled the police from a phone box. Newell was already dead. The previous morning his body had been found lying on the verge of a lonely road north of Crossmaglen.

Newell was the 197th and last serving UDR soldier to be murdered, although another six have died by terrorist act while serving in the Royal Irish Regiment, and in the last six months of the UDR there were three more attempted murders.

On 22 January 1992 the former commander of the Castlederg Company, by now retired from the UDR, was driving to school through country that ran close to the border.

Five days earlier the IRA had blown up a bus-load of construction workers at Teebane Cross on the Omagh–Cookstown road. They had been working at Lisanelly Barracks in Omagh. Eight died. Among the injured were two part-time soldiers in 1/9UDR. One lost an eye. After Teebane the former Company Commander realized that he had become complacent in his retirement and that he must start again to vary his daily route to Castlederg.

"It's not easy in schools to vary your timing and because I was the Principal I liked to be in assembly in the morning to deliver administrative instructions to the pupils and staff and also to participate in assembly. That particular week, on the Tuesday morning I had gone on quite circuitous routes. On the Wednesday morning I intended to go through Barons Courts which is even more circuitous, but I was thinking about school and not thinking about my security, and I passed the Barons Court turn-off before I realized my mistake. I was driving along, not thinking about an ambush, when suddenly I saw some uniformed men, what I thought to be a black-faced patrol of the Army, although they looked a bit odd. I was out of it a year and I thought maybe this was their way of doing things now. They didn't seem to have any berets on but they did have combat jackets. There was at least one ran across the road in front of me and then I suddenly heard a bang. As I drew level with a gateway into a bungalow there were three or four men blazing at me – straight at my car at a range of about five metres. All I could see was a haze of cordite, and they were firing very rapidly at me. I wasn't aware for about five seconds that I had been hit, then the pain hit me in the hand and shoulder. When the blood started to flow I lost the power in my arm and I realized I was shot and badly wounded. I kept on going with my one good arm. I had to ram the car down into a lower gear with my right arm through the steering wheel which was damaged as well. Then I just thought I would make for a house that I knew. I formed a picture of one in my mind, a parent whom I know very well. She stood at the sitting room window each morning getting the children ready for school and waiting for the bus. I used to see her head in the window quite regularly. I went there and honked the horn as I went through the gate. I staggered out of the car saying I'd been shot and shouted to her to ring for a doctor, the police, the school and my home."

He made a fair recovery but had to retire from the headmastership. The Garda arrested two Castlefinn men, but there was no evidence against them and they were released. One of them is now back living openly in Castlederg.

While the weary struggle continued in the North little changed and the light at the end of the tunnel seemed as far away as ever. Then a light came flooding in to Western Europe from the East. In the last months of 1989 the Communist régime fell apart. In November exultant crowds broke their way through the Berlin Wall and, bowing to the inevitable, the East German politburo announced that the people were free to leave the country wherever they wished, through the Iron Curtain or across the Wall. Within a fortnight the politburo in Czechoslovakia had resigned and in the last days of the year Ceaucescu, the Romanian dictator, and his wife were executed by firing squad. On 3 December the Russian President Gorbachev and the American, George Bush, meeting in Malta, agreed to sign an arms control pact, halving strategic nuclear weapons and reducing conventional forces in Europe. After forty-four years the

Cold War was over. The Western nations began drawing up plans to scale down their armed forces, the 'peace dividend' of greatly reduced defence expenditure.

By July 1990 King, the Defence Secretary, had told the Commons that the British review was under way under the title 'Options for Change'. Details had still to be worked out, but the strength of the Army would be run down to 116,000, a reduction of over 40,000.

General John Wilsey, who was GOC at the time, saw this as a perfect opportunity to resolve some of the most intractable problems of the UDR. He had previously been Chief of Staff at HQ Northern Ireland and he had a good feel for what these problems were. He maintained that the UDR had too many battalions and too many bases to defend and that it could be scaled down, relieving more soldiers for operational duties without any loss of operational effectiveness. Furthermore, and importantly, he saw as a *quid pro quo* the opportunity to give the UDR arguably what it wanted most: recognition, acceptance and a permanent place within the British Army – something it had been denied until now.[8]

In this he was helped by Colonel David Strudley who was already in post when Wilsey arrived and came at the problem from another direction. Strudley had returned to Northern Ireland in the latter part of 1989 as Assistant Chief of Staff in HQNI. He was determined to ensure that the problems he had experienced as CO 2UDR in trying to administer without sufficient staff an attached UDR company in the Keady-Middletown TAOR as well as Regular companies under operational control should be resolved once and for all. In the beginning it was a relatively modest aim, but in time his ideas developed into a wholesale review of the structure of the Regiment. The result which emerged from HQNI was a revolutionary proposal: the merger of the UDR and the Royal Irish Rangers into one regiment of the Regular Army; 'Project Infancy' as it was called. Initial reaction in the MOD tended to be sceptical; the inclusion of part-time soldiers in the Regular Army had never been attempted before. The NIO, who had been briefed on the plan but had no input into it, foresaw difficulties in selling the idea. However, when all the parties involved realized the advantages, the development of the proposal into a firm plan moved very quickly.

Secrecy was absolute. The initial proposal was circulated in the Ministry on a very restricted basis. Only a few nominated senior officers in the Rangers and the UDR were privy to it. Both sides welcomed the idea. From the Rangers' point of view the Regiment was certain to lose its second battalion under 'Options for Change'. It had never felt at home under the King's Division of infantry, the odd one out in a division composed of North Country battalions. A decision had been taken that adult recruit training at the Depot in Ballymena would be moved out of the Province in 1992. The concentration of junior soldier training at the Junior Infantry Battalion in England had already proved to be a mistake with a worrying number, far from home, dropping out without completing their training. If adult training was also moved to England, it was feared the move would have the same effect. Furthermore if the Depot was to leave Ballymena the Rangers would no longer have a foothold in Northern Ireland, apart from the TA, whose future was under threat. In short there was a very real danger that the Regiment, the last Irish infantry regiment of the line, would cease to exist.

Likewise for the UDR the principal attraction of the proposal was that it would ensure the future of the Regiment, albeit in a different, though not a markedly different, form. From its beginning it had had a separate status unique in the British Army, founded by an Act of Parliament, neither TA nor Regular Army – "like a fish with feathers," as one Commander described it. Under 'Project Infancy' the Regiment would become an integral part of the Regular Army, with the officers and soldiers serving on as nearly as possible the same terms of service as the Regulars, with the same career structure and opportunities for promotion and the same privileges.

The new Regiment would consist of one Regular or General Service battalion, to be formed by merging the two Ranger battalions, and seven Home Service battalions, formed from the existing nine UDR battalions. The Home Service battalions, still made up of full-time and part-time soldiers, would come under the command of the operational brigades, HQUDR would be replaced by a Regimental Headquarters, and the Brigadier by a full Colonel, responsible for regimental policy, posting of officers, recruiting, welfare and training. Training of both the General and Home Service recruits would continue to be carried out at the Ranger depot in Ballymena.

By the early summer of 1991 the plan had been approved. Despite the fact that it was still shrouded in secrecy, it was inevitable that some hint of what was being proposed should leak out and in July, four days before King was due to make his statement in the Commons revealing the details of 'Options for Change', *The Times* reported that the merger of the two regiments had been discussed as one of the ways of reducing the Regular Army order of battle from fifty-five to thirty-eight infantry battalions. Reaction in Northern Ireland was predictable. By breakfast time on the morning of publication Ken Maginnis was on the telephone to the Commander to ask him if the reports were true and to voice his misgivings. Ramsay decided to take him into his confidence and persuaded him of the advantages of 'Infancy' to the UDR. Thereafter the MP and former UDR Company Commander loyally and publicly supported it, despite the doubts of some of his colleagues. Faulkner briefed Molyneaux and, in Paisley's absence, his deputy, Peter Robinson, who refused to be convinced, maintaining that the plan had nothing to do with defence cuts and everything to do with Dublin's demand to get rid of the UDR. The day before the Commons announcement the GOC briefed his Advisory Council. It was the first the members had heard of 'Infancy', but they forthwith expressed their unanimous support. On 23 July, twenty-four days after the Queen had presented the Colours, King made his detailed Commons statement on the restructuring of the Army, including the decision "to bring the Ulster Defence Regiment more fully into the Army by merging it with the Royal Irish Rangers".

Meanwhile, in Lisburn Wilsey was holding a briefing for the media. He told them that the decision to merge the two regiments had been a military one. Under it the UDR would be fully integrated into the Regular Army. There were no plans to phase out the part-time element "at present", but, he added, "Who can say what will happen in three or four years time?" Some bases would be closed and Glenanne would not be rebuilt. Before the year's end 2 and 11UDR and 4 and 6UDR would be amalgamated, reducing the UDR to seven battalions. He hoped that the new Regiment would attract recruits from the Nationalist community and would be supported by the Cardinal. The Rangers had always recruited from the whole of Ireland and at present 30% of their soldiers were Catholics and 15% of the two battalions were from the Republic. (Later these somewhat confusing figures were amended by the MOD. Only eighty-three of the soldiers in the Rangers were from the Republic, and 6% of the Regiment was Catholic.) The new Regiment would come into being on 1 July 1992, a year hence, with the title The Royal Irish Regiment. "Infancy was probably the most significant and tricky challenge of my career," Wilsey said. "Even the day before the official announcement there were people trying to persuade me not to go ahead with it."

Over the next few days Ramsay and Faulkner flew round the Province visiting all the battalions to explain the plan to the soldiers and to answer their questions. The overall reaction was to welcome the decision. While there was some regret at losing the 'Ulster' title, this was offset by becoming a Royal regiment, and furthermore one that had fought at the Boyne and Aughrim in the Williamite War.[9] The full-time soldiers welcomed the improved career prospects. The part-timers were relieved to know that, despite rumours emanating from some politicians, their future was secure, at least for the time being. For all that there was a general concern in battalions that there might be a 'hidden agenda'. They had noted the GOC's remark that the part-timers were safe 'at present'. How long was 'at present'? Their fears proved groundless; the part-time element continues to be an indispensable part of the new Regiment to this day.

The only concerted discord came from soldiers in 7/10UDR, but that had more to do with reaction to a CO intent on applying more rigorous standards of fitness in his battalion than with opposition to the merger. Some of the officers and men talked to Sammy Wilson, the DUP spokesman, passing on to him wild rumours that were in most cases totally without foundation, in others a mischievous misrepresentation of the facts. Wilson passed his information on to the press, leading to such banner headlines as the *Sunday News* "Storm in the ranks. UDR on edge of revolt".[10] He claimed that a purge was taking place and that resignations were on the increase. In fact resignations over the last fifteen months of the Regiment followed the trend of the previous two years, a steady decline in the number of part-time soldiers; there was no reason to suppose that the loss of 135 part-time men and women was due to the merger.[11] In any case the reduction was small compared to the cuts imposed on the Army as a whole. On a visit to the MOD the CGS told Faulkner, "I like seeing you here. You're the only person around this place with a smile on his face."

At its annual party conference the DUP launched a campaign to 'save' the Regiment, including the posting up again of the 1989 'Hands off the UDR' posters across the province and collecting signatures for a petition to the Queen. Paisley castigated the Ulster Unionists for supporting the merger. Both parties agreed that the designation 'Ulster' should be retained and, during the Commons debate, tried and failed to persuade the government to change its mind about the title. Many of the serving soldiers would have preferred Royal Ulster Regiment, but, the new Regiment hoped to continue to draw recruits from the whole of Ireland. In the initial discussions the title Royal Regiment of Ireland had been preferred, but constitutionally that would have been unacceptable, as the Queen herself was said to have pointed out.

Only 16,000 signed the DUP's petition, probably because many people, while agreeing with the aim, realized that it would change nothing and that the DUP was using the UDR to score political points against the Ulster Unionists in the run up to the April General Election.

The detailed discussions on the implementation of the merger began at HQUDR in August. Considering that some of the other regiments faced with a merger under 'Options for Change' were barely on speaking terms, they went remarkably smoothly. The UDR was happy to adopt traditions that the Rangers had inherited over the centuries. The Ranger uniform was smart and distinctive and needed minimum alteration. The march past 'Killaloe' and the poignant slow march 'Eileen Allanagh' were generally agreed to be the best in the Army. For their part the Rangers, who had great difficulty in recruiting pipers, were delighted to inherit the pipes and drums of the UDR battalions, numbering around a hundred players. Both regiments were proud of their distinctive headdress. A happy compromise was agreed – the Ranger caubeen, the traditional headdress of the Irish soldier, for ceremonial and barrack dress, the UDR green beret on operations and training. The UDR crown and harp badge was retained, in gold on the berets and in silver on the caubeens. On flags, notice boards and the officers' crossbelts, the crest was wreathed in shamrocks.

The preliminary amalgamation of the four battalions announced by the GOC at his press conference took place before the year's end – 2 and 11UDR on 30 September and 4 and 6UDR on 25 November. Nobody doubted that the former made good sense. Both battalions were based in County Armagh. The numbers in 2UDR had fallen so low that the Battalion was no longer viable and 11UDR had been short of manpower since losing its Lisburn companies to 1/9UDR. The new battalion, 2/11 (Co Armagh), was based at Mahon Road, with companies there and at Drumadd Barracks outside Armagh. Despite the fact that their recruiting areas overlapped and the two towns are only eight miles apart, it was not an entirely happy amalgamation, the Armagh soldiers being country folk and the Craigavon townspeople, and not long after the formation of the Royal Irish a reorganization of the new battalions merged the Armagh and East Tyrone battalions, both country-based.

The Regiment regretted the merger of 4 and 6UDR. Because of the comparative remoteness of their county, Fermanagh people have always been a proud but separate community. Now the Battalion was to lose its TAOR to the Fermanagh Roulement Battalion, with most of its companies under the Regulars' operational control and the whole Battalion to come under command of 6UDR in Omagh. Unlike 2 and 11 it was an amalgamation across county boundaries. However the GOC was insistent. From next April control of budgets was to be decentralized to Commands and, though there was no intention to reduce the money available to combat terrorism, HQNI, like all headquarters, was required to avoid any unnecessary expenditure. The existence of a UDR and a Regular battalion headquarters in Grosvenor Barracks and St Angelo was an unnecessary expense, and at a time of large reductions in the Army as a whole such duplication of manpower could not be acceptable.

As 6UDR had not yet received their Colours and would have lost their separate identity by the time of the next presentation in April, the Queen agreed that the Lord Lieutenant, the Duke of Abercorn, a former officer in the battalion, should hand over the Colours on the day before the amalgamation. The parade took place at St Lucia Barracks on a dismal November day. It was a good, smart parade, the men and women steady despite appalling weather conditions, darkened skies and the rain blown hard on the wind across the Square. Before the consecration the Chaplain General, accompanied by Monsignor Mallon, the Senior Roman Catholic Chaplain to the Forces, dedicated a memorial stone to the dead of the Battalion. A piper played a lament and in the silence the chapel bells were ringing for Mass on the hill across the Strule.

There is a fashion in Northern Ireland to produce buttonhole badges to mark historic events. One such badge shows an axe slicing into the UDR. In fact the UDR was not axed, it was saved by the 'Infancy' plan, albeit under different command arrangements and a different, but Royal, title. Something had had to be done. The Regiment could not go on being a political football. Constant criticism and denigration of its motives were having an adverse effect on morale. The criticism was overstated, fuelled by occasional but widely publicized lapses of discipline by individuals and, occasionally, patrols. It was apparent that nothing the Regiment could do would ever persuade the Nationalist community and the Irish Government to accept the UDR. The pressure to disband it would go on. But once it became an integral of the Regular Army there could no longer be any question of disbanding it or of replacing it by raising the ceiling of the RUC. As time passed and peace broke out, there might well be a case for reducing the number of battalions, but the continued existence of the Regiment had been assured. The UDR has never received the credit it deserved for the commonsense way in which it accepted the merger, determined to soldier on and make it work.

Once the decision to merge had been made public, word had gone out that the last months of the Regiment should be as muted as possible. The UDR had always been a political factor, part of the problem of Northern Ireland, as the RUC was part of the problem. Now the Regiment must be 'depoliticized', and so far as possible kept out of the public eye, to ensure that nothing was said or done that might impede the success of the merger.

Happily, for all that, the Regiment went out on a high note.

7/10UDR won the Sword of Peace, awarded by Wilkinson Sword Ltd to the unit in each of the three Services considered to have contributed most to the cause of peace by establishing good and friendly relations with any community at home or overseas. The citation recorded that the Battalion during 1990 had helped fifty-nine organizations with assistance, money, or equipment and that many of the projects had been undertaken by part-time soldiers. "The soldiers, men and women, are at risk from terrorist attack at all times, on and off duty. To carry out community work which identified them as members of the security forces demanded a level of courage and dedication above and beyond the call of duty."

The sword was handed over to the Battalion by the Secretary of State in a ceremony held at Stormont. Inevitably there was controversy. The *Irish News* headline read "More an insult than a joke". It was sad because the soldiers had worked hard, mostly in their limited spare time, not just in 1990 but over many years to raise money for such organizations as Muscular Dystrophy and Children's Cancer Research, funds which helped children from whatever community. There were numerous instances of practical assistance – lending and erecting marquees for fetes, helping to run activities for the old, the disabled and the handicapped, not at a distance but working with people from both communities. All battalions had been involved. Sadly it did not fit in with the Nationalist image of the UDR to attribute to the soldiers such qualities as kindness and generosity to others in adversity.

Borough Councils queued up to award their Freedoms to the Regiment – North Down, Larne, when 1/9 UDR's Colours were carried in public for the first time, and Ards – but as the battalions had to remain operational, the ceremonies took a great deal of planning and rehearsal, and there simply was not time to fit in a ceremony to receive the Freedom of Ballymena. Belfast City Council installed a memorial window in stained glass in the main corridor of the City Hall, unveiled by the Lord Mayor, followed by dinner in the Banqueting Hall for representative officers, soldiers and wives.[12] In November the officers held their last Regimental dinner in the Royal Artillery mess at Woolwich, the only occasion on which all eleven Commanders were brought together. The guests were Sir Dennis and Lady Thatcher. The former Prime Minister was in forthright mood. As the dinner progressed she was seen to be making notes on the back of an envelope and after the toasts had been drunk she spoke in words of unstinted praise for the UDR:

"Out of your 22 years I have served as Prime Minister for eleven and a half and so I have seen on many, many occasions the marvellous work the Regiment does, and have had the pleasure and privilege of paying tribute to your integrity, your honour, your loyalty, your belief in all that is best and your unfailing bravery against terrorism. The figures speak for themselves. You have lost 197 people in those 22 years, most of them off duty, but you have never faltered in all that time. Duty to all that is best has always come first. The main thing is that we continue to uphold all that is best in our country's values. The United Kingdom stands for a great deal in the world, and always will, for the best values belong not only to history, they are forever contemporary. I know no better example of that than the Ulster Defence Regiment for although there are many other marvellous regiments in the United Kingdom army, this Regiment is unique, a unique service that has set a new tradition which will never be surpassed in the annals of bravery. So Mr Chairman, may I say thank you once again for upholding everything that we believe in. We are citizens of a remarkable country. May we hand on to coming generations traditions, values as great as the inheritance we have received. There is no one who has done more for that than The Ulster Defence Regiment. I thank you from the bottom of my heart and wish you well in all your endeavours in the future."

In April the colours of the three remaining battalions, 2/11, 7/10 and 8UDR were presented by Prince Andrew, Duke of York. His appointment as Colonel-in-Chief of the Royal Irish Regiment had been announced two months earlier. He was a popular choice. As a serviceman who had flown a helicopter on operations during the Falklands battles, he had an affinity with the UDR soldiers and a connection with Northern Ireland through one of his titles, Baron Killyleagh.

In the Province the level of violence was running high and, on grounds of security, it was decided that the parade must take place outside Northern Ireland. From several alternatives Edinburgh was chosen. By now Peter Graham, the former Commander UDR, was GOC Scotland and the old Cavalry Barracks at Redford was available. It was a complicated operation, planning a parade on the other side of the Irish Sea and moving across the guards and some 700 spectators. The ceremony was held on a soft spring morning with snow on the Pentlands Hills. Again the drill was immaculate. Afterwards the Duke mingled with the soldiers and families, establishing a rapport that bode well for his future role as Colonel-in-Chief.

1992 began with two major car bomb attacks in the centre of Belfast. In six months the city had suffered six such attacks. Brian Mawhinney, the Minister of State responsible for security, was reported to have told the Chief Constable and the GOC that, if another attack took place, heads would roll. On 10 January 1/9 and 7/10UDR were placed on call-out for a week, manning static roads blocks on the roads in to the city. It was the last time a UDR battalion was called out. For 7/10UDR, responsible for the security of the city centre, that winter was an intensely busy time. Not only were they dealing with major bomb incidents but also with frequent co-ordinated multiple hoaxes, vehicles abandoned at strategic points, intended to block the main arteries and cause chaotic traffic jams. Sitting in traffic jams had become a way of life in Belfast. Each hoax had to be dealt with on the basis that a vehicle contained a genuine device. Usually one of them did.

By now the full-time soldiers were regularly working in excess of 100 hours a week and an increasing number were transferring from permanent cadre to part-time. At least as a part-time soldier one had a chance of spending some time with one's children. In the case of the single soldiers, who would want a boyfriend who was for ever breaking a date? Married soldiers would ask their welfare officer to ring their wives to assure them that they really were on extra duty again, not keeping some illicit assignation.

Corporal Eric Glass had come under attack twice since joining 4UDR as a part-time soldier. His house in Newtownbutler had been burnt out and gunmen had ambushed his van as he was driving a party of his fellow Council workers out along the Garrison road. Despite the front seat passenger falling dead across him, he had managed to retain control, driving out of the ambush and thereby saving the lives of the others, an act for which he had been awarded the Queen's Gallantry Medal.

Glass was employed by Fermanagh District Council as its dog warden. On 6 February 1992 he received a phone call at his office.

> "This man came on and said to me, 'Did you hear about my dog?' I said, 'No, I didn't.' He says, 'A black labrador. My niece was down at the weekend, and it bit her in the face. She's not too bad now, but what should I do?' I told him if it was my dog I would get rid of it. 'I was afraid of that, but she will be staying pretty often, and I am afraid it would have taken a spite against her. Would you put it down for me?' I said I would, and that I would be out with him in about an hour."

Glass called at his home to collect some sandwiches and his personal protection pistol and set off for the address the caller had given him, a house up a lane by Leggs Post Office on the road to Belleek and close to the Border. Nearing the Post Office he pulled into the side to answer a radio call from the office, cocked his PPW, placed it under his anorak on the passenger seat and turned into the lane.

"About half-way up there was an old shed on the left-hand side, and there was a barrow sitting out a wee bit into the lane, so I thought he must be working there. I pulled up by the barrow. Nobody came out; nobody moved. So I reversed back, got out to move the barrow, drove up to the house and turned down into the street. Just as I stopped two men came running at me from either side of the van. The boy at the passenger side shouted, 'IRA. Get out of that f . . . ing van!' He was completely masked, just slits for the two eyes and the mouth. He had a pistol. I picked up my gun and cocked it, and one round popped out. I fired three shots through the door. He seemed to fall. I wasn't sure, but he seemed to disappear. I swung round in the seat, and there was a fella opening the driver's door. He had his rifle slung across his chest. I pushed the door open at him, and as I pushed, he ran. I jumped out the van and lay down at the front, just beside the wheel. One man was between the hedge and the wall, and another at the corner of the house. They were firing at me lying on the ground. Someone fired a shot and it burst the wheel of the van. I was firing back, till I realized the way I was doing I was actually wasting ammunition."

Glass realized that if he was not to run out of rounds he must fire carefully aimed shots. He waited until the head of the gunman appeared round the corner of the house, took deliberate aim and pressed the trigger. Nothing happened. The magazine was empty. If he had not forgotten in the first moments of the ambush that he had already cocked his weapon and cocked it again, wasting a round, he would in all probability have shot the gunman at the corner of the house.

"Empty magazine! So I jumped up at the open door of the van, ran round the door, got the spare magazine, back down on the ground again. At that one of them must have realized what was wrong, a man appeared at the corner of the house and came running down. I popped on the magazine. The boy at the corner fired again, then gave a shout and started to run up the side of the house and got round the corner. Somebody else roared, 'Two, three and four, run for it!'"

His attackers fled, but one of their last shots had ricochetted off the ground and struck Glass in the leg.

"I called them at work on the radio and said, 'This is Eric. I am badly injured in the leg', but the problem was they thought I said I was at Legg's Post Office. I thought I could get up beside the van, but the bone was sticking out of my leg. I was completely off balance, I could not get up. At that the old man who lived there appeared out of the house. He said to me was I badly injured? I said, 'No, it's not too bad'. He said, 'There's blood coming out of your boot. You can use the phone in the house if you can get in'. So I said, 'That's ok.

Can you get me a stick or something?' So he came back with a wee short stick. I got up beside the van by holding its side and the stick, but I could not get across to the house. I looked over at the house and saw he had a sweeping brush and told him to bring me that, and I used it like a crutch under my arm to get across to the house. I started to think my number was up. I couldn't remember the day, I couldn't remember anything, but then the RUC Beleek phone number came into my head. I talked to the sergeant, and with his local knowledge he knew where I was. He said he would be with me as soon as possible. 'Put down the phone. There's only the two lines into Belleek, the army's using one and I need to use this one.' I was feeling really down in the dumps then. I was feeling at my lowest point. I looked out the window and could see a man coming back up the field. He came up to this wee wall in front of the van and sat there for a minute or two. The next thing he hopped over the wall and round behind the van. I was panicking then. I thought he was going to come into the house and finish me off. I remember trying the trigger of my pistol, and I didn't even have the strength to pull it. He jumped back over the wall and away back down the field as hard as he could go."

A helicopter sent to fetch Glass flew in low over the house and landed beside the lane. The downdraught from the rotors caused the van to run forward and for the first time he saw the body lying on the ground. It was 22-year-old Joe McManus, son of a Sligo family prominent in the Republican movement. Gardai arrested the other three as they escaped over the Border. Glass was flown down to Dublin to give evidence at their trial. They were convicted and imprisoned, but now are out again. Glass recovered well, but is no longer able to work, and was unwilling to return to the scene. At first he had felt deeply sorry for the death of McManus.

"I had a son the same age. A son of yours is your child, no matter what age. I was worried in my head, thinking how I would have felt if my son had joined some illegal organization and been shot by the army. The more I turned it over in my head, the more I felt I had murdered someone's son. But then I read a notice in an Irish paper that said his mother and father were proud of him, and that he had died for Ireland."

"It's hard to think of a less glorious act," Toolis wrote in his book *Rebel Hearts*. "Four young men, two of them armed with automatic weapons, the others with handguns, lying in wait for a 49-year-old dog warden who had been tricked into visiting a remote farm one and a half miles from the Border; waiting with the intention of shooting him in the head, killing him in the cause of Irish freedom. But Joe McManus was accorded a hero's funeral imbued with the symbolism of martyrdom. Hundreds visited the family home across the border in the town of Sligo where he lay 'in state'; thousands turned out for his funeral, orations and eulogies were declaimed at the graveside; a few months later a memorial committee raised five thousand pounds for a gigantic headstone."

Gerry Adams was among the mourners. Toolis records in his book how he interviewed first Eric Glass and then the McManus family.

"In the memorial leaflet Sean was recorded at his son's graveside as saying he had no personal animosity towards the man who killed his son . . . Throughout our interview he constantly talked about 'the British soldier', not the man, the Northern Irish-born dog warden, Eric Glass.

"It was hard to reconcile this abstraction, the British soldier, with the man I had left hours earlier. What did they think of the man Joe had tried to kill? 'A faceless form to me, that's what he is,' said Sean. 'Joe would not have been shooting him as a person. He would have seen him as a member of an occupying force, which he is.'"

Thus it was that the IRA depersonalized their intended victims. They were not ordinary flesh and blood, people in essentials much like themselves, people who would suffer terrible pain, die or be crippled for life, people with families, young children, people whose death would send waves of anger and sorrow through a whole community. They were no more than the wooden targets set up on a range for target practice. And yet, as Toolis wrote, the ambushing of Glass was "not a war between soldiers, but a very personalized assassination".

When he had recovered sufficiently from his wounds Glass and his wife were summoned to Buckingham Palace where he received his Distinguished Conduct Medal at a private investiture with the Queen. She sat talking with them for quarter of an hour and then an equerry showed them round the Duke of York's apartments. Already awarded the QGM for the earlier ambush, he was the most decorated soldier in the Regiment.

What sort of man was he? In the aftermath of the shooting a three-man army team interviewed him to establish what lessons could be learnt from the ambush. "I am confused," one of them, a member of the SAS, said afterwards. "I don't know what I expected, some sort of Rambo type, I suppose, and what do I find, a slight, quiet, modest, gentle countryman. You must train them very well."

As he lay at the wheel of his van exchanging fire with his attackers the thought had flashed through Glass's mind, "This is just like anti-ambush drill at Magilligan". He had rehearsed the drills again on a training day a fortnight earlier.[13]

On the last day of May a Service of Remembrance and Thanksgiving was held in St Anne's Cathedral, attended by 1,200 people, including representatives drawn from all battalions, widows and members of the Regimental Association. The guests included the Lord Lieutenant, representing the Queen, the Secretary of State, Michael Mates the Minister of

State, the GOC and the Chief Constable. The service was taken by the Dean, the Very Reverend Jack Shearer, assisted by the Moderator of the Presbyterian and the President of the Methodist Church, and a Roman Catholic priest nominated by the Diocesan Office led the congregation in the Regimental Collect. The Regimental Secretary read the first lesson, Donne's Sonnet 'Death be not proud', and Prince Andrew read the second, 1 Corinthians Chapter 13, in the Authorised Version, read from his own Bible. Archbishop Eames gave the address.

> "We have come by many different paths to the Cathedral this afternoon. We have brought with us many different thoughts and emotions. From the lakes of Fermanagh, the hills of Down, the fields of Armagh, the farmland of Antrim, from city streets or the intimacy of town or village communities: from homes which have known years of service in uniform as well as homes where memories of a loved one will never die: from places of danger where the price of service has been great. The paths we have trod this afternoon have reflected most vividly the myriad of lives and experiences which during the past 22 years have made up the Ulster Defence Regiment. 22 years which will go down in history as a living reminder of what the poet called 'that kaleidoscope of contradictions' which make up our island home. But we have come to this Cathedral with one common purpose: to remember before Almighty God those who in the service of the whole community have made the supreme sacrifice, to recall the cost of service of a multitude of men and women of so many backgrounds and to place all our thoughts of change in the future in the hands of God."

In November when the Royal Irish Ranger chapel in the Cathedral was retitled the Chapel of the Royal Irish Regiment, the UDR Roll of Honour Book was laid up and a simple memorial dedicated to the memory of the men and women who had served in the fifteen UDR battalions.[14]

On the evening of the Thanksgiving Service the GOC held a farewell dinner for the members of the Advisory Council. The Council had met 157 times and nineteen people, influential members of the civilian community, Protestant and Catholic, had served on it at some time during its existence. Two had served throughout – Sir Robin Kinahan and Sir Ian Fraser, whose 90th birthday his fellow Council members had celebrated in the previous year. Sir John Wilsey told the members that the minutes of meetings

> "tell the story of the extraordinary development of the Regiment. At that first meeting the GOC of the time, Sir Ian Freeland, described the new Regiment as 'the perfect example of a home defence, part-time citizen force whose job will be to help the Regular Army to secure the Province against any attack'. He spoke of the role of the Council in helping to 'establish the Regiment as an effective,

non-sectarian force and to get it accepted by all parts of the community'. This theme re-emerges time and again in the Minutes, and attempts to enlist Roman Catholic recruits into the Regiment and to secure the support of the minority community have been top priorities. The record shows, and one day I hope it will be published to prove the point, that you and your predecessors have done so much to try and achieve these goals. At the very least, you have succeeded in keeping open the lines of communication with the Catholic leadership – and I know how difficult that has been at times – even to the extent of failing to secure this very day the support of the Cardinal or any other Catholic bishop at this afternoon's service.

"It will be up to future historians to assess definitively the overall contribution the Ulster Defence Regiment has made to securing government objectives in Northern Ireland over the past two decades. Militarily, however, I can say with certainty that, without the work of the Regiment, the Regular Army alone could never have contained the violence of these years. I am greatly impressed, and so have been many other Regular officers and soldiers who have served with and alongside the UDR, by the way in which the Regiment has developed into the highly professional force it is today whilst retaining its base as a 'Citizens' Army'.

"You have identified yourselves fully and most loyally with the Regiment and with the cause of the security forces in Northern Ireland. I know full well that at many times it cannot have been easy; always time-consuming for busy people, disruptive of family life and with a high degree of attendant risk. Nevertheless, you have spoken up on the Regiment's behalf, representing them and their side of the story in influential quarters and, if I may say so, done it splendidly."

The main parade to mark the formation of the new Regiment was organized by 1st Battalion The Royal Irish Rangers at their barracks at Warminster. Following the example of the Royal Inniskilling Fusiliers who, exactly 24 years earlier, had held a midnight parade to mark their reincarnation as a battalion of The Royal Irish Rangers, Tony Potter, the Rangers CO, decided that this parade too should take place at midnight. It incorporated two guards of Rangers and two of UDR, a total of some 600 men and women. The UDR were drawn from all battalions, but mainly 1/9UDR, who provided the Colour Party. Back in Ballykinlar on 1 July the GOC took the salute at the passing out of the first recruits for the new Regiment, thirteen for the General Service battalions, twenty for the Home Service. All had successfully completed a 21-week course.

In Thiepval Barracks the staff has gathered for the hand-over of the Headquarters building. The building is already empty, the records, the Roll of Honour boards, the pictures and Freedom silver moved up to the new Regimental Headquarters in Ballymena. The Headquarters Corporal, for years the faithful factotum and Man Friday to the staff, lowers the

Regimental flag, the flag that has flown at half-mast for the dead 197 times. He folds it and hands it over to Brigadier Ramsay. The staff turn and walk away, some to go to Ballymena, some like Ramsay to other climes and other experiences, one to civilian life.

Midnight in Warminster. Across the empty parade ground, slicked with rain, a bugler sounds the Last Post, a piper plays the lament 'Oft in the Stilly Night'. In the silence, broken by a train clattering by, the two regimental flags are lowered for the last time. A Greenfinch puts on her new caubeen with the green hackle, looks down at her UDR beret screwed up in her hands and weeps. The new flag is raised over the ramparts of the mock fort, the green and red of the UDR, blue for the old Order of St Patrick, and the UDR harp, now wreathed in shamrock, at its centre. Trumpeters sound a new fanfare, 'The Royal Irish Regiment'.

Fireworks explode in expanding bursts of galaxies, a set piece in fire of the Regimental badge. The gates open and the four guards march out, all now wearing the same dress, khaki jackets, green trousers, caubeens.[15] The Duke, accompanied by Major General Roger Wheeler and Colonel Sir Dennis Faulkner, the only person on parade still wearing a UDR beret, walks down the ranks of the four guards. The Chaplain General to the Forces and the Principal Roman Catholic Chaplain conduct a drumhead service, ending with the new Regimental Collect. Before the guards march past to the strains of 'The Grand Old Duke of York' and the new regimental march, 'Killaloe', Prince Andrew addresses the parade.

> "I know that many of you will be sad at the passing of your old Regiments, and rightly so, for both the Rangers and the UDR have established an enviable reputation throughout the Army for the highest professional standards, courage and determination in the face of the enemy; but above all, loyalty to your comrades and to The Queen. You are known too for that special Irish character, the spark of humour that will endure and foster friendship even under the most difficult of conditions. All these qualities have sustained the UDR in their campaign against the terrorist in which they have played a crucial role and for which they have had to pay a high price, throughout their short but distinguished history. They are also the qualities that have sustained the Royal Irish Rangers and their predecessors over the last 300 years.
>
> "But on this vesting night, I urge you to look ahead and go forward from here to build on the honour and distinction of your forebears."

Exactly 76 years previously the minutes were ticking away to Zero Hour on the Somme.

CHAPTER TWENTY

Conclusions

When the Ulster Defence Regiment was formed in 1970 two centuries had passed since the British in Ireland had raised a civilian force to oppose insurrection in their own land. It was a bold innovation. There was no recent precedent to draw on. Inevitably mistakes were made. Was the Regiment a success? What were the mistakes?

OPERATIONAL EFFECTIVENESS

The first criterion in judging any military force must be its operational effectiveness. For the first five years the UDR battalions were finding their feet, dedicated, working long hours but inadequately trained. Had it not been for the experience of those former Servicemen and members of the USC who joined the new Regiment, the experiment could have been stillborn. It was not until the end of the decade when, as a result of 'The Way Ahead' policy, the establishment of full-time soldiers was greatly increased, giving the battalions a 24-hour capability, that the Regiment was able to develop its full potential.

From then on the UDR was an unqualified success, with the part-time and full-time soldiers together providing the first line of military support to the police in the greater part of the Province. At a time when the army as a whole was seriously over-committed, successive GOCs emphasized that without the UDR the British Army would have been unable to contain the violence of the terrorists. The part-time soldiers always remained an essential element in the operational capability of the Regiment. Operationally battalions were highly professional. In terms of experience, their intimate knowledge of their country, of those who were involved in terrorism, of where previous attacks had taken place and previous finds had been made, they were better versed than the Regular units sent to Northern Ireland on three, four or six month tours.

TRAINING

Throughout the lifetime of the Regiment there were very few serious incidents that could be attributed to a lack of training, though in the early years the soldiers were almost alarmingly under-trained. If a man could handle a weapon in safety that was about the sum of it. To them training was a distraction from the main business of defending their people. The fact that in the early years time spent training earned no pay and the annual bounty was far below that awarded to the Territorial Army were a disincentive to attending the training sessions. Once the UDR Training Camp was opened at Ballykinlar and the recruits' courses for the permanent cadre were centralized and increased in length, the standard of permanent cadre training improved, and, within the limitations of what was required for service in Northern Ireland, was well up to Regular Army standards, despite the fact that pressure of operations frequently prevented battalions from reaching the target for training days set by Commander Land Forces. Part-time soldiers underwent only a week's recruits' course, followed by a week's continuation training. They had to complete an annual training cycle to retain their pay grade and earn their, greatly improved, bounty. Ultimately they were adequately trained within the limitations of their role, but with the demands of operations there was less time and opportunity for them to achieve the same high standards as the permanent cadre.

ADMINISTRATION

Battalions were always to suffer from a shortage of administrative staff. Initially the establishment of officers and soldiers for administrative duties was remarkably small. The fact that battalions somehow managed to get by led to a reluctance to authorize increases. As time went on, battalions could no longer rely on collocated Regular units to administer them. They took Regular sub-units under command and had to keep them supplied. The lack of administrative personnel became a serious weakness and the operational capability of battalions was reduced because of the need to use trained infantrymen for administrative duties. It was a weakness that was never resolved. Right up to the end the establishment of soldiers for administrative tasks was far below that of a Regular infantry battalion.

Despite this shortage the UDR was efficiently administered. The organization of battalion and regimental occasions, social functions, parades, beating retreats, services of remembrance, involving attention to detail and meticulous planning, were well up to Regular Army standards. The organization of the Colours presentation at Lisburn in two months and under conditions of strictest secrecy was a remarkable achievement that earned the praise of The Queen.

THE GREENFINCHES

The introduction of women soldiers into the ranks of the UDR, the way in which they were fully integrated into companies, going on patrol and taking the same risks as men, providing the staffs for operations rooms and supplementing the administrative staffs, was an unqualified success. Although over the years the number of male part-time soldiers gradually dwindled, the number of women remained more or less constant.

Many were involved in shooting and bombing incidents. Four were killed by terrorist action, two of them while on patrol. Others were wounded. Their successful integration into the Regiment led in 1992 to the Women's Royal Army Corps being integrated into the corps and regiments of the Regular Army.

CATHOLIC MEMBERSHIP

From the outset Westminster politicians and not a few members of the Regiment saw the UDR as an organization wich could perform the unique role of uniting the two communities side by side in the defence of their country. It was a laudable aim and, for the first eighteen months, it seemed that it might be achieved. In some battalions, notably Belfast and Down, the number of Catholic soldiers made up not far short of a third of their strength. Every battalion, even those that recruited from areas with a Republican tradition, attracted an encouraging number of Catholics.

Sadly the early optimism was premature. Within three or four years the number of Catholics had dwindled to about 3% of the whole and never rose above that figure again. The reasons were outside the control of the UDR. Mainly the Regiment lost its Catholic members for the same reasons that the security forces as a whole lost the confidence of the Catholic community – the Falls Road curfew in 1971, followed a year later by the one-sided application of internment, and then the tragedy of Bloody Sunday. In the aftermath of these events the Church and Nationalist leaders no longer encouraged their people to enlist. Soldiers still serving came under insidious intimidation from within their own community. The IRA singled out Catholic soldiers to be murdered. In nine months of 1972 a third of the dead were Catholics. Without the support of their community leaders, shunned by their own people and under threat for their lives, the great majority resigned or drifted away. Who could blame them?

Their loss was regretted within the Regiment. Apart from other considerations, it was inevitable that the Regiment would be branded with the same sectarian image as the USC.

Research has not brought to light a single case of a Catholic soldier being forced to leave as a result of intimidation by Protestant members of the company. Indeed the companies admired their courage and did all they could to protect them and to persuade them to serve on. There was no policy of discrimination against them. The only factor that could have been misinterpreted as discrimination was that in the beginning the most experienced men had to be selected for commissions and senior NCO posts, and the majority of these came from the ranks of the USC or ex-servicemen. Nevertheless a significant number of officers and NCOs were Catholic.

As a result of the loss of Catholics, the UDR became, much against its will, uneven in composition. It was not sectarian in its actions. It was part of the Regular Army, the battalions commanded by Regular officers, with Regular Training Majors and Regimental Sergeant Majors. None would have permitted any policy of sectarianism. For the same reasons the charge, often repeated, that the UDR was the 'B Specials' under another name was without foundation. Apart from any other factors, it was, as those who had served in the USC were the first to admit, infinitely more efficient, better led, better equipped and better administered.

The UDR never lost sight of the need to persuade Catholics to enlist, right up to the end. Various methods were tried – contacts with the Church, from the Cardinal to the parish priest, talks to headmasters and career masters of Catholic schools, community relations projects and public relations endeavours. But the hard fact was that, so long as the Church and the politicians withheld their support, all attempts to redress the balance were doomed to failure.

DUAL UDR/UDA MEMBERSHIP

The failure in the early years to issue clear and unequivocal orders that a member of the UDR could not also belong to or be associated with the UDA or any other paramilitary organization was to prove a serious error and caused the reputation of the Regiment much harm. Such men were not wanted and by the end of 1975 171 suspected of paramilitary involvement had been discharged, less than 2% of the Regiment.

The discharges did not entirely eradicate the problem. As events were to show, there were a few individuals who were prepared to take the law into their own hands and thereby betray their comrades by giving their first loyalty to the Loyalist paramilitaries.

DISCHARGE OF UNDESIRABLES

Ryder's claim that there was "a distinct lack of vigour in weeding out bad apples" had some justification. Battalions had no use for such people. They were unreliable and sullied the reputation of the Regiment, and there was no love lost between the UDR and the paramilitaries. The problem was not a lack of vigour. Army regulations did not allow for the straightforward discharge of disloyal soldiers. Disloyalty and military service were a contradiction in terms. Although soldiers could be put up for discharge because of paramilitary involvement, the process took a long time and every soldier had the right of appeal to the GOC and even on up to the Army Board, while those who thought they had been unjustly treated appealed to their MP. It was therefore essential that applications for discharge were accompanied by absolute proof of paramilitary involvement. Sometimes there was no proof, only suspicion or association. Many of the soldiers, particularly in the Belfast and Craigavon Battalions, lived on estates dominated by the UDA. They knew paramilitaries, they met them in the pubs and clubs, sometimes they were members of their own families. There was no reason to assume that such contracts made them disloyal to the UDR. On occasions there might be suspicion but no absolute proof, and often Special Branch and the Army Security Services were, for whatever reason, reluctant to provide the proof that would sustain an application for discharge.

COLLUSION

Over the years a number of soldiers were brought before the courts on charges involving collusion with Loyalist paramilitaries. Although these charges always showed the UDR in a bad light and gave ammunition to its accusers, bearing in mind that 40,000 men and women served in the Regiment, the numbers were very small.

Some of the charges concerned the passage of information. Such information was low level. Claims that detailed intelligence files were passed on are highly unlikely to be true. The files were tightly controlled and kept in secure cupboards behind bars in intelligence cells, manned by soldiers who had been specially vetted. In the report of his thorough and impartial investigation into allegations of collusion between the security forces and the Loyalist paramilitaries, Stevens stated that, of all the 2,600 documents recovered from these organizations, all were of the lowest security grading. He went on: "It would be wrong to conclude that a significant proportion of Ulster Defence Regiment soldiers . . . are involved with paramilitaries. This is not the case . . . The security forces documents recovered during the Enquiry and the evidence secured make it clear that the passing of information to paramilitaries by the Security Force members has been restricted to a small number of individuals. It is neither widespread nor institutionalized." The Enquiry resulted in only one member of the UDR being found guilty of a charge involving collusion.

In his study into the Loyalist paramilitaries, Steve Bruce, Professor of Sociology at the University of Aberdeen, came to the same conclusion: "A very, very small number of junior and marginal members of the Security Forces have actively aided the UDA and UVF. A very small number have given slight assistance in the form of weapons and information. Despite sharing a common enemy, recruiting from the same population and living in the same areas, the security forces and the paramilitaries have not enjoyed a cosy relationship."[1]

VETTING

No system of vetting can be wholly effective. Inevitably an applicant for any job will choose as his referees people whom he has reason to believe will give him a clean reference. At times, and in particular in the rush of applicants following internment, the vetting teams were under extreme pressure and people were cleared for enlistment who should have been turned down. The failure to vet Regular soldiers on transfer to the UDR proved a grave mistake. The murder that led directly to the Stevens Enquiry was committed by two soldiers who, not long before, had transferred into the UDR from the Regular Army, two men who, if they had been put through the vetting system, would never have been cleared.

It was wrong to accept for enlistment people with police records, except where the offences were of a minor nature. Within the UDR local people remembered those who had been in trouble with the law, and when they saw them patrolling the streets in Army uniforms that harmed the reputation of the Regiment.

However, the vetting system was controlled by the Regular Army; the decision as to whether an applicant was fit or not fit to serve was out of the UDR's hands.

COMPLAINTS

Soldiers on duty at check-points, the main point of contact with the public, were frequently subject to abuse by people who hated them. To ignore such behaviour required a very high standard of self-discipline, particularly when there was a strong suspicion that the individual had been involved in the murder of a member of the soldier's battalion, even of his family. Ritchie witnessed occasions when "before the UDR soldier had opened his mouth, a stream of vitriol came from the driver, swearing and f . . . ing and blinding about the UDR. That makes it extremely difficult for even the most patient and courteous soldier to say 'Good evening, sir' and treat him correctly."

The Commanding Officer of 1/9UDR recorded that in 1987/88, a year in which his patrols had searched 51,000 vehicles, the battalion had received six complaints, one of which had been substantiated, the following year eight, five of which had been groundless. In that year in the Army as a whole there had been 230 formal complaints, of which ten per cent were substantiated, an average of one in every 146,000 contacts with the public.[2] Sometimes tempers flared. When the complaint was of a serious nature, soldiers were taken to court. In lesser cases they were disciplined by the battalion. All complaints were investigated by the Military Police. There is no doubt that the number of complaints was exaggerated for political ends. Not that politicians and others were knowingly passing on spurious complaints, but they were too ready to believe the stories of the complainants, since every complaint added ammunition to the case for the disbandment of the UDR. There must be a strong suspicion that members of the public manufactured complaints or over-exaggerated minor incidents in order to provide the ammunition for this campaign. It is significant that, according to FitzGerald, the Taoiseach, in the year after the signing of the Anglo-Irish Agreement there was "a notable reduction in complaints of harassment", and that, once the UDR had ceased to exist as a separate regiment in 1992, though the same men were performing

378

the same operational tasks, there was again a dramatic reduction in the level of complaints.

It was in the interests of Sinn Fein to damage the operational effectiveness of the security forces by undermining the public's faith, as well as wasting time on investigations. Frequently complaints were not made to the Army or the police but straight to local politicians, the Irish Government and the press. What mattered was that the complaint should receive publicity rather than it be resolved, and inevitably such complaints told only one side of the story. A rebuttal could not be issued until the complaint had been investigated. By then it was questionable whether it was worth doing so, for the rebuttal served as a reminder of the complaint.

DISCIPLINE

Seventeen soldiers were convicted of eighteen murders, fourteen of which were committed for sectarian or terrorist reasons. Another eleven were convicted of manslaughter; two of these arose from the careless handling of personal protection weapons. One was sectarian.

A study by the Irish Information Partnership[3] quotes comparative statistics for terrorist-related offences in the period 1985–89 by the civilian population, the Army, the UDR and the RUC. The figures per thousand are respectively 5.9, 1.7, 9.1 and 0.9. However, as Bruce points out,[4] the statistics are based on a false premise. The majority of people serving in the UDR were males between the ages of 18 and 35. When the figures are adjusted for civilian males between these ages, the rate per thousand increases from 5.9 to 23, in other words two and a half times greater than for the UDR.

This does not alter the fact that the statistic for the UDR is appreciably worse than for the Regular Army and the police. There is no excuse for this but there is an explanation. The Regular soldier served in the Province for a limited tour. He was here to do a job, an outsider, skilled, efficient and committed to the task, as he would have been in Cyprus or Bosnia, but not personally committed by his roots and heritage. Most of them lived a semi-monastic life behind the wire and had little contact with the civilian population other than on patrol. The UDR soldiers were ordinary members of their community, a community whose very future was under threat. By the act of enlisting they did not become divorced from their own people. They knew what they were saying and thinking, they read the same newspapers, listened to their politicians complaining that security measures were inadequate and that the British government was not to be trusted. They saw their comrades killed, and all too often no one was held responsible for their killing. It was inevitable that some, and they were few compared with the numbers who served, would be tempted to take the law into their own hands.

Over 22 years of intense terrorist attacks just nine people are recorded

379

as having been shot dead by UDR patrols or off-duty soldiers in self-defence – three members of the IRA, a Loyalist hijacker, two joyriders, an alleged thief, a deaf youth who failed to stop when challenged in the aftermath of an explosion and a young man accidentally shot during a fracas with a patrol. It was by far the lowest total for any branch of the security forces.

RECRUITING

Despite determined recruiting campaigns in the media, television and local press and talks to university graduates and secondary schools, from 1973 onwards, when the strength reached its highest point, the Regiment was never able to arrest, except once briefly, the steady decline in numbers of part-time male soldiers. It was not for the want of trying, rather it was the fault of the male population of Northern Ireland. Based on the 1981 census figures, only 6% of male Protestants between the ages of 18 and 49 were serving in the UDR at that time.

The failure of the executive and traditional officer class to take commissions led to a serious shortage of junior officers. There were reasons, mainly that they were young men in the process of establishing themselves in their professions who could not afford to take on the added demanding responsibility of being an officer in the UDR, but was that necessarily sufficient excuse when the very future of their country was at risk?

PUBLIC RELATIONS

The raising of a part-time, home-based force from the civil population was an experience that any nation faced with internal insurrection might have to emulate. There were lessons to be learnt. As a result the UDR was subject to intense worldwide media scrutiny. Feature programmes were shown on the television networks, at home and overseas, including RTE. There were frequent, almost daily, news reports, leading articles, in-depth studies in the Sunday press, snide four-liners in the local *Sunday World*, illustrated articles in military journals, scurrilous reports in Sinn Fein's *An Phoblacht*, whose manipulation of the news was not restricted by the need to tell the truth. Much of the material was critical, particularly in the Nationalist press and in the United States. No other regiment of the British Army has ever come under such sustained, unrelenting criticism.

From 1977 onwards, when the RUC took over the lead in security, the role of the Army in the Province, including the UDR, was played down until by 1980, in the words of one experienced journalist, "it had just about disappeared out of sight". Battalions felt on the one hand that they were being deprived of the credit for their successes and on the other that the rebuttal of criticisms and spurious accusations was insufficiently robust. Successive Commanders recognized this, but it was mainly Brigadier Bray who between 1987 and 1989 fought publicly for the UDR's reputation – and received little credit for his efforts outside the UDR.

MORALE

Military formations and units are judged by their esprit de corps. It is a compilation of shared tragedies and shared successes; of shared dangers and a way of life that only those who have experienced it can understand; of pride, in themselves, in their achievements and in their battalions; of loyalty, to a cause and to their comrades, and a determination never to give in. The UDR battalions possessed all this, but they also possessed something even stronger, an intense sense of belonging. It was born out of two circumstances that other regiments had never experienced. In the first place, once a man or woman enlisted, the whole family became involved. Not only because husbands and wives, sons and daughters and even in a few cases grandparents served in its ranks, but also because even the family at home was at risk; even the children had to be taught the need for security.

Secondly the Regiment was the butt of constant, frequently unjustified and exaggerated criticism. The accusations that offended most were those that denigrated the motives of the men and women who, while setting their lives at risk, working exceedingly long hours and forfeiting a normal family life, were accused of being the armed wing of the Unionists and the oppressors of the Nationalists. It is doubtful whether there has ever been another time when units came under such sustained criticism. It had the effect of uniting the battalions in a way that was unique. This sense of belonging was very strong. It had to be. Only those who were part of it can understand its strength. To those who had that privilege they were the best years of their lives. The years when the morale of the Protestant community as a whole was at a low ebb did have an effect, but it was never a major problem. Indeed in a remarkable way, though they were mainly drawn from that community, the soldiers were able to rise above their people's fears and doubts. The performance of the battalions during the two Loyalist strikes was admirable, as was their acceptance of the decision to merge the Regiment. The only time that morale was damaged to a significant but temporary degree was during the Stevens Enquiry, the unjustified arrests and the manner in which they were carried out, the BBC "Panorama" programme and the failure to put forward a more immediate and robust defence.

NON OPERATIONAL SUCCESSES

From 1980 onwards the UDR achieved a remarkable degree of success in competition shooting and sporting contests, dominating some of the Northern Ireland unit championships and going on to make its mark in Army and Inter-Service Championships. Battalion teams and individuals taking part each year in the Regular Army Skill-at-Arms meeting at Bisley in competitions for rifle, light machine gun and pistol were regularly placed in the top twenty-five out of some 6–700 competitors. A team from 2UDR won the Infantry Championship once and the Major Units twice. In 1988 the Regimental team were narrowly beaten by the Gurkhas in the Methuen Cup, open to teams from all three services and regarded as the most prestigious Service Rifle match in all the United Kingdom.

In each of the last three years twenty of the places in the Army Hundred were won by UDR soldiers and in 1988 a Private from 6UDR won the Queen's Medal as the champion rifle shot from among the whole of the Regular Army. On several occasions members of the Regiment were selected to shoot for the Army in contests in Canada and Australia.

In football UDR battalions won the UK Infantry Challenge Cup on seven occasions and the Army Cup once. The golfers of 3UDR won the Northern Ireland Challenge Cup in every year from 1982 to 1990 and the Army Inter-Unit Cup on two occasions. For years UDR teams dominated the Army and Inter-Service Tug of War Championships, the latter being held during the Royal Tournament with teams from the Royal Navy, the Royal Air Force and the United States Navy. The Greenfinches won the Northern Ireland Womens Services Orienteering on five occasions, the UKLF Championship once and were runners up on four occasions. Other Greenfinches won trophies in volley ball, table tennis, cross country, squash, swimming, canoeing, athletics and tennis. Each year battalion teams represented the Regiment in the Nijmegen marches in Holland. Some battalions entered teams in the tough Cambrian Marches, a test of endurance and military skills, and in 1991 the 4UDR team won a Bronze medal. For soldiers, most of them part-time, committed to operational duties and with very little time for training, these results were a remarkable achievement and brought credit to the Regiment throughout the Army.

THE PIPES AND DRUMS

The Regimental Pipes and Drums, the members drawn from the battalion bands, made their first public appearance when they led the Lord Mayor's show through Belfast in 1974. Thereafter this became an annual engagement. They became known to a national audience when they took part for the first time at the Royal British Legion Festival of Remembrance at the Albert Hall in 1975 and again seven years later. In 1981 they appeared for the first time on Horse Guards Parade in Central London, participating in the Irish Massed Bands parade in the presence of the Queen Mother.

In one year they paraded before four different members of the Royal family in four days. They took part in the Colchester Tattoo, the Queen's Birthday ceremony in York, an International Air show at Aldergrove and in a tour of BAOR, and played before the Queen at the presentation of Colours in 1999. In 1978 5UDR won the Royal Scottish Pipe Band

Association World Championship against 126 entrants, repeating the success in the following year by winning the world title in Marching and Discipline, whilst 7/10UDR came second in the European Championships in 1990 and 1991.

It was the Pipes and Drums who provided the primary means of keeping the Regiment in the public eye in a non-operational role.

THE COST

One hundred and ninety-seven members of the Regiment were killed by terrorist action. As a result 120 wives were widowed and two husbands lost their wives. Some 158 children lost a father, and one her mother. Fifty-eight former members were murdered, fourteen of whom had transferred to the RUC. Another five former members have been killed while serving in The Royal Irish Regiment. Some 444 men and women were wounded. Of these thirty-five lost one or more limbs or in other ways were signifi-cantly disabled. 228 ex-members are receiving support from the charity Combat Stress as a result of the effects of stress, induced by a traumatic incident or accumulated over their years of service. No records exist for the number of cases of intimidation but they must run into hundreds. Since the scheme to rehouse families coming under threat was introduced in 1988, some 200 have had to give up their homes and move elsewhere. Some have left the country.

SUMMARY

There is no knowing how many lives were saved by the 40,000 men and women who served in the Ulster Defence Regiment. By their presence, in city streets and country roads and across the rural areas of the Province, they forced the paramilitaries of both hues to abort planned attacks. On many occasions they recovered weapons and explosives, including mines already emplaced and awaiting detonation. They provided an example of steadfastness through days of political turmoil and civil unrest. They remained loyal to the end. Without them life in the Province would have been overwhelmed by the violence of terrorism. Without them there would have been no peace. Fifteen soldiers were decorated for acts of gallantry; over one thousand received other awards.

The story of the Regiment is one of sacrifice, of steadfast loyalty and selfless endurance in the cause of peace. It is a testimony to great courage.

BALLYKINLAR
June 2000

APPENDIX A

Roll of Honour

SERVING SOLDIERS KILLED BY TERRORIST ACT

	BATTALION
1971	
Pte W Donnell	6
Pte F W R P Veitch	4
Pte W D Wilson	6
Pte J Russell	7
Sgt K Smyth	6
1972	
Sgt M Crawford	9
Pte T Callaghan	5
Sgt H D Dickson	2
Pte T J Fletcher	4
Capt M E McCausland	5
Lcpl J Jardine	3
Pte S L S Trainor	10
Cpl J D Elliott	3
Lcpl W H Gillespie	8
Pte E A Megahey	6
Cpl R Stanton	9
Pte H J Russell	9
Pte R McComb	10
Lcpl W H Creighton	4
Lcpl A Johnston	4
Pte J E Eames	4
Lcpl V Smyth	11
Pte T R Bullock	4
Csgt J Ruddy	3
Pte T T Maguire	10
Pte J R Bell	4
2Lt R I Long	11
Pte S Porter	5
Pte W J Bogle	6

Pte F D Greeves	8
Pte G E Hamilton	5

1973

Capt J Hood	5
Cpl D W Bingham	9
Ssgt D C Deacon	5
Pte W L Kenny	10
Cpl H F Caddoo	8
Pte S Watt	2
Pte J K Hill	2
Pte M Lilly	4

1974

Pte R N Jameson	6
Capt C M J McCabe	8
Cpl R T Moffett	8
WO2 D H B Sinnamon	8
Fpte E Martin	6
Cpl J Conley	5
Pte T J McCready	3

1975

Sgt A Doyle	11
Cpl J A Fraser	2
Lcpl J Reid	2
Lcpl D J Bell	2
Csgt J Nesbitt	2
Pte R Scott	5

1976

Pte J Arrell	5
Pte J A McCullough	2
Pte W J McCutcheon	5
Ssgt R H Lennox	5
Cpl R W McConnell	2
Flcpl G J B Leggett	2
Pte E R L Stewart	8
Pte R J Scott	5
Lt J Wilson	2
Lcpl S D Adams	8
Capt W R Bond	5
Lcpl J J Speer	5
Lcpl W C McCaughey	5

Pte G Lutton	11
Cpl W D Kidd	6

1977

Maj J P Hill	5
Pte J Reid	8
Pte D McQuillan	5
Cpl D Graham	8
Cpl G C Cloete	5
Capt W E Shiells	8
Cpl J Geddis	10
Lcpl G W D Tucker	10
Cpl J McFall	10
Cpl H A Rogers	10
2Lt R G Smyrl	8
Pte R J Bloomer	8
Fpte M A Hearst	2
Lt W C Kerr	5

1978

Cpl A C Grills	3
Sgt J B Eaglesham	8
Cpl W J Gordon	5
Cpl W J McKee	6
Pte A R Ferguson	4
Capt C Henning	2
Sgt R L Batchelor	10

1979

Pte R J McNally	11
Lcpl T J Armstrong	2
Pte J J Graham	6
Pte S G Gibson	8
Pte A Gore	10
Pte J A Hannigan	6
Pte J J Porter	2
Cpl H G Kernaghan	4
Pte J A Robinson	6
Cpl F H Irwin	8

1980

Pte R Smyth	3
Pte J J Cochrane	3
Pte R J S Wilson	3

Cpl A A Abercrombie	4
Pte W R Latimer	4
Pte W J Clarke	6
Pte M J Hewitt	2
Pte N H Donaldson	4
Pte C H Quinn	3

1981

Maj W E I Toombs	3
Lcpl S D Montgomery	5
Pte J D Smith	7
Pte W J Donnelly	8
Lcpl R W J McKee	3
Pte T A Ritchie	5
Lcpl T R Graham	4
Pte A Clarke	5
Pte M A Stockman	10
Sgt J P Connolly	10
Pte C Graham	4
Cpl T A E Beacom	4
Lcpl J McKeegan	6

1982

Pte S A Carleton	9
Lt J L Hamilton	6
Pte H A Cummings	6
Lcpl F A Willaimson	2
Sgt T G Cochrane	2
Cpl C H Spence	2
Cpl A Smith	2

1983

Lcpl C W McNeill	8
Pte A F Stinson	8
Cpl T Harron	6
Pte J Roxborough	6
Pte R R Alexander	6
Pte O Neely	6
Cpl R D Finlay	6
Pte T C Campbell	8
Maj F C Armstrong	2
Lcpl B V McKeown	5

1984

Pte R G Elliott	6
Pte L C Houston	UDR TC
Lcpl T A Loughlin	6
Pte S D Montgomery	11
Pte N J Johnston	8
Csgt I E Hillen	6
Pte D Chambers	11
Pte N J McKinlay	6
Fcpl H C J Kerrigan	6
Pte R D Bennett	8

1985

Pte J A Graham	4
Pte T W Harkness	8
Sgt R F Boyd	5
Capt G Hanna	3

1986

Pte W V Foster	6
Pte J F Earley	4
Pte T J Irwin	6
Pte W C Pollock	6
Cpl D B Brown	3
Pte R W Hill	3
Sgt D D M Taggart	7/10
Pte M A J Blaney	8

1987

Maj G Shaw	8
Cpl T J Oldman	4
Pte W T Graham	8
Capt I R K Anderson	6
Pte J J McIlwaine	7/10
Pte G J Tracey	7/10
Pte W R Megrath	11
Pte S W Megrath	7/10

1988

Capt T D Armstrong	8
Pte W J R Stewart	8
Cpl A T Johnston	3
Pte J Cummings	7/10

Pte F Starrett	7/10
Cpl W T Burleigh	4
Pte E Gibson	8
Lcpl M Darcy	6
Lcpl R W Butler	7/10
Pte R A McNicol	8
Pte S McKinney	2
Pte W J Moreland	3

1989

Pte T J Hardy	8
Lcpl S D Halligan	2

1990

Pte O F Kilpatrick	6
Sgt T A Jamison	5
Pte J Birch	3
Pte M D Adams	3
Pte S S Smart	3
Lcpl J Bradley	3
Pte C J McCullough	11
WO2 A D Cooper	8

1991

Pte P D Sutcliffe	2
Pte R J Love	2
Pte P R Blakely	2
Pte S Hamilton	2
Lcpl R W Crozier	2
Pte B M Lawrence	7/10
Pte M Boxall	5
Lcpl K A Newell	4/6

EX-SOLDIERS KILLED BY TERRORIST ACT

1971

Pte D J McCormick	6

1972

Pte I Scott	3

1973
Pte J I Vennard   11

1974
LtCol G W Saunderston   4
Pte W D J Hutchinson   6

1975
Lcpl G McCall   2

1976
Pte N Campbell   3
Pte K Worton   2
Pte D W McDowell   2
Pte W J Freeburn   11

1977
Ssgt R J Harrison   11

1978
Pte M Riley   10
Pte G Johnston   2

1979
Pte S Wray   5
Pte J McClenaghan   4
Pte A Dunne   2
Pte R G Hawthorne   2
Pte J Fowler   6
Pte R A Lockhart   2

1980
Cpl C Lundy   2
Pte H Livingstone   2
Pte R V Morrow   4
Pte W G Elliott   8

1981
Pte J Robinson   8
Pte J Proctor   5
Pte H R Hall   5
Sgt C D Neville   2
Cpl J McClintock   5

1982

Pte N Hanna	3
Pte T C I Cunningham	6
Pte W McIlveen	2
Pte J Eagleson	8
Cpl C Crothers	5
Pte S Corkey	2
Pte R Irwin	2
Pte J Gibson	8

1983

Capt J R E Truckle	11

1984

Pte R A Funston	4
Pte H Gallagher	6
Pte M Simpson	2

1985

Pte G Campbell	3
LCpl J D McElhinney	5
Pte D P Topping	11

1986

WO2 H McConville	3

1987

CSgt N Cush	7/10
Pte W C Finlay	5
Pte H Henry	5

1989

Pte R J Glover	5
Pte J Griffiths	2

1990

Pte D Sterritt	2
Pte D M Pollock	6
Pte N Kendall	11
Pte H B Gilmore	5

1991

Pte W J E Boyd	8
Cpl R M A Finlay	6

1993

Pte D H Martin	8
Sgt J Lyness	11
Lcpl J A Burns	5

1994

Pte S W E Smyth	2
Pte M A Smyth	5

EX-UDR SOLDIERS KILLED WHILST SERVING IN ROYAL IRISH BATTALIONS

Sgt R J Irvine	9
Lcpl I R Warnock	6
Lcpl M Johnson	7
Pte C Wren	8
Cpl T T Withers	3

APPENDIX B

Welfare

A November afternoon in 1997. "Mary" sits by the window of her home on the edge of the village and talks about her life as the wife of a member of the UDR.

"It was very lonely. You felt you were always coping alone. 'Jimmy' gave so much time to them that you felt you were always second best. The children missed him terribly as they were growing up. It was so scary always waiting for a phone call coming. On the nights he was on duty you would have dozed and wakened and dozed again until he came in, and then the relief would go and you would be angry. 'What kept you till this time of the morning?' I was always very careful about checking under the car and watching for any stranger coming to the door. We had no security. You just looked out the window to see if the caller was a stranger or someone you knew. The children would get down on their knees and look under the car the same as me, though they didn't know what they were looking for. They were very very protective with 'Jimmy'. Just after he was shot the twins were due to do their Eleven Plus, and I think what happened had a bad effect on them, they weren't able to concentrate and they didn't pass. For all that they have gone on to university.

"They still think the IRA will come for him. I actually dreamt last night that they came and took him and me away. Maybe it was thinking about you coming to talk about it today.

"You had this terrible worry all the time. I used to cry at night. Then when he was shot I felt strong. You wait for it for so long that it is almost a relief when it happens. I had felt very uneasy that night. The girls were at Girls Brigade so I had gone to my sister-in-law who lived a few doors away, but I couldn't settle and I came home. The phone rang twice, someone from the company looking for 'Jimmy'. Then it rang a third time. It was an officer from the Company. He said, 'Now Mary, don't panic. 'Jimmys' been involved in an incident up the road but he's alright.' I went and told my sister-in-law. A neighbour came with a car and we went to the hospital in Magherafelt. I was allowed to see 'Jimmy'. He put his hand out and took mine and said, 'It's just one of those things'. I just coped. I don't know how I did it. It wasn't until he went to the military hospital at

Woolwich that we learnt he would be permanently disabled. I cried for him, because he had been such an active man, but he was so relieved that he wasn't left more disabled that he was quite content. He never complained, never said, 'Why me?'

"I don't feel bitter. The people I would probably want to be bitter about, I don't know them, they are faceless. You can't be bitter about someone you can't see, and I'm glad because it would probably tear me up inside."

The disablement of her husband was not 'Mary's' only tragedy out of the troubles, her two brothers-in-law were murdered, one in the RUC, the other in the UDR.

The welfare problems of the UDR were very different from those of the Regular Army. The UDR soldier was always at risk, on duty, at work and in his home. The family shared the risks; the wives and children too had to be on their guard. Long hours of duty and sudden call-outs, resulting in broken promises, placed a strain on marriages. On average the Regular soldier worked longer hours, but he knew when his Northern Ireland tour would end and he could go home. The UDR soldier had no such end point. Even when he left the Regiment he was still under threat; of the fifty-eight former soldiers to be murdered, forty-four no longer had any involvement with the security forces.

Some 300 members of the Regiment came under threat and had to leave their homes, abandoning home improvements and gardens and starting again from scratch in a strange neighbourhood. Sometimes the house or farm had been in the family for generations. Such moves were traumatic. On occasions the threat was deemed to be so imminent that the family had to get out overnight. Married quarters and caravans were earmarked in Army barracks where the family could live until such time as they could find a place of their own. The new home must be sufficiently distant to ensure that the soldier could no longer be traced by the terrorist organization. New carpets and curtains must be bought, telephones re-connected. Children had to be entered into new schools, new uniforms bought, new friends made. Grandparents who had helped with the family were no longer on hand and soldiers would be faced with longer journeys to duty. For soldiers intimidated from their civilian jobs, it was often hard to find another at a time of high unemployment and some employers were reluctant to take on men whose UDR membership could put the rest of the workforce at risk.

Then there were the bereaved families. In the Regular units they would have been moved out of their married quarters within days and become the responsibility of their Regimental Headquarters; in the UDR the battalions must remain responsible for them for the rest of their days. For the soldiers the knowledge that, if they were killed, their families would be well cared for and never forgotten was an essential element in the maintenance of morale.

As time went on and the number of bereaved families multiplied, more soldiers were forced out of their homes and stress began to take its toll, it became apparent that the traditional Army system of company and platoon commanders being responsible for the welfare of their soldiers was no longer practical. In the case of part-time officers in particular, they simply did not have the time to hold down civilian jobs, supervise the operations and training of their soldiers and still look after their welfare and the welfare of their families and their widows. The then Commander UDR, Brigadier Michael Bray, directed that a co-ordinated welfare service be set up, consisting of a full-time Regimental Welfare Officer at HQUDR and a Battalion Welfare Officer on part-time/full-time service, usually a Greenfinch, with a small staff and an office in each battalion.

The system worked well, resulting in a great improvement in the care of the soldiers, the families and the widows. However, it was clearly wrong that the service should be organized on an ad hoc unofficial basis, with battalions already short of officers being expected to find a welfare officer without establishment cover, and for the officers to be given work that was becoming increasingly stressful and demanding while serving on part-time/full-time terms of service.

By chance the member of the British Red Cross responsible for welfare support for Services hospitals in Germany had been invited to speak at one of the annual joint seminars organized by HQUDR for the Regimental welfare staffs and the case workers from the Soldiers, Sailors, and Airmen's Families Association. Barbara Townsend had been responsible for counselling Service families involved in the Zeebrugge ferry disaster and was quick to understand the strain under which the part-time UDR welfare officers were working. She proposed that the UDR and the Red Cross Society should set up a joint working party to support the case for a full-time welfare service. By the end of 1991 the Working Party had submitted its report to the MOD, strongly supported by the Vice President of the Joint Committee of St John's and the Red Cross, Countess Mountbatten of Burma. Peter Brooke, the Secretary of State for Northern Ireland, who had taken a personal interest in UDR welfare after a meeting with widows organized by Ken Maginnis, had already agreed to speak to the Secretary for Defence. Thanks to this influential support and to a well-argued proposal by HQUDR, the MOD agreed to provide establishment cover for a full-time Welfare Service, an organization unique in the Army.

That welfare became so effective was due primarily to two factors – the dedication of the battalion welfare staffs and the generosity of the public within Northern Ireland, the rest of the United Kingdom and in countries further afield in supporting the Benevolent Fund. The Fund was established as a charitable trust in 1972, with the members of the Advisory Council as the trustees. Its aim was to provide grants paid out immediately to bereaved families and to help serving and ex-soldiers and their families in need, primarily but not solely as a result of their UDR service. There was already £10,000 in the fund, including £3,000 contributed by the readers of *The Daily Telegraph*, when an appeal was launched that November. This was reasonably successful. The soldiers agreed to contribute half a day's pay annually, increased to one day's pay in 1980 and in one year, '88/'89, when the demands on the fund were particularly heavy, two days. By March 1973 the total had reached £50,000. From then on an immediate grant of £200 was paid to the widow of every soldier killed by terrorist act and £25 to each of the children.

The grants were increased several times over the next eleven years but did not keep pace with inflation and were far below those awarded to RUC widows. Accordingly the trustees decided in 1983 to mount a national appeal, launched at a dinner in the Mansion House in London, attended by Prince and Princess Michael of Kent, the Lord Mayor of London, Service chiefs and leaders of industry and commerce. The target was £1 million. Each battalion was given a target and many novel fund-raising ventures were organized. The Greenfinches of 3UDR combed the pages of *Who's Who* and wrote to famous people – musicians, pop stars, television and radio personalities, authors and poets and sportsmen – asking them to send some personal item to be sold at an auction. Almost without exception they replied. Colonel Maurice Buckmaster who ran the Special Operations Executive in Occupied Europe during the war sent his Légion d'Honneur and Croix de Guerre medals, Frederick Forsyth the Paris street map he had used to plot the route of the assassin in his best selling novel *The Day of the Jackal*, James Galway a tin whistle with a book of instructions, Ken Dodd a tickling stick, Chris Bonnington the hammer axe he used on the 1975 Everest Expedition, whilst an officer who had served in the Falklands sent a plate from the dinner service belonging to General Menendez, commander of the defeated Argentine forces. One of the most touching gifts came from Jimmy Logan, the Scottish comedian. He commissioned a bowl decorated with a thistle at its centre and round its rim a poem to the Greenfinches, specially composed by himself.[1] The auction raised over £4,000. Overall the appeal was a huge success. By the following summer £1.25 million had been raised. Thereafter, thanks to judicious investment and the continuing generosity of the public, including church congregations, very many of whom took up special collections, the fund went from strength to strength. Grants were substantially increased and by 1990/1991 the total paid out in the financial year amounted to £212,500.

The fund was used in numerous ways – grants towards the cost of third-level education, purchase of lightweight wheelchairs and orthopaedic beds for the wounded, loans against Criminal Damage Compensation for houses and cars damaged in terrorist attacks, payment of expenses for a deaf child to attend a clinic in Israel as a result of which her hearing was partially restored. There were many such heart-warming stories and both inside and outside the Regiment it became well known that the UDR really did look after its own.

In each battalion the widows and parents who had lost a son or daughter serving in the Regiment met at regular intervals, enabling them to discuss their problems and draw strength from each other, particularly the newly bereaved. The Benevolent Fund financed outings and holidays for the groups. Caravans were purchased and placed on a site on the north coast where those with children could spend a summer holiday and a well-known English holiday camp firm provided free holidays at its camps across the water.

For teenage sons and daughters more ambitious holidays were arranged. Each year the Peace People offered one or two places on their group outings to Norway; a few went sailing with the Ocean Youth Club and group holidays were organized abroad in Bavaria, Switzerland, Holland, Belgium and Disneyworld. On five occasions a group was hosted by American families in the United States. Through the good offices of the American Embassy in London contact was made with the Adjutant General of the Veterans of Foreign Wars, the equivalent of the Royal British Legion, with its headquarters in Kansas City.

Twice the Veterans' families took the children into their homes and gave them holidays they would never forget. One group was entertained by the local Ancient Order of Hibernians, plaques were exchanged and a teenager from the Shankill Road made a pact that she would drink their health each St Patrick's Day if they would drink her health on the Twelfth of July. The arranging of these holidays led to a very happy and rewarding association between the UDR and a succession of US Defence Attachés at the Embassy in London. Some of the attachés paid private visits to the battalions, accompanied by their wives. Friendships developed and other holidays were arranged for groups of teenagers in the States. Colonel Rich Neal, USAF, arranged for his Methodist congregation in Memphis, Tennessee, to host a group. They visited Elvis Presley's home, Graceland, stayed free of charge as the guests of a luxurious hotel in Nashville courtesy of the owners, and spent two days enjoying the delights of Opryland, appearing on television. Other groups went to Gainsville in Florida, spending a day at Disneyland, and to Cookeville in Tennessee. Lasting friendships were made between the children and their hosts, who learnt an enduring lesson about terrorism, that the IRA was an organization that murdered the fathers of children very much like their own.

Other uses of the fund included the payment of Christmas grants to enable battalions to buy gifts for their bereaved families and the disabled, the financing of outings for disabled soldiers and the presentation to the next of kin of each soldier killed by terrorist act a memorial medallion to be worn on remembrance services, specially commissioned from Spinks, the London medal makers. In later years the disabled set up their own Disabled Soldiers Branch of the Royal British Legion, based in Antrim. They take part in paraplegic tournaments, in shooting and in bowls. One Greenfinch, wheelchair-bound as a result of a traffic accident, competed in the Paraplegic Olympics in South Africa in 1996 and won several medals.

In time the Regimental Welfare Service was expanded to include the appointment of a Legal Adviser, primarily to assist the serving soldiers and the bereaved in making claims for compensation under the Criminal Injury and Criminal Damage Legislation, and a Financial Adviser to advise the bereaved how best to invest this compensation, coupled in some instances with substantial life insurance. In the early years some widows used the money unwisely, not appreciating that they should invest the capital and use the interest to help keep them going over the lonely years ahead. One or two married unscrupulous men who left them when the money ran out, by which time they had lost their pensions. One, encouraged by a woman friend, became an alcoholic and her children had to be taken into care. Others paid off mortgages and left themselves with insufficient funds to pay for the upkeep of their homes thereafter.

Service in the UDR placed a strain on what, in less stressful circumstances, would have been stable and lasting marriages. Battalion Welfare Officers were ready to listen as always, to offer sympathy and help where they could, but they were not trained marriage counsellors. Service families in Northern Ireland were reluctant to use Relate, the volunteer marriage counselling service, for interviews with a counsellor must lead to the revealing of details about the husband's service and his routine. Though strict confidentiality was observed there would always be concern that a counsellor, unfamiliar with Service life, might not appreciate to the full the security implications of the interview records, even the risk to a soldier's life if the documents were not carefully handled.

When Relate was approached they were sympathetic and quick to appreciate the problem. Agreement was reached that one counsellor would be nominated to deal with all the UDR couples, with interviews being held at a house outside a military base, and that a contribution towards the fees would be paid by the Benevolent Fund. The system worked well and was later adopted for married couples of all three services in Northern Ireland.

The welfare staffs worked closely with other agencies and service charities. The Chief Executive of the War Pensions agency in Belfast became a personal friend of battalion welfare officers, visiting the battalions and giving talks to audiences of soldiers to ensure they understood their pension rights, and he and his staff were tireless in their efforts to ensure that widows and ex-soldiers who fell ill as a result of their service received their proper pensions.

The voluntary workers in SSAFA and Forces Help across the United Kingdom passed on cases of hardship they came across among ex-soldiers and dependants; in some cases the Royal British Legion could provide additional financial assistance from the Irish Soldiers Fund and the Leopardstown Hospital Trust, based in the Republic. Combat Stress took under its wing ex-soldiers suffering from the stressful effects of years of service under threat, providing fortnight holidays at its holiday home in Ayrshire; the Army Benevolent Fund paid for the expenses for families travelling to the holiday camps across the water; St Dunstan's and BLESMA were ready to help the blinded and limbless. The UDR was very fortunate in its friends.

In the '80s two compensation schemes were introduced to help families intimidated out of their homes. A MOD scheme, Home Moves on Security Grounds (HMSG), covered the cost of an enforced move, the legal expenses of selling a house, estate agents fees, removal and storage expenses and the replacement of carpets and curtains that no longer fitted in the new home, plus a not overly generous grant to cover such incidental expenses as reconnecting a telephone and buying school uniforms. Special Procurement of Evacuated Dwellings (SPED) was a government scheme under which home owners, military and civilian, forced to give up their house as a result of terrorist threat, were offered a fair market price for their former homes. The two schemes were a help, but did not cover all the expenses of an enforced move, while the price of a house in a safe area was likely to be more than the valuation of the old home in an area now considered unsafe. Nor did these schemes compensate the soldier forced out of a civilian job, such people as the part-time officer who had to give up a well-paid post in the GPO sorting office after a colleague had been killed by a vehicle booby trap meant for him and at 47 was unable to find another position. Eventually in 1991, late in the day, the Treasury did approve a scheme of compensation for loss of earnings for a maximum of three years.

During the UDR'S 22 years of service fifty-one soldiers died by their own hand and another 220 died of natural causes, a substantial number of these as a result of heart attacks. It would be wrong to over-emphasize the statistics; the main cause of suicide was probably the ready availability of personal protection weapons. However, there was no doubt that long hours of duty under constant threat in dangerous areas and involvement in traumatic incidents did have a cumulative adverse effect on some of the soldiers. In 1990 the Regiment set up a Stress Management system, working closely with the Command Psychiatrist, a retired Royal Navy officer. Within 48 hours of an incident he would visit the battalion and interview those who had been involved directly or on the periphery, recovering casualties, those on duty in the operations room or members of the platoon who had lost comrades. He also interviewed every soldier who came under attack, on or off duty. Further interviews would follow as necessary and, for those he considered needed longer term counselling, the psychiatrist ran panels attended by serving and former soldiers and in some instances wives and widows. When the soldier left the Regiment Combat Stress took over his care and counselling. At the moment it has some 228 former members of the Regiment on its books.

At first the new policy met with some resistance from COs who looked upon stress as a fashionable new concept and reckoned that their soldiers should pick themselves up, dust themselves down and get on with the battle, as they had done in previous wars. But as cases occurred of good soldiers breaking down, some falling foul of the law after being involved in an incident, they came to accept the need for Stress management.

One of the tasks of the psychiatrist was to visit battalions and talk to the welfare staffs, to make sure that they too were not becoming over-stressed. He was a gentle, caring man and they welcomed these visits. Their job was very demanding, demanding of their time and of their emotions. Some were married with families of their own. they were required to fill the roles of bereavement, debt and marriage guidance counsellors, initiate applications for Benevolent Fund grants, liaise with War Pensions, organize outings and holidays for their widows groups, visit homes damaged in bomb attacks, advise soldiers with domestic problems and, above all, to listen. Their great strength was that, unlike the RUC who used a central team of Civil Servants, the UDR welfare officers were serving members of the Regiment, living with their battal-ions, sharing the same dangers and the same problems. They were members of the family. When a soldier was killed they were required to go at once to the house, to console and help establish the family's wishes regarding the funeral and stay close to them until the funeral was over. In the following days they would pay regular visits, arranging legal and financial advice, and when in time the widows felt able they welcomed them into the battalion group. Sometimes the list of tasks and the heavi-ness of the burden seemed to be more than one officer and an assistant should be asked to bear. One had to cope with the death of five soldiers in nine weeks, four as a result of heart attacks, the fifth murdered. Late at night she had to break the news to his mother. On the day of the funeral another soldier committed suicide; two months later a seventh died in a traffic accident.

All the members of the welfare staff had received some limited training, but they were not trained counsellors. Given that their main task was to provide comfort and sympathy in tragic circumstances to families whose lives they shared, that was no bad thing, but they did lack the detachment that enables highly trained counsellors to help without becoming too emotionally involved themselves. Some of the UDR welfare officers came close to a breakdown. Welfare in the UDR was of a very high order, practical, generous, caring, immediate and continuing. That it worked so well was primarily due to the dedication of a devoted band of part-time officers and their assistants.

Bibliography

Books

Adams, Morgan and Bambridge, *Ambush. The war between the SAS and the IRA*, Pan Books Ltd, 1988. Includes an account of the Drumnakilly ambush on 29 August 1988.

Arthur, Max, *Northern Ireland. Soldiers talking*, Sidgwick and Jackson, 1987.

Barzilay, David, *The British Army in Ulster*, volumes 1 to 4, Century Services Ltd, 1973, '75, '78 and '81.

Bell, J Bowyer, *The Irish Troubles. A generation of violence 1967–1992*, Gill & Macmillan, 1994.

Bew, Paul and Gillespie, Gordon, *Northern Ireland, a Chronology of the Troubles 1968–1993*, Gill & Macmillan, 1993.

Bloomfield, Ken, *Stormont in Crisis. A Memoir*, Blackstaff Press, 1994.

Bruce, Steve, *The Red Hand. Protestant Paramilitaries in Northern Ireland*, Oxford University Press, 1992.

Callaghan, James, *A House Divided*, Collins, 1973.

Collins, Eamon with Mick McGovern, *Killing Rage*, Granta Books, 1997. Includes an account of the planning and murder of Major Ivan Toombs.

Collins, Frank, *Baptism of Fire*, Doubleday, 1997.

Coogan, Tim Pat, *The IRA*, Fontana, eleventh impression 1987.

Devlin, Bernadette, *The Price of my Soul*, Pan, 1969.

Devlin, Paddy, *Straight Left. An autobiography*, Blackstaff, 1993.

Dillon, Martin, *The Shankill Butchers*, Arrow, 1990.
    The Dirty War, Arrow, 1991.
    Stone Cold, Hutchinson, 1992.
    The Enemy Within, Doubleday, 1986.

Faulkner, Brian, *Memoirs of a Statesman*, Weidenfeld and Nicolson, 1978.

Flackes W D and Elliott, Sydney, *Northern Ireland. A political directory*, revised and updated Blackstaff Press, 1994.

FitzGerald, Garret, *All in a Life*, Gill & Macmillan, 1991.

Geragthy, Tony, *Who Dares Wins*, Warner Books, 1993.

Hamill, Desmond, *Pig in the Middle. The Army in Northern Ireland, 1969–1984*, Methuen, 1985.

Hermon, Sir John, *Holding the Line, an autobiography*, Gill & Macmillan, 1997.

Hezlet, Sir Arthur, *The B Specials*, Stacey, 1972.

Holland, Jack and McDonald, Henry, *INLA. Deadly divisions*, Poolbeg, 1994.

Holland, Jack and Pheonix, Susan, *Policing the Shadows*, Hodder & Stoughton, 1996.

Holt, Edgar, *Protest in Arms. The Irish Troubles 1916–1923*, Putnam, 1960.

Kemp, Anthony, *The SAS. Savage Wars of Peace*, Penguin Group, 1995.

Maudling, Reginald, *Memoirs*, Sidgwick and Jackson, 1978.

McNab, Andy DCM MM, *Immediate Action*, Bantam, 1995. Includes an account of the failed SAS ambush at Tamnamore.

Moloney, Ed and Pollak, Andy, *Paisley*, Poolbeg, 1986.

Morton, Peter, *Emergency Tour. 3 PARA in South Armagh*, Kimber, 1989. CO recounts his contacts with the UDR.

O'Neill, Terence, *Autobiography*, Hart-Davis Ltd, 1972.

Paisley, Ian Jr, *Reasonable Doubt. The case for the UDR Four*, Mercier Press, 1991.

O'Callaghan, Sean, *The Informer*, Bantam, 1998. Account of the attack on the deanery, Clogher.

Patrick, Lieutenant Colonel Derrick OBE, *Fetch Felix. The Fight Against the Ulster bombers 1976–1977*, Hamish Hamilton, 1979.

Rees, Merlyn, *Northern Ireland. A personal perspective*, Methuen, 1985.

Ryan, Meda, *The Day Michael Collins was Shot*, Poolbeg, 1989.

Ryder, Chris, *The Ulster Defence Regiment. An instrument of peace?*, Methuen, 1991. Updated and published in paperback, Mandarin 1992. This is the only book devoted to the Regiment. It acknowledges the courage of its soldiers, but contains the author's personal opinion and assumptions that are not always accurate. The UDR declined to assist him in his research. In a letter to the Army Information Services he stated that the book was "unavoidably one-sided because of the willingness of critics to cooperate more readily than the Regiment itself."

Ryder, Chris, *The RUC, a force under fire*, revised paperback edition, Mandarin, 1992.

Styles, Lieutenant Colonel George GC, *Bombs have no pity*, Luscombe, 1975.

Sutton, Malcolm, *An Index of Deaths from the Conflict in Ireland, 1969–1993*, Beyond the Pale publications, 1994.

Thatcher, Lady, *The Downing Street Years*, Harper Collins, 1993.

Toibin, Colm, *A Walk along the Border*, Macdonald, 1987.

Toolis, Kevin, *Rebel Hearts. Journeys within the IRA's soul*, Picador, 1995. Written from the Republican point of view, this book illustrates their hatred for the UDR, and includes an interview with Cpl Eric Glass after he had been involved in a shoot-out with an ASU in Fermanagh.

Urban, Mark, *Bigboys' Rules*, Faber & Faber, 1992.

Whitelaw, William, *The Whitelaw Memoirs*, Aurum Press, 1989.

Other Sources

National British and Irish newspapers
Local newspapers
Church of Ireland Gazette

HMSO publications

Disturbances in Northern Ireland. The Report of the Cameron Commission
Cmd 532 Sep '69
Report of the Advisory Committee on Police in Northern Ireland. The Hunt
Report Cmd 535 Oct '69
The Scarman Tribunal Feb '72
Report of Tribunal appointed to inquire into events in Londonderry on 30
Jan '72. The Widgery Tribunal Apr '72
Defence White Paper "The formation of the Ulster Defence Regiment"
Cmd 4188 November 1969 Hansard 1969

UDR sources

Battalion historical records
Minutes of the Advisory Council
Minutes of Commander UDRs' conference with his COs
Papers of General Sir John Anderson
Papers of Brigadier Dennis Ormerod

Publications

'Defence', a UDR internal news sheet published quarterly from 1972–76.
'Checkpoint', a UDR magazine of excellent quality published annually
1985–91.

Headquarters Northern Ireland publications

'Visor' published weekly and latterly fortnightly for distribution to all units
in the Province from February 1972–June 1985, running to 548
editions.

Reference Notes

Chapter One
(pp1–17)

1   *Protest in Arms* by Edgar Holt. Putnam 1960, p210. *The B Specials* by Sir Arthur Hezlet. Tom Stacey 1972, p4.
2   Hezlet ibid, p20, 27, 82.
3   Holt ibid p252.
4   *The IRA* by Tim Pat Coogan. Fontana 1971, p44.
5   Holt ibid, p303.
6   Holt ibid, p307.
7   "Disturbances in Northern Ireland." The report of the Cameron Commission. Cmd 532, Sep '69.
8   Hezlet ibid, p201.
9   *Daily Telegraph*, 14 Jun '90.
10 Interview Sir Robert Porter QC, Minister of Home Affairs, Mar '69–Aug '70, 31 Oct '93.
11 *A House Divided*, James Callaghan. Collins 1973, p42.
12 Porter ibid.
13 Interview Lieutenant Colonel D A Woods MC, 25 Mar '93.
14 Interview Dr G Chambers CBE, 11 Mar '93.
15 Interview Lieutenant Colonel J. S. T. Reilly OBE DL, 6 Apr '93.
16 Report of the Advisory Committee on Police in Northern Ireland Cmd 535, Oct '69.
17 Porter ibid.
18 Submission to the Hunt Committee by the RUC Central Representative Body, Aug '69.
19 Callaghan ibid p123.

Chapter Two
(pp18–33)

1   The decisions of the Working Party are taken from an undated account written by Captain M. H. Armstrong 2UDR.
2   Interview with General Sir John Anderson, 24–25 Mar '81.

3   Government Defence White Paper 'Formation of the Ulster Defence Regiment', Cmnd 4188, Nov '69.
4   Hansard 1969, pp1229–1240.
5   Lieutenant Colonel S. Miskimmin USC Staff Officer, Headquarters RUC, to all serving USC members, dated 12 Nov '69.
6   *Hansard* p1383 et seq.
7   From a speech given by Sir John Anderson on his dining out from the Regiment, 10 Dec '79.
8   Anderson papers. Script for talk to Belfast Rotary Club on 23 Aug '71.
9   Interview Major General L. Scott-Bowden CBE DSO MC, 5 May '93.
10 From an unclassified article by Scott-Bowden describing his experiences. *Royal Engineer Journal*, Apr '94.
11 Personal account by Major A. J. French, Royal Irish, GSO2, HQUDR, Jan '70–Aug '71.
12 Unclassified written account by Major G. B. Hill MBE, King's Own Borderers.
13 Anderson papers, 13 Jun '70.
14 'Raising of 5 (Co Londonderry) Battalion', an unpublished article by Lieutenant Colonel K. B. L. Davidson dated 1 May '74.
15 Unclassified written account by Lieutenant Colonel A. D. Woods MC undated.
16 Scott-Bowden interview, ibid.
17 By 17 Jun '71, the percentage of Catholics in each battalion were as follows: 1UDR 7%: 2UDR 8%: 3UDR 29%: 4UDR 3%: 5UDR 18%: 6UDR 11%: 7UDR 21%.
18 Interview Major A. J. French, 6 May '93.
19 Scott-Bowden interview ibid.
20 Interview Brigadier H. J. P. Baxter CBE GM, 6 Oct '93.
21 Hill, ibid.
22 Porter, ibid.
23 Unclassified written account Colonel K. W. Battson OBE, 31 Mar '93.

Chapter Three
(pp 34–51)

1   Interview Lieutenant Colonel J. A. Adams MBE 1 Mar '93.
2   Adams ibid.
3   A Bus Driver with six children and in receipt of families income supplement, as a result of the pay he earned on UDR duty lost his supplement and entered the tax bracket. He would have had to do 104 days duty with the UDR to make up what he had lost.
4   Coogan ibid p425 and 464.
5   Coogan ibid p429.
6   Callaghan ibid.

7   Barzilay, David, *The British Army in Ulster*, Volume 1 Century
     Services Limited 1973 pp16–18.
8   *Memoirs of a Statesman*, Brian Faulkner, Weidenfeld and Nicolson
     1978 p69.
9   Written account Lieutenant Colonel D.P.C. Beard dated 6 Jan '94.
10   French ibid. In accordance with the UDR Act, the Training Major was
     the only person in the battalion authorized to order an emergency
     call-out.
11   Written account by Lieutenant Colonel K. B. L. Davidson dated 1 May
     '74.
12   A new Regimental Flag was adopted to distinguish it from the one
     flown by the Rangers, made up of a horizontal infantry red stripe
     between two piper green stripes, with the Battalion title and UDR
     Badge superimposed in gold. Thereafter the Regimental Colours
     were red, green and gold.

Chapter Four
(pp52–66)

1   Callaghan ibid p164.
2   B Faulkner ibid pp115–116.
3   Interview with Gen Sir Harry Tuzo GCB OBE MC on 23 Aug '93.
4   Beard ibid.
5   Report by late 2/Lt T. W. R. Clarke in 3UDR Scrapbook.
6   Interview with Sir Graham Shillington CBE, Chief Constable 70–73,
     26 Aug '93.
7   Compton Report Nov '71.
8   Coogan ibid p434.
9   Original in 3UDR scrapbook.
10   Article "When you are a Catholic in the UDR" by John Burns, *Belfast
     Telegraph*, reprinted in Spring '73 edition of unclassified UDR news
     sheet "Defence".
11   Letter from CO 3UDR to each member of the battalion, 26 Aug '71.
12   Letter from Brigadier D. L. Ormerod CBE to Cardinal Conway, 17 Sep
     '71.
13   Interview Ormerod, 24–25 Aug '93.
14   One CO kept a flock of geese to provide an early warning system.
15   Written account by Mrs Lisa de Candole, 20 Oct '93.

Chapter Five
(pp67–88)

1   Anderson interview ibid.
2   Ormerod papers.

3   B Faulkner ibid p142.

4   Tuzo ibid.

5   *Irish News*, Sep '88.

6   3UDR historical record.

7   *Memoirs* by Reginald Maudling. Sidgwick and Jackson 1978 pp185–187.

8   B Faulkner ibid p152.

9   Inaccurate press reports such as this occurred throughout the lifetime of the Regiment. Some may have been planted deliberately to do the UDR harm, others came from disgruntled soldiers talking directly to journalists.

10 Beard ibid.

11 The .38 revolver was cumbersome and bulky, difficult to conceal on the person or to fire with one hand, an important factor if a soldier was ambushed whilst driving his car. Later it was replaced by a .22 Walther. This lacked penetrative power and the service issue ammunition was unreliable, though this was later replaced by a high-velocity .22 round. Soldiers considered to be at very high risk were issued with a 9mm Browning service pistol, but these too were large, difficult to conceal, were not designed to be carried with a round in the chamber, needed two hands to cock and made an audible noise when being made ready. Eventually in the late '80s the problem was resolved by a special MOD purchase of 9mm Walther P5 Compacts, with a magazine capacity of eight rounds. It was the ideal weapon; it was small and easily concealed, and was designed to be carried with a round in the chamber and to be cocked and fired one-handed.

12 *The Whitelaw Memoirs* by William Whitelaw. Aurum Press 1989 pp123–125.

13 Whitelaw pp128–129.

14 Whitelaw p134.

15 A survey carried out in Sep '72 showed the percentage by counties of males in the eligible age bracket serving in the UDR as follows:

Antrim	2.17
Armagh	4.38
Down	1.09
Fermanagh	7.00
Tyrone	5.50
Londonderry	2.26
Belfast	2.59
Overall Average	3.19

Chapter Six
(pp89–98)

1   *Northern Ireland. A political directory 1968–93* by W. D. Flackes & Sydney Elliott, published by Blackstaff Press, fourth edition 1994.
2   Flackes and Elliott ibid.
3   Interview with Operations Officer 11UDR. According to Dillon in *The Dirty War*, p218, the Sergeant, whom he wrongly describes as a serving UDR Captain, was a leading member of the UVF, "closely connected with UVF operations in South Armagh and intricately involved in assisting the UDA/UVF to plan and coordinate the bombing of Dublin and Monaghan in 1974." He was shot dead by the UVF a week before the Miami Showband murders, in the belief that he was about to turn informer and reveal the murder plan. Dillon, Martin, *The Dirty War*, Hutchinson/Arrow 1991. Used by permission of The Random House Group Ltd.
4   3UDR Special Part One order 64 dated 31 Oct '72.
5   Letter from Sir Oliver Napier to Adjutant 3UDR, 3 Nov '72. Included with Sir Oliver's permission.
6   In Lisbellaw during a scuffle between the UDA and a patrol of 4UDR, the UDA commander was found to be a Corporal in the Battalion. He was promptly discharged.
7   The new policy was spelt out on 31 January '73 by Peter Blacker, Under Secretary of State for the Army, during a wide-ranging debate in the Commons on the Supplementary Estimates for the UDR.
8   Ryder, Chris, *The Ulster Defence Regiment. An Instrument of Peace?*, Methuen 1991.
9   Written account by Brigadier R. V. Ockenden, dated 20 Jan '95.
10 Battalion historical records. "Defence", an unclassified UDR newspaper. Summer '73 edition.
11 Tuzo, ibid.
12 Dillon, Martin, *Stone Cold*, Arrow/Hutchinson, 1992 p77.

Chapter Seven
(pp99–114)

1   Interview Brigadier D. F. Ryan OBE, 6 May '93.
2   Ormerod interview, ibid.
3   During one attack on Belcoo a UDR guard commander gave what was quoted on courses at the School of Infantry as a classic example of a simple, succinct fire order: "Fire like f—k".

Chapter Eight
(pp115–121)

1   In all a succession of twelve WRAC officers filled the post.

Chapter Nine
(pp122–145)

1   Newsletter 9 Mar '74.

2   *The Irish Troubles. A generation of violence 1967–1992*, J. Bowyer Bell. Gill and Macmillan 1994.

3   1 RTR News sheet "First Edition".

4   Interview Brigadier H. J. P. Baxter CBE GM 6 Oct '93.

5   *Sunday Times* 1 and 8 Dec '96. O'Callaghan became disillusioned with the IRA's violence and moved to England where he set up a legitimate business. In '79 the IRA asked him to return. He did so, but contacted the Garda in Tralee and became a high level informer. He rose through the ranks of the IRA, becoming OC Southern Command and a Sinn Fein councillor. A senior detective described him as "The most important intelligence agent in the history of the Irish State". By '85 he was beginning to come under suspicion from the IRA, returned to England and later surrendered to the Kent police. He was charged and found guilty of over forty terrorist offences, including the murder of Eva Martin and a Catholic police officer. He was sentenced to two terms of life imprisonment but after eight years was granted the Queen's Pardon. He now uses his intimate knowledge of the workings and thought processes of Sinn Fein and the Provisionals to write articles for the media on the organization's probable future intentions, and has lectured in the United States.

    Safely across the border the raiding party tuned into the late news. When they heard that a Greenfinch had been killed there were "cheers and hand clapping". "Got one stiff anyway," someone said. Everybody had been happy with the operation. "Now there was near euphoria." Years later O'Callaghan met Richard Martin whilst the two of them were being interviewed for an Australian documentary. He "couldn't have been more forgiving or understanding," O'Callaghan recalled, "and just kept repeating 'It was an awful black night' and 'we must do something for the kids'."

O'Callaghan, Sean. *The Informer*, Bantam 1998, p65 and 308.

6   B. Faulkner ibid p262.

7   Article 'Mistakes Were Made in Security Policy' by Merlyn Rees. *Belfast Telegraph* 11 Aug '94.

8   Baxter ibid.

9   Incident report included in 3UDR historical record. The OP was
     finally abandoned in Jan '75.
10   In the first half of the '70s both Regular and UDR battalions made use
     of what were in effect propaganda leaflets, drawn up in the Battalion
     and printed in the Army printing press. Many battalions issued their
     own 'courtesy cards' which they handed out to motorists at VCPs,
     giving them the name of their unit and thanking them for their co-
     operation. For several years 3UDR produced their own 'courtesy'
     Christmas cards.
11   This was the first successful use of a 'critpit', named after Colonel I.
     R. Critchley, Deputy Commander of 3 Brigade.
12   According to the book *An Index of Deaths from the Conflict in Ireland*
     (Malcolm Sutton, Beyond the Pale, 1994) between 1969 and 1993
     the Security Forces killed 141 republican military activists. In the same
     period Republicans killed 950 serving and former members of the
     Army, including the UDR, the RUC and the Prison Service.
13   The husband of one of the Greenfinches was killed in the Enniskillen
     Remembrance Sunday bomb.
14   4UDR historical record.
15   *Daily Express*, 18 Nov '74.
16   Interview late Major A. S. Turner MBE, 3 Sep '93.

Chapter Ten
(pp146–161)

1   During the previous year Coen and Sean O'Callaghan had run a
     bomb-making factory in a semi-derelict cottage near Ballinamore
     in County Leitrim. Their task was to supply the Mid-Ulster PIRA
     each week with two tons of ammonium nitrate, distilled from
     agricultural fertilizer. Mixed with diesel oil, it made up ANFO, the
     IRA's effective home-made explosive. O'Callaghan ibid.
2   Information that 3UDR was using civilianized vans was quickly
     leaked by a local councillor, who told the press that they were
     being used to spy on Catholic communities. The story was
     published in the front page of the *Irish Times* and *Irish News*.
3   *Emergency Tour. 3 Para in South Armagh*, Peter Morton, William
     Kimber, 1989.
4   2UDR historical record and Visor, an unclassified newssheet
     published by AIS, HQNI, copy 56.
5   *Straight Left*, Paddy Devlin. Blackstaff 1993 p254. In a letter to *The
     Times* in July '83 Rees admitted that the Cabinet's Ireland
     Committee had seriously considered withdrawal. *Northern Ireland.
     A chronology of the troubles 1968–1993*, Bew, Paul and Gillespie,
     Gordon, Gill and Macmillan 1993, p99.

6   *Belfast Telegraph*, 16 and 17 Jun '75.
7   A year later LMGs were reissued to battalions.
8   Dillon describes the Miami Showband murders in *The Dirty War*, pages 216–217. He claims that the man who set up the attack was a former member of the UDR, who had been questioned about numerous murders and bombings. It has not been possible to verify this claim. His statement that the two UVF men killed by their own bomb were members of the UDR is untrue.
9   Baxter ibid.
10   The weapons used were two .45 and one .38 revolver. .45 calibre ammunition was not used in any Service weapons.
11   *Irish Times*, 28 Aug '75. The fact that the condolence notices purported to come from members of the UDR was, of course, no proof that they did.
12   *Guardian* article by Derek Brown, the Northern Ireland correspondent, republished in *Defence*, Winter '75.
13   According to an article on Father Faul, published in *Hibernia* in Nov '77, in six years he had made 400 complaints against the RUC, 100 against the Army, and fifty against the UDR. In all cases the Director of Public Prosecution had found insufficient evidence to proceed with his allegations "which is not surprising since the evidence is provided by the RUC", the article added.
14   Cogan, ibid, p565.
15   The tradition has continued with the Royal Irish Regiment, who, alone of the Regular Army, are given their own place in the muster.
16   Letter from Major General J. H. Page CB, OBE, MC, to the Colonel Commandant, quoted in *Defence*, Winter '75.

Chapter Eleven
(pp162–179)

1   Rees, Merlyn, *Northern Ireland. A personal perspective*, Methuen, 1985, p109.
2   Rees, ibid p294.
3   Rees, ibid p91.
4   Interview Sir John Hermon OBE QPM, 29 Jul '94.
5   Written account by Brigadier M. N. S. McCord CBE MC, Oct '94.
6   2UDR Historical record.
7   Interview Brigadier R. G. Elliot OBE, 1 Nov '94.
8   Article 'Families at War' by Doreen Brooks in the *Gloucestershire Echo*, republished in *Defence*, Summer '76.
9   3UDR Historical Record.
10   Interview Lieutenant General Sir David Young KBE CB DFC 30 Jun '94.
11   *Visor* 127.

12   *Fetch Felix* by Lieutenant Colonel Derrick Patrick OBE, Hamish Hamilton, 1981, p125.
13   Interview Lieutenant Colonel I. K. McBain, 1 Jul '94.
14   Newsletter 20 Nov '76.

Chapter Twelve
(pp180–197)

1   Whereas the combined Loyalist paramilitaries carried out 713 sectarian murders over twenty-four years, they killed only twenty-eight Republican military activists, twenty of them Provisionals.
2   *Londonderry Sentinel*, 12 Mar '77.
3   *Daily Express*, 16 Mar '77.
4   *Tyrone Courier*, 4 May '77.
5   Interview Brigadier M. N. S. McCord CBE MC on 30 Oct '94.
6   McBain ibid.
7   McCord ibid.
8   Hermon ibid.
9   Written account by Colonel M. J. Campbell-Lamerton OBE, 1995.
10   Campbell-Lamerton ibid.
11   McCord written account ibid. Campbell-Lamerton played rugby for Scotland twenty-three times, captaining the Lions team on their 1966 tour of Australia and New Zealand.
12   McCord interview ibid.
13   3UDR historical record 2 Dec '77.

Chapter Thirteen
(pp198–220)

1   Coogan ibid p578/579.
2   *The Dundee Courier*, Sep '79.
3   *Visor*, 276. At the annual Regular Army Skill at Arms meeting at Bisley the hundred soldiers who obtain the highest total of scores in the four major rifle competitions are awarded medals – The Army Hundred. In the twenty-one years that teams from the Regiment took part, a total of 138 Army Hundred medals were awarded to the UDR soldiers. In each of the final three years twenty out of the Hundred were members of the UDR. In 1986 the 2UDR team won the Major Units Championship, beating 2/2 Gurkhas by one point. It was, someone said, "like Northern Ireland winning the World Football Cup", but for security reasons at the time the success could not be publicized. Three years later a Private in 6UDR won the coveted Queen's Medal as Champion Rifle Shot. He received a personal message of congratulations from Her Majesty.

4   *Visor*, 280.
5   *Visor*, 278.
6   *Visor*, 287.
7   Since Nov '77 all permanent cadre soldiers had been required to pass an annual Basic Fitness Test (BFT).
8   Bruce, Steve, *The Red Hand*, Oxford University Press, 1992; *Belfast Telegraph*, 25 May '78; *Newsletter*, 26 May '78. According to Bruce, Davis's colleague who first informed the police was both a former Loyalist paramilitary and a member of the UDR, whilst one of the men convicted of the Post Office robbery was also in the UDA and had served briefly in 5UDR.
9   At the Ard Fheis in '81, Danny Morrison, PSF's director of publicity, said in his speech, "Who here really believes we can win the war through the ballot box? But will anyone here object if, with a ballot paper in this hand and an armalite in this hand, we take power in Ireland?" Flackes and Elliott, ibid p285.
10 In 1976 seven M60s had been stolen from a National Guard armoury in the United States. By the beginning of 1978 they were in PIRA's hands.
11 *Tyrone Constitution*, 25 Apr, '78.
12 *Newsletter*, 9 Oct '78.
13 JP 12 Sep '78.
14 Wier, who suffered brain damage, now attends a Special Care school. In 1984 a rug he had made was chosen as the winning exhibit from more than 500 entries at the War Pensions Welfare Services annual home craft exhibition in London. (*Visor*, 530).
15 *Ulster Herald*, 14 Aug '79.
16 Much of what follows concerning the Warrenpoint disaster and the subsequent briefing of Mrs Thatcher at Portadown is taken from an interview with Major General Sir David Thorne KBE on 15 Sep '95 and a private account of his two years as Commander 3 Brigade, written for his family in 1981.
17 An entry in the 3UDR historical record of 6 Sep '76 reads:

"Thanks to a tip off from the Garda, a 250lb IED was discovered in a culvert under the Newry Warrenpoint dual carriageway close to Narrow Water Castle. The command wires ran across the river into the wood on the southern side of the Border. Fortunately the device was discovered in time and successfully neutralized. One of our patrols had been in the area the night before, but had taken the upper road, otherwise it could have been a different story, although we have been well aware of the dangers of this stretch of road and have avoided deploying VCPs in the vicinity."

18 The definitive account of the whole incident was printed in *Visor*, 284.

19 Hamill, Desmond, *Pig in the Middle, The Army in Northern Ireland*, Methuen, 1985, pp253–258.

20 In her memoirs describing the visit the Prime Minister wrote: "It is difficult to convey the courage of the security forces whose job it is to protect the lives of us all from terrorism. In particular, members of the UDR, who do their military duty living in the community where they and their families are always vulnerable, show a quiet, matter-of-fact heroism which I have never ceased to admire." Margaret Thatcher, *The Downing Street Years*, HarperCollins, 1993, pp57–58.

21 Thorne, ibid.

22 Toibin, Colm, *A Walk along the Border*, Macdonald, 1987, pp116–117.

Chapter Fourteen
(pp221–242)

1 *Down Recorder*, 10 Jan '80.

2 Jonathan Harsch in the *Christian Science Monitor*, 3 Apr '80.

3 Interview Brigadier P. F. B. Hargrave CBE DL, 16 Oct '95.

4 *Visor*, 318.

5 *Belfast Telegraph*, 29 Feb '80.

6 *Newsletter*, 10 Jun '80.

7 Interviews Lieutenant Colonel R. A. D. Kells MBE UD 1 Aug and 3 Oct '94 and 5 Jan '96.

8 *Newsletter*, 8 Jul '80.

9 *Newsletter*, 11 Jul '80.

10 Interview IO Larne Company, 7 Jul '95.

11 IO ibid.

12 Interview Mrs Sylvia Deacon, 13 Feb '97.

13 Hamill ibid p263.

14 *Newsletter*, 17 Jan '81.

15 *Belfast Telegraph*, 17 Jan '81.

16 *Killing Rage* by Eamon Collins with Mick McGovern, Granta Books, '97, pp18–20.

17 Collins, ibid p148.

18 Collins, ibid p152.

19 In Sep '93 Kells was the subject of one of a series of television programmes on BBC2, 'Plain Tales from Northern Ireland. Business as Usual'. In the Omagh atrocity in August 1998 nine of the dead were killed in his shop in that town.

20 Holland and McDonald, *INLA. Deadly Divisions*, Torc, 1994, p181.

21 7UDR historical record: *Visor*, 384: *Irish News*, 13 Aug '81.

22 Ten years later one of her grandsons was killed in a mortar attack on

the RUC station at Keady while carrying out building work on the base. In the following year a second grandson was abducted, tortured and murdered by the IRA in Armagh.

23 Thatcher, ibid p393.
24 Hargrave, ibid.

Chapter Fifteen (pp243–268)

1 Toolis, Kevin, *Rebel Hearts*, Picador, '95, p62.
2 The UDR was the only unit of the British Army for whom the names and details of officers, serving and retired, were not listed in the Army List.
3 3UDR historical record.
4 Interview, Lieutenant General Sir Peter Graham KCB CBE, 21 Feb '96.
5 Report by CO 3UDR to HQ UDR, 5 Nov '84.
6 *Daily Telegraph*, 21 Sep '82.
7 A report by Independent Consumer Research (London) 'UDR Recruitment Advertising. Qualitative Research' dated Jul '84.
8 3UDR historical record, 18 Aug '83.
9 3UDR historical record, 9 Mar '84.
10 *Visor*, 467 and Kells, ibid.
11 3UDR historical record 25 Sep–6 Oct '84.
12 3UDR historical record 19 Mar '84.
13 Arthur, Max, *Northern Ireland. Soldiers talking*, Sidgwick and Jackson, London, 1987, page 235.
14 McNabb, Andy, *Immediate Action*, Bantam Press, 1996, pp163–173. Collins, Frank, *Baptism of Fire*, Doubleday, 1997, pp305–310. In later years Collins left the SAS, was ordained and appointed padre to 23SAS, the Territorial Army Regiment. Tragically in 1998 he took his own life.
15 Urban, Mark, *Big Boys Rules*, Faber and Faber, 1992, p190.
16 3UDR historical record 19–26 May '84.
17 10UDR historical record; Urban pp181–182.

Chapter Sixteen (pp269–291)

1 New Ireland Forum report.
2 2UDR historical report.
3 Foreword by Robert Kee to *Reasonable Doubt. The case for the UDR Four* by Ian Paisley Jnr, Mercier Press, Dublin, 1992.
4 Interview Sir John Bourn, KCB 2 Nov '94.

5   *Irish News*, 16 Jan '85.

6   *Belfast Telegraph*, 26 Jan '85. "Croppies lie down" is a 19th century Orange Order ballad, croppies being a dismissive name for Catholics.

7   *Belfast Telegraph*, 24 Feb '85.

8   *Belfast Telegraph*, 6 Feb '85.

9   3UDR Historical Record.

10 The 290 members of the Regiment who had enlisted at its inception and were still serving were presented with commemorative certificates.

11 *Irish News*, 28 Sep '86.

12 *Irish News*, 26 Jan '85. In all 203 serving UDR and Royal Irish solders were killed in terrorist attacks. In only 26% of the subsequent murder investigations were charges brought (information supplied by HQ RUC, 11 Nov '99).

13 Bruce, ibid p221.

14 Garret FitzGerald, *All in a Life*, Gill and Macmillan, Dublin, 1991, p516.

15 Fitzgerald ibid pp547–550.

16 *Fortnight*, 20 Oct '85.

17 Fitzgerald p552.

18 In his autobiography Hermon wrote:

"On Sunday 17 November I was infuriated to hear Taoiseach Garret FitzGerald state publicly on RTE radio that the Agreement was already bearing fruit in that *all* future UDR patrols would be accompanied by a RUC officer. Such a proposition had never been agreed by me with the NIO. I was silently critical of him for what I regarded as an erroneous claim. It was only years later, when reading his memoirs, that I realised that each of us had been misled by the British negotiators on this and other issues."

Hermon, *Holding the Line*, Gill and Macmillan, 1997, p180.

19 FitzGerald p552.

20 FitzGerald p574.

21 Verbal account by Lieutenant Colonel J. R. Dallow QLR.

22 *Irish Times*, 11 Nov '85.

23 *Irish Times*, 10 Oct '87.

24 Kells ibid: *Death on the Border* by Neil McCaffrey, Magill 4 Apr '85: 4UDR historical record.

25 8UDR Incident Report 2/86.

26 3UDR historical record.

27 *Newsletter*, 22 Apr '86.

28 3UDR Serious Incident Report, 3 Jun '86.

29 8UDR Incident Report 10/86, 24 Oct '86.

30 5UDR Incident Report 145, 14 Oct '86.

31 Ryder, Chris, *The RUC. A Force under Fire*, Methuen, 1989, p330.

32 1/9UDR historical record.

33 In October a soldier found guilty of theft and sentenced to sixty days' detention and stoppages of pay of £200 was the first member of the UDR to be sent to the Army jail, the Military Corrective Training Centre in Colchester.

34 Thatcher, ibid p415.

35 *Newsletter*, 8 Apr '86.

36 *Irish Times*, 18 Dec '85.

37 *Belfast Telegraph*, 28 Jun '86.

Chapter Seventeen
(pp292–320)

1   Interview Brigadier M. R. N. Bray CBE, 2 Oct '96.

2   *Newsletter*, 1 Dec '86.

3   5UDR historical record, 22 Feb '87.

4   *Irish Times*, 21 Dec '87.

5   *Derry Journal*, 9 Oct '87.

6   6UDR report on Aid to the Civil Power, "Flooding West Tyrone," 30 Oct '87 in 6UDR historical record: Checkpoint 88: *Newsletter* and *Irish News*, 23 Oct '87.

7   Checkpoint 88.

8   *Dromore Leader*, 28 Oct '87.

9   *Newsletter*, 20 Feb '88.

10 Interview with Brigadier D. Strudley CBE on 4 Sep '96.

11 CO's report 87/88 and 88/89 in 1/9UDR historical record.

12 Adams, Morgan, Bambridge, *Ambush. The War Between the SAS and the IRA*, Pan Books Ltd, 1988, pp108–117.

13 Strudley ibid.

14 Bowyer Bell ibid p738.

15 2UDR Increp 1/87.

16 8UDR Increp 8/87.

17 *Newsletter* 27 Jun, '87.

18 6UDR historical record, Jul '87.

19 5UDR historical record 6 Aug '87.

20 6UDR historical record, 6–13 Oct '87.

21 Over a period of five months in five separate finds 5UDR recovered some 2300lb of explosives.

22 4UDR historical record. Written account by Captain I. S. McDonald RAMC, Nov '87.

23 *Sunday Times* Insight article "Another Bloody Sunday", 15 Nov '87.

24   4UDR historical record. CO's report for 88/89.
25   Interview Mr and Mrs Stewart, 19 Nov '97, Eighteen months later the headstone on Stewart's grave was smashed with a concrete block.
26   Adams, Morgan, Bambridge, ibid. Chapter 1 gives a detailed account.
27   *Irish News*, 3 Aug '88.
28   *Irish News*, 26 Sep '88.
29   Bowyer Bell ibid p757.
30   *Daily Telegraph*, 29 Jun '88.
31   *Times*, 19 Apr '88.
32   5UDR historical record Annex L, 6 Nov '88.
33   1/9UDR Increp 11/88.
34   2UDR Increp 5/88. Checkpoint 1989.
35   11UDR historical record Annex O, CO's comments.

Chapter Eighteen
(pp321–346)

1   *Belfast Telegraph*, 15 Jan '91.
2   2UDR historical record.
3   *Belfast Telegraph*, 15 Jun '89.
4   3UDR historical record 6 Aug '88.
5   *Down Recorder*, 13 Sep '89.
6   Interview with Brigadier C. D. M. Ritchie CBE ADC, 7 Feb '97.
7   *Daily Telegraph*, 12 Sep '89.
8   *Newsletter*, 13 Sep '89.
9   *Belfast Telegraph*, 26 Sep '89.
10   Ritchie ibid.
11   *Belfast Telegraph*, 23 Oct '89.
12   Extract from Presidential address at AGM of Superintendent's Association, 2 May '90.
13   Flackes & Elliott, ibid p452.
14   Ritchie ibid.
15   *Irish Independent*, 22 Feb '90.
16   *Independent*, 22 Feb '90.
17   *Guardian*, 20 Feb '90.
18   *Irish News*, 23 Feb '90.
19   *Belfast Telegraph*, 20 Feb '90.
20   *Daily Mirror*, 14 Jun '90.
21   *Belfast Telegraph*, 17 May '90.
22   Summary of the report of the Deputy Chief Constable of Cambridgeshire John Stevens into allegations of collusion between members of the Security Forces and Loyalist Paramilitaries.
23   *The Times*, 31 Mar '90.
24   *Down Recorder*, 27 Feb '91.

25 *Irish News*, 12 Apr '90.
26 The nurse was found guilty of murder and sentenced to life imprisonment. Normally she would have expected to serve sixteen years, but under the early release scheme incorporated in the Good Friday Agreement she should have been released in July 2000. In the event she was released in December 1998 on the grounds that by then she was the last inmate in the women's prison at Maghaberry and, so it was said, it would have been inhuman to keep her locked up alone.
27 *Irish News*, 3 Dec '90.
28 Holland and McDonald, ibid, p318.
29 *Belfast Telegraph*, 20 Oct '90.

Chapter Nineteen
(pp347–372)

1 The date is significant. Some critics have suggested that the award of Colours was a sop to the UDR to soften the blow of its merger with the Royal Irish Rangers. In fact the award had been agreed over a year before the decision to make dramatic cuts in defence expenditure.
2 The presentation to 2UDR was postponed as a decision had already been taken to merge the Armagh and Craigavon battalions in November. As a result the Colour bearing the Craigavon Arms, though approved, was never made.
3 Facsimile copies were presented to every soldier on parade. Some battalions also produced a commemorative medallion.
4 *Irish News*, 1 Jul '91.
5 Interview Brigadier A. I. Ramsay CBE, 17 Feb '97.
6 John Potter 12 Nov '95.
7 *Newsletter*, 16 Nov '91.
8 Written account by General Sir John Wilsey, GCB CBE DL dated 12 Jan '00.
9 The new Royal Irish Regiment inherited the Battle Honours of the three precursors of the Rangers; the Royal Inniskilling Fusiliers, the Royal Irish Fusiliers and the Royal Ulster Rifles. The first had been raised to take part in William III's Irish campaign. As a result the ancestry of the Rangers stretched back 300 years, making it one of the oldest regiments in the British Army. It had celebrated its tercentenary three years before the merger. The new Regiment's full title incorporated all its precursors, and is given in the Army List as 'The Royal Irish Regiment (27th (Inniskilling) 83rd, 87th and The Ulster Defence Regiment).' The correct abbreviation is 'R IRISH', not 'RIR' as the media persist in using.

10 Sunday News, 27 Oct '91.
11 At the time of the merger the regimental strength was 5,885, made up of 2,888 part-time and 2,997 permanent cadre, the latter having finally overtaken the former.
12 The window is the first on the right along the left hand corridor from the main entrance.
13 Toolis, Kevin, *Rebel Hearts*, Picador, '95 p357. Interview Cpl Eric Glass DCM QGM, 14 Jun '00.
14 The fifteen battalions are:

1	(County Antrim)	6	(County Tyrone)
1/9	(County Antrim)	7	(City of Belfast)
2	(County Armagh)	7/10	(City of Belfast)
2/11	(County Armagh)	8	(County Tyrone)
3	(County Down)	9	(County Antrim)
4	(County Fermanagh)	10	(City of Belfast)
4/6	(County Fermanagh and Tyrone)	11	(Craigavon)
5	(County Londonderry)		

15 The problem of how the Greenfinches were going to change into their uniforms with decorum behind the wooden fence among all the men was solved when their new uniforms did not arrive in time.

Chapter Twenty
(pp373–383)

1 Bruce ibid, p225.
2 GOC at SSAFA annual meeting on 31 May '89.
3 Information Service on Northern Ireland and Anglo-Irish relations, issued by Irish Information Partnership, 1990, pp249–251; quoted by Bruce, p219 (Footnote).
4 Bruce ibid 219–220.

Appendix B
(p393)

1 Logan's poem reads as follows:

"In tears and in sorrow,
In sadness, in pain,
The Greenfinch of Ulster,
Come sunshine, come rain,
Stands guard in the night,

Stands watch through the day,
Protecting the weak
In her own special way.
So come fly little Greenfinch,
Fly high in the sky,
For the joy of tomorrow
Will be yours by and by,
And the pain of today
Will in time only be
An old song from the past,
But a proud memory."

Index